SOUTH-WESTERN
CENGAGE Learning™

**Intermediate MACRO,
First Edition**
Robert J. Barro

Editorial Director:
Jack W. Calhoun

Editor-in-Chief:
Joe Sabatino

Executive Editor:
Michael Worls

Developmental Editor:
Jennifer Thomas

Senior Marketing Manager:
John Carey

Marketing Communications Manager:
Sarah Greber

Content Project Manager:
Jacquelyn K. Featherly

Publisher/Director 4 Letter Press:
Neil Marquardt

4 Letter Press Research Coordinator:
Clara Goosman

Media Editor:
Deepak Kumar

Senior Manufacturing Coordinator:
Sandee Milewski

Production House/Compositor:
S4Carlisle Publishing Services

Senior Art Director:
Michelle Kunkler

Cover and Internal Designer:
Beckmeyer Design

Cover Image:
© Tatiana Popova/Shutterstock

For product information and technology assistance, contact us at
Cengage Learning Customer & Sales Support, 1-800-354-9706

For permission to use material from this text or product,
submit all requests online at **www.cengage.com/permissions**

Further permissions questions can be e-mailed to
permissionrequest@cengage.com

ExamView® and ExamView Pro® are registered trademarks of FSCreations, Inc. Windows is a registered trademark of the Microsoft Corporation used herein under license. Macintosh and Power Macintosh are registered trademarks of Apple Computer, Inc. used herein under license.

Library of Congress Control Number: 2009931868

Student Edition ISBN 13: 978-1-439-03913-7
Student Edition ISBN 10: 1-439-03913-5
Package ISBN 13: 978-1-439-04009-6
Package ISBN 10: 1-439-04009-5

South-Western Cengage Learning
5191 Natorp Boulevard
Mason, OH 45040
USA

Cengage Learning products are represented in Canada by Nelson Education, Ltd.

For your course and learning solutions, visit **www.cengage.com**

Purchase any of our products at your local college store or at our preferred online store **www.ichapters.com**

Printed in the United States of America
1 2 3 4 5 6 7 13 12 11 10 09

To Rachel, Zac, and Wiggles.

PREFACE

Sound Theory and a Unified Approach

Macroeconomics and microeconomics are the two pillars of economics. Yet, there is a wide gulf between the two pillars in the undergraduate curriculum. Micro courses teach material that is easier but basically consistent with the content taught to graduate students and used by economists in their research. In contrast, macro courses often bear little resemblance to graduate courses or academic research. Undergraduate macro textbooks and courses seem frequently to compromise good economics for presentations that are breezy, closely linked to arguments found in the popular press, and not very intellectually challenging. But sacrificing solid economics to capture student interest is not necessary—sound theory can be clearly written with vivid examples to reinforce it.

In addition to providing a more accurate presentation of the current state of macroeconomic thought, this text provides a unified approach that most macro textbooks lack. Rather than presenting a completely new model when shifting from a discussion of long-run theory to short-run theory, this book develops short-run and long-run models that build on one another in a natural, comprehensible, and elegant way. And all this is done *without* ignoring the important differences between the economy in the long run and the short run. Similarly, I bring in the Keynesian idea of sticky prices as a new idea but one that builds coherently on the structure of the basic equilibrium model.

Organizational Structure

Long-Term Growth

I now begin with long-run macroeconomics—that is, with the determinants of long-term economic growth. Great advances in theory and empirical analysis took place in this area since the late 1980s. Fortunately, it is possible to convey these important findings to undergraduates in a manageable and interesting way. Students can understand the exciting results (in Chapters 3 through 5) without having to first master the details of the underlying microeconomic foundations (which come in Chapters 6 and 7). This early consideration of results with important policy implications helps to drive home the impact and relevance of macroeconomics.

The Equilibrium Business-Cycle Model

A complete microeconomic framework is more important for satisfactory analyses of economic fluctuations. Therefore, I apply the micro foundations from Chapters 6 and 7 to the development of an equilibrium business-cycle model in Chapters 8 and 9. This model generalizes the real business-cycle model, which has become a centerpiece of macroeconomic research since the mid-1980s. Chapters 10 through 14 extend the equilibrium model to allow for money and inflation and for the government sector (expenditure, taxes, transfers, and public debt). These chapters on government were always viewed as strengths of my textbooks, and I believe that characterization still applies.

Incomplete Information and Sticky Prices

The next part focuses on interactions between money and the real economy. Chapter 15 extends the equilibrium business-cycle model to allow for incomplete information about prices in a setting of rational expectations. The exposition of this model is far superior to that in my previous books. Chapter 16 introduces the Keynesian idea of sticky prices and wages, with a focus on the new Keynesian model, another major development since the mid-1980s. This model recognizes that, rather than being perfect competitors, producers typically set prices, which represent markups on costs of production. Most importantly, these prices adjust only infrequently to changed circumstances. Chapters 15 and 16 together usefully supplement the equilibrium business-cycle model to allow for significant real effects from monetary policy.

The Open Economy –Web Chapters

In the interest of brevity that is a hallmark of *Intermediate MACRO*, Chapters 17 and 18 covering the open economy and international macroeconomics are now available to students and instructors online at http://4LTRpress.cengage.com/macro. Chapters 17 and 18 extend the equilibrium model to an open economy. I deal first with a purely real setting in which the home and foreign countries share a common currency. One significant topic is the current-account deficit, a great concern for the United States in recent years. The next chapter introduces different moneys and allows for the determination of exchange rates. An important issue here—relevant today to debates about China's currency—concerns the relative merits of fixed versus flexible exchange rates.

You'll also find many additional resources at http://4LTRpress.cengage.com/macro, including videos, quizzes, instructor resources, and more!

Acknowledgements

Throughout the writing and development of this book, many dedicated professors have generously contributed their time and comments to help improve its presentation. I am grateful for their consideration and assistance.

James Ahiakpor
  California State University, Hayward
Francis Ahking
  University of Connecticut
David Aschauer
  Bates College
Javed Ashraf
  University of West Florida
Scott Baier
  Clemson University
J. Ulysses Balderas
  Sam Houston State University
Christopher Baum
  Boston College
James Butkiewicz
  University of Delaware
Marco Cagetti
  University of Virginia
Rob Catlett
  Emporia State University
Byron Chapman
  University of Georgia

Amaresh Das
  Tulane University
A. Edward Day
  University of Texas, Dallas
Dennis Debrecht
  Carroll College
Larry Fu
  Illinois College
Michael Goode
  University of North Carolina, Charlotte
David B. Gordon
  Clemson University
John Grether
  Northwood University
David Hakes
  University of Northern Iowa
David Hammes
  University of Hawaii, Hilo
Joe Haslag
  University of Missouri
Peter Hess
  Davidson College

Jeanne Hey
  Lebanon Valley College
William Horace
  Syracuse University
Dennis Jansen
  Texas A&M University
Bryce Kanago
  University of Northern Iowa
Manfred Keil
  Claremont McKenna College
Doug Kinnear
  Colorado State University
Todd Knoop
  Cornell College
Robert Krol
  California State University, Northridge
Paul Lau
  University of Hong Kong
Joshua Lewer
  West Texas A&M University
Tony Lima
  California State University, Hayward
Ming Lo
  St. Cloud State University
Prakash Loungani
  Georgetown University
Paul Mason
  University of North Florida
B. Starr McMullen
  Oregon State University
Stephen O. Morrell
  Barry University
John J. Nader
  Grand Valley State University
Nick Noble
  Miami University of Ohio
Farrokh Nourzad
  Marquette University
Salvador Ortigueira
  Cornell University
Christopher Otruk
  University of Virginia

Stephen Parente
  University of Illinois, Champaign
Peter Pedroni
  Williams College
Jaishankar Raman
  Valparaiso University
Robert Reed
  University of Kentucky
William R. Reed
  University of Oklahoma
Bernard Rose
  Rocky Mountain College
Esteban Rossi-Hansberg
  Princeton University
William Seyfried
  Winthrop University
Mohamad Shaaf
  University of Central Oklahoma
Nicole Simpson
  Colgate University
Rodney Smith
  University of Minnesota
John Stiver
  University of Connecticut
Jack Strauss
  St. Louis University
Mark Strazicich
  Appalachian State University
James Swofford
  University of South Alabama
Mark Toma
  University of Kentucky
David Torgerson
  USDA Economics Research Service
Dosse Toulaboe
  Fort Hays State University
Fred Tyler
  Marist College
Bijan Vasigh
  Embry-Riddle Aeronautical University
Christian Zimmerman
  University of Connecticut

BRIEF CONTENTS

CONTENTS

ABOUT THE AUTHOR

Robert J. Barro

I was born in New York City, then moved to Los Angeles, where I attended high school. After studying physics at Caltech, including classes from Richard Feynman, I switched to economics for graduate school at Harvard. The change to economics was a great move for me! After jobs at Brown, Chicago, and Rochester, I returned to Harvard as a professor in 1987. I am presently a senior fellow of Stanford's Hoover Institution and a research associate of the National Bureau of Economic Research. I co-edit Harvard's *Quarterly Journal of Economics* and was recently president of the Western Economic Association and vice president of the American Economic Association. I have been visiting China a lot recently and am now honorary dean of the China Economics & Management Academy of the Central University of Beijing. My research has focused on macroeconomics and economic growth but includes recent work with my wife, Rachel, on the economics of religion. I am also studying the economic effects of rare disasters, such as depressions, world wars, epidemics, and natural disasters. Aside from academic research, I enjoy more popular writing, including work as a viewpoint columnist for *Business Week* from 1998 to 2006 and as a contributing editor of the *Wall Street Journal* from 1991 to 1998. My recent books include *Economic Growth* (second edition, with Xavier Sala-i-Martin, who astoundingly served for a time as acting president of the famous soccer team F.C. Barcelona), *Nothing Is Sacred: Economic Ideas for the New Millennium, Determinants of Economic Growth,* and *Getting It Right: Markets and Choices in a Free Society,* all from MIT Press.

CHAPTER 1

© Anyka/Fotolia

Thinking About Macroeconomics

Macroeconomics deals with the overall, or aggregate, performance of an economy. We study the determination of the economy's total production of goods and services, as measured by the real **gross domestic product (GDP)**. We analyze the breakdown of GDP into its major components: consumption, gross investment (purchases of new capital goods—equipment and structures—by the private sector), government purchases of goods and services, and net exports of goods and services. We also examine the aggregates of **employment** (persons with jobs) and **unemployment** (persons without jobs who are seeking work).

These terms refer to quantities of goods or labor. We are also interested in the prices that correspond to these quantities. For example, we consider the dollar prices of the goods and services produced in an economy. When we look at the price of the typical or average item, we refer to the **general price level**. We also study the **wage rate**, which is the dollar price of labor; the **rental price**, which is the dollar price paid to use capital goods; and the **interest rate**, which determines the cost of borrowing and the return to lending. When we consider more than one economy, we can study the **exchange rate**, which is the rate at which one form of money (e.g., the euro) exchanges for another form of money (e.g., the U.S. dollar).

We will set up an economic model, which will allow us to study how the various quantities and prices are determined. We can use the model to see how the quantities and prices respond to technological advances, government policies, and other variables. For example, we will consider monetary policy, which involves the determination of the quantity of money and the setting of interest rates. We will also study fiscal policy, which describes the government's expenditures, taxes, and fiscal deficits.

The performance of the overall economy matters for everyone because it influences incomes, job prospects, and prices. Thus, it is important for us—and even more important for government policymakers—to understand how the macroeconomy operates. Unfortunately, as is obvious from reading the newspapers, macroeconomics is not a settled scientific field. Although there is consensus on many issues—such as some of the determinants of long-run economic growth—there is also controversy about many topics, such as the sources of economic fluctuations and the short-run effects of monetary policy. The main objective of this book is to convey the macroeconomic knowledge that has been attained, as well as to point out areas in which a full understanding has yet to be achieved.

Output, Unemployment, and Prices in U.S. History

To get an overview of the subject, we can look at the historical record of some of the major macroeconomic variables in the United States. Figure 1.1 shows the total output or production of goods and services from 1869 to 2005. (The starting date is determined by the available data.) Our measure of aggregate output is the **real gross domestic product (GDP)**.[1] This concept expresses quantities in terms of a base year—in our case, 2000. Chapter 2 considers **national-income accounting** and thereby provides the conceptual details for measuring **real GDP**.

The general upward trend of real GDP in Figure 1.1 reflects the long-term growth of the U.S. economy. Figure 1.2 plots the growth rate of real GDP for each year, from 1870 to 2005. A simple way to compute the growth rate for year t is to take the difference between the levels of real GDP in years t and $t-1$, $Y_t - Y_{t-1}$, divide by year $t-1$'s level of real GDP, Y_{t-1}, and then subtract 1:

$$growth\ rate\ of\ real\ GDP\ for\ year\ t = (Y_t - Y_{t-1})/Y_{t-1} - 1$$

If we then multiply by 100, we get the growth rate of real GDP in percent per year.

The mean growth rate of real GDP from 1870 to 2005 was 3.5% per year. This growth rate meant that the level of real GDP, shown in Figure 1.1, expanded 121-fold from 1869 to 2005. If we divide through by population to determine real per capita GDP, it turns out that the mean per capita growth rate was 2.0% per year. This rate equals the 3.5% per-year growth rate of real GDP less the 1.5% per-year growth rate of population. The growth rate of real per capita GDP by 2.0% per year meant that real GDP per capita increased 16-fold from 1869 to 2005.

Figure 1.2 shows that the year-to-year growth rates of real GDP varied substantially around their mean of 3.5%. These variations are called **economic fluctuations** or, sometimes, the **business cycle**.[2] When real GDP falls toward a low point or trough, the economy is in a **recession**, or an economic contraction. When real GDP expands toward a high point or peak, the economy is in a **boom**, or an economic expansion.

The dates marked in Figure 1.2 correspond to the major U.S. recessions since 1870. There are many ways to classify periods of recession. In this graph, we mark as years of recession the years of low economic growth. In Chapter 8, we use a more sophisticated method to classify recessions. However, most of the classifications are the same as those shown in Figure 1.2.

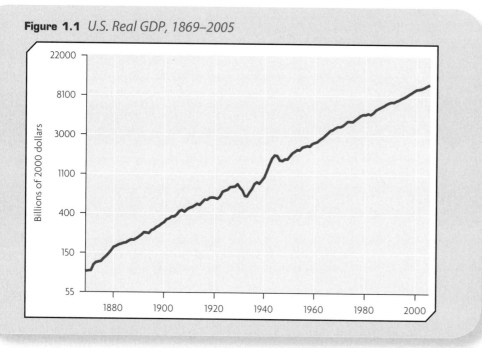

Figure 1.1 *U.S. Real GDP, 1869–2005*

The graph shows the real gross domestic product (GDP) on a proportionate (logarithmic) scale. Data before 1929 are for real gross national product (GNP). The numbers are in billions of 2000 U.S. dollars.

Sources: Data since 1929 are from Bureau of Economic Analysis (*http://www.bea.gov*). Values from 1869 to 1928 are based on data from Christina Romer (1988, 1989).

---

[1] The graph uses a proportionate scale, so that each unit on the vertical axis corresponds to the same percentage change in real GDP. Because of data availability, the numbers before 1929 refer to real gross national product (GNP). We discuss the relation between GDP and GNP in Chapter 2.

[2] The term "business cycle" can be misleading because it suggests a more regular pattern of ups and downs in economic activity than actually appears in the data.

Note in Figure 1.2 the **Great Depression** from 1930 to 1933, during which real GDP declined at 8% per year for four years. Other major recessions before World War II occurred in 1893–94, 1907–8, 1914, 1920–21, and 1937–38. In the post–World War II period, the main recessions occurred in 1958, 1974–75, and 1980–82.

For economic booms, note first in Figure 1.2 the high rates of economic growth during World Wars I and II and the Korean War. Peacetime periods of sustained high economic growth before World War II were 1875–80, 1896–1906, much of the 1920s, and the recovery from the Great Depression from 1933 to 1940 (except for the 1937–38 recession). After World War II, periods of sustained high economic growth occurred in 1961–1973 (except for the brief recession in 1970), 1983–89, and 1992–2000.

Another way to gauge recessions and booms is to consider the **unemployment rate**—the fraction of persons seeking work who have no job. Figure 1.3 shows the unemployment rate for each year from 1890 to 2005. The mean unemployment rate was 6.3%, and the median was lower—5.5%. During recessions, the unemployment rate typically rises above its median. The extreme example is the Great Depression, during which the

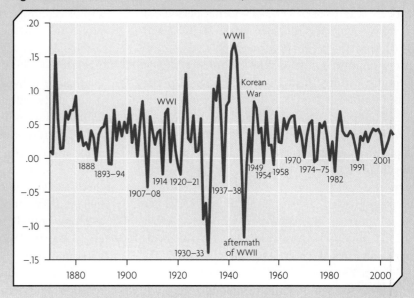

Figure 1.2 *Growth Rate of U.S. Real GDP, 1870–2005*

The graph shows the annual growth rate of real GDP (real GNP before 1929). The growth rates are calculated from the values of real GDP (or real GNP) shown in Figure 1.1. Aside from the years of major war, the years marked are recession periods. These periods have low (typically negative) rates of economic growth.

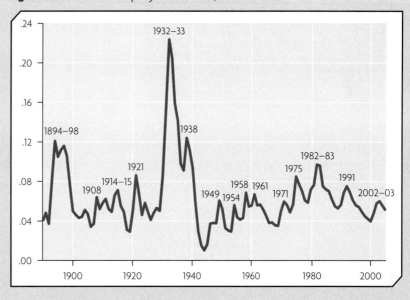

Figure 1.3 *U.S. Unemployment Rate, 1890–2005*

The graph shows the U.S. unemployment rate.

Sources: Data since 1929 are from Bureau of Labor Statistics (*http://www.bls.gov*). Values from 1890 to 1928 are based on data from Christina Romer (1986, Table 9). Values for 1933 to 1943 were adjusted to classify federal emergency workers as employed, as discussed in Michael Darby (1976).

unemployment rate reached 22% in 1932. Also noteworthy in the pre–World War II period are the average unemployment rates of 18% for 1931–35, 12% for

1938–39, 11% for 1894–98, and 8% for 1921–22. In the post–World War II period, the highest unemployment rate was 10% in 1982–83. Other periods of high unemployment rates included 1975–76 (8%) and 1958, 1961, and 1991–93 (7%).

Figures 1.2 and 1.3 show the turbulence of the U.S. economy during the two world wars and the 1930s. But suppose that we abstract from these extreme episodes and compare the post–World War II period with the period before World War I. Then the major message from the data is the similarity between the post–World War II and pre–World War I periods.

The mean growth rate of real GDP was 3.4% per year from 1948 to 2005, compared with 3.8% from 1870 to 1914 and 3.4% from 1890 to 1914. The mean unemployment rates were 5.6% from 1948 to 2005 and 6.4% from 1890 to 1914. The extent of economic fluctuations—in the sense of the variability of growth rates of real GDP or of unemployment rates—was only moderately larger in the pre–World War I period than in the post–World War II period.[3] The economy has, of course, changed greatly over the 136 years from 1869 to 2005—including a larger role for government, a diminished share of agriculture in the GDP, and dramatic changes in the monetary system. Nevertheless, the U.S. data do not reveal major changes in the intensity of economic fluctuations or in the average rate of economic growth.

Figure 1.4 shows the evolution of the U.S. price level from 1869 to 2005. This graph measures the price level as the deflator for the GDP (we discuss the details of this price index in Chapter 2). For present purposes, the important point is that the GDP deflator is a broad index, corresponding to the prices of all the items that enter into the gross domestic product.

One striking observation is the persistent rise in the price level since World War II, contrasted with the up and down movements before World War II. There are long periods in the earlier history—1869 to 1892 and 1920 to 1933—during which the price level fell persistently.

Figure 1.5 shows the annual **inflation rate** from 1870 to 2005. Each year's inflation rate is calculated as the growth rate in percent per year of the price level shown in Figure 1.4. A simple way to compute the inflation rate for year t is to take the difference between the price levels in years t and $t-1$, $P_t - P_{t-1}$, divide by year $t-1$'s price level, P_{t-1}, and then subtract 1:

$$\textit{inflation rate for year } t = (P_t - P_{t-1})/P_{t-1} - 1$$

If we then multiply by 100, we get the inflation rate in percent per year.

Notice from Figure 1.5 that the inflation rates after World War II were all greater than zero, except for 1949. In contrast, many of the inflation rates before World War II were less than zero. Note also in the post–World War II period that the inflation rate fell sharply from a peak of 8.8% in 1980–81 to means of 2.5% from 1983 to 2005 and only 2.0% from 1992 to 2005.

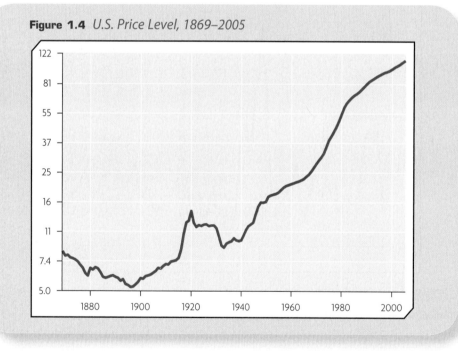

Figure 1.4 *U.S. Price Level, 1869–2005*

The graph shows the price deflator for the GDP (GNP before 1929). The numbers are on a proportionate (logarithmic) scale, with the value for the year 2000 set at 100. The sources are those indicated for GDP in Figure 1.1.

---

[3] For a detailed comparison of real GDP and unemployment rates for the two periods, see Christina Romer (1986, 1988, 1989).

In subsequent chapters, we will relate the changing behavior of the inflation rate to the changing character of monetary institutions and monetary policy. A key element of the pre–World War II period was the **gold standard**, a system in which the dollar price of gold was nearly constant. The United States adhered to this system from 1879 until World War I and, to some extent, from World War I until 1933. A key element of the post–World War II period was the changing monetary policy of the U.S. Federal Reserve. Notably, since the mid-1980s, the Federal Reserve and other major central banks have successfully pursued a policy of low and stable inflation.

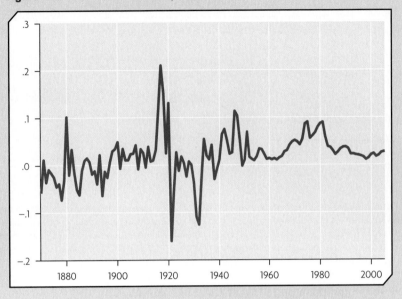

Figure 1.5 *U.S. Inflation Rate, 1870–2005*

The graph shows the annual inflation rate based on the GDP deflator (GNP deflator before 1929). The inflation rate is the annual growth rate of the price level shown in Figure 1.4.

Economic Models

As mentioned, we want to understand the determinants of major macroeconomic variables, such as real GDP and the general price level. To carry out this mission, we will construct a macroeconomic model. A model can be a group of equations or graphs, or a set of conceptual ideas. We will use all of these tools in this book—some equations but, more often, graphs and ideas.

An economic model deals with two kinds of variables: endogenous variables and exogenous variables. The **endogenous variables** are the ones that we want the model to explain. For example, the endogenous variables in our macroeconomic model include real GDP, investment, employment, the general price level, the wage rate, and the interest rate.

The **exogenous variables** are the ones that a model takes as given and does not attempt to explain. A simple example of an exogenous variable is the weather (at least in models that do not allow the economy to affect the climate). In many cases, the available technologies will be exogenous. For a single country's economy, the exogenous variables include the world prices of commodities such as oil and wheat, as well as levels of income in the rest of the world. In many cases, we will treat government policies as exogenous—for example, choices about monetary policy and the government's spending and taxes. We also treat as exogenous war and peace, which have important macroeconomic consequences.

The central idea of a model is that it tells us how to go from the exogenous variables to the endogenous variables; Figure 1.6 illustrates this process. We take as given the group of exogenous variables shown in the left box in the diagram. The model tells us how to go from these exogenous variables to the group of endogenous variables, shown in the right box in the diagram. Therefore, we can use the model to predict how changes in the exogenous variables affect the endogenous variables.

In macroeconomics, we are interested in the determination of macroeconomic—that is, economy-wide aggregate—variables, such as real GDP. However, to construct a useful macroeconomic model, we will find it helpful to build on a microeconomic approach to the actions of individual households and businesses. This microeconomic approach investigates individual decisions about how much to

Figure 1.6 *The Workings of an Economic Model*

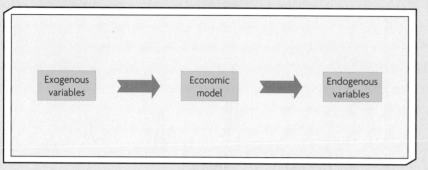

A model is a theory that tells us how to go from a group of exogenous variables to a group of endogenous variables. The model may be a list of equations or graphs or a set of conceptual ideas. The exogenous variables come from outside the model and are therefore not explained by the model. The endogenous variables are the ones that the model seeks to explain. With the help of the model, we can predict how changes in the exogenous variables affect the endogenous variables.

consume and save, how much to work, and so on. Then we can add up, or aggregate, the choices of individuals to construct a macroeconomic model. This underlying microeconomic analysis is called **microeconomic foundations**.

A Simple Example— The Coffee Market

To illustrate general ideas about models and markets, we can examine the market for a single product, such as coffee. Our analysis will focus on three key tools used by economists: demand curves, supply curves, and market-clearing conditions (quantity demanded equals quantity supplied).

Individuals decide how much coffee to buy—that is, the quantity of coffee to demand. Influences on this demand include the individual's income; the price of coffee, P_c; and the price of a substitute good, say, P_T, the price of tea. Since each individual is a negligible part of the coffee and tea markets, it makes sense that each individual would neglect the effect of his or her coffee and tea consumption on P_c and P_T. That is, each individual is a **price taker**; he or she simply decides how much coffee and tea to buy at given prices, P_c and P_T. Economists use the term **perfect competition** to describe a market in which there are so many buyers and sellers that no individual can noticeably affect the price.

Reasonable behavior for an individual household dictates that each household's quantity of coffee demanded would rise with income; fall with the coffee

price, P_c; and rise with the price of the substitute good, P_T. These results for individual households are examples of microeconomic analysis. When we add up across all households, we determine the aggregate quantity of coffee demanded as a function of aggregate income, denoted by Y, and the prices P_c and P_T. We can isolate the effect of the coffee price, P_c, on the total quantity of coffee demanded by drawing a market **demand curve**. This curve shows the total quantity of coffee demanded, Q_c^d, as a function of P_c.

Figure 1.7 shows the market demand curve for coffee. As already noted, a decrease in P_c increases Q_c^d. Recall, however, that the demand curve applies for given values of aggregate income, Y, and the price of tea, P_T. If Y rises, the quantity of coffee demanded, Q_c^d, increases for a given price, P_c. Therefore, the demand curve shown in Figure 1.7 shifts to the right. If P_T falls, the quantity of coffee demanded, Q_c^d, decreases for a given price, P_c. Therefore, the demand curve shifts to the left.

We also have to consider how individual producers of coffee decide how much to offer for sale on the

Demand and Supply Curves Are Functions

The market demand for coffee can be written as a function:

$$Q_c^d = D(P_c, Y, P_T)$$

The function $D(\cdot)$ determines the quantity of coffee demanded, Q_c^d, for any specified values of the three demand determinants: P_c, Y, and P_T. We assume that the function $D(\cdot)$ has the properties that Q_c^d decreases with the price of coffee, P_c; rises with income, Y; and rises with the price of tea, P_T. Figure 1.7 graphs Q_c^d against P_c for given values of the other demand determinants, Y and P_T. It is important to distinguish the demand curve, $D(\cdot)$, shown in Figure 1.7, from the quantity demanded, Q_c^d, at a given price, P_c (and for given Y and P_T). The demand curve refers to the whole functional relationship between quantity demanded and price, $D(\cdot)$, whereas the quantity demanded, Q_c^d, refers to one of the points along the curve.

The market supply of coffee is also a function, which can be written as

$$Q_c^s = S(P_c, weather)$$

We assume that the function $S(\cdot)$ has the properties that the quantity supplied, Q_c^s, rises with P_c and with better weather in coffee-producing areas. Figure 1.8 graphs the quantity supplied, Q_c^s, against P_c, for given weather conditions. It is important to remember that the supply curve, $S(\cdot)$, refers to the whole functional relationship between quantity supplied and price, whereas the quantity supplied, Q_c^s, refers to one of the points along the curve.

market—that is, how much coffee to supply. Influences on this supply include the price of coffee, P_c, and the cost of producing additional coffee. We assume, as in our analysis of demand, that the suppliers of coffee are price takers with respect to P_c. This assumption could be questioned because some producers of coffee are large and might consider the effects of their actions on P_c. However, an extension to allow for this effect would not change our basic analysis of the market for coffee.

Reasonable behavior by an individual producer dictates that the quantity of coffee supplied would rise with the price of coffee, P_c, and fall with an increase in the cost of producing additional coffee. For example, bad weather that destroys part of the coffee crop in Brazil would raise the cost of producing coffee and, thereby,

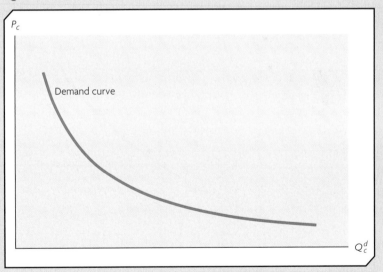

Figure 1.7 *Demand Curve for Coffee*

The market demand curve shows the total quantity of coffee demanded, Q_c^d, as a function of the price of coffee, P_c. A decrease in P_c raises Q_c^d. The demand curve applies for given aggregate income, Y, and the price of tea, P_T. If Y rises, the quantity of coffee demanded, Q_c^d, increases for a given P_c. Therefore, the demand curve in the diagram shifts to the right. If P_T falls, the quantity of coffee demanded, Q_c^d, decreases for a given P_c. Therefore, the demand curve shifts to the left.

reduce the coffee supplied by Brazilians. These results for individual producers are examples of microeconomic analysis.

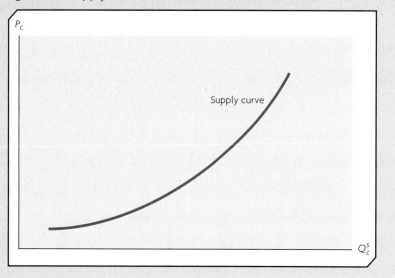

Figure 1.8 *Supply Curve for Coffee*

The market supply curve shows the total quantity of coffee supplied, Q_c^s, as a function of the price of coffee, P_c. An increase in P_c raises Q_c^s. The supply curve applies for given conditions that affect the cost of producing coffee. For example, a harvest failure in Brazil would decrease the total quantity of coffee supplied, Q_c^s, for a given price, P_c. Therefore, the supply curve shifts to the left.

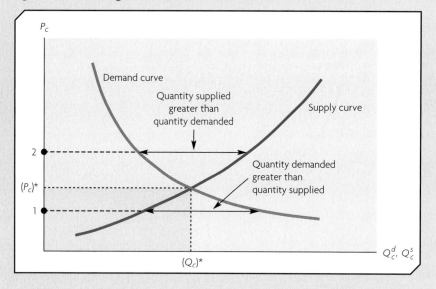

Figure 1.9 *Clearing of the Market for Coffee*

The coffee market clears at the price $(P_c)^*$ and quantity $(Q_c)^*$. At this point, the quantity of coffee supplied equals the quantity demanded.

areas, such as Brazil and Colombia.

As in our analysis of demand, we can isolate the effect of the coffee price, P_c, on the total quantity of coffee supplied by drawing a market **supply curve**. This curve, shown in Figure 1.8, gives the total quantity of coffee supplied, Q_c^s, as a function of P_c. As already noted, an increase in P_c raises Q_c^s. This supply curve applies for given cost conditions for producing coffee and, in particular, for given weather in coffee-producing areas. If bad weather destroys part of Brazil's coffee crop, the market quantity of coffee supplied, Q_c^s, decreases for a given price, P_c. Therefore, the supply curve shown in Figure 1.8 shifts to the left.

Figure 1.9 shows the clearing of the market for coffee. The price of coffee, P_c, is assumed to adjust to equate the quantity supplied, Q_c^s, to the quantity demanded, Q_c^d. This market-clearing price is the value $(P_c)^*$ shown in the figure. The corresponding market-clearing quantity of coffee is $(Q_c)^*$.

Why do we assume that the coffee price, P_c, adjusts to the market-clearing value, $(P_c)^*$? For any other price, the quantities supplied and demanded would be unequal. For example, at point 1 in Figure 1.9, where P_c is less than $(P_c)^*$, the quantity demanded, Q_c^d, would be greater than the quantity supplied, Q_c^s. In that case, some coffee drinkers

When we add up across all producers, we determine the aggregate quantity of coffee supplied. One result is that a rise in P_c increases the aggregate quantity of coffee supplied, Q_c^s. The total quantity supplied also depends on weather conditions in coffee-producing

must be unsatisfied; they would not be able to buy the quantity of coffee that they want at the price P_c. That is, suppliers would be unwilling to provide enough coffee to satisfy all of the desired purchases at this low price. In this circumstance, we would think that competition among the eager demanders of coffee would raise the market price, P_c, toward $(P_c)^*$.

Conversely, at point 2 in Figure 1.9, where P_c is higher than $(P_c)^*$, the quantity demanded, Q_c^d, would be less than the quantity supplied, Q_c^s. In this case, some coffee producers must be unsatisfied; they would not be able to sell the full quantity of coffee that they want to sell at the price P_c. That is, coffee drinkers would be unwilling to buy all the coffee that the producers offer at this high price. In this situation, we would expect that competition among the eager suppliers of coffee would reduce the market price, P_c, toward $(P_c)^*$.

The market-clearing price, $P_c = (P_c)^*$, is special because only at this price is there no pressure for the coffee price to rise or fall. In this sense, the market-clearing price is an **equilibrium** price. This price tends to remain the same unless there are shifts to the demand curve or the supply curve.

We can think of our market-clearing analysis of the coffee market as a model of how the coffee market operates. The two endogenous variables in the model are the price, P_c, and quantity, Q_c, of coffee. We can use the market-clearing analysis from Figure 1.9 to see how changes in exogenous variables affect the endogenous variables in the model. The exogenous variables are the outside forces that shift the demand and supply curves for coffee. For demand,

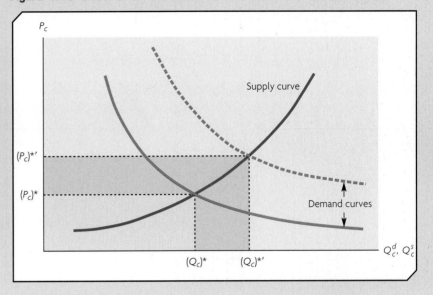

Figure 1.10 *Effect of an Increase in Demand on the Coffee Market*

In Figure 1.9, the coffee market cleared at the price $(P_c)^*$ and quantity $(P_c)^*$. An increase in income, Y, or in the price of tea, P_T, raises the demand for coffee. Therefore, the demand curve shifts rightward from the solid red curve to the dashed red curve. The market-clearing price of coffee rises to $(P_c)^{*\prime}$, and the market-clearing quantity of coffee rises to $(Q_c)^{*\prime}$.

we referred to two exogenous variables: income, Y, and the price of tea, P_T.[4] For supply, we mentioned as exogenous variables the weather conditions in coffee-producing areas, such as Brazil.

Figure 1.10 shows how an increase in demand affects the coffee market. The rise in demand could reflect an increase in income, Y, or the price of tea, P_T. We represent the increase in demand by a rightward shift of the demand curve. That is, consumers want to buy more coffee at any given price, P_c. We see from the diagram that the market-clearing price rises from $(P_c)^*$ to $(P_c)^{*\prime}$, and the market-clearing quantity increases from $(Q_c)^*$ to $(Q_c)^{*\prime}$. Thus, our model of the coffee market predicts that increases in Y or P_T raise P_c and Q_c. As in the diagram in Figure 1.6, the model tells us how changes in the exogenous variables affect the endogenous variables.

Figure 1.11 shows how a decrease in supply affects the coffee market. The reduction in supply could reflect poor weather conditions in coffee-producing areas, such as Brazil and Colombia. We represent the decrease in supply by a leftward shift of the supply curve. That is,

---

[4] From a broader perspective that encompasses the tea market and the overall economy, the price of tea, P_T, and incomes would also be endogenous variables. This broader analysis is called general-equilibrium theory—that is, it considers the conditions for the clearing of all markets simultaneously. The limitation to a single market, such as the one for coffee, is an example of partial-equilibrium analysis. In this case, we assess the clearing of the coffee market while taking as given the outcomes in the other markets.

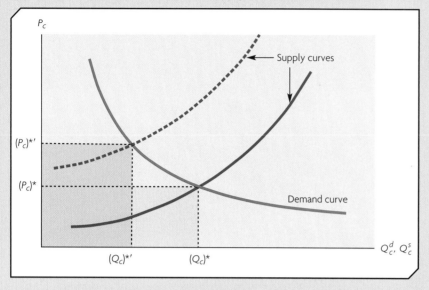

Figure 1.11 *Effect of a Decrease in Supply on the Coffee Market*

In Figure 1.9, the coffee market cleared at the price $(P_c)^*$ and quantity $(Q_c)^*$. A harvest failure in Brazil reduces the supply of coffee. Therefore, the supply curve shifts leftward from the solid blue curve to the dashed blue curve. The market-clearing price of coffee rises to $(P_c)^{*\prime}$, and the market-clearing quantity of coffee falls to $(Q_c)^{*\prime}$.

producers want to sell less coffee at any given price, P_c. We see from the diagram that the market-clearing price rises from $(P_c)^*$ to $(P_c)^{*\prime}$, and the market-clearing quantity decreases from $(Q_c)^*$ to $(Q_c)^{*\prime}$. Thus, our model of the coffee market predicts that a poor coffee harvest raises P_c and lowers Q_c.

Table 1.1 summarizes the results from the market-clearing model of the coffee market. As in Figure 1.6, the model tells us how changes in the exogenous variables affect the endogenous variables.

Our macroeconomic model will use this kind of market-clearing analysis to predict how changes in exogenous variables affect the endogenous macroeconomic variables. However, we will not study an array of goods, such as coffee, tea, and so on. Rather, we will consider the aggregate demand for and supply of a composite good that corresponds to the economy's overall output, the real GDP. We will also analyze the demand for and supply of factors of production—labor and capital services.

Flexible Versus Sticky Prices

When we studied the market for coffee, we focused on market-clearing conditions. Therefore, when an exogenous variable changed, we based our predictions on how

this change altered the market-clearing price and quantity. The assumption that underlies this analysis is that the price of coffee adjusts rapidly to clear the market for coffee—that is, to equate the quantity demanded to the quantity supplied. We observed that, if the price differed from its market-clearing value, either demanders or suppliers of coffee could not be satisfied in their offers to buy or sell at the established price. Consequently, there was always pressure for the coffee price to adjust toward its market-clearing value—the market-clearing price was the only equilibrium price.

Although most economists accept the focus on market-clearing prices when analyzing coffee or similar products, there is less agreement on whether macroeconomics should focus on market-clearing conditions. In particular, not all economists agree that we should consider only situations of market clearing in the market for the composite good that represents real GDP or in the market for labor. For long-run analysis, there is a consensus that the market-clearing framework provides the best guide to how an economy operates. Therefore, in our study of long-run economic growth in Chapters 3–5, we use a market-clearing, equilibrium approach. However, for analyses of short-run macroeconomic fluctuations, there is a sharp divide among economists as to whether a market-clearing model provides useful insights.

The famous economist John Maynard Keynes, writing in the wake of the Great Depression in the 1930s, argued that the labor market typically did not clear—he thought that the labor market was usually in a state of **disequilibrium**, by which he meant a discrepancy between the quantities of labor demanded and supplied. In particular, he argued that wage rates were sticky and adjusted only slowly to generate equality between the quantities

Table 1.1 *Effects of Changes in Exogenous Variables on the Endogenous Variables in the Coffee Market*

Change in Exogenous Variable	Effect on P_c	Effect on Q_c
Increase in income, Y	rises	rises
Increase in price of tea, P_T	rises	rises
Poor coffee harvest	*rises*	*falls*

of labor demanded and supplied. More recently, some macroeconomists have emphasized instead the tendency of some goods markets to be in disequilibrium. This approach, called the **new Keynesian model**, argues that some prices are sticky and move only slowly to equate the quantities of goods demanded and supplied.

Other economists argue that an equilibrium approach, which relies on market-clearing conditions, gives us the best insights into short-run economic fluctuations. This approach applies the same methodology to short-run fluctuations that most economists apply to long-run economic growth. Wages and prices are viewed as sufficiently flexible in the short run so that a useful macroeconomic analysis can concentrate on market-clearing situations. As in our analysis of the coffee market (summarized in Table 1.1), we can then focus on how changes in exogenous variables affect market-clearing quantities and prices.

One point that seems clear is that we cannot understand or evaluate sticky-price models unless we have the flexible-price, market-clearing model as a benchmark. After all, macroeconomists agree that the economy is always approaching the market-clearing position—that is why this setting is the one typically used to study long-run economic growth. A reasonable inference is that, whatever the ultimate verdict on the significance of sticky prices in the short run, it is best to begin macroeconomic analysis with a market-clearing model.

We set out the basic market-clearing model of economic fluctuations in Chapters 6–10. We call this model an equilibrium business-cycle model (a broader term than "real business-cycle model," which often appears

AP Images

in the economics literature). We extend the model to allow for inflation in Chapter 11 and for government spending, taxes, and fiscal deficits in Chapters 12–14. Chapter 15 allows for misperceptions about prices and wages but continues to assume a market-clearing framework. Only in Chapter 16 are we ready to assess the sticky wages and prices that are the hallmarks of Keynesian and new Keynesian models.

CHAPTER 2

National-Income Accounting: Gross Domestic Product and the Price Level

© iStockphoto.com/Scott Leigh

I n Chapter 1, we used terms such as "gross domestic product (GDP)" and the "price level" without defining them precisely. Now, by looking at national-income accounting, we develop the meanings of these terms. Many challenging issues arise in the construction of the national-income accounts. However, for our purposes, we will deal only with the basic concepts.

Nominal and Real GDP

We begin with the gross domestic product (GDP). **Nominal GDP** measures the dollar (or euro, etc.) value of all the goods and services that an economy produces during a specified period, such as a year. For example, in 2005, the U.S. nominal GDP was US$12.5 trillion. The nominal GDP is a **flow variable**: It measures the dollar amount of goods produced per unit of time, such as a year.

Consider the definition of nominal GDP one step at a time. The word "nominal" means that the goods produced during a year are measured as values in dollars (or in units of another currency, such as euros). For most goods and services—pencils, automobiles, haircuts, and so on—the dollar value is determined by the price at which these items sell in the marketplace.

Some goods and services, including many produced by governments, are not exchanged on markets. For example, the government does not sell its services for national defense, the justice system, and police. These items enter into nominal GDP at their nominal (dollar) cost of production. This treatment is problematic because it amounts to assuming that government employees experience no changes over time in their productivity. However, in the absence of market prices, it is unclear what alternative approach would be more accurate.

Another item, owner-occupied housing, enters into GDP as an estimate of what this housing would fetch on the market if the owner rented the property to another person. This amount is called the **imputed rental income** on owner-occupied housing. Conceptually, the same approach ought to apply to consumer durables, such as households' automobiles, furniture, and appliances. However, this treatment has not been followed; that is, the GDP does not include the estimated rental income on consumer durables.[1] For government-owned

---

[1] The capital owned by businesses (such as factories and machinery) contributes to the goods and services produced by the businesses. Therefore, the market value of output already includes the rental income on business capital. For this reason, it is unnecessary for measures of GDP to include an imputed rental income on business capital.

property, the assumption in the national accounts is that the imputed rental income equals the estimated depreciation. This assumption is troublesome, but, again, a preferred alternative method is not obvious.

It is important to understand that the nominal GDP includes the value of the goods and services produced during a specified time interval, such as a year. That is, GDP measures current production. For example, if an automaker manufactures and sells a new car in 2007, the full value of the car counts in the GDP for 2007. However, if someone sells in 2007 a used car that was built in 2006, this sale does not count in the GDP for 2007.

The nominal GDP can be misleading because it depends on the overall level of prices, as well as on the physical quantity of goods produced. Table 2.1 illustrates this problem. Think about a simple economy that produces only butter and golf balls. The table shows the hypothetical quantities and prices of these goods in 2006 and 2007. In 2006, the economy produces 50 pounds of butter, which sell at $2.00 per pound. Thus, the dollar value of 2006's butter output is $100. In 2006, the economy also produces 400 golf balls, priced at $1.00 per ball, for a golf-ball output of $400. The nominal GDP for 2006 is the sum of the

Table 2.1 *The Calculation of Nominal and Real GDP: A Simple Example*

	2006a	**2006b**	**2007a**	**2007b**
Prices				
butter	$2.00 per pound	$2.00 per pound	$3.00 per pound	$1.50 per pound
golf balls	$1.00 per ball	$1.00 per ball	$1.10 per ball	$0.89 per ball
Quantities				
butter	50 pounds	50 pounds	40 pounds	70 pounds
golf balls	400 balls	400 balls	391 balls	500 balls
Nominal Market Values				
butter	100	100	120	105
golf balls	400	400	430	445
nominal GDP	500	500	550	550
2006–07 Average Price				
butter	$2.50 per pound	$1.75 per pound	$2.50 per pound	$1.75 per pound
golf balls	$1.05 per ball	$0.945 per ball	$1.05 per ball	$0.945 per ball
Market Values at 2006–07 Average Prices				
butter	125.0	87.5	100.0	122.5
golf balls	420.0	378.0	410.6	472.5
total	545.0	465.5	510.6	595.0
ratio to 2005	1.0	1.0	0.937	1.278
Chained Real GDP, 2006 Base	500.0	500.0	468.5	639.0
Implicit GDP Deflator, 2006 Base	100	100	117	86

dollar values of butter and golf-ball output: $100 + $400 = $500.

The columns labeled 2007a and 2007b show two possibilities for prices and quantities in 2007. In case *a*, the prices of both goods rise—to $3.00 per pound of butter and $1.10 per golf ball. In case *b*, the prices of both goods decline—to $1.50 per pound of butter and $0.89 per golf ball. In case *a*, the quantities of both goods decline—to 40 pounds of butter and 391 golf balls. In case *b*, the quantities of both goods rise—to 70 pounds of butter and 500 golf balls.

We have assumed numbers so that the nominal GDP in 2007 is the same in both cases. In case *a*, the nominal GDP is $120 for butter plus $430 for golf balls, for a total of $550. In case *b*, the nominal GDP is $105 for butter plus $445 for golf balls, for a total again of $550. However, the quantities of both goods are higher in case *b* than case *a*. Thus, any sensible measure of real GDP in 2007 would show a higher value in case *b* than case *a*. Thus, the equality of the nominal GDPs is misleading. Identical figures on nominal GDP can conceal very different underlying differences in levels of production.

Calculating Real GDP

Economists solve the problem of changing price levels by constructing measures of real GDP. Until recently, the most common way to compute real GDP was to multiply each year's quantity of output of each good by the price of the good in a base year, such as 2000. Then all of these multiples were added to get the economy's aggregate real GDP. The resulting aggregate is called "GDP in 2000 dollars" (if 2000 is the base year). Or, sometimes, the result is called **GDP in constant dollars**, because we use prices (for the base year, 2000) that do not vary over time. In contrast, the nominal GDP is sometimes called **GDP in current dollars**, because this calculation of GDP uses each good's price in the current year.

Since the prices from the base year (say, 2000) do not vary over time, the method just described provides a reasonable measure of changes over time in the overall level of production. That is, it provides a sensible measure of real GDP. However, a shortcoming of this approach is that it weights the outputs of the various goods by their prices in the base year, which happened to be 2000. For example, suppose that a personal computer costs more than a couch in 2000.

In this case, each computer produced in 2007 (of the same quality as ones produced in 2000) would count more than each couch for 2007's real GDP, even though computers were then cheaper than couches. More generally, the base-year weights become less relevant over time as relative prices of goods change. The response of the Bureau of Economic Analysis (BEA, a part of the U.S. Commerce Department) had been to make frequent shifts in the base year. However, a more accurate solution, called the chain-weighted method, was adopted in the mid-1990s to get a better measure of real GDP. The resulting variable is called **chain-weighted real GDP**. This chain-weighted measure is the one publicized in the media, and it is the one we shall use in this book to measure real GDP.

To illustrate how chain-weighting works, we can again use our hypothetical data for a simple economy from Table 2.1. The method starts by computing the average price of each good for two adjacent years—2006 and 2007 in the table. For example, in scenario *a*, the average price of butter for 2006 and 2007 is $2.50 per pound. In scenario *b*, it is $1.75 per pound.

In each year—2006 and 2007 in the table—the quantities produced of each good are multiplied by the average prices for the two adjacent years. For example, in case *a*, the value of the butter produced in 2006 is $125 when calculated at the average price for 2006 and 2007, compared to $100 when the (lower) price for 2006 is used. For 2007, in case *a*, the value of the butter is $100 when computed at the average price, compared to $120 when the (higher) price for 2007 is used.

Using these average-price numbers, we sum the values of the goods produced in each year to get the totals shown in Table 2.1. For example, for 2006, in case *a*, the total dollar value is $545, compared to $500 when we used prices for 2006. For 2007, in case *a*, the total dollar value is $510.60, compared to $550 when we used prices for 2007.

Next we compute the ratios of each of these totals to the totals for 2006. Thus, the ratios are 1.0 for the two cases (*a* and *b*) that apply to 2006. For 2007, the ratio is 0.937 in case *a* and 1.278 in case *b*.

To get chained real GDP on a 2006 base, we multiply the ratios just calculated by the nominal GDP ($500) for 2006. Thus, chained real GDP for 2006 on a 2006 base is the same as nominal GDP—$500 (for cases *a* and *b*). For 2007, chained real GDP on a 2006 base is $468.5 in case *a* and $639.0 in case *b*.

Thus, although the nominal GDPs for 2007 are the same, the chained real GDP is substantially higher in case *b*. This result makes sense because the quantities of butter and golf balls are both higher in case *b* than in case *a*.

We can proceed the same way for other years. For example, when we get data for 2008, we can calculate the ratio of the value of output in 2008 to that for 2007. These ratios are analogous to those calculated for 2007 compared to 2006 in Table 2.1. We then want to express the results for 2008 on a 2006 base, so that all the chained values apply to the same base year. To do this, we multiply the ratio for 2008 compared to 2007 by the ratio for 2007 compared to 2006. This gives us the ratio of 2008 values to 2006 values. Finally, we multiply the last ratio by nominal GDP for 2006 to get the chain-weighted GDP for 2008 on a 2006 base. This procedure is called *chain-linking*. If we carry out this procedure from one year to the next, we end up with a time series for chain-weighted real GDP expressed in terms of a single base year.

In Table 2.1, the base year for chain-weighted real GDP is 2006. However, the actual base year used by the Bureau of Economic Analysis in the early 2000s was 2000. With the chain method, the choice of which year to use for the base is not important. We use a single base year only to ensure that the real GDPs for each year are comparable. (The ratio of chain-weighted real GDPs for two years, such as 2006 and 2007, is the same for any choice of base year.)

We can use the results on real GDP to construct an index for the overall level of prices. In Table 2.1, where 2006 is the base year, we can think of the overall price level for 2006 as "100." This number is arbitrary; it just serves as a comparative position that can be related to price levels in other years.

For case *a* in 2007, the nominal GDP is $550, and the chain-weighted real GDP on a 2006 base is $468.50. We can think of an implicit price level used to convert a dollar value—the nominal GDP of $550—into a real value—the real GDP of $468.50:

$$(nominal\ GDP)/(implicit\ price\ level) = real\ GDP$$

If we rearrange the terms in the equation, we have

$$implicit\ price\ level = (nominal\ GDP)/(real\ GDP)$$

For example, for 2007 in case *a*, in Table 2.1, we have

$$implicit\ price\ level = (550/468.50) = 1.17$$

In contrast, for 2007 in case *b*, we have

$$implicit\ price\ level = (550/639.0) = 0.86$$

The numbers 1.17 and 0.86 do not mean anything as absolute magnitudes. However, they have meaning when compared with similarly calculated price levels for other years. As mentioned, the usual convention is to think of a price index that takes on the value 100 for the base year, which is 2006 in our example. When compared to this base, the price level for 2007 in case *a* is $1.17 \times 100 = 117$, whereas in case *b* it is $0.86 \times 100 = 86$. These values are shown in Table 2.1. The usual name for these price indexes is the **implicit GDP deflator** (on a 2006 base). That is, these values are the ones implicitly used to convert from nominal GDP to real GDP (on a 2006 base).

Real GDP as a Measure of Welfare

Although real GDP reveals a lot about an economy's overall performance, it is not a perfect measure of welfare. Some of the shortcomings of real GDP from a welfare standpoint include:

- The aggregate real GDP does not consider changes in the distribution of income.
- The calculated real GDP excludes most nonmarket goods. The exclusions include legal and illegal transactions in the "underground economy," as well as services that people perform in their homes. For example, if a person cares for his or her child at home, the real GDP excludes this service. But if the person hires someone to care for the child at home or at a day-care center, the real GDP includes the service.
- Real GDP assigns no value to leisure time.
- Measured real GDP does not consider environmental damage, such as air and water quality, except to the extent that this pollution affects the market value of output.

Despite these shortcomings, the real GDP tells us a lot about how an economy's standard of living changes over time. It also allows us to compare standards of living across countries. Measured real GDP helps us to understand short-run economic fluctuations as well as long-term economic development.

Alternative Views of GDP—Expenditure, Income, and Production

e can think about GDP in three different ways. First, we can consider expenditure on goods and services produced domestically by households, businesses, government, and foreigners. Second, we can calculate the incomes earned domestically in the production of goods and services—compensation of employees, rental income, corporate profits, and so on. Finally, we can measure the domestic production of goods and services by industry—agriculture, manufacturing, wholesale and retail trade, and so on. An important point is that all three approaches will end up with the same totals for nominal and real GDP. To see this, we take up each approach in turn, beginning with the breakdown by type of expenditure.

Measuring GDP by Expenditure

The national accounts divide GDP into four parts, depending on who or what buys the goods or services. The four sectors are households, businesses, all levels of government, and foreigners. Table 2.2 shows the details of this breakdown for 2005. The first column lists values in current (2005) dollars, and the second column expresses each amount as a percentage of nominal GDP. The third column shows each value as chained real dollars in terms of the base year, 2000. The nominal GDP for

Table 2.2 *Expenditure Components of U.S. Gross Domestic Product in 2005*

Category of Expenditure	Trillions of Dollars	% of Nominal GDP	Trillions of Chained 2000 Dollars
Gross domestic product	**12.49**	**100.0**	**11.13**
Personal consumption expenditure	**8.75**	**70.0**	**7.86**
durable goods	1.03	8.2	1.14
nondurable goods	2.56	20.5	2.30
services	5.15	41.3	4.44
Gross private domestic investment	**2.10**	**16.9**	**1.92**
fixed investment	2.09	16.7	1.90
nonresidential	1.33	10.7	1.29
residential	0.76	6.1	0.60
change in business inventories	0.02	0.0	0.02
Government purchases*	**2.36**	**18.9**	**1.99**
federal	0.88	7.0	0.74
state and local	1.49	11.9	1.25
Net exports of goods and services	**−0.73**	**−5.8**	**−0.63**
exports	1.30	10.4	1.20
imports	2.03	16.2	1.83

Source: Bureau of Economic Analysis (*http://www.bea.gov*).

* This category corresponds in the national accounts to government consumption and investment. The national-accounts category includes depreciation of government capital stocks.

2005 of $12.49 trillion corresponds to $11.13 trillion in 2000 dollars. If we make these calculations for other years, we can compare across years to see how real GDP has changed over time.

1. Personal consumption expenditure. The purchases of goods and services by households for consumption purposes are called **personal consumption expenditure**. This variable, like GDP, is a flow concept. Thus, nominal personal consumption expenditure has units of dollars per year. This spending typically accounts for more than half of GDP. For example, Table 2.2 shows that, in 2005, the nominal personal consumption expenditure of $8.75 trillion was 70% of the nominal GDP of $12.49 trillion.

The national accounts distinguish purchases of consumer goods that are used up quickly, such as toothpaste and various services, from those that last for a substantial time, such as automobiles and furniture. The first group is called **consumer nondurables and services**, and the second is called **consumer durables**. An important point is that consumer durables yield a flow of services for an extended period. An automobile, for instance, can be used by the owner for many years or can be sold or rented to another driver. Therefore, purchases of consumer durables can be viewed as a type of investment. Table 2.2 shows the division of personal consumption expenditure among durable goods, nondurable goods, and services. In 2005, the nominal spending on durables of $1.03 trillion constituted 12% of total nominal personal consumption expenditure.

The third column of Table 2.2 reports the components of GDP in chained 2000 dollars. For example, the nominal personal consumption expenditure of $8.75 trillion in 2005 corresponds to $7.86 trillion in 2000 dollars. If we apply this calculation to other years, we can compute the changes over time in real personal consumption expenditure or in the other real components of GDP. However, there are difficulties in comparing the level of real personal consumption expenditure in a given year with the level of real GDP in the same year. As already mentioned, the nominal personal consumption expenditure for 2005 was 70% of nominal GDP. However, a comparison of real personal consumption expenditure with real GDP depends on which base year one happens to use. The reason is that the comparison of real consumer expenditure with real GDP depends on the changes in relative prices that occurred between the base year (say, 2000) and the comparison year (say, 2005). In particular, the results depend on how prices of items contained in personal consumption expenditure changed compared to the prices of the other items that entered into GDP.

2. Gross private domestic investment. The second major category of GDP is **gross private domestic investment**. Investment, like personal consumption expenditure, is a flow variable, measured in dollars per year. The "fixed" part of gross private domestic investment comprises purchases by domestic businesses of new capital goods, such as factories and machinery. These capital goods are durables, which serve as inputs to production for many years. Thus, these goods are analogous to the consumer durables that we already mentioned. In fact, in the national accounts, an individual's purchase of a new home—which might be considered the ultimate consumer durable—is counted as part of fixed business investment, rather than personal consumption expenditure.

Gross private domestic investment is the sum of fixed investment and the net change in businesses' **inventories** of goods. In 2005, this net inventory change was a comparatively small amount, $0.02 trillion. The total nominal gross private domestic investment was $2.10 trillion, which constituted 17% of nominal GDP.

One common error about national-income accounting arises because the spending on new physical capital is called "investment." This terminology differs from the concept of investment used in normal conversation, where investment refers to the allocation of financial assets among stocks, bonds, real estate, and so on. When economists refer to a business's investment, they mean the business's purchases of newly produced goods, such as a factory or machine.

Another point about investment concerns **depreciation**. The stock of capital goods is the outstanding quantity of goods in the form of factories, machinery, and so on. Thus, the capital stock is a **stock variable**, measured as a quantity of goods. Since capital goods wear out or depreciate over time, a part of gross investment merely replaces the old capital that has depreciated. Depreciation is a flow variable—the dollar value of the goods that wear out per year. Depreciation is comparable in units to GDP and gross private domestic investment.

The difference between gross private domestic investment and depreciation—called **net private domestic investment**—is the net change in the value of the stock of physical capital goods. The GDP includes gross private domestic investment. If we replace this gross investment by net investment (by subtracting depreciation), we also subtract depreciation from

GDP. The difference between GDP and depreciation is called **net domestic product (NDP)**. The NDP is a useful concept because it measures GDP net of the spending needed to replace worn-out or depreciated capital goods.

3. Government purchases of goods and services. The third component of GDP is government purchases of goods and services.[2] This category includes consumption outlays (such as salaries of military personnel and public-school teachers), as well as public investment (such as purchases of new buildings). One important point is that the government sector includes all levels of government, whether federal, state, or local. Another point is that government purchases of goods and services exclude transfers, such as payments to Social Security retirees and welfare recipients. These transfers do not represent payments for currently produced goods and services. Therefore, these outlays do not appear in GDP. In 2005, nominal government purchases of goods and services totaled $2.36 trillion, or 19% of nominal GDP.

4. Exports and imports. Some of the goods and services produced domestically are exported to foreign users. These **exports** of goods and services must be added to domestic purchases to compute the economy's total domestic production (GDP). Foreigners also produce goods and services that are imported into the home country—for use by households, businesses, and government. These **imports** of goods and services must be subtracted from domestic purchases to calculate the economy's total production (GDP). The foreign component therefore appears in GDP as **net exports**: the difference between spending of foreigners on domestic production (exports) and spending by domestic residents on foreign production (imports). Net exports may be greater than zero or less than zero. Table 2.2 shows that, in 2005, net nominal exports were −$0.73 trillion, or −5.8% of nominal GDP. The net export component breaks down into $1.30 trillion of exports (10.4% of GDP) less $2.03 trillion of imports (16.2% of GDP).

Economists often use a theoretical model that omits net exports. Then the model applies to a **closed economy**, which has no trade linkages to the rest of the world. In contrast, an economy that is linked through trade to the rest of the world is called an **open economy**. Reasons for using a closed-economy model include the following:

- It simplifies the analysis.
- At least for the United States, exports and imports have been small compared to GDP, so that not too much error arises from ignoring international trade. This point was reasonably persuasive in 1950, when exports and imports were each only 4% of GDP. However, the point is less convincing for 2005, when exports were 10% of GDP and imports were 16% of GDP.
- The world as a whole really is a closed economy, so we have to carry out a closed-economy analysis to assess the world economy.

We follow the closed-economy tradition of macroeconomics until Chapter 17, which allows for international trade.

Measuring GDP by Income

Another way to look at GDP is in terms of the income earned by various factors of production. This concept is called **national income**. To make clear the relation between production and income, we can think of a simple

© Juice Images/Fotolia

[2] The national accounts refer to this category as "government consumption and investment." Government consumption includes an estimate of rental income on existing government capital. However, as already mentioned, the assumption is that this rental income coincides with the estimated depreciation of government capital stocks. Therefore, "government consumption and investment" in the national accounts adds depreciation of government capital to the category "government purchases of goods and services."

Table 2.3 *Hypothetical Data for Calculation of National Income*

Type of Revenue	Amount	Type of Cost or Profit	Amount
Bakery (produces final good)			
Sale of bread	$600	Labor	$200
		Flour	350
		Profit	50
		Total cost & profit	$600
Mill (produces intermediate good)			
Sale of flour	$350	Labor	$250
		Profit	100
		Total cost & profit	$350

closed economy that has only two businesses. One, a mill, uses only labor to produce flour. The second, a bakery, uses flour and labor to produce bread. Bread is the only final product. Flour is the only intermediate product—it is used up entirely in the production of the final good, bread. Notice that, to simplify matters, we are ignoring capital inputs, such as factories and machines.

Income statements for the two businesses appear in Table 2.3. The nominal GDP for this economy is the value of the final product, bread, of $600. This amount is also the revenue of the bakery. The income statement shows that the costs and profit for the bakery break down into $350 for flour, $200 for labor (for workers in the bakery), and $50 for profit (of the bakery). For the mill, the $350 of revenue goes for $250 of labor (for workers at the mill) and $100 for profit (of the mill). The national income equals the total labor income of $450 plus the total profit of $150, or $600. Thus, in this simple economy, national income equals GDP.

Notice that the GDP counts the value of the final product, bread, of $600, but does not count separately the value of the flour, $350. The flour is used up in the production of bread—that is, the $600 in bread sales already takes into account the $350 cost of the intermediate good, flour. If we added the $350 in sales of flour to the $600 in sales of bread, we would *double-count* the contribution of the intermediate good, flour. To put it another way, the **value added** by

the bakery is only $250—sales of $600 less payments for flour of $350. The value added by the mill is the full $350, because we assumed that the mill uses no intermediate goods. Therefore, if we combine the value added of $350 for the mill with the value added of $250 for the bakery, we get the GDP of $600. Hence, GDP equals the sum of value added from all sectors. The national income in this simple economy equals the GDP and, therefore, also equals the sum of value added from all sectors.

Table 2.4 shows the breakdown of U.S. national income in 2005. The total nominal national income was $10.90 trillion. Although the method for computing national income is conceptually the same as that in Table 2.3, the U.S. economy includes additional forms of income. The largest part of U.S. national income was compensation of employees—$7.13 trillion, or 65% of the total. This component is analogous to the labor income shown in Table 2.3.

Several parts of the U.S. national income in Table 2.4 represent income that accrues to capital. These amounts did not appear in Table 2.3 because we did not consider that the bakery and mill each have capital equipment, such as machinery, that contributes to the production of goods. In the U.S. national accounts, the categories of income from capital comprise rental income of persons, corporate profits, and net interest. The total of $1.92 trillion represented 18% of national income.

Table 2.4 *U.S. National Income by Type in 2005*

Type of Income	Trillions of Dollars	% of National Income
National income	**10.90**	**100.0**
Compensation of employees	7.13	65.3
Proprietors' income	0.94	8.6
Rental income of persons	0.07	0.7
Corporate profits	1.35	12.4
Net interest	0.50	4.6
Taxes on production	0.90	8.3
Less: subsidies	(0.06)	(0.5)
Business transfers	0.08	0.7
Surplus of government enterprises	(0.01)	0.0

Source: Bureau of Economic Analysis (*http://www.bea.gov*).

The U.S. national income for 2005 also includes proprietors' income of $0.94 trillion (9% of the total). This income represents payments to self-employed persons, including unincorporated businesses. This income represents a mix of payments to labor and capital. The breakdown into labor and capital is unknown, although economists have made estimates.

Taxes on production—sales, excise, and value-added (VAT)[3]—are included in market prices of goods. Therefore, these taxes on production appear in GDP, which is calculated from market values of output. The tax revenues are also part of government revenue—therefore, these revenues enter into national income as income of the government sector. Subsidies paid to producers by government amount to negative production taxes. Therefore, subsidies enter with a negative sign in national income. In 2005, the total of taxes on production less subsidies was $0.85 trillion, or 8% of national income.[4]

1. Differences between GDP and national income. In the simplified economy of Table 2.3, GDP and national income were equal. In practice, divergences between GDP and national income reflect two main items: income receipts and payments involving the rest of the world, and depreciation of capital stocks. We take up these two items in turn.

The U.S. GDP is the value of goods and services produced within the United States. The U.S. national income is the income received by all sectors residing in the United States. One source of divergence between GDP and national income is that residents of the United States receive income from the rest of the world. The main item is the income on capital (assets) owned by U.S. residents but located abroad. A secondary part is labor income of U.S. residents working abroad. The total of this "factor income from abroad" in 2005 was $0.51 trillion, as shown in Table 2.5. The counterpart to the U.S. factor income from abroad is the U.S. payments to factors located abroad. These payments are to capital (assets) located in the United States but owned by foreigners and to foreigners working in the United States. The total of these payments to the rest of the world in 2005 was $0.47 trillion. The **net factor income from abroad** is the difference between U.S.

---

[3] The value-added tax is important in many countries but does not exist in the United States.

[4] The U.S. national income for 2005 also includes two minor components: business's net transfers to households and government ($0.08 trillion, or 1% of national income) and the surplus of government enterprises (which was close to zero).

Table 2.5 *Relations Between U.S. GDP and Income in 2005*

Category of Product or Income	Trillions of Dollars
Gross domestic product (GDP)	**12.49**
Plus: income receipts from rest of world	0.51
Less: income payments to rest of world	(0.47)
Equals: Gross national product (GNP)	**12.52**
Less: depreciation of capital stock	(1.57)
Equals: Net national product (NNP)	**10.95**
Less: statistical discrepancy	(0.04)
Equals: National income	**10.90**
Less: corporate profits, taxes on production, contributions for social insurance, net interest, business transfers, surplus of government enterprises	(3.64)
Plus: personal income receipts on assets, personal transfer payments	2.98
Equals: Personal income	**10.25**
Less: personal taxes	(1.21)
Equals: Disposable personal income	**9.04**

Source: Bureau of Economic Analysis (*http://www.bea.gov*).

income receipts from the rest of the world and U.S. income payments to the rest of the world: $0.51 trillion less $0.47 trillion, or $0.04 trillion. The addition of this amount to the GDP of $12.49 trillion yields the **gross national product (GNP)** of $12.52 trillion, as shown in Table 2.5. The GNP gives the total gross income to U.S. factors of production, whether located in the United States or abroad.

One part of U.S. GDP covers the depreciation of the fixed capital stock located in the United States. This depreciation does not show up as income for factors of production. In particular, depreciation is subtracted from gross business revenue to calculate corporate profits or proprietors' income. If we subtract from GNP the estimated depreciation of $1.57 trillion, we get the net national product (NNP) for 2005 of $10.95 trillion. Aside from a statistical discrepancy (–$0.04 trillion in 2005), the NNP corresponds to national income. Thus, Table 2.5 shows how we get to the national income of $10.90 trillion, the number that we saw before in Table 2.4.

2. Personal income and personal disposable income. We can also calculate the income that households

receive directly, a concept called **personal income**. The route from national income to personal income involves a number of adjustments. First, only a portion of corporate profits are paid out as dividends to households. The other part is called *retained earnings*. Second, personal income excludes contributions for government social-insurance programs, because individuals do not receive these contributions directly as income. Other adjustments involve transfer payments and the surplus of government enterprises. Table 2.5 lists the various items. The personal income for 2005 of $10.25 trillion turned out to be $0.65 trillion less than national income.

We can also compute the income that households have left after paying personal taxes, which include individual income taxes and property taxes. (Some other levies—production taxes and contributions for social insurance—were already deducted to calculate personal income.) Personal income after taxes is called **disposable personal income**. In 2005, personal taxes were $1.21 trillion. Deducting this amount from the personal income of $10.25 trillion leads to the disposable personal income of $9.04 trillion, as shown in Table 2.5.

Measuring GDP by Production

We can also break down national income in accordance with the sectors of production that generate the income. Table 2.6 shows this breakdown for the United States in 2005.

The total national income of $10.89 trillion[5] in 2005 breaks down into $10.86 trillion from domestic industries and $0.03 trillion from the rest of the world. The last item is the net factor income from abroad. For the domestic industries, $9.56 trillion, or 88% of national income, comes from the private sector, and $1.30 trillion, or 12%, comes from government (federal, state, and local).

Table 2.6 shows how the $9.56 trillion of income from private industries divides into 14 sectors. The largest shares are 19% in finance, insurance, and real estate; 16% in professional and business services; 14% in manufacturing; 10% in education, health care, and social assistance; 9% in retail trade; 7% in wholesale trade; 6% in construction; 4% in arts, entertainment, recreation, accommodation, and food services; 4% in information; and 3% in transportation. Note that agriculture and mining together constitute only 2.5% of the total.

Table 2.6 *U.S. National Income by Sector in 2005*

Sector of Production	Trillions of Dollars	% of National Income
National income	10.89	100.0
Net factor income from abroad	0.03	0.3
Domestic industries	10.86	99.7
Government	1.30	12.0
Private industries	9.56	87.7
		% of Private National Income
Agriculture, forestry, fishing, hunting	0.08	0.8
Mining	0.16	1.7
Utilities	0.18	1.9
Construction	0.61	6.4
Manufacturing	1.34	14.0
Wholesale trade	0.68	7.2
Retail trade	0.84	8.8
Transportation, warehousing	0.32	3.3
Information	0.39	4.1
Finance, insurance, real estate, rental, leasing	1.86	19.4
Professional and business services	1.48	15.5
Education, health care, social assistance	0.95	9.9
Arts, entertainment, recreation, accommodation, food services	0.40	4.2
Other private services	0.26	2.9

Source: Bureau of Economic Analysis (*http://www.bea.gov*).

[5] This total differs slightly from the national income of $10.90 trillion shown in Tables 2.4 and 2.5 because of a differing treatment of depreciation.

Seasonal Adjustment

Data on GDP and its components are available for the United States and most other countries on a quarterly basis. These data allow us to study economic fluctuations at a quarterly frequency. However, one problem with the raw data is that they include sizeable systematic variations due to seasonal factors. The typical pattern is that U.S. real GDP rises during a calendar year and reaches a peak in the fourth quarter (October–December). Then real GDP usually falls sharply in the first quarter of the next year (January–March) before rebounding from the second to the fourth quarters.

The seasonal fluctuations in real GDP and other macroeconomic variables reflect the influences of weather and holidays (notably the Christmas period and summer vacations). For most purposes, we want to use the national-accounts data to study economic fluctuations that reflect factors other than normal seasonal patterns. For this reason, the BEA adjusts real GDP and its components to filter out the typical seasonal variation. Variables adjusted this way are called **seasonally adjusted data**. The national-accounts information reported in the news media and used for most macroeconomic analyses comes in this seasonally adjusted form. We use seasonally adjusted quarterly data in this book to analyze economic fluctuations.

Seasonal adjustments apply also to many of the monthly variables reported in the news media and used for macroeconomic analyses. These variables include employment and unemployment, labor earnings, industrial production, retail sales, and the consumer price index.[6] When we discuss these monthly variables in this book, we refer to seasonally adjusted data.

Prices

We already discussed how the computation of chained real GDP generates an implicit price deflator for the GDP. The resulting series gives us a good measure of an overall price index. That is, we get a price index that matches up with the overall market basket of goods and services produced domestically. We can also use this approach to get implicit price deflators for the components of GDP. For example, we have a deflator for personal consumption expenditure, one for gross private domestic investment, and so on.[8]

In addition to these implicit price deflators, we have broad price indexes that the Bureau of Labor Statistics (BLS) computes directly. The most important examples are the **consumer price index (CPI)** and the **producer price index (PPI)**, which is also called the **wholesale price index**.

by*the*numbers

Gross State Product for U.S. States

We have focused on the overall U.S. GDP. It is also possible to break down GDP into amounts produced within each of the 50 U.S. states plus the District of Columbia. The value of the gross output produced in a state is called **gross state product (GSP)**. Table 2.7 shows how the total nominal U.S. GDP of $11.7 trillion in 2004 broke down by state.[7] California contributed 13.3% of U.S. GDP, New York 7.7%, Texas 7.6%, and Florida 5.1%. At the low end, Vermont, North Dakota, Wyoming, Montana, and South Dakota each had only 0.2% of U.S. GDP.

---

[6] The seasonal variation in the consumer price index turns out to be minor but is substantial in the other variables. Seasonal variation is not detectable in various interest rates, and these variables are not seasonally adjusted.

[7] The total of gross state product for the states, $11.67 trillion, is slightly less than the U.S. GDP for 2004, $11.73 trillion, because GDP includes compensation of government employees and depreciation of military capital stocks located abroad (and, therefore, not within any state).

[8] However, the deflator for government purchases of goods and services is not very useful. Since most of the government output is not sold on markets, this price deflator reflects arbitrary assumptions about costs of providing public services. The main assumption is that the productivity of government employees does not vary over time.

Table 2.7 *Gross State Product by U.S. State in 2004*

State	Gross State Product ($ billion)	% of U.S. Total	State	Gross State Product ($ billion)	% of U.S. Total
U.S.	11,666*	100.0	Missouri	203	1.7
Alabama	140	1.2	Montana	27	0.2
Alaska	34	0.3	Nebraska	68	0.6
Arizona	200	1.7	Nevada	100	0.9
Arkansas	81	0.7	New Hampshire	52	0.4
California	1551	13.3	New Jersey	416	3.6
Colorado	200	1.7	New Mexico	61	0.5
Connecticut	186	1.6	New York	897	7.7
Delaware	54	0.5	North Carolina	336	2.9
D.C.	77	0.6	North Dakota	23	0.2
Florida	599	5.1	Ohio	420	3.6
Georgia	343	2.9	Oklahoma	108	0.9
Hawaii	50	0.4	Oregon	128	1.1
Idaho	44	0.4	Pennsylvania	468	4.0
Illinois	522	4.5	Rhode Island	42	0.4
Indiana	228	2.0	South Carolina	136	1.2
Iowa	111	1.0	South Dakota	29	0.2
Kansas	99	0.8	Tennessee	218	1.9
Kentucky	136	1.2	Texas	884	7.6
Louisiana	153	1.3	Utah	83	0.7
Maine	43	0.4	Vermont	22	0.2
Maryland	228	2.0	Virginia	329	2.8
Massachusetts	318	2.7	Washington	262	2.2
Michigan	372	3.2	West Virginia	49	0.4
Minnesota	224	1.9	Wisconsin	212	1.8
Mississippi	76	0.7	Wyoming	24	0.2

Source: Bureau of Economic Analysis (*http://www.bea.gov*).

* Total is less than the 2004 GDP of $11,734 because GDP includes compensation of government employees and depreciation of military capital stocks located abroad.

The main CPI series comes from monthly and bimonthly surveys of prices of goods and services in 87 urban areas. Data are collected on roughly 80,000 items from 23,000 retail and service establishments. The CPI also includes data on rents, which come from a survey of 50,000 landlords or tenants. The index that receives the most attention applies to urban consumers, estimated to cover 87% of the overall U.S. population. The CPI is a weighted average of individual prices, where the current weights reflect expenditure shares found in the Consumer Expenditure Survey of over 30,000 individuals and families in 1993–95. These weights remain fixed from month to month, until a new survey is taken.[9]

---

[9] The CPI, which weights individual prices by the importance of goods in a prior year (such as 1993–95), is called a Laspeyres index of prices. In contrast, a price index that weights prices by the importance of goods in the current year is called a Paasche index. The old-style implicit GDP deflator, which weighted current expenditure in accordance with prices from a prior base year, turns out to be a Paasche index of prices. However, the modern version of the implicit GDP deflator is a chain-linked index, where the weights effectively change with each observation. The PPI is another example of a Laspeyres index of prices.

The CPI computed in 2006 was defined to equal 100 for the average of months in 1982–84. Thus, the CPI for March 2006 of 199.8 meant that the price of the average item rose by 99.8% from mid-1983 to March 2006. This cumulative increase in the price level corresponded to an average growth rate of the price level by 3.1% per year over the 23 years since mid-1983. That is, the inflation rate measured by the CPI was 3.1% per year. In contrast, the inflation rate computed from the implicit GDP deflator over the same period was 2.5% per year. As discussed in the box below, the higher CPI inflation rate—by 0.6% per year—probably reflects an upward bias created by the maintenance of fixed weights for long periods in the CPI market basket.

BACK TO REALITY

Problems with the Consumer Price Index

The CPI receives a lot of attention because it provides monthly information on the prices of a broad market basket of goods and services bought by households. Part of the attention arises because some public and private contracts index nominal payments to the CPI. For example, benefits paid under Social Security, payments made on the U.S. Treasury's inflation-protected securities, and bracket limits in the U.S. individual income tax adjust automatically for changes in the CPI.

Many economists think that the reported increases in the CPI overstate inflation and, hence, that the automatic adjustments of Social Security benefits and some other payments have been too large to keep the outlays fixed in real terms. Naturally, this assessment is controversial, because any repairs would have significant consequences for real transfer payments, real tax collections, and so on. The idea that changes in the CPI seriously overstate inflation was expressed in 1996 by the President's Commission on the Consumer Price Index (see Michael Boskin et al. [1996]). The Commission's conclusion was that the growth rate of the CPI exaggerated inflation on average by over one percentage point per year.

One reason for the overstatement of inflation is called *substitution bias*. The idea is that changes in supply conditions shift the relative prices of various goods and services, and households respond by shifting expenditure toward the goods and services that have become relatively cheaper. However, because the weights in the CPI are fixed for long intervals, the formula for computing the CPI responds only with a substantial lag to changes in the pattern of purchases. In particular, the CPI fails to give increasing weight to the cheaper items that tend to become more important in the typical household's expenditures. This problem is conceptually easy to fix by shifting to the chain-weighting approach described previously for the calculation of the implicit GDP deflator. This deflator is free of substitution bias because the weights change nearly continuously over time.

The BLS has constructed a chain-weighted measure of the CPI since December 1999. This series showed an annual inflation rate of 2.45% per year from December 1999 to April 2006, compared to 2.84% per year for the standard CPI over the same period. The inflation rate from the implicit GDP deflator (a chain-weighted index) over the same period was 2.41% per year—close to the chain-weighted CPI. These comparisons suggest that the substitution bias in the standard CPI led to an overstatement of inflation by around 0.4% per year.

Another, more challenging problem—which applies to the implicit GDP deflator as well as the CPI—involves quality change. Despite attempts to measure improvements in quality, these changes tend to be underestimated. Therefore, some of the price increases that are recorded as inflation should actually be viewed as increases in money spent to get better quality products.

© Kathy deWitt/Alamy

A full accounting for quality improvements would therefore lower the inflation rate. Some improved measurement has been made for goods such as automobiles, computers, houses, and television sets. Interesting proposals for measuring quality change have also been offered in the medical area, where technical advances that save lives or improve the quality of life tend to be labeled as inflation.

A different kind of quality improvement involves the retail revolution associated with the rise of Wal-Mart and other big-box stores. Because of improved efficiencies in distribution and sales, customers get merchandise at lower prices than those offered by traditional outlets. However, BLS procedures do not count the substitution of low-priced Wal-Mart goods for high-priced alternative products as decreases in prices.

Another problem is that the various price indexes do not consider the effective reductions in the price level due to the introduction of new products. For example, when personal computers or DVD players became available, households were made better off for a given dollar income—even if the new goods were initially "expensive." The same idea applies to the invention of new prescription drugs, even if the prices of these drugs are "high" at the outset. The creation of useful new products tends to raise households' real income or, equivalently, lower the effective price level. Thus, a proper accounting for new products would lower the average inflation rate. The economy's real economic growth would also look stronger if the effects of new products were properly considered.

The PPI is computed in a manner conceptually similar to that of the CPI. However, the PPI does not cover services and primarily includes goods that are raw materials and semifinished products. Each month the PPI survey collects about 100,000 prices from about 30,000 businesses. One shortcoming of the PPI is that it is too narrow a concept to reflect the general level of prices in an economy.

Questions and Problems

A. Review questions

1. Define nominal and real GDP. Are these flow or stock concepts? Explain why the differences between nominal and real GDP are important.

2. Define the implicit price deflator. Where does this concept come from? How does it relate to nominal and real GDP? How does the implicit price deflator differ from the consumer price index (CPI)?

3. We discussed alternative views of GDP from the perspectives of expenditure, income, and production. What are the basic differences in these approaches? Why do they add to the same total for GDP?

B. Problems for discussion

4. What are some of the shortcomings of real GDP from a welfare perspective? Do you have any practical suggestions for revising the computation of GDP to achieve a better measure of welfare?

5. Table 2.5 shows the relation between GDP and income for the United States in 2005. Replicate this table for any European country.

Introduction to Economic Growth

n 2000, the real GDP per person in the United States was $34,800 (valued in U.S. dollars for the year 2000). This high output per person meant that the typical U.S. resident had a high **standard of living**, which refers to the quantity and quality of the goods and services consumed. Most families had their own home, at least one car, several television sets, education at least through high school and often college, and a level of health that translated into a life expectancy at birth of nearly 80 years. Nearly as high standards of living applied to most Western European countries—including the United Kingdom, Germany, France, and Italy—and a few other places, such as Canada, Australia, New Zealand, Japan, Singapore, and Hong Kong.

The residents of most other countries were not nearly as well off in 2000. For example, the real GDP per person was $9,100 in Mexico, $3,900 in China, $2,600 in India, and $740 in Nigeria, the most populous country in Africa.[1] Lower real GDPs per person meant lower standards of living. The typical resident of Mexico could afford food, shelter, and basic health care but could not attain the range and quality of consumer goods available to most Americans. Even more seriously, the typical Nigerian had concerns about nutrition and housing, and faced a life expectancy at birth of less than 50 years.

How can countries with low real GDP per person catch up to the high levels enjoyed by the United States and other rich countries? The only answer is to have a high **rate of economic growth**—the rate at which real GDP per person increases—over long periods, such as 20 or 40 years. To illustrate, Table 3.1 shows the level of real GDP per person that China would attain in 2020, based on its growth rate of real GDP per person from 2000 to 2020. It would take a growth rate of 10% per year—an unprecedented accomplishment for 20 years—for China's real GDP per person in 2020 to approach $30,000, nearly the U.S. level in 2000. Moreover, since the U.S. real GDP per person will likely be growing, even a 10% growth rate would leave China's real GDP per person in 2020 far short of the U.S. level. Worse yet, if China's real GDP per person grew at only 2% per year, its level of real GDP per person in 2020 would be only $5,800, 17% of the U.S. level in 2000. Thus, differences in rates of economic growth, when sustained for 20 years or more, make an enormous difference in standards of living, measured by levels of real GDP per person.

The benefits of sustained economic growth apply to all nations, not just China. Thus, the universal question is, what can we—or our governments—do to increase the rate of economic growth? The importance of this question inspired economist Robert Lucas (1988) to ask: "Is there some action a government of India could take that would lead the Indian economy to grow like Indonesia's or Egypt's? If so, what, exactly? If not, what is it about the 'nature of India' that makes it so? The consequences for human welfare involved in questions like these are simply staggering: once one starts to think about them, it is hard to think about

---

[1] These GDP numbers adjust for purchasing-power differences across countries. The data are from Alan Heston, Robert Summers, and Bettina Aten (2002).

Table 3.1 *Economic Growth and China's Real GDP per Person in 2020**

Growth Rate of Real GDP per Person from 2000 to 2020	Real GDP per Person in 2020 (in 2000 dollars)
2% per year	5,820
5% per year	10,600
10% per year	28,800

*China starts with real per capita GDP of $3,900 in 2000. We calculate the level of real GDP per person in 2020 as follows. Start with the natural logarithm of real GDP per person in 2000: ln (3,900) = 8.269. Then multiply the number of years, 20, by the growth rate—for example, 0.02 if the growth rate is 2% per year: 20 × 0.02 = 0.40. Add this to 8.269 to get 8.669. Then take the exponential of 8.669 to get the answer, 5,820.

anything else" (p. 5).[2] Questions like these underline the challenge of developing policies that promote economic growth. This challenge motivates the study that we begin in this chapter and continue in the following two chapters.

We start by presenting key facts about economic growth, first for a large number of countries since 1960 and, second, for the United States and other rich countries for over a century. These observations bring out patterns that we need to understand to design policies to promote economic growth. As a way to gain this understanding, we construct a model of economic growth, called the Solow model. In Chapters 4 and 5, we extend this model and see how these extensions relate to patterns of economic growth and to Lucas's policy challenge.

Facts About Economic Growth

Economic Growth Around the World from 1960 to 2000

We start our study of economic growth by comparing living standards—gauged by real GDP per person—for a large number of countries. This comparison will allow us to see at a glance which countries are rich and which are poor. In Figure 3.1, the horizontal axis plots real GDP per person (in U.S. dollars for the year 2000), and the vertical axis shows the number of countries with each real GDP per person in 2000. The graph applies to 151 countries with data, and representative countries are labeled for each bar.

The United States, with a real GDP per person of $34,800, was only the second richest country in 2000—the number one spot went to Luxembourg, a very small country, with $45,900. More generally, the top positions were dominated by the long-term members of the rich countries' club, which is known as the Organization for Economic Cooperation and Development (OECD). This elite group includes most of Western Europe, the United States, Canada, Australia, New Zealand, and Japan. Overall, 20 of the richest 25 economies in 2000 were OECD members. The other five were Singapore (ranked 3rd), Hong Kong (6th), Macao (14th), Cyprus (23rd), and Taiwan (25th). (Hong Kong and Macao are parts of China, and Taiwan's status is in dispute.)

The poorest country in Figure 3.1 is Congo (Kinshasa), a sub-Saharan African country, with a real GDP per person of $238, again in 2000 U.S. dollars. Therefore, in 2000, the richest country (Luxembourg) had a real GDP per person that was 193 times that of the poorest country. If we exclude Luxembourg because of its small size and compare instead with the United States, we find that the United States had a real GDP per person

---

[2] When Lucas wrote these words in the mid-1980s, India had been growing more slowly than Egypt and Indonesia for some time. The growth rates of real GDP per person from 1960 to 1980 were 2.5% per year in Egypt, 3.5% in Indonesia, and 1.6% in India. However, India did manage to surpass the other two countries in terms of growth rates from 1980 to 2000: The growth rates of real GDP per person were 2.7% per year for Egypt, 3.3% for Indonesia, and 3.8% for India. Thus, the Indian government may have met Lucas's challenge.

that was 146 times as large as Congo's.

Economists use the term **poverty** to describe low standards of living. A person or family living in poverty has difficulty affording the basic necessities of life—food, clothing, shelter, and health—and can only dream about automobiles and television sets. Poverty reflects low real incomes of individuals and families. According to one definition used by international organizations such as the United Nations and the World Bank, an individual was living in poverty in 2000 if his or her annual income was less than $570 per year in 1996 prices.

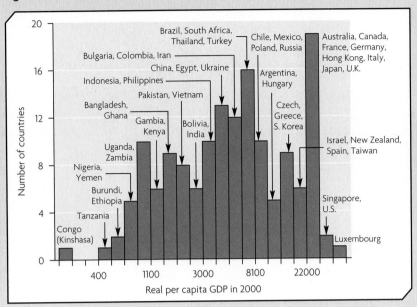

Figure 3.1 *World Distribution of Real GDP per Person in 2000*

The graph shows the distribution of real gross domestic product (GDP) per person for 151 countries in 2000. The horizontal axis is in 2000 U.S. dollars and uses a proportionate scale. Representative countries are indicated for the ranges of real GDP per person.

The value of $570 per year is a modification of a well-known standard established in the 1980s that viewed the poverty line as an income of $1 per person per day. Therefore, we can refer to $570 per year as the $1-per-day poverty standard.

The number of persons living in poverty in a country depends on two things. One is the way that the country's income is distributed among persons; for example, the total income might be distributed nearly evenly, or a small fraction of the population might have most of the income. The second is the country's average real income, which can be approximated by real GDP per person. If this average is very low, the typical resident will be living in poverty even if income is distributed evenly.

In practice, the second factor—a country's real GDP per person—is the most important determinant of the number of people living in poverty. Countries with very low real GDP per person are the ones in which a large fraction of the population lives in poverty. Therefore, the data plotted in Figure 3.1 tell us that world poverty in 2000 was dominated by sub-Saharan Africa—an amazing 23 of the lowest 25 real GDPs per person were in this region. The two other countries in this poorest group were Yemen (9th from the bottom) and Tajikistan (25th).

Real GDP per person in 2000 gives us a snapshot of the standard of living at a point in time. The rich countries, such as the OECD members, were rich in 2000 because their levels of real GDP per person rose for a long period. Similarly, the levels of real GDP per person in poor countries in 2000—especially in sub-Saharan Africa—had not been growing. In fact, as we shall see, many of these growth rates were negative, so that real GDP per person fell over time.

To measure economic growth, we have to compare the levels of real GDP per person in 2000 with those from earlier years. Figure 3.2 begins this comparison by showing a graph of real GDP per person 40 years earlier, in 1960. This graph is similar to the one in Figure 3.1. The horizontal axis again shows real GDP per person, still using U.S. dollars in the year 2000. The vertical axis shows the number of countries with each real GDP per person in 1960. The total number of countries is only 113, given the availability of data for 1960.

In 1960, Switzerland was at the top with a real GDP per person of $15,600, and the United States was again second, at $12,800. The top 25 was dominated by the long-term members of the OECD—again, 20 of the richest 25 countries were OECD members. One difference from 2000 was that no Asian countries were in the top 25 in 1960. Several Latin American countries (Argentina,

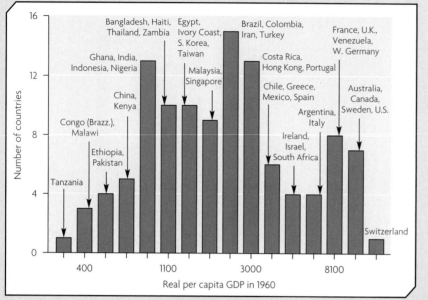

Figure 3.2 *World Distribution of Real GDP per Person in 1960*

The graph shows the distribution of real GDP per person for 113 countries in 1960. The horizontal axis is in 2000 U.S. dollars and uses a proportionate scale. Representative countries are indicated for the ranges of real GDP per person.

one in 2000, where the U.S. real GDP per person was 146 times that of Congo (Kinshasa).

If we compare the levels of real GDP per person in 2000 and 1960 for each country, we can compute the country's growth rate of real GDP per person over the 40 years.[3] Figure 3.3 shows the distribution of these growth rates for the 112 countries with the necessary data. The construction of this graph is similar to those in Figures 3.1 and 3.2. The horizontal axis now shows the growth rate of real GDP per person from 1960 to 2000, and the vertical axis shows the number of countries with each growth rate.

Uruguay, and Venezuela) were in the top group, but none remained in 2000. Israel and South Africa were also in this group in 1960 but not in 2000 (at which point Israel was ranked 27th, and South Africa 55th).

The low end for real GDP per person was dominated somewhat less by sub-Saharan Africa in 1960 than in 2000. The poorest country in 1960 was Tanzania, at $400, but "only" 19 of the 25 countries with the lowest real GDPs per person were in sub-Saharan Africa. Five of the poorest 25 in 1960 were in Asia—Pakistan, China, Nepal, India, and Indonesia. The other member of the lowest 25 was Romania (25th from the bottom). The six non-African countries grew rapidly enough over the next 40 years to escape the lowest category. In fact, the high growth in Asia and the low growth in sub-Saharan Africa from 1960 to 2000 were major parts of the story about world standards of living in 2000. In the next section, we discuss how these developments affected world poverty.

In 1960, the richest country (Switzerland) had a real GDP per person that was 39 times that of the poorest country (Tanzania). This spread was lower than the

The average growth rate of real GDP per person from 1960 to 2000 for 112 countries was 1.8% per year. The fastest-growing country was Taiwan, with a rate of 6.4%. More generally, many of the fast growers from 1960 to 2000—8 of the top 12—came from East Asia. Aside from Taiwan, the East Asian countries in the top 20 were Singapore, South Korea, Hong Kong, Thailand, China, Japan (which grew rapidly mainly up to the early 1970s), Malaysia, and Indonesia. Some long-term OECD countries were among the top 20 for economic growth: Ireland, Portugal, Spain, and Luxembourg. The other members of the top 20 were Botswana (the star performer of sub-Saharan Africa), Cyprus, Barbados, Mauritius, Romania, Cape Verde, and Congo (Brazzaville).

At the bottom end, 18 of the 20 worst performers for economic growth from 1960 to 2000 were in sub-Saharan Africa. The two non-African slow growers were Nicaragua (−1.2% per year) and Venezuela (−0.5%). Among the 18 African countries,

---

[3] The easiest way to compute the growth rate of real GDP per person from 1960 to 2000 is to calculate $(1/40) \cdot \log$ (real GDP per person in 2000/real GDP per person in 1960), where log is the natural logarithm.

15 experienced negative growth of real GDP per person, with Congo (Kinshasa) the worst at −3.6% per year. Thus, the reason for low levels of real GDP per person in 2000 is partly that countries in this region started off badly in 1960 (around the time of independence for most of the countries) and, even more so, that they performed so poorly in terms of the growth of real GDP per person from 1960 to 2000. The poorest countries in 2000—especially in sub-Saharan Africa—were poor mainly because they had grown at low or negative rates since 1960. Thus, to go further, we have to understand why these countries failed to grow at higher rates.

We have also learned that a group of countries in East Asia grew at high rates from 1960 to 2000. This strong growth enabled these countries to move from low levels of real GDP per person in 1960 to much higher levels in 2000. To understand this change, we have to understand why these countries grew at high rates.

To appreciate the high levels of real GDP per person in the OECD countries in 2000, we have to look at data before 1960. That is, these countries were rich in 2000 partly because they grew from 1960 to 2000 but, even more so, because they were already rich in 1960. To get a feel for these longer-term developments in currently rich countries, we will look at historical data for the United States and other OECD countries later in this chapter.

World Poverty and Income Inequality

We noted that poverty refers to a minimally acceptable level of real income, such as the World Bank's $1-per-day standard (which actually corresponds to

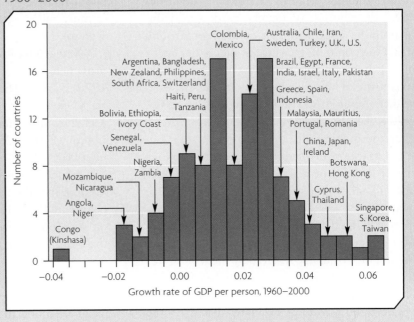

Figure 3.3 *World Distribution of Growth Rates of Real GDP per Person, 1960–2000*

The graph shows the distribution of the growth rate of real GDP per person for 112 countries from 1960 to 2000. Representative countries are indicated for the ranges of growth rates. The unweighted average growth rate was 1.8% per year.

$570 per year in 1996 dollars). The term **inequality** is often used interchangeably with "poverty" but is actually different in meaning. Inequality describes an unequal distribution of income across individuals at a point in time within a country or around the world. One common measure of inequality is the fraction of a nation's income received by persons in the lowest fifth of the distribution. If income were equally distributed, this number would be 20%. The greater the shortfall of this share from 20%, the higher the income inequality. Similarly, we can look at the fraction of income received by persons in the upper fifth of the distribution. The greater the excess of this share above 20%, the higher the income inequality.

In practice, the distribution of income is far from equal—for 73 countries with data around 1990, the average amount of the income received by the lowest fifth was 6.6%, whereas the average for the highest fifth was 45%. These income shares were 6.5% and 39% for the United States (about average inequality based on the lowest fifth, and lower than average inequality based on the highest fifth), 7.8% and 41% for the United Kingdom (less unequal than the United States at the bottom but slightly more unequal at the top), 9.4% and 28% for Canada (a country with relatively little inequality), and 4.4% and 60% for Brazil (a country with a lot of inequality).

For a given average income per person, the degree of inequality determines the fraction of the population that falls below the $1-per-day poverty line. Unless average real income is extremely low, more inequality means that a higher fraction of the population falls below the poverty line. However, when average real income changes—for example, when real GDP per person rises—inequality and poverty behave differently.

To understand why, suppose that everyone's real income were to double. In this case, inequality would not change—for example, if the lowest fifth of the distribution started with 6% of total income, the lowest fifth would still have 6% after everyone's income doubled. In contrast, poverty would fall sharply if everyone's real income doubled—because more people's real incomes would exceed the $1-per-day

standard. If we think that a person's welfare depends on his or her real income, rather than income measured relative to that of other persons, then poverty is more meaningful than inequality as a measure of welfare.

Xavier Sala-i-Martin (2006) showed that economic growth led to a dramatic fall in world poverty from 1970 to 2000. The estimated number of people below the $1-per-day poverty line ($570 per year in 1996 prices) fell from 700 million, or 20% of the world's population in 1970, to 398 million, or 7% of the population in 2000.[4]

Figure 3.4 shows how these changes occurred. Part (a) describes the distribution of income for the world's people in 1970. The horizontal axis plots real income on a proportionate scale, and the vertical axis shows the number of people with each level of income. The vertical lines marked $1 show the income levels that correspond to the $1-per-day poverty line. Consider the area below the upper curve and to the left of the $1 line. To find the fraction of the world's population with incomes below $1 per day, we take the ratio of this area to the total area under the upper curve. The result is 20%.

World economic growth from 1970 to 2000 led to a shift from Figure 3.4a to Figure 3.4b. Notice that the whole distribution of income shifted to the right, because larger proportions of the world's people had higher real incomes. Hence, the fraction of the world's population with incomes below the $1-per-day poverty line was much smaller in 2000 than in 1970. The percentage for 2000 was 7%, compared to 20% in 1970. This sharp decline in poverty rates shows the dramatic progress over three decades as a result of economic growth.

The graphs also show how some of the world's largest countries fared from 1970 to 2000. For poverty, the biggest changes occurred in China and India, which accounted for nearly 40% of world population in 2000. In 1970, many residents of China and India and other Asian countries were below the $1-per-day poverty line—Asia accounted for 80% overall of persons living in poverty. However, Figures 3.4a and 3.4b show that the income distribution curves for China and India (and also Indonesia, another large

---

[4] The fraction of the population living in poverty is called the *poverty rate*, whereas the number of people living in poverty is called the *poverty headcount*. The decrease in the poverty rate from 1970 to 2000 was so sharp that the world poverty headcount decreased, despite the substantial rise in world population.

Asian country) shifted dramatically to the right from 1970 to 2000. This change reflected the strong economic growth in Asia, particularly since the late 1970s for China and the mid-1980s for India. Consequently, by 2000, Asia accounted for only 19% of persons living in poverty.

We also know that recent decades saw very low economic growth in sub-Saharan Africa. Consequently, the poverty numbers soared. In 1970, sub-Saharan Africa accounted for only 13% of persons living in poverty. However, in 2000, this region accounted for 74% of persons in poverty. Thus, poverty shifted from primarily an Asian problem to mainly an African problem.

The results are more complicated for world inequality. We can think of the changes in two parts: the first is within countries and the second is across countries. Inequality rose from 1970 to 2000 within several large countries, including the United States, the United Kingdom, and China. However, Sala-i-Martin showed that these changes within countries had only minor effects on inequality across persons in the entire world.

The second factor is the dispersion of average incomes across countries. We know from Figures 3.1 and 3.2 that the ratio of the highest real GDPs per person (concentrated in the OECD countries) to the lowest (primarily in sub-Saharan Africa) rose from 1960 to 2000. However, since world inequality involves numbers of people, rather than numbers of countries, we have to give more weight to the larger countries. The

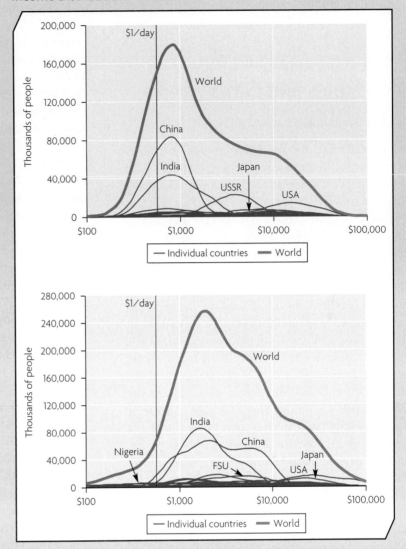

Figure 3.4 *(a) World Income Distribution in 1970; (b) World Income Distribution in 2000*

Figure 3.4a is for 1970 and Figure 3.4b is for 2000. In each case, the horizontal axis plots real income in 1985 U.S. dollars on a proportionate scale. For the upper curves in the two figures, the vertical axis shows the number of people in the world with each level of income. The vertical lines marked $1 show the annual real incomes that correspond to the standard poverty line of $1 per day ($570 per year in 1996 prices). The income distributions for a few large countries are shown separately. FSU is the former Soviet Union. (Nigeria is hidden beneath the Asian countries in Figure 3.4a.) The values shown on the upper curves for numbers of people in the world are the vertical sums of the numbers of people in all of the individual countries. However, only a few of the countries can be discerned in these graphs.

Source: These graphs come from Xavier Sala-i-Martin (2006).

income changes in the larger countries, especially China and India, matter a lot more than the changes in the smaller countries. Since China and India had very low average real incomes in 1970, their strong economic growth from 1970 to 2000 contributed heavily to a reduction of world income inequality. It

Long-Term Growth in the United States and Other Rich Countries

We mentioned that, for the United States and other OECD countries, the main reason for high real GDP per person in recent years is that these countries already had high real GDP per person in 1960. Therefore, to understand U.S. prosperity, we have to take a long-term view that starts well before 1960.

If we go back more than a century, we find that U.S. real GDP per person in 1869 (the first year for which reliable annual data are available) was $2,311, measured in 2000 U.S. dollars. Therefore, the real GDP per person of $37,600 in 2005 was 16 times that of 1869. An increase in real GDP per person and, hence, in the typical person's real income by a factor of 16, makes an enormous difference in the standard of living. In 2005, unlike in 1869, the typical U.S. family not only owned a comfortable home and had ample food and clothing but also possessed many things not even imagined in 1869: automobiles, television sets, telephones, personal computers, and a connection to the Internet. Also, compared with 136 years earlier, education levels were much higher, life expectancy was substantially longer, and a much larger fraction of the population lived in cities.

The average growth rate of real GDP per person in the United States from 1869 to 2005 was 2.0% per year. This growth rate does not seem all that impressive—it is only slightly higher than the average rate of 1.8% per year from 1960 to 2000 for the 112 countries shown in Figure 3.3. Moreover, the long-term U.S. growth rate is much less than the 6.0% per year achieved by some East Asian countries from 1960 to 2000. Nevertheless, the U.S. growth rate of 2.0% per year—when sustained for such a long time—was enough to make the United States the world's second richest country in 2005.

Living standards in the United States in 2005 would have been very different if the average growth rate of real GDP per person since 1869 had been much lower or higher than 2.0%. If the growth rate had been 1.0% per year, real GDP per person in 2005 would have been $9,004, only four times the value in 1869. In this case,

the typical American family would have possessed reasonable food and health care but would lack a comfortable home and a fine automobile, would be missing an array of pleasant consumer products, and would have lower levels of education. Alternatively, if the growth rate had been 3.0%, the level of real GDP per person in 2005 would have been $136,700, 59 times the level in 1869. A real GDP per person of $136,700 means that the typical family would have had a grand home, a couple of nice cars, expensive private schooling, health care, and so on.

Similar calculations apply to other OECD countries, many of which are now nearly as rich as the United States. These countries also came to be rich because their real GDP per person grew for a long time at the unspectacular rate of around 2% per year.

Although average growth rates of real GDP per person over a century or more were around 2% per year, the growth rates were not constant over time. To see this, consider Table 3.2, which shows growth rates for 17 OECD countries, including the United States. The table shows unweighted averages for the 17 countries of the growth rates of real GDP per person over 20-year periods from 1820 to 2000. The average growth rate over the full 180 years was 1.8% per year, with no clear trend. However, the average growth rates since 1940 were somewhat higher: 2.4% per year.

The decline in the growth rate of real GDP per person from 3.1% per year for 1960–1980 to 1.8% per year for 1980–2000 is sometimes called the **productivity slowdown**. Measures of productivity—such as output per person and per worker—did not grow as fast from 1980 to 2000 as in the previous 20 years. However, the growth rate of 1.8% per year for 1980–2000 equaled the average growth rate since 1820. Thus, the high growth rate for 1960–1980 (and, it turns out, for 1950–1960) may have been the outlier. A reasonable guess from the numbers in Table 3.2 is that future growth rates of real GDP per person will average something close to 2% per year.

Patterns of World Economic Growth

In looking at the data, we observed some important patterns in economic growth. First, some countries, such as those in East Asia, grew rapidly from 1960 to 2000 and thereby raised their levels of real GDP per person substantially over 40 years. Second, over the

Table 3.2 *Long-Term Economic Growth in OECD Countries*

Period	Growth Rate of Real GDP per Person (Percent per Year)	Number of Countries
1820–1840	1.2	10
1840–1860	2.1	10
1860–1880	1.3	14
1880–1900	1.4	17
1900–1920	0.8	17
1920–1940	1.8	17
1940–1960	2.4	17
1960–1980	3.1	17
1980–2000	1.8	17

Note: The data are from Angus Maddison (2003). The 17 countries included are Australia, Austria, Belgium, Canada, Denmark, Finland, France, Germany, Italy, Japan, Netherlands, New Zealand, Norway, Sweden, Switzerland, the United Kingdom, and the United States. The growth rates are unweighted averages for the countries with available data. Fewer countries have data for the earlier periods.

same period, other countries—especially in sub-Saharan Africa—grew at low or negative rates and therefore ended up with low levels of real GDP per person in 2000. Third, the United States and other OECD countries had high levels of real GDP per person in 2000 mostly because they grew at moderate rates—around 2% per year—for a century or more.

These observations suggest questions that we would like to answer about economic growth:

- What factors caused some countries to grow fast and others to grow slow over periods such as 1960 to 2000? In particular, why did the East Asian countries do so much better than the sub-Saharan African countries?
- How did countries such as the United States and other OECD members sustain growth rates of real GDP per person of around 2% per year for a century or more?
- What can policymakers do to increase growth rates of real GDP per person?

The answers to these questions could contribute a great deal to the living standards of future generations. The theories about economic growth that we turn to next bring us closer to finding these answers.

Theory of Economic Growth

 ow we will build a model of economic growth to help understand the patterns found in the international data. We start by considering the *production function*, which tells us how goods and services are produced.

The Production Function

We begin our theoretical study of economic growth by considering how a country's technology and factors of production—or factor inputs—determine its output of goods and services, measured by real GDP. The relation of output to the technology and the quantities of factor inputs is called a **production function**.

We will build a simplified model that has two factor inputs: **capital stock**, K, and labor, L. In this model, capital takes a physical form, such as machines and buildings used by businesses. A more complete model would include **human capital**, which embodies the effects of education and training on workers' skills, and the effects of medical care, nutrition, and sanitation on workers' health. In our simplified model, the amount of labor input, L, is the quantity of work-hours per year for labor of a standard quality and effort. That is, we imagine that, at a point in time, each worker has the same skill. For convenience, we often refer to L as the **labor force** or the number of workers—these interpretations are satisfactory if we think of each laborer as working a fixed number of hours per year.

We use the symbol A to represent the **technology level**. For given quantities of the factor inputs, K and L, an increase in A raises output. That is, a more technologically advanced economy has a higher level of overall **productivity**. Higher productivity means that output is higher for given quantities of the factor inputs.

Mathematically, we write the production function as

Key equation (production function):

(3.1) $Y = A \bullet F(K, L)$

One way to see how output, Y, responds to the variables in the production function—the technology level, A, and the quantities of capital and labor, K and L—is to change one of the three variables while holding the other two fixed. Looking at the equation, we see that Y is proportional to A. Hence, if A doubles, while K and L do not change, Y doubles.

For a given technology level, A, the function $F(K, L)$ determines how additional units of capital and labor, K and L, affect output, Y. We assume that each factor is productive at the margin. Hence, for given A and L, an increase in K—that is, a rise in K at the margin—raises Y. Similarly, for given A and K, an increase in L raises Y.

The change in Y from a small increase in K is called the **marginal product of capital (MPK)**. The MPK tells us how much Y rises when K increases by one unit, while A and L do not change. The corresponding change in Y from a small increase in L is called the **marginal product of labor (MPL)**. The MPL tells us how much Y rises when L increases by one unit, while A and K do not change. We assume that the two marginal products, MPK and MPL, are greater than zero.

Figure 3.5 shows how output, Y, responds to an increase in capital input, K. This figure is a graph of the production function, $A \bullet F(K, L)$, from equation (3.1). The special feature of this graph is that we are holding constant the values of A and L. Therefore, the graph shows how increases in K affect Y when A and L do not change.

The curve in Figure 3.5 goes through the origin, because we assume that output, Y, is zero if the amount of capital stock, K, is zero. The slope of the curve at any point is the MPK—that is, the change in Y from a small increase in K. Since we have assumed that this marginal product, MPK, is always greater than zero, the slope of the curve is positive throughout. We also assume that the slope flattens as K rises. The curve has this shape because we assume that the MPK declines as K rises, for given A and L. This property is known as **diminishing marginal product of capital**. As an example, at a low K, such as point a in the graph, an increase in K by one unit might raise Y by 0.1 units

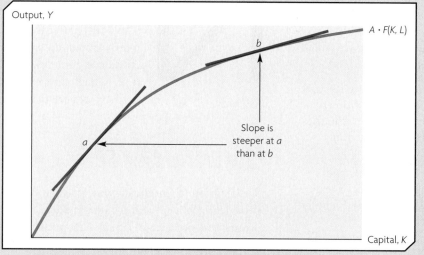

Figure 3.5 *The Production Function in Terms of Capital Input*

Output, Y

$A \bullet F(K, L)$

b

Slope is steeper at a than at b

a

Capital, K

The curve shows the effect of capital input, K, on output, Y. We hold fixed the technology level, A, and the quantity of labor input, L. Therefore, the slope of the curve at any point is the marginal product of capital, MPK. This slope gets less steep as K rises because of diminishing marginal product of capital. Therefore, the slope at point a is greater than that at point b.

per year. However, at a high K, such as point b, an increase in K by one unit might raise Y by only 0.05 units per year.

Figure 3.6 shows the corresponding graph for output, Y, as a function of labor input, L. This figure is again a graph of the production function, $A \cdot F(K, L)$, from equation (3.1). The special feature now is that we are holding constant the values of A and K. This graph shows how increases in L affect Y when A and K do not change. Again, the curve goes through the origin, because we assume that Y is zero if L is zero. The positive slope of the curve at any point is the MPL. The flattening of the curve as L rises indicates that the MPL falls as L increases, for given A and K. Hence, we are assuming **diminishing marginal product of labor**. As an example, at a low L, such as point a in the graph, an increase in L by one unit might raise Y by 0.1 units per year. However, at a high K, such as point b, an increase in L by one unit might raise Y by only 0.05 units per year.

Another assumption is that the production function in equation (3.1) exhibits **constant returns to scale** in the two factor inputs, K and L. The idea is that if we double the scale of inputs—double K and L—the output, Y, doubles. As an example, assume that a business starts with 5 machines, $K = 5$, and 5 workers, $L = 5$. The business has a given technology level, A, and is able to produce an output, Y, of, say, 100 widgets per year. Now, suppose that K and L double, so that the business has $K = 10$ machines and $L = 10$ workers. The technology level, A, is the same as before. Our assumption is that, with twice as many machines and workers and the same technology level, the business can produce twice as much output. That is, Y is now 200 widgets per year.

More generally, if the production function exhibits constant returns to scale, a multiplication of the two factor inputs, K and L, by any positive number leads to a multiplication of output, Y, by the same number.

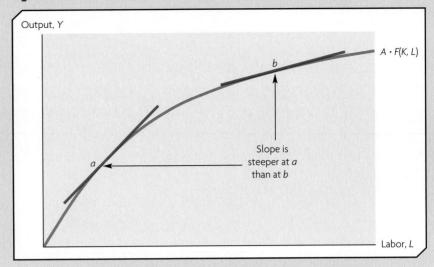

Figure 3.6 *The Production Function in Terms of Labor Input*

Output, Y

$A \cdot F(K, L)$

b

a

Slope is steeper at a than at b

Labor, L

The curve shows the effect of labor input, L, on output, Y. We hold fixed the technology level, A, and the quantity of capital input, K. Therefore, the slope of the curve at any point is the marginal product of labor, MPL. This slope gets less steep as L rises because of diminishing marginal product of labor. Therefore, the slope at point a is greater than that at point b.

Therefore, if we multiply K and L by the quantity $1/L$ in equation (3.1), we also multiply Y by $1/L$ to get

$$Y/L = A \cdot F(K/L, L/L)$$

The value L/L on the right-hand side equals one (a constant) and can, therefore, be ignored. By writing the production function this way, we see that output per worker, Y/L depends only on the technology level, A, and the quantity of capital per worker, K/L. We can show this property more clearly by defining $y \equiv Y/L$ to be output per worker and $k \equiv K/L$ to be capital per worker, and then defining a new function, f, that relates y to k:

(3.2) $$y = A \cdot f(k)$$

Figure 3.7 shows the graph of output per worker, y, versus capital per worker, k, for a given technology level, A. This graph looks the same as the one in Figure 3.5. The slope of the curve in Figure 3.7 again tells us the effect of more capital on output; that is, it measures the MPK. Note that the marginal product of capital diminishes as capital per worker, k, rises.

Growth Accounting

The production function in equation (3.1) determines the level of output or real GDP, Y, at a point in time for given values of its three determinants: the technology

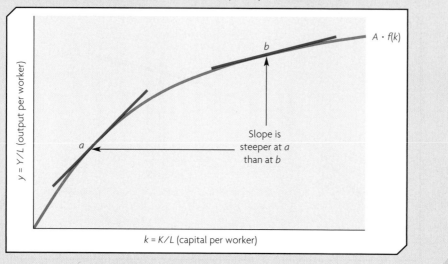

Figure 3.7 *Output per Worker Versus Capital per Worker*

This method for showing the production function plots output per worker, $y = Y/L$, against capital per worker, $k = K/L$. We hold fixed the technology level, A. The slope of the curve at any point is the marginal product of capital, MPK. This slope gets less steep as k rises because of diminishing marginal product of capital. Therefore, the slope at point a is greater than that at point b.

level, A, and the quantities of capital and labor, K and L. However, the production function is also the starting point for our investigation of economic *growth*. To use the production function to study growth, we use a method called **growth accounting** to consider how growth in Y depends on growth in A, K, and L. Whereas *the production function is a relation between the level of Y and the levels of A, K, and L, growth accounting is a relation between the growth rate of Y and the growth rates of A, K, and L.*

To begin the analysis of growth accounting, let ΔY represent the change in Y over an interval of time—say, a year. (The symbol Δ, the Greek letter capital delta, represents the change in a variable.) The growth rate of Y over the year is given by $\Delta Y/Y$. For example, if $Y = 100$ and $\Delta Y = 1$ over a year, the growth rate is $\Delta Y/Y = 1\%$ per year. Similarly, if we use ΔA, ΔK, and ΔL to represent the changes in technology, capital, and labor, the growth rates of each are $\Delta A/A$, $\Delta K/K$, and $\Delta L/L$, respectively.

Our next task is to explain precisely how $\Delta A/A$, $\Delta K/K$, and $\Delta L/L$, contribute to the growth rate of real GDP, $\Delta Y/Y$. Start with the contribution of technology. We see from the production function

(3.1) $\qquad Y = A \bullet F(K, L)$

that Y would grow at the same rate as A if K and L were unchanged. For example, if $\Delta A/A = 1\%$ per year

and K and L are constant, then $\Delta Y/Y = 1\%$ per year. Even if K and L are changing, equation (3.1) tells us that a higher growth rate of A would contribute to a higher growth rate of Y. If $\Delta A/A$ is higher by 1% per year, $\Delta Y/Y$ is higher by 1% per year, for given growth rates of capital and labor, $\Delta K/K$ and $\Delta L/L$.

Now consider the contributions to the growth of real GDP from growth in capital and labor. We know that $\Delta Y/Y$ increases when $\Delta K/K$ and $\Delta L/L$ increase. To be more precise, suppose that the contribution of growth in capital to the growth of real GDP is given by $\alpha \bullet \Delta K/K$, where α (the Greek letter alpha) is greater than zero. Similarly, suppose that the contribution of growth in labor to the growth of real GDP is given by $\beta \bullet \Delta L/L$, where β (the Greek letter beta) is also greater than zero. In this case, we can write that the growth rate of real GDP is given by

(3.3) $\qquad \Delta Y/Y = \Delta A/A + \alpha \bullet (\Delta K/K) + \beta \bullet (\Delta L/L)$

That is, the growth rate of real GDP, $\Delta Y/Y$, equals the growth rate of technology, $\Delta A/A$, plus the contributions from the growth of capital, $\alpha \bullet (\Delta K/K)$, and labor, $\beta \bullet (\Delta L/L)$. Notice that, since Y is proportional to A in the production function, equation (3.1), the coefficient on $\Delta A/A$ in equation (3.3) is one.

To think about the effects from the growth rates of capital, $\Delta K/K$, and labor, $\Delta L/L$, let's simplify for the moment by neglecting growth of technology, so that $\Delta A/A = 0$. If $\Delta K/K$ and $\Delta L/L$ were the same, say, 1% per year, the condition of constant returns to scale tells us that the growth rate of real GDP, $\Delta Y/Y$, would also be 1% per year. But we see from equation (3.3) that, if $\Delta K/K$ and $\Delta L/L$ each equal one, $\Delta Y/Y$ must equal $\alpha + \beta$. Therefore, we must have

$$\alpha + \beta = 1$$

The condition of constant returns to scale implies that α and β add up to one.

Since the coefficients α and β add up to one, and each coefficient is greater than zero, we know that α and β are each less than one. That is, the coefficients satisfy

$$0 < \alpha < 1$$

and

$$0 < \beta < 1$$

Notice that, if $\Delta K/K = 1\%$ per year and $\Delta L/L = 0$, the effect on $\Delta Y/Y$ is given by α in equation (3.3). Thus, if K grows while L stays fixed, Y grows at a rate slower than the growth rate of K (because $\alpha < 1$). Similarly, if $\Delta L/L = 1\%$ per year and $\Delta K/K = 0$, the effect on $\Delta Y/Y$ is given by β in equation (3.3). Thus, if L grows while K stays fixed, Y grows at a rate slower than the growth rate of L (because $\beta < 1$).

We know from Chapter 2 that—if we neglect net flows of income from the rest of the world—the economy's total real income equals real GDP, Y, less depreciation of capital stocks. If the depreciation of capital is small, Appendix A to this chapter shows that the coefficient α approximates the share of capital income in the economy's total real income. For example, if $\alpha = 1/3$—a commonly assumed value for the share of capital income—then a growth rate of capital, $\Delta K/K$, of 1% a year would contribute $(1/3)\%$ per year to the growth rate of real GDP, $\Delta Y/Y$.

Similarly, under the conditions explored in Appendix A to this chapter, β approximates the share of labor income in the economy's total real income. For example, if $\beta = 2/3$—a commonly assumed value for the share of labor income—a growth rate of labor, $\Delta L/L$, of 1% a year would contribute $(2/3)\%$ per year to $\Delta Y/Y$.

The interpretations of α and β as shares of capital and labor in total real income fit with our result that $\alpha + \beta = 1$. That is, we have

share of capital income + share of labor income = 1

$$\alpha + \beta = 1$$

Thus, payments to capital and labor exhaust all of the real income in the economy.

We can rearrange the condition $\alpha + \beta = 1$ to substitute $1 - \alpha$ for β on the right-hand side of equation (3.3) to get

Equation (3.4) says that we can break down the growth rate of real GDP, $\Delta Y/Y$, into the growth rate of technology, $\Delta A/A$, and a weighted average of the growth rates of capital and labor, $\alpha \cdot \Delta K/K$ and $(1 - \alpha) \cdot \Delta L/L$. The growth rate of capital gets the weight α (corresponding to capital's share of income), and the growth rate of labor gets the weight $1 - \alpha$ (corresponding to labor's share of income).

We now simplify by assuming that the coefficient α, which we interpret as capital's share of income, is fixed. That is, we assume that this coefficient does not change as the economy grows. The constancy of income shares does not always apply in the real world, but it does work as a reasonable approximation for the United States and many other countries. In Appendix C to this chapter, we show that the constancy of α holds for a commonly assumed form of the production function, $A \cdot F(K, L)$.

The Solow Growth Model

We learned from growth accounting in equation (3.4) that the growth rate of real GDP, $\Delta Y/Y$, depends on the growth rate of technology, $\Delta A/A$, and a weighted average of the growth rates of capital and labor, $\Delta K/K$ and $\Delta L/L$. To go from growth accounting to a theory of economic growth, we have to explain the growth rates of technology, capital, and labor. We begin this explanation by constructing the **Solow growth model**.

The Solow model makes several simplifying assumptions. First, labor input, L, equals the labor force, which is the number of persons seeking work. That is, the model does not allow for unemployment—labor input equals the labor force, all of which is employed. However, the important assumption is that the unemployment rate is constant, not necessarily zero. For example, if 96% of the labor force is always employed, labor input would always be a fixed multiple of the labor force and would grow at the same rate as the labor force.

The relation between the labor force, L, and population is given by

labor force, L =
(labor force/population) • population

The ratio of labor force to population is the **labor-force participation rate**. In the United States, in recent years, the labor-force participation rate has been close to one-half. For example, in March 2006, the sum of the civilian labor force (150.6 million) and active-duty

Key equation (growth-accounting formula):

(3.4) $\Delta Y/Y = \Delta A/A + \alpha \cdot (\Delta K/K) + (1 - \alpha) \cdot (\Delta L/L)$

military (1.4 million) was 51% of the total population.[5] The second assumption in the Solow model is that this participation rate does not change over time. In this case, the equation tells us that the growth rate of labor input, L, equals the growth rate of population.

Third, the model ignores a role for government, so that there are no taxes, public expenditures, government debt, or money. Fourth, the model assumes a closed economy; that is, there is no international trade in goods and services or in financial assets.

To begin our analysis of the Solow model, consider again the growth-accounting equation:

(3.4)
$$\Delta Y/Y = \Delta A/A + \alpha \bullet (\Delta K/K) + (1 - \alpha) \bullet (\Delta L/L)$$

BACK TO REALITY

Intellectual Origin of the Solow Growth Model

The Solow model was created during the 1950s by the MIT economist Robert Solow. This research led eventually to a Nobel Prize in 1987 for "contributions to the theory of economic growth." The Solow model was extended during the 1960s, especially by David Cass (1965) and Tjalling Koopmans (1965), and became known as the neoclassical growth model. The Solow model and the 1960's extensions were actually anticipated in theoretical work done by the mathematician Frank Ramsey in the 1920s. Hence, this growth model is often called the Ramsey model. Unfortunately, Ramsey's brilliant career was cut short by his death in 1930 at age 26.

© Crandall/The Image Works

We focus initially on growth of the two inputs, K and L, and ignore changes in the technology level, A. That is, we assume $\Delta A/A = 0$. In this case, the growth-accounting equation simplifies to

(3.5)
$$\Delta Y/Y = \alpha \bullet (\Delta K/K) + (1 - \alpha) \bullet (\Delta L/L)$$

Hence, in this version of the Solow model, the growth rate of real GDP, $\Delta Y/Y$, is a weighted average of the growth rates of capital, $\Delta K/K$, and labor, $\Delta L/L$.

We will find it useful to focus on real GDP per worker, $y = Y/L$, rather than the level of real GDP, Y. If Y were fixed, growth in L means that y would decline over time. For example, with a fixed Y, growth in workers at 1% per year implies that y falls by 1% per year. More generally, we have the formula:

(3.6)
$$\Delta y/y = \Delta Y/Y - \Delta L/L$$
growth rate of real GDP per worker =
growth rate of real GDP − growth rate of labor

Using the same reasoning, the growth rate of capital per worker, $\Delta k/k$, falls short of the growth rate of capital, $\Delta K/K$, by the growth rate of the number of workers:

(3.7)
$$\Delta k/k = \Delta K/K - \Delta L/L$$
growth rate of capital per worker =
growth rate of capital − growth rate of labor

Hence, for a given $\Delta K/K$, a higher $\Delta L/L$ means that, over time, each worker has less capital to work with.

If we rearrange the terms on the right-hand side of equation (3.5), we get

$$\Delta Y/Y = \alpha \bullet (\Delta K/K) - \alpha \bullet (\Delta L/L) + \Delta L/L$$

Then, if we move $\Delta L/L$ from the right side to the left side and combine the two terms on the right side that involve α, we get

$$\Delta Y/Y - \Delta L/L = \alpha \bullet (\Delta K/K - \Delta L/L)$$

We see from equation (3.6) that the left-hand side is the growth rate of real GDP per worker, $\Delta y/y$, and from equation (3.7) that the term in parentheses on the right-hand side is the growth rate of capital per worker, $\Delta k/k$. Therefore, the key result is that the growth rate of real GDP per worker depends only on the growth rate of capital per worker:

(3.8)
$$\Delta y/y = \alpha \bullet (\Delta k/k)$$

We see from equation (3.8) that, to analyze the growth rate of real GDP per worker, $\Delta y/y$, we need only

[5] The BLS computes a different measure of the labor-force participation rate—the ratio of the civilian labor force to the civilian noninstitutional population, which is the population (aged 16 and over) not on active military duty and not in institutions such as prisons. Defined this way, the labor-force participation rate in March 2006 was (150.6/228.0) = 66%.

determine the growth rate of capital per worker, $\Delta k/k$. Moreover, we know from equation (3.7) that $\Delta k/k$ is the difference between the growth rate of capital, $\Delta K/K$, and the growth rate of labor, $\Delta L/L$. We first assess $\Delta K/K$ and then turn to $\Delta L/L$.

The Growth Rate of the Capital Stock

The change in the stock of capital, ΔK, will depend on the economy's **saving**, which is the income that is not consumed. In our analysis in Chapter 7, we analyze saving behavior by considering the optimal choices of individual households. However, we simplify here by using Solow's assumption that each household divides up its real income in a fixed proportion s to saving and $1 - s$ to consumption, C.

For the economy as a whole, we know from our study of national-income accounting in Chapter 2 that national income equals NDP, which equals GDP less depreciation of capital stocks. In our model, some of the national income is labor income, which goes to workers, and some is capital income, which goes to owners of capital. However, all income must flow eventually to households, partly in their role as workers and partly in their role as owners of capital (or owners of businesses). We assume that saving depends only on households' total income, not on how this income divides up between labor income and capital income.

Depreciation arises because capital stocks wear out over time. Buildings need repairs, machines deteriorate, and vehicles require new parts. We capture depreciation in a simple way by assuming that all forms of capital depreciate at the same constant rate, δ (the Greek letter delta). Therefore, the flow quantity δK is the amount of capital that depreciates or disappears each year. In practice, the value of δ depends on the type of building or machine, but a reasonable average number is 5% per year. For example, if the stock of capital, K, is 100 machines, and δ is 5% per year, depreciation equals 5 machines per year.

The economy's real national income equals real NDP, which equals real GDP, Y, less depreciation, δK. From now on, we shorten the term national income to income. If households save the fraction s of all income, the economy's total real saving is

$$real\ saving = s \bullet (Y - \delta K)$$

$$real\ saving = (saving\ rate) \bullet (real\ income)$$

Since household real income, $Y - \delta K$, goes either to consumption, C, or real saving, $s \bullet (Y - \delta K)$, we can also write

(3.9) $$Y - \delta K = C + s \bullet (Y - \delta K)$$

$$real\ income = consumption + real\ saving$$

In a closed economy with no government sector, real GDP, Y, must be either consumed or invested. That is, the goods and services produced are used for only two purposes: consumption and outlays on capital goods or **gross investment**, I. Therefore, we have

$$Y = C + I$$

$$real\ GDP = consumption + gross\ investment$$

If we subtract depreciation, δK, from both sides, we get

(3.10) $$Y - \delta K = C + (I - \delta K)$$

$$real\ NDP = consumption + net\ investment$$

Notice on the right-hand side that we have defined **net investment** as gross investment, I, less the part of that investment, δK, needed to make up for the depreciation of existing capital.

Equations (3.9) and (3.10) have the same variable on the left-hand side (because real national income equals real NDP). Consequently, the right-hand sides must be equal:

$$C + s \bullet (Y - \delta K) = C + I - \delta K$$

If we cancel out the variable C on the two sides of the equation, we get a key equality between real saving and net investment:

(3.11) $$s \bullet (Y - \delta K) = I - \delta K$$

$$real\ saving = net\ investment$$

The change in the capital stock equals gross investment, I—the purchases of new capital goods—less the depreciation of existing capital:

$$\Delta K = I - \delta K$$

$$change\ in\ capital\ stock =$$
$$gross\ investment - depreciation$$

$$change\ in\ capital\ stock = net\ investment$$

Since net investment equals real saving from equation (3.11), we also have

(3.12) $$\Delta K = s \bullet (Y - \delta K)$$

$$change\ in\ capital\ stock = real\ saving$$

If we divide through each side of equation (3.12) by K, we get the formula we are seeking for the growth rate of the capital stock:

(3.13) $$\Delta K/K = s \bullet Y/K - s\delta$$

This result for $\Delta K/K$ is one of the two pieces needed to determine the growth rate of capital per worker:

(3.7) $$\Delta k/k = \Delta K/K - \Delta L/L$$

We now turn to the second piece—the growth rate of labor, $\Delta L/L$.

The Growth Rate of Labor Given our previous assumptions (a constant labor-force participation rate and a constant unemployment rate), the growth rate of labor, $\Delta L/L$, equals the growth rate of population. Thus, we now consider **population growth**.

Population growth rates vary across countries and over time. In the United States, the population growth rate has been about 1% per year for several decades. In many Western European countries, population growth rates fell from around 1% per year in the 1960s to roughly zero in 2000. In China and India, population growth rates declined from over 2% per year in the 1960s to recent values between 1 and 1.5% per year. Many low-income countries still have population growth rates above 2% per year. However, there has been a worldwide tendency for population growth rates to decline over time.

In the model, we assume that population grows at a constant rate, denoted by n, where n is a positive number ($n > 0$). At this point, we do not attempt to explain the population growth rate within the model; that is, we take n to be exogenous. We assume that labor, L, begins at an initial year, denoted by year 0, at the quantity $L(0)$, as shown in

Figure 3.7. Thereafter, the growth rate of L, $\Delta L/L$, equals the exogenous population growth rate, n:

(3.14) $$\Delta L/L = n$$

Since n is constant, Figure 3.8 shows the time path of L as a straight line (using a proportionate scale on the vertical axis).

The Growth Rate of Capital and Real GDP per Worker We can substitute our result for the growth rate of capital, $\Delta K/K$, from equation (3.13) and for the growth rate of labor, $\Delta L/L$, from equation (3.14) into equation (3.7) to determine the growth rate of capital per worker, $\Delta k/k$. We get

(3.15) $$\Delta k/k = \Delta K/K - \Delta L/L$$
$$\Delta k/k = s \bullet (Y/K) - s\delta - n$$

Equation (3.15) is a key result in the Solow growth model. Because of the importance of this equation, we will examine the various terms. On the left-hand side, the growth rate of capital per worker has units of per year. For example, a value for $\Delta k/k$ of 0.02 per year means that capital per worker is growing at 2% per year.

The terms on the right-hand side of equation (3.15) are determinants of the growth rate of capital per worker. Hence, each of these terms must also have units of per year. Consider the term $s \bullet (\Delta Y/K)$, which is the product of the saving rate, s, and Y/K. The saving rate, s, is a pure number—that is, a number without units of time or goods. For example, if $s = 0.2$, households save 20% of their income. The term Y/K—output per unit of capital—is called the **average product of capital**. The units for Y—a flow variable—are goods per year, and those for K—a stock variable—are goods. Therefore, the average product of capital has units of

*(goods per year)/
goods = per year*

Since s is a pure number, the units of $s \bullet (Y/K)$ are the same as the units of Y/K, which are per year, just like $\Delta k/k$.

The other terms on the right-hand side of

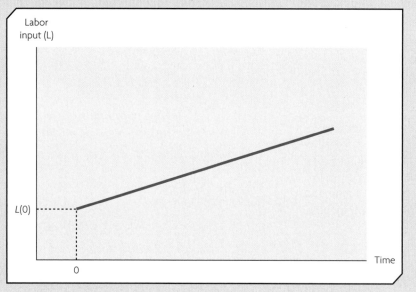

Figure 3.8 *Time Path of Labor Input*

Labor input (L)

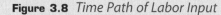

L(0)

Time

0

Labor input, L, starts at time 0 at L(0). Labor input then grows with population at the constant rate n. On a proportionate scale, L follows a straight line, as shown in the figure.

equation (3.15) also have units of per year. The term $s\delta$ is the product of a pure number, s, and δ, which has units of per year. The population growth rate, n, also has units of per year.

We will find it useful to express the average product of capital, Y/K, in terms of real GDP per worker, y, and capital per worker, k. The relation is

$$Y/K = \frac{Y/L}{K/L} \quad \text{or}$$

$$Y/K = \frac{y}{k}$$

If we substitute this result for Y/K into equation (3.15), we get the central relation of the Solow model:

Key equation (Solow growth model):

(3.16) $\qquad \Delta k/k = s \bullet (y/k) - s\delta - n$

Finally, once we know the growth rate of capital per worker from equation (3.16), we can use equation (3.8) to determine the growth rate of real GDP per worker:

(3.17) $\qquad \Delta y/y = \alpha \bullet (\Delta k/k)$

$$\Delta y/y = \alpha \bullet [s \bullet (y/k) - s\delta - n]$$

If the capital-share coefficient, α, is fixed, we can go readily from the growth rate of capital per worker, $\Delta k/k$, in equation (3.16) to the growth rate of real GDP per worker, $\Delta y/y$, in equation (3.17). Since the number of workers grows at the same rate, n, as population, $\Delta y/y$ also equals the growth rate of real GDP per person.

The Transition and the Steady State The key to the Solow growth model is equation (3.16), which determines the growth rate of capital per worker, $\Delta k/k$. The equation shows that $\Delta k/k$ depends on the saving rate, s, the depreciation

rate, δ, the population growth rate, n, and the average product of capital, y/k. We have assumed that s, δ, and n are constants. Therefore, the only reason that $\Delta k/k$ varies over time is that the average product of capital, y/k, varies. We will now consider how this average product depends on capital per worker, k. In this way, we will find that changes over time in k lead to changes in y/k and, thereby, to changes in $\Delta k/k$.

We considered before the MPK, which is the ratio of a change in real GDP, ΔY, to a change in capital, ΔK. Geometrically, the marginal product was given by the slope of the production function, shown in Figure 3.7. We reproduce this construction in Figure 3.9. In this new graph, we compute the average product of capital, y/k, as the ratio of y (the variable on the vertical axis) to k (the variable on the horizontal axis). This ratio equals the slope of a straight line from the origin to the production function. The graph shows two such lines, one from the origin to point a and another from the origin to point b. The first line corresponds to capital per worker k_a and the second to the larger capital per worker k_b. The graph shows that the average product of capital, y/k, declines as capital per worker, k, rises, for example, from k_a to k_b. This **diminishing average product of capital** is analogous to the diminishing marginal product of capital, which we discussed before.

We can show diagrammatically how equation (3.16) determines the growth rate of capital per worker,

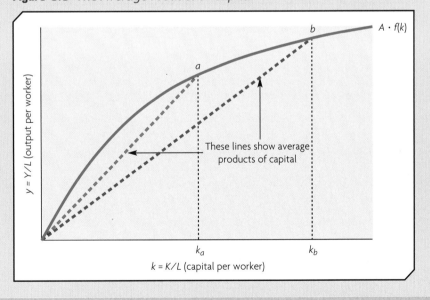

Figure 3.9 *The Average Product of Capital*

The graph shows the production function for output per worker, $y = Y/L$, versus capital per worker, $k = K/L$, as in Figure 3.7. The slope of a straight line from the origin to the production function gives the average product of capital, y/k, at the associated value of k. As k rises, for a given technology level, A, the average product of capital falls. For example, the slope of the dashed red line, from the origin to point a, is greater than that of the dashed blue line, from the origin to point b. Therefore, the production function exhibits diminishing average product of capital.

$\Delta k/k$, by graphing the terms on the right-hand side of the equation versus capital per worker, k. In the first term, $s \bullet (y/k)$, the crucial property is the one just derived: the average product of capital, y/k, diminishes as k rises. Hence, the curve for $s \bullet (y/k)$, slopes downward versus k, as shown in Figure 3.10.

The remaining terms on the right-hand side of equation (3.16) can be written as $-(s\delta + n)$. The term $s\delta + n$ is described by the horizontal line in Figure 3.10. Since $s\delta + n$ enters with a minus sign in equation (3.16), we have to subtract the position along the horizontal line from that of the curve (which gives $s \bullet [y/k]$) to determine $\Delta k/k$.

To study how the growth rate of capital per worker, $\Delta k/k$, changes over time, we have to know the capital per worker that the economy has initially—that is, at year 0. The economy begins with an accumulated stock of capital in the forms of machines and buildings. We represent this starting stock by $K(0)$. Since the initial labor is $L(0)$, the initial capital per worker is

$$k(0) = K(0)/L(0)$$

Recall that the production function in per-worker form is

(3.2) $$y = A \bullet f(k)$$

Therefore, the initial level of real GDP per worker is given by

$$y(0) = Y(0)/L(0)$$
$$y(0) = A \bullet f[k(0)]$$

In Figure 3.10, the growth rate of capital per worker, $\Delta k/k$, is the vertical distance between the $s \bullet (y/k)$ curve and the horizontal line, $s\delta + n$ (see equation [3.16]). We assume that, when $k = k(0)$, the curve lies above the line. In this case, capital per worker grows initially. That is, $\Delta k/k$ is greater than zero and is given by the distance marked by the green arrows. This positive growth rate means that capital per worker, k, increases over time—that is, k moves rightward in Figure 3.10. Notice that the distance between the curve and the horizontal line diminishes over time. Since this distance equals $\Delta k/k$, we have shown that the growth rate of capital per worker slows down over time. This result is an important property of the Solow model.

Eventually, the increase in capital per worker, k, eliminates the gap between the $s \bullet (y/k)$ curve and the $s\delta + n$ line in Figure 3.10. The gap gets close to zero when k approaches the value k^* on the horizontal axis. When $k = k^*$, $\Delta k/k$ equals zero. Therefore, k no longer moves to the right—with $\Delta k/k = 0$, k stays fixed at the value k^*. For this reason, we call k^* the capital per worker in the **steady state**. The corresponding real GDP per worker in the steady state is given from the production function in per-worker form in equation (3.2) by

$$y^* = f(k^*)$$

The results tell us that capital per worker, k, follows a **transition path** from its initial value, $k(0)$, to its steady-state value, k^*. Figure 3.11 shows this transition path as the red curve. Note that k starts at $k(0)$, rises over time, and eventually gets close to k^*, shown as the dashed blue line.

Recall that the formula for the growth rate of capital per worker is

Figure 3.10 *Determination of the Growth Rate of Capital per Worker in the Solow Model*

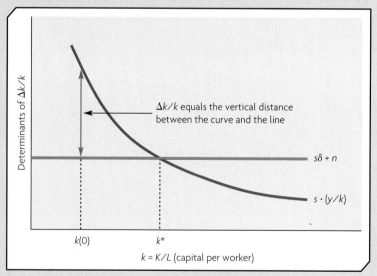

The technology level, A, is fixed. The vertical axis plots the two determinants of the growth rate of capital per worker, $\Delta k/k$, from the right-hand side of equation (3.16). $\Delta k/k$ equals the vertical distance between the negatively sloped $s \bullet (y/k)$ curve (in blue) and the horizontal line at $s\delta + n$ (in red). At the steady state, where $k = k^*$, the curve and line intersect, and $\Delta k/k = 0$. The initial capital per worker, $k(0)$, is assumed to be less than k^*. Therefore, when $k = k(0)$, $\Delta k/k$ is greater than zero and equal to the vertical distance shown by the green arrows.

(3.16) $\qquad \Delta k/k = s \bullet (y/k) - s\delta - n$

In the steady state, $\Delta k/k$ equals zero. Therefore, the right-hand side of equation (3.16) must also be zero in the steady state:

$$s \bullet (y^*/k^*) - s\delta - n = 0$$

If we move n to the right-hand side, combine the terms involving s on the left-hand side, and multiply through by k^*, we get

(3.17) $\qquad s \bullet (y^* - \delta k^*) = nk^*$

steady-state saving per worker = steady-state capital provded for each new worker

The left-hand side is saving per worker in the steady state. The right-hand side is the capital provided to each new worker in the steady state. Recall that k^* is the steady-state quantity of capital for each worker. The investment per worker needed to generate the necessary new capital is k^* multiplied by the growth rate, n, of the labor force. Therefore, the steady-state investment per worker, nk^*, on the right-hand side of equation (3.17) equals the steady-state saving per worker on the left-hand side of the equation.

Our analysis allows us to think of the process of economic growth in the Solow model as having two phases. In the first phase, there is a transition from an initial capital per worker, $k(0)$, to its steady-state value, k^*. This transition is shown by the red curve in Figure 3.11. During this transition, the growth rate of capital per worker, $\Delta k/k$, is greater than zero but declining gradually toward zero. In the second phase, the economy is in (or near) the steady state, represented by the dashed blue line in Figure 3.11. In this phase, $\Delta k/k = 0$.

Our goal was to determine how the growth rate of real GDP per worker (and per person), $\Delta y/y$, varies over time. We can now reach this goal, because $\Delta y/y$ equals the growth rate of capital per worker, $\Delta k/k$, multiplied by α, which we assume to be constant (with $0 < \alpha < 1$):

(3.8) $\qquad \Delta y/y = \alpha \bullet (\Delta k/k)$

Therefore, everything that we said about $\Delta k/k$ applies also to $\Delta y/y$, once we multiply by α. In particular, starting at the initial capital per worker $k(0)$ shown in Figure 3.10, we have that $\Delta y/y$ starts out positive, then declines as capital per worker, k, and real GDP per worker, y, rise. Eventually, when k reaches its steady-state value, k^*, $\Delta y/y$ falls to zero (because equation [3.8] implies $\Delta y/y = 0$ when $\Delta k/k = 0$). In the steady state, real GDP per worker, y, equals its steady-state value, y^*.

In Figure 3.11, we can view the transition as applying to real GDP per worker, y, as well as to capital per worker, k. That is, the red curve also describes the transition from the initial real GDP per worker, $y(0)$, to its steady-state value, y^*.

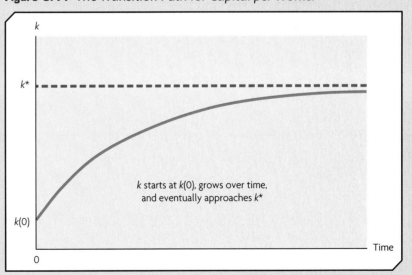

Figure 3.11 *The Transition Path for Capital per Worker*

k starts at k(0), grows over time, and eventually approaches k*

In the Solow model, described by Figure 3.10, capital per worker, k, starts at k(0) and then rises over time. The growth rate of k slows down over time, and k gradually approaches its steady-state value, k*. The transition path from k(0) to k* is shown by the red curve. The dashed blue line shows the steady-state value, k*.

dothemath

We have seen how Figure 3.10 determines the steady-state capital per worker, k^*. We can also determine k^* algebraically. If we set $\Delta k/k = 0$ in equation (3.16), the right-hand side of the equation must be zero, so that

$$s \bullet (y^*/k^*) - s\delta - n = 0$$

If we rearrange the terms in this equation and divide by s, we find that the average product of capital in the steady state is

(3.18) $$y^*/k^* = \delta + n/s$$

If we use equation (3.2) to substitute $A \cdot f(k^*)$ for y^*, we find that the steady-state capital per worker, k^*, must satisfy

(3.19) $$A \bullet f(k^*)/k^* = \delta + n/s$$

This algebraic result for k^* will be helpful in the next chapter, when we work further with the Solow model.

Questions and Problems

A. Review questions

1. What is a production function? In what way does it represent a relation between factor inputs and the level of output?

2. Explain the concepts of marginal and average products of capital. What is the difference between the two? Is the average product always greater than the marginal product?

3. Does a positive saving rate, $s > 0$, mean that capital per worker, k, rises over time? Explain by referring to equation (3.16).

4. Does a positive saving rate, $s > 0$, mean that output per worker, y, and capital per worker, k, grow in the long run? Explain.

5. Explain why an increase in capital per worker, k, reduces the growth rate of capital per worker, $\Delta k/k$. How does this result depend on diminishing productivity of capital?

B. Problems for discussion

6. Constant returns to scale
We have assumed that the production function, $A \bullet F(K, L)$, exhibits constant returns to scale.

That is, if we multiply the inputs, K and L, by any positive number, we multiply output, Y, by the same number. Show that this condition implies that we can write the production function as in equation (3.2):

$$y = A \bullet f(k)$$

where $y = Y/L$ and $k = K/L$.

7. Cobb-Douglas production function
The Cobb-Douglas production function, discussed in the appendix to this chapter, is given by

$$Y = AK^\alpha L^{1-\alpha}$$

where $0 < \alpha < 1$

a. Define A, K, and L.

b. What does it mean that Y is proportional to A?

c. What does it mean that the marginal product of capital (or labor), MPK (or MPL), is greater than zero? Show that the marginal products are positive in the Cobb-Douglas case.

d. What does it mean that the marginal product of capital (or labor), MPK (or MPL), is decreasing? Show that the marginal products are diminishing in the Cobb-Douglas case.

e. Does the Cobb-Douglas production function satisfy the property of constant returns to scale, discussed in Problem 6? Explain your answer.

8. Determination of steady-state capital per worker
Consider the steady-state capital per worker, k^*, determined in Figure 3.10. How is k^* affected by the following?

a. An increase in the saving rate, s.

b. An increase in the technology level, A.

c. An increase in the depreciation rate, δ.

d. An increase in the population growth rate, n.

9. Growth with a Cobb-Douglas production function
Suppose that the production function takes the Cobb-Douglas form, discussed in Problem 7:

$$Y = A \bullet F(K, L) = AK^{\alpha}L^{1-\alpha} \text{ where } 0 < \alpha < 1.$$

a. In the steady state, $\Delta k/k$, given by equation (3.16), equals zero. Use this condition, along with the form of the production function, to get a formula for the steady-state capital and output per worker, k^* and y^*.

b. Let $c = C/L$ be consumption per worker. What is steady-state consumption per worker, c^*?

c. Use equation (3.16) to work out a formula for the growth rate of capital per worker, $\Delta k/k$. Can you show that $\Delta k/k$ falls during the transition as k rises? What happens during the transition to the growth rate of output per worker, $\Delta y/y$?

10. Growth without diminishing productivity of capital
Suppose that the production function is $Y = AK$ (the so-called AK model).

a. What is the condition for the growth rate of capital per worker, $\Delta k/k$, in equation (3.16)? What does the $s \bullet (y/k)$ curve look like in Figure 3.10?

b. What are the growth rates of capital and output per worker, $\Delta k/k$ and $\Delta y/y$? Are these growth rates greater than zero? Do these growth rates decline during a transition?

c. Discuss how your results relate to diminishing productivity of capital. Is it plausible that diminishing productivity would not apply?

chapter appendix

This appendix has three parts. Part A provides a formal derivation of the growth-accounting equation, given in equation (3.4). Part B shows how to use the growth-accounting equation to analyze productivity growth. Part C discusses a common form of the production function, known as the Cobb-Douglas production function.

Part A: The Growth-Accounting Equation

The growth-accounting equation is

(3.4)
$$\Delta Y/Y = \Delta A/A + \alpha \cdot (\Delta K/K) + (1 - \alpha) \cdot (\Delta L/L)$$

We derive this equation more formally here and work out a formula for the coefficient α.

The production function is

(3.1)
$$Y = A \cdot F(K, L)$$

The form of this equation tells us that, for given K and L, an increase in the growth rate of technology, $\Delta A/A$, by 1% per year raises the growth rate of real GDP, $\Delta Y/Y$, by 1% per year. This reasoning explains why the term $\Delta A/A$ appears as it does in equation (3.4).

Consider now the effect from changes in K, when A and L are held fixed. If K increases by the amount ΔK, while A and L do not change, the increase in real GDP equals ΔK multiplied by the marginal product of capital, MPK:

$$\Delta Y = MPK \cdot \Delta K$$

To get the growth rate of Y, divide each side by Y:

$$\Delta Y/Y = (MPK/Y) \cdot \Delta K$$

Then, if we multiply and divide by K on the right-hand side, we get

$$\Delta Y/Y = \left(\frac{MPK \cdot K}{Y}\right) \cdot (\Delta K/K).$$

This result determines $\Delta Y/Y$ when K is growing but A and L are held fixed. More generally, it tells us the contribution of $\Delta K/K$ to $\Delta Y/Y$, even when A and L are changing. That is, to get the contribution of $\Delta K/K$ to $\Delta Y/Y$, multiply $\Delta K/K$ by the term $(MPK \cdot K)/Y$. Therefore, in equation (3.4), we must have that the coefficient α is given by

(3.20)
$$\alpha = (MPK \cdot K)/Y$$

In a competitive economy, capital's marginal product, MPK, equals the real rental price paid per unit of capital. (We work out this result in Chapter 6.) In that case, the term $MPK \cdot K$ equals the amount paid per unit of capital, MPK, multiplied by the quantity of capital, K, and therefore equals the total real rental payments to capital. Therefore, α is given by

$$\alpha = (MPK \cdot K)/Y$$
$$\alpha = \text{(real rental payments to capital)/(real GDP)}$$

If depreciation of capital stocks were zero, the real rental payments would equal the real income on capital and real GDP would equal the economy's total real income (that is, real national income). In this case, equation (3.20) implies that α equals the *capital share of income*. More generally, depreciation of capital stocks has to be subtracted from real rental payments and real GDP to compute real incomes. In this case, the capital share of income will be less than α. In any event, since the real rental payments to capital have to be smaller than real GDP, we have $0 < \alpha < 1$.

Now we consider the contribution to the growth of real GDP from growth in labor input. If L increases by the amount ΔL, while A and K are held fixed, the increase in real GDP equals ΔL multiplied by the marginal product of labor:

$$\Delta Y = MPL \cdot \Delta L$$

If we divide through by Y, we get

$$\Delta Y/Y = (MPL/Y) \cdot \Delta L$$

Then, if we multiply and divide by L on the right-hand side, we get

$$\Delta Y/Y = \left(\frac{MPL \cdot L}{Y}\right) \cdot (\Delta L/L).$$

Therefore, to get the contribution of $\Delta L/L$ to $\Delta Y/Y$, we have to multiply $\Delta L/L$ by the term $(MPL \cdot L)/Y$. Hence, in equation (3.4), we must have

(3.21)
$$1 - \alpha = (MPL \cdot L)/Y$$

In a competitive economy, labor's marginal product, MPL, equals the real wage rate. (We work out this result in Chapter 6.) Therefore, the term $MPL \cdot L$ equals the amount paid per unit of labor, MPL, multiplied by the quantity of labor, L, and therefore equals the total real wage payments to labor. If depreciation of capital stocks were zero, real GDP, Y, would equal total real income. In this case, equation (3.21) implies that $1 - \alpha$ equals the *labor share of income*. More generally, since total real income is less than Y, the labor share of income will be greater than $1 - \alpha$.

Part B: The Solow Residual

We know that the growth rate of technology, $\Delta A/A$ contributes to the growth rate of real GDP, $\Delta Y/Y$. Since the technology level, A, is not directly observable, we need some way to measure it from national-accounts data. A common approach is to rearrange the growth-accounting formula, equation (3.4), to get

(3.22)
$$\Delta A/A = \Delta Y/Y - \alpha \cdot (\Delta K/K) - (1 - \alpha) \cdot (\Delta L/L)$$
$$\text{growth rate of A} = \text{growth rate of real GDP} - \text{contribution of capital and labor}$$

The terms on the right-hand side can be measured from national-accounts data. Therefore, we can use this equation to measure the left-hand side, which equals the growth rate of technology, $\Delta A/A$.

The term $\Delta A/A$ in equations (3.4) and (3.22) is often called **total factor productivity (TFP) growth**. This concept comes from Robert Solow (1957) and is also often called the **Solow residual**. This terminology arises because equation (3.22) shows that we can compute $\Delta A/A$ as the *residual* after we take the growth rate of real GDP, $\Delta Y/Y$, and subtract out the contributions to growth from the changing factor inputs, $\alpha \cdot (\Delta K/K)$ for capital and $(1 - \alpha) \cdot (\Delta L/L)$ for labor. Economists have calculated these Solow residuals for various countries and time periods.

Part C: The Cobb-Douglas Production Function

We assumed in our analysis of the Solow model that α (which equals the capital share of income if depreciation can be neglected) was constant. That is, α did not change as capital per worker, k, varied. We can show that this assumption is valid for a particular form of the production function:

(3.23)
$$Y = A \cdot F(K, L)$$
$$Y = AK^{\alpha} L^{1-\alpha}$$

In this form, the constant α appears as the exponent on capital, K, whereas $1 - \alpha$ appears as the exponent on labor, L. We assume that α is a fraction, so that $0 < \alpha < 1$. This form of the production function has been used by economists in many theoretical and empirical studies.

The function in equation (3.23) is called the **Cobb-Douglas production function**, named after the economist and U.S. Senator Paul Douglas, who apparently teamed up with a mathematician named Cobb. It is easy to show that the Cobb-Douglas production function satisfies constant returns to scale. (Multiply K and L each by two and see what happens to Y.) In terms of real GDP and capital per worker, y and k, the Cobb-Douglas production function is

(3.24)

$$y = Y/L$$
$$= AK^\alpha L^{1-\alpha} \cdot (1/L)$$
$$= AK^\alpha L^{1-\alpha} \cdot L^{-1}$$
$$= AK^\alpha L^{-\alpha}$$
$$= A \cdot (K/L)^\alpha$$
$$y = AK^\alpha$$

We can show using calculus that the exponent α that appears in the Cobb-Douglas production function in equation (3.23) satisfies equation (3.20):

(3.20)

$$\alpha = (MPK \cdot K)/Y$$

To verify this result, recall that MPK is the effect on Y from a change in K, while holding fixed A and L. If we take the derivative of $Y = AK^\alpha L^{1-\alpha}$ with respect to K, for given A and L, we get

$$MPK = dY/dK$$
$$= \alpha AK^{\alpha-1} L^{1-\alpha}$$
$$= \alpha AK^\alpha K^{-1} L^{1-\alpha}$$
$$= \alpha AK^\alpha L^{1-\alpha} \cdot (1/K)$$
$$= \alpha \cdot (Y/K)$$

Therefore, we have

$$(MPK \cdot K)/Y = [\alpha \cdot (Y/K) \cdot K]/Y = \alpha$$

as in equation (3.20).

CHAPTER 4

© Monkey Business/Fotolia

Working with the Solow Growth Model

N ow that we have constructed the Solow growth model, we can put it into action by seeing how various economic changes affect growth in the short and long run. We begin by studying variations in the saving rate, the technology level, the level of labor input, and the population growth rate. Then we explore convergence, or a tendency for poor countries to catch up to rich ones.

We found in the Solow model that the growth rate of capital per worker, $\Delta k/k$, was given from equation (3.16). We repeat this key equation here:

(4.1)
$$\Delta k/k = s \cdot (y/k) - s\delta - n$$

where k is capital per worker, y is real gross domestic product (real GDP) per worker, y/k is the average product of capital, s is the saving rate, δ is the depreciation rate, and n is the population growth rate. We assumed that everything on the right-hand side was constant except for y/k. We found that, in the transition to the steady state, the rise in k led to a fall in y/k and, hence, to a fall in $\Delta k/k$. In the steady state, k was constant and, therefore, y/k was constant. Hence, $\Delta k/k$ was constant and equal to zero.

The production function in per-worker form was given in equation (3.2). We repeat this equation here:

(4.2)
$$y = A \cdot f(k)$$

If we substitute for y from equation (4.2) into equation (4.1), we get a revised version of the basic Solow equation:

(4.3)
$$\Delta k/k = sA \cdot f(k)/k - s\delta - n$$

Up to now, we assumed that the saving rate, s, the technology level, A, and the population growth rate, n, were fixed. Now we allow for changes in s, A, and n. We also consider changes in the level of labor input, L. We analyze the effects of these changes on the two phases of the Solow model. What are the effects on the transition to the steady state, and what are the effects on the steady state? We can think of the first part as representing the short-run effects and the second part as representing the long-run effects.

A Change in the Saving Rate

How do differences in the saving rate, s, affect economic growth? As an example of differences in saving rates, we can compare nations in which the residents regularly save at a high rate—such as Singapore and South Korea, or some other East Asian countries—with places in which the residents typically save at a low rate—such as most countries in sub-Saharan Africa or Latin America. Some of the differences in saving rates result from government policies and some may stem from cultural differences. The important point is that saving rates differ across societies and over time.

Figure 4.1 extends the Solow model from Figure 3.9 to consider two saving rates, s_1 and s_2, where s_2 is greater than s_1. Each saving rate determines a different curve for $s \cdot (y/k)$—the one with s_2 lies above that for s_1. Recall that the growth rate of capital per worker, $\Delta k/k$, equals the vertical distance between the $s \cdot (y/k)$ curve and the horizontal line, $s\delta + n$. There are also two positions for this horizontal line, one for s_1 and the other for s_2. However, this shift in the horizontal line turns out to be minor. Therefore, we can see from the Figure 4.1 that $\Delta k/k$ is higher at any capital per worker, k, when the saving rate is s_2 rather than s_1.[1] Specifically, at $k(0)$, $\Delta k/k$ is higher when the saving rate is s_2, rather than s_1. (We have assumed that $\Delta k/k$ is greater than zero for both saving rates.)

For either saving rate, the growth rate of capital per worker, $\Delta k/k$, declines as capital per worker, k, rises above $k(0)$. When the saving rate is s_1, $\Delta k/k$ reaches zero when k attains the steady-state value k_1^* in Figure 4.1. However, at k_1^*, $\Delta k/k$ would still be greater than zero if the saving rate were higher—for example, if it equaled s_2. If the saving rate is s_2, capital per worker, k, rises beyond k_1^* until it reaches the higher steady-state value, k_2^*. Since capital per worker is higher, we also know that real GDP per worker is greater when the saving rate is s_2—that is, $y_2^* > y_1^*$.

To summarize, in the short run, an increase in the saving rate raises the growth rate of capital per worker. This growth rate remains higher during the transition to the steady state. In the long run, the growth rate of capital per worker is the same—zero—for any saving rate. In this long-run or steady-state situation, a higher saving rate leads to higher steady-state

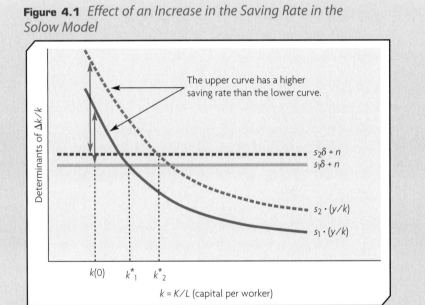

Figure 4.1 *Effect of an Increase in the Saving Rate in the Solow Model*

This graph comes from Figure 3.9. The curves for $s \cdot (y/k)$ are for the saving rates s_1 and s_2, where s_2 is greater than s_1. Similarly, the horizontal lines for $s\,\delta + n$ are for the saving rates s_1 and s_2. The growth rate of capital per worker, $\Delta k/k$, is higher at any k when the saving rate is higher. For example, at $k(0)$, when the saving rate is s_1, $\Delta k/k$ equals the vertical distance shown by the green arrows. When the saving rate is s_2, $\Delta k/k$ equals the vertical distance shown by the red arrows. In the steady state, $\Delta k/k$ is zero, regardless of the saving rate. The higher saving rate yields a higher steady-state capital per worker; that is, k_2^* is greater than k_1^*.

---

[1] The rise in the $s \cdot (y/k)$ curve is greater than the increase in the $s\,\delta + n$ line as long as $y/k > \delta$; that is, as long as real GDP per worker, y, is greater than depreciation per worker, δk. Thus, we need only to be sure that the net domestic product is greater than zero, as is surely the case.

We can determine the steady-state capital per worker, k^*, algebraically from the steady-state condition given in equation (3.19). We repeat this result here:

(4.4) $$A \cdot f(k^*)/k^* = \delta + n/s$$

An increase in s lowers the right-hand side. Hence, the left-hand side must be lower, and this reduction can occur only through a decrease in the average product of capital, $A \cdot f(k^*)/k^*$. We know from Figure 3.8 that, if A is fixed, a decrease in the average product of capital requires an increase in capital per worker, k. Therefore, an increase in s raises k^*.

capital per worker, k^*, not to a change in the growth rate (which remains at zero).

One important extension of the Solow model—carried out in the mid-1960s by David Cass (1965) and Tjalling Koopmans (1965)—allowed households to choose the saving rate, s. To study this choice, we need the microeconomic analysis of how households determine consumption at different points in time. We defer this analysis to Chapter 7.

A Change in the Technology Level

We have assumed, thus far, that the technology level, A, was fixed. In reality, technology varies over time and across locations. For examples of improvements in technology over time, we can think of the introductions of electric power, automobiles, computers, and the Internet. For differences across locations, we can think of businesses in advanced economies, such as the United States and Western Europe, as having better access to leading technologies than their counterparts in poor countries. To assess the influences from differences in technologies, we begin by considering the effects in the Solow model from a change in the technology level, A.

The formula for the growth rate of capital per worker is again

(4.3) $$\Delta k/k = sA \cdot f(k)/k - s\delta - n$$

where $A \cdot f(k)/k$ is the average product of capital, y/k. Note that a higher A means that y/k is higher at a given k.

Figure 4.2 compares two levels of technology, A_1 and A_2, where A_2 is greater than A_1. Each technology level corresponds to a different curve for $s \cdot (y/k) = sA \cdot f(k)/k$. The curve with the higher technology level, A_2, lies above the other one. Notice that the positions of the two curves are similar to those in Figure 4.1, which considered two values of the saving rate, s. Hence, our analysis of effects from a change in A is similar to that for a change in s.

At the initial capital per worker, $k(0)$, in Figure 4.2, the growth rate of capital per worker, $\Delta k/k$, is higher with the higher technology level, A_2, than with the lower one, A_1. In both cases, $\Delta k/k$ declines over time. For the lower technology level, $\Delta k/k$ falls to zero when capital per worker, k, attains the steady-state value k_1^*. For the higher technology level, k rises beyond k_1^* to reach the higher steady-state value k_2^*. Thus, an increase in A results in a higher $\Delta k/k$ over the transition period. In the long run, $\Delta k/k$ still falls to zero, but the steady-state capital per worker, k^*, is higher. That is, k_2^* is greater than k_1^*.

An increase in the technology level, A, raises the steady-state real GDP per worker, $y^* = A \cdot f(k^*)$, for two reasons. First, an increase in A raises real GDP per

dothemath

We can derive the effect of A on k^* algebraically from the condition we used before:

(4.4) $$A \cdot f(k^*)/k^* = \delta + n/s$$

An increase in A does not affect the right-hand side. Therefore, the steady-state capital per worker, k^*, must adjust on the left-hand side to keep the steady-state average product of capital, $A \cdot f(k^*)/k^*$, the same. Since the increase in A raises this average product, k^* must change in a way that reduces the average product. As we know from Figure 3.8, a reduction in the average product of capital requires a rise in k^*. Therefore, an increase in A raises k^*.

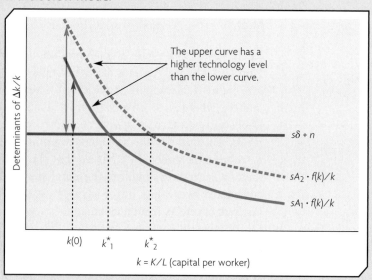

Figure 4.2 *Effect of an Increase in the Technology Level in the Solow Model*

The upper curve has a higher technology level than the lower curve.

$s\delta + n$

$sA_2 \cdot f(k)/k$

$sA_1 \cdot f(k)/k$

Determinants of $\Delta k/k$

$k(0)$ k_1^* k_2^*

$k = K/L$ (capital per worker)

The upper curve has a higher technology level than the lower curve. This graph comes from Figure 3.9. The two curves for $s \cdot (y/k) = sA \cdot f(k)/k$ are for the technology levels A_1 and A_2, where A_2 is greater than A_1. The growth rate of capital per worker, $\Delta k/k$, is higher at any k when the technology level is higher. For example, at $k(0)$, when the technology level is A_1, $\Delta k/k$ equals the vertical distance shown by the blue arrows. When the technology level is A_2, $\Delta k/k$ equals the vertical distance shown by the red arrows. In the steady state, $\Delta k/k$ is zero, regardless of the technology level. The higher technology level yields a higher steady-state capital per worker; that is, k_2^* is greater than k_1^*.

worker, y, for given capital per worker, k. Second, the steady-state capital per worker, k^*, is higher when A is higher. On both counts, an increase in A raises y^*.

To summarize, in the short run, an increase in the technology level, A, raises the growth rates of capital and real GDP per worker. These growth rates remain higher during the transition to the steady state. In the long run, the growth rates of capital and real GDP per worker are the same—zero—for any technology level. In this long-run or steady-state situation, a higher technology level leads to higher steady-state capital and real GDP per worker, k^* and y^*, not to changes in the growth rates (which remain at zero).

Consumption in the Solow Model

Recall that real income equals real net domestic product, $Y - \delta K$, which equals consumption, C, plus saving, $s \cdot (Y - \delta K)$. Therefore, in terms of quantities per worker, we have

$$y - \delta k = c + s \cdot (y - \delta k)$$

where c is consumption per worker. An increase in the saving rate, s, means that c must fall for given $y - \delta k$. However, since higher saving leads in the long run to higher real GDP, consumption may increase in the long run. Here, we consider what the Solow model says about the effect of saving on consumption in the long run.

We found that an increase in the saving rate, s, raises the steady-state capital and real GDP per worker, k^* and y^*. The rise in real GDP per worker leads to an increase in the typical person's real income. However, people care about their consumption, not their income, per se. Thus, we want to know how a rise in the saving rate affects steady-state consumption per person.

Consumption per person is given by

$$consumption\ per\ person = (consumption\ per\ worker)$$
$$\times\ (workers/population)$$

The ratio of workers to population is the labor-force participation rate, which we have assumed to be constant. Therefore, consumption per person always moves along with consumption per worker, c. This result means that we can focus on c to see what happens to consumption per person.

Since consumption equals the real income not saved, and saving per worker in the steady state is $s \cdot (y^* - \delta k^*)$, we have

(4.5) $\qquad c^* = y^* - \delta k^* - s \cdot (y^* - \delta k^*)$

where c^* is the steady-state value of c. We also know from Chapter 3 that steady-state saving per worker is just enough to provide new workers with capital to work with:

(3.17) $\qquad s \cdot (y^* - \delta k^*) = nk^*$

Therefore, we can substitute nk^* for $s \cdot (y^* - \delta k^*)$ on the right-hand side of equation (4.5) to get

(4.6) $\qquad c^* = y^* - \delta k^* - nk^*$

We know that a rise in the saving rate, s, raises k^*, say, by the amount Δk^*. The change in c^* follows from equation (4.6) as

$$\Delta c^* = \Delta y^* - (\delta + n) \cdot \Delta k^*$$

We can compute Δy^* by noting that it must equal Δk^* multiplied by the marginal product of capital, MPK:

$$\Delta y^* = MPK \cdot \Delta k^*$$

Therefore, if we substitute $MPK \cdot \Delta k^*$ for Δy^*, we get that the change in c^* is given by

(4.7) $\qquad \Delta c^* = MPK \cdot \Delta k^* - (\delta + n) \cdot \Delta k^*$
$\qquad\qquad \Delta c^* = (MPK - \delta - n) \cdot \Delta k^*$

We see from equation (4.7) that Δc^* is greater than zero if MPK is greater than $\delta + n$. The part $MPK - \delta$ is the net marginal product of capital—that is, the MPK net of depreciation. This term gives the rate of return on additional capital. Hence, equation (4.7) says that an increase in steady-state capital per worker, k^*, raises steady-state consumption per worker, c^*, as long as the rate of return on capital, $MPK - \delta$, is greater than the population growth rate, n. Typical estimates of rates of return on capital are around 10%, whereas population growth rates are around 0–2%. Therefore, in normal circumstances, Δc^* is greater than zero.

The positive effect of the saving rate, s, on steady-state consumption per worker, c^*, and, therefore, on steady-state consumption per person, does not necessarily mean that the typical person is better off by saving more. In order to achieve the higher steady-state capital per worker, k^*, households have to save more during the transition to the steady state. Hence, levels of consumption per person during part of the transition have to be reduced. Thus, there is a trade-off—less consumption per person in the short run and more consumption per person in the long run. Whether the typical person is better or worse off depends on, first, how much consumption is gained in the long run in comparison with how much is lost in the short run and, second, on how patient people are about deferring consumption.

Changes in Labor Input and the Population Growth Rate

We can consider two types of changes in labor input, L. First, L could change at a point in time because of a sudden shift in the size of the labor force. Second, a change in the population growth rate could affect the long-term time path of labor input. We begin with a one-time change in L.

A Change in Labor Input

Changes in labor input, L, can result from shifts in the labor force. For example, the labor force could decline precipitously due to an epidemic of disease. An extreme case from the mid-1300s is the bubonic plague, or Black Death, which is estimated to have killed about 20% of the European population. The potential loss of life due to the ongoing AIDS epidemic in Africa may be analogous, and there is also a lot of concern about avian flu. In these examples, physical capital does not change initially, and the starting capital per worker, $k(0) = K(0)/L(0)$, rises because of the drop in $L(0)$.

Wartime casualties are another source of decrease in the labor force. However, since wartime tends also to destroy physical capital, the effect on capital per worker depends on the circumstances. Migration can also change the labor force. One example is the Mariel boatlift of over 100,000 Cuban refugees, mostly to Miami, in 1980. Another case is the large in-migration to Portugal in the mid-1970s by its citizens who had been residing in African colonies. When these colonies became independent, many residents returned to Portugal, and this inflow raised the domestic Portuguese population by about 10%. Finally, in Israel in the 1990s, the roughly 1,000,000 Russian Jewish immigrants constituted about 20% of Israel's 1990 population.

Figure 3.8 showed the path of labor input, L, starting at $L(0)$ and then growing at the constant rate n. In Figure 4.3, we assume that the initial level of labor input rises from $L(0)$ to $L(0)'$ while n does not change. Thus, we are considering a proportionate increase in the level of labor input, L, in each year. Since the initial stock of capital, $K(0)$, does not change, the increase in $L(0)$ decreases the initial capital per worker, $k(0) = K(0)/L(0)$.

Figure 4.4 considers the effects of an increase in the level of labor input. The rise in initial labor from $L(0)$ to $L(0)'$ reduces the initial capital per worker from $k(0)$ to $k(0)'$. However, a key point is that the curve for $s \cdot (y/k)$ and the horizontal line at $s\delta + n$ do not change. The reduction in $k(0)$ raises the initial average product of capital, y/k (see Figure 3.9) and leads, thereby, to a higher $s \cdot (y/k)$ along the unchanged curve. Consequently, the growth rate of capital per worker, $\Delta k/k$, rises initially. We can see this result in Figure 4.3 because the vertical distance between the $s \cdot (y/k)$ curve and the $s\delta + n$ line is greater at $k(0)$

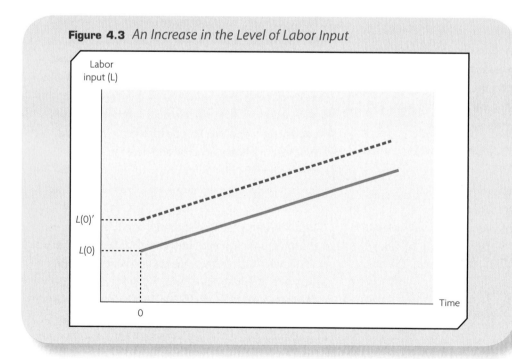

Figure 4.3 *An Increase in the Level of Labor Input*

In year 0, labor input jumps upward from $L(0)$ to $L(0)'$. The population growth rate, n, does not change.

We can again work out the steady-state results algebraically from the condition

(4.4)
$$A \cdot f(k^*)/k^* = \delta + n/s$$

Note that A, s, n, and δ are constant, and the level of labor input, L, does not enter into the equation. Therefore, the steady-state capital per worker, k^*, does not change when L changes.

(the red arrows) than at $k(0)$ (the blue arrows). The growth rate $\Delta k/k$ remains higher during the transition to the steady state. However, $\Delta k/k$ still declines toward its long-run value of zero. Moreover, the steady-state capital per worker, k^*, is the same whether labor input starts at $L(0)'$ or $L(0)$. Thus, if $L(0)'$ is twice as large as $L(0)$, the long-run level of capital, K, is also twice as large (so that capital per worker remains the same). Since k^* is unchanged, we also have that real GDP per worker, y^*, does not change. In the long run, an economy with twice as much labor has twice as much real GDP, Y.

To summarize, in the short run, an increase in labor input, $L(0)$, raises the growth rates of capital and real GDP per worker. These growth rates remain higher during the transition to the steady state. In the long run, the growth rates of capital and real GDP per worker are the same—zero—for any level of labor input, $L(0)$. Moreover, the steady-state capital and real GDP per worker, k^* and y^*, are the same for any L. Thus, in the long run, an economy with twice as much labor input has twice as much capital and real GDP.

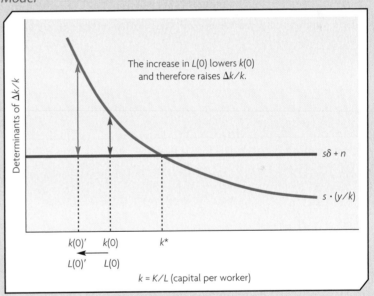

Figure 4.4 *Effect of an Increase in Labor Input in the Solow Model*

This graph comes from Figure 3.10. If the initial level of labor input rises from $L(0)$ to $L(0)'$, the initial capital per worker declines from $k(0) = K(0)/L(0)$ to $k(0)' = K(0)/L(0)'$. Therefore, the growth rate of capital per worker, $\Delta k/k$, rises initially. Note that the vertical distance shown by the red arrows is larger than that shown by the blue arrows. The steady-state capital per worker, k^*, is the same for the two values of $L(0)$.

A Change in the Population Growth Rate

Figure 4.5 shows an increase in the population growth rate from n to n'. We assume now that the initial population and, hence, level of labor input, $L(0)$, do not change. Thus, the initial capital per worker, $k(0)$, does not change.

Figure 4.5 *An Increase in the Population Growth Rate*

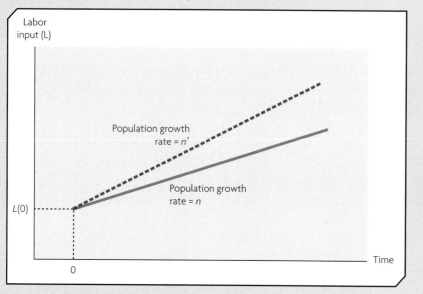

The population growth rate rises in year 0 from n to n'. The initial level of labor input, $L(0)$, does not change.

In Figure 4.6, the higher population growth rate corresponds to a higher horizontal line for $s\delta + n$. Recall that the growth rate of capital per worker, $\Delta k/k$, equals the vertical distance between the $s \bullet (y/k)$ curve and the $s\delta + n$ line. Therefore, $\Delta k/k$ is lower at any capital per worker, k, when the population growth rate is n' rather than n. We can also see this result from the formula for the growth rate of capital per worker:

(4.3) $\quad \Delta k/k = sA \bullet f(k)/k - s\delta - n$

A higher n—the yellow shaded term—lowers $\Delta k/k$ for given k. The reason that $\Delta k/k$ is lower when n is higher is that a larger portion of saving goes to providing the growing labor force, L, with capital to work with.

For either population growth rate in Figure 4.6, the growth rate of capital per worker, $\Delta k/k$, declines as capital per worker rises above $k(0)$. When the population growth rate is n' $\Delta k/k$ reaches zero when k attains the steady-state value $(k^*)'$. However, at $(k^*)'$, $\Delta k/k$ would still be greater than zero if the population growth rate were lower—in particular, if it equaled n. Thus, if the population growth rate is n, capital per worker rises beyond $(k^*)'$—k increases until it reaches the steady-state value k^*, which is greater than $(k^*)'$.

Figure 4.6 *Effect of an Increase in the Population Growth Rate in the Solow Model*

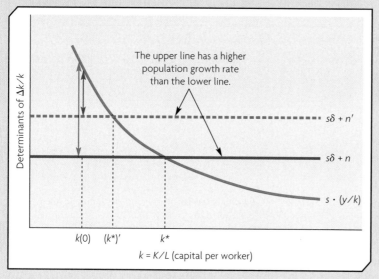

This graph comes from Figure 3.10. An increase in the population growth rate from n to n' raises the horizontal line from $s\delta + n$ to $s\delta + n'$. The growth rate of capital per worker, $\Delta k/k$, is lower at any k when the population growth rate is higher. For example, at $k(0)$, when the population growth rate is n, $\Delta k/k$ equals the vertical distance given by the red arrows. When the population growth rate is n', $\Delta k/k$ equals the vertical distance given by the blue arrows. In the steady state, $\Delta k/k$ is zero, regardless of the population growth rate. A higher population growth rate yields a lower steady-state capital per worker; that is, $(k^*)'$ is less than k^*.

As usual, we can find the effect of n on k^* algebraically from the condition

(4.4) $$A \cdot f(k^*)/k^* = \delta + n/s$$

An increase in n raises the right-hand side of the equation. Hence, the steady-state average product of capital, $A \cdot f(k^*)/k^* = y^*/k^*$, has to rise on the left-hand side. Because of diminishing average product of capital (Figure 3.9), this change requires a decrease in k^*. Therefore, as we already found, an increase in n reduces k^*.

Figure 4.6 shows that, at the initial capital per worker, $k(0)$, an increase in the population growth rate from n to n' lowers the growth rate of capital per worker, $\Delta k/k$. The growth rate of real GDP per worker, $\Delta y/y$, falls correspondingly. Thus, in the short run, a higher n lowers $\Delta k/k$ and $\Delta y/y$. These growth rates remain lower during the transition to the steady state. However, in the steady state, $\Delta k/k$ and $\Delta y/y$ are zero for any n. That is, a higher n leads to lower steady-state capital and real GDP per worker, k^* and y^*, not to changes in the growth rates, $\Delta k/k$ and $\Delta y/y$ (which remain at zero). A change in n does affect the steady-state growth rates of the levels of capital and real GDP, $\Delta K/K$ and $\Delta Y/Y$. An increase in n by 1% per year raises the steady-state values of $\Delta K/K$ and $\Delta Y/Y$ by 1% per year.

We can see from Figure 4.6 that an increase in the depreciation rate, δ, affects the steady-state capital per worker in the same way as an increase in the population growth rate, n. This result follows because equation (4.3) involves the term $s\delta + n$, which can rise either from an increase in n or an increase in δ. The kind of analysis that we carried out for an increase in n tells us that an increase in δ lowers the growth rates of capital and real GDP per worker, $\Delta k/k$ and $\Delta y/y$, in the short run. In the steady state, an increase in δ leads to lower capital and real GDP per worker, k^* and y^*, not to changes in $\Delta k/k$ and $\Delta y/y$, which remain at zero.[2]

Convergence

ne of the most important questions about economic growth is whether poor countries tend to converge or catch up to rich countries. Is there a systematic tendency for low-income countries like those in Africa to catch up to the rich OECD countries? We will start our answer to this question by seeing what the Solow model says about **convergence**. Then we will look at how the facts on convergence match up with the Solow model.

Convergence in the Solow Model

To study convergence, we focus on the transition for capital per worker, k, as it rises from its initial value, $k(0)$, to its steady-state value, k^*. In Figure 3.11, we see that k^* works like a target or magnet for k during the transition. Therefore, an important part of our analysis of convergence concerns the determination of k^*. We have studied how k^* depends on the saving rate, s, the technology level, A, the population growth rate, n, the depreciation rate, δ, and the initial level of labor input, $L(0)$. We can summarize these results in the form of a function for k^*:

(4.7) $$k^* = k^*[s, A, n, \delta, L(0)]$$
$$(+)(+)(-)(-)(0)$$

---

[2] One difference is that an increase in n raises the steady-state growth rates of the levels of capital and real GDP, $(\Delta K/K)^*$ and $(\Delta Y/Y)^*$, whereas an increase in ffl does not affect these steady-state growth rates.

Table 4.1 *Effects on Steady-State Capital per Worker, k**

Increase in this Variable	Effect on k^*
saving rate, s	increase
technology level, A	increase
depreciation rate, δ	decrease
population growth rate, n	decrease
level of labor force, $L(0)$	no effect

Note: The right-hand column shows the effect of an increase in the variable in the left-hand column on the steady-state ratio of capital to labor, k^*. These results come from equation (4.7).

The sign below each variable indicates the effect on k^*. Thus, equation (4.7) shows that k^* rises with s and A, falls with n and δ, and does not depend on the level of labor input, represented by $L(0)$. Table 4.1 summarizes these results.

To apply the Solow model to convergence, we have to allow for more than one economy. In making this extension, we assume that the economies are independent of each other. Specifically, they do not engage in international trade in goods and services or in financial assets. In other words, we still think of each economy as closed.

Think now of two economies, 1 and 2, and suppose that they start with capital per worker of $k(0)_1$ and $k(0)_2$, respectively, where $k(0)_1$ is less than $k(0)_2$. Each economy is assumed to have the same production function, $y = A \bullet f(k)$. Thus, economy 2 is initially more advanced in the sense of having higher capital and real GDP per worker, $k(0)$ and $y(0)$. Imagine that each economy has the same values for the determinants of k^* listed in Table 4.1, so that they have the same steady-state capital per worker, k^*.

We show this situation in Figure 4.7, which has been adapted from Figure 3.10. The only difference between the two economies is that one starts at $k(0)_1$ and the other at $k(0)_2$. Therefore, the differences in the transition paths of k depend only on the differences in these starting values. The graph in Figure 4.7 shows that the vertical distance between the $s \bullet (y/k)$ curve and the $s\delta + n$ line is greater at $k(0)_1$ than at $k(0)_2$. That is, the distance marked with red arrows is greater than that marked with blue arrows. Therefore, the growth rate of capital per worker, $\Delta k/k$, is higher initially for economy 1 than economy 2. Because k grows at a faster rate in economy 1, its level of k converges over time toward economy 2's level.

Figure 4.8 shows the transition paths of capital per worker, k, for economies 1 and 2. Note that $k(0)_1$ is less than $k(0)_2$, but k_1 gradually approaches k_2. (At the same time, k_1 and k_2 both gradually approach k^*.) Thus, economy 1 converges toward economy 2 in terms of the levels of k.

We can express the results in terms of real GDP per worker, y. The capital per worker, k, determines y from the production function:

(4.2) $$y = A \bullet f(k)$$

Since economy 1 starts with lower capital per worker, $k(0)$, it must also start with lower real GDP per worker—$y(0)_1$ is less than $y(0)_2$. The growth rate of real

GDP per worker relates to the growth rate of capital per worker from equation (3.8), which we repeat:

(4.8)
$$\Delta y/y = \alpha \bullet (\Delta k/k)$$

where α is the capital-share coefficient. (We assume that α is the same in the two economies.) We showed in Figure 4.7 that $\Delta k/k$ was higher initially in economy 1 than in economy 2. Therefore, $\Delta y/y$ is also higher initially in economy 1. Hence, economy 1's real GDP per worker, y, converges over time toward economy 2's real GDP per worker. The transition paths for y in the two economies look like those shown for k in Figure 4.8.

To summarize, the Solow model says that a poor economy—with low capital and real GDP per worker—grows faster than a rich one. The reason is the diminishing average product of capital, y/k. A poor economy, such as economy 1 in Figure 4.7, has the advantage of having a high average product of capital, y/k. This high average product explains why the growth rates of capital and real GDP per worker are higher than in the initially more advanced economy, economy 2. Thus, the Solow model predicts that poorer economies tend to

Figure 4.7 *Convergence in the Solow Model*

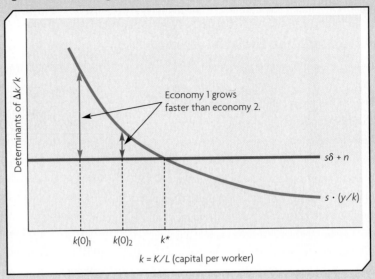

This graph comes from Figure 3.10. Economy 1 starts with lower capital per worker than economy 2—$k(0)_1$ is less than $k(0)_2$. Economy 1 grows faster initially because the vertical distance between the $s \bullet (y/k)$ curve and the $s\delta + n$ line is greater at $k(0)_1$ than at $k(0)_2$. That is, the distance marked by the red arrows is greater than that marked by the blue arrows. Therefore, capital per worker in economy 1, k_1, converges over time toward that in economy 2, k_2.

Figure 4.8 *Convergence and Transition Paths for Two Economies*

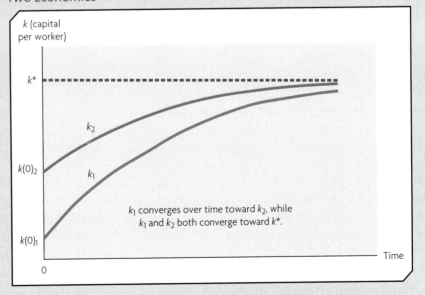

Economy 1 starts at capital per worker $k(0)_1$, and economy 2 starts at $k(0)_2$, where $k(0)_1$ is less than $k(0)_2$. The two economies have the same steady-state capital per worker, k^*, shown by the dashed blue line. In each economy, k rises over time toward k^*. However, k grows faster in economy 1 because $k(0)_1$ is less than $k(0)_2$. (See Figure 4.7.) Therefore, k_1 converges over time toward k_2.

Endogenous Population Growth

Our analysis treated the population growth rate, n, as exogenous—determined outside of the model. However, since the writings of Thomas Malthus (1798), economists have argued that population growth responds to economic variables. Malthus was a British economist and minister who wrote his *Essay on Population* in 1798. He argued that an increase in real income per person raised population growth by improving life expectancy, mainly through better nutrition but also through improved sanitation and medical care. Another influence, Malthus believed, was that higher income encouraged greater fertility. He thought that birth rates would rise as long as real income per person exceeded a **subsistence level**, which is the amount needed to pay for the basic necessities of life.

We can incorporate Malthus's ideas about population growth into the Solow model. In Figure 3.10, for a given population growth rate, n, the economy approaches a steady-state capital per worker, k^*, and a corresponding real NDP per worker, $y^* = A \cdot f(k^*) - \delta k^*$, which equals real national income per worker. The real income per person is then

$$real\ income\ per\ person =$$
$$(real\ NDP\ per\ worker) \times (workers/population)$$

The last term on the right-hand side is the labor-force participation rate, which we assume to be fixed.

When household real income per person rose above the subsistence level, Malthus believed that the population growth rate would rise. Figure 4.6 showed the effect from a rise in the population growth rate; this change lowered the

steady-state capital and real GDP per worker. According to Malthus, this process would continue until the steady-state real income per person fell to the subsistence level.

Malthus's view on the relation between real income per person and life expectancy is reasonable. Data across countries show that higher real GDP per person matches up closely with higher life expectancy at birth.[3] However, Malthus's idea about fertility seems unreasonable. At least in the cross-country data since 1960, higher real GDP per person matches up with lower fertility.[4] In fact, this relation is so strong that higher real GDP per person matches up with a lower population growth rate, even though countries with higher real GDP per person have higher life expectancy.

We can modify the Solow model to include Malthus's idea that population growth is endogenous. However, contrary to Malthus, we should assume a negative effect of real GDP per person—and, hence, of capital per worker, k—on the population growth rate, n.

The condition for the growth rate of capital per worker is again

(4.3) $\qquad \Delta k/k = sA \cdot f(k/k) - s\delta - n$

During the transition to the steady state, a rise in k reduced the average product of capital, y/k, and thereby decreased the growth rate of capital per worker, $\Delta k/k$. Now we have that a rise in k also lowers n. This change raises $\Delta k/k$ and, thus, offsets the effect from a reduced average product of capital. Hence, a declining population growth rate is one reason why rich societies can sustain growing capital and real GDP per worker for a long time.

converge over time toward richer ones in terms of the levels of capital and real GDP per worker.

Facts About Convergence

The main problem with these predictions about convergence is that they conflict with the evidence for a broad

group of countries. We already looked, in Figure 3.3, at growth rates of real GDP per person from 1960 to 2000. To apply the Solow model to these data, we have to translate from amounts per worker to amounts per person. The formula for real GDP per person is again

$$real\ GDP\ per\ person =$$
$$(real\ GDP\ per\ worker) \bullet (workers/population)$$

[3] Although this relation is suggestive, it does not prove that the causation is from higher real income per person to greater life expectancy, rather than the reverse. In fact, both directions of causation seem to be important.

[4] This relation does not prove that the causation is from higher real income per person to lower fertility, rather than the reverse. In fact, the reverse effect is predicted by the Solow model. If a society chooses, perhaps for cultural reasons, to have higher fertility and population growth, the model predicts lower steady-state real GDP per worker. In practice, both directions of causation seem to be important.

The ratio of workers to population is the labor-force participation rate, which we have assumed to be constant. For example, if the ratio is around one-half, as in recent U.S. experience, real GDP per person is about one-half of real GDP per worker.

With this translation, we find that the Solow model predicts convergence for real GDP per person. Specifically, the model predicts that a lower level of real GDP per person would match up with a higher subsequent growth rate of real GDP per person.

Figure 4.9 uses the data for countries from Figure 3.3 to plot growth rates of real GDP per person from 1960 to 2000 against levels of real GDP per person in 1960. If the convergence predictions from the Solow model were correct, we should find low levels of real GDP per person matched with high growth rates, and high levels of real GDP per person matched with low growth rates. Instead, it is difficult to discern any pattern in the data—if anything, there is a slight tendency for the growth rate to rise with the level of real GDP per person.

The sample of countries included in Figure 4.9 is very broad; it includes the richest and poorest economies in the world. The convergence prediction of the Solow model accords better with the data if we limit the observations to economies that have more similar economic and social characteristics. Figure 4.10 on page 65 is the same as Figure 4.9, except that the sample is limited to 18 advanced OECD countries. For this limited sample, lower levels of real GDP per person in 1960 do match up, on average, with

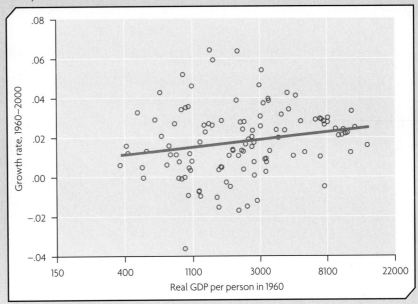

Figure 4.9 *Growth Rate Versus Level of Real GDP per Person for a Broad Group of Countries*

The horizontal axis shows real GDP per person in 1960 in 2000 U.S. dollars on a proportionate scale for 112 countries. The vertical axis shows the growth rate of real GDP per person for each country from 1960 to 2000. The red line is the straight line that provides a best fit to the relation between the growth rate of real GDP per person (the variable on the vertical axis) and the level of real GDP per person (on the horizontal axis). Although this line slopes upward, the slope is—in a statistical sense—negligibly different from zero. Hence, the growth rate is virtually unrelated to the level of real GDP per person. Thus, this broad group of countries does not display convergence.

higher growth rates from 1960 to 2000. This pattern reflects especially the catching up of some of the initially poorer OECD countries—Greece, Ireland, Portugal, and Spain—to the richer ones.

Figure 4.11 on page 65 shows an even clearer pattern of convergence for a still more homogenous group of economies—the states of the United States. The figure plots the average growth rate of personal income per person from 1880 to 2000 against the level of personal income per person in 1880.[5] This graph shows a dramatic tendency for the initially poorer states to grow faster than the initially richer ones over the 120 years after 1880. This convergence tendency does not reflect only the recovery of the southern states, which were defeated during the U.S. Civil War (1861–1865). The convergence pattern applies if we examine economic performance within any of the four main regions—Northeast, South, Midwest, and West. Researchers have found results similar to those in

---

[5] We use personal income because data on gross state product are unavailable for the U.S. states for the period since 1880.

Figure 4.10 *Growth Rate Versus Level of Real GDP per Person for OECD Countries*

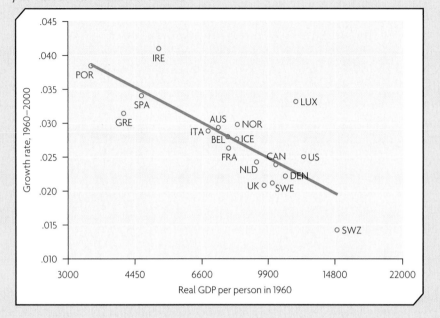

The horizontal axis shows real GDP per person in 1960 in 2000 U.S. dollars on a proportionate scale for 18 of the 20 founding members of the OECD (excluding Germany and Turkey). The abbreviation identifies each country. (AUS stands for Austria; Australia was not a founding member of the OECD.) The vertical axis shows the growth rate of real GDP per person for each country from 1960 to 2000. The red line is the straight line that provides a best fit to the relation between the growth rate of real GDP per person (the variable on the vertical axis) and the level of real GDP per person (on the horizontal axis). The line has a clear negative slope—therefore, a lower level of real GDP per person in 1960 matches up with a higher growth rate of real GDP per person from 1960 to 2000. Thus, the group of OECD countries exhibit convergence.

Figure 4.1 for regions of some other advanced countries.

Figures 4.9 to 4.11 tell us that similar economies tend to converge, whereas dissimilar economies display no relationship between the level of real GDP per person and the growth rate. Thus, the convergence pattern is strongest for regions of an advanced country (Figure 4.11), next strongest among a group of rich countries (Figure 4.10), and weakest—in fact, absent—for the full worldwide sample of countries (Figure 4.9).

Conditional Convergence in the Solow Model

The Solow model's prediction of convergence seems to explain growth patterns in similar economies, and it seems to fail when we examine a dissimilar array of economies. Do these findings mean that the model is flawed? Are there changes we can make to improve its predictions?

To find the flaw and try to correct it, let's reexamine the Solow model. One key assumption was that the determinants of the steady-state capital per worker, k^*, were the same for all economies. This assumption is reasonable for similar economies but is less plausible for a broad sample of countries with sharply different economic, political, and social characteristics. In particular, the assumption is unreasonable for the worldwide sample of countries considered in Figure 4.9. To explain the lack of convergence for this group, we have to allow for differences in the steady-state positions, k^*.

Suppose that countries differ with respect to some of the determinants of k^* in equation (4.7) and Table 4.1. For example, k^* could vary because of differences in saving rates, s, levels of technology, A, and population growth rates, n.[6] Figure 4.12 on page 66 modifies Figure 4.7 to show how differences in saving rates affect convergence. Economy 1 has the saving rate s_1, and economy 2 has the higher saving rate s_2. We assume, as in Figure 4.7, that economy 1 has lower initial capital per worker; that is, $k(0)_1$ is less than $k(0)_2$. Remember that the growth rate of capital per worker, $\Delta k/k$, equals the vertical distance between the $s \cdot (y/k)$ curve and the $s\delta + n$ line. We see from Figure 4.12 that it is uncertain whether the distance between the $s \cdot (y/k)$ curve and the $s\delta + n$ line is greater initially for economy 1 or economy 2. The lower capital per worker, $k(0)$, tends to make the distance greater for economy 1, but the lower saving rate, s, tends to make the distance smaller for economy 1. In the graph, these two forces roughly balance, so that $\Delta k/k$ is about the same for the two economies. That is, the distance marked with the blue arrows is similar to the one marked with the red arrows. Therefore, the poorer economy, economy 1, does not necessarily converge toward the richer economy, economy 2.

To get the result in Figure 4.12, we had to assume that the economy with lower $k(0)$—economy 1—had a lower saving rate, s. This assumption is reasonable because an economy with a lower s has a lower steady-state capital per worker, k^*. In the long run, an economy's capital per worker, k, would be close to its steady-state value, k^*. Therefore, it is likely when we examine countries at an arbitrary date, such as date 0, that $k(0)$ will be lower in the economy with the lower s—$k(0)$ tends to be lower in economy 1 than in economy 2. Thus, the pattern that we assumed—a low saving rate matched with a low $k(0)$—is likely to apply in practice.

We get a similar result if we consider other reasons for differences in the steady-state capital per worker, k^*. Suppose that the two economies have the same saving rates but that economy 1 has a lower technology level, A, than economy 2. In this case, the two curves for $s \cdot (y/k)$ again look as shown in Figure 4.12.[7] Therefore, it is again uncertain whether the vertical distance between the $s \cdot (y/k)$ curve and the $s\delta + n$ line is greater for economy 1 or economy 2. The lower capital per worker, $k(0)$, tends to make the distance greater for economy 1, but the lower A tends to make the distance smaller for economy 1. As before, it is possible that the two forces roughly balance, so that $\Delta k/k$ is about the same for the two economies. Thus, the

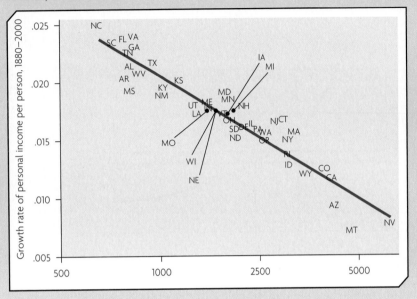

Figure 4.11 *Growth Rate Versus Level of Income per Person for U.S. States, 1880–2000*

The horizontal axis shows real personal income per person in 1982–1984 U.S. dollars on a proportionate scale for 47 U.S. states. The two-letter abbreviation identifies the state. (Alaska, the District of Columbia, Hawaii, and Oklahoma are excluded.) The vertical axis shows the growth rate of real personal income per person for each state from 1880 to 2000. The solid line is the straight line that provides a best fit to the relation between the growth rate of income per person (the variable on the vertical axis) and the level of income per person (on the horizontal axis). The line has a clear negative slope—therefore, a lower level of income per person in 1880 matches up with a higher growth rate of income per person from 1880 to 2000. Thus, the U.S. states exhibit convergence.

---

[6] Levels of population and the labor force vary greatly across countries, but the level of labor input, represented by $L(0)$, does not affect k^* in the model. The depreciation rate, δ, probably does not vary systematically across countries.

[7] In this case, unlike in Figure 4.12, the $\delta s + n$ lines are the same for the two countries.

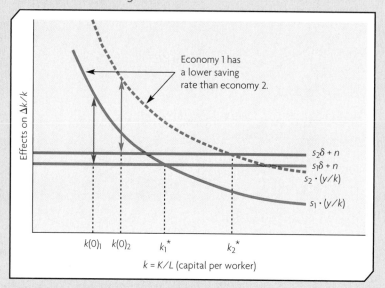

Figure 4.12 *Failure of Convergence in the Solow Model: Differences in Saving Rates*

As in Figure 4.7, economy 1 starts with lower capital per worker than economy 2—$k(0)_1$ is less than $k(0)_2$. However, we now assume that economy 1 also has a lower saving rate; that is, s_1 is less than s_2. The two economies have the same technology levels, A, and population growth rates, n. Therefore, k_1^* is less than k_2^*. In this case, it is uncertain which economy grows faster initially. The vertical distance marked with the blue arrows may be larger or smaller than the one marked with the red arrows.

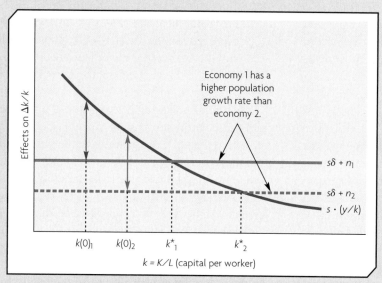

Figure 4.13 *Failure of Convergence in the Solow Model: Differences in Population Growth Rates*

As in Figure 4.12, economy 1 starts with lower capital per worker than economy 2—$k(0)_1$ is less than $k(0)_2$. The two economies now have the same saving rates, s, and technology levels, A, but economy 1 has a higher population growth rate, n; that is, n_1 is greater than n_2. Therefore, as in Figure 4.12, k_1^* is less than k_2^*. It is again uncertain which economy grows faster initially. The vertical distance marked with the blue arrows may be larger or smaller than the one marked with the red arrows.

poorer economy, economy 1, need not converge toward the richer economy, economy 2.

To get this result, we had to assume that the economy with the lower starting capital per worker, $k(0)$—economy 1—had the lower technology level, A. This assumption is reasonable because an economy with a lower A has a lower steady-state capital per worker, k^*. Therefore, it is again likely when we look at the two economies at date 0 that $k(0)$ will be lower in economy 1 than economy 2.

The same conclusions apply if we consider differences in population growth rates. In Figure 4.13, the two economies have the same saving rates and technology levels, but economy 1 has a higher population growth rate, n. Hence, the $s\delta + n$ line is higher for economy 1. It is again uncertain whether the vertical distance between the $s \cdot (y/k)$ curve and the $\delta s + n$ line is greater for economy 1 or economy 2. The lower capital per worker, $k(0)$, for economy 1 tends to make the distance greater for economy 1, but the higher n tends to make the distance smaller for economy 1. As in our other cases, it is possible that the two forces roughly balance, so that $\Delta k/k$ would be about the same in the two economies—the distance marked with the blue arrows is similar to the one marked with the red arrows. Thus, economy 1 again need not converge toward economy 2.

To get this result, we had to assume that the economy

with the lower starting capital per worker, $k(0)$—economy 1—had the higher population growth rate, n. This assumption makes sense because an economy with a higher n has a lower steady-state capital per worker, k^*. Therefore, it is again likely when we look at the two economies at date 0 that $k(0)$ will be lower in economy 1 than economy 2.

Now let's generalize the conclusions from our three cases. In each case, economy 1 had a characteristic—lower saving rate, s, lower technology level, A, higher population growth rate, n—that led to a lower steady-state capital per worker, k^*. For a given starting capital per worker, $k(0)$, each of the three characteristics tended to make country 1's initial growth rate less than economy 2's initial growth rate. We see these effects in Figures 4.12 and 4.13. At a given $k(0)$, the vertical distance between the $s \cdot (y/k)$ curve and the $s\delta + n$ line is smaller if s or A is lower or if n is higher.

Since economy 1 has lower k^*, it is also likely to have lower initial capital per worker, $k(0)$. The lower $k(0)$ tends to make economy 1 grow faster than economy 2—the convergence force shown in Figure 4.7. Whether economy 1 grows faster or slower overall than economy 2 depends on the offset of two forces. The lower $k(0)$ generates faster growth in economy 1, but the lower k^* generates slower growth in economy 1. It is possible that the two forces roughly balance, so that the two economies grow at about the same rate. That is, we need not find convergence.

Figure 4.14 shows the transition paths of capital per worker, k, for the two economies. We assume that economy 1 starts with a lower capital per worker—$k(0)_1$ is less than $k(0)_2$—and also has a lower steady-state capital per worker—k_1^* is less than k_2^*. The graph shows that capital per worker in each economy converges

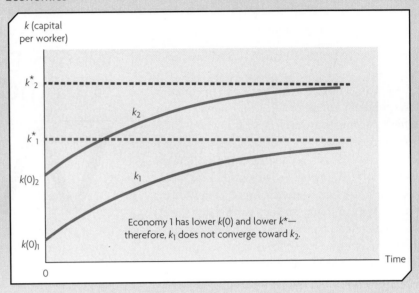

Figure 4.14 *Failure of Convergence and Transition Paths for Two Economies*

As in Figures 4.12 and 4.13, economy 1 has a lower starting capital per worker—$k(0)_1$ is less than $k(0)_2$—and also has a lower steady-state capital per worker—k_1^* (the dashed brown line) is less than k_2^* (the dashed blue line). Each capital per worker converges over time toward its own steady-state value: k_1 (the red curve) toward k_1^*, and k_2 (the green curve) toward k_2^*. However, since k_1^* is less than k_2^*, k_1 does not converge toward k_2.

toward its own steady-state level—k_1 toward k_1^*, and k_2 toward k_2^*. However, since k_1^* is less than k_2^*, k_1 does not converge toward k_2.

We can summarize our findings for the growth rate of capital per worker in an equation:

Key equation (conditional convergence in the Solow model):

(4.9)
$$\Delta k/k = \varphi[k(0), k^*]$$
$$(-)\ (+)$$

growth rate of capital per worker = function of initial and steady-state capital per worker

The function φ indicates how $\Delta k/k$ depends on the initial capital per worker, $k(0)$, and the steady-state capital per worker, k^*. The minus sign under $k(0)$ signifies that, for given k^*, a decrease in $k(0)$ raises $\Delta k/k$. The plus sign under k^* means that, for given $k(0)$, a rise in k^* increases $\Delta k/k$.

We can interpret the effects in equation (4.9) from the perspective of our equation for the growth rate of capital per worker:

(4.3) $$\Delta k/k = sA \bullet f(k)/k - s\delta - n$$

The negative effect of $k(0)$ in equation (4.9) corresponds in equation (4.3) to a lower initial average product of capital, $A \bullet f(k)/k$. The positive effect of k^* in equation (4.9) corresponds in equation (4.3) to a higher saving rate, s, a higher technology level, A, or a lower population growth rate, n.

One important result in equation (4.9) is that the negative effect of $k(0)$ on the growth rate, $\Delta k/k$, holds only in a conditional sense—that is, for a given k^*. This pattern is called **conditional convergence**: A lower $k(0)$ predicts a higher $\Delta k/k$, conditional on k^*. In contrast, the prediction that a lower $k(0)$ raises $\Delta k/k$ without any conditioning is called **absolute convergence**.

Recall from Figure 4.9 that we do not observe absolute convergence for a broad group of countries. We see from equation (4.9) that we can use the Solow model to explain the lack of convergence in this diverse group. Suppose that some countries have low saving rates, low technology levels, or high population growth rates and, therefore, have low steady-state capital per worker, k^*. In the long run, capital per worker, k, will be close to k^*. Therefore, when we look at date 0 (say, 1960), we tend to find that low values of $k(0)$ match up with low values of k^*. A low value of $k(0)$ makes the growth rate of capital per worker, $\Delta k/k$, high, but a low value of k^* makes $\Delta k/k$ low. Thus, the data may show little relation between $k(0)$ and $\Delta k/k$. This pattern is consistent with the one found in Figure 4.9 for growth rates and levels of real GDP per person.

Where Do We Stand with the Solow Model?

When we first considered convergence, we observed that the lack of absolute convergence for a broad group of countries, as in Figure 4.9, was a failing of the Solow model. Then we found that an extension of the model to consider conditional convergence explained this apparent failure. We show in the next chapter that conditional convergence allows us to understand many other features of economic growth in the world.

Although the Solow model has many strengths, we should be clear about what the model does not explain. Most important is the failure to explain how real GDP per person grows in the long run—for example, at a rate of about 2% per year for well over a century in the United States and other advanced countries. In the model, capital per worker—and, hence, real GDP per worker and per person—are constant in the long run. Thus, a key objective of the next chapter is to extend the model to explain long-run economic growth.

Questions and Problems

A. Review questions

1. If the initial level of labor input, $L(0)$, doubles, why does the steady-state capital stock, K^*, double? That is, Figure 4.4 implies that steady-state capital per worker, k^*, does not change. How does this result depend on constant returns to scale in the production function?

2. Does population growth, $n > 0$, lead to growth of output in the long run? Does it lead to growth of output per worker in the long run?

3. What is the meaning of the term *convergence*? How does absolute convergence differ from conditional convergence?

4. For 112 countries, Figure 4.9 shows that the growth rate of real per capita GDP from 1960 to 2000 bears little relation to the level of real GDP in 1960. Does this finding conflict with the Solow model of economic growth? How does this question relate to the concept of conditional convergence?

B. Problems for discussion

5. Variations in the saving rate
Suppose that the saving rate, s, can vary as an economy develops.

a. The equation for the growth rate of capital per worker, k, is given by

(4.1) $$\Delta k/k = s \bullet (y/k) - s\delta - n$$

Is this equation still valid when s is not constant?

b. Suppose that s rises as an economy develops; that is, rich countries save at a higher rate than poor countries. How does this behavior affect the results about convergence?

c. Suppose, instead, that s falls as an economy develops; that is, rich countries save at a lower rate than poor countries. How does this behavior affect the results about convergence?

d. Which case seems more plausible—b or c? Explain.

6. Variations in the population growth rate
Suppose that the population growth rate, n, can vary as an economy develops.

a. The equation for the growth rate of capital per worker, k, is again given from

(4.1) $$\Delta k/k = s \bullet (y/k) - s\delta - n$$

Is this equation still valid when n is not constant?

b. Suppose that n falls as an economy develops; that is, rich countries have lower population growth rates than poor countries. How does this behavior affect the results about convergence?

c. Suppose, instead, that n rises as an economy develops; that is, rich countries have higher population growth rates than poor countries. How does this behavior affect the results about convergence?

d. Which case seems more plausible—b or c? Explain, giving particular attention to the views of Malthus about endogenous population growth.

chapter appendix

We assess here how fast convergence takes place in the Solow model. Figure 4.15 starts by reproducing the construction from Figure 3.10. The horizontal line is again at $s\delta + n$, and the capital per worker starts at $k(0)$. The saving curve is shown in blue as $s \cdot (y/k)^{\mathrm{I}}$. The growth rate of capital per worker, $\Delta k/k$, equals the vertical distance between the $s \cdot (y/k)^{\mathrm{I}}$ curve and the $s\delta + n$ line.

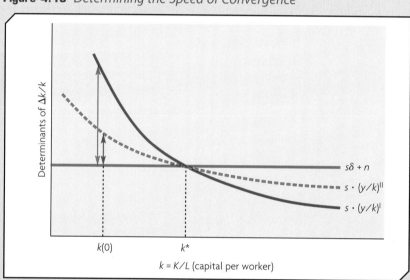

Figure 4.15 *Determining the Speed of Convergence*

This graph modifies Figure 4.4. The first saving curve, $s \cdot (y/k)^{\mathrm{I}}$, is the same as before. The second saving curve, $s \cdot (y/k)^{\mathrm{II}}$, does not slope downward as much as the first one. The reason is that the average product of capital, y/k, diminishes less rapidly with k in the second case. At $k(0)$, the distance between the $s \cdot (y/k)$ curve and the $s\delta + n$ line is greater in the first case (the red arrow) than in the second (the blue arrow). Therefore, the initial $\Delta k/k$ is higher in the first case, and the convergence to the steady state is faster. The conclusion is that convergence is faster when the average product of capital diminishes more rapidly with k.

As stressed before, the source of convergence in the Solow model is the diminishing average product of capital, y/k. Recall that this average product is given by

$$y/k = A \cdot f(k)/k$$

The tendency for the average product to fall as k increases is the reason that the $s \cdot (y/k)^{\mathrm{I}}$ curve slopes downward. The slope of the curve determines how fast convergence occurs, and this slope will depend on the form of the function $f(k)/k$.

To understand the role of the slope of the $s \cdot (y/k)$ curve, Figure 4.15 includes a second saving curve, $s \cdot (y/k)^{\mathrm{II}}$, shown in red. In comparison with the first curve, the second one has the same saving rate, s, and technology level, A, but a different form of the function $f(k)k/k$. This different form means that the relation between k and y/k is different for curve II than for curve I. Specifically, at any value of k, the second curve does not slope downward as much as the first one. That is, the average product of capital, y/k, diminishes less rapidly with k in the second case than in the first one.

To ease the comparison, we set up the graph so that the two saving curves intersect the $s\delta + n$ line at the same point. Hence, the steady-state capital per worker, k^*, is the same in the two cases. However, at the initial capital per worker, $k(0)$, the vertical distance between the saving curve and the $s\delta + n$ line is larger in the first case than in the second. In the graph, the first distance is shown by the brown arrows, and the second distance by the green arrows. Therefore, at $k(0)$, $\Delta k/k$ is higher in the first case. The higher growth rate means that k converges more rapidly toward its steady-state level, k^*. Hence, we have shown that the rate of convergence is higher when the average product of capital diminishes more rapidly with k.

For a given technology level, A, the relation between the average product of capital, y/k, and k depends on the form of the function $f(k)/k$. To take a concrete example, consider the Cobb-Douglas production function, introduced in the Appendix, Part C to Chapter 3, where $f(k) = k^\alpha$. In this case, the average product of capital is

(4.10)
$$y/k = A \cdot f(k)/k$$
$$= Ak^\alpha/k$$
$$= Ak^\alpha \cdot k^{-1}$$
$$= Ak^{(\alpha - 1)}$$
$$y/k = Ak^{-(1 - \alpha)}$$

Since $0 < \alpha < 1$, the average product of capital, y/k, falls as k rises. The value of α determines how fast y/k falls as k rises. If α is close to 1, equation (4.10) says that y/k falls slowly as k rises (curve II in Figure 4.15 is like this). If α is close to zero, y/k falls quickly as k rises (curve I is like this). Generally, the lower α is, the more quickly y/k falls as k rises. To get a quantitative idea about the rate of convergence, consider an intermediate case in which $\alpha = 0.5$. In this case, the average product of capital is

$$y/k = Ak^{-(1/2)}$$
$$y/k = A/\sqrt{k}$$

That is, the average product of capital declines with the square root of k.

Recall that the growth rate of k is given by

(4.1)
$$\Delta k/k = s \cdot (y/k) - s\delta - n$$

If we substitute $y/k = A/\sqrt{k}$, we get

(4.11)
$$\Delta k/k = sA/\sqrt{k} - s\delta - n$$

If we specify values for the saving rate, s, the technology level, A, the depreciation rate, δ, the rate of population growth, n, and the initial capital per worker, $k(0)$, we can use equation (4.11) to calculate the time path of k. Since we know $k(0)$, equation (4.11) determines k at the next point in time, $k(1)$. Then, given $k(1)$, we can use the equation to calculate $k(2)$. Proceeding in this way, we can calculate $k(t)$ at any time t.

Table 4.2 shows the solution for the path of $k(t)$. The calculations assume that the initial capital per worker, $k(0)$, is one-half of its steady-state value, k^*. The table reports the values of k/k^* and y/y^* that prevail after 5 years, 10 years, and so on. Note that it takes about 25 years—roughly a generation—to eliminate half of the initial gap between k and k^*. By analogy to radioactive decay in physics, we can define the time for half of the convergence to the steady state to occur as the *half-life*. Since the ratio k/k^* starts at 0.5 and the half-life of the convergence process is 25 years, the ratio reaches 0.75 in 25 years and 0.875 in 50 years. Hence, although capital per worker, k, converges toward k^*, the Solow model predicts that this process takes a long time. The same numerical results on half-lives turn out to apply to the adjustment of real GDP per worker, y, to its steady-state level, y^*.

Table 4.2 *The Transition Path in the Solow Model*

Year	k/k*	y/y*
0	0.50	0.71
5	0.56	0.75
10	0.61	0.78
15	0.66	0.81
20	0.71	0.84
25	0.74	0.86
30	0.78	0.88
35	0.81	0.90
40	0.83	0.91
45	0.86	0.93
50	0.88	0.94

Note: The table shows the solution of the Solow model for capital per worker, k, and real GDP per worker, y. The results are expressed as ratios to the steady-state values, k/k^* and y/y^*. The transitional behavior of k and y comes from equation (4.11), which assumes $y = A \cdot \sqrt{k}$. The calculations assume that k/k^* starts at 0.5 and uses the values $n = 0.01$ per year and $\delta = 0.05$ per year. The values of s, A, and $L(0)$ turn out not to affect the results. The initial value for k/k^* also does not matter for the speed of convergence.

If α is greater than 0.5, the average product of capital, y/k, declines more slowly as k rises, and the convergence to the steady state is less rapid. Therefore, the half-life is more than 25 years. Conversely, if α is less than 0.5, y/k declines more quickly as k rises, and the convergence to the steady state is more rapid. In this case, the half-life is less than 25 years.

Many interesting applications have been made for speeds of convergence and half-lives calculated from the Solow model. One implication involves the aftermath of the U.S. Civil War, which ended in 1865. The model says that the southern states from the defeated Confederacy would converge only slowly in terms of real income per person to the richer northern states. (The war reduced the income per person in the south from roughly 80% of the northern level to about 40%.) The quantitative prediction, which turns out to be accurate, is that the convergence process would take more than two generations to be nearly complete.

Similarly, with the unification of Germany in 1990, the model predicts that the poor eastern parts from the formerly Communist East Germany would converge, but only slowly, to the richer western regions. (In 1990, the GDP per person of the eastern regions was about one-third of the western level.) This prediction for gradual convergence of real GDP per person accords with the German data for the 1990s.

CHAPTER 5

Conditional Convergence and Long-Run Economic Growth

I n the previous two chapters, we developed and extended the Solow model of economic growth. The most important results for short-run analysis concerned convergence during the transition to the steady state. We show in the first part of this chapter how to use these results to understand patterns of economic growth in the world.

We observed at the end of Chapter 4 that the major deficiency of the Solow model was its failure to explain long-run economic growth. In the steady state, the growth rate of real GDP per worker was zero. In the second part of this chapter, we extend the model to analyze long-run growth.

Conditional Convergence in Practice

We found that the Solow model predicted convergence across economies in capital per worker, k. We summarized this conclusion in an equation for the growth rate of capital per worker, $\Delta k/k$:

(4.9) $$\Delta k/k = \varphi[k(0), k^*],$$
$$(-) \quad (+)$$

where k^* is the steady-state value of k. For a given k^*, a lower $k(0)$ matches up with a higher $\Delta k/k$. Thus, the model has a convergence property for k. The convergence is conditional in the sense of depending on variables that affect k^*. For given $k(0)$, an increase in k^* raises $\Delta k/k$.

The production function relates real GDP per worker, y, to capital per worker, k:

(4.2) $$y = A \bullet f(k)$$

We can use equation (4.2) in equation (4.9) to replace $\Delta k/k$ by $\Delta y/y$, $k(0)$ by $y(0)$, and k^* by y^* to get

> **Key equation (conditional convergence for real GDP per worker):**
>
> **(5.1)** $$\Delta y/y = \varphi[y(0), y^*]$$
> $$(-) \quad (+)$$
>
> growth rate of real GDP per worker = function of initial and steady-state real GDP per worker

Equation (5.1) shows that the Solow model determines the growth rate of real GDP per worker, $\Delta y/y$, as a function of initial real GDP per worker, $y(0)$, and steady-state real GDP per worker, y^*. For given y^* an increase in $y(0)$ lowers $\Delta y/y$. For given $y(0)$, an increase in y^* raises $\Delta y/y$. This relation exhibits the convergence property because a poorer economy—with lower $y(0)$—has a higher growth rate, $\Delta y/y$. However, the convergence is conditional in the sense of depending on variables that influence the steady-state position, y^*.

In our discussion in Chapter 4, we focused on three variables that influenced the steady-state capital and real GDP per worker, k^* and y^*: the saving rate, s, the technology level, A, and the population growth rate, n. Economists have extended the Solow model to allow for additional variables that affect k^* and y^*. We can understand these effects, without working through the details, by taking a broader view of the technology level, A. The important feature of a higher A is that it raises productivity; that is, it allows real GDP to rise for given inputs of capital and labor. Many variables that are not strictly technological also influence an economy's productivity. These other influences affect economic growth in ways analogous to changes in A.

As an example, productivity depends on the degree of market efficiency. Economies can enhance efficiency by removing restrictions due to government regulations, by lowering tax rates, and by promoting competition, possibly through antitrust enforcement. Another way for markets to work better, discussed in Chapter 17, is for governments to allow free trade in goods and services across international borders. This kind of international openness allows countries to specialize in the production of the goods and services in which they have natural advantages. Hence, greater international openness tends to raise world productivity. A country's legal and political system also influences its productivity. Productivity tends to rise if governments do better at enforcing property rights, if the judicial system runs more smoothly, and if official corruption declines.

Recent Research on the Determinants of Economic Growth

Recent research has used the equation for conditional convergence, given in equation (5.1), as a framework to analyze the determinants of economic growth across countries. The idea is to measure an array of variables

that influence a country's steady-state real GDP per worker, y^*. Equation (5.1) then tells us two things. First, if we hold fixed y^* (by holding fixed the variables that influence y^*), the growth rate of real GDP per worker, $\Delta y/y$, should exhibit convergence. That is, for given y^*, a lower $y(0)$ should match up with a higher $\Delta y/y$. Second, any variable that raises or lowers y^* should correspondingly raise or lower $\Delta y/y$ for given $y(0)$. In practice, because of difficulties in measuring numbers of workers, most studies have measured y by real GDP per person, rather than real GDP per worker.

Figure 5.1 shows empirical results for the relation between the growth rate and level of real GDP per person. The cross-country data are for a broad group of countries and are essentially the same as those plotted in Figure 4.9.[1] However, because we are holding fixed variables that determine the steady-state real GDP per worker, y^*, the graph looks very different from before. With the other variables held constant, the convergence pattern becomes clear—low levels of real GDP per person match up with high growth rates of real GDP per person, and high levels of real GDP per person match up with low growth rates. Thus, there is evidence for conditional convergence across a broad group of countries.

The relation shown in Figure 5.1 applies when we hold constant a list of variables that influence y^*. The particular list used to construct the graph is

- a measure of the saving rate
- the fertility rate for the typical woman (which influences population growth)
- subjective measures of maintenance of the rule of law and democracy
- the size of government, gauged by the share of government consumption purchases in GDP
- the extent of international openness, measured by the volume of exports and imports
- changes in the terms of trade (the ratio of prices of exported goods to prices of imported goods)
- measures of investment in education and health
- the average rate of inflation, which is an indicator of macroeconomic policy

One reason that we considered these variables is to isolate conditional convergence, as shown in Figure 5.1. Equally important, however, is that we learn how the variables in the list affect economic growth. The research shows that the growth rate of real GDP per person rises

---

[1] One new feature is that the data are for the three 10-year periods from 1965 to 1995. A country's real GDP per person in 1965 is matched with its growth rate of real GDP per person from 1965 to 1975; the real GDP per person in 1975 is matched with the growth rate of real GDP per person from 1975 to 1985; and so on. If the data are available, each country appears three times in the graph. In contrast, in Figure 4.9, a country's real GDP per person in 1960 is matched with its growth rate of real GDP per person from 1960 to 2000. Therefore, each country appeared only once in this graph.

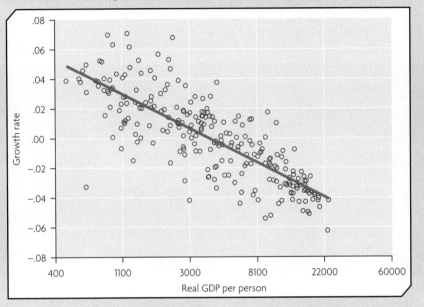

Figure 5.1 *Growth Rate Versus Level of Real GDP per Person: Conditional Convergence for a Broad Group of Countries*

The horizontal axis shows real GDP per person in 2000 U.S. dollars on a proportionate scale. The data are for 71 countries in 1965, 85 countries in 1975, and 82 countries in 1985. (The sample was based on the availability of data—86 countries appear at least once.) The vertical axis shows the corresponding growth rates of real GDP per person—for 1965–75, 1975–85, and 1985–95. Each of the growth rates filters out (and, therefore, holds constant) the estimated effects of the variables discussed in the text. The red line is the straight line that provides a best fit to the relation between the growth rate of real GDP per person (the variable on the vertical axis) and the level of real GDP per person (on the horizontal axis). The line has a clear negative slope. Therefore, once we hold constant the other variables, a lower level of real GDP per person matches up with a higher growth rate of real GDP per person. This relation is called "conditional convergence."

in response to a higher saving rate, lower fertility, better maintenance of the rule of law, smaller government consumption purchases, greater international openness, improvement in the terms of trade, greater quantity and quality of education, better health, and lower inflation. Democracy has a less clear effect—if a country starts from a totalitarian system, increases in democracy seem to favor economic growth. However, after a country reaches a midrange of democracy (characteristic in recent years of Indonesia, Turkey, and several countries in Latin America), further democratization seems to reduce growth.

Research on the determinants of economic growth has been lively since the early 1990s. This research has suggested numerous additional variables that influence growth. The variables considered include the scope of banking and financial markets, the degree of income inequality, the extent of official corruption, the role of colonial and legal origins, and the intensity of religious participation and beliefs. In the Back to Reality box, we consider two other variables: debt relief and foreign aid.

These kinds of empirical results have raised our understanding of the determinants of economic growth, but our knowledge remains incomplete. For one thing, economists have isolated only some of the variables that influence growth. The problems relate partly to data—for example, it is difficult to quantify government distortions from regulations and taxation or to measure various aspects of legal and political systems. Another problem is that many variables influence economic growth, and it is impossible to isolate all of these effects with the limited data available. Moreover, it is often difficult to be sure whether a variable—for example, maintenance of the rule of law or the levels of investment in education and health—affects economic growth or is affected by growth. In practice, both directions of causation are often important.

Examples of Conditional Convergence

If we look at history, we find examples of conditional convergence. At the end of World War II, the economies of many nations were destroyed. Cities were leveled, factories bombed, and farmland used as battlefields. By 1946, Japan, Germany, France, and other countries in Europe suffered sharp reductions in physical capital. Human capital also fell sharply, but the reductions in physical capital were larger. In our model, these events generated low starting values of capital and real GDP per worker, $k(0)$ and $y(0)$. But these countries also had characteristics that were favorable to rapid economic recovery—including strong human capital in the forms of education and health, and good legal and political traditions that encouraged markets and trade. We can represent these favorable characteristics as high values of steady-state capital and real GDP per worker, k^* and y^*. Hence, conditional convergence—summarized in equation (5.1)—predicts that these countries would have high growth rates of real GDP per person in the aftermath of World War II. This prediction fits the facts.

BACK TO REALITY

A Rock Star's Perspective on Debt Relief and Foreign Aid

In the summer of 1999, I met Bono, the lead singer of the rock group U2. Bono wanted to discuss the Jubilee 2000 campaign, which was a global movement aimed at canceling the international debts of the world's poorest countries. I told him that I was an unlikely candidate to support Jubilee 2000. Bono said that was precisely why he wanted to talk with me. He wanted to see whether a hard-thinking economist could be persuaded of the soundness of the campaign.[2] In particular, he was not interested in a global welfare project but rather wanted to push debt relief as a way to promote sound economic policies and rapid economic growth. He even said that the relief would be conditioned on a country's commitment to use the freed-up money for productive investments.

I was shocked to hear these arguments from a rock star. Nevertheless, I recovered to say that this commitment was unenforceable and that debt relief would not be on the top 10 list of policies for growth promotion in poor countries. More important were well-functioning legal and political systems, openness to markets at home and abroad, investments in education and health, and sound macroeconomic policy. I mentioned the musical line "money for nothing" (from a song by Dire Straits) and said that it applied to a number of ways in which a country received unearned money. These included debt relief, debt default, foreign aid, and natural resources such as oil. Experience showed that all of these forms of free money tended to reduce economic growth. I also argued that growth would be encouraged if a country gained a reputation for honoring foreign debts and other contracts.

Bono agreed that it was important for a country to fulfill its debt obligations, especially those that originated from sensible commercial transactions. However, he argued that most of the international debts of African and other poor countries derived from poorly designed projects conceived by the World Bank, other international organizations, and donor countries such as the United States. Many of these loans were made to corrupt dictators, who diverted the funds for personal gain. He noted that these debts could never be repaid. Bono said that the idea of the term Jubilee 2000 was that it was a one-time happening and would, therefore, not encourage default on newly incurred debts. (I was a little worried here, because the Bible says that Jubilees are supposed to occur every 50 years.)

In the end, I was not convinced to put debt relief on the top 10 list of growth-promoting policies for poor countries. But, since the arguments I heard were better than I had anticipated, I was pleased at the time to offer two restrained cheers for Jubilee 2000.

In retrospect, my response was two cheers too many. William Easterly (2001) has argued convincingly that the problem of high foreign debt for poor countries is not new and that the remedy of debt relief is neither new nor effective. Easterly noted that we have already been trying debt forgiveness for two decades, with little of the salutary results promised by Jubilee 2000. He also documented that the main response to debt relief has been for countries to run up new debts, most used to finance nonproductive projects. There is no evidence that past debt relief operations helped the poor, who were Bono's intended target. So, why would one expect new debt relief to work any better?

Although I had doubts about the efficacy of Bono's proposals, he nevertheless achieved many successes since our meeting in summer 1999. His campaign brought him into contact with numerous world leaders, including then President Bill Clinton and Pope John Paul II (who is said

---

[2] The "hard-thinking" phrase was Bono's.

to have tried on Bono's famous sunglasses). Bono swayed numerous politicians and economists to his cause, and his great exercise in persuasion culminated in the $435 million U.S. debt relief legislation of November 2000.

Because I hold Bono in high esteem, I wish I could believe that this and future programs of debt relief would help to spur economic growth. But economic analysis keeps me from believing these things. I wonder what would happen if Bono, instead, directed his persuasive talents to furthering ideas that seem to matter for economic growth. I have in mind property rights, the rule of law, free markets, and small government. And, I would be happy to include investments in education and health. But, of course, this is just a dream.

ShowBizIreland/Getty Images

As another example of conditional convergence, in the 1960s, many East Asian countries, such as South Korea and Taiwan, were poor and, therefore, had low values of capital and real GDP per worker, $k(0)$ and $y(0)$. However, these countries also had reasonably good legal systems, satisfactory programs in education and health, and relatively high openness to international trade. Therefore, the steady-state values, k^* and y^*, were high. Hence, we predict the high growth rates of real GDP per person from 1960 to 2000.

The typical sub-Saharan African country was also poor in the 1960s; that is, capital and real GDP per worker, $k(0)$ and $y(0)$, were low. Hence, from the perspective of absolute convergence, we would predict high growth rates of real GDP per person in Africa—whereas, in fact, the growth rates were the lowest in the world from 1960 to 2000. Conditional convergence can explain this outcome, because the African countries had poorly functioning legal and political systems, weak education and health programs, high rates of population growth, and large corrupt governments. Thus, the steady-state values, k^* and y^*, were low, and the sub-Saharan African countries failed to grow.

We see from these examples that the idea of conditional convergence allows us to understand many apparently dissimilar experiences about economic growth. This idea helps us to understand growth rates of real GDP per person in rich countries after World War II, as well as in East Asian and sub-Saharan African countries from 1960 to 2000. More generally, the idea of conditional convergence helps to explain the range of growth rates experienced by a broad group of countries since 1960.

Long-Run Economic Growth

Thus far, the Solow model does not explain how capital and real GDP per worker, k and y, grow in the long run. In the model, these variables are fixed in the long run at their steady-state values, k^* and y^*. Thus, the model does not explain how real GDP per person grew at around 2% per year for well over a century in the United States and other currently rich countries.

We will now consider extensions of the Solow model that explain long-run growth of capital and real GDP per worker, k and y. We begin with a model in which the average product of capital, y/k, does not diminish as k rises. Then we allow for technological progress in the sense of continuing growth of the technology level, A. We will consider first a model in which this technological progress is just assumed—that is, A grows in an exogenous manner. Then we will consider theories in which technological progress is explained within the model—that is, endogenous growth models. We will also consider models of technological diffusion, in which a country's technology level, A, rises through imitation of advanced technologies from other countries.

Models with Constant Average Product of Capital

The diminishing average product of capital, y/k, plays a major role in the Solow model's transition to the steady state. As capital per worker, k, increases, the decline in y/k reduces the growth rate of capital per worker, $\Delta k/k$. Eventually, the economy approaches a steady state, in which k reaches a fixed value, k^*, and $\Delta k/k$ is zero. This sketch of the transition suggests that the conclusions would differ if y/k did not decline as k rose. Thus, we now consider a modified model in which y/k does not change as k rises. We are particularly interested in whether this modification can explain long-run growth of capital and real GDP per worker.

Recall that, in the Solow model, the growth rate of capital per worker, k, is given by

(4.1) $\qquad \Delta k/k = s \bullet (y/k) - s\delta - n$

Now we want to reconsider our assumption that the average product of capital, y/k, falls as k rises. This diminishing average product makes sense if we interpret capital narrowly—for example, as machines and buildings. If a business keeps expanding its machines and buildings, without adding any workers, we would expect the marginal and average products of capital to fall. In fact, if labor input does not increase, we would expect the marginal product of capital eventually to get close to zero. If no one is available to operate an extra machine, the marginal product of that machine would be nil.

Another view is that we should interpret capital more broadly to include human capital in the forms of formal education, on-the-job training, and health. Human capital is productive, and the quantity of this capital can be increased by investment. Hence, human capital is analogous to machines and buildings. We might go further to include **infrastructure capital**, which is the capital often owned by government to provide services such as transportation, electric power, and water.

The tendency for capital's marginal and average products to fall as capital per worker, k, rises is less pronounced and may be absent if we view capital in this broad sense. That is, if we double not only machines and buildings but also human and infrastructure capital, real GDP may roughly double. All we are holding constant here, aside from the technology level, A, is the quantity of raw labor, L. If raw labor is not a critical input to production, capital's marginal and average products may not decline as capital accumulates.

To see the consequences of this modification, consider a case in which capital—broadly defined to include human and infrastructure capital—is the only factor input to production. Then, instead of the usual production function,

(4.2) $\qquad y = A \bullet f(k)$

we might have

(5.2) $\qquad y = Ak$

Equation (5.2) is the special case of equation (4.2) in which $f(k) = k$. For obvious reasons, the new model is called the ***Ak* model**.

In the Ak model, the average product of capital is constant. If we divide both sides of equation (5.2) by capital per worker, k, we get

(5.3) $\qquad y/k = A$

Hence, the average product of capital equals the technology level, A. (The marginal product of capital also equals A.) If we substitute $y/k = A$ into equation (4.1), we get that the growth rate of k is

(5.4) $\qquad \Delta k/k = sA - s\delta - n$

We can use a graph analogous to Figure 3.9 to study the determination of the growth rate of capital per worker, $\Delta k/ks$, in the Ak model. The new feature in Figure 5.2 is that the term $s \bullet (y/k) = sA$ is not downward sloping versus k—instead, it is a horizontal line at sA. The other horizontal line, at $s\delta + n$, is the same as before. Also as before, $\Delta k/k$ equals the vertical distance between the two lines. However, now this distance is constant, rather than diminishing as k rises.

Two important conclusions follow from Figure 5.2. First, instead of being zero, the long-run growth rate of capital per worker, $\Delta k/k$, is greater than zero and equal to $sA - s\delta - n$, as shown in the graph and in equation (5.4). This growth rate is greater than zero because we assumed that sA was greater than $s\delta + n$. This condition is more likely to hold the higher the saving rate, s,[3] and the technology level, A, and the lower the population growth rate, n, and the depreciation rate, δ.

---

[3] We are assuming $A > \delta$; otherwise, real net domestic product is less than zero.

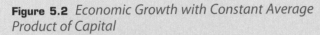

Figure 5.2 *Economic Growth with Constant Average Product of Capital*

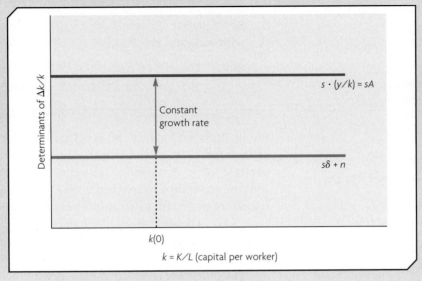

This graph modifies Figure 3.9 to allow for an unchanging average product of capital, y/k. In this Ak model, y/k equals the technology level, A. Therefore, the s · (y/k) curve becomes the horizontal line sA. If sA is greater than sδ + n, as shown, the growth rate of capital per worker, Δk/k, is a positive constant equal to the vertical distance between the two horizontal lines. This distance is shown by the red arrows.

If sA is greater than $s\delta + n$, as assumed in Figure 5.2, growth of capital per worker, k, continues forever at the rate $sA - s\delta - n$. Moreover, since $y = Ak$, real GDP per worker, y, grows forever at the same rate. In this case, a higher saving rate, s, or a higher technology level, A, raises the long-run growth rates of capital and real GDP per worker, $\Delta k/k$ and $\Delta y/y$. Conversely, a higher population growth rate, n, or a higher depreciation rate, δ, lowers the long-run values of $\Delta k/k$ and $\Delta y/y$. In contrast, in the standard Solow model, $\Delta k/k$ and $\Delta y/y$ were zero in the steady state and, therefore, did not depend on s, A, δ, and n. The reason for the different result is that the standard model assumed diminishing average product of capital, y/k.

The second important result from Figure 5.2 and equation (5.4) is the absence of convergence. The growth rates of capital and real GDP per worker, $\Delta k/k$, and $\Delta y/y$, do not change as capital and real GDP per worker, k and y, rise. Consequently, poor economies—with low k and y—do not tend to grow faster than rich economies.

Economists have developed more sophisticated models in which the average product of capital does not change as capital accumulates. Some models distinguish human from nonhuman capital and allow for an education sector that produces human capital. However, two basic shortcomings apply to most of these models. First, the loss of the convergence prediction is a problem,

because we do observe conditional convergence in cross-country data. Therefore, we cannot be satisfied with a growth model that fails to predict conditional convergence. Second, a common view among economists is that diminishing marginal and average products of capital apply eventually to the accumulation of capital even when interpreted in a broad sense to include human and infrastructure capital. If we reintroduced diminishing average product of capital, growth of capital and real GDP per worker could not continue in the long run just by accumulating capital. Therefore, we now turn to another explanation for long-run economic growth: technological progress.

Exogenous Technological Progress

In Chapter 4, we studied the effects of a one-time increase in the technology level, A. This change raised the growth rates of capital and real GDP per worker, $\Delta k/k$ and $\Delta y/y$, during the transition to the steady state. However, the economy still approached a steady state in which $\Delta k/k$ and $\Delta y/y$ were zero. Thus, we cannot explain long-run growth in k and y from a single increase in A. Rather, we have to allow for continuing increases in A. This regular process of improvement in technology is called **technological progress**.

Solow did extend his growth model to allow for technological progress, but he did not try to explain the sources of this progress. He just assumed that technological progress occurred and then examined the consequences for economic growth. In other words, he assumed **exogenous technological progress**—the improvements in technology were not explained within the model. This approach would be reasonable if most improvements in technology came by luck—in particular, if they did not depend much on purposeful effort by businesses (including nonprofit enterprises, such as universities), workers, and the government. In this section, we follow Solow's practice by assuming that the technology level, A, grows exogenously at a constant rate g:

$$\Delta A/A = g$$

In a later section, we discuss **endogenous growth theory**, which tries to explain the rate of technological progress within the model.

The Steady-State Growth Rate

The growth-accounting equation worked out in Chapter 3 is again

(3.3)
$$\Delta Y/Y = \Delta A/A + \alpha \bullet (\Delta K/K) + (1 - \alpha) \bullet (\Delta L/L)$$

where Y is real GDP, K is the capital stock, and L is labor input. If we substitute $\Delta A/A = g$ and $\Delta L/L = n$, the population growth rate, we get

(5.5)
$$\Delta Y/Y = g + \alpha \bullet (\Delta K/K) + (1 - \alpha) \bullet n$$

Recall that the growth rate of real GDP per worker, $\Delta y/y$, is given by

(3.6)
$$\Delta y/y = \Delta Y/Y - \Delta L/L$$

so that, with $\Delta L/L = n$,

(5.6)
$$\Delta y/y = \Delta Y/Y - n$$

If we substitute for $\Delta Y/Y$ from equation (5.5), we get

$$\Delta y/y = g + \alpha \bullet (\Delta K/K) + (1 - \alpha) \bullet n - n$$
$$= g + \alpha \bullet (\Delta K/K) + \cancel{n} - \alpha n - \cancel{n}$$
$$= g + \alpha \bullet (\Delta K/K - n)$$

The growth rate of capital per worker, $\Delta k/k$, is given by

(3.7)
$$\Delta k/k = \Delta K/K - \Delta L/L$$

so that, with $\Delta L/L = n$,

(5.7)
$$\Delta k/k = \Delta K/K - n$$

If we substitute $\Delta k/k$ for $\Delta K/K - n$ in the formula for $\Delta y/y$, we get

(5.8)
$$\Delta y/y = g + \alpha \bullet (\Delta k/k)$$

Therefore, real GDP per worker grows because of technological progress, g, and growth of capital per worker, $\Delta k/k$.

The growth rate of capital per worker, $\Delta k/k$, is still determined in the Solow model by

(4.3)
$$\Delta k/k = sA \bullet f(k)/k - s\delta - n$$

If we substitute this expression for $\Delta k/k$ into equation (5.8), we get

Key equation (growth rate of real GDP per worker with technical progress):

(5.9)
$$\Delta y/y = g + \alpha \bullet [sA \bullet f(k)/k - s\delta - n]$$

In our previous analysis, where A was fixed, increases in k led to reductions in the average product of capital, $y/k = A \bullet f(k)/k$. Consequently, in the long run, the economy approached a steady state in which the average product of capital was low enough so that $\Delta k/k$ equaled zero in equation (4.3). Then, with $g = 0$, $\Delta y/y$ also equals zero in equations (5.8) and (5.9).

The difference now is that each increase in A raises the average product of capital, $y/k = A \bullet f(k)/k$, for given k. Hence, the negative effect of rising k on y/k is offset by a positive effect from rising A. The economy will tend toward a situation in which these two forces balance. That is, k will increase in the long run at a constant rate, and y/k will be unchanging. We call this situation **steady-state growth**.

Since the average product of capital, y/k, does not change during steady-state growth, the numerator of the ratio, y, must grow at the same rate as the denominator, k. Therefore, we have

(5.10)
$$(\Delta y/y)^* = (\Delta k/k)^*$$

where the asterisks designate values in steady-state growth.

We know from equation (5.10) that capital and real GDP per worker, k and y, grow at the same rate in steady-state growth. Now we want to determine the steady-state growth rate. Equation (5.8) implies that, in steady-state growth:

(5.11)
$$(\Delta y/y)^* = g + \alpha \bullet (\Delta k/k)^*$$

Using equation (5.10), we can replace $(\Delta k/k)^*$ on the right-hand side by $(\Delta y/y)^*$ to get

$$(\Delta y/y)^* = g + \alpha \bullet (\Delta y/y)^*$$

If we move the term $\alpha \bullet (\Delta y/y)^*$ from the right side to the left side, we get

$$(\Delta y/y)^* - \alpha \bullet (\Delta y/y)^* = g$$

which implies, after we combine the terms on the left,

$$(1 - \alpha) \bullet (\Delta y/y)^* = g$$

If we divide both sides by $1 - \alpha$, we get the steady-state growth rate of real GDP per worker:

Key equation (steady-state growth rate with technological progress):

(5.12) $\qquad (\Delta y/y)^* = g/(1 - \alpha)$

Since $0 < \alpha < 1$, equation (5.12) tells us that *the steady-state growth rate of real GDP per worker, $(\Delta y/y)^*$, is greater than the rate of technological progress, g.* As an example, if $\alpha = 1/2$, we have

$$(\Delta y/y)^* = 2g$$

Thus, when $\alpha = 1/2$, $(\Delta y/y)^*$ is twice the rate of technological progress, g.

The reason that the growth rate of real GDP per worker, $(\Delta y/y)^*$, is greater than g is that the steady-state growth rate of capital per worker, $(\Delta k/k)^*$, is greater than zero, and this growth rate adds to g to determine $(\Delta y/y)^*$—see equation (5.11). In fact, we know from equation (5.10) that the growth rates of k and y are the same in steady-state growth:

$$(\Delta k/k)^* = (\Delta y/y)^*$$

Therefore, equation (5.12) implies

(5.13) $\qquad (\Delta k/k)^* = g/(1 - \alpha)$

The important finding from equations (5.12) and (5.13) is that exogenous technological progress at the rate $\Delta A/A = g$ leads to long-term growth in real GDP and capital per worker, k and y, at the rate $g/(1 - \alpha)$. The technological progress offsets the tendency for the average product of capital, y/k, to fall when k rises and, thereby, allows for long-term growth of k and y.

Recall from our discussion in Chapter 3 that the growth rate of real GDP per person in the United States averaged 2% per year from 1869 to 2005. Similar long-term growth rates of real GDP per person applied to other advanced economies. To explain this long-term growth within the Solow model, we have to look at the model's predictions for steady-state growth.

Since the labor-force participation rate is constant in the model, the growth rate of real GDP per person equals the growth rate of real GDP per worker. Therefore, to get long-term growth of real GDP per person at around 2% per year, we need the steady-state growth rate of real GDP per worker, which equals $g/(1 - \alpha)$ from equation (5.12), to be around 2% per year. If we think of α as the

share of capital income and use values for α between 1/3 and 1/2, the required value for g is a little over 1% per year. In other words, if the technology improves exogenously at a rate around 1% per year, the Solow model's prediction for the long-term growth rate of real GDP per person matches the long-term growth rates observed in the United States and other advanced countries.

Steady-State Saving Now we consider how technological progress affects steady-state saving. The growth rate of capital per worker, $\Delta k/k$, is again

(4.1) $\qquad \Delta k/k = s \bullet (y/k) - s\delta - n$

In steady-state growth, we can replace $\Delta k/k$ from equation (5.13) with $g/(1 - \alpha)$ to get

$$g/(1 - \alpha) = s \bullet (y/k) - s\delta - n$$

We can then rearrange the terms to get

$$s \bullet [(y/k) - \delta] = n + g/(1 - \alpha)$$

If we multiply through by k, we determine saving per worker, $s \bullet (y - \delta k)$, in steady-state growth:

In steady-state growth:

(5.14) $\qquad s \bullet (y - \delta k) = nk + [g/(1 - \alpha)] \bullet k$

When $g = 0$, steady-state saving per worker equals nk, the amount required to provide the growing labor force with capital to work with. When g is greater than zero, steady-state saving also includes the term $[g/(1 - \alpha)] \bullet k$. Since $g/(1 - \alpha)$ equals the steady-state growth rate of capital per worker, $\Delta k/k$ (equation [5.13]), this term is

$$[g/(1 - \alpha)] \bullet k = (\Delta k/k) \bullet k$$
$$= \Delta k$$

Therefore, this term is the saving per worker needed in the steady state to provide for increasing capital per worker.

The Transition Path and Convergence In Figure 3.11, we analyzed the transition path for capital per worker, k, in the Solow model without technological progress. We found that k gradually approached its steady-state value, k^*. Thus, k^* was the target that k was approaching. The model with exogenous technological progress still has a transition path for k. However, we have to think of k^* as a moving target, rather than a fixed point. That is, k^* moves over time along a steady-state path.

In steady-state growth, equation (5.13) says that capital per worker rises at the rate $(\Delta k/k) = g/(1 - \alpha)$.

Figure 5.3 *The Transition Path for Capital per Worker in the Solow Model with Technological Progress*

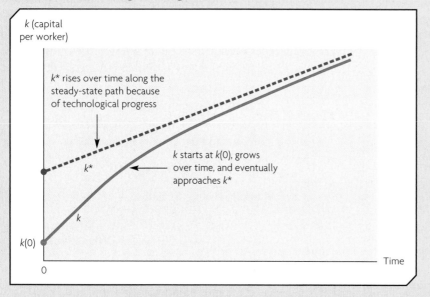

k (capital per worker)

k* rises over time along the steady-state path because of technological progress

k*

k starts at k(0), grows over time, and eventually approaches k*

k

k(0)

0   Time

In the Solow model with technological progress at the rate *g*, the steady-state level of capital per worker, *k**, is not fixed; *k** rises over time along the steady-state path shown by the blue line. (Since we use a proportionate scale on the vertical axis, the straight line means that *k** grows along the steady-state path at a constant rate, given by *g*/[1 − α]). In the transition, capital per worker, *k*, starts at *k*(0), rises over time along the red curve, and gradually approaches the *k** line. (We assume that *k*[0] lies below the *k** line.)

paths, k^*. Economy 1 begins at the capital per worker $k(0)_1$, and economy 2 at the higher capital per worker $k(0)_2$. The graph shows that k_1 and k_2 converge toward the steady-state path, k^*, and that k_1 also converges toward k_2. Therefore, economy 1 has a higher growth rate of capital per worker, $\Delta k/k$, than economy 2 during the transition to the steady-state path. In other words, if the two economies have the same steady-state paths, absolute convergence holds, and the poorer economy (with lower $k[0]$) has a higher $\Delta k/k$. These results are similar to those found in Figure 4.8 for the model without technological progress, where $g = 0$.

Figure 5.5 considers a case in which the two economies have different steady-state paths, k^*. We assume that economy 1—with lower $k(0)$—also has a lower k^*. We discussed in Chapter 4 why an economy with low k^* tends also to have low k when observed at an arbitrary time, such as date 0. The graph shows that each economy converges over time toward its own steady-state path—k_1 toward k_1^*, and k_2 toward k_2^*. Since $k_1(0)$ is less than $k_2(0)$, and k_2^* is less than k_2^*, we cannot be sure which economy has the higher growth rate of capital per worker, $\Delta k/k$, during the transition. The lower $k(0)$ tends to make $\Delta k/k$ higher in economy 1, but the lower k^* tends to make $\Delta k/k$ lower in economy 1. Thus, convergence need not hold in an absolute sense. However, conditional convergence still applies—if we hold fixed the steady-state path, k^*, a lower $k(0)$ leads to higher growth rates of capital per worker, $\Delta k/k$, during the transition.

We expressed all the results about convergence in terms of capital per worker, k. However, the results also hold for real GDP per worker, y, once we make use of the production function, $y = A \bullet f(k)$. Therefore, we can also use Figures 5.4 and 5.5 to assess convergence of real GDP per worker across economies.

Hence, capital per worker, k, varies over time in the steady state—it grows at the rate $g/(1 − α)$. We now define k^* to be the value that k takes at each point in time along the steady-state path. We just have to remember that k^* rises over time when g is greater than zero.

Capital per worker, k, again starts at some initial value, $k(0)$. The model still has a transition in which k moves from $k(0)$ to its steady-state path. However, we have to represent the steady-state path not by a fixed point, but rather by the blue line labeled k^* in Figure 5.3. This line has a positive slope because capital per worker grows in the steady state. The graph shows that k begins at $k(0)$, rises over time along the red curve, and gradually approaches its moving target, k^*.

Along the steady-state path, $k = k^*$ grows at the rate $g/(1 − α)$ (equation [5.13]). Therefore, in order for k to approach k^* as shown in Figure 5.3, the growth rate of k, $\Delta k/k$, must be greater than $g/(1 − α)$, the growth rate of k^*. Otherwise, k could not catch up during the transition to its moving target, k^*.

The results for the transitional behavior of k again tell us about convergence across economies. As before, convergence depends on whether different economies have the same or different steady states. Figure 5.4 shows a case in which two economies have the same steady-state

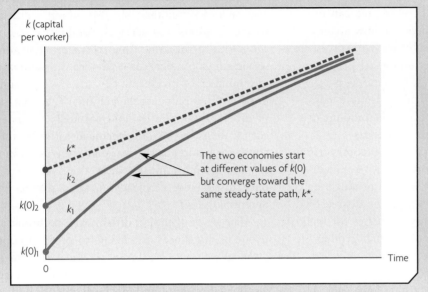

Figure 5.4 *Convergence and Transition Paths for Two Economies in the Solow Model with Technological Progress*

The two economies start at different values of $k(0)$ but converge toward the same steady-state path, k^*.

As in Figure 5.3, the steady-state capital per worker, k^*, rises over time along the steady-state path shown by the dashed blue line. The first economy starts at $k(0)_1$, and the second economy starts at the higher value $k(0)_2$. During the transitions, capital per worker in each economy, k_1 or k_2, gradually approaches the common steady-state path, k^*. The first economy (the red curve) has a higher growth rate of capital per worker, $\Delta k/k$, than the second economy (the green curve), so that k_1 converges toward k_2. Therefore, absolute convergence applies.

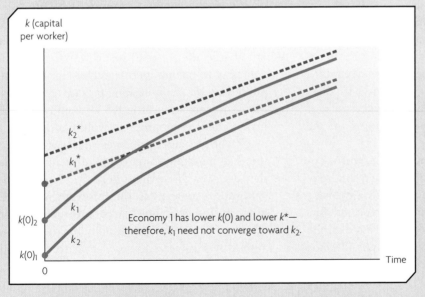

Figure 5.5 *Failure of Convergence and Transition Paths for Two Economies in the Solow Model with Technological Progress*

Economy 1 has lower $k(0)$ and lower k^*—therefore, k_1 need not converge toward k_2.

As in Figure 5.4, the first economy starts at $k(0)_1$, and the second economy starts at the higher value $k(0)_2$. However, economy 1 now has a lower steady-state path of capital per worker; that is, the dashed brown line for k_1^* lies below the dashed blue line for k_2^*. During the transitions, k_1 and k_2 gradually approach their respective steady-state paths, k_1^* and k_2^*. However, the growth rate of capital per worker, $\Delta k/k$, need not be higher in economy 1 than economy 2. Therefore, k_1 (the red curve) does not necessarily converge toward k_2 (the green curve). Hence, absolute convergence need not hold.

Endogenous Growth Theory

The inclusion of exogenous technological progress allows the Solow model to match the long-term growth rates of real GDP per person observed in the United States and other advanced countries. However, many economists have criticized this fix of the model because the technological progress comes from nowhere—it is not explained by the model. For that reason, economists led by Paul Romer in the late 1980s and early 1990s tried to extend the model to explain why technological progress occurs. The models that Romer and others developed are called endogenous growth theory because, first, the models explain the rate of technological progress, and, second, as in the Solow model, the technological progress leads to long-run growth of real GDP and capital per worker.

Most endogenous growth models focus on investments in **research and development (R&D).** Successful R&D projects lead to the discovery of new products, better products, or superior methods of production. In the Solow growth model, we can think of these research successes as increases in the technology level, A. However, in contrast to the Solow model with exogenous technological progress, the growth rate of A is explained within the model. Therefore, we can use endogenous growth models to understand how government policies and other variables influence R&D investment and, thereby, the rate of technological progress and the long-run growth rate of real GDP per person.

Theories of technological progress specify a connection between R&D investment and the amount of technological advance, represented by increases in A. Because research entails discovery, the outcomes are uncertain. For example, when working on new medicines, computer designs, or other original products or processes, a researcher does not know the degree of success in advance. This uncertainty is greater for basic research than for refinements of existing products or methods of production. However, we can say generally that a greater amount of R&D investment leads to a larger expected increase in the technology level, A. Therefore, to have more technological progress on average, innovators must be motivated to raise R&D outlays. For private businesses, the motivation comes from greater prospective profit. The government may affect the profit motive by subsidizing research, some of which is carried out by nonprofit organizations, such as universities. The government may also contract directly for research projects, such as in defense industries and the space program.

In many respects, R&D investment resembles the familiar investment in physical capital. The R&D outlays correspond to investment expenditure, and the technology level, A, corresponds to the stock of capital, K. However, there are two important differences between technological progress and increases in the stock of capital. One has to do with diminishing returns and the other with ownership rights.

A key question is whether diminishing returns apply to R&D investment. Specifically, as the technology level, A, grows, does it become increasingly expensive in terms of R&D outlays to generate expected further increases in A? If so, the R&D process exhibits diminishing returns, and it may be impossible for R&D investments to sustain technological progress and long-run growth of real GDP per worker. If not, it may be possible for R&D investments to maintain technological progress and long-run growth of real GDP per worker.

To understand how ownership rights differ between technology and the stock of capital, think of the technology level, A, as representing an idea about how

to use factor inputs, K and L, to produce output, Y. In contrast, think of the stock of capital, K, as a machine or a building. If A represents an idea, all producers can use the idea simultaneously. If producer 1 uses the idea to create goods and services, producer 2 can use the same idea at the same time to create other goods and services. In a physical sense, an idea is a **nonrival good**— any number of producers can use the idea simultaneously without reducing the amount of the idea available to others. Examples of nonrival ideas are mathematical formulas in calculus, chemical formulas for drugs, codes for computer software, and the notes in a song. An important point about a nonrival idea is that, once discovered, efficiency dictates sharing with all potential users.

The stock of capital differs from the stock of ideas. If one business uses a machine to produce goods, it is physically impossible for other businesses to use the same machine at the same time. This property holds also for labor input and most other goods and services. Economists say that each of these is a **rival good**.

Suppose, however, that all ideas were freely available once discovered. In this case, profit-seeking businesses would devote few resources to making inventions. The learning of an idea typically requires R&D investment, but there is no individual payoff— no profit motive—for making the discovery. As an example, the invention of a chemical formula for a new drug typically entails substantial R&D outlays. If the formulas for successful drugs were distributed widely and all firms were allowed to use these formulas without charge, there would be no way for the innovating company to recoup its research expenses. Then—if we are relying on profit-seeking private enterprises, rather than governments—little R&D would take place, and little technological progress would occur.

Profit-seeking companies invest in R&D only if they can maintain some rights in the (good) ideas that they discover. These rights are called **intellectual property rights**. In some areas, the enforcement of intellectual property rights involves a **patent** (typically for 17 or 20 years) or a **copyright** (usually for the lifetime of the author plus 50 years). These legal protections are especially important for pharmaceuticals, software, books, music, and movies.

Many basic discoveries have no patent protection, partly because of legal limitations and partly because of practical considerations in defining the scope of an idea. For example, Isaac Newton did not have patent protection for his mathematical innovations in calculus, Solow did not have property rights in his growth model, and

Henry Ford did not have exclusive use over the assembly line. For a more recent example, Toyota Motors did not have property rights over the idea of just-in-time inventory management, the practice of having suppliers deliver product components just before they're needed in a production process instead of storing raw materials in physical inventory. Other automobile manufacturers, Dell Computer, and many other companies copied this idea to reduce their inventory costs.

In many cases, businesses that make patentable inventions do not seek patents, sometimes because the approval process is costly and, more often, because businesses do not want to reveal the information needed to gain approval. Such information tends to aid competitors even when patents are granted. In the absence of formal patent protection, the main methods of maintaining intellectual property rights are secrecy and the advantages gained from moving first into a new area.

Paul Romer (1990) constructed the first model that linked R&D investment and intellectual property rights to a theory of technological progress and economic growth. In his model, an inventor retained perpetual monopoly rights over his or her invention. However, this extreme form of intellectual property rights is not necessary for Romer's main results. The basic idea is that some form of intellectual property rights ensured that successful innovators were rewarded for their discoveries.

The Romer model distinguishes the return to society from an invention from the private return, which is the reward to the inventor. The private return is greater than zero because of the intellectual property rights, but the social return tends to exceed the private one. For example, the social benefits from the invention of the transistor or the microchip were much greater than the payoffs to the individuals and businesses that made the discoveries.[4] For this reason, the resources devoted to R&D and the resulting rate of technological progress tend to be too low from a social perspective. This reasoning is often used to justify government subsidy of innovative activity, especially basic research. However, government subsidies also create problems, including the politics of choosing what to subsidize and the necessity to raise revenues to pay for the subsidies.

Romer equated technology with ideas, and he assumed that the returns from generating new ideas did not diminish as the technology level advanced. His reasoning was that the number of potentially good ideas was unlimited, so the stock of remaining ideas would not be depleted as more things were discovered. Thus, at least as a working hypothesis, we might assume that the returns to the creation of ideas are constant. This assumption turns out to be consistent with a constant, steady-state growth rate of real GDP per worker, driven by technological progress at a constant rate. That is, the results look like those in the Solow model when the technology level, A, grows exogenously at the constant rate g.

In the Romer model, where R&D investment is carried out by profit-seeking businesses, the rate of technological progress depends on the private rewards from making discoveries. These rewards depend on a number of factors:

- The private return to R&D investment is higher if the costs of R&D are lower. Some of these costs depend on government policies. Costs are lower if the government subsidizes R&D. Costs are higher if there are large expenses for gaining government approval (of new drugs, for example) or satisfying government regulations.

- The reward from successful innovations depends on how much they raise sales revenue or reduce production costs. One consideration is the size of the market over which the benefits from a discovery can be spread. A bigger market, which includes domestic and foreign sales, encourages more R&D.

- The private return is higher if intellectual property rights over the use of an invention are more secure and long lasting. In many cases, these rights will be better protected domestically than internationally. Another consideration is the ease with which competitors, domestic or foreign, can imitate successful innovations. The easier the imitation, the lower the intellectual property rights over an innovation and, hence, the smaller the incentive for R&D investment.

Changes in any of these factors influence the rate of technological progress and, therefore, the economy's steady-state growth rate of real GDP per worker. These effects are analogous to those from changes in the rate of exogenous technological progress, g, in the Solow model.

Advanced countries spend the most on R&D. They have the most scientists and engineers, and are granted most of the patents. (India is an exception to the usual pattern, as a poor country with many innovations in computer software.) One reason for the concentration of R&D in rich countries is the complementary

---

[4] Theoretically, the private returns could exceed the social ones. This situation can apply if resources are wasted when competing researchers strive to be the first to make a discovery, or if the main consequence from an improved product is the transfer of monopoly profits from the old industry leader to the new one. However, it is hard to present convincing empirical examples of this theoretical possibility.

The Story of Napster and Viagra

What do Napster (the once popular Internet site for copying music) and proposals to limit prescription drug prices have in common? Both seek to reduce prices of goods that cost little to produce now but were expensive to create initially. Cutting prices today looks great for users and, arguably, for society as a whole. If it costs virtually nothing to copy a CD over the Internet, why should people not be able to copy and listen to the music, rather than having to pay $10 at the local store? If it costs only a few dollars to produce and distribute a standard quantity of Viagra, why should people not be able to use the drug if they are willing to pay $10, rather than $100?

The problem is that the "high" prices are the rewards for the costly efforts that came before. Music companies and artists expend time and money to create hits, and the bulk of the expenses are for failed projects. To compensate for these efforts and to provide incentives for future hits, the industry has to reap large profits on its few successes.

Piracy is a problem for producers of music and similar products, such as books, movies, and computer software. The incentive to abridge intellectual property rights reflects the big gap between the prices charged by the copyright owners and the actual costs of copying and distribution. Innovations in the Internet and computer technology have dramatically lowered these costs. On the one hand, these advances are desirable, because they allow products to reach a vastly expanded audience. On the other hand, the down side is the threat to intellectual property rights. These rights are partly a matter of fairness, in the philosophical sense that inventors ought to be able to control the use of their discoveries. But, more concretely, if intellectual property rights disappear and no other effective means of compensating creativity is implemented, society will see much less future greatness in music, books, movies, and software.

It may be that the Internet makes impossible the effective enforcement of intellectual property rights in certain areas. If so, we are likely to be in trouble with respect to future creativity. However, the best policy would be to try to maintain some degree of property rights, and the pursuit of the legal case in 2001 against Napster's Internet-based copying facility was probably a helpful part of this policy.

Prescription drugs are similar in many respects. One way to see that retail prices of patented drugs exceed current costs of production is to compare U.S. prices with the lower ones prevailing in some other countries. For example, many drugs sell in Canada at about one-half the U.S. price. Some people conclude that the United States ought to adopt Canada's policies for pricing of prescription drugs or, alternatively, allow reimportation of the cheaper drugs into the United States. A more reasonable view is that the incentives for drug research and innovation created by high U.S. prices give Canada, Mexico, and other small markets what economists call a *free ride*. The idea of a free ride is that it allows some people—in this case, Canadians and Mexicans—to enjoy the fruits of someone else's labor without having to share fully in the costs. Specifically, these small countries can benefit from low prices of prescription drugs without having to worry about the effects on the overall market and, hence, on the incentives for companies to develop new drugs.

The United States does not have the option to free ride because it is such a large part of the market for prescription drugs. If the United States were to follow Canada's lead, fewer new drugs would be available for the whole world. Thus, for the United States, the choice is whether to have many effective new drugs at high prices or to have few new drugs at low prices. This choice is the relevant one for society as a whole, but many people fantasize that they can have low prices *and* many new drugs. Unfortunately, it just ain't so.

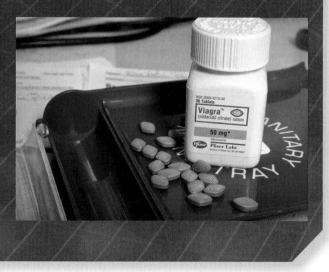

resources that support research, including a large supply of skilled workers and strong educational institutions. The large domestic market available to wealthy countries is also significant. However, a small country can successfully innovate if it is well connected to other markets through international trade, and if intellectual property rights are respected in foreign countries. As examples, Sweden and Finland have been leaders in pharmaceuticals and telecommunications.

At the start of this chapter, we discussed cross-country empirical research on convergence and other aspects of economic growth. These empirical findings match up well with the version of the Solow growth model that includes exogenous technological progress. Thus far, less cross-country empirical work has been done on the endogenous growth models. One finding, however, is that countries that spend more on R&D investment tend to have higher growth rates of real GDP per person.[5]

The Diffusion of Technology

For the world as a whole, the only way to raise the technology level, A, is for someone to discover something new. However, for an individual country or producer, it is possible to raise A—the technology level available to that country or producer—by imitating or adapting someone else's innovation. For example, color television sets were invented in the United States by RCA (Radio Corporation of America), but the technology for producing televisions was copied and improved in Japan. Similarly, the technology for operating steel mini-mills in the United States was based on innovations in Germany and elsewhere.

The term **diffusion of technology** describes the imitation and adaptation of one country's technology by another country. For low-income countries, imitation and adaptation tend to be less expensive than invention as ways to improve methods of production and introduce new and better products. Therefore, low-income countries tend to focus on diffusion of technology as the way to raise technology levels.

Businesses have used many methods to imitate leading technologies. A multinational firm from an advanced country can use an advanced technology in a foreign subsidiary. Domestic entrepreneurs then learn from the foreign-owned operations about products and production processes. These channels of technological diffusion were important in the textile industries in Hong Kong and Mauritius (an economically successful island off the east coast of Africa).

Sometimes the transfer of technology occurs through observation and analysis of products exchanged in international trade. For example, an importer of a good may be able to deduce how the good was produced by taking it apart (through a process of "reverse engineering"). In other cases, a foreign company licenses or sells its processes to domestically owned businesses. For example, Nucor—the first steel mini-mill producer in the United States—purchased technological designs from a German company. In still other cases, domestic residents work or study at a business or university in an advanced country and bring back the technology to their home countries.

The diffusion of technology is another mechanism for poor countries to converge toward rich ones. Low-income countries are poor partly because they lack access to leading technologies. Therefore, these countries can grow rapidly by imitating better technologies from advanced countries. However, as imitation proceeds, the supply of useful uncopied technologies decreases, and the cost of further imitation tends to rise. This rising cost of imitation is similar to the decreasing average product of capital, y/k, in the Solow model. Therefore, growth rates of follower countries tend to decline, and their levels of real GDP per worker tend to converge toward those in the advanced countries.

Studies show that the rate of technological diffusion to a developing country is high when the country trades a lot with rich countries, has high education levels, and has well-functioning legal and political systems, as in some East Asian countries.[6] Therefore, these characteristics help to explain the high rates of economic growth in East Asia since the 1960s.

What Do We Know About Economic Growth?

We began our study of economic growth in Chapter 3 with the Solow growth model. In the first phase of this model, capital and real

---

[5] See David Coe and Elhanan Helpman (1995). For evidence on the relation between R&D and productivity at the level of industries and firms, see Zvi Griliches (1998).
[6] See, for example, Florence Jaumotte (2000) and Francesco Caselli and Wilbur Coleman (2001).

BACK TO REALITY

Hybrid Corn: A Case of Technological Diffusion

In 1957, Zvi Griliches published one of the first studies of the diffusion of technology. He investigated the spread of hybrid corn. The basic idea—crossing specially selected strains of corn to develop types suitable to local conditions—was familiar to agricultural scientists since the early twentieth century. However, the first successful commercial application did not occur until the 1930s in Iowa. Researchers then needed time to develop hybrids that grew well in other states. The delay in application to a new state depended on the costs of the necessary refinements and on the potential gains in crop yields

and market sizes. The speed of acceptance within a state also depended on the economic benefits from the hybrids. Figure 5.6 shows the time of introduction of hybrid corn in various states and the speed with which each state adopted the new strain. One reason for the delay in the southern states was that these hybrids had to be substantially modified from those used in Iowa. Applications of the Griliches model to technological diffusion in other industries include Michael Gort and Steven Klepper (1982) and Boyan Jovanovic and Saul Lach (1997).

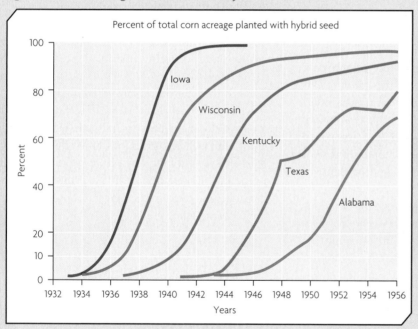

Figure 5.6 *Technological Diffusion for Hybrid Corn*

The innovations in hybrid corn began in the United States in Iowa in the early 1930s. This innovation spread later to other agricultural states, as shown in the graphs. Each curve shows the fraction of corn acreage planted in various years with hybrid seed.

to growth of capital and real GDP per worker in the steady state.

In Chapter 4, we used the Solow model to predict short- and long-run effects from changes in the saving rate, the technology level, the size of the labor force, and the population growth rate. The transition phase of the model predicted convergence—poor economies tend to grow faster than rich ones and, therefore, tend to catch up over time to rich ones. Although this prediction conflicted with observations for a broad group of countries, a modified concept—conditional convergence—fit well with the data. Conditional convergence allows for differences in steady-state positions, due to variations in saving rates, technology levels, and population growth rates. In extended models, the differences can reflect other variables, including legal and political systems, openness to international

GDP per worker rise from their initial levels to their steady-state levels. The second phase is the steady state. In Chapters 3 and 4, capital and real GDP per worker did not grow in the steady state. However, in the present chapter, the inclusion of technological progress led

trade, and the efficiency of education and health programs.

In the present chapter, we showed that the concept of conditional convergence explains many historical patterns of economic growth. We can understand why some war-ravaged OECD countries grew rapidly after World War II. We can also explain why, from 1960 to 2000, most East Asian countries grew fast but most sub-Saharan African countries grew slowly or not at all.

The basic Solow model does not explain long-run growth of real GDP per person, a pattern that applies for well over a century to the United States and other advanced countries. The model does explain long-term per capita growth at around 2% per year if we assume exogenous technological progress at about 1% per year. Endogenous growth models rely on R&D investment as the source of improvements in technology. These models predict how intellectual property

rights, research subsidies, and other variables affect the rate of technological progress and, hence, the long-run growth rate of real GDP per person.

Technological diffusion is the main method by which low-income countries raise their technology levels. This diffusion helps to explain convergence of poor countries toward rich countries but does not explain technological progress for the whole world.

Although we understand a lot about economic growth, there is much that remains unexplained. For example, economists have isolated only some of the variables that underlie differences across countries in steady-state positions. In the long-run context, we are still uncertain about the sources of technological progress. In particular, we cannot say with confidence how government policies that affect incentives for R&D investment influence long-run economic growth in a single country or in the world. Thus, although we have learned a lot, there is still much to do.

Questions and Problems

A. Review questions

1. Suppose that the technology level, A, grows exogenously at a positive rate, $g > 0$. Does the level of output, Y, grow in the long run? Does output per worker, Y/L, grow in the long run?

2. Most countries in sub-Saharan Africa grew at a low rate from 1960 to 2000, while many countries in East Asia grew at a high rate. How can the concept of conditional convergence help to explain these observations?

B. Problems for discussion

3. Convergence and the dispersion of income (difficult) Consider a group of economies that satisfies absolute convergence; that is, poor economies tend to grow faster than rich ones.

a. Does this convergence property imply that a measure of the dispersion of income per person—or income inequality—across the economies will narrow over time? (This question relates to Galton's fallacy, an idea applied by Galton to the distribution of heights and other characteristics in a population. If a parent

is taller than average, the child tends to be taller than average but shorter than the parent. That is, there is reversion to the mean, an effect that parallels the idea of absolute convergence. Does the presence of reversion to the mean imply that the distribution of heights across the population will narrow over time? The answer is no, but you are supposed to explain why.)

b. We found in Figure 4.11 that absolute convergence held for the U.S. states from 1880 to 2000. A measure of the dispersion of per capita income across the states declined for most of the period from 1880 to 1970 (except for the 1920s and 1930s). Dispersion did not change a great deal from 1970 to 2000. Can you relate these observations to your answer from question a?

c. We found in Figure 4.9 that absolute convergence did not hold for a broad group of countries from 1960 to 2000. We did find in Figure 5.1 that conditional convergence held for these countries. A measure of the dispersion of per capita real GDP across these countries shows a mild, but persistent, increase from 1960 to 2000. How would you account for this pattern?

chapter appendix

The Steady-State Path in the Solow Model with Exogenous Technological Progress

We now derive the steady-state path, k^*, in the model with exogenous technological progress. The path is shown graphically in Figure 5.3. This appendix provides an algebraic derivation.

The growth rate of capital per worker is given by

(4.1)
$$\Delta k/k = s \cdot (y/k)^* - s\delta - n$$

Hence, along a steady-state path, the growth rate is

(5.15)
$$(\Delta k/k)^* = s \cdot (y/k)^* - s\delta - n$$

where $(y/k)^*$ is the unchanging average product of capital in a position of steady-state growth. We also know that, in a situation of steady-state growth, k grows at the rate

(5.13)
$$(\Delta k/k)^* = g/(1 - \alpha)$$

Therefore, if we substitute $g/(1 - \alpha)$ for $(\Delta k/k)^*$ on the left-hand side of equation (5.15), we get

$$g/(1 - \alpha) = s \cdot (y/k)^* - s\delta - n$$

We can rearrange the terms to get

$$s \cdot (y/k)^* = s\delta + n + g/(1 - \alpha)$$

Then, if we divide by s, we get a formula for the steady-state average product of capital:

(5.16)
$$(y/k)^* = \delta + (1/s) \cdot [n + g/(1 - \alpha)]$$

Note that the right-hand side of the equation is constant. Therefore, this result verifies that the average product of capital, $(y/k)^*$, does not change in steady-state growth.

Since the production function is

$$y = A \cdot f(k)$$

We can write the average product of capital, y/k, as

$$y/k = A \cdot f(k)/k$$

Therefore, if we define k^* to be the time-varying value for k during steady-state growth, the steady-state average product of capital is

(5.17)
$$(y/k)^* = A \cdot f(k^*)/k^*$$

Equations (5.16) and (5.17) give us two expressions for $(y/k)^*$. Therefore, the two right-hand sides must be equal:

(5.18)
$$A \cdot f(k^*)/k^* = \delta + (1/s) \cdot [n + g/(1 - \alpha)]$$

The right-hand side is constant, and the technology level, A, on the left-hand side grows over time at the rate g. Therefore, if we specify the form of the production function, f, we can use equation (5.18) to determine the steady-state path, k^*.

Suppose that the production function, $f(k)$, takes the Cobb-Douglas form,

(3.24)
$$y = Ak^\alpha$$

which we discussed in the Appendix, Part C to Chapter 3. In this case,

$$A \cdot f(k)/k = Ak^{\alpha}/k$$
$$= Ak^{\alpha} k^{-1}$$
$$= Ak^{\alpha-1}$$
$$A \cdot f(k)/k = Ak^{-(1-\alpha)}$$

Therefore, we can substitute $A \cdot f(k^*)^{-(1-\alpha)}$ in equation (5.18) to get

$$A \cdot (k^*)^{-(1-\alpha)} = \delta + (1/s) \cdot [n + g/(1-\alpha)]$$

If we multiply through by $(k^*)^{1-\alpha}$ and s, divide through by $[sd + n + g/(1-a)]$, and rearrange terms, we get

(5.19)
$$(k^*)^{1-\alpha} = \frac{sA}{[s\delta + n + g/(1-\alpha)]}$$

On the right-hand side, everything except A does not vary over time. If A were constant, k^* would be constant, as in the Solow model without technological progress ($g = 0$). If A grows at the rate g, equation (5.19) implies that k^* grows at the rate $g/(1-\alpha)$, consistent with the result in equation (5.13).

Markets, Prices, Supply, and Demand

P*eople care a lot about whether the economy is expanding or contracting. During a boom, when real GDP rises, consumption and investment tend to be strong, employment tends to rise, and unemployment tends to fall. Conversely, during a recession, when real GDP falls, consumption, investment, and employment tend to be weak, and unemployment tends to increase. During recessions, people find it hard to locate good jobs, and more workers lose jobs than find them. The inability to keep or find a good job causes hardship for job seekers and their families.*

In this part of the book, our main goal is to understand these economic fluctuations—that is, the increases of real GDP during booms and the decreases during recessions. These fluctuations typically apply to relatively short periods, such as 1 or 2 years. In contrast, our study of economic growth in Chapters 3 through 5 focused on the long term: 5–10 years or even 20–30 years or longer.

To build a model of economic fluctuations, we start by working out the model's microeconomic foundations. These foundations describe how individual consumers and producers make choices. In the present chapter, we will focus on the markets for labor and capital services. In Chapter 7, we extend the analysis to consumption and saving.

An example of a microeconomic choice is a worker's decision about how much to work. Another example is a producer's decision about how many workers to hire. In these decisions, an individual worker or producer takes as given the prices that it faces. One of these prices is the real wage rate, which specifies the quantity of goods that a worker can buy with an hour of labor.

A key assumption in our model is that individual workers, consumers, and producers are too small to have a significant impact on the prices that influence their decisions. To take a concrete example—which we detail later—consider a simple analysis of the labor market. Suppose that, in choosing how much labor to supply, each worker takes as given the real wage rate. Similarly, in deciding how much labor to demand, each producer takes as given the real wage rate. Thus, the individual choices of quantities supplied and demanded are made at given market prices. Economists say that this assumption applies under perfect competition. With perfect competition, each market participant assumes that he or she can sell or buy any quantity desired at the going price. In particular, each participant is small enough that changes in his or her quantity supplied and demanded have a negligible impact on the market price.

When we add up the individual choices, we determine aggregate or market supply and demand functions. For example, we determine the market supply of and demand for labor as a function of the real wage rate, w/P; Figure 6.1 shows this case. The aggregate quantity of labor supplied, L^s, is assumed to rise as w/P increases (along the blue curve). Therefore, the L^s curve slopes upward. The aggregate quantity of labor demanded, L^d is assumed to decline as w/p rises (along the red curve). Therefore, the L^d curve slopes downward.

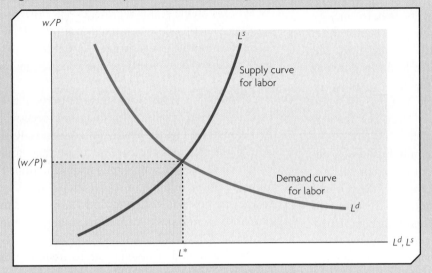

Figure 6.1 *An Example of Market Clearing: The Labor Market*

This figure gives a simple example of how a market—in this case, the labor market—clears. The labor-demand curve, L^d, slopes downward versus the real wage rate, w/P. The labor-supply curve, L^s, slopes upward versus w/P. Market clearing corresponds to the intersection of the two curves. The market-clearing real wage rate is $(w/P)^*$, and the market-clearing quantity of labor is L^*.

We simplify by assuming that households perform all of the functions in the economy. Each household runs a family business and uses labor, L, and capital, K, to produce goods, Y, through the production function, which we introduced in Chapter 3:

(3.1)

$$Y = A \cdot F(K, L)$$

More realistically, the production of goods might take place in a large corporation or a small business. However, if we included these private businesses in our model, we would have to take into account that they must ultimately be owned by households, possibly through shares traded on a **stock market**. When we think of businesses as parts of households, we avoid the complexities of ownership structure. Since we end up with the same macroeconomic results, this simplification is worth making.

Once we know the market supply and demand functions, we have to consider how these functions determine the quantities and prices in the economy. Our main approach relies on **market-clearing conditions**. As an example, in Figure 6.1, the market supply of and demand for labor each depends on the real wage rate, w/P. Our assumption is that w/P adjusts to clear the labor market—that is, to equate the quantity of labor supplied to the quantity demanded. Thus, the market-clearing real wage rate is the value (w/P^*) on the vertical axis, and the market-clearing quantity of labor is the value L^* on the horizontal axis.

With this background about markets in mind, we will now start the construction of the microeconomic foundations for our macroeconomic model. We begin by specifying the structure of the markets in the model.

Markets in the Macroeconomy

ur macroeconomic model contains several markets on which exchanges occur. In this section, we describe the participants in each market and identify the goods and services exchanged on each market.

The Goods Market

In the real world, the typical household uses little of the goods that it helps to produce in the marketplace. Usually, a person works on one or a few products and receives income from the sale of these products, or from the sale of labor services, which help to produce the products. The person then spends this income on an array of goods. The model would become too complex if we tried to capture this variety of goods.

We simplify by imagining that households sell all the goods they produce on a **goods market**. Then households buy back from this market the goods that they want. One reason that a household buys goods is for *consumption*. Another reason is to increase the stock of goods in the form of capital—machines and buildings—used for production. This use of goods is called *investment*.

The Labor Market

Households supply labor on a **labor market**. To simplify at the outset, we assume that the quantity supplied, L^s, is a constant, L. This assumption is not harmless, and we eventually change it in Chapter 8. As in previous chapters, we measure labor as the flow quantity of person-hours per year. For example, if a person works 40 hours per week, 52 weeks per year, the flow of person-hours per year is 2,080.

Households, as managers of family businesses, demand labor in the quantity L^d from the labor market. The labor demanded is used as an input to the production of goods. Notice that each household wears two hats in our simplified economy. When wearing the first hat, the household supplies labor and, thereby, looks like an employee, hired by the person who buys the labor. When wearing the second hat, the household demands labor and, thereby, looks like an employer, who hires the person who sells the labor.

The Rental Market

Next we consider the capital input to production. Households own the capital stock, K. An individual household can add to its stock by buying goods from the goods market and can lower its stock by selling goods on the goods market. We can think of these trades as resales of used capital goods. For example, a household might sell a used automobile or house, which are forms of capital goods. In our model, where households run businesses, we also imagine that households might sell a used machine or a whole used factory.

The stock of capital, K, is measured in units of goods—for example, numbers of automobiles or numbers of machines. Conceptually, we should distinguish this stock of goods from the flow of capital services. For example, suppose that a household owns a single machine. If the machine operates 8 hours per day, 5 days per week, 52 weeks per year, the machine is used for 2,080 hours per year. We think of these 2,080 machine-hours per year—a flow variable—as the quantity of capital services. This flow is analogous to the flow of labor services, measured in person-hours per year.

We simplify at the outset by assuming that each unit of capital—say, each machine—is used for a fixed number of hours per year, perhaps 2,080. In this case, the flow of capital services is a constant multiple of the capital stock—each machine represents 2,080 machine-hours per year. Therefore, in this case, we will not get

into any trouble if we enter the capital stock, K, as an input to the production function, as we did in equation (3.1). This stock really represents the flow of capital services, but this flow is a fixed multiple of the stock. Since the multiple is a constant—say, 2,080—we do not have to show it explicitly in the production function, $F(K, L)$.

Although a household owns a particular unit of capital—say, a machine—it does not necessarily use that capital for its own production of goods. Rather, the household can rent the capital to another household, which then uses it as an input to production. For example, a household might rent its house or automobile to another household. In our model, we extend this idea of rentals to all types of capital, including machines and factories.

We shall find it convenient to assume that each household rents out all of the capital that it owns on a **rental market**. Thus, if a household owns a machine, it offers for rent all of the capital services—say, 2,080 machine-hours per year—that this machine provides. In the real world, we can think of Hertz as owning automobiles and renting them to users. Other real-world examples are rentals of furniture from a company such as Cort Furniture, rentals of tools from a store such as Home Depot, and rentals of taxis and truck cabs from their owners. The important assumption in our model is that households do not allow any of their capital to sit idle and, rather, provide all of it for use on the rental market.

The amount of capital offered on the rental market is analogous to the amount of labor offered or supplied to the labor market, L^s. Therefore, we think of the capital offered on the rental market as the supply of capital services, K^s. Since we have assumed that each household rents out all of its capital, we have $K^s = K$. (More precisely, we should multiply by 2,080 to convert from capital stock—numbers of machines—to capital services—machine-hours per year. But since 2,080 is a constant, we can ignore it.) Our assumption that the supply of capital services is constant is analogous to our assumption that the supply of labor is constant. Again, the assumption is not harmless, and we change our assumption about capital services in Chapter 9.

So far, we have assumed that each household rents out all the capital that it owns. However, households, as managers of family businesses, also use capital services to produce goods. To get this capital input, households rent it from the rental market. The amount of capital rented on the rental market is analogous to the amount of labor purchased or demanded from the labor market, L^d. Therefore, we think of the capital rented on the rental market as the demand for capital services, K^d.

Notice that we are assuming that each household rents out all of its capital, $K^s = K$ and then rents back the quantity K^d. If K^s is greater than K^d, we could think instead of the household as retaining the quantity K^d of its own capital for use in production of goods and then renting out only the remainder, $K^s - K^d$. Analogously, if K^s is less than K^d, we can think of the household as using the entire quantity K^s of its own capital for use in production of goods, and then renting the additional amount, $K^d - K^s$. The results would be the same under these alternative assumptions. Therefore, we shall find it convenient to stick with the assumption that the household rents out all of its capital, $K^s = K$, and then rents back the quantity, K^d, that it uses as an input to production.

The Bond Market

The last market that we introduce is one in which households borrow or lend. A borrowing household receives a loan from another household, whereas a lending household provides a loan to another household. In the real world, this lending and borrowing would typically occur through financial institutions, such as banks. However, as in our neglect of private businesses, we simplify by assuming that households carry out all lending and borrowing directly.

We assume that a household that makes a loan receives a piece of paper—a form of contract—that specifies the terms of the loan. We call this piece of paper a *bond*, and we call the market on which households borrow or lend the **bond market**. The holder of a bond—the lender—has a claim to the amount owed by the borrower.

Money as a Medium of Exchange

Households buy and sell goods on the goods market, labor on the labor market, capital services on the rental market, and bonds on the bond market. We assume that the exchanges on each of these markets use a single form of **medium of exchange**. In general, a medium of exchange is an object held, not for its own sake, but rather to trade fairly soon for something else, such as goods and services. We call the medium of exchange in our model **money**. Historically, money has taken many forms, including precious commodities such as gold and silver, or sometimes beads and shells. However, in our model, we assume that

money is just a piece of paper, analogous to a paper **currency** issued by a government.

Money is denominated in an arbitrary unit, such as a "dollar." For example, a household may have $100 of U.S. currency. Dollar amounts are in **nominal** terms. Thus, $100 is the value of the household's currency in dollar or nominal units. One important property of paper money is that it bears no interest. That is, if a household has $100 of money and just leaves it under the mattress, the amount of money held is still $100 the following week and the following year (assuming that it is not lost). In contrast, bonds will earn interest.

We use the symbol M for the dollar quantity of money that a household holds. The sum of the individual holdings of money equals the aggregate quantity of money in the economy. We assume, for now, that this aggregate quantity of money is a given constant. Therefore, the total money held by all households must end up equaling this constant.

Markets and Prices

The key macroeconomic variables in our model will be determined by the interactions of households who trade on the various markets. We will now describe the details of each market.

The Goods Market

We assume that there is a single type of good, which can be used for consumption or investment. The goods market is the place in which households exchange goods for money. The price in this market, denoted by P, expresses the number of dollars that exchange for one unit of goods. We call P the **price level**. The consumer price index (CPI) which we discussed in Chapter 2, is a real-world counterpart of the price level. The CPI measures the dollar cost of a representative market basket of goods and services.[1] Alternatively, we can think of the deflator for the gross domestic product (the GDP deflator), which is a price index related to the economy's overall production of goods and services (the real GDP). In the model, which has just one type of good, the price level, P, corresponds to the CPI or the GDP deflator. We assume, for now, that there is no inflation,

which is the change over time in the price level. That is, we assume that P does not change over time.

Recall that households produce goods in the flow quantity Y per year, where Y is given from the production function as

(3.1) $$Y = A \bullet F(K, L)$$

Since all of these goods are sold on the goods market, the variable Y will also represent the quantity of goods per year sold and bought on the goods market. The quantity PY is the dollar value per year of the goods bought and sold on the goods market.

For a seller of goods, the price level, P, is the number of dollars obtained for each unit of goods sold. In contrast, for a buyer, P is the number of dollars paid per unit of goods. Since P dollars buy 1 unit of goods, $1 buys $1/P$ units of goods. The expression $1/P$ is, therefore, the value of $1 in terms of the goods that it buys. Similarly, M dollars exchange for

$$(M) \bullet (1/P) = M/P$$

units of goods. The quantity M is the value of money in dollars, and the quantity M/P is the value of this money in terms of the goods that it buys. An expression like M/P is in **real terms**—in units of goods—whereas a quantity like M is in dollar or nominal terms.

As an example, if a household has $100 of money and the price level is 5, the real value of the household's money is

$$100/5 = 20$$

That is, the household could buy 20 units of goods with its $100 of money. Hence, 100 is the dollar or nominal value of the household's money, and 20 is the real value of this money, measured in terms of the quantity of goods that it buys. To put it another way, each $1 of money can buy one-fifth of a unit of goods. Hence, one-fifth is the real value of each dollar.

The Labor Market

Households buy and sell labor in the labor market at the dollar or **nominal wage rate**, w. Since we measure labor, L, in units of hours worked per year, the wage rate, w, has the units of dollars per hour worked. A household that buys the amount of labor L^d pays the nominal amount wL^d per year, and then gets to use the labor as an input to production. A household that sells

---

[1] More precisely, the CPI measures the dollar cost of a market basket of goods in a particular year—say, 2007—expressed relative to the dollar cost of the market basket of goods in a base year—say, 1996.

the quantity of labor L^s receives the nominal wage income of wL^s per year.

The **real wage rate** is w/P. This real wage rate is the value in goods per hour received by a supplier of labor and paid by a demander of labor. For example, if the dollar wage rate is $w = \$10$ per hour and the price level is $P = 5$, the real wage rate is

$$w/P = 10/5 = 2$$

This real wage rate—2 goods per hour worked—determines the quantity of goods that can be bought with the nominal wage ($\$10$) paid for an hour of work. Since people care about the goods that they get, we shall find that household decisions depend on the real wage rate, w/P, rather than the nominal wage rate, w.

The Rental Market

In the rental market, households rent out capital, K, for dollars at the dollar or **nominal rental price**, R. The price R is expressed in dollars per unit of capital per year. For example, if $R = \$100$ per year, a household receives $\$100$ per year for each unit of capital (say, a machine or an automobile) that the household rents out on the rental market.

A household that rents the amount of capital K^d pays the nominal amount RK^d per year and then gets to use the capital as an input to production. A household that rents out the quantity of capital K^s receives the nominal rental income of RK^s per year.

The **real rental price** is R/P. This real rental price is the value in goods per unit of capital per year received by the supplier and paid by the demander. For example, if the dollar rental price is $R = \$100$ and the price level is $P = 5$, the real rental price is

$$R/P = 100/5 = 20$$

This real rental price—20 goods per unit of capital per year—gives the quantity of goods that can be bought with the rental payments ($\$100$) for each unit of capital over a year. Again, since people care about the goods that they get, we shall find that household decisions depend on the real rental price, R/P, rather than the nominal rental price, R.

The Bond Market

Our model has a simple form of bond market in which households borrow and lend from each other. For example, a household might make a loan to another

household that wants to buy a car, a house, a machine, or a factory. A **bond** is the piece of paper that lays out the terms of the loan contract.

A bond could be an IOU that says that household a owes a certain number of dollars to the holder of the bond. Initially, the borrower owes the money to household b, which is the household that advanced the money. However, we assume that bonds can be sold on the bond market to another household, perhaps household c, which becomes the holder of the bond. Household a then owes the money to household c.

We define units so that each unit of bonds commits the borrower to repay $\$1$ to the holder of the bond. This $\$1$ is the **principal** of each bond. The principal is the initial amount advanced on a loan.

We simplify by thinking of all bonds as having very short **maturity**, by which we mean the time at which the principal must be paid back. At any point in time, the issuer of a bond—the borrower—is entitled to buy back the bond for the fixed $\$1$ of principal. That is, the borrower can retire the loan by giving back the $\$1$ to the holder of the bond. Similarly, the holder of the bond is entitled to return the bond to the borrower at any time in exchange for $\$1$. That is, the holder can cancel the loan by demanding the $\$1$ of principal.

These assumptions are not so realistic. For example, with a student loan, the lender (which might be a bank) cannot demand repayment until many years in the future; that is, the maturity is long. Similarly, home mortgages often have long maturities, although borrowers can usually pay back the principal at any time. Despite these real-world complications, our assumption that maturities are very short will capture the most important aspects of interest rates in a tractable way.

We assume that, as long as a bond is neither retired nor cancelled, each unit of bonds commits the borrower to pay the holder a flow of interest payments of $\$i$ per year. The variable i is the interest rate, which is the ratio of the interest payment, $\$i$, to the principal, $\$1$. The interest rate, i, can vary over time.

As an example, suppose that a household borrows $\$1,000$, so that the principal amount outstanding is $\$1,000$. Assume that the interest rate, i, is 5% per year. In this case, the annual interest payment is

$$\text{Interest payment} = \text{interest rate} \cdot \text{principal}$$
$$\$50 \quad = \quad 5\% \quad \cdot \quad \$1000$$

For the holder of a bond, the interest rate, i, determines the return per year to lending. For the issuer of a bond, i determines the cost per year of borrowing.

One complication is that a borrower receives dollars today—say, $1,000—and pays interest over time—say, $50 per year—with dollars in the future. If the price level, P, were changing—that is, if the inflation rate were not zero—today's dollars and future dollars would differ in their real values. Thus, when we allow for inflation in Chapter 11, we have to distinguish two concepts of interest rates—the *nominal interest rate* and the *real interest rate*. However, for now, we do not have to worry about this complication because the inflation rate is zero.

We simplify by assuming that all bonds are alike, regardless of the household that issued the bond. Most importantly, we neglect differences among issuers in the risk that payments of interest and principal will not be made. One type of risk is that a borrower will default on a loan by refusing to pay or by disappearing. Since we ignore these risks, the interest rate, i, will have to be the same on all bonds. Otherwise, borrowers would want to do all their borrowing at the lowest interest rate, whereas lenders would want to do all their lending at the highest interest rate. Since all bonds are identical, borrowers and lenders can be matched only if the interest rates on all bonds are the same.

Let B represent the number of bonds in dollar or nominal units that a household holds. This amount may be greater than zero or less than zero for an individual household. Notice, however, that for any dollar borrowed by one household, there must be a corresponding dollar lent by another household. Hence, the total of positive bond holdings for lenders must exactly match the total of negative bond holdings for borrowers. Therefore, when we sum up over all households, the total of the Bs must always be zero.

Finally, we consider the price of bonds. One unit of bonds was defined to have a principal of $1—that is, each unit can always be exchanged for $1 by canceling the loan. Therefore, the nominal price of these bonds must always be $1 per unit.[2] However, the important variable for our analysis is the interest rate, i. We can think of i as the cost or price of credit. A higher i means that obtaining credit—borrowing—is more expensive in terms of the interest that has to be paid. At the same time, a higher i means that extending credit—lending—is more rewarding in that it yields a higher flow of interest income.

Constructing the Budget Constraint

The quantities and prices determined on the four markets will determine household income. Households will receive income from managing the family business, wages, rentals of capital services, and interest received. These flows of income are **sources of funds** for households. Households use their sources of funds to buy goods or increase their assets—that is, to *save*. The purchases of goods and assets are **uses of funds** for households. The important point is that the total sources of funds must equal the total uses of funds. This equality is called the household **budget constraint**, which we derive in this chapter. In Chapter 7, we use the budget constraint to understand how households choose consumption and saving.

Income

Begin by considering household income. Households receive income in four forms: profit from the family business, wage income, rental income, and interest income. We consider each of these in turn.

Profit Households may earn **profit**—an excess of revenue over costs—from their business activities. If a household uses the quantity of labor L^d and the quantity of capital K^d as inputs to production, the amount of goods produced, Y, is given by the production function:

(6.1) $$Y = A \bullet F(K^d, L^d)$$

Since all goods sell at the price level, P, the nominal income from sales is PY per year.

Households pay the nominal amounts wL^d per year for labor input and RK^d per year for capital input. The difference between the income from sales and the payments to labor and capital is the nominal profit per year from running the family business. This nominal profit, which we represent by Π, is given by

profit = income from sales − wage and rental payments
$$\Pi = PY - (wL^d + RK^d)$$

---

[2] The price is fixed at $1 per unit because we are considering bonds with very short maturity. Longer-term bonds commit the borrower to pay the bondholder a stream of nominal payments (in interim payments called *coupons* and in a final payment called the *principal*) over a period, up to the maturity date. We can define the units so that each unit of bonds commits the borrower to pay the holder $1 at the maturity date. The nominal price of these bonds will vary when the interest rate, i, changes.

If we substitute $A \cdot F(K^d, L^d)$ for Y, we get

(6.2) $\Pi = PA \cdot F(K^d, L^d) - (wL^d + RK^d)$

This expression is useful because it shows how profit, Π, depends on households' business decisions, which are the quantities demanded of capital and labor input, K^d and L^d.

Wage Income   If households supply the quantity of labor L^s to the labor market, they receive the nominal wage income of wL^s per year. As already mentioned, we assume for now that the quantity of labor supplied is the fixed amount L. Therefore, the nominal wage income is wL.

Rental Income   If households supply the quantity of capital K^s to the rental market, they receive the nominal rental income of RK^s per year. Since households supply all of their available capital, K, to the rental market, so that $K^s = K$, the nominal rental income is RK.

We assume, as in Chapter 3, that capital depreciates at the rate δ. Therefore, the quantity δK of capital disappears each year. The dollar value of this lost capital is $P \cdot \delta K$ per year. Hence, the net nominal rental income from ownership of capital is

net nominal rental income =
nominal rental income − value of depreciation
$= RK - \delta PK$

We want to calculate the rate of return that households get by owning capital. To compute this rate of return, we have to manipulate the expression for net nominal rental income. Start by dividing and multiplying the first term by P to get

net nominal rental income = $(R/P) \cdot PK - \delta PK$

Next, combine the terms on the right-hand side to get

(6.3)   *net nominal rental income = $(R/P - \delta) \cdot PK$*

The right-hand side expresses the net nominal rental income as the product of two terms: $R/P - \delta$ and PK. The second term, PK, is the dollar value of the capital owned by households. The first term, $R/P - \delta$, is the rate of return on each dollar held in the form of capital. The important result is the formula for the rate of return on capital:

(6.4)   *rate of return on owning capital = $R/P - \delta$*

The rate of return on owning capital is the real rental price, R/P, less the rate of depreciation, δ.

Interest Income   If a household's nominal bond holdings are B, the flow of nominal interest income received is iB per year. Notice that interest income is greater than zero for a holder of bonds (when B is greater than zero) and less than zero for an issuer of bonds (when B is less than zero). That is, an issuer of bonds—someone who owes money to another person—has to pay out interest rather than receive it. Since B equals zero for the whole economy, we have that the total of interest income equals zero. The amount paid to holders of bonds (lenders) exactly balances the amount paid by issuers of bonds (borrowers).

Total Income   We can put the four types of income together to calculate households' total nominal income per year. The result is

household nominal income =
nominal profit + nominal wage income +
nominal net rental income + nominal interest income

If we substitute Π for nominal profit (from equation [6.2]), wL for nominal wage income, $(R/P - \delta) \cdot PK$ for nominal net rental income (from equation [6.3]), and iB for nominal interest income, we get

(6.5)   *household nominal income =*
$\Pi + wL + (R/P - \delta) \cdot PK + iB$

Consumption

So far, we have discussed household income. Now we will consider household expenditures on goods. Households consume goods in the quantity C per year. Since the price level is P, the nominal amount spent on consumption per year is

$$household\ nominal\ consumption = PC$$

Assets

Now we will work out how households' incomes and expenditures relate to households' assets. Households hold assets in three forms: money, M; bonds, B; and ownership of capital, K. Money pays no interest. Bonds pay interest at the rate i per year. Ownership of capital yields the rate of return $R/P - \delta$ per year (from equation [6.4]). We assume that households can divide their assets any way they wish among the three forms. That is, at any point in time, households can exchange dollars of money for dollars of bonds and can exchange dollars of money for units of capital at the price level, P. So, when would households choose to hold all three forms of assets?

Bonds seem to be more attractive than money if the interest rate, i, is greater than zero. Households would, however, hold some money for convenience, because they use money as a medium of exchange—for example, to buy or sell goods and labor. In contrast, our assumption is that bonds are not readily accepted in exchange for goods or labor—usually, the holder of a bond has to sell the bond for money before buying goods or labor. The special role of money in making exchanges motivates households to have a positive *demand for money*. We will postpone our study of this demand for money until Chapter 10. For now, we assume that households hold a fixed amount of money in dollar terms; that is, we assume that the change over time of a household's nominal money holdings is zero. If we use the symbol Δ to represent a change over time, we have

$$\Delta M = 0$$

As an example, a family might want to hold $200 on average to cover expenses for groceries, gasoline, and other goods. The amount of money held by an individual household would vary over time, sometimes rising above $200 and sometimes falling below $200. However, if the average money held by each household is always $200, then the total money held at every point in time by all households would tend not to vary much. Our assumption is that the change in the total amount of money held by all households, ΔM, is zero.

In considering whether to hold assets as bonds or capital, households would compare the rate of return on bonds—the interest rate, i—with the rate of return on ownership of capital—$R/P - \delta$. Would households be willing to hold both forms of assets if the rates of return differed? They might be willing to hold both types if the assets differed by characteristics other than the rate of return. In the real world, the most important difference is the *riskiness* of the returns. Some types of bonds, such as U.S. Treasury Bills with three-month maturity, are nearly risk-free.[3] Forms of owning capital, such as stock in Ford Motor Company, provide uncertain returns. In these situations, the risky asset (stock in Ford) typically has to pay an expected rate of return greater than the interest rate on U.S. Treasury Bills to induce people to hold the risky asset.

To keep things manageable in our model, we do not consider risk in the returns paid on bonds or capital. That is, we assume that, aside from rates of return, bonds and capital look the same to households as ways to hold assets. In this case, if bonds offered a higher rate of return, households would hold no capital. In contrast, if capital offered a higher rate of return, households would want to borrow a lot to hold a lot of capital (actually, an infinite amount). Since the economy's stock of capital is greater than zero but less than infinity, the two rates of return must be equal. This condition is

Key equation:

rate of return on bonds = rate of return on ownership of capital

(6.6) $$i = R/P - \delta$$

If we use this result to substitute i for $R/P - \delta$ in the expression for household nominal income in equation (6.5), we get

(6.7) $$household\ nominal\ income = \Pi + wL + i \bullet (B + PK)$$

---

[3] The holder of a three-month U.S. Treasury Bill has virtual certainty of receiving the promised dollar amount three months in the future. However, the real value of this payment is uncertain because the future price level is unknown; that is, the inflation rate is uncertain. Thus, U.S. Treasury Bills have risk in their real returns. Since 1997, the U.S. Treasury has issued inflation-protected securities (indexed bonds). These assets, if held to maturity, provide a guaranteed real return.

The last term shows that assets held as bonds or ownership of capital yield the same rate of return per year, given by the interest rate, i.

Household Budget Constraint

Now we will use the results on household income to construct the household budget constraint. This constraint relates changes in households' assets to the flows of income.

At a point in time, a household has assets in the form of money, bonds, and ownership of capital:

$$nominal\ value\ of\ assets = M + B + PK$$

We define **nominal saving** to be the change over time in the nominal value of assets. Therefore, if we again use the symbol Δ to represent a change over time, we have

$$nominal\ saving = \Delta(nominal\ assets)$$
$$= \Delta M + \Delta B + P \bullet \Delta K$$

If we use our assumption that $\Delta M = 0$, we get

(6.8) $$nominal\ saving = \Delta B + P \bullet \Delta K$$

That is, a household's saving corresponds to changes in its holdings of bonds and capital.

A household's nominal saving depends on its income and consumption. If income is greater than consumption, the difference will be saved and, therefore, added to assets. If income is less than consumption, nominal saving is less than zero, and the difference will subtract from nominal assets. Therefore, we have

$$nominal\ saving =$$
$$nominal\ income - nominal\ consumption$$

If we substitute for nominal income from equation (6.7) and replace nominal consumption by PC, we get

(6.9) $$nominal\ saving =$$
$$\Pi + wL + i \bullet (B + PK) - PC$$

Equations (6.8) and (6.9) are two ways of representing nominal saving. Therefore, the right-hand sides of the equations must be equal:

(6.10) $$\Delta B + P \bullet \Delta K =$$
$$\Pi + wL + i \bullet (B + PK) - PC$$

This equation says that nominal saving, $\Delta B + P \bullet \Delta K$ on the left-hand side, equals the difference between nominal income, $\Pi + wL + i \bullet (B + PK)$, and nominal consumption, PC, on the right-hand side.

If we rearrange equation (6.10) to put nominal consumption, PC, on the left-hand side, we get

> Key equation (household budget constraint in nominal terms):
>
> **(6.11)** $$PC + \Delta B + P \bullet \Delta K =$$
> $$\Pi + wL + i \bullet (B + PK)$$
>
> nominal consumption + nominal saving = nominal income

EXTENDING THE MODEL

Allowing for a Risk Premium on Ownership of Capital

We can make our model more realistic by allowing for a difference between the rate of return on ownership of capital, $R/P - \delta$, and the interest rate on bonds, i. We can write the relationship between the two rates of return as

$$R/P - \delta = i + risk\ premium$$
$$rate\ of\ return = interest\ rate + risk\ premium\ on\ capital$$

Thus, the **risk premium** is the excess of the anticipated rate of return on capital—for example, the expected rate of return on holding corporate stock—over the expected rate

of return on a nearly risk-free asset, such as U.S. Treasury Bills. The risk premium normally has to be greater than zero to induce households to hold the riskier asset. If the risk premium is constant, our analysis would not change by allowing for this premium. More interesting (and more difficult) would be to allow the risk premia to vary over time. Some reasons that risk premia change are: First, the perceived riskiness of capital changes; second, households become more or less willing to absorb risk; and, third, innovations in the financial markets or the legal system make it easier for households to reduce the overall risk in their assets and incomes.

The right-hand side has total nominal income, $\Pi + wL + i \bullet (B + PK)$. Equation (6.11) says that households are constrained to divide this total nominal income between the two terms on the left-hand side: nominal consumption, PC, and nominal saving, $\Delta B + P \bullet \Delta K$. Thus, equation (6.11) is the **household budget constraint in nominal terms**.

We shall find it useful to express the household budget constraint in real terms by dividing all the terms in equation (6.11) by the price level, P. After we do this division, we get

> Key equation (household budget constraint in real terms):
>
> **(6.12)** $\quad C + (1/P) \bullet \Delta B + \Delta K =$
> $\qquad \Pi/P + (w/P) \bullet L + i \bullet (B/P + K)$
>
> consumption + real saving = real income

This equation is the **household budget constraint in real terms**. The right-hand side has total real income, $\Pi/P \bullet (w/P) \bullet L + i \bullet (B/P + K)$. The left-hand side has consumption, C, and the change in the real value of assets, $(1/P) \bullet \Delta B + \Delta K$. We refer to the change in the real value of assets as **real saving**. Notice that nominal saving, $\Delta B + P \bullet \Delta K$, which appears on the left-hand side of equation (6.11), gives the change in the nominal value of assets. In contrast, real saving, $(1/P) \bullet \Delta B + \Delta K$, which appears on the left-hand side of equation (6.12), gives the change in the real value of assets.

Figure 6.2 shows graphically the household budget constraint from equation (6.12). Suppose that a household has a given total real income, $\Pi/P + (w/P) \bullet L + i \bullet (B/P + K)$, on the right-hand side of the equation. The budget constraint says that this real income must be divided between consumption, C, and real saving, $(1/P) \bullet \Delta B + \Delta K$. One possibility is that the household sets real saving to zero, so that C equals the total real income. This choice corresponds to point 1, shown on the horizontal axis where C equals total real income. Another possibility is that the household sets C to zero, so that real saving equals total real income. This choice corresponds to point 2, shown on the vertical axis where real saving equals total real income. More commonly, the household would choose an intermediate point, such as point 3, where C and real saving are both greater than zero. The full range of possibilities is shown by the downward-sloping red line in the figure. This line is called a **budget line**. The budget constraint in equation (6.12) tells us that, along a budget line, each increase in C by one unit corresponds to a decrease in real saving by one unit. Hence, the slope of a budget line is -1.

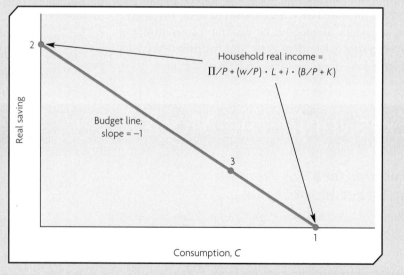

Figure 6.2 *The Household Budget Constraint*

Household real income = $\Pi/P + (w/P) \cdot L + i \cdot (B/P + K)$

Budget line, slope = -1

Real saving

Consumption, C

Households have a given total of real income, $\Pi/P + (w/P) \bullet L + i \bullet (B/P + K)$. This total must be divided between consumption, C, and real saving, $(1/P) \bullet \Delta B + \Delta K$. Thus, if real saving is zero, C equals the total of real income along the horizontal axis at point 1. If C is zero, real saving equals the total of real income along the vertical axis at point 2. The budget constraint in equation (6.12) allows the household to select any combination of consumption and real saving along the budget line, shown in red, such as point 3. The budget line has a slope of -1. Therefore, along this line, one unit less of consumption corresponds to one unit more of real saving.

Clearing of the Markets for Labor and Capital Services

ow that we have worked out the household budget constraint, we can consider the choices that households make. We begin by considering decisions about the family business. These decisions determine the demands for labor and capital services. Once we know these demands, we can study the clearing of the markets for labor and capital services.

Profit Maximization

The two business decisions that households make are the quantities of labor and capital services to demand, L^d and K^d. These decisions determine the amount of goods produced and sold on the goods market, $A \cdot F(K^d, L^d)$, and, therefore, the amount of nominal profit from

(6.2) $$\Pi = P A \cdot F(K^d, L^d) - wL^d - RK^d$$

To calculate real profit, we can divide through equation (6.2) by the price level, P, to get

(6.13) $$\Pi/P = A \cdot F(K^d, L^d) - (w/P) \cdot L^d - (R/P) \cdot K^d$$

real profit = output − real wage payments − real rental payments

We can see from the right-hand side of the household budget constraint in equation (6.12) that an increase in real profit, Π/P, raises household real income. Figure 6.3 shows how an increase in real income affects households. An increase in real income moves the budget line outward from the red line to the blue one. In comparison with the red budget line, the blue line allows households to choose higher consumption, C, for any given value of real saving, $(1/P) \cdot \Delta B + \Delta K$. Therefore, as long as households like more consumption, they prefer more real income to less. This result tells us that households, as managers of family businesses, will seek to make real profit, Π/P, as high as possible. That is, households will choose their demands for labor and capital services, L^d and K^d, to maximize Π/P, as given in equation (6.13).

We assume that an individual household takes as given the real wage rate for labor, w/P, and the real rental price for capital, R/P. As mentioned before, these assumptions are standard for competitive markets—an individual household is too small to have a noticeable effect on the market prices. In this situation, each household can buy or sell whatever quantity of labor it wants at the going real wage rate, w/P, and can rent or rent out whatever amount of capital it wants at the going real rental price, R/P. Therefore, the household will demand quantities of labor and capital services, L^d and K^d, that maximize real profit, Π/P, for given values of w/P and R/P.

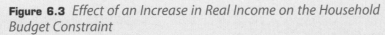

Figure 6.3 *Effect of an Increase in Real Income on the Household Budget Constraint*

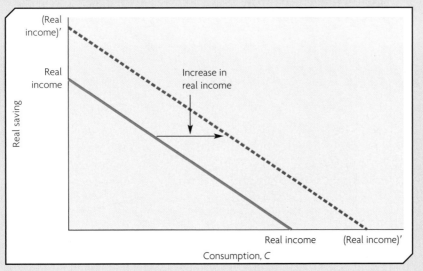

If household real income, $\Pi/P + (w/P) \cdot L + I \cdot (B/P + K)$ rises, the budget line moves outward from the red line to the blue line. That is, in the graph, (real income)′ is larger than (real income). In comparison with the red line, the blue line allows the household to have more consumption, C, for any given value of real saving, $(1/P) \cdot \Delta B + \Delta K$. Since households like more consumption, they prefer more real income to less.

The Labor Market

We will now consider the demand for labor and the supply of labor. Then we will determine the real wage rate, w/P, from the market-clearing condition for the labor market: The quantity of labor demanded equals the quantity supplied.

Demand for Labor   The demand for labor, L^d, comes from the objective of profit maximization. Consider the effect of an increase in labor input, L^d, by one unit on real profit, Π/P, as given in equation (6.13). The increase in L^d raises output, $A \bullet F(K^d, L^d)$, on the right-hand side by increasing production and, hence, sales of goods on the goods market. We know from Chapter 3 that an increase in L^d by one unit raises production by the marginal product of labor (MPL). An increase in L^d also raises the second term on the right-hand side, the real wage payments, $(w/P) \bullet L^d$. For a given real wage rate, w/P, an increase in L^d by one unit raises these payments by the amount w/P. Therefore, the overall effect from an increase in L^d by one unit is to change real profit by

$$\Delta(\Pi/P) = \Delta[A \bullet F(K^d, L^d)] - w/P$$
$$= MPL - W/P$$

change in real profit =
marginal product of labor − real wage rate

We know from Chapter 3 that the MPL depends on the quantity of labor input, L^d. As L^d rises, the MPL falls. This relation is shown by the downward-sloping red curve in Figure 6.4. This curve applies for a given technology level, A, and capital input, K^d.

Suppose that the household selects a low labor input, such as L_1 in Figure 6.4, where the marginal product of labor, MPL_1, is greater than w/P. In this case, an increase in L^d by an additional unit would raise real profit, Π/P. The reason is that the addition to output— by MPL_1 units—is larger than the addition to wage payments—by w/P units.

However, as L^d rises, the MPL falls and eventually gets as low as w/P. If the household continues to raise L^d, the MPL falls below w/P, such as at L_2 in the figure. In that situation, further increases in L^d lower Π/P. Thus, to maximize real profit, the household should stop at the point where the MPL equals w/P. The graph shows that this equality occurs where the value along the curve for the MPL equals w/P.

For a given real wage rate, w/P, on the vertical axis, the graph in Figure 6.4 shows on the horizontal axis the quantity of labor demanded, L^d. We can see that a decrease in w/P raises L^d. Hence, if we graph L^d versus w/P, we map out a downward-sloping demand curve. That is, the labor-demand curve looks as shown in Figure 6.1.

Each household determines its labor demand, L^d, as shown in Figure 6.4. Therefore, when we add up across all the households, we end up with an aggregate or market demand for labor that also looks like the curve shown in the figure. In particular, a decrease in the real wage rate, w/P, raises the market quantity of labor demanded, L^d.

Supply of Labor   We are assuming that each household supplies a fixed quantity of labor to the labor market. Therefore, the aggregate or market supply of labor, L^s, is the given amount L. More realistically, the quantity

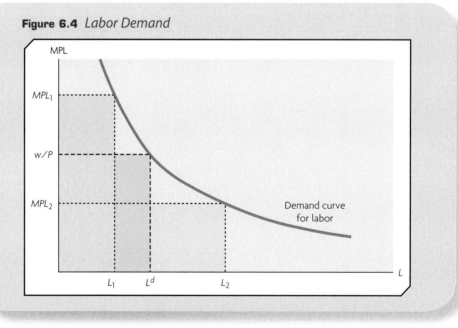

Figure 6.4 *Labor Demand*

For a given technology level, A, and capital input, K^d, the marginal product of labor, MPL, decreases as labor input, L, increases. Therefore, the MPL, given by the red curve, declines on the vertical axis as L rises on the horizontal axis. The household chooses labor input, L^d, where the MPL equals the real wage rate, w/P. At a lower labor input, such as L_1, MPL_1 is greater than w/P, and at a higher labor input, such as L_2, MPL_2 is less than w/P. If w/P decreases, L^d increases.

of labor supplied would depend on the real wage rate, w/P. For example, we might have the upward-sloping labor-supply curve shown in Figure 6.1. However, we neglect until Chapter 8 this dependence of L^s on w/P.

Clearing of the Labor Market The market labor demand, L^d, is determined from Figure 6.4 as a downward-sloping function of the real wage rate, w/P. We reproduce this curve in Figure 6.5. The market labor supply, L^s, is assumed to be the constant L. We show this fixed labor supply as the vertical line at L. Now we can determine the equilibrium value of w/P from the market-clearing condition for the labor market. Specifically, we assume that w/P is determined to equate the aggregate quantity of labor demanded, L^d, to the aggregate quantity supplied, L. This market-clearing value of w/P corresponds in Figure 6.5 to the intersection of the L^d curve with the vertical line at L. The market-clearing value for w/P is denoted by $(w/P)^*$ on the vertical axis. The corresponding market-clearing quantity of labor input, L^*, equals L on the horizontal axis.

The equality between L and L^d means that the market-clearing real wage rate, $(w/P)^*$, equals the marginal product of labor, MPL:

(6.14) $\quad (w/P)^* = MPL \ (evaluated \ at \ L)$

By *MPL* (evaluated at L), we are referring in Figure 6.4 to the value for the marginal product of labor that corresponds to the quantity of labor L.[4]

Why do we assume that the labor market clears? The idea is that only at this market-clearing position would the real wage rate, w/P, tend neither to rise nor fall. If w/P were below $(w/P)^*$, for example, at $(w/P)_1$ in Figure 6.5, the aggregate quantity of labor demanded would exceed the quantity supplied in the amount shown by the green arrows. In this case, demanders of labor would compete to hire scarce workers by raising w/P.[5] Conversely, if w/P were above $(w/P)^*$, for example, at $(w/P)_2$ in Figure 6.5, the aggregate quantity of labor demanded would fall short of the quantity supplied in the amount shown by the brown arrows. In this case, the eager suppliers of labor would bid down w/P. In equilibrium, w/P will be determined to clear the labor market—that is, so that the aggregate quantity of labor supplied, L, equals the quantity demanded, L^d.

The Market for Capital Services

We will now consider the demand for capital services and the supply of capital services. Then we will determine the real rental price, R/P, from the market-clearing condition for the market for capital services: The

Figure 6.5 *Clearing of the Labor Market*

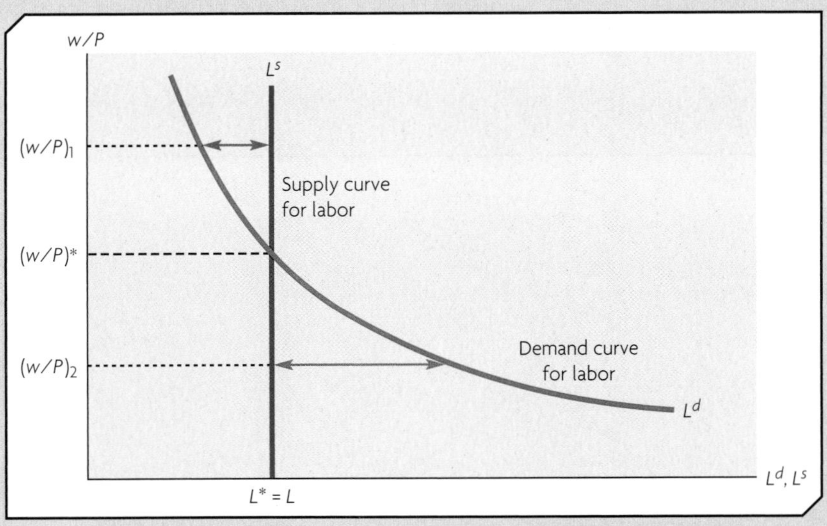

The downward-sloping labor-demand curve, L^d, comes from Figure 6.4. We assume that labor supply, L^s, is fixed at L. The market-clearing real wage rate is $(w/P)^*$. The market-clearing quantity of labor input is $L^* = L$. At a higher real wage rate, such as $(w/P)_1$, the quantity of labor supplied, L^s, exceeds the quantity demanded, L^d, in the amount shown by the green arrows. At a lower real wage rate, such as $(w/P)_2$, the quantity of labor supplied, L^s, falls short of the quantity demanded, L^d, in the amount shown by the brown arrows.

---

[4] Note that the curve for MPL in Figure 6.4 applies for a given capital stock, K. A change in K would shift the MPL associated with a given value of L and would therefore change $(w/P)^*$ in Figure 6.5.
[5] This description views the participants in the labor market as directly setting the real wage rate, w/P. However, our story would be the same if, instead, the price level, P, were given, and the participants in the labor market adjusted the nominal wage rate, w.

quantity of capital services demanded equals the quantity supplied.

Demand for Capital Services

As with the demand for labor, the demand for capital services, K^d, comes from the objective of profit maximization. Consider the effect of an increase in K^d by one unit on a household's real profit, as given again by

(6.13) $\Pi/P = A \bullet F(K^d, L^d) - (w/P) \bullet L^d - (R/P) \bullet K^d$

real profit =
output − real wage payments − real rental payments

We know from Chapter 3 that an increase in capital input, K^d, by one unit raises output, $A \bullet F(K^d, L^d)$, the first term on the right-hand side, by the marginal product of capital (MPK). An increase in K^d also raises the real rental payments, $(R/P) \bullet K^d$, the last term on the right-hand side. For a given real rental price, R/P, an increase in K^d by one unit raises real rental payments by the amount R/P. Therefore, the overall effect from an increase in K^d by one unit is to change real profit by

$$\Delta(\Pi/P) = \Delta[A \bullet F(K^d, L^d)] - R/P$$
$$= MPL - R/P$$

change in real profit =
marginal product of capital − real rental price

We know from Chapter 3 that the MPK depends on the amount of capital input, K^d. As K^d rises, MPK falls. This relation is shown by the downward-sloping red curve in Figure 6.6. This curve applies for a given technology level, A, and labor input, L^d.

Suppose that the household selects a low value of capital input, K^d, such as K_1 in Figure 6.6, at which the marginal product of capital, MPK_1, is greater than R/P. In this case, an increase in K^d by an additional unit would raise real profit, Π/P. The reason is that the addition to output (by MPK_1 units) is greater than the increase

in real rental payments (by R/P units). However, as K^d rises, the MPK falls and eventually gets as low as R/P. If the household continues to raise K^d, the MPK falls below R/P, such as at K_2 in the figure. In that case, further increases in K^d lower Π/P. Thus, to maximize real profit, the household should stop at the point where the MPK equals R/P. The graph shows that this equality occurs where the value along the curve for the MPK equals R/P.

For a given real rental price, R/P, on the vertical axis, the graph in Figure 6.6 shows on the horizontal axis the quantity of capital services demanded, K^d. We can see that a decrease in R/P increases K^d. Hence, if we graph K^d versus R/P, we determine a downward-sloping demand curve.

Each household sets its demand for capital services, K^d, as shown in Figure 6.6. Therefore, when we add up across all the households, we end up with an aggregate or market demand for capital services that also looks like the curve shown in the figure. In particular, a decrease in the real rental price, R/P, raises the market quantity of capital services demanded, K^d.

Supply of Capital Services

For the economy as a whole, the aggregate quantity of capital, K, is given from past flows of investment. That is, in the short run, the economy has a given stock of houses, cars, machines,

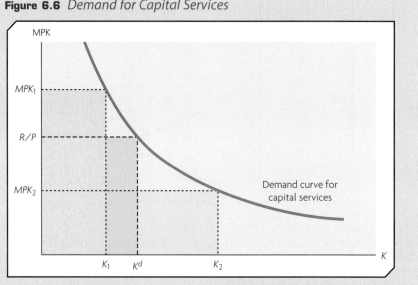

Figure 6.6 *Demand for Capital Services*

For a given technology level, A, and labor input, L^d, the marginal product of capital, MPK, decreases as capital input, K, increases. Therefore, the MPK, given by the red curve, declines on the vertical axis as K rises on the horizontal axis. The household chooses capital input, K^d, where the MPK equals the real rental price, R/P. In contrast, at a lower capital input, such as K_1, MPK_1 is greater than R/P, and at a higher capital input, such as K_2, MPK_2 is less than R/P. If R/P decreases, K^d increases.

and factories. This capital stock is owned by households, and all of the services from this stock are supplied to the rental market. Therefore, in the short run, the aggregate or market quantity of capital services supplied, K^s, equals K.

Clearing of the Market for Capital Services

The market demand for capital services, K^d, is determined from Figure 6.6 as a downward-sloping function of the real rental price, R/P. We reproduce this curve in Figure 6.7. The market supply of capital services, K^s, is the constant K. We show this fixed supply of capital services as the vertical line at K. As with the labor market, we assume that the equilibrium value of R/P is determined to clear the market—that is, so that the aggregate quantity of capital services supplied, K, equals the aggregate quantity demanded, K^d. This market-clearing value of R/P corresponds in Figure 6.7 to the intersection of the K^d curve with the vertical line at K. The market-clearing value for R/P is denoted by $(R/P)^*$ on the vertical axis. The corresponding market-clearing quantity of capital services, K^*, equals K on the horizontal axis.

The equality between K and K^d means that the market-clearing real rental price, $(R/P)^*$, equals the marginal product of capital, MPK:

(6.15) $(R/P)^* = MPK$ (*evaluated at* K)

By *MPK* (evaluated at K), we are referring in Figure 6.6 to the value for the marginal product of capital that corresponds to the capital input K.[6]

We can ask again why we assume that the market clears. The idea is that only at this market-clearing position would the real rental price, R/P, tend neither to rise nor fall. If R/P were below $(R/P)^*$ for example, at $(R/P)_1$ on the vertical axis in Figure 6.7, the aggregate quantity of capital services demanded would exceed the quantity supplied in the amount shown by the green arrows. In this case, demanders of capital services would compete to hire scarce capital by bidding up R/P. Conversely, if R/P were above $(R/P)^*$, for example, at $(R/P)_2$ on the vertical axis in Figure 6.7, the aggregate quantity of capital services demanded would fall short of the quantity supplied in the amount shown by the brown arrows. In this case, the suppliers of capital services would compete by lowering R/P. In equilibrium, R/P will be determined to clear the market—that is, so that the aggregate quantity of capital services supplied, K, equals the aggregate quantity demanded, K^d.

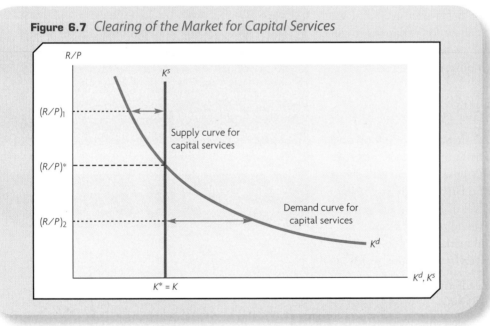

Figure 6.7 *Clearing of the Market for Capital Services*

The downward-sloping demand curve for capital services, K^d, comes from Figure 6.6. The supply of capital services, K^s, is fixed at K. The market-clearing real rental price is $(R/P)^*$. The market-clearing quantity of capital services is $K^* = K$. At a higher real rental price, such as $(R/P)_1$, the quantity of capital services supplied, $K^s = K$, exceeds the quantity demanded, K^d, in the amount shown by the green arrows. At a lower real rental price, such as $(R/P)_2$, the quantity of capital services supplied, $K^s = K$, falls short of the quantity demanded, K^d, in the amount shown by the brown arrows.

The Interest Rate

The market-clearing solution for the real rental price will allow us to determine the interest rate, *i*.

---

[6] Note that the curve for MPK in Figure 6.6 applies for a given labor input, L. A change in L would shift the MPK associated with a given value of K and would therefore change $(R/P)^*$ in Figure 6.7.

We found before that i equals the rate of return to owning capital:

(6.6)
$$i = R/P - \delta$$

rate of return on bonds =
rate of return on ownership of capital

Therefore, if we substitute for R/P from the formula for $(R/P)^*$ in equation (6.15), we get

> Key equation (equilibrium interest rate):
>
> **(6.16)** $i = MPK \, (evaluated \, at \, K) - \delta$

Thus, once we determine R/P, we also determine the interest rate, i.

This last result is important. It says that the interest rate, i, cannot change unless something changes the MPK. For a given technology level, A, the MPK depends on the inputs of capital services, K, and labor, L. In our present setting, K and L are given. Therefore, i will also be given. In the real world, the interest rate, i, tends to fluctuate a good deal. Thus, to capture this aspect of reality, we have to extend our model to allow for variations in the MPK. We introduce in Chapters 8 and 9 some sources of changes in the MPK and, therefore, in the interest rate, i.

Profit in Equilibrium

We determined households' demands for labor and capital services, L^d and K^d, from the objective of profit maximization. Households as business managers chose L^d and K^d to make real profit, Π/P, as high as possible. Now we will consider the level of Π/P that households receive when the labor and rental markets clear.

When the labor and rental markets clear, so that $L^d = L$ and $K^d = K$, real profit is given from equation (6.13) by

(6.17) $\Pi/P = A \cdot F(K, L) - (w/P) \cdot L - (R/P) \cdot K$

Since the labor and rental markets clear, we also have, from equations (6.14) and (6.15),

$$w/P = MPL$$
$$R/P = MPK$$

BACK TO REALITY

Economic Profit Versus Accounting Profit

Our definition of profit differs from the standard accounting definition. The reason for the difference is the treatment of rental payments on capital. Suppose, for example, that a household (or, more realistically, a business) owns capital and uses the capital to produce goods. In that case, the household pays no explicit rental payments on the capital that it uses in production. The rental payments are only implicit—the household should think of paying rentals to itself on the capital that it owns and uses. These implicit rental payments represent the income that the household could have received by renting the capital to another producer. Thus, the foregone rental payments should be treated as a cost (called an *opportunity cost*) of using one's own capital to produce goods.

However, standard accounting practices, including the national-income accounts, do not include most forms of implicit rental payments as costs.[7] For this reason, the usual accounting measure of rental payments understates the rental payments that are appropriate from an economic perspective. Since rental payments are a negative item for real profit, Π/P, in equation (6.17), we also get that the accounting measure overstates real profit from an economic standpoint. Since the economic profit is zero in equilibrium, the accounting measure of profit must be greater than zero in equilibrium. The accounting measure of profit really measures the uncounted part of the rental income on capital.

where MPL and MPK are evaluated at the given values of L and K. If we substitute these formulas for w/P and R/P into equation (6.17), we get

(6.18) $\Pi/P = A \cdot F(K, L) - MPL \cdot L - MPK \cdot K$

---

[7] If a business borrows money to finance purchases of capital goods, the usual accounting practice treats the interest payments on the business's debt as costs. Therefore, interest expenses—which represent the rental payments on debt-financed capital—enter as a negative item into the accounting definition of profit. Thus, standard accounting procedures include rental payments on capital as costs when the capital is debt financed but not when the capital is owned outright by a business. In the case of corporations, this ownership corresponds to finance of capital by issue of equity shares (corporate stock) or *retained earnings* (after-tax profit not paid out as dividends to shareholders).

We show in the Appendix that the expression on the right-hand side of equation (6.18) equals zero. That is, when the values for w/P and R/P satisfy the market-clearing conditions for labor and capital services, the real profit, Π/P, ends up being zero. Another way to say this is that real GDP, which equals $A \bullet F(K, L)$, just covers the payments to the two factor inputs, $(w/P) \bullet L$ for labor and $(R/P) \cdot K$ for capital services. Output equals the total of these real factor incomes, and all of this income goes to either labor or capital. Nothing is left over for profit.

We therefore have something of a paradox. Households as business managers select their demands for labor and capital services, L^d and K^d, to maximize profit. However, when w/P and R/P satisfy market-clearing conditions, the resulting real profit, Π/P, is zero. That is, the highest real profit that households can attain is zero. The Back to Reality box notes that accounting measures of profit include part of rental payments to capital and tend, therefore, to be greater than zero.

From an economic perspective, the reason that profit ends up being zero in our model is that profit represents the return to a household from managing a business. We have assumed that all households are equally good at business management and that the process of managing takes no effort. Therefore, in equilibrium, business management receives zero compensation (profit is nil).

Another point is that households as business owners are the *residual claimants* on business earnings. That is, profit income is the residual after subtracting from sales the costs of factor inputs, labor and capital. In our model, profit is not risky—it equals zero in equilibrium with complete certainty. More realistically, profit involves uncertainties about sales and costs. In most circumstances, the average profit has to be greater than zero to compensate business owners for assuming the risks of being a residual claimant.

Questions and Problems

A. Review questions

1. Why would households be interested only in the real values of consumption, income, and assets such as bonds? Think about how households would feel if the nominal values of consumption, income, and assets all doubled, and the price level, P, also doubled.

2. Distinguish clearly between a household's initial asset position and the change in that position. If a household has negative saving, is that household necessarily a borrower in the sense of having a negative position in bonds?

3. Derive the budget line shown in Figure 6.2. What does this line show?

4. How does an increase in the real wage rate, w/P, affect the quantity of labor demanded, L^d? Where does the assumption of diminishing marginal product of labor (MPL) come in?

5. How does an increase in the real rental price, R/P, affect the quantity of capital services demanded, K^d? Where does the assumption of diminishing marginal product of capital (MPK) come in?

B. Problems for discussion

6. Discount bonds
   The bonds in our model have a maturity close to zero; they just pay interest in accordance with the current interest rate, i, as a flow over time. We could consider, instead, a discount bond, such as a U.S. Treasury Bill. This type of asset has no explicit interest payments (called *coupons*) but pays a principal of, say, $1,000 at a fixed date in the future. A Bill with one-year maturity pays off one year from the issue date, and similarly for three-month or six-month Bills. Let P^B be the price of a discount bond with one-year maturity and principal of $1,000.

a. Is P^B greater than or less than $1,000?

b. What is the one-year interest rate on these discount bonds?

c. If P^B rises, what happens to the interest rate on these bonds?

d. Suppose that, instead of paying $1,000 in one year, the bond pays $1,000 in two years. What is the interest rate per year on this two-year discount bond?

7. Term structure of interest rates

Suppose that the economy has discount bonds (discussed in question 6) with one- and two-year maturities. Let i_t^1 be the interest rate on a one-year bond issued at the start of year t, and i_{t+1}^1 the interest rate on a one-year bond issued at the start of year $t + 1$. Let i_t^2 be the interest rate (per year) on a two-year bond issued at the start of year t. We can think of i_t^1 as the current short-term interest rate and i_t^2 as the current long-term interest rate.

a. Assume that, at the start of year t, everyone knows not only i_t^1 and i_t^2, but also the next year's one-year rate, i_{t+1}^1. What must be the relation of i_t^2 to i_t^1 and i_{t+1}^1? Explain the answer by considering the incentives of lenders and borrowers.

b. If $i_{t+1}^1, > i_t^1$ what is the relation between i_t^2, the long-term interest rate, and i_t^1, the short-term interest rate? The answer is an important result about the term structure of interest rates.

c. How would the results change if we assumed, more realistically, that there was uncertainty in year t about the future one-year interest rate, i_{t+1}^1?

8. Financial intermediaries

Consider a financial intermediary, such as a bank, that participates in the credit market. This intermediary borrows from some households and lends to others. (The loan from a customer to a bank often takes the form of a deposit account.)

a. Does the existence of intermediaries affect the result that the aggregate amount of loans is zero?

b. What interest rates would the intermediary charge to its borrowers and pay to its lenders? Why must there be some spread between these two rates?

c. Can you provide some reasons to explain why intermediaries might be useful?

chapter appendix

Output Equals Real Factor Incomes and Profit Equals Zero

We show here that, when capital and labor are each paid their marginal products, the total of real income payments to capital and labor equals the output or real GDP. Hence, profit is zero. These results are shown most easily using calculus.

Start with the production function for real GDP, Y:

(3.1)
$$Y = A \cdot F(K, L)$$

In Chapter 3, we assumed that the production function satisfied constant returns to scale in capital and labor, K and L. Therefore, if we multiply K and L each by $1/L$, we also multiply Y by $1/L$:

$$Y/L = A \cdot F(K/L, 1)$$

Thus, output per unit of labor, Y/L, depends only on capital per unit of labor, K/L. If we multiply through each side of the equation by L, we get another way to write the production function:

(6.19)
$$Y = AL \cdot F(K/L, 1)$$

We can use calculus to calculate the MPK from equation (6.19). The MPK is the derivative of Y with respect to K, while holding fixed A and L:

$$MPK = AL \cdot F_1 \cdot (1/L)$$

where F_1 is the derivative of the function F with respect to its first argument, K/L. We get the last term, $1/L$, from the chain rule for differentiation. That is, $1/L$ is the derivative of K/L with respect to K, while holding fixed L. If we cancel out L and $(1/L)$, we get

(6.20)
$$MPK = AF_1$$

The MPL is the derivative of Y with respect to L, while holding fixed A and K. Since L appears in two places on the right-hand side of equation (6.19), we have to calculate the derivative with respect to L of the product of two terms, AL and $F(K/L, 1)$. The first part of the answer is the derivative of the first term, A, multiplied by the second term, $F(K/L, 1)$. The second part is the first term, AL, multiplied by the derivative of the second term. This derivative is $F_1 \cdot (-K/L^2)$ where F_1 is again the derivative of the function F with respect to its first argument, K/L. The term $-K/L^2$ comes from the chain rule for differentiation. That is, $-K/L^2$ is the derivative of K/L with respect to L, while holding fixed K. Putting the results together, we get

(6.21)
$$MPL = A \cdot F(K/L, 1) + AL \cdot F_1 \cdot (-K/L^2)$$
$$MPL = A \cdot F(K/L, 1) - A \cdot (K/L) \cdot F_1$$

If the factor inputs are each paid their marginal products, so that $w/P = MPL$ and $R/P = MPK$, we can use equations (6.20) and (6.21) to calculate the total payments to labor and capital:

$$(w/P) \cdot L + (R/P) \cdot K = MPL \cdot L + MPK \cdot K$$
$$= [A \cdot F(K/L, 1) - A \cdot (K/L) \cdot F_1] \cdot L + (AF_1) \cdot K$$
$$= AL \cdot F(K/L, 1) - AK \cdot F_1 + AK \cdot F_1$$
$$= AL \cdot F(K/L, 1)$$

Equation (6.19) tells us that the last term equals real GDP Y, which equals $A \cdot F(K, L)$. Therefore, we have shown:

(6.22)
$$(w/P) \cdot L + (R/P) \cdot K = A \cdot F(K, L)$$

Thus, the total real payments to labor and capital, $(w/P) \cdot L + (R/P) \cdot K$ equal real GDP, $A \cdot F(K, L)$.[8]

Recall that real profit is given by

(6.17)
$$\Pi/P = A \cdot F(K, L) - (w/P) \cdot L - (R/P) \cdot K$$

Therefore, the result in equation (6.22) proves that Π/P is zero in equilibrium, as claimed in the text.

---

[8] This result is called Euler's Theorem.

Image Copyright Aaron Wood, 2009. Used under license from Shutterstock.com

CHAPTER 7

Consumption, Saving, and Investment

T he previous chapter introduced the four markets in our model of the macro economy—goods, labor, capital services, and bonds. We related household income to the prices and quantities in the four markets. We began the construction of the model's microeconomic foundations by considering how households, as managers of family businesses, determined their demands for labor and capital services. Then we investigated the clearing of the markets for labor and capital services. For given values of labor, L, and capital, K, these market-clearing conditions determined the real wage rate, w/P, the real rental price of capital, R/P, and the interest rate, i.

In this chapter, we extend our microeconomic analysis of households to the choices of consumption and saving. Then we will use these results to determine economy-wide levels of consumption, saving, and investment. These results will form the basis for an equilibrium business-cycle model, which we will use in Chapters 8 and 9 to analyze macroeconomic fluctuations.

Consumption and Saving

I n this section, we study an individual household's choice of consumption, C. In making this decision, the household also determines how much to save.

Start with the household budget constraint from equation (6.12) of Chapter 6:

(6.12)
$$C + (1/P) \bullet \Delta B + \Delta K = \Pi/P + (w/P) \bullet L + i \bullet (B/P + K)$$

We showed in Chapter 6 that real profit, Π/P, equaled zero when the markets for labor and capital services cleared. Therefore, we can set $\Pi/P = 0$ to get a simplified form of the household budget constraint:

(7.1)
$$C + (1/P) \bullet \Delta B + \Delta K = (w/P) \bullet L + i \bullet (B/P + K)$$

$$consumption + real\ saving = real\ income$$

Recall that the expression $(1/P) \bullet \Delta B + \Delta K$ represents real saving—the change in the real value of assets held as bonds, B, and ownership of capital, K. Real income consists of real wage income, $(w/P) \bullet L$, plus real asset income, $i \bullet (B/P + K)$.

We want to explore how the household chooses consumption and real saving. In making these choices, we assume, as in Chapter 6, that an individual household takes as given the real wage rate, w/P. This assumption is standard for a competitive market—the individual household is too small to have a noticeable effect on w/P. Now we go further by assuming that an individual household takes the interest rate, i, as given. This assumption is also standard for a competitive market—the individual household is too small to have a noticeable effect on i. Notice that, in this setup, each household can lend or borrow as much as it wants at the going interest rate. A household would borrow by issuing a bond that pays the interest rate, i. A household would lend by buying a bond that pays the interest rate, i.

Suppose that a household has given labor, L, and real assets, $(B/P + K)$. Then, since the real wage rate, w/P, and the interest rate, i, are given by the market to an individual household, the total of household real income, $(w/P) \cdot L + i \cdot (B/P + K)$, is determined on the right-hand side of equation (7.1).

With a given real income, the household's only choice is how to divide this income between consumption, C, and real saving, $(1/P) \cdot \Delta B + \Delta K$. That is, the household budget constraint in equation (7.1) constrains the total of consumption and real saving on the left-hand side. A household would like to have more of both, but this desire cannot be met for a given real income.

Figure 7.1 (similar to Figure 6.2 in Chapter 6) shows how the budget constraint from equation (7.1) allows the household to choose between consumption, C, and real saving, $(1/P) \cdot \Delta B + \Delta K$. One option is to set real saving to zero, so that C equals the total real income. This choice corresponds to point 1, shown on the horizontal axis where C equals total real income. Another option is to set C to zero, so that real saving equals total real income. This choice corresponds to point 2, shown on the vertical axis where real saving equals total real income. More typically, the household would opt for an intermediate position, where C and real saving are both greater than zero. For example, the household could pick point 3 in the graph.

The full range of possibilities is shown by the downward-sloping red budget line in Figure 7.1. The budget constraint in equation (7.1)

tells us that, along a budget line, each increase in C by one unit of goods corresponds to a decrease in real saving by one unit. Hence, the slope of a budget line is -1. The important point is that if the household wants one unit more of consumption, it must give up one unit of real saving.

So far, we have considered only the choice between consumption and saving at a point in time. But the reason for saving is to raise future assets, which will allow for higher consumption in the future. Thus, the essence of the household's choice between today's consumption and today's saving is the choice between today's consumption and tomorrow's consumption. By today and tomorrow, we mean that today's consumption has to be considered as part of a long-term plan—perhaps a lifetime plan, or even a longer one that considers the well-being of one's children. The key idea is that, to understand the choice between consumption and saving, we have to study the household's choices of consumption at different points in time.

The household budget constraint, equation (7.1), applies at every point in time. The link between today's budget constraint and tomorrow's budget constraint comes from the effect of today's real saving, $(1/P) \cdot \Delta B + \Delta K$, on tomorrow's real assets, $B/P + K$. We can go a long way in exploring this linkage by considering

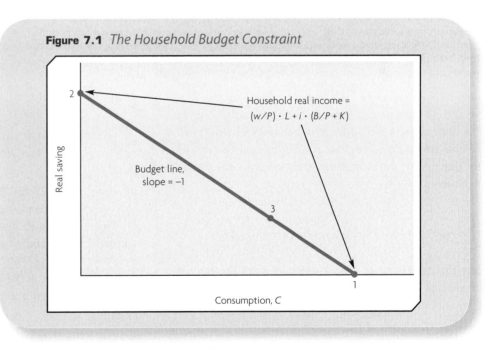

Figure 7.1 *The Household Budget Constraint*

Households have a given total of real income, $(w/P) \cdot L + i \cdot (B/P + K)$. This total must be divided between consumption, C, and real saving, $(1/P) \Delta B + \Delta K$. Thus, if real saving is zero, C equals the total of real income along the horizontal axis at point 1. If C is zero, real saving equals the total of real income along the vertical axis at point 2. The budget constraint in equation (7.1) allows the household to select any combination of consumption and real saving along the budget line, shown in red, such as point 3. The budget line has a slope of -1. Along this line, one unit less of consumption corresponds to one unit more of real saving.

Figure 7.2 Change in Real Assets in Year 1

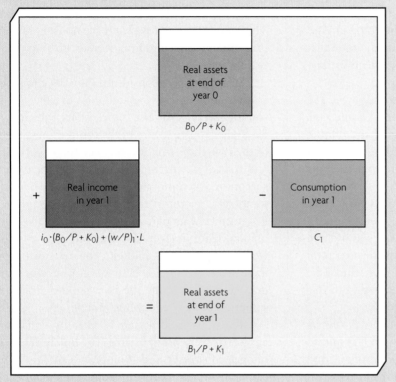

The red bin has the real assets at the end of year 0, $B_0/P + K_0$, the first term on the right-hand side of equation (7.4). The real income for year 1, $i_0 \bullet (B_0/P + K_0) + (w/P)_1 \bullet L$ in the blue bin, corresponds to the second term on the right-hand side of equation (7.4) and adds to the red bin. The consumption for year 1, C_1 in the green bin, corresponds to the third term on the right-hand side of equation (7.4) and subtracts from the red bin. The final result is the real assets at the end of year 1, $B_1/P + K_1$ in the yellow bin. This amount is the left-hand side of equation (7.4).

at the end of the previous year, year 0, and therefore also the amounts held at the *beginning* of year 1. Thus, $(B_1/P + K_1) - (B_0/P + K_0)$ is the change in real assets—or real saving—in year 1.

On the right-hand side of equation (7.2), the real wage rate for year 1 is $(w/P)_1$ and the real wage income for the year is $(w/P)_1 \bullet L$. Since we assume that labor, L, is fixed over time, we do not include a year subscript. The interest rate for assets held at the end of year 0 is i_0. Thus, the real asset income for year 1 is $i_0 \bullet (B_0/P + K_0)$. When we add real wage income to real asset income, we get total real income for year 1 on the right-hand side.

The budget constraint in equation (7.2) is for year 1. The same form of budget constraint applies to year 2:

(7.3)
$$C_2 + (B_2/P + K_2) - (B_1/P + K_1) = \\ (w/P)_2 \bullet L + i_1 \bullet (B_1/P + K_1)$$

consumption in year 2 + real saving in year 2 = real income in year 2

Our next task is to combine the budget constraints in equations (7.2) and (7.3) to describe a household's choice between consuming this year, C_1, and next year, C_2. Notice that both budget constraints include the assets held at the end of year 1, $B_1/P + K_1$. We can use equation (7.2) to solve out for this term by moving C_1 and $B_0/P + K_0$ from the left-hand side to the right-hand side and rearranging terms to get

(7.4)
$$B_1/P + K_1 = \\ B_0/P + K_0 + i_0 \bullet (B_0/P + K_0) + (w/P)_1 \bullet L - C_1$$

$$\frac{\text{real assets}}{\text{end year 1}} = \frac{\text{real assets}}{\text{end year 0}} + \frac{\text{real income}}{\text{year 1}} - \frac{\text{consumption}}{\text{year 1}}$$

Figure 7.2 shows this relation visually. The red bin has the real assets at the end of year 0, $B_0/P + K_0$, which is the first term on the right-hand side of equation (7.4).

just two periods. To be concrete, think of the first period as the current year and the second period as the following year. Once we understand this two-period framework, we can readily extend the model to determine consumption and saving over many periods.

Consumption over Two Years

For the current year, year 1, we can write the budget constraint from equation (7.1) as

(7.2)
$$C_1 + (B_1/P + K_1) - (B_0/P + K_0) = \\ (w/P)_1 \bullet L + i_0 \bullet (B_0/P + K_0)$$

consumption in year 1 + real saving in year 1 = real income in year 1

On the left-hand side, C_1 is year 1's consumption. The real assets B_1/P and K_1 are the amounts held at the end of year 1. The real assets B_0/P and K_0 are the amounts held

Add to this amount the blue bin, which contains the real income in year 1, $i_0 \cdot (B_0/P + K_0) + (w/P)_1 \cdot L$. This income is the second term on the right-hand side of equation (7.4). Then subtract the green bin, which contains consumption in year 1, C_1, the final term on the right-hand side. We end up with the yellow bin, which contains the real assets at the end of year 1, $B_1/P + K_1$, the term on the left-hand side of equation (7.4).

The same analysis applies to year 2. The analog to equation (7.4) is

(7.5)
$$B_2/P + K_2 = $$
$$B_1/P + K_1 + i_1 \cdot (B_1/P + K_1) + (w/P)_2 \cdot L - C_2$$

$$\frac{real\ assets}{end\ year\ 2} = \frac{real\ assets}{end\ year\ 1} + \frac{real\ income}{year\ 2} - \frac{consumption}{year\ 2}$$

Figure 7.3, similar to Figure 7.2, shows this relationship visually.

Going back to equation (7.4), we can combine the two terms involving $B_0/P + K_0$ on the right-hand side to get

(7.6)
$$B_1/P + K_1 = $$
$$(1 + i_0) \cdot (B_0/P + K_0) + (w/P)_1 \cdot L - C_1$$

Notice, on the right-hand side, that we multiply $B_0/P + K_0$ by the term $1 + i_0$. The "1" represents the principal of year 0's assets, and the "i_0" represents the interest paid on these assets.

We see on the right-hand side of equation (7.6) that, if the household lowers year 1's consumption, C_1, by one unit, the real assets held at the end of year 1, $B_1/P + K_1$, rise by one unit on the left-hand side. Visually, in Figure 7.2, suppose that we take one unit of goods out of the green C_1 bin and do not change the red and blue bins. Since the green bin enters with a minus sign, taking one unit out of it means that there will be one unit more left in the yellow bin, which has $B_1/P + K_1$.

If we combine the two terms involving $B_1/P + K_1$ on the right-hand side of

the second year's budget constraint in equation (7.5), we get

(7.7)
$$B_2/P + K_2 = $$
$$(1 + i_1) \cdot (B_1/P + K_1) + (w/P)_2 \cdot L - C_2$$

This expression takes the same form as equation (7.6), except that everything is updated by one year. Notice, on the right-hand side, that a higher value of $B_1/P + K_1$, the assets held at the end of year 1, allows the household to raise year 2's consumption, C_2, also on the right-hand side. Visually, in Figure 7.3, an increase in $B_1/P + K_1$ by one unit means that we add one unit to the red bin (which has the assets at the end of year 1) and i_1 units to the blue bin (which includes the interest income on the assets from the end of year 1). Suppose that we do not change the yellow bin, which has the assets held at the end of year 2, $B_2/P + K_2$. In this case, we must have $1 + i_1$ units more in the green bin, which contains C_2. Note that C_2 can be increased by $1 + i_1$ units without having to change the assets held at the end of year 2, $B_2/P + K_2$.

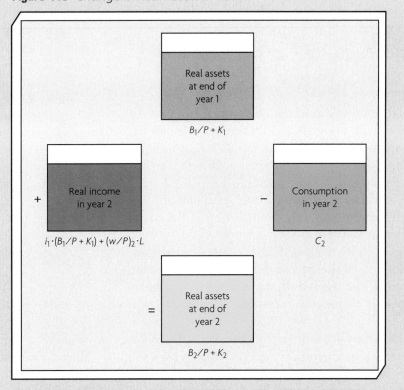

Figure 7.3 *Change in Real Assets in Year 2*

Real assets at end of year 1

$B_1/P + K_1$

+ Real income in year 2

$i_1 \cdot (B_1/P + K_1) + (w/P)_2 \cdot L$

− Consumption in year 2

C_2

= Real assets at end of year 2

$B_2/P + K_2$

The red bin has the real assets at the end of year 1, $B_1/P + K_1$ the first term on the right-hand side of equation (7.5). The real income for year 2, $i_1 \cdot (B_1/P + K_1) + (w/P)_2 \cdot L$ in the blue bin, corresponds to the second term on the right-hand side of equation (7.5) and adds to the red bin. The consumption for year 2, C_2 in the green bin, corresponds to the third term on the right-hand side of equation (7.5) and subtracts from the red bin. The final result is the real assets at the end of year 2, $B_2/P + K_2$ in the yellow bin. This amount is the left-hand side of equation (7.5).

We now have the building blocks to establish the link between consuming this year, C_1, and next year, C_2. Recall from equation (7.6) and Figure 7.2 that a reduction in C_1 by one unit allows the household to increase assets at the end of year 1, $B_1/P + K_1$, by one unit. We also have from equation (7.7) and Figure 7.3 that an increase in $B_1/P + K_1$ by one unit can be used to raise C_2 by $1 + i_1$ units. Thus, if C_1 decreases by one unit, the household can increase C_2 by $1 + i_1$ units. Moreover, the household can make this switch between C_1 and C_2 without changing $B_2/P + K_2$, the real assets carried over to year 3 (and shown as the yellow bin in Figure 7.3). Thus, the household can change the timing of consumption between this year and next year, C_1 and C_2, without shortchanging or enriching the future—that is, without altering the assets available for year 3 and beyond.

To construct the full two-year budget constraint algebraically, first replace $B_1/P + K_1$ on the right-hand side of equation (7.7) by the right-hand side of equation (7.6) to get

$$B_2/P + K_2 = (1 + i_1) \cdot [(1 + i_0) \cdot (B_0/P + K_0) + (w/P)_1 \cdot L - C_1] + (w/P)_2 \cdot L - C_2$$

If we multiply the terms inside the large brackets by $1 + i_1$, we get

(7.8) $B_2/P + K_2 = (1 + i_1) \cdot (1 + i_0) \cdot (B_0/P + K_0) + (1 + i_1) \cdot (w/P)_1 \cdot L - (1 + i_1) \cdot C_1 + (w/P)_2 \cdot L - C_2$

Notice the effects of the interest-rate terms on the right-hand side of equation (7.8). The first term includes the assets from the end of year 0, $B_0/P + K_0$, which pay the return $i_0 \cdot (B_0/P + K_0)$ in year 1. If the household holds these assets, it ends up with $(1 + i_0) \cdot (B_0/P + K_0)$ in assets at the end of year 1. Hence, each unit of assets from the end of year 0 is multiplied by $1 + i_0$ to get assets at the end of year 1.

Equivalently, in Figure 7.2, if $B_0/P + K_0$ rises by one unit, the red bin rises by one unit and the blue bin rises by i_0 units. Therefore, if the green bin, which contains C_1, does not change, the yellow bin increases by $1 + i_0$ units.

The same calculation applies for year 2. Each unit of assets held at the end of year 1 is multiplied by $1 + i_1$ to get assets at the end of year 2. In Figure 7.3, if $B_1/P + K_1$ rises by one unit, the red bin rises by one unit and the blue bin rises by i_1 units. Therefore, if the green bin,

which contains C_2, does not change, the yellow bin increases by $1 + i_1$ units. If we put this result together with the result for year 1, we find that each unit of assets held for two periods—from the end of year 0 to the end of year 2—ends up as $(1 + i_1) \cdot (1 + i_0)$ units of assets. This interest-rate term is the one that multiplies $B_0/P + K_0$ on the right-hand side of equation (7.8).

Similarly, the household could save its wage income in year 1, $(w/P)_1 \cdot L$, and thereby have more assets at the end of year 1. (In Figure 7.2, the blue and yellow bins each rise by one unit.) Each unit of these assets becomes $1 + i_1$ units at the end of year 2. (In Figure 7.3, the red bin rises by one unit, the blue bin rises by i_1 units, and the yellow bin increases by $1 + i_1$ units.) Therefore, $(w/P)_1 \cdot L$ is multiplied by $1 + i_1$ in equation (7.8). In contrast, the wage income $(w/P)_2 \cdot L$ appears by itself because the household receives this income too late to get any asset returns in year 2.

To think about the consumption terms, notice in equation (7.6) that year 1's consumption, C_1, enters in the same way as year 1's real wage income, $(w/P)_1 \cdot L$, but with a minus sign.[1] The reason is that real saving is the difference between real income and consumption. We therefore find in equation (7.8) that C_1, like $(w/P)_1 \cdot L$, is multiplied by $1 + i_1$. Similarly, year 2's consumption, C_2, enters into equation (7.7) in the same way as year 2's real wage income, $(w/P)_2 \cdot L$, except for the sign.[2] Therefore, C_2, like $(w/P)_2 \cdot L$, appears in equation (7.8) without any interest-rate terms.

If we divide through everything in equation (7.8) by $1 + i_1$ and rearrange the terms to put the ones involving consumption on the left-hand side, we get

Key equation (two-year household budget constraint):

(7.9) $C_1 + C_2/(1 + i_1) = (1 + i_0) \cdot (B_0/P + K_0) + (w/P)_1 \cdot L + (w/P)_2 \cdot L/(1 + i_1) - (B_2/P + K_2)/(1 + i_1)$

We get this result by using the budget constraints for years 1 and 2, as given in equations (7.2) and (7.3). Therefore, we call equation (7.9) the **two-year budget constraint**.

---

[1] Equivalently, in Figure 7.2, an increase by one unit in the blue bin, which contains $(w/P)_1 \cdot L$, has the same effect as a decrease by one unit in the green bin, which contains C_1.

[2] Equivalently, in Figure 7.3, an increase by one unit in the blue bin, which contains $(w/P)_2 \cdot L$, has the same effect as a decrease by one unit in the green bin, which contains C_2.

Observe how the wage incomes, $(w/P)_1 \bullet L$ and $(w/P)_2 \bullet L$, enter on the right-hand side of equation (7.9). We do not add the two together but rather divide $(w/P)_2 \bullet L$ by $1 + i_1$ before combining it with $(w/P)_1 \bullet L$. Similarly, on the left-hand side, we make the same adjustment to C_2 before combining it with C_1. To understand these adjustments, we have to explore the concept of **present value**.

Present Value   If the interest rate, i_1, is greater than zero, \$1 held as assets in year 1 becomes more than \$1 in year 2. Therefore, \$1 received or spent in year 1 is equivalent to more than \$1 in year 2. Or, viewed in reverse, dollars received or spent in year 2 must be **discounted** to make them comparable to dollars in year 1. The general idea of discounting is that dollars received later are not worth as much as dollars received earlier. Here we apply the general notion of discounting to a comparison of year 1 with year 2.

To be concrete, suppose that the interest rate is $i_1 = 5\%$ per year. Assume that a household has \$100 of income in year 1 but plans to spend this income a year later, in year 2. Then the household can buy \$100 of bonds at the start of year 1 and have \$105 at the start of year 2. Hence, \$100 received in year 1 is worth as much as \$105 received in year 2. Equivalently, the \$105 from year 2 has to be discounted to get the income needed in year 1 to generate \$105 in year 2. We find this amount by solving the equation:

income needed in year $1 \times (1 + 5\%) = \$105$

The required amount of income in year 1 is \$105/1.05 = \$100.

More generally, if we substitute i_1 for 5%, the income for year 2 has to be divided by $1 + i_1$ to find the equivalent amount for year 1. Hence, if the wage income received in year 2 is $(w/P)_2 \bullet L$, the present value (or year 1 value) of this income is $(w/P)_2 \bullet L/(1 + i_1)$. The term $1 + i_1$ is an example of what economists call a **discount factor**. When we discount by this factor—that is, divide by $1 + i_1$—we determine the present value of year 2's income. If we went beyond year 2, we would have a different discount factor for each year.

The two-year budget constraint in equation (7.9) shows that we express year 2's wage income as a present value, $(w/P)_2 \bullet L/(1 + i_1)$, before combining it with year 1's income, $(w/P)_1 \bullet L$. The sum, $(w/P)_1 \bullet L + (w/P)_2 \bullet L/(1 + i_1)$, is the total present value of wage income for years 1 and 2. Similarly, we express year 2's consumption as the present value $C_2/(1 + i_1)$ before combining it with year 1's consumption, C_1. The sum, $C_1/(1 + i_1)$, is the total present value of consumption for years 1 and 2.

Our next task is to analyze a household's choices of how much to consume in year 1 and year 2. We know that these choices have to respect the two-year budget constraint, given in equation (7.9). But the household still has a lot of leeway in deciding among the feasible combinations of C_1 and C_2. We have to figure out which combination the household will prefer among those that satisfy the two-year budget constraint.

Choosing Consumption: Income Effects   To understand choices of consumption, we have to bring in *household preferences* about consuming at different points in time. By preferences, we mean a ranking of time paths of consumption in terms of the satisfaction that the household gets. Economists use the term **utility** as a synonym for satisfaction or happiness.[3] Our assumption is that the household chooses the time path of consumption—in this case, C_1 and C_2—to maximize utility, subject to the budget constraint in equation (7.9).

We assume that, other things being the same, utility increases if C_1 or C_2 (or consumption in any other year) rises. We assume further that a household likes to consume at similar levels at different points in time, rather than consuming at high levels some of the time and at low levels other times. For example, a household prefers having C_1 and C_2 both equal to 100, rather than having C_1 equal to 0 and C_2 equal to 200. These preferences motivate a household to *smooth consumption* even when income is irregular. By "smooth," we mean that the planned levels of consumption chosen for different years, such as C_1 and C_2, tend to be close to each other, rather than varying greatly from one year to the next.

Consider some intuitive examples of consumption smoothing. Suppose that a person gets an unexpected windfall of income, perhaps from winning the lottery or receiving a surprise check in the mail. The usual response is to spread the extra money over consumption at various dates, rather than spending it all at once. Similarly, because people anticipate that their incomes will go down when they retire, they tend to save in advance to avoid sharply lower consumption during retirement.

---

[3] The term **utility function** is used to express the relation between the utility obtained and the time path of consumption—in this case, the values of C_1 and C_2.

To see how the household chooses C_1 and C_2, return to the two-year budget constraint:

(7.9)
$$C_1 + C_2/(1 + i_1) =$$
$$(1 + i_0) \bullet (B_0/P + K_0) + (w/P)_1 \bullet L$$
$$+ (w/P)_2 \bullet L/(1 + i_1) - (B_2/P + K_2)/(1 + i_1)$$

p.v. of consumption = value of initial assets
+ p.v. of wage incomes − p.v. of assets end year 2

where we use *p.v.* as an abbreviation for present value. The first term on the right-hand side, $(1 + i_0) \bullet (B_0/P + K_0)$, is the value in year 1 of initial assets. This term adds to the present value of wage incomes received in years 1 and 2, $(w/P)_1 \bullet L + (w/P)_2 \bullet L/(1 + i_1)$. We shall find it convenient to combine these two terms into a single measure, V, of the present value of the household's sources of funds received through year 2. Thus, we define V by

(7.10)
$$V = (1 + i_0) \bullet (B_0/P + K_0) + (w/P)_1 \bullet$$
$$L + (w/P)_2 \bullet L/(1 + i_1)$$

p.v. of sources of funds = value of initial assets
+ p.v. of wage incomes

If we substitute this definition of V into equation (7.9), we get

(7.11)
$$C_1 + C_2/(1 + i_1) =$$
$$V - (B_2/P + K_2)/(1 + i_1)$$

p.v. of consumption = p.v. of sources of funds
− p.v. of assets end year 2

The last term on the right-hand side of equation (7.11), $(B_2/P + K_2)/(1 + i_1)$, is the present value of the real assets held at the end of year 2. These assets will help to pay for consumption in years 3 and later. We assume, for now, that this term is fixed. That is, we analyze the choices of C_1 and C_2 while holding constant the assets that a household provides for year 3 and beyond. This simplifying device allows us to carry out a two-period analysis, where we study just the choices of C_1 and C_2.

Suppose that V, the present value of the sources of funds, increases due to a rise in initial assets, $(B_0/P + K_0)$, or wage incomes, $(w/P)_1 \bullet L$ and $(w/P)_2 \bullet L$. Since we are holding fixed the term $(B_2/P + K_2)/(1 + i_1)$, equation (7.11) tells us that the total present value of consumption, $C_1 + C_2/(1 + i_1)$, must rise by the same amount as V. Since households like to consume at similar levels in the two years, we predict that C_1 and C_2 will rise by similar amounts. These responses of consumption to increases in initial assets or wage incomes are called **income effects**. An increase in V, the present value of the sources of funds, leads to higher consumption in each year, C_1 and C_2.

Choosing Consumption: The Intertemporal-Substitution Effect

The income effects that we just studied tell us about the overall level of consumption—for example, the responses of C_1 and C_2 to a change in initial assets and wage incomes. The other major decision is how much to consume in one year compared to the other year. We have already assumed that households like to have similar levels of C_1 and C_2. However, this preference is not absolute. Households would be willing to deviate from equal consumption levels if there were an economic incentive to deviate. The interest rate, i_1, provides this incentive.

Consider again the two-year budget constraint:

(7.11)
$$C_1 + C_2/(1 + i_1) = V - (B_2/P + K_2)/(1 + i_1)$$

p.v. of consumption = p.v. of sources of funds
− p.v. of assets end year 2

The left-hand side has the present value of consumption, $C_1 + C_2/(1 + i_1)$. This expression shows that C_2 is discounted by $1 + i_1$ before adding it to C_1. This discounting means that a unit of C_2 is effectively cheaper than a unit of C_1. The reason is that, if a household defers consumption from year 1 to year 2, it can hold more assets (or borrow less) at the end of year 1. Since each unit of assets becomes $1 + i_1$ units in year 2 (see equation [7.7]), one unit less of C_1 can be replaced by $1 + i_1$ units more of C_2.

As an example, suppose that you are considering taking a vacation this summer. If the interest rate is $i_1 = 5\%$, you might prefer to postpone the vacation until next summer. The reward is that you could spend 5% more and have a better vacation.

We can also use this example to see how the household responds to an increase in the interest rate. If the interest rate rises to $i_1 = 10\%$, the reward for waiting increases—now you could spend 10% more on the delayed vacation. Thus, our prediction is that the vacation is more likely to be postponed when the interest rate, i_1, rises. Hence, C_1, consumption of vacations in year 1, falls, and C_2, consumption of vacations in year 2, rises.

The general point is that an increase in the interest rate, i_1, lowers the cost of C_2 compared to C_1. That is, a higher i_1 provides a greater reward for deferring consumption. Therefore, the household responds to an increase in i_1 by lowering C_1 and raising C_2. Economists call this response an **intertemporal-substitution effect**. By "intertemporal," we mean that the effect refers to substitution *over time*. The household shifts consumption away from one point in time, such as year 1, and toward another point, such as year 2.[4] The By the Numbers box describes empirical estimates of the strength of the intertemporal-substitution effect in U.S. data.

Although we analyzed the intertemporal-substitution effect in terms of consumption in different years, we can view the results through a different lens to determine the responses of saving. That is, we can figure out the effects of the interest rate on the household's saving.

Return to the household budget constraint for year 1:

(7.2)
$$C_1 + (B_1/P + K_1) - (B_0/P + K_0) = (w/P)_1 \cdot L + i_0 \cdot (B_0/P + K_0)$$

consumption in year 1 + *real saving in year* 1 = *real income in year* 1

We know from the intertemporal-substitution effect that an increase in the interest rate, i_1, motivates the household to postpone consumption, so that this year's consumption, C_1, falls on the left-hand side. Since year 1's real income, $(w/P)_1 \cdot L + i_0 \cdot (B_0/P + K_0)$ on the right-hand side of equation (7.2), is given, the decline in C_1 must be matched by a rise in year 1's real saving, $(B_1/P + K_1) - (B_0/P + K_0)$. That is, the intertemporal-substitution effect motivates the household to save more when the interest rate rises.

Our analysis of interest rates is incomplete because we have considered only the intertemporal-substitution effect. We have not yet considered whether a change in the interest rate also has an income effect.

bythenumbers

Empirical Evidence on Intertemporal Substitution of Consumption

The intertemporal-substitution effect predicts that a higher interest rate motivates households to reduce current consumption compared to future consumption. A study by David Runkle (1991) isolated the effect of interest rates on consumption by examining food outlays for 1,100 U.S. households from 1973 to 1982. (The data are from the *Panel Study of Income Dynamics* (PSID), conducted at the University of Michigan.) Runkle found that an increase in the annual interest rate by one percentage point raises the typical family's growth rate of consumption by about one-half percentage point per year.

The isolation of intertemporal-substitution effects in aggregate consumption data has proven to be more difficult, as discussed by Robert Hall (1989). However, a study of U.S. nondurable consumption by Joon-Ho Hahm (1998) estimated that a rise in the annual interest rate by one percentage point increases the growth rate of

aggregate consumption by around one-third percentage point per year. Thus, the intertemporal-substitution effect does apply to aggregate consumption data.

Image Copyright Joy Brown, 2009. Used under license from Shutterstock.com

---

[4] Economists usually assume that households prefer to consume earlier rather than later. In this case, the interest rate, i_1, has to be greater than zero—perhaps 2% per year—to motivate households to choose equal values of C_1 and C_2. If i_1 is greater than 2%, the household sets C_1 below C_2, whereas if i_1 is less than 2%, the household sets C_1 above C_2. The main point is still that an increase in i_1 reduces C_1 and raises C_2.

The Income Effect from a Change in the Interest Rate We can understand the income effect from a change in the interest rate, i_1, by examining the household budget constraint for year 2:

(7.3) $$C_2 + (B_2/P + K_2) - (B_1/P + K_1) = (w/P)_2 \cdot L + i_1 \cdot (B_1/P + K_1)$$

consumption in year 2 + real saving in year 2 = real income in year 2

We can see the income effect from i_1 in the yellow shaded term, $i_1 \cdot (B_1/P + K_1)$, which gives the income on assets in year 2. We can break this term down into its two parts, $i_1 \cdot (B_1/P)$ and $i_1 K_1$.

Consider first the part $i_1 \cdot (B_1/P)$, which is the interest income on bonds. This interest income is greater than zero for a holder of bonds (the lender), for whom B_1/P is greater than zero. However, this term is less than zero for an issuer of bonds (the borrower), for whom B_1/P is less than zero. For a holder of bonds, the income effect from an increase in i_1 is positive, because the interest income received on a given amount of bonds, B_1/P, is larger. For an issuer of bonds, the income effect from an increase in i_1 is negative, because the interest paid on a given amount of bonds, B_1/P, is larger. For the economy as a whole, lending and borrowing must balance—any outstanding bond has both a holder and an issuer. Therefore, for the average household, B_1/P has to be zero. Hence, for the average household, the income effect from the term $i_1 \cdot (B_1/P)$ is zero.

Households also hold assets in the form of ownership of capital, and the $i_1 K_1$ part of the yellow shaded term in equation (7.3) represents the income received on these assets in year 2. For the economy as a whole, the capital stock, K_1, is, of course, greater than zero. Thus, in contrast to bonds, the average household's holding of claims on capital, K_1, is greater than zero. Therefore, when we consider the term $i_1 K_1$, the income effect from an increase in i_1 is positive.

To put the results together, in the aggregate, the income effect from an increase in i_1 consists of a zero effect from the term $i_1 \cdot B_1/P$ and a positive effect from the term $i_1 K_1$. Therefore, the full income effect from an increase in i_1 is positive.

Figure 7.4 *Effects of the Interest Rate on Consumption and Saving*

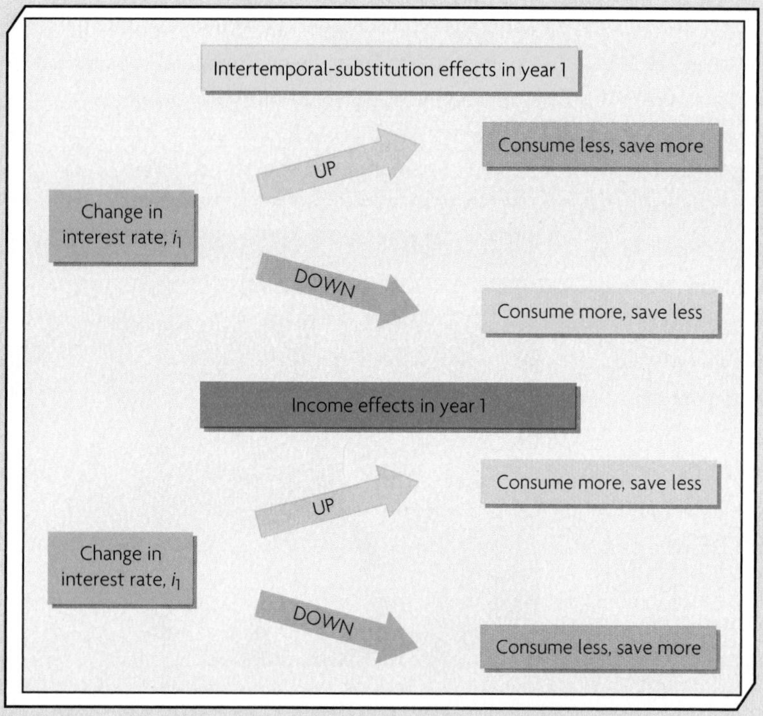

Intertemporal-substitution effects in year 1

Change in interest rate, i_1

UP → Consume less, save more

DOWN → Consume more, save less

Income effects in year 1

Change in interest rate, i_1

UP → Consume more, save less

DOWN → Consume less, save more

If year 1's interest rate, i_1, goes up, the intertemporal-substitution effect predicts that year 1's consumption, C_1, will rise, and year 1's real saving, $(B_1/P + K_1) - (B_0/P + K_0)$, will fall. These intertemporal-substitution effects are in the opposite direction if i_1 goes down. The income effects always offset the intertemporal-substitution effects. For example, if i_1 goes up, the income effect predicts that consumption, C_1, will rise, and real saving, $(B_1/P + K_1) - (B_0/P + K_0)$, will fall.

Combining Income and Substitution Effects In many circumstances, an economic change will involve both income and substitution effects. Consider, for example, the effect of an increase in the interest rate, i_1, on year 1's consumption, C_1. The intertemporal-substitution effect motivates the household to reduce C_1. However, an increase in i_1 also has a positive income effect, which motivates the household to raise C_1. Therefore, the overall effect from an increase in i_1 on C_1 is ambiguous. Year 1's consumption, C_1, falls if the intertemporal-substitution effect dominates but rises if the income effect dominates. In the next section, we will use the *multiyear budget constraint* to assess the strength of the income effect. In some cases, this analysis allows us to determine whether the income effect is likely to be stronger or weaker than the substitution effect.

Figure 7.4 provides a visual summary of the intertemporal-substitution and income effects from a change in the interest rate, i_1. The upper part shows that the intertemporal-substitution effect predicts that an increase in i_1 will lower year 1's consumption, C_1, and, therefore, raise year 1's real saving, $(B_1/P + K_1) - (B_0/P + K_0)$. If i_1 falls, these intertemporal-substitution effects are in the opposite direction. The lower part shows that the income effects always offset the intertemporal-substitution effects. For example, if i_1 rises, the income effects predict that C_1 will rise and, hence, real saving, $(B_1/P + K_1) - (B_0/P + K_0)$ will fall.

Consumption over Many Years

We now extend the household budget constraint to include consumption over many years. We start with the two-year budget constraint:

(7.9)
$$C_1 + C_2/(1 + i_1) =$$
$$(1 + i_0) \cdot (B_0/P + K_0) + (w/P)_1 \cdot L + (w/P)_2 \cdot$$
$$L/(1 + i_1) - (B_2/P + K_2)/(1 + i_1)$$

p.v. of consumption = value of initial assets
+ p.v. of wage incomes − p.v. of assets end year 2

We now relax our simplifying assumption that the household could not change the present value of assets held at the end of year 2—that is, the yellow shaded term, $(B_2/P + K_2)/(1 + i_1)$ in equation (7.9). These assets are, in fact, not fixed. A change in $(B_2/P + K_2)$ means that the household provides more or less assets for consumption in years 3 and beyond. To understand the choice of $(B_2/P + K_2)$ we have to consider consumption and income in future years. The Appendix describes in detail how to make this extension. Here we provide an intuitive analysis.

The left-hand side of equation (7.9) is the present value of consumption for years 1 and 2. When we consider many years, the left-hand side becomes the present value of consumption over these many years. The first term added is the present value of year 3's consumption, which is $C_3/[(1 + i_1) \cdot (1 + i_2)]$. We divide C_3 by $(1 + i_1) \cdot (1 + i_2)$ because this term measures the cumulation of interest earnings over two years, from year 1 to year 3. That is, one unit of assets in year 1 becomes $1 + i_1$ units in year 2, and each of these units becomes $1 + i_2$ units in year 3.

If we continue to include years farther into the future, we end up with the overall present value of consumption:

overall present value of consumption =
$$C_1 + C_2/(1 + i_1) + C_3/[(1 + i_1) \cdot (1 + i_2)] + \cdots$$

The ellipses (…) indicate that we include the present values of C_4, C_5, and so on. The multiyear budget constraint has this overall present value of consumption on the left-hand side.[5] In contrast, equation (7.9) included this present value only for years 1 and 2.

The right-hand side of equation (7.9) includes the year-one value of initial assets, $(1 + i_0) \cdot (B_0/P + K_0)$. This term still appears in the multiyear setting. However, equation (7.9) includes the present value of wage incomes only for years 1 and 2. When we consider many years, we end up with the present value of wage incomes over these many years. By analogy to the results for consumption, we end up with

oveall present value of wage incomes =
$$(w/P)_1 \cdot L + (w/P)_2 \cdot L/(1 + i_1) + (w/P)_2 \cdot$$
$$L/[(1 + i_1) \cdot (1 + i_2)] + \cdots$$

Again, the ellipses indicate that we include the present values of $(w/P)_3 \cdot L$, $(w/P)_4 \cdot L$, and so on. Notice that the interest-rate terms—needed to calculate present values—are the same as those for consumption.

The final point is that the right-hand side of equation (7.9) includes the present value of assets held at the end of year 2, $(B_2/P + K_2)/(1 + i_1)$. When we consider many years, this term becomes the present value of assets held in the distant future. Because of the discounting used to calculate present values, we can safely neglect this term. (See the Appendix for a discussion.) Therefore, we end up with the **multiyear budget constraint**:

> Key equation (multiyear budget constraint):
>
> **(7.12)** $C_1 + C_2/(1 + i_1) + C_3/[(1 + i_1) \cdot (1 + i_2)] + \cdots =$
> $(1 + i_0) \cdot (B_0/P + K_0) + (w/P)_1 \cdot L + (w/P)_2 \cdot$
> $L/(1 + i_1) + (w/P)_3 \cdot L/[(1 + i_1) \cdot (1 + i_2)] + \cdots$
>
> *present value of consumption =*
> *value of initial assets + present*
> *value of wage incomes*

---

[5] Year 4's consumption, C_4, is divided by $(1 + i_1) \cdot (1 + i_2) \cdot (1 + i_3)$ and so on.

The multiyear budget constraint is useful because it allows us to compare the effects of temporary and permanent changes in income. For a temporary change, we can consider an increase in year 1's wage income, $(w/P)_1 \bullet L$, by one unit while leaving unchanged the initial assets, $(B_0/P + K_0)$, and the wage incomes for the other years, $(w/P)_2 \bullet L$, $(w/P)_3 \bullet L$, and so on. An example would be a bonus that an employee does not expect to be repeated. One possibility, which satisfies the multiyear budget constraint in equation (7.12), is that the household would spend all of its extra income on year 1's consumption, C_1. However, households tend not to react this way, because they like to have similar levels of consumption in each year. Thus, we predict that the household would respond to a rise in $(w/P)_1 \bullet L$ by raising consumption by similar amounts in each year: C_1, C_2, C_3, and so on. This response means, however, that consumption in any particular year, such as year 1, cannot increase very much. Therefore, if $(w/P)_1 \bullet L$ rises by one unit, we predict that C_1 increases by much less than one unit. To put it another way, the **propensity to consume** in year 1 out of an extra unit of year 1's income tends to be small when the extra income is temporary.

We can interpret the results in terms of saving by looking again at the household's budget constraint for year 1:

[7.2] $\quad C_1 + (B_1/P + K_1) - (B_0/P + K_0) =$
$$(w/P)_1 \bullet L + i_0 \bullet (B_0/P + K_0)$$

consumption in year 1 + *real saving in year* 1 =
real income in year 1

If $(w/P)_1 \bullet L$ rises by one unit on the right-hand side, C_1 rises by much less than one unit on the left-hand side. Therefore, year 1's real saving, $(B_1/P + K_1) - (B_0/P + K_0)$, must rise by nearly one unit on the left-hand side. That is, the **propensity to save** in year 1 out of an extra unit of year 1's income is nearly one when the extra income is temporary. Saving goes up so much because additional assets are needed to provide for the planned increases in consumption in future years.

Consider, as a contrast, a permanent increase in wage income, where $(w/P)_1 \bullet L$, $(w/P)_2 \bullet L$, $(w/P)_3 \bullet L$, and so on each rise by one unit. An example would be a wage increase that an employee expects to be permanent. The multiyear budget constraint in equation (7.12) shows that it would be possible for the household to respond by increasing consumption by one unit in each year—in that case, for any $t = 1, 2, 3$, and so on, each rise in C_t would match each rise in $(w/P)_t \bullet L$. Moreover, we predict that the household would respond roughly this

way because this behavior is consistent with the desire to have similar levels of consumption each year. Thus, the prediction is that the propensity to consume out of an extra unit of year 1's income would be high—close to one—when the extra income is permanent.

For the response of saving, we can again look at year 1's budget constraint in equation (7.2). If $(w/P)_1 \bullet L$ rises by one unit on the right-hand side, and C_1 rises by roughly one unit on the left-hand side, year 1's real saving, $(B_1/P + K_1) - (B_0/P + K_0)$ must change by little or not at all. In other words, the propensity to save in year 1 out of an extra unit of year 1's income is small when the extra income is permanent. Saving does not change much because, in this case, the household does not need additional assets to provide for the planned increases in future consumption. These increases can be paid for by the higher future wage incomes: $(w/P)_2 \bullet L$, $(w/P)_3 \bullet L$, and so on.

Our findings about temporary and permanent changes of income correspond to Milton Friedman's famous concept of **permanent income**.[6] His idea was that consumption depends on a long-term average of incomes—which he called permanent income—rather than current income. If a change in income is temporary, permanent income and, hence, consumption change relatively little. Therefore, as in our analysis, the propensity to consume out of temporary income is small. The By the Numbers box discusses empirical evidence on the propensity to consume.

We can also assess the effects from changes in anticipated future incomes. The multiyear budget constraint is again

[7.12] $\quad C_1 + C_2/(1 + i_1) + C_3/[(1 + i_1) \bullet$
$$(1 + i_2)] + \cdots =$$
$$(1 + i_0) \bullet (B_0/P + K_0) + (w/P)_1 \bullet L + (w/P)_2 \bullet$$
$$L/(1 + i_1) + (w/P)_3 \bullet L/[(1 + i_1) \bullet (1 + i_2)] + \cdots$$

overall present value of consumption = *value of initial
assets* + *overall present value of wage incomes*

Suppose, to begin, that real wage incomes, $(w/P)_t \bullet L$, for $t = 1, 2$, and so on, are all the same. Then, assume in year 1 that the household learns that it will be getting a permanent raise the following year. Hence, expected future wage incomes, $(w/P)_2 \bullet L$, $(w/P)_3 \bullet L$ and so on, all rise. Alternatively, the household might learn in year 1 that it would be receiving in the future an inheritance payment or an insurance settlement.

The household would react to higher expected future incomes by raising consumption by similar amounts in each year: C_1, C_2, and so on. In particular,

[6] See Friedman (1957), Chapters 2 and 3.

by*the*numbers

Empirical Evidence on the Propensity to Consume

Economists have found strong evidence that the propensity to consume out of permanent changes in income is much larger than that for temporary changes. Some of the clearest evidence comes from special circumstances in which people received windfalls of income, which were clearly temporary and at least partly unanticipated.

One example is the receipt by Israeli citizens of lump-sum, nonrecurring restitution payments from Germany in 1957–58 (see Mordechai Kreinin [1961] and Michael Landsberger [1970]). The payments were large and roughly equal to an average family's annual income. The typical family increased its consumption expenditure during the year of the windfall by about 20% of the amount received. However, consumption expenditure includes consumer durables, which last for many years and should be regarded partly as saving rather than consumption. Therefore, the true propensity to consume was less than 20%.

Another example is the payment in 1950 to U.S. World War II veterans of an unanticipated, one-time life insurance dividend of about $175, roughly 4% of an average family's annual income at the time. In this case, consumption expenditure rose by about 35% of the windfall (see Roger Bird and Ronald Bodkin [1965]). However, since consumption expenditure includes consumer durables, the true propensity to consume was less than 35%.

Broader studies of consumer behavior show that the propensity to consume out of permanent changes in income is large and not much different from unity. In contrast, the propensity to consume out of temporary income is about 20% to 30% (see Robert Hall [1989]). Although this response to temporary changes is greater than that predicted by our theory, the important point is that the response of consumption to permanent changes in income is much larger than that to temporary changes.

---

year 1's consumption, C_1, increases even though no higher income has yet shown up.

Consider a case where wage incomes starting in year 2—$(w/P)_2 \cdot L$, $(w/P)_3 \cdot L$, and so on—increase by one unit. Because these increases in wage incomes were anticipated in year 1, we predicted that C_1, C_2, C_3, and so on would rise by similar amounts. Therefore, although year 2 has higher wage income than year 1—$(w/P)_2 \cdot L$ is greater than $(w/P)_1 \cdot L$—we do not predict that the rise in wage income in year 2 will be matched by a rise in consumption. That is, we predict that C_1 and C_2 will be similar. We get this result because the anticipated increase in income from year 1 to year 2 was already reflected in a higher C_1. The important prediction is that the household's consumption will not respond to an increase in income when that increase was already expected. The By the Numbers box discusses empirical evidence on this proposition.

Consumption, Saving, and Investment in Equilibrium

 e will now use our analysis of a single household's choices of consumption and saving to determine the aggregate quantities of consumption and saving. This analysis will allow us to determine the aggregate quantity of investment. Once we finish this section, we will have all the building blocks in place to study economic fluctuations. Our analysis of that topic begins in Chapter 8.

bythe**numbers**

The Response of Consumption to Anticipated Income Changes

In our model, the household's consumption would not respond to changes in income that were anticipated beforehand. To assess this prediction empirically, we have to isolate variations in income that households would have predicted in advance. The most convincing tests of this hypothesis involve responses of individual consumption in special circumstances where income variations are clearly predictable.

A study by Chang-Tai Hsieh (2003) examines the response of consumption by Alaskans to predictable payments from the Alaska Permanent Fund, which was created in 1976 as a device to distribute part of the state's oil royalties to Alaskan residents. These payments have been substantial; $1,964 per person ($7,856 for a family of four) in 2000. Since 1994, the payments have been made each October through a system of direct deposits to individuals' bank accounts. Hsieh's main finding is that individual consumption expenditure on a quarterly basis did not respond to the sizeable income variations created by the large royalty payments in the fourth quarter of each year. Thus, as predicted, households smoothed their consumption over the year—effectively using their high fourth quarter income to pay for roughly the same amount of consumption in each quarter.

Empirical results are different for seemingly predictable variations in income that are smaller and, perhaps, less easy to forecast accurately. For example, Jonathan Parker (1999) found that household consumption reacted to increases in after-tax income associated with reaching the ceiling on income subject to the Social Security payroll tax. We discuss this tax in Chapter 13; for present purposes, the important point is that the tax for the main Social Security program applies only to wage earnings up to a maximum amount each year—in 2006, the ceiling was $94,200. Parker's estimate was that nondurable consumption expenditure rose by about

20 cents for each dollar of predictable increase in after-tax income. This result departs from our model if most individuals knew in advance that their wage incomes would rise enough later in the year so that they would not have to pay the Social Security payroll tax for the rest of the year.

Similarly, Nicholas Souleles (1999) found that household consumption responded to the receipt of refunds from the federal individual income tax. This result conflicts with our model if a substantial part of these tax refunds were anticipated. However, Souleles's estimated propensities to consume for nondurable consumption were not large—less than 10%.

Overall, the empirical evidence supports the model's prediction that households would react in advance to forecastable variations in income. The data are inconsistent with the proposition that consumption is invariant to all predictable income changes. However, the departures are not that large and seem to arise mainly in cases where the income involved is relatively minor.

Ken Graham/Getty Images

We have discussed how a household divides its real income between consumption and real saving. Now we will determine the aggregates of consumption and real saving. These quantities are the amounts that arise when the various markets clear. That is, as in Chapter 6, we go from microeconomic foundations—the behavior of individual households—to aggregate variables by using market-clearing conditions.

Consider again the household budget constraint at a point in time:

(7.1)
$$C + (1/P) \bullet \Delta B + \Delta K = (w/P) \bullet L + i \bullet (B/P + K)$$

$$\textit{consumption + real saving = real income}$$

If we separate real income on assets, $i \bullet (B/P + K)$ into its two parts, $i \bullet (B/P)$ and iK, we get the revised budget constraint:

$$C + (1/P) \bullet \Delta B + \Delta K = (w/P) \bullet L + i \bullet (B/P) + iK$$

We know from Chapter 6 that the interest rate, i, is determined from

(6.6)
$$i = (R/P - \delta)$$

$$\textit{rate of return on bonds =}$$
$$\textit{rate of return on ownership of capital}$$

If we substitute $(R/P - \delta)$ for i in the iK term of the budget constraint, we get

$$C + (1/P) \bullet \Delta B + \Delta K = (w/P) \bullet L + i \bullet (B/P) + (R/P) \bullet K - \delta K$$

Since this equation applies for each household, it also applies when we add up across all the households. That is, the equation can be applied to the aggregate variables. However, we know for the aggregate of households that the total quantity of bonds, B, must be zero. That is, when the bond market clears, households in the aggregate hold a zero net quantity of bonds. The condition that $B = 0$ at every point in time also implies that the change in aggregate bond holdings, ΔB, must always be zero. If we substitute $B = 0$ and $\Delta B = 0$ into the equation, we find that, in the aggregate, the household budget constraint becomes

$$C + \Delta K = (w/P) \bullet L + (R/P) \bullet K - \delta K$$

We know from Chapter 6 that, when the labor and rental markets clear, the total payments to factors—$(w/P) \bullet L$ for labor plus $(R/P) \bullet K$ for capital—equal real gross domestic product (real GDP), Y. (See the Appendix to Chapter 6.) If we substitute Y for $(w/P) \bullet L + (R/P) \bullet K$ in the equation, we find that the aggregate household budget constraint becomes

Key equation (aggregate form of household budget constraint):

(7.13)
$$C + \Delta K = Y - \delta K$$
$$\textit{consumption + net investment =}$$
$$\textit{real GDP - depreciation =}$$
$$\textit{real net domestic product}$$

Recall that the real gross domestic product is determined from the production function by $Y = A \bullet F(K, L)$. Therefore, on the right-hand side of equation (7.13), the real net domestic product, $Y - \delta K$, is determined, for a given technology level, A, by the given values of K and L. Therefore, the left-hand side of the equation implies that the economy's net investment, ΔK, is determined by households' choices of consumption, C. Given the real net domestic product, one unit more of consumption, C, means one unit less of net investment, ΔK. In Chapter 8, we investigate how much households choose to consume, C, given that the interest rate, i, is determined from equation (6.6) to equal the rate of return on capital, $R/P - \delta$. This choice of C determines ΔK from equation (7.13).

Notice that, when the bond market clears, net investment, ΔK, equals economy-wide real saving. For an individual household, real saving equals $(1/P) \bullet \Delta B + \Delta K$—the change in the real value of assets held as bonds or capital. However, for the economy as a whole, ΔB equals zero, and real saving equals ΔK.

Questions and Problems

A. Review questions

1. Derive the two-year household budget constraint shown in equation (7.9). According to this constraint, if a household reduces this year's consumption, C_1, by one unit, how much would next year's consumption, C_2, rise (if nothing else changes in the equation)?

2. Show how taking a present value gives different weights to income and consumption in different years. Why is a unit of real income in the present more valuable than a unit of real income next year? Why is a unit of consumption next year cheaper than a unit this year?

3. What factors determine whether the propensity to consume out of an additional unit of income is less than or equal to one? Can the propensity be greater than one?

4. Discuss the effects on this year's consumption, C_1, from the following changes:

a. An increase in the interest rate, i_1

b. A permanent increase in real wage income, $(w/P) \bullet L$

c. An increase in current real wage income, $(w/P)_1 \bullet L$, but no change in future real wage incomes

d. An increase in future real wage income, $(w/P)_t \bullet L$ for $t = 2, 3$, and so on

e. A one-time windfall, which raises initial real assets, $(B_0/P + K_0)$

B. Problems for discussion

5. Permanent income

The idea of permanent income is that consumption depends on a long-run average of income, rather than current income. Operationally, we can define permanent income as the hypothetical, constant income that has the same present value as a household's sources of funds on the right-hand side of the multiyear budget constraint:

(7.12) $C_1 + C_2/(1 + i_1) + C_3/[(1 + i_1) \bullet (1 + i_2)] + \cdots =$
$(1 + i_0) \bullet (B_0/P + K_0)$
$+ (w/P)_1 \bullet L + (w/P)_2 \bullet$
$L/(1 + i_1) + (w/P)_3 \bullet L/[(1 + i_1) \bullet (1 + i_1)] + \cdots$

a. Use equation (7.12) to get a formula for permanent income, when evaluated in year 1.

b. What is the propensity to consume out of permanent income?

c. If consumption, C_t, for $t = 1, 2$, and so on is constant over time, what is the value of permanent income?

6. Income effects

Consider again the household's multiyear budget constraint in equation (7.12). What are the income effects from the following:

a. An increase in the price level, P, for a household that has a positive value of initial nominal bonds, B_0. What if B_0 is zero or negative?

b. An increase by 1% per year in every year's interest rate, i_t. Assume here that $B_0 = 0$.

chapter appendix

The Multiyear Budget Constraint and the Planning Horizon

We show here how to calculate the household budget constraint over many years. When we considered two years, we got the budget constraint

(7.9) $$C_1 + C_2/(1 + i_1) = (1 + i_0) \cdot (B_0/P + K_0) + (w/P)_1 \cdot L + (w/P)_2 \cdot L/(1 + i_1) - (B_2/P + K_2)/(1 + i_1)$$

To extend to many years, we will begin with year 3.

The real assets held at the end of year 2 are given by

(7.5) $$(B_2/P + K_2) = (1 + i_1) \cdot (B_1/P + K_1) + (w/P)_2 \cdot L - C_2$$

The real assets held at the end of year 3 are given by an analogous formula, with everything updated by one year:

(7.14) $$(B_3/P + K_3) = (1 + i_2) \cdot (B_2/P + K_2) + (w/P)_3 \cdot L - C_3$$

We found before that we could express the real assets held at the end of year 2 by

(7.8) $$(B_2/P + K_2) = (1 + i_1) \cdot (1 + i_0) \cdot (B_0/P + K_0) + (1 + i_1) \cdot (w/P)_1 \cdot L - (1 + i_1) \cdot C_1 + (w/P)_2 \cdot L - C_2$$

If we replace $(B_2/P + K_2)$ on the right-hand side of equation (7.14) by the right-hand side of equation (7.8), we get

$$(B_3/P + K_3) = (1 + i_2) \cdot [(1 + i_1) \cdot (1 + i_0) \cdot (B_0/P + K_0) + (1 + i_1) \cdot (w/P)_1 \cdot L - (1 + i_1) \cdot C_1 + (w/P)_2 \cdot L - C_2] + (w/P) \cdot L - C_3$$

If we multiply the terms inside the brackets by the term $1 + i_2$, we get

(7.15) $$(B_3/P + K_3) = (1 + i_2) \cdot (1 + i_1) \cdot (1 + i_0) \cdot (B_0/P + K_0) + (1 + i_2) \cdot (1 + i_1) \cdot (w/P)_1 \cdot L - (1 + i_2) \cdot (1 + i_1) \cdot C_1 + (1 + i_2) \cdot (w/P)_2 \cdot L - (1 + i_2) \cdot C_2 + (w/P)_3 \cdot L - C_3$$

The important result involves interest rates. The initial real assets, $(B_0/P + K_0)$ now accumulate interest over three years, up to the end of year 3. Thus, these assets are multiplied on the right-hand side of equation (7.15) by $(1 + i_2) \cdot (1 + i_1) \cdot (1 + i_0)$. Year 1's real wage income, $(w/P)1 \cdot L$ accumulates interest over two years and is therefore multiplied by $(1 + i_2) \cdot (1 + i_1)$. The other real income and consumption terms enter in an analogous way.

If we divide through everything in equation (7.15) by $(1 + i_2) \cdot (1 + i_1)$ and rearrange the terms to put only those involving consumption on the left-hand side, we get the three-year budget constraint.

(7.16) $$C_1 + C_2/(1 + i_1) + C_3/[(1 + i_1) \cdot (1 + i_2)] =$$
$$(1 + i_0) \cdot (B_0/P + K_0) + (w/P)_1 \cdot L + (w/P)_2 \cdot L/(1 + i_1) + (w/P)_3 \cdot L/[(1 + i_1) \cdot (1 + i_2)] - (B_3/P + K_3)/[(1 + i_1) \cdot (1 + i_2)]$$

This result extends the two-year budget constraint from equation (7.9) to three years. Everything in equation (7.16) appears as a present value (or year 1 value). But now the budget constraint includes the real wage income and consumption from year 3, $(w/P)_3 \cdot L$ and C_3, and these amounts are discounted for the accumulation of interest over two years—that is, by $(1 + i_1) \cdot (1 + i_2)$. The real assets held at the end of year 3, $(B_3/P + K_3)$, now appear on the right-hand side and are also discounted by $(1 + i_1) \cdot (1 + i_2)$.

By now, we see how to extend the budget constraint to any number of years. Each time we push forward one more year, we bring in the real income and consumption from that year. We also bring in the real assets held at the end of the new year and drop the real assets held at the end of the previous year. All the new terms are discounted to reflect the accumulation of interest from year 1 up to the future year. For example, if we consider j years, where j is greater than 3, we get the j-year budget constraint.

(7.17)

$$C_1 + C_2/(1 + i_1) + C_3/[(1 + i_1) \cdot (1 + i_2)] + \cdots$$
$$+ Cj/[(1 + i_1) \cdot (1 + i_2) \cdots \cdot (1 + i_{j-1})] = (1 + i_0) \cdot (B_0/P + K_0)$$
$$+ (w/P)_1 \cdot L + (w/P)_2 \cdot L/(1 + i_1) + (w/P)_3 \cdot L/[(1 + i_1) \cdot (1 + i_2)]$$
$$+ \cdots + (w/P)_j \cdot L/[(1 + i_1) \cdot (1 + i_2) \cdots \cdot (1 + i_{j-1})]$$
$$- (B_j/P + K_j)/[(1 + i_1) \cdot (1 + i_2) \cdots \cdot (1 + i_{j-1})]$$

We want to use equation (7.17) to understand how the household chooses year 1's consumption, C_1. That is, the household now makes this choice as part of a long-term plan that considers future consumptions and real incomes out to year j. These future values relate to the current choice through the j-year budget constraint. We can think of the number j as the **planning horizon**—that is, the number of years over which the household plans its choices of consumption and saving.

How long is the horizon that the typical household considers when making decisions? Because we are dealing with households that have access to borrowing and lending, a long horizon is appropriate. By borrowing or lending, households can effectively use future income to pay for current consumption, or current income to pay for future consumption. When expressed as a present value, future incomes are as pertinent for current decisions as today's income.

Economists often assume that the typical household's planning horizon is long but finite. For example, in theories called **life-cycle models**, the horizon, j, represents an individual's expected remaining lifetime.[7] If people do not care about things that occur after their death, they have no reason to carry assets beyond year j. Accordingly, they plan so as to set to zero the final stock of assets, $(B_j/P + K_j)$, in equation (7.17).[8] That is, each person plans to end up with no assets when he or she dies.

It is straightforward to define the anticipated lifetime and, thereby, the planning horizon for an isolated individual. The appropriate horizon is, however, not so obvious for a family in which individuals have spouses and children. Since a person cares about his or her spouse and children, the applicable horizon extends beyond a person's expected lifetime, and households give weight to the expected future real incomes and consumptions of children. Further, since children care about their prospective children, should they have any, there is no clear point at which to draw the line.

Instead of imposing a **finite horizon** (where j is a finite number), we can think of each household's plan as having an **infinite horizon**. That is, the planning period, j, extends arbitrarily far out into the future and can be thought of as being infinite. There are two good reasons to make this assumption:

- First, if we think of the typical person as part of a family that cares about members of future generations—children, grandchildren, and so on—into the indefinite future, this setup is appropriate.

- Second, although it is not obvious at this point, an infinite horizon is the simplest assumption.

If we use an infinite horizon, we allow the number j to become arbitrarily large in equation (7.17). In that case, there is no final year, j, and we do not have to worry about the last term on the right-hand side, which involves $(B_j/P + K_j)$.[9] Thus, the **infinite-horizon budget constraint**—the constraint that applies to an infinite planning period—is the one we used before:

(7.12)

$$C_1 + C_2/(1 + i_1) + C_3/[(1 + i_1) \cdot (1 + i_2)] + \cdots =$$
$$(1 + i_0)] \cdot (B_0/P + K_0) + (w/P)_1 \cdot L + (w/P)_2 \cdot L/(1 + i_1) + (w/P)_3 \cdot L/[(1 + i_1) \cdot (1 + i_2)] + \cdots$$

The ellipses signify that we are including terms involving C_t and $(w/P)_t \cdot L$ for $t = 1, 2$, and so on—that is, extending out to arbitrarily large values of t.

---

[7] Life-cycle models are associated particularly with the economist Franco Modigliani. See Franco Modigliani and Richard Brumberg (1954), and Albert Ando and Franco Modigliani (1963).

[8] We have to rule out the possibility of dying with negative assets. Otherwise, each person would like to set $(B_j/P + K_j)$ to be a large negative number.

[9] Because of the discounting by $(1 + i_1) \cdot (1 + i_2) \cdot ? \cdot (1 + i_{j-1})$, the present value of the assets left over, $(B_j/P + K_j)$, tends to become negligible as j gets very large.

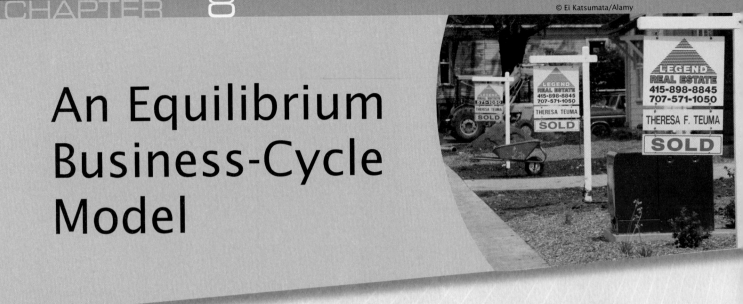

CHAPTER 8

© Ei Katsumata/Alamy

An Equilibrium Business-Cycle Model

This chapter uses the framework developed in Chapters 6 and 7 to study the short-term economic fluctuations called business cycles. A business cycle involves phases in which real gross domestic product (real GDP) is expanding or contracting. A period of expanding real GDP—a boom—is typically accompanied by increases in other macroeconomic variables, such as consumption, investment, and employment, and with decreases in the unemployment rate. Conversely, a period of contraction—a recession—tends to feature decreases in consumption, investment, and employment, along with rises in the unemployment rate.

The economy's total output, real GDP, is the key indicator of whether the economy is in a phase of expansion or contraction. Thus, to understand the nature of economic fluctuations, we will look first at the behavior of U.S. real GDP during the post–World War II period.

Cyclical Behavior of Real GDP—Recessions and Booms

The blue graph in Figure 8.1 shows U.S. real GDP on a quarterly basis from 1947.1 (the first quarter of 1947) to 2006.1 (the first quarter of 2006). This graph is analogous to the one showing annual data since 1869 in Figure 1.1 of Chapter 1.

If we look at the graph of real GDP in Figure 8.1, we can think of the movements as reflecting two forces. First, there is the overall upward movement or *trend* in real GDP from 1947 to 2006. We think of this trend

as reflecting long-term economic growth, the subject of Chapters 3 through 5. Second, there are shorter-term fluctuations of real GDP around its trend. We think of these economic fluctuations as stemming from the business cycle—that is, from booms and recessions. In this and the next chapter, we seek to understand these economic fluctuations.

We imagine that real GDP has two parts:

(8.1) $$real\ GDP = trend\ real\ GDP + cyclical\ part\ of\ real\ GDP$$

To break down real GDP into trend and cycle, we start by estimating the trend. A good measure of the trend is a reasonably smooth curve fit to the data on real GDP. In Figure 8.2, the blue graph shows real GDP. **Trend real GDP** is the red curve.[1] This graph is a smooth curve drawn through the blue graph.

---

[1] The trend is called a Hodrick-Prescott filter (H-P filter), named after the economists Robert Hodrick and Edward Prescott. The general idea is to determine the position of the trend to fit the movements in real GDP without fluctuating too much. The procedure allows the slope of the trend to change slowly over time in response to observed changes in the growth rate of real GDP.

Figure 8.1 *U.S. Real GDP, 1947–2006*

The graph shows U.S. real GDP from 1947.1 to 2006.1. The data are quarterly, seasonally adjusted, and measured in dollars from the base year, 2000. We use a proportionate (or logarithmic) scale. Therefore, each change along the vertical axis represents the same proportionate or percentage change in real GDP.

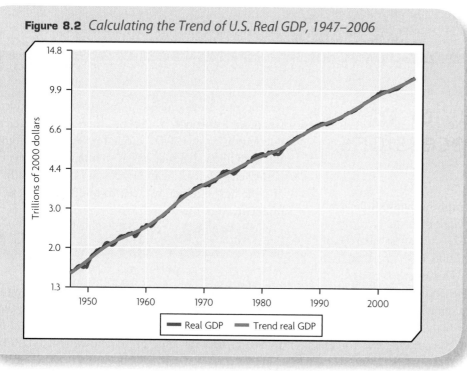

Figure 8.2 *Calculating the Trend of U.S. Real GDP, 1947–2006*

Real GDP   Trend real GDP

The blue graph shows U.S. real GDP from Figure 8.1. The red curve is a smooth trend drawn through the GDP data. We think of this trend curve as reflecting long-run economic growth.

Once we know trend real GDP, displayed in red in Figure 8.2, we can calculate the deviation from the trend. If we rearrange the terms in equation (8.1), we get

(8.2) *cyclical part of real GDP = real GDP − trend real GDP*

We call the difference between real GDP and its trend the **cyclical part of real GDP**, because we view this part as coming from the business cycle—that is, from short-term economic fluctuations.

Figure 8.2 demonstrates that the most important property of U.S. real GDP from 1947 to 2006 is the overall upward trend, shown in red. In fact, it is not so easy in this graph to discern the cyclical part, which is the difference between real GDP and its trend. In subsequent graphs, we magnify the cyclical part to get a clearer picture. However, we should remember that the trend in real GDP is the main determinant of how the typical person's standard of living in the United States in 2006 compares with that 10, 20, or 50 years earlier. Therefore, in the long run, economic growth is more important than economic fluctuations.

Although economic fluctuations are typically small compared to long-term trends, the fluctuations do influence the typical person's well-being. For example, people are harmed during recessions because they have lower real incomes and less consumption, and often lose their jobs. Most discussions in the news media focus on fluctuations rather than trends. This focus probably exists because trends represent long-term forces that are usually not news, whereas fluctuations reflect recent events that do constitute news. In addition, it is easier (even if usually wrong) to blame economic fluctuations, especially an ongoing recession, on the current political administration. It is more difficult to assign responsibility for long-term economic growth.

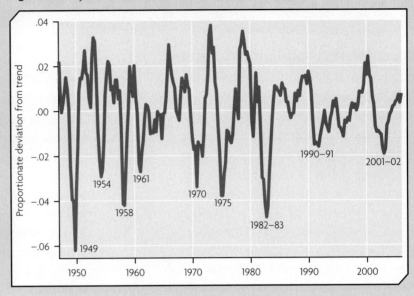

Figure 8.3 *Cyclical Part of U.S. Real GDP, 1947–2006*

The graph plots the difference between real GDP (the blue graph in Figure 8.2) and its trend (the red graph in Figure 8.2). The resulting series—the cyclical part of real GDP—shows the deviations of real GDP from its trend. This cyclical part is measured in a proportionate sense; for example, 0.02 means that real GDP is 2% above trend, and −0.02 means that real GDP is 2% below trend. The recession years marked are those in which the cyclical part of real GDP was negative and reached at least 1.5% in magnitude.

© Photos 12/Alamy

Figure 8.3 shows a magnified version of the cyclical part of real GDP. This cyclical part is the difference between real GDP and its trend from Figure 8.2. By changing the scale on the vertical axis, we get a clear picture in Figure 8.3 of when real GDP was above or below its trend.

The variability of the cyclical part of real GDP is a good way to gauge the extent of economic fluctuations. To get a quantitative measure, we use a statistic called the **standard deviation**.[2] In Figure 8.3, the standard deviation of the cyclical part of real GDP is 1.7%. This value means that the typical range of fluctuation of U.S. real GDP from 1947 to 2006 was between 1.7% below and 1.7% above trend.[3]

The low points, or troughs, in Figure 8.3 pick out the nine U.S. recessions from 1947 to 2006. The general notion of a recession is a period of low economic activity, gauged by real GDP and other macroeconomic variables. In our case, we make this definition operational by looking at periods in which the cyclical part of real GDP was negative and reached at least

[2] The standard deviation is the square root of the variance. The variance is the average of the squared deviation of a variable from its mean. In the present case, the mean of the cyclical part of real GDP is close to zero (because of the way we constructed the trend in Figure 8.2). Therefore, the variance is just the average squared value of the cyclical part of real GDP.

[3] If a variable is normally distributed (a reasonable approximation for the cyclical part of real GDP), about two-thirds of the time the variable is between one standard deviation below and one standard deviation above its mean. About 95% of the time, the variable is between two standard deviations below and two standard deviations above its mean.

bythenumbers

Recessions in Long-Term U.S. History

The recessions of the post–World War II period, shown in Figure 8.3, were mild compared to some earlier ones, especially the Great Depression of the early 1930s. We can measure U.S. recessions back to 1869 using the annual data on real GDP from Figure 1.1 of Chapter 1.

Figure 8.4 shows the cyclical part of real GDP from 1869 to 2005. The method for calculating the cyclical part is the same as that used for post–World War II data in Figures 8.2 and 8.3, except that the long-term data are annual. To focus on major contractions, we label as recessions in Figure 8.4 only cases in which the cyclical part of real GDP was negative and at least 3% in magnitude. With this more stringent cutoff (compared to 1.5% in Figure 8.3), some of the post–World War II recessions—including those for 1990–91 and 2001–02—are too mild to be marked.

The Great Depression dwarfs any of the recessions experienced since World War II. In the worst year, 1933, real GDP fell short of trend by 19%. Two other large recessions during the interwar period occurred in 1920–22 and 1938–40—real GDP was 9% below trend in both cases.

The pre–World War I period does not contain any recessions as large as those of the interwar years. In fact, the period from 1869 to 1914 does not differ greatly from the period since 1947, in terms of the extent of economic fluctuations. It is hard to be precise, however, because the pre-1929 national-accounts data are less reliable.[4]

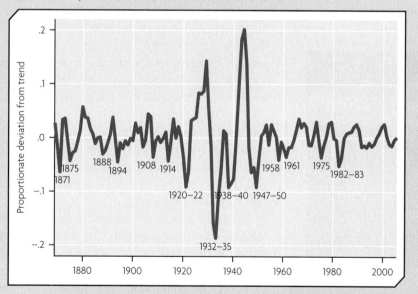

Figure 8.4 *Cyclical Part of U.S. Real GDP, 1869–2005*

The graph plots the cyclical part of real GDP, which is the difference between real GDP (real GNP before 1929) and its trend. The procedure is analogous to that used in Figures 8.2 and 8.3, except that the underlying data are now annual. The recession years marked are those in which the cyclical part of real GDP was negative and reached at least 3% in magnitude.

1.5% in magnitude. By this definition, recessions occurred in 1949, 1954, 1958, 1961, 1970, 1975, 1982–83, 1990–91, and 2001–02. The departures of real GDP from trend ranged from the mild recessions of 1990–91 (where the largest shortfall from trend was 1.6%), 2001–02 (1.9%), and 1961 (2.7%), to the more severe recessions of 1949 (6.2%), 1982–83 (4.7%), 1958 (4.2%), and 1975 (3.8%).

The semi-official arbiter of when U.S. recessions begin and end is the National Bureau

---

[4] Christina Romer's (1986, 1988) analysis shows that the pre–World War I period was only slightly more variable than the post–World War II period in terms of the extent of economic fluctuations.

of Economic Research (NBER), which is a think tank located near Harvard University in Cambridge, Massachusetts. The NBER does not have a strict definition of what constitutes a recession but does take into account a number of macroeconomic variables observed at monthly frequencies, including employment, retail sales, personal income, and industrial production. Despite the differences between our definition of a recession and the NBER concept, the dates shown in Figure 8.3 correspond well to those announced by the NBER.

We can also use Figure 8.3 to isolate economic booms, represented by the high points, or peaks, in the cyclical part of real GDP. The most recent peak was at 2.4% above trend in the second quarter of 2000. This peak coincided with large investments in the Internet and other forms of advanced technology.

An Equilibrium Business-Cycle Model

Conceptual Issues

To model economic fluctuations, we start by assuming that these fluctuations reflect **shocks** to the economy. An example of a shock is a change in the technology level, A, which enters into the production function introduced in equation (3.1) of Chapter 3 and repeated here:

(8.3)
$$Y = A \bullet F(K, L)$$

An increase in A means that the economy is more productive—it can produce more output, Y, with given inputs of capital and labor, K and L. Conversely, a decrease in A means that the economy is less productive. In the present chapter, we focus on shocks to A as sources of economic fluctuations.

We call our model an **equilibrium business-cycle model** because it uses equilibrium conditions to determine how the shocks affect real GDP, Y, and other macroeconomic variables, such as consumption, C, investment, I, and the quantity of labor input, L. The model assumes that the supply and demand functions, such as those for labor and capital services, accord with the underlying microeconomic foundations worked out in Chapters 6 and 7. Given these functions, the key equilibrium conditions are that markets have to clear. For example, the total quantity of labor supplied equals the total quantity demanded, and the total quantity of capital services supplied equals

the total quantity demanded. In Chapter 16, we explore models in which some markets do not clear.

A famous example of an equilibrium business-cycle model is the **real business-cycle model** (RBC model) developed by the 2004 Nobel laureates Finn Kydland and Edward Prescott (1982). The RBC model emphasizes shocks to the technology level, A, and uses the same kind of equilibrium conditions that we employ. Hence, the equilibrium business-cycle model in this chapter is a real business-cycle model. However, in subsequent chapters we generalize the model to include different forms of shocks; for example, Chapter 15 considers disturbances that are monetary, rather than real. Since our basic approach remains the same, we can use the broader label, equilibrium business-cycle model, to cover these extensions as well as the model in this chapter.

Our model will predict patterns of fluctuations in real GDP and other macroeconomic variables. After working out these predictions, we compare them to macroeconomic data. Since we focus in this chapter on shocks to the technology level, A, the model will have a chance to work well only if we allow for shifts in A to be sometimes positive and sometimes negative. The positive shocks will generate booms, and the negative shocks will generate recessions.

If we think of A as the technology level, it is easy to imagine increases in A—for example, from discoveries of new goods or methods of production. Examples from our discussion of technological progress in Chapter 5 are the invention and adaptation of electric power, the transistor, computers, and the Internet.[5] However, many smaller discoveries contributed to the economic booms shown in Figure 8.3.

If we view A as the technology level, it is hard to imagine important decreases in A. After all, producers would not usually forget previous technological advances. However, we mentioned in our study of the Solow growth model in Chapter 5 that events other than technological discoveries can affect productivity and, thereby, influence the economy in ways similar to changes in the technology level. Moreover, these other events can be negative—amounting to decreases in A—or positive.

Some events that resemble changes in the technology level, A, are shifts in legal and political systems, changes in the degree of competition, and variations in the volume of international trade. Adverse events that have effects similar to reductions in A include harvest failures, wartime destruction, natural disasters, and strikes.

Our analysis of economic fluctuations takes a broad view of A to encompass these examples. In this case,

---

[5] For a more complete list, including innovations such as just-in-time inventory management, see the discussion in Jones (2005).

changes in *A* can sometimes be positive and sometimes negative. However, we shall find it convenient still to refer to *A* as the "technology level."

In the equilibrium business-cycle model developed in this chapter, we explain economic fluctuations as short-term responses to shocks to the technology level, *A*. The main feature that makes the analysis short term is that we assume, as an approximation, that we can hold fixed the stock of capital, *K*. That is, in thinking about the relatively brief duration of a recession or a boom, we do not allow enough time to elapse for the changes in machines and buildings—the goods included in *K*—to be significant. In contrast, for long-term analyses of economic growth, as in Chapters 3 through 5, the changes in *K* are a central part of the story.

The Model

Now we will work out the short-run effects from a shift in the technology level, *A*. Real GDP, *Y*, is given by the production function

(8.3) $$Y = A \bullet F(K, L)$$

In addition to treating the capital stock, *K*, as fixed in the short run, we also assume initially that labor input,

L, is fixed. In this case, changes in *Y* will reflect only changes in *A*. When *A* rises, *Y* rises, and when *A* falls, *Y* falls. Later in this chapter we make the model more realistic by allowing for short-run variations in *L*. In Chapter 9, we will extend further to allow for variations in the utilization rate of capital.

In practice, many shifts to *A* will not be observable; that is, we will not be able to tell what changes have occurred in the variables that influence the economy's productivity. The problem is that if we are free to make assumptions about which unobservable changes have occurred, we will be able to match any observed fluctuations in real GDP, such as those shown in Figure 8.3. Given how easy it is to fit these data, we should not give our model any credit for "explaining" the fluctuations in real GDP in this way.

The real challenge for the model is to predict how other macroeconomic variables move along with real GDP during economic fluctuations. As an example, we want to see what the model predicts for the changes in consumption and investment during booms and recessions. Similarly, we can assess the behavior of the real wage rate, the real rental price of capital, and the interest rate. Later, when we drop the assumption that *L* is fixed, we can look at the behavior of employment and unemployment. The general idea is that we will test our equilibrium business-cycle model by making predictions about the relationship between real GDP and other macroeconomic variables, and then looking at the data to see if these predictions are accurate. We will now start our analysis of macroeconomic variables.

The Marginal Product of Labor and the Real Wage Rate We know from the production function in equation (8.3) that an increase in the technology level, *A*, raises the marginal product of labor (MPL) for given inputs of capital, *K*, and labor, *L*. We show the effects from a higher schedule for the MPL in Figure 8.5. We consider two technology levels, *A*

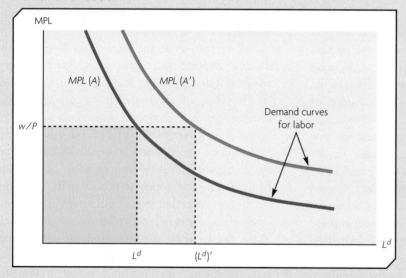

Figure 8.5 *Effect of an Increase in the Technology Level on the Demand for Labor*

When the technology level is *A*, the MPL is given by the blue curve, labeled *MPL* (*A*). At the real wage rate *w/P*, shown on the vertical axis, the quantity of labor demanded is L^d on the horizontal axis. The technology level *A'* is greater than *A*. Therefore, the MPL, given by the red curve labeled *MPL* (*A*), is higher at any labor input than the value along the blue curve. When the technology level is *A'* and the real wage rate is *w/P*, the quantity of labor demanded is $(L^d)'$, which is greater than L^d.

and A' where A' is greater than A. We assume that the capital stock is fixed at K. The downward-sloping blue curve shows how the MPL varies with L when the technology level is A. If the real wage rate is w/P, on the vertical axis, the quantity of labor demanded is the amount L^d on the horizontal axis. The downward-sloping red curve shows the MPL when the technology level is A'. The MPL is higher for any L on this second curve than on the first one. Therefore, at the given real wage rate, w/P, the quantity of labor demanded, $(L^d)'$ on the horizontal axis, is greater than L^d.

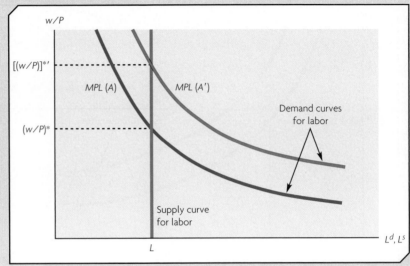

Figure 8.6 *Effect of an Increase in the Technology Level on the Real Wage Rate*

Labor supply is the given value L, shown on the horizontal axis. If the technology level is A, the schedule for the MPL determines the blue labor-demand curve, labeled *MPL* (A). Therefore, the market-clearing real wage rate is $(w/P)^*$, shown on the vertical axis. The technology level A' is greater than A, as in Figure 8.5. Therefore, the schedule for the MPL is given by the red labor-demand curve, labeled *MPL* (A). In this case, the market-clearing real wage rate is $[(w/P)^*]'$, which is greater than $(w/P)^*$.

The two labor-demand curves in Figure 8.6 come from Figure 8.5. For labor supply, we assume for now that the quantity of labor supplied is fixed at the value L on the horizontal axis. That is, the labor-supply curve is a vertical line at L.

If the technology level is A, the labor-demand curve is given in Figure 8.6 by the downward-sloping blue curve. Therefore, the labor market clears—the quantity of labor demanded equals the quantity supplied—when the real wage rate, w/P, equals the market-clearing value $(w/P)^*$, shown on the vertical axis. The real wage rate $(w/P)^*$ equals the MPL evaluated at L (when the technology level is A and the capital stock is fixed at K).

If the technology level rises to A', the labor-demand curve is given in Figure 8.6 by the downward-sloping red curve. In this case, the market-clearing real wage rate equals $[(w/P)^*]'$ on the vertical axis. Since the MPL is higher, at the given L, on the red curve than on the blue one, the market-clearing real wage rate is higher. That is, $[(w/P)^*]'$ is greater than $(w/P)^*$.

One way to think about the result is that, at the initial real wage rate, $(w/P)^*$, the rise in the MPL means that the quantity of labor demanded, $(L^d)'$, exceeds the quantity supplied, which is fixed at L. Therefore, employers (households in their role as business managers)

compete for the scarce labor and drive up the real wage rate to $[(w/P)^*]'$.

We found that an increase in the technology level, A, raises the real wage rate, w/P. Hence, the model predicts that an economic boom—where real GDP is high because A is high—will have a relatively high w/P. In contrast, a recession will have a relatively low w/P.

Marginal Product of Capital, Real Rental Price, and the Interest Rate We know from the production function in equation (8.3) that an increase in the technology level, A, raises the MPK for given inputs of capital, K, and labor, L. We show the effects of a higher MPK in Figure 8.7. This figure again considers two technology levels, A and A', where A' is greater than A. We still assume that labor input is fixed at L. The downward-sloping blue curve shows how the MPK varies with K when the technology level is A. If the real rental price is R/P on the vertical axis, the quantity of capital demanded is the amount K^d on the horizontal axis. The downward-sloping red curve shows the MPK when the technology level is A'. The MPK is higher at any given K on this second curve than on the first one. Therefore, at the given real rental price, R/P, the quantity of capital demanded, $(K^d)'$ on the horizontal axis, is greater than K^d.

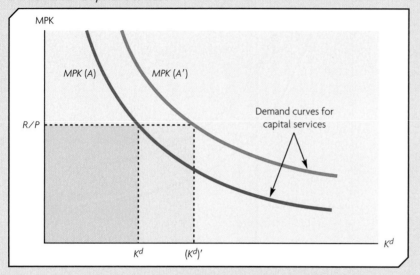

Figure 8.7 *Effect of an Increase in the Technology Level on the Demand for Capital Services*

When the technology level is *A*, the MPK is given by the blue curve, labeled *MPK* (*A*). At the real rental price *R/P*, shown on the vertical axis, the quantity of capital demanded is *K^d* on the horizontal axis. The technology level *A'* is greater than *A*. Therefore, the MPK, given by the red curve labeled *MPK* (*A*), is higher at any capital input than the value along the blue curve. When the technology level is *A'* and the real rental price is *R/P*, the quantity of capital demanded is (*K^d*)', which is greater than *K^d*.

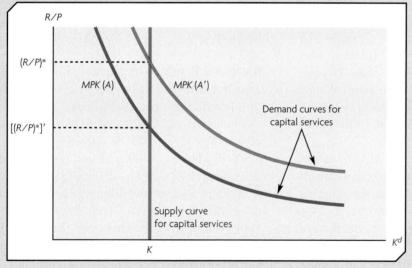

Figure 8.8 *Effect of an Increase in the Technology Level on the Real Rental Price of Capital*

The supply of capital services is the given value *K*, shown on the horizontal axis. If the technology level is *A*, the schedule for the MPK is given by the blue curve, labeled *MPK* (*A*). This curve gives the demand for capital services when the technology level is *A*. The market-clearing real rental price is (*R/P*)*, shown on the vertical axis. The technology level *A'* is greater than *A*, as in Figure 8.7. Therefore, the schedule for the MPK is given by the red curve, labeled *MPK* (*A*). This curve gives the demand for capital services when the technology level is *A'*. In this case, the market-clearing real rental price is [(*R/P*)*]', which is greater than (*R/P*)*.

The two demand curves for capital services in Figure 8.8 come from Figure 8.7. We assume that the quantity of capital services supplied is fixed at *K* on the horizontal axis. That is, the supply curve is a vertical line at *K*.

If the technology level is *A*, the demand curve for capital services is given in Figure 8.8 by the downward-sloping blue curve. Therefore, the market for capital services clears—the quantity of capital services demanded equals the quantity supplied—when the real rental price, *R/P*, equals the market-clearing value (*R/P*)* on the vertical axis. The real rental price (*R/P*)* equals the MPK evaluated at *K* (when the technology level is *A* and labor input is fixed at *L*).

If the technology level rises to *A'*, the demand curve for capital services is given in Figure 8.8 by the downward-sloping red curve. In this case, the market-clearing real rental price equals [(*R/P*)*]' on the vertical axis. Since the MPK is higher, at the given *K*, on the red curve than on the blue one, the market-clearing real rental price is higher. That is, [(*R/P*)*]' is greater than (*R/P*)*.

We conclude that an increase in the technology level, A, raises the real rental price of capital, R/P. Hence, the model predicts that an economic boom—where real GDP is high because A is high—will have a relatively high R/P. In contrast, a recession will have a relatively low R/P.

Recall from our analysis in Chapter 6 that the interest rate is given by

$$(6.6) \qquad i = R/P - \delta$$

rate of return on bonds = rate of return on ownership of capital

We know from Figure 8.8 that, when the market for capital services clears, the real rental price, R/P, equals the MPK evaluated at the given values of capital, K, and labor, L. Therefore, the interest rate is given by

$$(8.4) \qquad i = MPK \text{ (evaluated at given } K \text{ and } L) - \delta$$

An increase in the technology level raises the MPK at given inputs of capital, K, and labor, L. Therefore, equation (8.4) implies that the interest rate, i, rises. Hence, the model predicts that an economic boom will have a relatively high interest rate, whereas a recession will have a relatively low interest rate.

Consumption, Saving, and Investment

Now we will use our microeconomic analysis from Chapter 7 to determine how much households consume and save. A rise in the technology level, A, raises the interest rate, i, and a higher i motivates households to defer consumption from the present to the future (the intertemporal-substitution effect). On this ground, we predict that current consumption would fall. However, our analysis is incomplete, because we have to allow for income effects.

Consider the household budget constraint at each point in time from Chapter 7:

$$(7.1) \qquad C + (1/P) \cdot \Delta B + \Delta K = (w/P) \cdot L + i \cdot (B/P + K)$$

consumption + real saving = real income

Income effects enter through real wage income, $(w/P) \cdot L$, and real asset income, $i \cdot (B/P + K)$. An increase in A raises real wage income, because w/P rises and L does not change. An increase in A also raises real asset income, because i rises, B/P is unchanged (at zero in the aggregate), and K does not change in the short run. Therefore, an increase in A raises overall household real income.

Another way to see the effect on overall income is to use the aggregate household budget constraint from Chapter 7 that applies when the markets for bonds, labor, and capital services clear:

$$(7.13) \qquad C + \Delta K = Y - \delta K$$

consumption + net investment = real GDP − depreciation

= real net domestic product

If we substitute $Y = A \cdot F(K, L)$ from the production function (equation [8.3]), we get

$$(8.5) \qquad C + \Delta K = A \cdot F(K, L) - \delta K$$

Since depreciation, δK, is fixed in the short run, the income effect from a change in A boils down to its effect on real GDP, $Y = A \cdot F(K, L)$. Since an increase in A raises real GDP for given K and L, we again see that a rise in A raises overall real income.

The increase in real income motivates households to raise current consumption (as well as future consumption). This response is the familiar income effect. This effect works against the intertemporal-substitution effect, which tends to reduce current consumption. Therefore, we are unsure whether an increase in the technology level, A, leads to more or less current consumption, C. The net change depends on whether the income effect is stronger or weaker than the intertemporal-substitution effect.

We can sharpen our prediction because the size of the income effect depends on how long the change in the technology level, A, lasts. For the rest of this section, we assume that the change in A is permanent. This situation would apply to a literal technological advance, because producers tend not to forget these advances. In this case, the increases in real income tend also to be permanent. Therefore, we should consider the case from Chapter 7 in which real income rises by similar amounts each year. The prediction for this case was that the propensity to consume out of higher income would be close to one. Hence, if an increase in A raises real GDP, $Y = A \cdot F(K, L)$, by one unit, then—from the standpoint of the income effect—current consumption, C, would rise by roughly one unit.

To compute the overall effect on current consumption, we have to balance the income effect—whereby consumption rises by roughly as much as real GDP—against the intertemporal-substitution effect, which lowers current consumption. Quantitative estimates of the intertemporal-substitution effect show that it has less of an impact than this large income effect. Hence, when the increase in A is permanent, current consumption will rise. However, as long as the intertemporal-substitution operates at all, the increase in current consumption will be less than the increase in real GDP.

In equation (7.1), the change on the left-hand side in C is less than the change on the right-hand side in real income, which corresponds to the change in real GDP, Y. Therefore, household real saving must rise on the left-hand side. That is, part of the extra household real income goes to consumption and another part goes to real saving.

In the aggregate household budget constraint in equation (7.13), we found that current consumption, C, rises, but by less than the increase in real GDP, Y. Therefore, net investment, ΔK, must increase—the increase in real GDP shows up partly as more C and partly as more ΔK. Since net investment, ΔK, equals real saving, this result is consistent with our finding that real saving increased.

Matching the Theory with the Facts

ur equilibrium business-cycle model makes a number of predictions about how fluctuations in macroeconomic variables match up with variations in real GDP. Now we will examine the predictions for consumption, investment, the real wage rate, the real rental price of capital, and the interest rate. We will focus on U.S. data since 1954; the difference from Figures 8.1 to 8.3 is that we are leaving out the years 1947 to 1953. That period is unusual because of the heavy influences from the aftermath of World War II and the Korean War. We will consider the economic effects of wartime in Chapter 12.

Consumption and Investment

We can measure consumption, C, from the national-income accounts by real consumer expenditure. This expenditure accounted, on average, for 64% of U.S. GDP from 1954 to 2006. We calculate the cyclical part of real consumer expenditure by using the method applied to real GDP in Figure 8.2. The result is the blue graph in Figure 8.9. This graph shows the proportionate deviation of real consumer expenditure from its trend. We

also show, as the red graph, the cyclical part of real GDP (copied from Figure 8.3).

Two important findings emerge from Figure 8.9. First, real consumer expenditure typically fluctuates in the same direction as real GDP.[6] When a variable fluctuates, like real consumer expenditure, in the same direction as real GDP, we say that the variable is **procyclical**. A procyclical variable moves in the same direction as the business cycle—it tends to be high relative to its trend in a boom and low relative to its trend in a recession. (A variable that fluctuates in the opposite direction from real GDP is **countercyclical**. One that has little tendency to move in a particular direction during a business cycle is **acyclical**.) Second, real consumer expenditure fluctuates in a proportional sense by less than real GDP. From 1954.1 to 2006.1, the standard deviation of the cyclical part of real consumer expenditure was 1.2%, compared with 1.6% for the cyclical part of real GDP. Thus, in a proportionate sense, real consumer expenditure varies by less than real GDP in booms and recessions.

We can measure gross investment, I, from the national-income accounts by real gross domestic private investment. This expenditure accounted, on average, for 16% of GDP from 1954 to 2006. We again use the method from Figure 8.2 to calculate the cyclical part of real gross investment. The result is the blue graph in Figure 8.10. This graph shows the proportionate deviation of real investment from its trend. The cyclical part of real GDP is again the red graph.

One finding from Figure 8.10 is that, like real consumer expenditure, real gross investment is procyclical; that is, it typically fluctuates in the same direction as real GDP.[7] Hence, investment is high relative to its trend in a boom and low relative to its trend in a recession. Another finding is that real gross investment fluctuates, in a proportional sense, much more than real GDP. In terms of the standard deviations of the cyclical parts, the one for gross investment was 7.2%, compared to 1.6% for real GDP.[8] Thus, in a proportionate sense, real investment fluctuates much more than real GDP in booms and recessions. The volatility of investment means that it represents far more of the fluctuations in real GDP than we would expect from the average ratio of gross investment to GDP (16%).

---

[6] From 1954.1 to 2006.1, the correlation of the cyclical part of real consumer expenditure with the cyclical part of real GDP was 0.88.

[7] From 1954.1 to 2006.1, the correlation of the cyclical part of real gross domestic private investment with the cyclical part of real GDP was 0.92.

[8] Consumer expenditure includes purchases of consumer durables, such as automobiles, furniture, and appliances, as well as spending on nondurables and services. We should think of consumer durables as forms of capital owned by households. Therefore, we should view the purchases of these durables as forms of gross investment. Hence, we could combine the purchases of consumer durables with gross investment to get a broader measure of investment. We would then represent consumption by a narrower measure—real consumer expenditure on nondurables and services. If we make these changes, we find that the narrower measure of real consumer expenditure fluctuates, in a proportional sense, less than the one shown in Figure 8.9—that is, we get a stronger pattern of consumption being less variable than real GDP.

Going back to the model, permanent shifts in the technology level, *A*, match up with some of the empirical patterns found in Figures 8.9 and 8.10. Specifically, increases in *A* generate economic booms, where real GDP increases, and these increases show up partly as more consumption and partly as more investment. In reverse, decreases in *A* create recessions, where real GDP, consumption, and investment all decline.

Does the model explain why investment fluctuates proportionately far more than consumption? Recall that, because the changes in the technology level, *A*, are permanent, the income effects are strong. On this ground, consumption would change by roughly the same amount as real GDP. However, we also found that an increase in *A* led to a rise in the interest rate, which reduced current consumption and raised current real saving. This effect means that, during a boom, consumption rises proportionately by less than real GDP. Analogously, during a recession, consumption falls proportionately by less than real GDP. Thus, to match the observation that consumption is less variable than real GDP, the model relies on the intertemporal-substitution effect

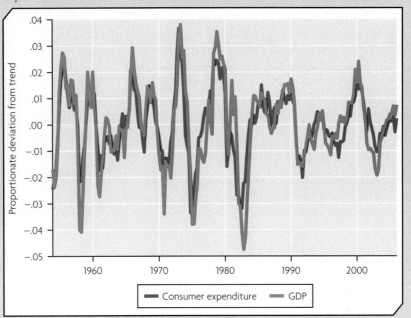

Figure 8.9 *Cyclical Behavior of U.S. Real GDP and Consumer Expenditure*

The red graph is the deviation of real GDP from its trend. The blue graph is the deviation of real consumer expenditure from its trend. These deviations are measured in a proportionate sense. The data on GDP and consumer expenditure are quarterly and seasonally adjusted. Real consumer expenditure is procyclical—it fluctuates closely with real GDP but is less variable than real GDP.

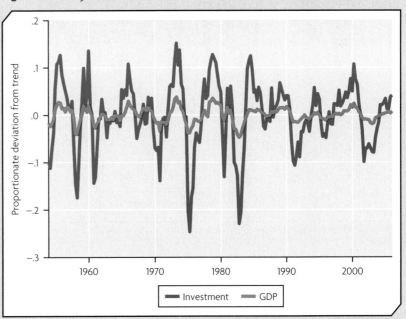

Figure 8.10 *Cyclical Behavior of U.S. Real GDP and Investment*

The red graph is the deviation of real GDP from its trend. The blue graph is the deviation of real gross private domestic investment from its trend. These deviations are measured in a proportionate sense. The data on GDP and investment are quarterly and seasonally adjusted. Real gross investment is procyclical—it fluctuates closely with real GDP but is far more variable than real GDP.

from the interest rate. One problem, however, is that empirical studies have found evidence only for small intertemporal-substitution effects on consumption and saving. Therefore, it may be important to find additional reasons to explain why consumption is proportionately less variable than real GDP. We explore an important reason in a later section, which allows for the change in the technology level, A, to be partly temporary.

The Real Wage Rate

The model predicts that the real wage rate, w/P, will be relatively high in booms and relatively low in recessions. A good measure of the nominal wage rate, w, is the average hourly nominal earnings of production workers in the total private economy (these data start in 1964). We can measure the real wage rate, w/P, by dividing nominal earnings by a broad measure of the price level, the deflator for the gross domestic product. The results are similar if we use the CPI.

We calculate the cyclical part of the real wage rate, w/P, by the procedure used for real GDP in Figure 8.2. The result is the blue graph in Figure 8.11. This graph shows the proportionate deviation of w/P from its trend. We again show as the red graph the cyclical part of real GDP (from Figure 8.3). We see that the real wage rate is procyclical—it tends to be above its trend during booms and below its trend during recessions.[9] This finding accords with the model's predictions.

The Real Rental Price

The model predicts that the real rental price of capital, R/P, will be relatively high in booms and relatively low in recessions. The main problem in testing this proposition is that the rental price is difficult to measure for the whole economy. The reason is that most forms of capital—such as structures and equipment owned by corporations—are not explicitly rented out. These types of capital are typically used by their owners. In effect, businesses rent capital to themselves, but we cannot observe the implicit rental price for this capital. (The national-income accounts estimate an implicit rental price for owner-occupied housing by calculating what the rental price would have been if the home owner had rented out the house.)

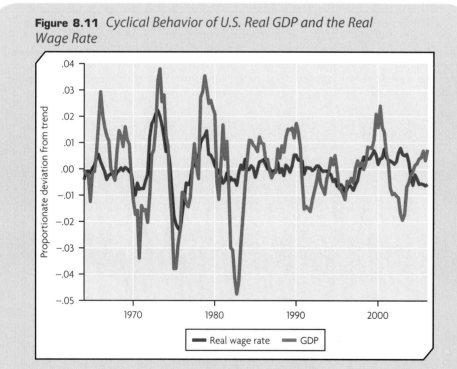

Figure 8.11 *Cyclical Behavior of U.S. Real GDP and the Real Wage Rate*

The red graph is the deviation of real GDP from its trend. The blue graph is the deviation of the real wage rate from its trend. These deviations are measured in a proportionate sense. The real wage rate is average hourly nominal earnings of production workers in the total private, nonagricultural economy divided by the price deflator for the GDP. The data on GDP and wage rates are quarterly and seasonally adjusted. (The underlying data on wage rates are monthly.) The real wage rate is procyclical—it fluctuates with real GDP but is not as variable as real GDP.

---

[9] From 1964.1 to 2006.1, the correlation of the cyclical part of the real wage rate with the cyclical part of real GDP was 0.58.

Casey Mulligan (2001) estimated the implicit real rental price, R/P, for capital owned by the U.S. corporate sector. He made this calculation by dividing total payments to corporate capital by the total quantity of this capital. The blue graph in Figure 8.12 is the cyclical part of Mulligan's R/P series. This graph shows the proportionate deviation of R/P from its trend. We again show as the red graph the cyclical part of real GDP. We see that R/P is procyclical—it tends to be above its trend in booms and below its trend during recessions.[10] This finding fits the model's predictions.

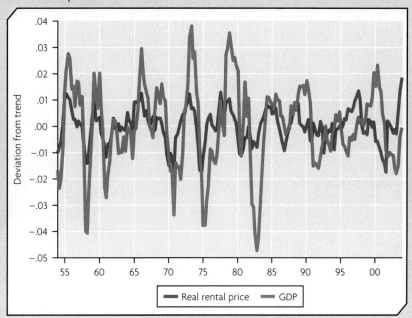

Figure 8.12 *Cyclical Behavior of U.S. Real GDP and the Real Rental Price of Capital*

The red graph is the deviation of real GDP from its trend (in a proportionate sense). The blue graph is the deviation of the real rental price of corporate capital from its trend. The real rental price was calculated by Casey Mulligan (2001), based on after-tax payments to capital per unit of capital in the U.S. corporate sector. The real rental price is procyclical—it fluctuates with real GDP.

The Interest Rate

The model predicts that booms will have a high interest rate, i, whereas recessions will have a low interest rate. This pattern looks right; that is, interest rates tend to be above trend during booms and below trend during recessions.[11] However, to get a full picture, we have to consider the effect of inflation on nominal and real interest rates. We will consider inflation in Chapter 11.

Temporary Changes in the Technology Level

n our model, all changes in the technology level, A, were permanent. This assumption is reasonable for technological advances but less compelling for other interpretations of A. For example, if a decrease in A represents a harvest failure or a general strike, the change would be temporary. To allow for these cases, we now assume that the change in A is temporary. Think of the change as lasting for one year.

The change in the assumption about the technology level, A, does not affect most of our analysis. If A increases temporarily, real GDP, $A \bullet F(K, L)$, still rises for fixed values of K and L. The MPK and the interest rate, i, also rise as before. The intertemporal-substitution effect from the higher i still motivates households to reduce current consumption, C, and raise current real saving.

There are some new results about income effects. The overall change in current consumption, C, again depends on the size of the income effect. In our previous case—where the increase in the technology level, A, was permanent—the income effect raised consumption by about as much as the increase in real GDP. This change worked against the intertemporal-substitution effect, which reduced current consumption. For a permanent rise in A, the income effect more than offset the intertemporal-substitution effect, and current consumption increased.

---

[10] From 1954.1 to 2003.4 (over which the data on the real rental price are available), the correlation of the cyclical part of the real rental price with the cyclical part of real GDP was 0.52.

[11] From 1954.1 to 2006.1, the correlation of the cyclical part of the interest rate on three-month U.S. Treasury Bills with the cyclical part of real GDP was 0.39.

When the increase in the technology level, A, is temporary, the income effect is weak. Therefore, the income effect now raises current consumption, C, by only a small amount. Since the income effect is weak, we can no longer be confident that it more than offsets the intertemporal-substitution effect. Hence, current consumption may rise or fall. In any event, current consumption does not rise by nearly as much as real GDP.

Consider again the aggregate budget constraint that applies when the markets for bonds, labor, and capital services clear:

(7.13)
$$C + \Delta K = Y - \delta K$$

consumption + net investment =
real GDP − depreciation

= real net domestic product

Real GDP, $Y = A \cdot F(K, L)$, rises, and consumption, C, either falls or rises by a small amount. Hence, net investment, ΔK, rises by nearly as much as—or possibly by even more than—real GDP. The model therefore predicts that an economic boom would feature high real GDP and investment. However, consumption would rise by, at most, a small amount. Conversely, a recession would have low real GDP and investment, but consumption would decline by, at most, a modest amount.

These patterns conflict with the data, because consumption is clearly procyclical—it rises well above trend during booms and falls well below trend in recessions. Thus, if the underlying shocks were purely temporary changes in the technology level, A, the model would not explain the behavior of consumption. Our conclusion is that we cannot rely solely on temporary changes in A as the main source of economic fluctuations. However, the model does work better if we allow for changes in A to be less than fully permanent, even if not purely temporary.

Consider again the empirical observation that consumption fluctuates proportionately by less than real GDP. When we assumed that the changes in the technology level, A, were permanent, the model could explain the smaller variability of consumption only if the intertemporal-substitution effect on consumption was substantial. However, if the changes in A are less than fully permanent, we have another reason why consumption is less variable than real GDP. If a change in A lasts for a long time, but not forever, the income effect will be strong. However, the income effect will not be strong enough to raise consumption by as much as the change in real GDP. Thus, consumption can fluctuate proportionately less than real GDP even if the intertemporal-substitution effect on consumption is

weak. This reasoning suggests that the model works best to fit the data when the underlying shocks to A are long lasting but less than fully permanent. This form of shock to technology has typically been assumed in real business-cycle models.

Variations in Labor Input

n important shortcoming of the model worked out thus far is its failure to fit the observed behavior of labor input during economic fluctuations. Labor input, L—measured by employment or total hours worked—varies with the business cycle. As we detail later, L is high in booms and low in recessions; that is, it is clearly procyclical. We cannot give our model a high grade unless we can use it to explain this important phenomenon.

To fit the facts on labor input, we will now extend the model to allow for a variable supply of labor, L^s. This extension will be important for two reasons. First, we will be able to explain short-term variations in labor input, L. Second, changes in real GDP will reflect the variations in L, as well as the direct effect from changes in the technology level, A. We first extend the microeconomic foundations of the model to allow for variable L^s. Then we will use our equilibrium business-cycle model to assess how labor input, L, moves during economic fluctuations.

Labor Supply

Start with a modified form of the household budget constraint worked out in equation (7.1) of Chapter 7:

(8.6)
$$C + (1/P) \cdot \Delta B + \Delta K =$$
$$(w/P) \cdot L^s + i \cdot (B/P + K)$$

consumption + real saving = real income

The left-hand side is the total of consumption, C, and real saving, $(1/P) \cdot \Delta B + \Delta K$. The right-hand side is household real income, which is the sum of real wage income, $(w/P) \cdot L^s$, and real asset income, $i \cdot (B/P + K)$. The difference from before is that we replaced L by the quantity of labor supplied, L^s, to allow for a variable labor supply.

Since each household has a fixed amount of time each year, a higher quantity of labor supplied, L^s, means a smaller amount of leisure time. From the perspective of a household, a higher L^s can mean either that working family members work more hours per year or that more members work. In the latter case, the rise in labor supply shows up as an increase in labor-force participation. Either way, more labor supplied means less leisure time for the family.

We have already assumed that households like consumption, C. Now we assume that households also like more leisure time. To put it differently, households dislike work effort, represented by the quantity of labor supplied, L^s.

As with consumption and saving, the choice of L^s involves substitution and income effects. We start with the *substitution effect for leisure and consumption*.

The Substitution Effect for Leisure and Consumption Consider the household budget constraint in equation (8.6). The right-hand side includes the real wage rate, w/P, and the interest rate, i, each of which an individual household takes as given. Suppose that we also hold fixed the real assets, $B/P + K$, on the right-hand side, and the real saving, $(1/P) \cdot \Delta B + \Delta K$, on the left-hand side. In this case, a household can raise or lower the quantity of labor supplied, L^s, and thereby raise or lower real wage income, $(w/P) \cdot L^s$. Since we are holding everything else fixed in equation (8.6), the higher or lower real wage income will increase or decrease consumption, C. In other words, if the household chooses to work one more hour and thereby have one less hour of leisure, the extra w/P of real wage income pays for w/P more units of consumption. Therefore, the household can substitute one less hour of leisure for w/P more units of consumption.

If the real wage rate, w/P, rises, the household gets a better deal by working more because it gets more consumption for each extra hour worked. Since the deal is better, we predict that the household responds to a higher w/P by working more. Another way to view the result is that a higher w/P makes leisure time more expensive compared to consumption: w/P tells the household how much consumption it gives up by taking an extra hour of leisure. An increase in w/P motivates the household to substitute away from the object that got more expensive—leisure time—and toward the one that got cheaper—consumption. Therefore, a higher real wage rate, w/P, raises the quantity of labor supplied, L^s.

Income Effects on Labor Supply As usual, we also have to consider income effects. Consider again the budget constraint

(8.6)
$$C + (1/P) \cdot \Delta B + \Delta K = (w/P) \cdot L^s + i \cdot (B/P + K)$$

consumption + real saving = real income

We see from the yellow shaded term that a change in the real wage rate, w/P, has an income effect. For a given quantity of labor supplied, L^s, a higher w/P means higher real wage income, $(w/P) \cdot L^s$. Our prediction is that the household spends the extra income on consumption and leisure time. Thus, on this ground, a higher w/P leads to a smaller quantity of labor supplied, L^s. Since the substitution effect from a higher w/P favors higher L^s, the overall effect is ambiguous. An increase in the real wage rate, w/P, raises L^s if the substitution effect is stronger than the income effect.

We may be able to resolve the ambiguity by considering whether the income effect is strong or weak. We found in Chapter 7 that the strength of the income effect depended on whether the change in income was permanent or temporary. To see how this works, consider a modified form of the multi-year budget constraint worked out in Chapter 7 in equation (7.12):

(8.7)
$$C_1 + C_2/(1 + i_1) + C_3/[(1 + i_1) \cdot (1 + i_2)] + \cdots = (1 + i_0) \cdot (B_0/P + K_0) + (w/P)_1 \cdot L_1^s + (w/P)_2 \cdot L_2^s/(1 + i_1) + (w/P)_3 \cdot L_3^s/[(1 + i_1) \cdot (1 + i_2)] + \cdots$$

present value of consumption = value of initial assets + present value of wage incomes

The difference from before is that we replaced the fixed quantity of labor, L, by the quantity of labor supplied in each year, L_1^s, where $t = 1, 2$, and so on.

When we examined income effects on consumption in Chapter 7, we found that households responded to higher real wage rates by consuming more each year. That is, the income effect was positive for each year's consumption. However, the income effect was much stronger if the change in the real wage rate was permanent and applied to $(w/P)_2$, $(w/P)_3$, and so on, rather than just to $(w/P)_1$.

The same reasoning applies to labor supply. A permanent increase in real wage rates results in a large income effect. In this case, we are unsure whether an increase in $(w/P)_1$ (accompanied by increases in future real wage rates, $[w/P]_2$, $[w/P]_3$, and so on) raises or lowers year 1's quantity of labor supplied, L_1^s. The income effect, which lowers labor supply, may be stronger or weaker than the substitution effect, which raises labor supply.

In contrast, if the change in year 1's real wage rate, $(w/P)_1$, is temporary, the income effect is small. In this case, we can be confident that the income effect will be weaker than the substitution effect. Therefore, a temporary increase in year 1's real wage rate, $(w/P)_1$ (when $[w/P]_2$, $[w/P]_3$, and so on do not change), would raise year 1's quantity of labor supplied, L_1^s.

Intertemporal-Substitution Effects on Labor Supply We found in Chapter 7 that a change in the

bythenumbers

Empirical Evidence on Intertemporal Substitution of Labor Supply

George Alogoskoufis (1987b) found, for U.S. household data from 1948 to 1982, that an increase in the expected growth rate of real wage rates by one percentage point per year raised the growth rate of employment by about one percentage point per year. Thus, employment was deferred when workers thought that future real wage rates would be higher than current real wage rates. Alogoskoufis also found that an increase in the annual interest rate by one percentage point lowered the growth rate of employment by 0.6 percentage points per year. For British household data from 1950 to 1982, Alogoskoufis (1987a) found weaker, but still statistically significant, intertemporal-substitution effects. An increase in the expected growth rate of real wage rates by one percentage point per year raised the growth rate of employment by 0.4 percentage points. An increase in the interest rate by one percentage point lowered the growth rate of employment by 0.2 percentage points per year.

The Alogoskoufis studies found no evidence that hours worked per worker responded to time-varying real wage rates or interest rates. This pattern is surprising—one would expect workers to work extra hours, including overtime and weekends, when real wage rates are temporarily high.

Casey Mulligan (1995) argued that it is hard to detect intertemporal-substitution effects from time-varying real wage rates in the Alogoskoufis data. One problem is that it is unclear when households perceive current real wage rates to be temporarily high or low. Therefore, Mulligan looked at unusual events for which the temporary nature of high real wage rates was clear.

One of the events that Mulligan observed was the construction of the Alaskan gas pipeline from 1974 to 1977. He found that the temporarily high real wage rates paid to construction workers elicited a substantial increase in labor supply. A temporary rise of real wage rates by 10% was estimated to raise average hours worked per week by 20%. The second event that Mulligan observed was the cleanup of the *Exxon Valdez* oil spill in Alaska in 1989. He found that the temporarily high real wage rates paid to workers in the transportation and public utilities industries induced a sharp increase in labor supply. The estimate was that a temporary rise in real wage rates by 10% raised average hours worked per week by even more than 20%. Thus, unlike Alogoskoufis, Mulligan found a substantial response of hours worked per worker to temporarily high real wage rates.

© Natalie Fobes/CORBIS

interest rate, i, had an intertemporal-substitution effect on consumption. Now we will study intertemporal-substitution effects on labor supply. We will first consider effects from interest rates and then study new effects from variations over time in real wage rates.

The multiyear budget constraint is again

(8.7)
$$C_1 + C_2/(1 + i_1) + C_3/[(1 + i_1) \cdot (1 + i_2)] + \cdots = (1 + i_0) \cdot (B_0/P + K_0) + (w/P)_1 \cdot L_1^s + (w/P)_2 \cdot L_2^s/(1 + i_1) + (w/P)_3 \cdot L_3^s/[(1 + i_1) \cdot (1 + i_2)] + \cdots$$

The yellow shaded terms show that an increase in year 1's interest rate, i_1, makes year 2's consumption, C_2, cheaper compared with year 1's, C_1. Therefore, an increase in i_1 lowered C_1 and raised C_2. In other words, households substituted away from the object that got more expensive—current consumption—and toward the one that got cheaper—future consumption.

The pink shaded terms in equation (8.7) show that year 2's real wage income, $(w/P)_2 \cdot L_2^s$, is discounted by $1 + i_1$ to get a present value before combining it with year 1's real wage income, $(w/P)_1 \cdot L_1^s$. If the interest rate, i_1, rises, a unit of year 2's real wage income, $(w/P)_2 \cdot L_2^s$, becomes less valuable as a present value compared to a unit of year 1's real wage income, $(w/P)_1 \cdot L_1^s$. We therefore predict that the household would increase L_1^s and decrease L_2^s. This change is an intertemporal-substitution effect on labor supply—a higher interest rate favors more labor supply today and less in the future.

Another way to view this result is through leisure time. A higher interest rate, i_1, means that future consumption and leisure time are cheaper in present-value terms compared to current consumption and leisure time. Therefore, the household substitutes toward the cheaper objects—future consumption and leisure time—and away from the more expensive ones—current consumption and leisure time.

There are also intertemporal-substitution effects from variations of the real wage rate over time. Start from equal real wage rates in each year—$(w/P)_1 = (w/P)_2 \cdots$, and assume that year 1's real wage rate, $(w/P)_1$, falls, while future real wage rates—$(w/P)_2$, $(w/P)_3$, and so on—do not change. This change motivates the household to supply less labor when the real wage rate is temporarily low (year 1) and more labor in future years. Hence, a fall in year 1's real wage rate, $(w/P)_1$, reduces year 1's quantity of labor supplied, L_1^s, because of this intertemporal-substitution effect. We can also say that current leisure time is relatively cheap when the real wage rate is temporarily low. In other words, a period of temporarily low real wage rates is a good time to take a vacation.

The previous By the Numbers box summarizes empirical evidence about intertemporal-substitution effects on labor supply. These results suggest that the quantity of labor supplied responds as predicted to interest rates and to variations in real wage rates over time.

Fluctuations in Labor Input

We want to incorporate the new analysis of labor supply into our equilibrium business-cycle model. However, before we make this extension, let's look at the data to see what we are trying to explain.

The Cyclical Behavior of Labor Input: Empirical
Figures 8.13 and 8.14 show two concepts of U.S. labor input. The first is employment (numbers of persons with jobs) and the second is **total hours worked** (which multiplies employment by the average weekly hours worked per employee).[12] We use the method from Figure 8.2 to calculate the cyclical part of each measure of labor input. We show the cyclical parts of employment and total hours worked as the blue graphs in Figures 8.13 and 8.14, respectively. These graphs show the proportionate deviation of employment or total hours worked from trend. As before, the red graphs show the cyclical parts of real GDP.

We see from the graphs that both measures of labor input are procyclical: They move in the same direction as real GDP during booms and recessions.[13] That is, employment and total hours worked are both high relative to trend during booms and low relative to trend during recessions. The variability of labor input is nearly as great as that of real GDP—the standard deviations of the cyclical parts were 1.3% for employment and 1.5% for total hours worked, compared with 1.6% for real GDP. Thus, in a proportionate sense, employment and total hours worked vary by nearly as much as real GDP during booms and recessions.

---

[12] The data are from the establishment survey of the BLS (www.bls.gov). The employment numbers exclude agricultural workers, the self-employed, and a few other types of labor input. Total hours worked is the product of employment and average weekly hours worked in the total private economy (available since 1964).

[13] From 1954.1 to 2006.1, the correlation of the cyclical part of employment with the cyclical part of real GDP was 0.81. From 1964.1 to 2006.1, the correlation of the cyclical part of total hours worked with the cyclical part of real GDP was 0.88.

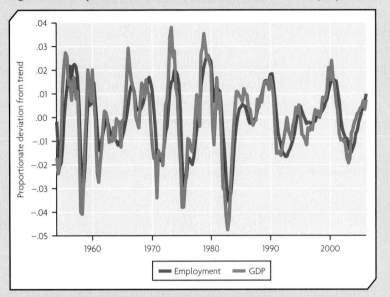

Figure 8.13 *Cyclical Behavior of U.S. Real GDP and Employment*

The red graph is the deviation of real GDP from its trend. The blue graph is the deviation of employment from its trend. These deviations are measured in a proportionate sense. Employment comes from the BLS payroll survey—it measures the total number of persons working on payrolls in the nonagricultural economy. The data on real GDP and employment are quarterly and seasonally adjusted. (The underlying data on employment are monthly.) Employment is procyclical—it fluctuates closely with real GDP and is nearly as variable as real GDP.

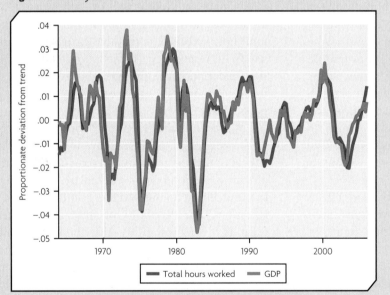

Figure 8.14 *Cyclical Behavior of U.S. Real GDP and Total Hours Worked*

The red graph is the deviation of real GDP from its trend. The blue graph is the deviation of total hours worked from its trend. These deviations are measured in a proportionate sense. Total hours worked is employment (from Figure 8.13) multiplied by average weekly hours of persons working. The data for weekly hours, available since 1964, come from the BLS payroll survey and refer to the private, nonagricultural economy. The data on real GDP and total hours are quarterly and seasonally adjusted. (The underlying data on total hours worked are monthly.) Total hours worked is procyclical—it fluctuates closely with real GDP and is about as variable as real GDP.

The Cyclical Behavior of Labor Input: Theory

We will now work out the equilibrium business-cycle model with variable labor supply. We assume again that economic fluctuations reflect shocks to the technology level, A. These shocks are long lasting but not permanent.

Figure 8.15 shows how an increase in the technology level, A, affects the labor market. The downward-sloping labor-demand curves come from Figure 8.5. The blue curve shows market labor demand, L^d, at an initial technology level, A. This curve slopes downward, as usual, because a decrease in the real wage rate, w/P, raises the quantity of labor demanded. The downward-sloping red curve is for a higher technology level, A'.

Figure 8.15 shows an upward-sloping curve for labor supply, L^s. This curve slopes upward because we assume that the substitution effect from a higher current real wage rate, w/P, dominates the income effect. We already noted that this upward slope is likely to apply if the changes in w/P are not fully permanent. The same curve for L^s applies for the two technology levels. That is, for a given w/P, we assume that the labor-supply curve does not shift when the technology level rises from A to A'. This assumption is not fully accurate because it neglects effects on L^s from an increase in the interest rate (which occur when the technology level rises).

However, the inclusion of an interest-rate effect would not change our main results.

We reach two important conclusions from Figure 8.15. First, as before, the real wage rate rises, from $(w/P)^*$ to $[(w/P)^*]'$ on the vertical axis. Second, aggregate labor input increases, from L^* to $(L^*)'$ on the horizontal axis. The second effect is new, and it depends on the upward slope of the labor-supply curve, L^s. If a higher current w/P induces a greater quantity of labor supplied, an increase in the technology level raises labor input, L. Hence, the model now matches the observation, from Figures 8.13 and 8.14, that labor input moves along with real GDP during economic fluctuations.

The increase in labor input also contributes to the rise in real GDP, $Y = A \cdot F(K, L)$. Hence, real GDP rises partly because of the direct effect from the higher technology level, A, and partly because of the increase in labor input, L.

The Cyclical Behavior of Labor Productivity

Another important macroeconomic variable is labor productivity. The definition of labor productivity used in popular media is the average product of labor, which is the ratio of real GDP, Y, to labor input, L. In the equilibrium business-cycle model, this concept of labor

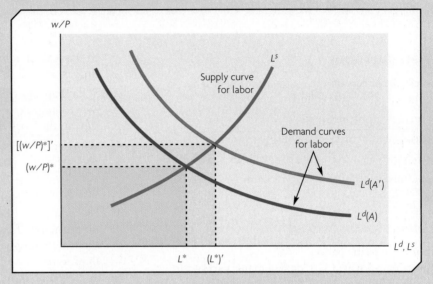

Figure 8.15 *Clearing of the Labor Market*

At the technology level A, the demand for labor, labeled $L^d(A)$ along the blue curve, slopes downward versus the real wage rate, w/P. At the higher technology level, A', the demand for labor, labeled $L^d(A')$ along the red curve, is larger at any given w/P. These two curves are from Figure 8.5. The supply of labor, L^s, shown in green, slopes upward versus w/P because we assume that the substitution effect from a change in w/P dominates the income effect. The increase in the technology level from A to A' raises the real wage rate from $(w/P)^*$ to $[(w/P)^*]'$ on the vertical axis, and increases labor input from L^* to $(L^*)'$ on the horizontal axis.

productivity tends to be procyclical—high in booms and low in recessions. The reason is that the average product of labor, Y/L, typically moves in the same direction as the marginal product of labor, MPL. We already know that the MPL—which equals the real wage rate, w/P, when the labor market clears—is procyclical.

To calculate labor productivity, we can measure labor input, L, by employment or total hours worked. The first measure of labor productivity, Y/L, is real GDP per worker, and the second is real GDP per worker-hour. Labor productivity turns out to be procyclical in both cases. The model matches this feature of labor productivity. However, a more detailed analysis suggests that there may be a quantitative puzzle in that real GDP per worker-hour is less procyclical than predicted by the model.

Questions and Problems

A. Review questions

1. Discuss the effects on this year's quantity of labor supplied, L_1^s, from the following changes:

a. An increase in the interest rate, i_1

b. A permanent increase in the real wage rate, w/P

c. A temporary increase in the real wage rate, w/P

d. A one-time windfall, which raises initial real assets, $(B_0/P + K_0)$

B. Problems for discussion

2. Labor-force participation
   In post–World War II U.S. data, a major part of the increase in labor input, L, reflects a rise in labor-force participation, particularly by women. The table shows how the overall participation rate changed from 1950 to 2000. (The participation rate is defined as the ratio of the civilian labor force to the noninstitutional population, which is the civilian population aged 16 and older and not residing in prisons and other institutions.)

Year	Participation Rate (%)
1950	59.2
1960	59.4
1970	60.4
1980	63.8
1990	66.5
2000	67.1

a. Is this behavior of labor-force participation consistent with our analysis of income and substitution effects?

b. Is the behavior consistent with the observation that average weekly hours of workers changed little during the post–World War II period?

c. Are there other factors that we should consider to explain the changing labor-force participation?

3. A change in population
   Assume a one-time decrease in population, possibly caused by an onset of disease or a sudden out-migration.

a. Use a variant of Figure 8.15 to determine the effects on the labor market. What happens to labor input, L, and the real wage rate, w/P?

b. Use a variant of Figure 8.8 to determine the effects on the market for capital services. What happens to the real rental price, R/P? What happens to the interest rate, i?

c. What happens to output, Y, and consumption, C? What happens to investment, I? What happens over time to the stock of capital, K?

4. A change in the capital stock
   Assume a one-time decrease in the capital stock, K, possibly caused by a natural disaster or an act of war. Assume that population does not change.

a. Use a variant of Figure 8.8 to determine the effects on the market for capital services. What happens to the real rental price, R/P? What happens to the interest rate, i?

b. Use a variant of Figure 8.15 to determine the effects on the labor market. What happens to labor input, L, and the real wage rate, w/P?

c. What happens to output, Y, and consumption, C? What happens to investment, I? What happens over time to the stock of capital, K?

5. A shift in desired saving
   Suppose that households change their preferences so that they wish to consume more and save less in the current year. That is, current consumption, C_1, rises for a given interest rate, and for given current and future income.

a. Use a variant of Figure 8.15 to determine the effects on the labor market. What happens to labor input, L, and the real wage rate, w/P?

b. Use a variant of Figure 8.8 to determine the effects on the market for capital services. What happens to the real rental price, R/P? What happens to the interest rate, i?

c. What happens to consumption, C, and investment, I? What happens over time to the stock of capital, K?

6. A change in the willingness to work
   Suppose that households change their preferences so that they wish to work and consume more in each year.

a. Use a variant of Figure 8.15 to determine the effects on the labor market. What happens to labor input, L, and the real wage rate, w/P?

b. Use a variant of Figure 8.8 to determine the effects on the market for capital services. What happens to the real rental price, R/P? What happens to the interest rate, i?

c. What happens to consumption, C, and investment, I? What happens over time to the stock of capital, K?

AP Images

CHAPTER 9

Capital Utilization and Unemployment

T he equilibrium business-cycle model from Chapter 8 explains a number of features of economic fluctuations. However, an important shortcoming is that the two factor inputs, capital and labor, are always fully employed. This chapter remedies these deficiencies by allowing for a variable utilization rate for capital and a variable employment rate for labor.

For the capital stock, we allow for a variable supply of capital services in the short run. This extension explains why the capital-utilization rate is less than 100% and tends to be relatively high in a boom and relatively low in a recession. This pattern helps us to understand the fluctuations of real GDP.

Similarly, the model does not explain why the labor force is less than fully employed; that is, it does not explain unemployment. To study the levels and variations in the unemployment rate, we extend the model to allow workers to search for good jobs and employers to search for productive workers. This process of job matching can explain the existence and variability of unemployment and job vacancies. We can explain why the unemployment rate is low in a boom and high in a recession. This pattern helps us to understand the fluctuations of labor input and real GDP.

Capital Input

I n Chapter 8, we assumed that households supplied all of their given capital stock, K, to the rental market, so that the supply of capital services, K^s, was a vertical line at K in Figure 8.8. The real rental price, R/P adjusted to equate the quantity of capital services demanded, K^d, to the quantity supplied, K^s. Therefore, the given capital stock, K, was always fully utilized in production. To put it another way, the **capital utilization rate**—the fraction of the capital stock used in production—was always 100%.

Now we extend the microeconomic foundations of the model to allow for a variable capital utilization

rate and, hence, for a variable supply of capital services. Then we use our market-clearing approach to the rental market to assess the determination of the quantity of capital services.

Up to now, we did not distinguish the stock of capital, K, from the quantity of capital services used in production. Think of K as the number of machines, and assume that each machine is utilized a fixed number of hours per year. For example, if businesses use each machine 8 hours per day, 5 days per week, and 52 weeks per year, then each machine yields 2,080 machine-hours per year. In this case, capital services—measured as machine-hours per year—would always be a fixed multiple, such as 2,080, of the capital stock.

In practice, the capital utilization rate can vary. If businesses operate each machine 16 hours per day, corresponding to two 8-hour shifts each weekday instead of one, then each machine would yield 4,160 machine-hours per year, rather than 2,080. Similarly, businesses can raise the utilization rate by operating on weekends.

Let the variable κ (the Greek letter kappa) represent the utilization rate for the capital stock, K. We measure κ in units of hours per year, and K as the number of machines (a stock of goods). The product of κ and K, κK, represents the flow of capital services. The term κK has units of

(hours per year) • *(number of machines) =*
machine-hours per year

We now modify the production function from equation (3.1) to replace the capital stock, K, by the quantity of capital services, κK:

> Key equation (prodution function with variable capital utilization):
>
> **(9.1)** $\qquad Y = A \bullet F(\kappa K, L)$

For given K, κK, rises with the utilization rate, κ. Therefore, an increase in κ raises real GDP, Y, for a given technology level, A, capital stock, K, and labor input, L.

Our assumption is that production depends only on the quantity of capital services per year, κK, and not on how these services break down between the utilization rate, κ, and the number of machines, K. Running 16 machines for 8 hours per day is assumed to be just as productive as running 8 machines for 16 hours per day.

The Demand for Capital Services

In Chapter 6, we worked out the demand for capital services, K^d, as an input to production. Households, as managers of family businesses, chose K^d to maximize real profit, given by

(6.13) $\qquad \Pi/P = A \bullet F(K^d, L^d) - (w/P) \bullet$
$L^d - (R/P) \bullet K^d$

The maximization of Π/P led to the equation of the MPK to the real rental price of capital, R/P. An increase in R/P reduced the quantity of capital services demanded, K^d, as shown by the downward-sloping curve in Figure 6.6.

This analysis is still valid if we revise equation (6.13) to allow for a variable capital utilization rate:

(9.2) $\qquad \Pi/P = A \bullet F[(\kappa K)^d, L^d)] - (w/P) \bullet$
$L^d - (R/P) \bullet (\kappa K)^d$

The real rental price, R/P, is now measured per unit of capital services. That is, since κK has units of machine-hours per year, R/P has units of goods per machine-hour.

As before, households choose the quantity of capital services demanded, now represented by $(\kappa K)^d$, to maximize real profit, Π/P. This maximization again implies that the MPK equals the real rental price, R/P. However, the MPK is now the additional goods produced by an extra machine-hour of capital services. The resulting demand curve for capital services, $(\kappa K)^d$, still looks like the one shown in Figure 6.6. We show this demand as the downward-sloping blue curve in Figure 9.1.

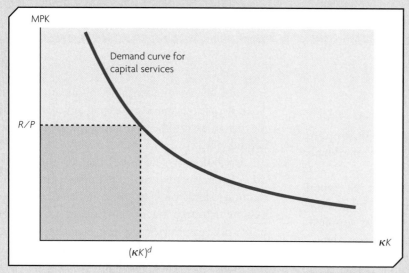

Figure 9.1 *Demand for Capital Services*

For a given technology level, *A*, and labor input, *L*, the marginal product of capital services, MPK on the vertical axis, decreases as the quantity of capital services, *κK*, rises on the horizontal axis. The household chooses the quantity of capital services, (*κK*)*ᵈ*, where the MPK equals the real rental price, *R/P*.

Assume that the technology level rises from A to A'. This change raises the MPK at a given quantity, κK. Figure 9.2 shows this change as the shift from the blue curve to the red one. At the given real rental price, R/P, the quantity of capital services demanded rises from $(\kappa K)^d$ to $[(\kappa K)^d]'$. These results are similar to those in Figure 8.7, which did not allow for a variable capital utilization rate.

The Supply of Capital Services

We assumed in Chapter 8 that owners of capital (households) supplied all of their capital, K, to the rental market. Now we extend this analysis to allow owners to choose the capital utilization rate, κ. For a given stock of capital, K, owners can supply more or less capital services per year by varying κ. Why would an owner ever set κ below its maximum possible value? This maximum rate, corresponding to the operation of machines 24 hours per day and 7 days per week, is 8,736 hours per year.

One reason to set the utilization rate, κ, below its maximum is that increases in κ tend to raise the depreciation rate, δ. Machines wear out faster if they are used more intensively. Moreover, as κ rises, the time available for maintenance declines, thereby contributing further to a higher depreciation rate. We can capture these effects by writing the depreciation rate as an upward-sloping function of κ:[1]

$$\delta = \delta(\kappa)$$

Owners of capital choose the utilization rate, κ, to maximize their net real income from supplying capital services:

net real income from supplying capital services =
real rental payments − depreciation

$$= (R/P) \bullet \kappa K - \delta(\kappa) \bullet K$$

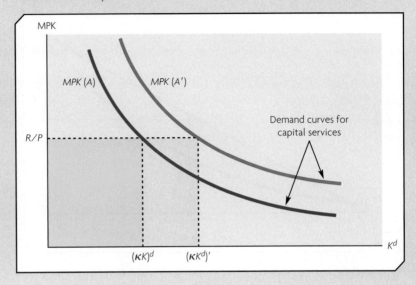

Figure 9.2 *Effect of an Increase in the Technology Level on the Demand for Capital Services*

When the technology level is A, the MPK is given by the blue curve, labeled MPK (A). At the real rental price, R/P shown on the vertical axis, the quantity of capital services demanded is $(\kappa k)^d$ on the horizontal axis. The technology level A' is greater than A. Therefore, the MPK, given by the red curve labeled MPK (A'), is higher at any capital input than the value along the blue curve. When the technology level is A' and the real rental price is R/P the quantity of capital services demanded is $(\kappa k)^d$, which is greater than $(\kappa k)^d$.

If we take the variable K outside, we can write the result as

(9.3) *net real income from supplying capital services = $K \bullet [(R/P) \bullet \kappa - \delta(\kappa)]$*

Thus, the net real income equals the capital owned, K, multiplied by the term $(R/P) \bullet \kappa - \delta(\kappa)$. To understand this term, note that the first part, $(R/P) \bullet \kappa$, is the product of the real rental per machine-hour, (R/P), and the machine-hours per year, κ, from each machine. Thus, $(R/P) \bullet \kappa$ is the real rental income per year on each unit of capital. When we subtract the depreciation rate, $\delta(\kappa)$, we get the net real rental income per unit of capital, $(R/P) \bullet \kappa - \delta(\kappa)$. This term gives the rate of return from owning capital:

Key equation (rate of return on capital):

(9.4) *rate of return from owning capital = $(R/P) \bullet \kappa - \delta(\kappa)$*

---

[1] This analysis was introduced by Jeremy Greenwood, Zvi Hercowitz, and Gregory Huffman (1988).

Figure 9.3 Choosing the Capital Utilization Rate

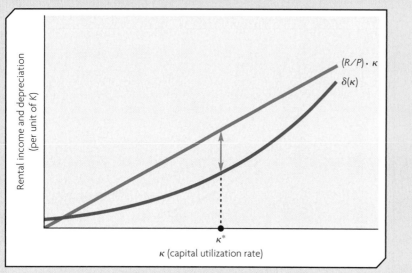

The green line from the origin is the real rental income per unit of capital, $(R/P) \cdot \kappa$. The blue curve shows the depreciation rate, $\delta(\kappa)$, as an upward-sloping function of the capital utilization rate, κ. The gap between the green line and the blue curve equals the rate of return from owning capital, $(R/P) \cdot \kappa - \delta(\kappa)$, given in equation (9.3). Owners of capital choose κ to maximize this vertical distance—this maximization occurs when $\kappa = \kappa^*$ on the horizontal axis.

For a given capital stock, K, the maximization of the net real income from supplying capital services boils down to maximizing the net real return from owning capital, $(R/P) \cdot \kappa - \delta(\kappa)$, in equation (9.4). Figure 9.3 graphs the two parts of this return against the capital utilization rate, κ. The straight green line shows the first part, $(R/P) \cdot \kappa$. This line starts from the origin, and its slope equals the real rental price, R/P. As in our previous analysis, an individual household takes R/P as given.

The second part of the rate of return from owning capital in equation (9.4) is the negative of the depreciation rate, $\delta(\kappa)$. We graph $\delta(\kappa)$ versus κ in Figure 9.3 as the blue curve. We assume that $\delta(\kappa)$ is greater than zero when κ equals zero; that is, capital depreciates even when it sits idle (perhaps because it gets rusty). Second, $\delta(\kappa)$ rises as κ increases above zero, so that a higher κ leads to a higher depreciation rate, $\delta(\kappa)$.[2]

The rate of return from owning capital, given by equation (9.4), equals the vertical distance between the green line and the blue curve in Figure 9.3. Owners of capital (households) select the utilization rate, κ, that maximizes this distance. In the graph, this maximization occurs when $\kappa = \kappa^*$ on the horizontal axis. At κ^*, the vertical distance between the line and the curve is shown by the red arrows. Typically, κ^* will be set below

its maximum feasible value of 8,736 hours per year. Owners avoid this extremely high rate of capital utilization because it leads to rapid depreciation of the capital stock. The Back to Reality box discusses other reasons for owners to choose a capital utilization rate less than 100%.

Now we have to figure out how a change in the real rental price, R/P changes the chosen capital utilization rate, κ^*. Suppose that the real rental price rises from R/P to $(R/P)'$. At R/P, the real rental payments per unit of capital, $(R/P) \cdot \kappa$, are given by the green line from the origin in Figure 9.4. At the higher real rental price, $(R/P)'$, the real rental payments per unit of capital, $(R/P)' \cdot \kappa$, are given by the brown line, which is steeper than the green line. The depreciation curve, $\delta(\kappa)$, shown in blue, comes from Figure 9.3. This curve does not shift because $\delta(\kappa)$ does not depend on R/P.

When the real rental price is R/P, households maximize the vertical distance between the green line and the blue curve by picking the capital utilization rate κ^*, shown on the horizontal axis in Figure 9.4. When the real rental price rises to $(R/P)'$, households maximize by choosing the higher utilization rate $(R/P)'$. Thus, an increase in the real rental price raises the capital utilization rate; the higher real rental price makes it worthwhile to raise κ despite the resulting increase in the depreciation rate, $\delta(\kappa)$.

Market Clearing and Capital Utilization

We considered in Chapter 8 the effects of an increase in the technology level, A, on real GDP, labor input, and other variables. Now we can include the effect on the capital utilization rate, κ, and, hence, on the quantity of capital services, κK.

---

[2] We also assume that $\delta(\kappa)$ gets more sensitive to κ as κ increases. Graphically, the curve $\delta(\kappa)$ has a convex shape—it bows out toward the horizontal axis.

Figure 9.5 puts together our analyses of the demand for, and supply of, capital services. The vertical axis shows the real rental price, R/P, and the horizontal axis shows the market demand for, and supply of, capital services. The two downward-sloping demand curves come from Figure 9.2. The blue curve corresponds to the technology level A, and the red curve to the higher technology level A'. Note that the increase in the technology level raises the market demand for capital services, $(\kappa k)^d$.

The upward-sloping supply curve in Figure 9.5 comes from Figure 9.4. The supply curve slopes up because an increase in the real rental price, R/P, motivates a higher capital utilization rate, κ. For a given stock of capital, K, the increase in κ raises the quantity of capital services supplied, $(\kappa k)^s$.

BACK TO REALITY

Multiple Shifts and Overtime Hours

We found that the capital utilization rate, κ, would typically be set at less than its maximum feasible value of 8,736 hours per year. We got this result by considering the positive effect of κ on the depreciation rate, $\delta(\kappa)$. We can bring in additional reasons for less than full utilization of factories and machines.

We have assumed that real GDP, γ, depends on capital services in the form κK:

(9.1) $$Y = A \bullet F(\kappa K, L)$$

where K is the number of machines and κ the hours per year that each machine operates. If we start with $\kappa = 2{,}080$ hours per year—where a business uses capital eight hours per day on weekdays—the business could raise κ by operating more than one shift per day or by opening on weekends. However, more hours of operation per week incur additional costs, including the electric power needed to keep the lights on. These kinds of expenses are called   —they arise only when capital is used. We should subtract these costs from the expression for real profit in equation (9.2) to get

$$\Pi/P = A \bullet F[\,(\kappa K)^d, L^d)] - (w/P) \bullet L^d$$
$$- (R/P) \bullet (\kappa K)^d - user\ costs\ of\ capital$$

The user costs—which increase with κ—can explain why capital operates less than full time. That is, a business may prefer to have 100 machines operated half the time, rather than 50 machines operated full time.

In addition, to raise k, businesses typically have to operate machines and factories at less convenient times, such as evenings and weekends. Typically, these times of operation are more expensive than standard business hours because workers require higher wage rates for night shifts or overtime hours. Complementary services from other businesses, such as suppliers and transporters, may also be unavailable at these times. (Lower electricity rates and less highway congestion at off-hours are offsetting factors.) If we allow for high costs of operation at unusual hours, we get another reason why businesses operate their capital at less than maximal capacity.

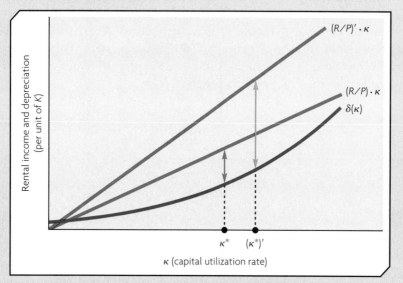

Figure 9.4 *Effect of an Increase in the Real Rental Price on the Capital Utilization Rate*

The blue curve is the depreciation rate, $\delta(\kappa)$, from Figure 9.3. The two lines from the origin are the real rental income per unit of capital. The green line is for the real rental price R/P, and the brown line is for the higher real rental price $(R/P)'$. At R/P owners of capital maximize the difference between the rental income line and the depreciation curve by choosing the capital utilization rate κ^* on the horizontal axis. At $(R/P)'$, they maximize the difference by choosing the higher utilization rate $(\kappa^*)'$. Therefore, an increase in R/P raises the capital utilization rate.

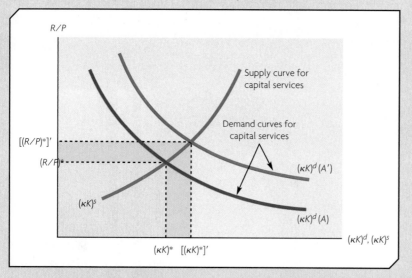

Figure 9.5 *Clearing of the Market for Capital Services*

At the technology level, the demand for capital services, labeled $(\kappa k)^d(A)$ along the blue curve, slopes downward versus the real rental price, R/P. At the higher technology level A', the demand for capital services, labeled $(\kappa k)^d(A')$ along the red curve, is larger at any given. These curves are from Figure 9.2. The supply of capital services, $(\kappa k)^s$, slopes upward versus R/P along the green curve because an increase in R/P raises the capital utilization rate, κ (as in Figure 9.4). Thus, an increase in the technology level from A to A' raises the market-clearing real rental price from $(R/P)^*$ to $[(R/P)^*]'$, and the quantity of capital services from $(\kappa k)^*$ to $[(\kappa k)^*]'$. Since the stock of capital, K, is fixed, the increase in capital services reflects the rise in the utilization rate from κ^* to $(\kappa^*)'$, as in Figure 9.4.

Figure 9.4 shows that, for a given R/P, the technology level, A, does not affect the choice of the capital utilization rate, κ. Therefore, the increase in A in Figure 9.5 does not shift the supply curve for capital services. (Ultimately, a rise in A will increase the quantity of capital services supplied. However, this increase works through an increase in R/P, which determines the reward to owners of capital from supplying more services. That is, we get a movement along the given supply curve, not a shift in the curve.)

When the technology level is A, Figure 9.5 shows that the market for capital services clears when the real rental price is $(R/P)^*$ on the vertical axis and the quantity of capital services is $(\kappa K)^*$ on the horizontal axis. When the technology level rises to A', the demand curve for capital services shifts to the right, and the supply curve does not shift. Therefore, the market clears at the higher real rental price, $[(R/P)^*]'$, and the larger quantity of capital services, $[(\kappa K)^*]'$.

We noted in Chapter 8 that an increase in the technology level raised the real rental price, R/P. The new effect in Figure 9.5 is the increase in the quantity of capital services, κK. Since the capital stock, K, is fixed in the short run, the increase in capital services reflects the rise in the utilization rate from κ^* to $(\kappa^*)'$. We therefore find that booms—where a high A causes real GDP to be high—will have a relatively high capital utilization rate, whereas recessions—where a low A causes real GDP to be low—will have a relatively low utilization rate.

Recall that the production function is

(9.1)
$$Y = A \bullet F(\kappa K, L)$$

We now have three reasons why real GDP rises in a boom and falls in a recession. First, a high or low technology level, A, causes real GDP to be correspondingly high or low. Second, as discussed in Chapter 8, a high or low A causes L to be correspondingly high or low. Third, the new effect is that a high or low A causes the capital utilization rate, κ, and, thereby, the quantity of capital services, κK, to be correspondingly high or low.

Recall that the rate of return on capital is given by

(9.4)
rate of return from owning capital =
$(R/P) \bullet \kappa - \delta(\kappa)$

For a given capital utilization rate, κ, equation (9.4) shows that an increase in the real rental price, R/P, raises the rate of return from owning capital. This effect is the one explored in Chapter 8, where κ did not vary. Now we get an additional effect from the adjustment of κ. We know that κ is chosen to maximize the rate of return shown in equation (9.4). Therefore, the change in κ—upward in our case, in response to the increase in R/P—raises the rate of return on capital. We therefore conclude, as in Chapter 8, that the rate of return from owning capital rises overall in response to an increase in the technology level, A.

We still have that the rate of return on bonds—the interest rate, i—must equal the rate of return on ownership of capital. In Chapter 6, this condition was

(6.6)
$$i = R/P - \delta$$
rate of return on bonds =
rate of return on ownership of capital

Now we use equation (9.4) to measure the rate of return on ownership of capital to get

(9.5)
$$i = (R/P) \bullet \kappa - \delta(\kappa)$$
rate of return on bonds =
rate of return on ownership of capital

We find that an increase in the technology level, A, raises the rate of return from owning capital, which

is the expression on the right-hand side of equation (9.5). Therefore, as in Chapter 8, the interest rate, i, increases. The interest rate is still procyclical in the model.

The Cyclical Behavior of Capacity Utilization

To check our prediction that the capital utilization rate, k, is procyclical, we can use the Federal Reserve's data on capacity utilization rates in manufacturing, mining, and public utilities. The Federal Reserve computes capacity utilization by expressing a sector's output of goods as a percentage of the estimated "normal capacity" of each sector to produce goods. The information on output comes from the Federal Reserve's data on industrial production. From January 1948 to March 2006, the average of the overall capacity utilization rate was 82%, with a range from 71% to 92%.

The blue graph in Figure 9.6 shows the deviation of the capacity utilization rate from its trend (using the method shown in Figure 8.2 to construct the trend). The red graph is again the deviation of real GDP from its trend. Note that the capacity utilization rate is clearly procyclical.[3] The rate is above trend in booms and below trend in recessions. Thus, the model's prediction about the cyclical behavior of the capital utilization rate matches up with the Federal Reserve's data on capacity utilization rates.

The Labor Force, Employment, and Unemployment

 e now explore how observed fluctuations in labor input, L, relate to variations in the labor force, employment, and hours worked per worker. First we look at empirical patterns in the U.S. data. Then we will extend our equilibrium business-cycle model to explain some puzzles, especially the fluctuations in the employment rate.

---

[3] From 1954.1 to 2006.1, the correlation of the cyclical part of the capacity utilization rate with the cyclical part of real GDP was 0.90.

Figure 9.6 *Cyclical Behavior of U.S. Real GDP and Capacity Utilization*

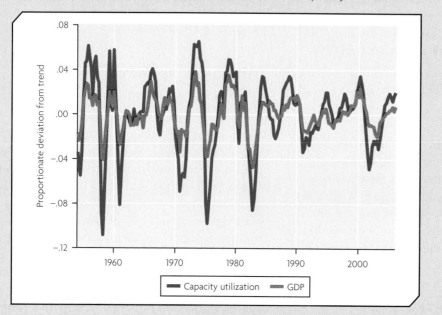

The red graph is the deviation of real GDP from its trend. The blue graph is the deviation of the capacity utilization rate from its trend. These data are based on industrial production and apply to manufacturing from 1948 to 1966, and to a broader index that includes mining and public utilities since 1967. The data on real GDP and capacity utilization are quarterly and seasonally adjusted. (The underlying data on capacity utilization are monthly.) The capacity utilization rate is procyclical—it fluctuates closely with real GDP but is more variable than real GDP.

Basic Concepts and Empirical Patterns

The U.S. data show that labor input, L, is procyclical; that is, it moves during economic fluctuations in the same direction as real GDP. For example, in Figure 8.13, we measured L by total hours worked per year. This concept of L is strongly procyclical—from 1964 to 2006, the correlation of the cyclical part of total hours worked with the cyclical part of real GDP was 0.88.

In Chapter 8, we allowed L to change by introducing variable labor supply. To get the right cyclical pattern, we relied on a positive response of the quantity of labor supplied, L^s, to the real wage rate, w/P. A high w/P in economic booms motivated households to raise L^s, and this response allowed L to expand.

Our analysis did not specify whether the changes in L resulted from shifts in the labor force, from changes in the employment rate, or from changes in hours worked per worker. Suppose, for now, that we continue to neglect variations in hours worked per worker, so that each job comes with a standard number of hours worked per year. Changes in total hours worked then reflect only changes in employment—the number of persons with jobs. In this environment, the quantity

of labor supplied, L^s, is the number of persons who offer themselves for work, given the real wage rate, w/P. This concept of labor supply fits with the BLS measure of the civilian labor force—the sum of persons with jobs plus persons self-described as looking for work. We can think of the quantity of labor demanded, L^d, as the number of jobs that employers want filled, given w/P.

In a market-clearing setting, the real wage rate, w/P, is determined, as usual, to equate the quantity of labor supplied, L^s, to the quantity demanded, L^d. Thus, the market-clearing employment, L, equals the labor force, L^s, and also equals the number of jobs that employers want filled, L^d. The real world departs from this environment in two major respects. First, the labor force is always greater than employment, and the difference between the two equals the number of persons unemployed.

Second, the number of jobs that employers want filled is always greater than employment, and the difference between these two equals the number of job **vacancies.**

One important variable from the supply side of the labor market is the *unemployment rate,* which equals the ratio of the number of persons unemployed to the labor force. Conversely, the **employment rate** is the ratio of the number of persons employed to the labor force.[4] If we let u be the unemployment rate, we have

u = number unemployed/labor force
= (labor force − number employed)/labor force
= 1 − (number employed/labor force)
= 1 − employment rate

Thus, if we rearrange terms, we get

$$employment\ rate = 1 - u$$

On the demand side of the labor market, the **vacancy rate** is the ratio of the number of job vacancies to the total number of jobs that employers want occupied. The employment rate from the employer perspective is the ratio of employment to the total number of jobs that employers want occupied. One reason that this side of the market is less emphasized is that data on job vacancies are not as accurate as data on unemployment. Typically, economists have relied on incomplete information on **help-wanted advertising** in newspapers. Recently, however, the BLS has improved its measures of job vacancies.

From the labor-supply side, we can think of employment as determined by:

employment = labor force •
(employment/
labor force)
= labor force •
employment rate
= labor force •
(1 − u)

Our previous analysis assumed that the unemployment rate, u, was zero, so that variations in

employment coincided with variations in the labor force. Now, changes in employment can also reflect changes in u.

We saw in Figure 8.13 that employment is nearly as variable as real GDP—from 1954 to 2006, the standard deviations of the cyclical parts were 1.3% for employment and 1.6% for real GDP. In addition, these cyclical parts were strongly positively correlated—the correlation was 0.81—so that employment is clearly procyclical.

Figures 9.7 and 9.8 show how the two variables that determine employment—the labor force and the employment rate, 1 − u—contribute to the variations in U.S. employment from 1954 to 2006.[5] Figure 9.7 shows that the labor force is relatively stable—from 1954 to 2006, the standard deviation of the cyclical part was 0.4%. Moreover, the correlation with the cyclical part of real GDP was only 0.31. In contrast, the employment rate shown in Figure 9.8 is more variable—the standard deviation of the cyclical part was 0.7%—and much more correlated with the cyclical part of real GDP— this correlation was 0.88. Thus, the procyclical variations in employment have more to do with changes in

Figure 9.7 *Cyclical Behavior of U.S. Real GDP and the Labor Force*

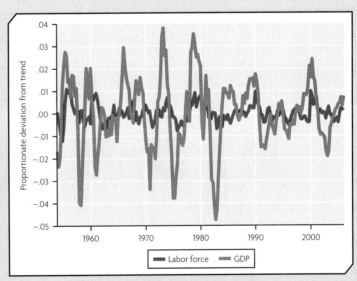

The red graph is the deviation of real GDP from its trend. The blue graph is the deviation of the civilian labor force from its trend. The civilian labor force—the number of persons employed or seeking employment—comes from the BLS Household Survey (www.bls.gov). The data on real GDP and the labor force are quarterly and seasonally adjusted. (The underlying data on the labor force are monthly.) The labor force is weakly procyclical—it fluctuates weakly with real GDP and is less variable than real GDP.

---

[4] The BLS instead defines the employment-population ratio to be the ratio of civilian employment to the civilian noninstitutional population, which is the population aged 16 and over that is not in an institution, such as a prison or mental hospital, or on active duty in the military.

[5] One problem is that the data on the labor force and the employment rate, shown in Figures 9.7 and 9.8, are from the BLS survey of households, whereas the employment numbers in Figure 8.13 are from the BLS survey of establishments (firms). (See www.bls.gov.) However, this discrepancy does not affect our main conclusions.

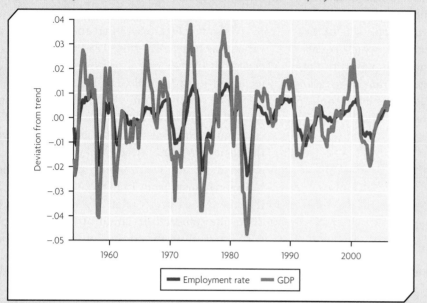

Figure 9.8 *Cyclical Behavior of U.S. Real GDP and the Employment Rate*

The red graph is the deviation of real GDP from its trend (in a proportionate sense). The blue graph is the deviation of the employment rate from its trend. The employment rate is the ratio of the number employed to the labor force. The measures of employment and labor force come from the BLS Household Survey (www.bls.gov). The data on real GDP and the employment rate are quarterly and seasonally adjusted. (The underlying data on the employment rate are monthly.) The employment rate is strongly procyclical—it fluctuates in the same direction as real GDP.

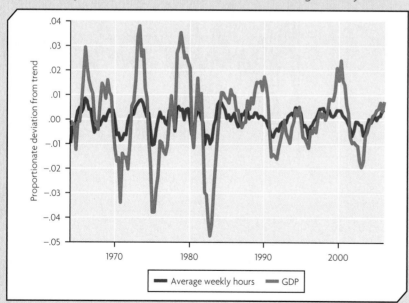

Figure 9.9 *Cyclical Behavior of U.S. Real GDP and Average Weekly Hours*

The red graph is the deviation of real GDP from its trend. The blue graph is the deviation of average weekly hours worked from its trend. The data for weekly hours come from the BLS payroll survey (www.bls.gov) and refer to the private, nonagricultural economy. The data on real GDP and weekly hours are quarterly and seasonally adjusted. (The underlying data on weekly hours are monthly.) Average weekly hours are procyclical—they fluctuate with real GDP but are less variable than real GDP.

the employment rate than with changes in the labor force. This finding means that our previous analysis—which focused on fluctuations in the labor force (a proxy for labor supply)—is missing something important.

We can also allow for variations in hours worked per worker. We can write

total hours worked = employment • (hours worked per worker)

We saw in Figure 8.14 that total hours worked is nearly as variable as real GDP—from 1964 to 2006, the standard deviation of the cyclical part was 1.5%, compared to 1.6% for real GDP. Total hours worked is also highly correlated with real GDP—the correlation between the cyclical parts was 0.88. Thus, total hours worked are more procyclical than employment.

Figures 9.7 and 9.8 considered the two variables that determine employment: the labor force and the employment rate. Figure 9.9 shows the additional variable, hours worked per worker, that determines total hours worked. From 1964 to 2006, the standard deviation of the cyclical part of hours worked per worker was 0.4%, and the correlation with the cyclical part of real GDP was 0.74. Thus, from the standpoint of accounting for the overall fluctuations of total hours worked, hours worked per worker is less important than the employment rate and more important than the labor force.

Our equilibrium business-cycle model from Chapter 8 is probably satisfactory for understanding fluctuations in the labor force and hours worked per worker. In these cases, we can think of the real wage rate, w/P, as adjusting to equate the quantity of labor supplied, L^s, to the quantity demanded, L^d. However, this approach leaves unexplained the most important factor—the fluctuations in the employment rate or, equivalently, in the unemployment rate.

To explain unemployment and vacancies, we have to introduce some "friction" into the workings of the labor market. That is, we have to explain why persons in the labor force who lack jobs take some time to find them, and why businesses with unfilled jobs take some time to fill them. Thus, the key to unemployment and vacancies is the process of persons searching for jobs and businesses searching for workers.

In our previous discussions of the labor market, we simplified by treating all workers and jobs as identical. However, in this world, the search process among workers and businesses would be trivial. Thus, for the analysis to be realistic, we have to allow for differences among workers and jobs. Then we can think of the labor market as operating to find good matches between jobs and workers. Because jobs and workers differ, this matching process is difficult and time consuming; unemployment and vacancies arise as parts of this process.

The next section extends our equilibrium business-cycle model to include a simple model of job matching. This extension has two main objectives. First, we want to explain why the levels of unemployment and vacancies are greater than zero. Second, we want to understand how unemployment and vacancies vary over time—in particular, why the employment rate is procyclical and the unemployment rate is countercyclical.

A Model of Job Finding

Consider a person, call her Hillary, who has just entered the labor force and is not yet employed. Hillary might be a student who just graduated from school or just reentered the labor force after raising a family. Suppose that Hillary searches for a position by visiting firms. Each firm interviews job candidates to assess their likely qualifications for a position. As a result of each inspection, the firm estimates the value of a candidate's potential marginal product, MPL. To keep things simple, assume that the firm offers Hillary a job with a real wage rate, w/P, equal to the estimated marginal product. We assume, only for simplicity, that each job entails a standard number of hours worked per week. In this case, w/P determines the real income received while employed (equal to the product of w/P and the number of hours worked per week).

Hillary decides whether to accept the job at the offered real wage rate, w/P. The alternative is to remain unemployed and continue to search. We assume that it does not pay to accept a job and nevertheless keep searching. This assumption is reasonable because the costs of getting set up in a new job usually make it undesirable to take positions with short expected durations. Furthermore, it is likely to be easier to search for jobs while unemployed.

More search pays off if a subsequent wage offer exceeds the initial one. One cost of rejecting an offer is the income foregone while not working. This income must, however, be balanced against any income that people receive because they are unemployed. We denote by ω (the Greek letter omega) the effective real income while unemployed. The amount ω includes **unemployment insurance** payments from the government and any value that Hillary attaches to time spent not working, rather than on the job.

In evaluating an offer, the first consideration is how it compares with others that may be available. In making this comparison, Hillary has in mind a distribution of likely wage offers, given her education, experience, and so on. We are assuming that the attractiveness of a job depends only on the real wage rate. The main results would not change if we extended the model to take into account the work location and working conditions.

Figure 9.10 shows a typical shape for the distribution of wage offers. For each real wage rate, w/P, on the horizontal axis, the value on the vertical axis shows the probability of receiving that offer. For the curve shown, offers usually fall in a middle range of w/P. There is, however, a small chance of getting a very high offer (in the right tail of the distribution) or one near zero.

Figure 9.10 shows the value , which is the effective real income received while unemployed. We know that Hillary would reject any offer that paid less than ω. For the case in the graph, ω lies toward the left end of the distribution of wage offers. This construction implies that most—but not all—offers exceed ω. Given the position of ω, Hillary's key decision is whether to accept a real wage, w/P, when it is greater than ω.

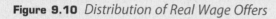

Figure 9.10 *Distribution of Real Wage Offers*

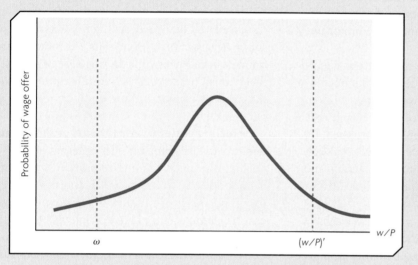

The curve shows the chances of receiving offers of real wages, *w/P*, of different sizes. The higher the curve, the more likely that real wage offers of that size will be received. On the horizontal axis, *ω* is the effective real income received while unemployed, and (*w/P*)' is the reservation real wage. Job offers are accepted if they pay at least as much as (*w/P*)', and are otherwise rejected.

She may refuse a real wage rate, *w/P*, that exceeds *ω* to preserve her chance of getting a still better offer. However, there is a trade-off, because she then foregoes real income while not working. The balancing of these forces generates what economists call a **reservation real wage**, denoted by (*w/P*)'. Offers below (*w/P*)' are rejected, and those above (*w/P*)' are accepted. If Hillary sets a high value of (*w/P*)', she will probably spend a long time unemployed and seeking work. Conversely, a low (*w/P*)' means that the time spent unemployed will usually be brief. However, a low (*w/P*)' also means that Hillary will likely end up in a job with a low (*w/P*)'.

The optimal reservation real wage, (*w/P*)', depends on the shape of the wage-offer distribution in Figure 9.10, as well as the effective real income while unemployed, and the expected duration of a job.[6] For our purposes, we do not have to go through the details of the determination of the optimal (*w/P*)'. We can get the main results by describing the important properties that come out of this analysis.

Since some job offers are unacceptable—that is, *w/P* < (*w/P*)' for some offers—it typically takes time for Hillary to find an acceptable position. In the interim, she is "unemployed," although engaged in a job search.

Thus, incomplete information about where to find the best job can explain why unemployment is greater than zero.

An increase in the effective real income while unemployed, *ω*, motivates Hillary to raise her standards for job acceptance; that is, (*w/P*)' increases. This effect is particularly strong if Hillary's likely offers of real wages, *w/P*, are not much above *ω*. For example, an increase in *ω* caused by a rise in unemployment insurance benefits will have a strong impact on (*w/P*)' if the benefits are high compared to usual wage offers. In the United States, where unemployment insurance benefits are not so high, a small increase in benefits would not have a major effect on (*w/P*)' for the typical job seeker. In contrast, in countries such as France and Germany, which have very generous unemployment insurance programs, a rise in benefits would have a much greater impact on the typical (*w/P*)'.

For a given distribution of wage offers in Figure 9.10, an increase in *ω* makes it more likely that *w/P* < (*w/P*)' will apply, because (*w/P*)' increases. Hence, job offers will be rejected more often. It follows that job searchers, such as Hillary, tend to take longer to find a position when *ω* increases. For a group of persons, we therefore predict that a rise in *ω* reduces the **job-finding rate**, which is the rate at which job seekers find positions. Correspondingly, a rise in *ω* raises the expected **duration of unemployment**, which is the amount of time that the typical unemployed person stays unemployed.

Suppose that the entire distribution of wage offers improves. For example, a favorable shock to the technology level, *A*, could raise the MPL of all workers—say, by 10%. Since each real wage offer, *w/P*, equals the value of a worker's potential marginal product, the distribution

---

[6] For a discussion of job search models that involve a reservation wage, see Belton Fleisher and Thomas Kniesner (1984, pp. 477–507).

of real wage offers in Figure 9.10 shifts to the right—the typical real wage offer, w/P, rises by 10%. Therefore, if the reservation real wage, $(w/P)'$, does not change, job offers fall more often in the acceptable range, where $w/P > (w/P)'$. Hence, the job-finding rate rises, and the expected duration of unemployment falls.

We have to consider, however, that a better distribution of wage offers tends to raise the reservation real wage, $(w/P)'$. Job seekers, such as Hillary, become more selective—raise $(w/P)'$—if they anticipate that the better distribution of real wage offers will persist into the future. For example, a permanent improvement in technology would tend to have a long-run impact on real wage offers. In this case, $(w/P)'$ would rise. The increase in $(w/P)'$ works against our predicted rise in the job-finding rate. In the example where all real wage offers, w/P, increase by 10%, the job-finding rate will rise only if the increase in $(w/P)'$ is by less than 10%.

There are two reasons why the increase in the reservation real wage, $(w/P)'$, tends to be smaller in proportion than the rise in the typical real wage offer, w/P. First, if the rise in workers' MPL is not permanent, future real wage offers will tend to rise by less than current offers. In this case, $(w/P)'$ will also rise proportionately less than the typical real wage, w/P, offered currently to job searchers.

Second, even if the improvement in real wage offers is permanent, $(w/P)'$ will rise proportionately by less than the typical real wage offer, w/P, if the effective real income received while unemployed, ω, does not change. To see why, we can compare three scenarios, as follows.

- Scenario 1 is the initial situation, where offers of real wage rates, w/P, are given by the distribution in Figure 9.10, and the effective real income received while unemployed is ω.
- Scenario 2 is the new situation, where the typical real wage offer, w/P is permanently higher by 10%, and ω is unchanged.
- Scenario 3 is a hypothetical situation, where the typical real wage offer, w/P, is permanently higher by 10%, and ω is also permanently higher by 10%.

Compare Scenario 1 with Scenario 3: The only difference is that everything is scaled upward by 10% in Scenario 3. Therefore, in weighing the trade-off between accepting or rejecting a job offer, it seems reasonable (and is, in fact, optimal) that a person would set the reservation real wage, $(w/P)'$, higher by 10% in Scenario 3. Therefore, the probability of receiving an acceptable job offer is the same in Scenario 3 as in Scenario 1. Hence, the job-finding rate is the same in these two cases.

Now compare Scenario 3 with Scenario 2. The only difference is that the real income received while unemployed, ω, is higher by 10% in Scenario 3. Therefore, a job seeker would set the reservation real wage, $(w/P)'$, higher in Scenario 3 than in Scenario 2, and the job-finding rate is lower in Scenario 3 than in Scenario 2.

Now put the results together. Scenario 3 has the same job-finding rate as Scenario 1. Scenario 2 has a higher job-finding rate than Scenario 3. We have therefore shown that the job-finding rate is higher in Scenario 2 than in Scenario 1. Thus, as claimed, a permanent improvement in real wage offers, w/P, raises the job-finding rate if the real income while unemployed, ω, does not change.

In our model, the increase in real wage offers could come from an improvement in the technology level, A. However, in a richer model, technological change might make some skills obsolete. For example, electric lights made worthless the value of the output of lamplighters, and the automobile lowered the value of the output of blacksmiths. Therefore, technological change can reduce the value of the MPL—and, hence, the real wage offered—for workers with obsolete skills. Nevertheless, it is still reasonable for the economy as a whole that an improvement in technology would raise the value of the MPL and, therefore, the real wage offered to the typical job seeker.

Search by Firms

Thus far, we have taken an unrealistic view of how firms participate in the job-search process. Firms received applications, evaluated candidates in terms of the likely value of their MPL, and then expressed real wage offers, w/P, that equaled these marginal products. This model does not allow firms to utilize their information about the characteristics of jobs, the traits of workers who tend to be productive on these jobs, and the real wages that typically have to be paid for such workers. Firms would communicate this information by advertising job openings that specify ranges of requirements for education, work experience, and so on, and also indicate a salary range. Such advertisements appropriately screen out most potential applicants and generate more rapid and better matches of workers to jobs.

Although search by firms is important in a well-functioning labor market, the allowance for this search does not change our major conclusions. In particular,

- It still takes time for workers to match with jobs, so that the expected durations of unemployment and vacancies are greater than zero.

- An increase in workers' effective real incomes while unemployed, ω, lowers the job-finding rate and raises the expected duration of unemployment.

- A favorable shock to productivity raises the job-finding rate and lowers the expected duration of unemployment.

Job Separations

Workers search for jobs that offer high real wages, and employers search for workers with high productivity. Although workers and firms evaluate each other as efficiently as possible, they often find out later that they made mistakes. An employer may learn that a worker is less productive than anticipated, or a worker may discover that he or she dislikes the job. When a job match looks significantly poorer than it did initially, firms are motivated to discharge the worker, or the worker is motivated to quit.

Separations arise because of changed circumstances, even when firms and workers accurately assessed each other at the outset. For example, an adverse shock to a firm's production function may lower a worker's MPL and lead to a discharge. If we distinguish the goods produced by different firms, we get a similar effect from a decline in the demand for a firm's goods. That is, the value of a worker's MPL would fall if the real value attached to each unit of output declined. For example, a blacksmith's physical marginal product might not change, but the automobile lowered the value attached to fitting a horse with a shoe.

Workers also experience changed circumstances— for example, in family status, schooling, location, and retirement, as well as alternative job prospects. Some of these shifts are surprises, whereas others are predictable. The important point is that these changes can induce workers to quit jobs.

The tendency for a job match to break up is sensitive to how good the match was at the outset. If the match was borderline, small changes in production conditions or worker circumstances are sufficient to make the match mutually unattractive.

Separations also occur because jobs were known to be temporary at the outset. Examples include seasonal workers in agriculture or at sports stadiums, or working for the Internal Revenue Service (which has high demand near April of each year).

We conclude that job separations take place for a variety of reasons. For a group of workers, we can identify determinants of the **job-separation rate**, the rate at which job matches dissolve. This rate is high, for example, among inexperienced workers who are hard to evaluate or among young persons who are likely to experience changes in family size or job preferences. The separation rate is also high in industries that are subject to frequent shocks to technology or product demand.

If there were no job separations, no new persons entering the labor force, and no new jobs, the search process would eventually eliminate unemployment and vacancies. But separations, new job seekers, and new positions mean that the finding of jobs is continually offset by the creation of new unemployment and vacancies. We will now illustrate this process with a simple example.

Job Separations, Job Finding, and the Natural Unemployment Rate

In Figure 9.11, the square labeled L denotes the number of persons employed, and the square labeled U shows the number unemployed. To simplify, assume that the labor force, $L + U$, does not change over time. To understand economic fluctuations,

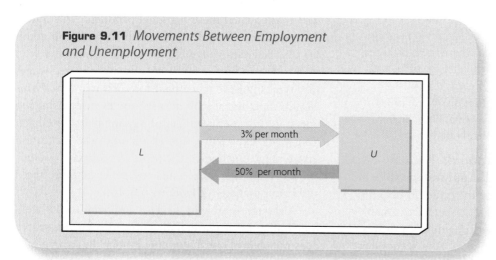

Figure 9.11 *Movements Between Employment and Unemployment*

In this example, 3% of those employed, L, lose their jobs each month, and 50% of those unemployed, U, find jobs. The net change in employment, ΔL, is $0.5\ U - 0.03 \bullet L$. The change in unemployment, ΔU, is the negative of ΔL.

the assumption of a constant labor force may be satisfactory because, empirically, variations in the labor force are a small part of short-run changes in labor input.

Some fraction of employed persons experiences a job separation each period—say, a month. In Figure 9.11, the arrow from L to U represents the number of job separations per month. Since the labor force is constant, all those who lose jobs move from category L to category U. We are ignoring the fact that many job losers find new jobs immediately, without ever becoming unemployed.

Since December 2000, the BLS has carried out the Job Openings and Labor Turnover Survey (JOLTS), which estimates the job-separation rate for the total nonfarm economy. This rate is the ratio of total job separations over a month to civilian employment. From December 2000 to February 2006, the separation rate averaged 3.1% per month, and the average number of monthly separations was 4.32 million. This number is staggering—the U.S. job market has an enormous flow of persons out of jobs (and, as we shall see, also into jobs).

Figure 9.12 shows how the job-separation rate varied from December 2000 to February 2006. Note that late 2000 was the end of a boom period (see Figure 8.3). The red graph in Figure 9.12 shows that the unemployment rate rose from 3.9% in December 2000 to a peak of 6.3% in June 2003. Then the economy recovered, and the unemployment rate fell to 4.7% in March 2006.

The blue graph in Figure 9.12 shows that the job-separation rate did not vary much from December 2000 to February 2006—only between 2.8% and

Figure 9.12 *Job-Separation Rate and the Unemployment Rate December 2000–February 2006*

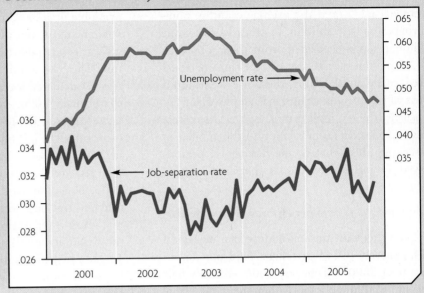

The graph covers the period of data availability for the Job Openings and Labor Turnover Survey (JOLTS) from the BLS (www.bls.gov). The blue graph and the left scale are for the job-separation rate, calculated as the ratio of monthly total job separations to the number of persons employed. The red graph and the right scale are for the unemployment rate.

3.5% per month. In particular, the job-separation rate changed little during the recession of 2001–02 and the strong economy of 2003–06. Thus, these data—though available only for a few years—suggest that the job-separation rate may not have a strong association with recessions and booms.[7]

The other part of the story is the rate at which people find jobs. In Figure 9.11, the arrow pointing from U to L represents the number of unemployed persons who find jobs during a month. We are again not being completely realistic, because we are ignoring movements out of and into the labor force. Some of the unemployed, U, may become discouraged about job prospects during a recession and therefore drop out of the labor force. This phenomenon is called **discouraged workers**. However, we are also neglecting opposing forces that motivate people to intensify job search during a recession. For example, if a person loses his or her job, the person's spouse might enter the labor force. As already mentioned, we know that variations in the labor force are a small part of short-run fluctuations in labor input. Therefore, the assumption of a constant labor force may be a satisfactory approximation.

---

[7] For a discussion of this behavior of the job-separation rate, see Robert Hall (2005).

We can use the BLS survey, JOLTS, to gauge the job-finding rate. From December 2000 to February 2006, the ratio of job hirings over a month to civilian employment averaged 3.2%, and the average monthly number of hirings was 4.45 million. In other words, while 4.32 million persons separated from their jobs each month, 4.45 million (not necessarily the same persons) were hired each month. Thus, there are tremendous gross flows of persons out of and into employment.

To measure the job-finding rate, we have to express the number of jobs found in relation to the number of persons seeking jobs—that is, the number of persons unemployed, U, rather than the number employed, L. Thus, we have

$job - finding\ rate = (number\ of\ hires\ per\ month)/U$

When defined this way, the job-finding rate measured by the BLS survey, JOLTS, averaged 0.58 per month from December 2000 to February 2006—roughly half of the unemployed found a job within one month. This number overstates the job-finding rate for the unemployed, because many job hires come from people who moved from one job to another (without becoming unemployed) and some came from people outside of the labor force (who were never recorded as unemployed). If we could adjust the number of hires per month to include only hirings that come from the unemployed,

we would calculate a smaller job-finding rate. However, we lack the data to make this adjustment.

Although the job-finding rate estimated from the available data likely overstates the level of the rate, the movements in the estimated rate over time probably give a good indication of changes in the job-finding rate. The blue graph in Figure 9.13 shows the pattern of the calculated job-finding rate from December 2000 to February 2006. By comparing with the red graph, we see that the job-finding rate mirrored the unemployment rate. The job-finding rate fell from a peak of 0.90 in December 2000 to a low point of 0.44 in spring 2003, then recovered along with the economy to 0.70 in early 2006. Thus, the data show clearly that the job-finding rate falls during a recession and rises in a boom.

The job-separation and job-finding rates determine the dynamics of persons employed and unemployed. To get a realistic example, we will use numbers for the job-separation and job-finding rates that mirror the U.S. data. Specifically, assume that the job-separation rate is 0.03 per month and the job-finding rate is 0.5 per month, as shown in Figure 9.11. We assume, for now, that these rates are constant. This assumption may be satisfactory for the job-separation rate but not for the job-finding rate, which tends to fall below average during a recession and rise above average during a boom.

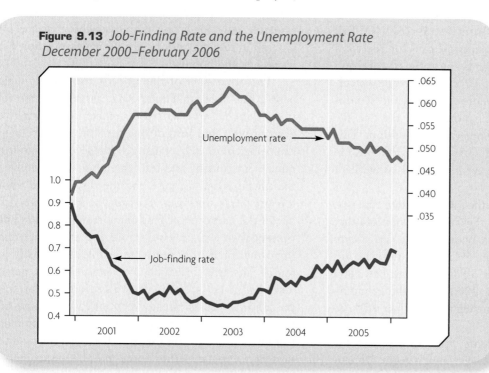

Figure 9.13 *Job-Finding Rate and the Unemployment Rate December 2000–February 2006*

The graph covers the period of data availability for the Job Openings and Labor Turnover Survey (JOLTS) from the BLS (www.bls.gov). The blue graph and the left scale are for the job-finding rate, calculated as the ratio of monthly job hires to the number of persons unemployed. The red graph and the right scale are for the unemployment rate.

Table 9.1 assumes that the labor force is fixed at 150 million people (roughly the U.S. number in 2006). Suppose that the economy starts in month 1 with an unemployment rate, u, of 10%, indicating a serious recession. Employment, L, starts at 135 million, and unemployment, U, starts at 15 million.

We can work through the process of job separation and finding to determine the time paths of employment and unemployment. In

Table 9.1 *Dynamics of Employment and Unemployment*

	Start of Month			During Month			
Month	Number Employed (L) (millions)	Number Unemployed (U) (millions)	Unemployment Rate (U)	Number Who Lose Jobs (millions)	Number Who Find Jobs (millions)	Change in L(ΔL) (millions)	Change in U(ΔU) (millions)
1	135.0	15.0	0.100	4.0	7.5	3.5	−3.5
2	138.5	11.5	0.077	4.2	5.8	1.6	−1.6
3	140.1	9.9	0.066	4.2	5.0	0.8	−0.8
4	140.9	9.1	0.061	4.2	4.6	0.4	−0.4
5	141.3	8.7	0.058	4.2	4.4	0.2	−0.2
6	141.5	8.5	0.057	4.2	4.2	0.0	0.0
8	141.5	8.5	0.057	4.2	4.2	0.0	0.0

Note: This example assumes that the economy starts with 135 million people employed, L, and 15 million unemployed, U. The labor force, $L + U$, is fixed at 150 million. The unemployment rate is $u = U/(L + U) = U/150$. As in Figure 9.11, 3% of those employed lose jobs each month, and 50% of those unemployed find jobs. The net change in employment, ΔL, is $0.5 \cdot U - 0.03 \cdot L$. The net change in unemployment, ΔU, is the negative of ΔL. When L reaches 141.5 million and U reaches 8.5 million, ΔL and ΔU equal zero. Thus, the natural unemployment rate is $u^n = 8.5/150 = 5.7\%$.

the first month, 3% of the 135.0 million employed—4.0 million persons—lose their jobs. At the same time, 50% of the 15.0 unemployed—7.5 million persons—find jobs. Hence, the net increase in employment during the month is 3.5 million—an enormous number that is not realistic. Correspondingly, unemployment falls by 3.5 million, and the unemployment rate declines to 7.7%.

As the number employed rises, job separations increase, but only slightly—to 4.2 million in the second month. As the number unemployed falls, job findings fall—to 5.8 million in the second month. Therefore, in month 2, employment rises on net by 1.6 million, and unemployment falls by 1.6 million. The unemployment rate is now down to 6.6%.

This process continues until the numbers of job separations and findings are the same. In our example, the economy gets close to this balance in month 6—when employment reaches 141.5 million and unemployment equals 8.5 million. The corresponding unemployment rate is 5.7%. Therefore, the **natural unemployment rate** is 5.7%. By natural, we mean that the economy tends toward this value automatically, given the rates at which people lose and find jobs.

This model, although not fully realistic, brings out some important points about the unemployment rate. First, although the unemployment rate eventually stays constant at the natural rate, there is still a large amount of job turnover. In the model (and the U.S. data), about 4 million people lose and find jobs each month when the unemployment rate equals its natural value of 5.7%. These large flows out of and into jobs are a normal part of the operation of the fluid U.S. labor market.

Second, the keys to the dynamics of employment and unemployment are the rates of job separation and finding. In our example, we assumed that these rates were fixed at 3% and 50%, respectively. Our earlier discussion suggested that these rates would depend on characteristics of workers and jobs. For example, we discussed effects from a person's age and job experience, from the effective real income while unemployed, ω, and from the variability of an industry's supply and demand conditions. The rates of job separation and finding depend also on shifts to economy-wide productivity, for example, shocks to the technology level, A.

We now generalize the model to bring out the roles of the job-separation and job-finding rates. Let σ (the Greek letter sigma) be the job-separation rate and φ (the Greek letter phi) the job-finding rate. The change in the number of persons employed over a month, ΔL, is given by

(9.6)
$$\Delta L = \varphi U - \sigma L$$
$$= job\ findings - job\ separations$$

The first term, φU, is the number of unemployed persons who find jobs over a month, and the second term, σL, is the number of employed persons who lose jobs over a month. (We assume that a person who finds a job stays employed for at least a month, and that a person who loses a job takes at least a month to find a new one.)

Equation (9.6) implies that employment, L, increases and unemployment, U, decreases if job findings, φU, are greater than job separations, σL. In the reverse case, L decreases and U increases. To determine the long-run levels of L and U, we have to find the situation where L and U are constant. This constancy requires $\Delta L = 0$, and equation (9.6) says that $\Delta L = 0$ when job findings equal job separations:

$$\varphi U = \sigma L$$

job findings = job separations

To find the long-run L and U, we use our assumption that the labor force, $L + U$, is constant at 150 million. Hence, we can substitute $L = 150 - U$ in the last equation to get

$$\varphi U = \sigma \bullet (150 - U)$$

If we combine the terms involving U and put them on the left-hand side, we get

$$U \bullet (\varphi + \sigma) = 150 \bullet \sigma$$

Therefore, the long-run number unemployed is given by

$$U = 150 \bullet \sigma/(\varphi + \sigma)$$

The natural unemployment rate, $u^n = U/150$, is therefore

> Key equation (natural unemployment rate):
>
> **(9.7)** $\qquad u^n = \sigma/(\varphi + \sigma)$

Equation (9.7) shows that a higher job-separation, σ, raises the natural unemployment rate, u^n, whereas a higher job-finding rate, φ, lowers u^n.[8] For example, an increase in the effective real income while unemployed, ω, lowers φ, and thereby raises u^n. Thus, more generous unemployment insurance programs increase the long-run unemployment rate. The Internet assists in the process of job matching and, thereby, likely raises φ. Hence, the Internet would lower u^n.

Economic Fluctuations, Employment, and Unemployment

We now combine the model of job search with our equilibrium business-cycle model to see how employment and unemployment behave during recessions and booms. Assume, as usual, that economic fluctuations result from shocks to the technology level, A. Suppose, as in Table 9.1, that the labor force is fixed at 150 million; the job-separation rate, σ, is 0.03 per month; and the job-finding rate, φ, is 0.50 per month. Employment, L, starts at 141.5 million; unemployment, U, at 8.5 million; and the unemployment rate, u, at 5.7%.

Suppose that an adverse shock to the technology level, A, reduces the marginal product of labor for the typical worker and job. The job-finding rate, φ, falls because market opportunities became poorer—probably temporarily—relative to the real income received while unemployed, ω. Figure 9.13 suggests that the decline in the job-finding rate during a recession is quantitatively important. We assume, for an example, that φ falls from 0.50 per month to 0.40.

Figure 9.12 shows that the job-separation rate, σ, did not change a lot as the economy moved from boom to recession to recovery. Therefore, we assume that σ stays fixed at 0.03 per month.

Table 9.2 shows that the drop in the job-finding rate, φ, causes employment, L, to fall gradually and unemployment, U, to rise gradually. In month 1, job finding falls to 3.4 million—still a large number, but more than offset by the 4.2 million job loss. Hence, L falls during the month by 0.8 million, and U expands accordingly. This process continues through month 5, when the cumulative fall in employment is 1.8 million, and the unemployment rate, u, reaches 6.9%.

Table 9.2 assumes that the job-finding rate, φ, returns to its normal value, 0.50, in month 5. In response, employment, L, and unemployment, U, return gradually to their long-run values. Since φ and σ now take on the values assumed in Table 9.1, the economy approaches the long-run position where $L = 141.5$ million and $U = 8.5$ million. By month 9, L and U are close to their long-run values, and the unemployment rate, u, is near the natural rate, 5.7%.

---

[8] For analyses of this type of model, see Robert Hall (1979), Chitra Ramaswami (1983), and Michael Darby, John Haltiwanger, and Mark Plant (1985).

Table 9.2 *Dynamics of Employment and Unemployment During a Recession*

	Start of Month			During Month			
Month	Number Employed (L) (millions)	Number Unemployed (U) (millions)	Unemployment Rate (u)	Job-finding Rate (φ) (monthly)	Number Who Lose Jobs (millions)	Number Who Find Jobs (millions)	Change in L (ΔL) (millions)
1	141.5	8.5	0.057	0.40	4.2	3.4	−0.8
2	140.7	9.3	0.062	0.40	4.2	3.7	−0.5
3	140.2	9.8	0.065	0.40	4.2	3.9	−0.3
4	139.9	10.1	0.067	0.40	4.2	4.0	−0.2
5	139.7	10.3	0.069	0.50	4.2	5.2	1.0
6	140.7	9.3	0.062	0.50	4.2	4.6	0.4
7	141.1	8.9	0.059	0.50	4.2	4.4	0.2
8	141.3	8.7	0.058	0.50	4.2	4.4	0.2
9	141.5	8.5	0.057	0.50	4.2	4.2	0.0
8	141.5	8.5	0.057	0.50	4.2	4.2	0.0

Note: In this example, the labor force is fixed at 150 million. The economy starts from the long-run position of Table 9.1, with employment, *L*, of 141.5 million; unemployment, *U*, of 8.5 million; and an unemployment rate, *u*, of 5.7%. These values correspond to a job-separation rate, σ, of 0.03 per month and a job-finding rate, φ, of 0.50 per month. In month 1, the start of a recession is assumed to lower φ to 0.40 but to leave σ unchanged at 0.03. These values generate a gradual decline in *L* and a gradual rise in *U*. In month 5, we assume that φ returns to 0.50. This change generates a gradual return of *L* toward 141.5 million and of *U* toward 8.5 million.

Although the example in Table 9.2 is not fully realistic, it brings out several features of real-world recessions. First, the buildup of a recession involves a period of gradually falling employment and rising unemployment. Second, even after an economic recovery begins, it takes a while for employment and unemployment to return to their prerecession levels. Third, even during a recession, large numbers of jobs are created each month—they are just outnumbered by jobs lost.

Vacancies

We can extend the model to allow for job vacancies. Suppose that firms have some idea about potential workers in the sense of the value of their MPL. Firms also have a sense of the real wage rate, *w/P*, needed to induce the typical qualified applicant to accept a job. Finally, there are costs for posting job openings and interviewing applicants. Given these considerations, firms determine how many job openings to advertise.

For our purposes, we do not have to work through a detailed model of job openings. We can just note some important properties that emerge from such a model. One result is that an increase in the value of prospective marginal products, MPL, raises the number of job openings. A second result is that an increase in the real wage rate, *w/P*, required to get workers to accept jobs lowers the number of job openings. Finally, a reduction in costs of posting jobs and processing applications—caused, for example, by the rise of the Internet—raises the number of job openings.

Suppose that an increase in the technology level, *A*, raises the MPL. For given real wage rates, *w/P*, firms post more job openings. Therefore, job vacancies increase. Conversely, an unfavorable shock reduces vacancies. Thus, our prediction is that vacancies are procyclical—high in booms and low in recessions.

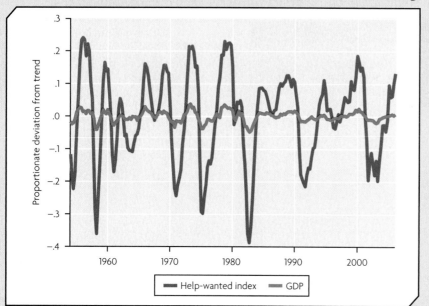

Figure 9.14 *Cyclical Behavior of U.S. Real GDP and Help-Wanted Advertising*

The red graph is the deviation of real GDP from its trend. The blue graph is the deviation of the help-wanted-advertising index from its trend. The data on help-wanted advertising in major newspapers come from the Conference Board. The data on real GDP and help-wanted advertising are quarterly and seasonally adjusted. (The underlying data on help-wanted advertising are monthly.) The help-wanted-advertising index is procyclical—it fluctuates with real GDP and is much more variable than real GDP.

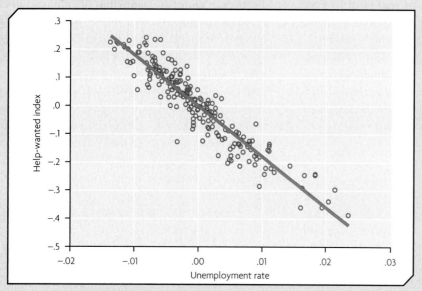

Figure 9.15 *The Unemployment Rate and Help-Wanted Advertising: A Beveridge Curve*

The horizontal axis is the deviation of the unemployment rate from its trend. This variable is the same, except for a minus sign, as the deviation of the employment rate from its trend, shown in Figure 9.8. The vertical axis is the proportionate deviation of the index of help-wanted advertising from its trend (from Figure 9.14). The plots use quarterly, seasonally adjusted data from 1954.1 to 2006.1. (The underlying data on both variables are monthly.)

As already mentioned, data on U.S. job vacancies have been inadequate until the introduction of the BLS survey, JOLTS, in December 2000. To fill this gap in the data, economists used as a proxy for job vacancies an index of help-wanted advertising in major newspapers.[9] This index has a number of shortcomings: It does not cover all job vacancies, is not representative of vacancies in the entire country, and the role of newspaper advertising in the job-search process has diminished over time (being replaced a good deal recently by the Internet). Despite these shortcomings, the cyclical part of the help-wanted advertising index is a useful proxy for fluctuations in job vacancies.

The blue graph in Figure 9.14 shows the cyclical part of the help-wanted index from 1954 to 2006. This variable is constructed by the method used for real GDP in Figure 8.3. The red graph is the cyclical part of real GDP. The main finding is that, as predicted, the help-wanted index is procyclical—the correlation with the cyclical part of real GDP was 0.91.

The procyclical pattern for vacancies (proxied by the

---

[9] This index is compiled by the Conference Board. For a discussion, see Katharine Abraham (1987).

help-wanted index) helps to explain why the job-finding rate is high in a boom and low in a recession. In our previous analysis, we argued that job seekers would be more likely to accept job offers in a boom because of the increase in the real wage rate, w/P. The increase in vacancies reinforces this response, because the greater availability of jobs makes it easier for workers to locate positions that look like good matches. Thus, in a boom, the rate of job acceptance increases partly because the wage offers are better and partly because good jobs are easier to find. Conversely, in a recession, the rate of job acceptance decreases because the pay is worse and attractive positions are harder to find.

We know, from Figure 9.8, that the employment rate is procyclical and, hence, that the unemployment rate is countercyclical. Thus, vacancies and unemployment move in opposite directions. Figure 9.15 describes this relation with a scatter plot for U.S. data from 1954 to 2006 between the cyclical parts of the unemployment rate and the help-wanted index. This plot is called a *Beveridge curve*, named after the British economist William Beveridge. For a discussion, see Robert Shimer (2003).

BACK TO REALITY

Seasonal Fluctuations

Our analysis views economic fluctuations as resulting from shocks to the technology level. Shocks other than technological changes, such as harvest failures and strikes, have effects that resemble those from changes in A. Seasonal changes also resemble shifts to the technology.

As noted in Chapter 2, economists usually use seasonally adjusted data to study economic fluctuations. The seasonal adjustment eliminates the normal change in a variable, such as real GDP, from winter (the first quarter) to spring (the second quarter), and so on. In the unadjusted data, real GDP tends to rise each year toward a peak in the fourth quarter. This systematic quarter-to-quarter pattern does not appear in the seasonally adjusted numbers.

Robert Barsky and Jeffrey Miron (1989) studied the seasonally unadjusted numbers. They found that the seasonal fluctuations in quantities—real GDP, consumption, investment, employment, and unemployment—are larger than the variations associated with typical recessions and booms. From 1948 to 1985, over 80% of the quarterly fluctuations in real GDP and over 60% of those in the unemployment rate reflected seasonal factors (Barsky and Miron, 1989, Table 1). Further, the seasonal patterns of co-movement among real GDP and its major components and between real GDP and employment look similar to those found in economic fluctuations (*ibid.*, Table 2). For example, in the seasonal pattern, investment and consumption move along with real GDP, and investment fluctuates much more than consumption. J. Joseph Beaulieu and Jeffrey Miron (1992) show that the U.S. findings apply also to 25 industrialized or semi-industrialized countries.

Seasonal fluctuations reflect influences of weather and holidays. We can think of some of these effects as variations in technology, such as the adverse impact of winter on the construction industry. Other effects correspond to variations in household preferences, such as the positive impact of Christmas on consumer demand and the negative impact of summer vacations on labor supply. The magnitude of the seasonal fluctuations shows that these kinds of disturbances can be quantitatively important in the short run. That is, the seasonal evidence weakens the argument made by some economists that shocks to technology and preferences are not large enough to account for the observed magnitude of recessions and booms.

The horizontal axis in Figure 9.15 shows the cyclical part of the unemployment rate, u. The vertical axis shows the cyclical part of the help-wanted advertising index. Note the clear downward slope—the correlation between the two series is -0.93. Thus, the data strongly confirm that a low unemployment rate matches up with high vacancies, whereas a high unemployment rate matches up with low vacancies.

Questions and Problems

A. Review questions

1. Explain how the quantity of capital services depends on the stock of capital, K, and the capital utilization rate, κ. Why is the rate of return on capital given by equation (9.4)?

2. Use Figure 9.4 to study the capital utilization rate, κ. How does κ change when

a. the real rental price, R/P, rises?

b. the depreciation rate, $\delta(\kappa)$, rises for each value of κ?

3. What is the definition of the unemployment rate? Since it does not include persons who are "out of the labor force," does it underestimate the true unemployment rate? Can you think of reasons why the reported numbers may overestimate the true unemployment rate?

4. Suppose that a job seeker receives a real wage offer, w/P, that exceeds his or her effective real income while unemployed, ω. Why might the person reject the offer?

5. Once a job seeker and a firm find a job match, why might they choose subsequently to end the match? List some influences on the job-separation rate.

6. What is the natural rate of unemployment, u^n? Why might the unemployment rate, u, differ from u^n? Can u^n change over time?

B. Problems for discussion

7. The job-finding rate
   Discuss the effects on the job-finding rate and the expected duration of unemployment from the following:

a. an increase in unemployment insurance benefits

b. an increase in the allowable duration of unemployment insurance benefits

c. a technological change, such as the Internet, that improves the matching of workers and jobs

8. The job-finding rate, the job-separation rate, and the dynamics of the unemployment rate
   Suppose that the labor force is fixed at 100 million people, of whom 92 million initially have jobs and 8 million are unemployed. Assume that the job-separation rate is 2% per month and the job-finding rate is 40% per month. Trace out the time paths of employment and unemployment. What is the natural unemployment rate?

9. Cyclical behavior of the labor force
   Figure 9.7 shows that the labor force is weakly procyclical. What pattern would you predict on theoretical grounds? (Hint: Think first about people's incentives to leave the labor force—that is, to stop looking for work—during a recession. Are there also incentives for people to enter the labor force during a recession?)

10. Job vacancies
    Suppose that economic fluctuations are caused by shocks to the technology level, A. What do you predict for the cyclical behavior of job vacancies? How then would fluctuations in vacancies relate to fluctuations in the unemployment rate? How does your answer relate to the Beveridge curve shown in Figure 9.15?

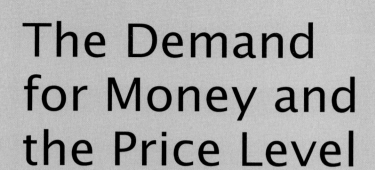

© Fotolia XII/Fotolia

The Demand for Money and the Price Level

O ur model has three forms of assets: money, bonds, and ownership of capital. So far, we have not analyzed how much money households hold or how these holdings change over time. We therefore carried out our analysis in Chapters 6 through 9 under the assumption that each household held a constant stock of money, M. Now we extend the microeconomic foundations of the model to explain why a household holds part of its assets as money; that is, we explain the **demand for money**. By demand for money, we refer to the quantity of money that a household decides to hold as a function of the price level, P, the interest rate, i, and other variables.

As mentioned in Chapter 6, we assume in the model that money is the sole medium of exchange in the economy. Households exchange money for goods on the goods market, money for labor on the labor market, money for capital services on the rental market, and money for bonds on the bond market. However, households do not directly exchange goods for goods (a process called **barter**), bonds for goods, and so on.

Concepts of Money

T he money in our model matches up with paper currency issued by a government. For example, the money could be U.S. dollar notes issued by the Federal Reserve, euro notes issued by the European Central Bank, and almost 200 other forms of paper currency issued by the world's governments. These currencies are sometimes called **fiat money** because they have value due to government fiat, rather than through intrinsic value. In earlier times, societies tended to rely more on **commodity money**, such as gold and silver coins, which do have intrinsic value. These coins are valued, in part, for their content of gold or silver. In the following box, we discuss how another commodity, the cigarette, served as money in a prisoner-of-war camp. In our model, money has no intrinsic value; it is just a piece of paper issued by the government. Therefore, we do not have to consider any resources used up when intrinsically valuable goods serve as money.

If we think of money as paper currency issued by the government, there are several reasons why this money might occupy the dominant position as an economy's medium of exchange. First, the government may impose legal restrictions that prevent private parties, such as Microsoft Corporation, from issuing small-size, interest-bearing bonds that could serve conveniently as hand-to-hand currency. Further, the government may enact statutes that reinforce the use of its money. As an

Money in a Prisoner-of-War Camp

R.A. Radford (1945) described his experience with the economy of a German prisoner-of-war (POW) camp during World War II. He observed that cigarettes became the primary medium of exchange, with many goods being exchanged for cigarettes, which were then used to buy other goods. In addition, most prices were expressed in units of cigarettes, for example, as four cigarettes per ration of treacle (a form of syrup).

Radford noted that cigarettes had several attractive characteristics as money (p. 194): "homogeneous, reasonably durable, and of convenient size for the smallest or, in packets, for the largest transactions." One drawback, applicable also to other commodity moneys, was the resource cost of using cigarettes as a medium of exchange. That is, the cigarettes used as money could not simultaneously be smoked and, worse yet, might deteriorate physically over time.

Radford discussed an attempt to introduce paper money as an alternative medium of exchange. This money was issued by the camp restaurant and was supposed to be redeemable for a fixed quantity of food. However, problems arose with respect to the credibility of the promised food value of the paper money, and cigarettes remained the primary medium of exchange. For our purposes, an interesting lesson from Radford's story is that a medium of exchange is important in any economy, even a POW camp.

© Steve Outram/Alamy

example, there is the proclamation that the U.S. dollar is "**legal tender** for all debts public and private." The term "legal tender" means that U.S. dollar currency has to be accepted in some forms of trade, such as payments of taxes to the government. However, since the legal-tender requirement does not specify the price, P, at which exchanges have to occur, the content of the legal-tender provision is unclear—what would legal tender mean if P were infinity? Perhaps more significant is that U.S. courts are more inclined to enforce contracts that are denominated in U.S. dollars rather than other units.

Another consideration is the cost of establishing one's money as reliable and convenient. These costs include prevention of counterfeiting, replacement of worn-out notes, willingness to convert notes into different denominations, and so on. Because of these costs, money would always tend to bear interest at a rate lower than bonds. In fact, because of the inconvenience of paying interest on hand-to-hand currency, the interest rate on currency is typically zero. That is, if one holds $1 of currency and does not lose it, one will still have $1 of currency in the future.

We can relate our abstract concept of money to conventional measures of the money stock. The theoretical construct corresponds most closely to currency held by the public. In the real world, currency held by the public differs from *total currency in circulation*, which includes currency held in the vaults of banks and other depository institutions. (Currency in circulation does not include amounts held by the U.S. Treasury or by Federal Reserve Banks.) A further distinction is between total currency in circulation and **high-powered money**, which adds the deposits held by banks and other depository institutions at the Federal Reserve. Another name for high-powered money is the **monetary base**.

In March 2006, the amount of (seasonally adjusted) currency held by the public in the United States was $735 billion, which amounted to 5.6% of nominal gross domestic product (GDP). This amount of currency is surprisingly large—about $2,500 per U.S. resident. In the box that follows, we note that much of the currency is in $100 bills, many of which are held abroad, rather than by U.S. residents.

The term "money" often refers to a **monetary aggregate** that is broader than currency. A monetary aggregate is the total dollar stock of a group of financial

Where Is All the Currency?

As mentioned, in March 2006, the amount of U.S. currency held by the public was about $2,500 per person in the United States. To understand this surprisingly large number, start with the observation that, at the end of 2005, 72% of currency in circulation by value, including coins, was in $100 bills. (The data on currency by denomination are in the *Treasury Bulletin*.) Thus, much of the currency is likely not used for ordinary transactions. Because currency is anonymous, it is attractive for illegal activities, such as the drug trade. Currency transactions also facilitate tax evasion. However, the amount of U.S. currency held for these purposes is unknown.

More is known about the amounts of U.S. currency held abroad, mostly in the form of $100 bills. Foreigners like U.S. money as a store of value and a medium of exchange because the money has a reasonably stable value and can readily be exchanged for goods or other assets. In addition, transactions carried out in currency can usually be hidden from local governments, and this secrecy is particularly attractive when the government is oppressive. The foreign demand for U.S. currency is especially high in countries experiencing economic and political turmoil. A recent joint study by the Federal Reserve and the U.S. Treasury estimated that 55–60% of the total U.S. currency in circulation in 2002 was held abroad. The geographical division was estimated to be 25% in Latin America (with Argentina the highest demander), 20% in the Middle East and Africa, 15% in Asia, and 40% in Europe (with Russia and other former Soviet republics as particularly high users). For additional discussion, see Richard Porter and Ruth Judson (2001) and Board of Governors of the Federal Reserve System (2003).

assets defined to be money. The most common definition, called **M1**, attempts to classify as money the assets that serve regularly as media of exchange. This concept adds to currency held by the public the **checkable deposits** issued by banks and other financial institutions. Checkable deposits are deposits held at financial institutions that can be withdrawn by writing a check. The amount of these checkable deposits (including travelers' checks) in the United States in March 2006 was $649 billion, or 5.0% of nominal GDP.[1] Therefore, M1—the sum of currency and checkable deposits—was $1,384 billion, or 10.6% of nominal GDP. The total M1 was 53% in currency and 47% in checkable deposits (including travelers' checks). In earlier times, a much smaller proportion of M1 was in currency, and a much larger proportion was in checkable deposits. For example, in 1960, only 19% of M1 was in currency, whereas 81% was in checkable deposits. This change illustrates the declining importance of checkable deposits held at banks and other financial institutions. These checking accounts have been replaced to a considerable extent by other forms of financial assets, such as money-market accounts, which have become much easier to access.

Table 10.1 shows ratios of currency to nominal GDP for OECD countries (the rich countries in the Organization for Economic Cooperation and Development), plus China, in 1960, 1980, and 2000. Notice that the ratio of currency to GDP declined over time in most countries—a typical case, for France, showed a decrease from 0.133 in 1960 to 0.052 in 1980 and 0.035 in 2000. However, in some countries, the ratio leveled off or even rose from 1980 to 2000—this pattern applied to Canada, Finland, Germany, Japan, Spain, and the United States. In 2000, the highest currency ratio was 0.121 in Japan, and the lowest was 0.019 in New Zealand. The United States, at 0.059, was close to the median. Table 10.2 shows comparable figures with money defined to be M1.

Still broader definitions of money add in other kinds of deposits held at financial institutions. For example, **M2** ($6,777 billion in the United States in March 2006) includes household holdings of savings deposits, small-time deposits, and retail money-market mutual funds. However, the M2 definition goes beyond the concept of money as a medium of exchange. In our model, it is best to use a narrower definition of money, for example, as currency held by the public.

---

[1] The standard definition of checkable deposits includes travelers' checks issued by banks and other depository institutions. Other travelers' checks, amounting to $6.9 billion in March 2006, are included separately in M1, not as part of checkable deposits. Our measure of checkable deposits departs from the standard definition by including all travelers' checks.

Table 10.1 *Ratios of Currency to Nominal GDP*

Country	1960	1980	2000
Australia	0.054	0.036	0.041
Austria	0.119	0.078	0.071
Belgium	0.220	0.110	0.054
Canada	0.046	0.034	0.034
China	—	—	0.072
Denmark	0.068	0.032	0.029
Finland	0.036	0.025	0.025
France	0.133	0.052	0.035
Germany	0.072	0.062	0.070
Greece	0.103	0.130	—
Ireland	0.117	0.077	0.052
Italy	—	0.070	0.066
Japan	0.069	0.072	0.121
Netherlands	0.125	0.064	0.047
New Zealand	0.061	0.025	0.019
Norway	0.112	0.060	0.030
Portugal	0.177	0.131	0.057
South Korea	0.059	0.049	0.034
Spain	0.120	0.083	0.099
Sweden	0.090	0.064	0.043
Switzerland	0.197	0.141	0.093
United Kingdom	0.081	0.044	0.025
United States	0.056	0.042	0.059

Note: The table shows the ratio of currency held by the public to nominal GDP. The data are from International Monetary Fund, *International Financial Statistics.*

The Demand for Money

We will now extend the microeconomic foundations of our model to consider the demand for money. Since we identify money with hand-to-hand currency, we assume that the interest rate paid on money is zero. In contrast, the rate of return on bonds and ownership of capital equals the interest rate, i, which we assume is greater than zero. Henceforth, we refer to bonds and ownership of capital as **interest-bearing assets**, because these assets pay a positive return to the holder. The important point is that these assets yield a higher rate of return than money and are therefore better than money as long-term **stores of value**. Nevertheless, since households use money to make exchanges, households will hold some money for convenience, rather than always cashing in earning assets immediately prior to each exchange. That is, the demand for money will be greater than zero.

Table 10.2 *Ratios of M1 to Nominal GDP*

Country	1960	1980	2000
Australia	0.228	0.126	0.211
Austria	0.197	0.151	0.280
Belgium	0.322	0.192	0.271
Canada	0.152	0.112	0.213
China	—	—	0.146
Denmark	0.246	0.201	—
Finland	—	0.080	0.307
France	0.468	0.280	0.224
Germany	0.160	0.170	0.288
Greece	0.151	0.196	0.288
Ireland	—	—	0.197
Italy	—	0.442	0.416
Japan	0.265	0.286	0.484
Netherlands	0.274	0.187	0.367
New Zealand	0.279	0.110	0.141
Norway	0.235	0.145	0.403
Portugal	—	0.390	0.427
South Korea	0.104	0.101	0.090
Spain	0.327	—	0.338
Sweden	—	—	—
Switzerland	0.489	0.362	0.396
United Kingdom	—	—	—
United States	0.294	0.169	0.146

Note: The table shows the ratio of M1 (currency held by the public plus checkable deposits) to nominal GDP. The data are from the International Monetary Fund, *International Financial Statistics*. Data on M1 were unavailable for Sweden and the United Kingdom.

In Chapter 6, we wrote the household budget constraint in nominal terms in equation (6.11), which we repeat here:

(10.1)
$$PC + \Delta B + P \bullet \Delta K =$$
$$\Pi + wL + i \bullet (B + PK)$$

nominal consumption + nominal saving =
nominal income

On the right-hand side, the household receives nominal profit, Π (which is zero in equilibrium), nominal wage income, wL, and nominal asset income, $i \bullet (B + PK)$, all in the form of money. On the left-hand side, the household uses money to buy consumption goods, in the nominal amount PC, and to add to interest-bearing

assets (that is, to save), in the nominal amount $\Delta B + P \bullet \Delta K$.

Although all of the income and spending terms in equation (10.1) use money, it would be possible for the household to hold little or no money at every point in time. If each inflow of income were perfectly synchronized with an equal outflow of expenditure on goods or purchases of interest-bearing assets, each household's money balance could always be close to zero. However, this synchronization would require a great deal of effort and planning. We assume, as a general matter, that the household can reduce its average money balance by incurring more **transaction costs**. By transaction costs, we mean any expenses of time or goods related to the timing and form of various exchanges. In the real world, examples of transaction costs are the time spent going to the bank or an automatic teller machine (ATM), and brokerage fees.

One way to maintain a low average money balance is to rush off to the store as soon as money wages are paid to spend one's entire weekly or monthly paycheck on goods. Another method would be to go immediately to a financial institution to convert all of one's wage income into interest-bearing assets. More realistically, a household might immediately deposit its paycheck into a bank account (or might arrange for the paycheck to be deposited directly into an account). In addition, if workers were paid wages more frequently—say, weekly rather than monthly—it would be easier for workers to maintain a lower average money balance.

The general idea is that, by putting more effort into money management and, thereby, incurring more transaction costs, the household can reduce its average holding of money, M. For a given total of nominal assets, $M + B + PK$, a reduction in the average level of M raises the average holding of interest-bearing assets, $B + PK$. Since asset income is $i \cdot (B + PK)$, the rise in $B + PK$ raises asset income. Thus, a household's average holding of money, M, emerges from a trade-off. With a frequent transaction strategy, M will be low and asset income will be high, but transaction costs will be high. With an infrequent transactions strategy, M will be high and asset income will be low, but transaction costs will be low. The household's choice of average money holdings entails finding the right balance between additional asset income and added transaction costs.

We use the term "demand for money," labeled M^d, to describe the average holding of money that results from the household's optimal strategy for money management. Many formal models of money management have been developed to assess this demand for money. For our purposes, we do not have to go through these models. Rather, we are mainly interested in how some key variables affect the quantity of money demanded, M^d. Specifically, we want to know how M^d depends on the price level, P, the interest rate, i, and real GDP, Y.

The Interest Rate and the Demand for Money

A higher interest rate, i, provides a greater incentive to hold down average holdings of money, M, in order to raise average holdings of interest-bearing assets,

$B + PK$. That is, with a higher i, households are more willing to incur transaction costs in order to reduce M. For example, households respond to a higher i by transacting more frequently between money and interest-bearing assets. We predict, accordingly, that an increase in i reduces the nominal demand for money, M^d. For a given price level, P, we can also say that a higher i lowers the real demand for money, M^d/P.

The Price Level and the Demand for Money

Suppose that the price level, P, doubles. Assume that the nominal wage rate, w, and the nominal rental price, R, also double, so that the real wage rate, w/P, and the real rental price, R/P, do not change. In this case, the household's nominal income, $\Pi + wL + i \cdot (B + PK)$ on the right-hand side of the budget constraint in equation (10.1), is twice as high as before.[2] However, the real value of this income, $\Pi/P + (w/P) \cdot L + i \cdot (B/P + K)$, is unchanged. Thus, we are considering a doubling of the nominal values of all variables, with no changes in the real values. In this circumstance, the household would want to double the average nominal quantity of money, M, held. This doubling of M means that the average real money balance, M/P, does not change.

To think about this result, suppose that a household's nominal income is $500 per week. Suppose that the initial plan for money management—involving some frequency of exchange between money and interest-bearing assets—dictates holding half a week's worth of income, on average, in the form of money. In this case, the household's average holding of money, M, is $250. After the doubling of the price level, P (along with the doubling of the nominal wage rate, w, and rental price, R), the household's nominal income is $1,000 per week. The household would not change its frequency of exchange between money and interest-bearing assets, because the trade-off for optimal money management—interest income versus transaction costs—is the same as before. Therefore, the household still holds half a week's worth of income in the form of money. With twice as much nominal income, half a week's worth of income is twice as much money in nominal terms—$500 instead of $250. Hence, the nominal demand for money, M^d, doubles. Since M^d and P have both doubled, the ratio, M^d/P, is the same. The result is that the **real demand for money**, M^d/P, does not change when P changes.

---

[2] We are assuming that $\Pi = 0$ and that, L, K, and i are unchanged. We are also considering the average household, so that $B = 0$.

Real GDP and the Demand for Money

Suppose again that the initial plan for money management dictates holding half a week's worth of income, on average, in the form of money. Hence, when nominal income is $500, the household's average holding of money, M, is $250. Assume now that nominal income doubles to $1,000, while the price level, P, is unchanged. Therefore, real income, $\Pi/P + (w/P) \bullet L + i \bullet (B/P + K)$, doubles. If its money-management plan were unchanged, each household would still hold half a week's worth of nominal income as money. However, half a week's worth of income is now twice as much money—$500 instead of $250. Thus, households would double their nominal demand for money, M^d. Since P is constant, the real demand for money, M^d/P, also doubles.

This result has to be modified because higher real income shifts the trade-off between interest income and transaction costs. Specifically, the larger real money balance, M/P, means that more real income on assets, $i \bullet (B/P + K)$, could be gained by spending additional effort on money management. The key point is that the real transaction costs for economizing on money have not changed. Thus, when real income doubles, households are motivated to incur more transaction costs to reduce their average money holding. For example, instead of holding 0.5 weeks' worth of income as money, households might hold only 0.4 weeks' worth of income as money. In this case, nominal money demand, M^d, rises from $250 to $400, rather than $500. That is, a doubling of real income raises M^d, but by less than 100%. The response of M^d is, in proportional terms, smaller than the change in real income. (This result is called **economies of scale in cash management**, because higher-income households hold less money in proportion to their income.) Since the price level, P, is unchanged, the real demand for money, M^d/P, rises, but less than proportionately, with real income.

In the aggregate, household real income moves along with real GDP, Y. That is, from Chapter 7, the aggregate form of the household budget constraint is

(7.13) $\qquad C + \Delta K = Y - \delta K$

$$consumption + net\ investment =$$
$$real\ GDP - depreciation$$
$$= real\ net\ domestic\ product$$

For given depreciation, δK, the aggregate of household real income is determined on the right-hand side of equation (7.13) by real GDP, Y. We therefore have that the aggregate real demand for money, M^d/P, rises, but less than proportionately, with Y.

Other Influences on the Demand for Money

For given values of the interest rate, i, the price level, P, and real GDP, Y, money demand depends on the payments technology and the level of transaction costs. As examples, increased use of credit cards and greater convenience of checkable deposits reduce the demand for currency. Expanded use of ATM machines makes currency easier to obtain but has an uncertain impact on the demand for currency; the machines make currency more attractive for payments but also make it easier to hold a smaller average currency balance by going more often to the ATM.

The Money-Demand Function

We can summarize the discussion by writing down a formula for nominal money demand for the aggregate of households:

> Key equation (money-demand function):
>
> **(10.2)** $\qquad M^d = P \bullet L(Y, i)$

We get the aggregate money-demand function in equation (10.2) by adding up the demands from individual households. We assume that the form of the aggregate money-demand function comes from the effect of each right-hand-side variable, such as the interest rate, i, on the average money held by each household.

We assume in equation (10.2) that the nature of the transactions technology is given. Then, for given real GDP, Y, and interest rate, i, the nominal money demand, M^d, is proportional to the price level, P. For given P, M^d increases with Y (though less than proportionately) and decreases with i. This dependence is summarized by the function $L(\bullet)$. Note that if we divide both sides of equation (10.2) by P, we get the real demand for money:

(10.3) $\qquad M^d/P = L(Y, i)$

We call $L(\bullet)$ the real money-demand function. From this perspective, equation (10.2) says

$$nominal\ demand\ for\ money =$$
$$price\ level \bullet (real\ demand\ for\ money)$$

The Payments Period and the Demand for Money

Irving Fisher (1926) stressed the dependence of the demand for money on the period between payments of wages. The general idea is that a shorter period makes it easier for workers to maintain a low average money balance. This effect is particularly important during extreme inflations—for example, the German hyperinflation after World War I. In such circumstances, the cost of holding money becomes very high—we can represent this effect in our model by a high interest rate, *i*. Because of the high cost of holding money, workers and firms are willing to incur more transaction costs—such as the costs of making more frequent wage payments—to reduce their average holdings of money. In 1923, the final year of the Germany hyperinflation, an observer reported: "It became the custom to make an advance of wages on Tuesday, the balance being paid on Friday. Later, some firms used to pay wages three times a week or even daily" (Costantino Bresciani-Turroni, 1937, p. 303).

Similarly, during the Austrian hyperinflation after World War I: "The salaries of the state officials, which used to be issued at the end of the month, were paid to them during 1922 in installments three times per month" (J. van Walre de Bordes, 1927, p. 163).

©Brooks Kraft/CORBIS

Empirical Evidence on the Demand for Money

Many statistical studies have analyzed the determinants of the demand for money. Most of these studies focus on M1, the monetary aggregate that comprises currency held by the public plus checkable deposits. However, some studies have examined separately the demand for currency.

The empirical results confirm negative effects of interest rates on the demand for money, whether money is measured by M1 or currency. For example, in his classic empirical studies for the United States, Steven Goldfeld (1973, 1976) found that a 10% increase in interest rates (for example, a rise from 5% to 5.5%) reduces the demand for M1 in the long run by about 3%. Goldfeld and Daniel Sichel (1990) and Ray Fair (1987) reported similar findings for a number of OECD countries. Jack Ochs and Mark Rush (1983) showed that the negative effect of interest rates on the demand for M1 in the

United States reflect similar proportionate effects on currency and checkable deposits.

Casey Mulligan and Xavier Sala-i-Martin (2000) showed that money demand becomes more sensitive to changes in interest rates when the level of interest rates rises. At low rates—say, 2%—an increase in the interest rate by 10% (to 2.2%) lowers money demand by 2%. However, at an interest rate of 6%, an increase by 10% (to 6.6%) reduces money demand by 5%.

There is strong evidence for a positive effect of real GDP on real money demand and weaker evidence for economies of scale in this relation. Goldfeld (1973, 1976) found that an increase in real GDP by 10% leads, in the long run, to an increase by about 7% in the real demand for M1. The change in M1 breaks down into an increase of checkable deposits by around 6% and an increase in currency by about 10%. Therefore, economies of scale in the demand for M1 apply to checkable deposits but not to currency.

Our analysis predicted that an increase in the price level would raise the nominal demand for money in the same proportion. This proposition receives strong empirical support. For example, Goldfeld (1973, 1976) found that an increase in the price level by 10% leads to a 10% increase in the nominal demand for M1.

We noted that changes in transactions technology can have important influences on the demand for money. This effect has been important in the United States since the early 1970s because of a variety of financial innovations. The innovations include the expanded use of credit cards, the development of money-market accounts that are convenient alternatives to checkable deposits held at banks, the introduction of ATM machines, and the widespread use of electronic funds transfers.

Before the 1980s, economists ignored financial innovations when fitting equations for money demand. The estimated equations worked well up to the mid-1970s, in the sense that their predictions for the demand for money were fairly accurate. However, after the mid-1970s, the estimates that ignored financial innovations started to fail. In particular, the actual amount of M1—especially checkable deposits—that people held fell well short of the amount predicted from earlier empirical relationships. Michael Dotsey (1985) showed that the volume of electronic funds transfers was a good measure of the extent of financial innovation. He found, first, that the spread of electronic funds transfers led to a substantial decline in the real demand for M1. Second, when the volume of electronic funds transfers was held constant, the demand for M1 became stable over time. In particular, the fitted equation showed effects from interest rates and real GDP that were similar to those, such as Goldfeld's, that ignored financial innovations but included data only up to the early 1970s.

Determination of the Price Level

e now extend the equilibrium business-cycle model to determine the price level, P. The central idea is to add a new equilibrium condition: The nominal quantity of money equals the nominal quantity demanded.

The Nominal Quantity of Money Supplied Equals the Nominal Quantity Demanded

We assume that money takes the form of currency and that the nominal quantity of money is determined by the monetary authority, for example, the Federal Reserve in the United States or the European Central Bank in the euro zone. Thus, the nominal quantity of money supplied, M^s, is a given amount, M.

The aggregate demand for nominal money is given from the function we worked out before:

(10.2) $$M^d = P \bullet L(Y, i)$$

This equation gives the nominal quantity of money, M^d, that households want to hold, whereas M^s is the actual amount of nominal money outstanding. We propose as another equilibrium condition for our model an equality between M^s and M^d:

(10.4) $$M^s = M^d$$

nominal quantity of money supplied =
nominal quantity of money demanded

If we substitute for M^d the form of the nominal demand-for-money function from equation (10.2), we can write the result as

> Key equation (nominal quantity of money supplied equals nominal quantity demanded):
>
> **(10.5)** $$M^s = P \bullet L(Y, i)$$

To see why we expect $M^s = M^d$ to hold in equation (10.4), consider what happens when M^s—the given quantity of money supplied—differs from M^d. If M^s is greater than M^d, households have more money than they want to hold. Therefore, they try to spend their excess money, for example, on goods.[3] We anticipate that the increased desire to buy goods would raise the price level, P. This process continues until P rises enough to equate the nominal quantity of money demanded, M^d, on the right-hand side of equation (10.4) to the nominal quantity supplied, M^s, on the left-hand side. That is, the equilibrium price level is high enough so that

---

[3] Another possibility is that households buy bonds and, thereby, affect the interest rate, i, paid on bonds. However, in the present setting, i turns out not to change in a full equilibrium. The result is different—that is, the interest rate may change—if we do not allow for full flexibility of the price level, P. We consider this possibility in Chapter 16.

households are willing to hold the nominal quantity of money supplied, M^s.

The same process works in reverse if M^s is less than M^d. In that case, households try to rebuild their money balances, for example, by reducing their spending on goods. In this case, P falls enough to equate the nominal quantity of money demanded, M^d on the right-hand side of equation (10.4), to the nominal quantity supplied, M^s on the left-hand side.

One important point is that we are assuming that goods prices are flexible, so that the price level, P, adjusts rapidly to ensure equality between the nominal quantity of money supplied, M^s, and the nominal quantity demanded, M^d. This assumption about price flexibility parallels our previous assumptions about market-clearing conditions in the markets for labor and capital services. For the labor market, we assumed that the real wage rate, w/P, adjusted to ensure equality between the quantities of labor supplied, L^s, and demanded, L^d. For the rental market, we assumed that the real rental price, R/P, adjusted to ensure equality between the quantities of capital services supplied, $(\kappa K)^s$, and demanded, $(\kappa K)^d$. If we put the equations together, we have that the three nominal prices—P, w, and R—adjust rapidly to ensure that three equilibrium conditions hold simultaneously: first, $M^s = M^d$; second, $L^s = L^d$; and third, $(\kappa K)^s = (\kappa K)^d$. Economists refer to this situation as one of **general equilibrium**. The word "general" in this expression means that the equilibrium conditions—supply equals demand—apply simultaneously in all the markets.

Figure 10.1 shows graphically the equation of the nominal quantity of money demanded, M^d, to the nominal quantity supplied, M^s. The vertical axis shows the price level, P. The nominal quantity of money demanded, M^d, is the product of P and the real quantity of money demanded, $L(Y, i)$—see equation (10.2). Recall that the real quantity of money demanded, $L(Y, i)$, is determined, for a given transactions technology, by real GDP, Y, and the interest rate, i. Hence, for given Y and i (and a given transactions technology), the nominal quantity of money demanded, M^d, is proportional to P. We graph M^d accordingly in Figure 10.1 as the upward-sloping red line, which starts from the origin.[4] It is important to realize that this graph applies for given determinants of the real demand for money, $L(Y, i)$. The nominal quantity of money supplied, M^s, is shown by the vertical blue line at the value M.

The equilibrium condition, $M^s = M^d$ in Figure 10.1, corresponds to equations (10.4) and (10.5). The graph for M^d applies for given determinants of the real demand for money, $L(Y, i)$. That is, we are taking as given real GDP, Y, the interest rate, i, and any other determinants of the real demand for money. We can then use Figure 10.1 to find the equilibrium price level, which is the value P^* shown on the vertical axis. At P^*, the upward-sloping M^d line intersects the vertical M^s line. That is,

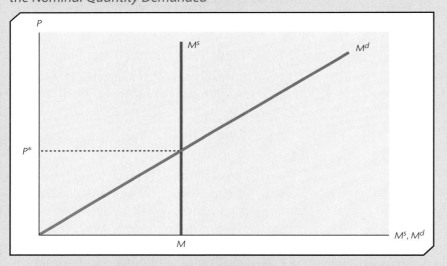

Figure 10.1 *The Nominal Quantity of Money Supplied Equals the Nominal Quantity Demanded*

The nominal quantity of money demanded is given by $M^d = P \cdot L(Y, i)$ from equation (10.2). For a given real quantity of money demanded, $L(Y, i)$, M^d is proportional to the price level, P. Therefore, the nominal quantity demanded, M^d, is given by the upward-sloping red line, which starts from the origin. The nominal quantity of money supplied is the constant $M^s = M$, shown by the vertical blue line. The equilibrium condition $M^s = M^d$ holds when the price level is P^* on the vertical axis. Thus, P^* is the equilibrium value of P.

---

[4] It may seem puzzling to have a demand curve with an upward slope, since economists are used to having demand curves with a downward slope. However, P is the price of a unit of goods in terms of money (dollars per good). The price of a unit of money in terms of goods is $1/P$ (goods per dollar). If we had placed $1/P$, rather than P, on the vertical axis, the money-demand function would have the conventional negative slope. However, since we want to think about the determinants of the price level, it is more convenient to have P on the vertical axis.

P^* is the price level, P, that equates the nominal quantity of money demanded, M^d, to the nominal quantity supplied, M^s.

A Change in the Nominal Quantity of Money

We now study the effects from a one-time change in the nominal quantity of money supplied, M^s. To be concrete, suppose that M^s doubles from M to $2M$. The simplest way this could happen is for the monetary authority, on a one-time basis, to print up a lot of extra currency and give it to people.

Figure 10.2 shows the effect from an increase in the nominal quantity of money supplied, M^s, from M to $2M$. Suppose that the money-demand line, M^d, does not shift. In this case, we can determine the change in the equilibrium price level, P^*, by looking at the intersections with the M^d line. The figure shows that the increase in M^s from M to $2M$ raises the equilibrium price level from P^* to $2P^*$ on the vertical axis.

We can verify the result from equation (10.5):

(10.5) $M^s = P \bullet L(Y, i)$

The nominal quantity of money supplied, M^s, doubles on the left-hand side. If the real quantity of money demanded, $L(Y, i)$, does not change, the doubling of the price level, P, doubles the nominal quantity of money demanded, $M^d = P \bullet L(Y, i)$ on the right-hand side. Thus, equation (10.5) still holds with M^s and P twice as high as they were initially.

Consider now how the doubling of M^s affects the labor market, described in Figure 8.15. Since the technology level, A, has not changed, the real wage rate, w/P, and labor input, L, do not change. Therefore, the price level, P, is twice as high, and w/P is unchanged. We conclude that, in general equilibrium, the nominal wage rate, w, has to double.

Consider next how the doubling of M^s affects the rental market for capital services, described in Figure 9.5. As in the labor market, the unchanged technology level, A, means that the real rental price, R/P, and the quantity of capital services, κK, do not change. The fixed κK corresponds to a given capital stock, K, and an unchanged capital utilization rate, κ. Thus, the price level, P, is twice as high, and R/P is unchanged. We must have, in general equilibrium, that the nominal rental price, R, doubles.

Remember from Chapter 9 that the interest rate, i, has to equal the rate of return on ownership of capital:

(9.5) $interest\ rate = rate\ of\ return$
$on\ ownership\ of\ capital$

$i = (R/P) \bullet \kappa - \delta(\kappa)$

Since the doubling of M^s does not change the real rental price, R/P, and the capital utilization rate, κ, the rate of return on ownership of capital does not change on the right-hand side of equation (9.5). Therefore, the interest rate, i, is also unchanged on the left-hand side of the equation. This result is important—in general equilibrium, with full adjustment of the price level, P, a one-time increase in the nominal quantity of money supplied, M^s, does not affect the interest rate.

Recall that real GDP, Y, is given from the production function used in Chapter 9:

(9.1) $Y = A \bullet F(\kappa K, L)$

Figure 10.2 *An Increase in the Nominal Quantity of Money*

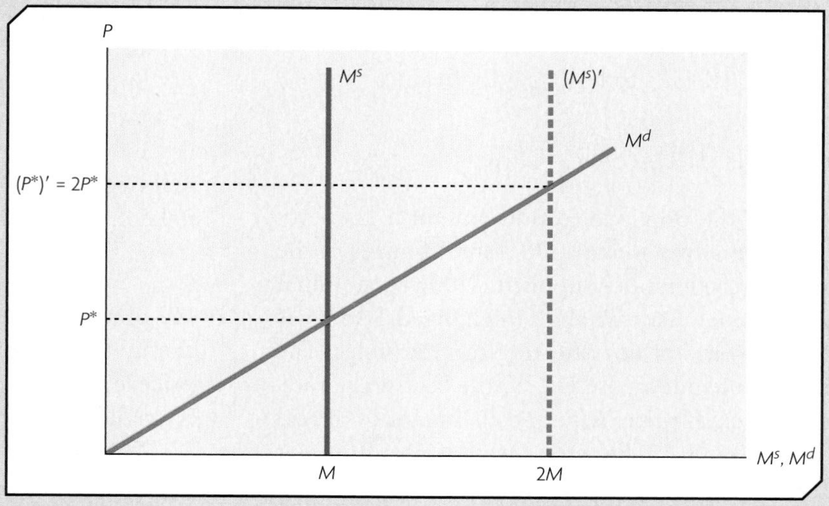

The nominal demand for money, M^d, shown by the red line, is the same as in Figure 10.1. The nominal quantity of money supplied, M^s, doubles from M (the vertical blue line) to $2M$ (the vertical green line). Therefore, the equilibrium price level doubles, on the vertical axis, from P^* to $(P^*)' = 2P^*$.

The technology level, A, is fixed, and we have shown that a doubling of M^s does not affect the quantities of capital services, κK, and labor, L. Therefore, equation (9.1) implies that Y is unchanged. In other words, in general equilibrium, a one-time increase in the nominal quantity of money supplied, M^s, does not affect real GDP.

We have verified that a doubling of M^s does not affect real GDP, Y, and the interest rate, i. These two variables are the determinants of real money demand, given by $L(Y, i)$ in equation (10.3). This result validates our assumption in Figure 10.2 that the money-demand line, $M^d = P \bullet L(Y, i)$, does not shift when M^s doubles. We conclude that our previous result—a doubling of M^s leads to a doubling of the price level, P—is correct.

To sum up, a doubling of the nominal quantity of money supplied, M^s, leads to a doubling of all of the nominal prices—the price level, P; the nominal wage rate, w; and the nominal rental price, R. There are no changes in real money balances, M/P; the real wage rate, w/P; and the real rental price, R/P. We also conclude that the determinants of the real demand for money, $L(Y, i)$, remain the same—the increase in M^s has no effect on real GDP, Y, or the interest rate, i. Note, however, that nominal GDP equals PY. Since P doubles and Y is unchanged, nominal GDP doubles.

The analogous conclusions hold for a decrease in the nominal quantity of money supplied, M^s. If M^s halved, going from M to $M/2$, P would halve, and real money balances, M/P, would again be unchanged. The nominal wage rate, w, and the nominal rental price, R, would halve, so that the real wage rate, w/P, and the real rental price, R/P, would stay the same. As before, the decrease in M^s has no effect on real GDP, Y. Hence, nominal GDP, PY, falls to half its initial value.

The Neutrality of Money

The results in the previous section exhibit a property called the **neutrality of money**. One-time changes in the nominal quantity of money supplied, M^s, affect nominal variables but leave real variables unchanged. Money is neutral in the sense of not affecting real variables. The real variables include real GDP, Y; the real wage rate, w/P; the real rental price, R/P; and the quantity of real money balances, M/P. The interest rate, i, also does not change. We should think of i as a real variable because it governs intertemporal-substitution effects for consumption and work. In Chapter 11, which introduces inflation, we distinguish the nominal interest rate from the real interest rate.

Almost all economists accept the neutrality of money as a valid long-run proposition. That is, in the long run, an increase or decrease in the nominal quantity of money supplied, M^s, influences nominal variables but not real ones. However, many economists believe that money is not neutral in the short run. In the short run, increases in M^s are usually thought to increase real GDP, Y, whereas decreases in M^s are thought to decrease Y. The main source of the difference in conclusions involves the flexibility of nominal prices—notably, the price level, P, and the nominal wage rate, w. These nominal prices are thought to be flexible up or down in the long run in response to increases or decreases in M^s. However, P and w are often viewed as less flexible in the short run, especially when decreases in M^s mean that P and w have to decrease. In some models, the assumption of price flexibility is replaced by an assumption that P or w is *sticky* in the short run. We discuss sticky-price and sticky-wage models in Chapter 16.

A Change in the Demand for Money

We mentioned that financial innovations could affect the real demand for money. To explore these effects, suppose that the nominal demand for money is again given initially by

(10.2) $$M^d = P \bullet L(Y, i)$$

where $L(Y, i)$ is the real demand for money. As before, the nominal money demand, M^d, is graphed versus the price level, P, as the upward-sloping red line in Figure 10.3.

Suppose now that an improvement in the technology for making financial transactions—perhaps increased use of credit cards or ATM machines—decreases the real demand for money to $[L(Y, i)']$, so that the nominal demand becomes

$$(M^d)' = P \bullet [L(Y, i)]'$$

We graph the new nominal money demand, $(M^d)'$, as the upward-sloping green line in Figure 10.3. At any price level, P, the nominal quantity of money demanded is smaller along the green line than along the red line.

We assume that the nominal quantity of money supplied, M^s, is fixed at M, shown by the vertical blue line in Figure 10.3. Therefore, the initial equilibrium price level is P^* on the vertical axis. At this point, M^s equals the nominal quantity of money demanded, M^d. After the fall in the real demand for money, the equilibrium price level is $(P*)'$ on the vertical axis. At this point, M^s equals the new nominal quantity of money demanded, $(M^d)'$. Note that the decrease in the real demand for money leads to a higher price level; that is, $(P*)'$ is above $P*$. (As before, we assume that the price level adjusts rapidly to its equilibrium level.)

A decrease in the real demand for money is similar to an increase in the nominal quantity of money supplied, M^s, in that the price level, P, rises in each case. However, one difference is that a change in M^s is fully neutral, whereas a change in the real demand for money is not fully neutral. To see why, note that the decrease in the real demand for money led to a rise in P, while M^s was fixed at M. Therefore, the real quantity of money, M/P, decreased. In addition, the change in transactions technology that led to the decline in the real demand for money—such as expanded use of credit cards or ATM machines—would itself have real effects. For example, the resources used up in transaction costs would change. However, in most cases, the effects on macroeconomic variables, such as real GDP, will be small enough to neglect.

The Cyclical Behavior of the Price Level

In Chapters 8 and 9, we used our equilibrium business-cycle model to study how shifts to the technology level, A, create economic fluctuations. Now we can use our analysis of the demand for money to determine how the price level, P, moves during economic fluctuations.

Recall that the nominal demand for money is given by

(10.2) $$M^d = P \bullet L(Y, i)$$

Think about a recession, in which real GDP, Y, falls. The decline in Y reduces the real quantity of money

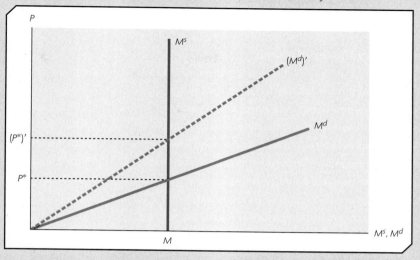

Figure 10.3 *A Decrease in the Real Demand for Money*

The nominal demand for money is initially given by the red line, $M^d = P \bullet \pounds(Y, i)$. We consider a decrease in the real demand for money, $\pounds(Y, i)$. This real demand is lower along the dashed green line, $(M^d)'$, than along the red line. The nominal quantity of money supplied, M^s, is the constant M, shown by the vertical blue line. The decrease in the real demand for money raises the equilibrium price level from $P*$ to $(P*)'$ on the vertical axis.

demanded, given by $L(Y, i)$ on the right-hand side of equation (10.2). However, we also found that the interest rate, i, tends to fall in a recession. The decrease in i raises the real quantity of money demanded, $L(Y, i)$. The overall change depends on the magnitudes of the decreases in Y and i, and on the sensitivity of $L(Y, i)$ to Y and i. Typical estimates indicate that the real quantity of money demanded, $L(Y, i)$, declines overall in this situation; the fall in i tends to be small, and $L(Y, i)$ is not very responsive to changes in i. Therefore, we assume that, in a recession, the real quantity of money demanded, given by $L(Y, i)$, decreases overall.

We can use Figure 10.3 to determine the effect of an economic contraction on the price level, P. Recall that this figure applied to a decrease in the real demand for money, $L(Y, i)$, caused by a change in the transactions technology. However, the same construction applies if $L(Y, i)$ decreases for other reasons. In the present case, the real quantity of money demanded, $L(Y, i)$, falls overall because of the decreases in real GDP, Y, and the interest rate, i. Thus, we can use Figure 10.3 to study how the price level, P, changes during a recession.

We see from Figure 10.3 that, for a given nominal quantity of money supplied, M^s, the decrease in the real quantity of money demanded, $L(Y, i)$, raises the price level, P. Hence, in a recession, a relatively high P tends to accompany the decrease in real GDP, Y. If we

Back to Reality

The Quantity Theory of Money

The quantity theory of money refers to a body of thinking about the relation between money and prices. This viewpoint goes back hundreds of years, with some of the more important statements coming from David Hume, Henry Thornton, and Irving Fisher.[5] There are two common elements in these analyses. First, increases in the nominal quantity of money raise the general level of prices. Second, as an empirical matter, movements in the nominal quantity of money account for the bulk of long-run changes in the price level.

Some economists refined the quantity theory to apply to changes in the nominal quantity of money measured relative to changes in the quantity of goods and services—real GDP—on which people spent their money. However, real GDP is only one variable that affects the real demand for money. Therefore, quantity theorists went further to argue that prices rose only when the nominal quantity of money expanded in relation to

the real money balances that people wanted to hold. Hence, most variations in the price level would reflect movements in the nominal quantity of money if the fluctuations in this quantity were much greater than the fluctuations in the real quantity of money demanded. Milton Friedman (1956) stressed the stability of the real demand for money as the hallmark of a modern quantity theorist.

Sometimes economists identify the quantity theory of money with the proposition that changes in the nominal quantity of money are neutral. This idea corresponds to our previous result that changes in nominal money have no effects on real variables. Many quantity theorists regard this result as valid in the long run but not for short-run variations in the nominal quantity of money. Thus, in some versions of the quantity theory, changes in the nominal quantity of money have temporary effects on real variables, such as real GDP.

---

had done the analysis in reverse—to consider a boom in which the real quantity of money demanded, $L(Y, i)$, increased—we would get the opposite conclusion. That is, the price level, P, would fall. Thus, our model has a new prediction: If the nominal quantity of money supplied, M^s, does not vary, the price level, P, will be relatively high in recessions and relatively low in booms. That is, we predict that P will be countercyclical.[6]

The result that the price level, P, is countercyclical may be counterintuitive. One might guess that, since real GDP is low in a recession, the low real income would lead to low consumer demand and tend, thereby, to reduce P. However, in our equilibrium business-cycle model, the underlying shocks come from the supply side, not the demand side. For example, a low technology level, A—the source of a recession in the model—means that goods and services are in low

supply. When looked at this way, it makes sense that P would tend to be high in a recession.

Now we will consider how the model's predictions about the price level, P, match up with the U.S. data. We measure P by the deflator for the GDP. We calculate the cyclical part of P by using the method applied to real GDP in Figure 8.2. The result is the blue graph in Figure 10.4. This graph shows the proportionate deviation of P from its trend. We also show as the red graph the cyclical part of real GDP (from Figure 8.3). We can see from Figure 10.4 that P typically fluctuates in the direction opposite to real GDP.[7] That is, as predicted, the price level is high—relative to trend—in recessions, and low—relative to trend—in booms. The results are similar if we use the consumer price index (CPI), rather than the GDP deflator, to measure the price level.

---

[5] See Hume's essay, "Of Money," in Eugene Rotwein (1970), Thornton (1802), and Fisher (1926).

[6] This result was first emphasized by Finn Kydland and Edward Prescott (1990).

[7] From 1954.1 to 2006.1, the correlation of the cyclical part of the GDP deflator with the cyclical part of real GDP was −0.61. The GDP deflator is less variable than real GDP: The standard deviation of the cyclical part of the GDP deflator was 0.8%, compared with 1.6% for real GDP.

We see from the blue graph in Figure 10.4 that two of the largest positive deviations of the GDP deflator from its trend were in 1974–75 and 1981–82. These increases in the price level reflected, in part, the sharp rises in oil prices generated by the oil cartel run by OPEC. These periods also featured recessions in the United States, so that real GDP was well below its trend, as seen on the red graph. Thus, the price level and real GDP moved in opposite directions at the times of these oil shocks. However, the inverse relation between the price level and real GDP is not just the result of oil shocks—the pattern applies more generally to the period 1954–2006, shown in Figure 10.4.[8]

Price-Level Targeting and Endogenous Money

A key assumption in our model is that the nominal quantity of money supplied, M^s, is independent of the nominal demand for money, $M^d = P \bullet L(Y, i)$. In other words, the monetary authority decides how much nominal money, M, to provide, and sticks with this quantity no matter what happens to nominal money demand, M^d. A formal way to say this is that the money-supply function, given in our case by $M^s = M$, is independent of the money-demand function.

This formulation is useful for studying exogenous changes in the nominal quantity of money supplied, M^s. By exogenous, we mean that the change comes from out of the blue, or at least from outside of the model. The trouble is that most changes in money supply are not like this in the real world.

The head of the central bank does not just wake up in the morning and happen to think that it would be nice if the nominal quantity of money were higher or lower by 10%. Usually, the changes in M^s are responses to economic events; the changes happen because the monetary authority is trying to accomplish some important economic objective. One common objective is to achieve a desired or *target* value of the price level, P. Related objectives, considered in later chapters, are to target the inflation rate and the nominal interest rate.

When the monetary authority seeks to attain a specified price level, P, it typically has to adjust the nominal quantity of money, M, in response to changes in the nominal quantity demanded, M^d. Another way to say this is that M will be endogenous, or determined within the model. We therefore have a setting of **endogenous money**. To see how this works, we now assume that the monetary authority wants the price level, P, to equal a target level, which we call $\bar{P}$. This objective is called **price-level targeting**.

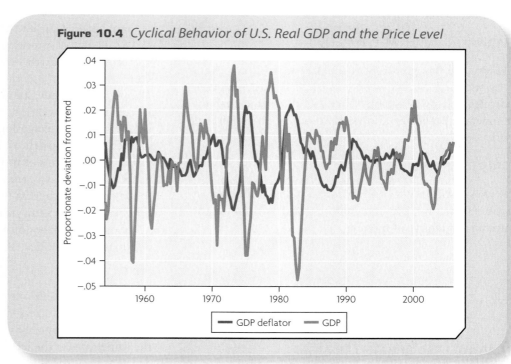

Figure 10.4 *Cyclical Behavior of U.S. Real GDP and the Price Level*

The red graph is the deviation of real GDP from its trend. The blue graph is the deviation of the GDP deflator from its trend. These deviations are measured in a proportionate sense. The GDP deflator is countercyclical—it fluctuates in the direction opposite to real GDP—and is less variable than real GDP.

[8] The pattern is different before World War II. From 1880 to 1940 (using the available annual data), the correlation of the cyclical part of the GNP deflator with the cyclical part of real GNP was positive: 0.39. The main difference in the earlier period is the high frequency of banking panics, which tended to reduce broad monetary aggregates, such as M1, and the price level, along with output. This effect was especially important from 1931 to 1934, during the Great Depression.

For present purposes, we assume that the monetary authority can determine the path of the nominal quantity of money, M, possibly subject to minor random errors. This assumption is reasonable in our model because we are taking a narrow view of money as currency. However, the assumption would be less satisfactory if we took a broader view of M, for example, to add the deposit accounts included in broader monetary aggregates, such as M1 and M2. Another reasonable assumption is that the monetary authority can control a monetary aggregate that is slightly broader than currency: the monetary base. This aggregate adds to total currency outstanding the reserves of financial institutions held at the central bank.

Since we assume that the monetary authority has no technical problems in controlling the quantity of nominal money, the changes in M will reflect only intentional policy, not technical errors. In particular, changes in M will occur because the underlying objective of price-level targeting, $P = \overline{P}$, dictates changes in M.

We still have equality at every point in time between the nominal quantity of money, M, and the nominal quantity demanded, M^d:

(10.6) $M = P \bullet L(Y, i)$

Before, we thought of M as equal to an arbitrary quantity supplied, M^s. Now we will let M be endogenous—determined by equation (10.6)—and assume that the monetary authority allows M to adjust to achieve its price-level target:

(10.7) $P = \overline{P}$

If we substitute $P = \overline{P}$ from equation (10.7) into equation (10.6), we get a condition for determining the nominal quantity of money:

Key equation (endogenous determination of money):

(10.8) $M = \overline{P} \bullet L(Y, i)$

nominal quantity of money = price-level target •
real quantity of money demanded

The idea in equation (10.8) is that the price level, P, can be constant at its target value $\overline{P}$ only if the nominal quantity of money, M, varies on the left-hand side to compensate for changes in the real quantity of money demanded, $L(Y, i)$, on the right-hand side. For example, if $L(Y, i)$ doubles but M stays the same, P would have to fall to satisfy equation (10.6). Alternatively, if $L(Y, i)$ stays the same but M doubles, P would have to rise. To keep P fixed at $\overline{P}$, proportionate changes in the real quantity of money demanded, $L(Y, i)$, have to be matched by equal proportionate changes in M. This condition tells us how price-level targeting determines the behavior of M in equation (10.8). The general point is that the nominal quantity of money, M, will be endogenous and will react to changes in variables that affect the real quantity of money demanded, $L(Y, i)$. We now apply this analysis to determine M in three settings: long-term growth, cyclical fluctuations, and seasonal movements.

Trend Growth of Money   To determine the trend in the nominal quantity of money, M, we have to allow for a long-run trend in the real quantity of money demanded, $L(Y, i)$, on the right-hand side of equation (10.8). The most important source of this trend is long-run economic growth—that is, an upward trend in real GDP, Y. We can use the Solow growth model from Chapter 5 to understand this trend. In the long-run or steady-state situation, real GDP, Y, grows at a constant rate due to technological progress and population growth.[9] This growth of Y produces a continuing rise in the real quantity of money demanded, $L(Y, i)$. If we think of money as currency, the empirical estimates of money demand suggest that the growth rate of $L(Y, i)$ will be about the same as the growth rate of Y.[10]

Consider our condition for determining the nominal quantity of money, M:

(10.8) $M = \overline{P} \bullet L(Y, i)$

Since the price-level target, $\overline{P}$, is constant, continuing growth of the real quantity of money demanded, $L(Y, i)$, on the right-hand side requires M to grow at the same rate on the left-hand side. Since $L(Y, i)$ grows at the same rate as real GDP, Y, we conclude that M must grow at the same rate as Y. Thereby, the growth rate of the nominal quantity of money, M, matches the growth rate of the real quantity demanded, $L(Y, i)$, and

---

[9] The interest rate, i, will be constant in this situation, because the marginal product of capital, MPK, will not be changing. Therefore, at least if we neglect financial innovations, the real quantity of money demanded, $L(Y, i)$, will be changing only because of the growth of real GDP, Y.

[10] With economies of scale in money demand, the real quantity of money demanded would grow at a slower rate than real GDP. As discussed before, the empirical evidence suggests that these economies of scale are important for checkable deposits but not for currency. We are also neglecting the possibility that continuing financial innovations affect the real demand for money.

allows the price level, P, to remain constant at its target level, $\overline{P}$.

The important conclusion is that a growing economy will have growth in its nominal quantity of money, M, assuming that the monetary authority seeks to stabilize the price level, P. This result accords with data considered in Chapter 11. We shall see there that growing M applies to almost all countries in the world. However, we also allow in Chapter 11 for inflation—that is, for a continual upward movement in P.

Cyclical Behavior of Money To study the cyclical behavior of money, we again use the condition for determining the nominal quantity of money, M:

(10.8) $$M = \overline{P} \bullet L(Y, i)$$

We know that the real quantity of money demanded, $L(Y, i)$, is high in a boom and low in a recession; this is because a change in real GDP, Y, moves $L(Y, i)$ in the same direction. (We assume that this effect dominates the impact from a change in the interest rate, i.) We also know that, if M did not fluctuate, the price level, P, would fall in a boom and rise in a recession. That is, P would be countercyclical—low relative to trend in booms and high relative to trend in recessions.

If the monetary authority wants to keep the price level, P, fixed at its target, $\overline{P}$, during economic fluctuations, it has to introduce a cyclical pattern into the nominal quantity of money, M. In particular, in equation (10.8), the cyclical fluctuations in M on the left-hand side have to match the cyclical fluctuations in the real quantity of money demanded, $L(Y, i)$, on the right-hand side. Thus, M will have to rise in a boom (along with the rise in $L[Y, i]$) and fall in a recession (along with the fall in $L[Y, i]$). In other words, M should be procyclical.

Recall that we found that the price level, P, is countercyclical in the U.S. data. This pattern fit with our equilibrium business-cycle model when we assumed that the nominal quantity of money, M, did not vary over the business cycle. In other words, the monetary authority (the Federal Reserve) has not pursued a monetary policy that completely eliminated the countercyclical behavior of P: M has not been sufficiently procyclical to avoid a countercyclical price level. Nevertheless, we would like to know whether the monetary authority has followed a policy that is somewhat procyclical; that is, whether nominal money, M, is high relative to trend during booms and low relative to trend during recessions. If so, this policy would have moderated the countercyclical pattern for P.

Empirically, the nominal quantity of money, M, is weakly procyclical. For example, from 1954 to 2006, the correlation of the cyclical part of currency held by the public with the cyclical part of real GDP was only 0.08. Broader monetary aggregates are somewhat more procyclical: from 1959 to 2006, the correlations with the cyclical part of real GDP were 0.14 for M1 and 0.31 for M2. The weak procyclical pattern in monetary aggregates is consistent with our finding that the price level, P, is countercyclical. The monetary aggregates would have had to be more procyclical to eliminate the countercyclical pattern in P.

Seasonal Variations in Money We have argued that, to achieve price-level stability, the monetary authority has to vary the nominal quantity of money, M, to match the changes in the real quantity demanded, $L(Y, i)$, that occur because of economic growth or fluctuations. An analogous argument applies to the variations in $L(Y, i)$ associated with the seasons.

Until the mid-1980s, the quantity of real currency held in December was about 2% higher than the average for the year, whereas the amount held in February was about 1% lower than average. If the monetary authority had kept the nominal quantity of currency, M, constant over the year, the price level, P, would have had the reverse seasonal pattern—low in December and high in February. To see how the monetary authority avoided this outcome, we can again use our condition for determining the nominal quantity of money, M:

(10.8) $$M = \overline{P} \bullet L(Y, i)$$

To avoid a seasonal pattern in the price level, P, the Federal Reserve engineered a relatively high nominal quantity of currency, M, when the real quantity of money demanded, $L(Y, i)$, was high—for example, December—and a relatively low nominal quantity when $L(Y, i)$ was low—for example, February. Thus, the nominal quantity of currency, M, has a pronounced seasonal pattern, whereas the price level, P, does not have a substantial seasonal pattern. (That is, before seasonal adjustments, P has little seasonal variation.)

The seasonal variations in the real demand for U.S. currency have declined substantially since the mid-1980s. For example, the December excess of real currency over the average for the year varied between 1.6% and 2.2% from 1950 to 1983, but then fell to an average of 0.9% in the 1990s and 0.7% from 2000 to 2005. A study by the Federal Reserve and the U.S. Treasury (Board of Governors of the Federal Reserve System, 2003) suggests that this change relates to the increased use of U.S. currency in foreign countries. The foreign demand for U.S. currency has less of a seasonal pattern than that found in domestic demand. Therefore, the full seasonal variation weakened when more of the currency was held by foreigners.

The pattern is different if we look at checkable deposits, the other main part of M1. The seasonal variations in the U.S. real demand for checkable deposits have not changed so much over time. For example, the December excess of real checkable deposits over the average for the year ranged between 2.4% and 3.3% from 1959 to 1997, then rose to an average of 3.6% from 1998 to 2005. The difference from currency probably arises because the foreign demand for U.S. checkable deposits is not nearly as important as the foreign demand for U.S. currency.

Questions and Problems

A. Review questions

1. What are the costs of transacting between money and alternative financial assets? You might make a list and include such items as the time spent going to the bank or waiting in line. How were these costs affected by the development of automatic teller machines (ATMs)?

2. Consider the following changes and state whether the effect on the real quantity of money demanded is an increase, decrease, or no change:

a. an increase in the nominal interest rate, i

b. an increase in real transaction costs

c. an increase in real GDP, Y, caused by a rise in per capita real GDP with population held constant

d. an increase in real GDP, Y, caused by a rise in population with per capita real GDP held constant

e. an increase in the price level, P

3. Suppose that the nominal quantity of money, M, doubles once and for all.

a. The rise in the price level, P, suggests that workers will be worse off. Is this correct?

b. The rise in the nominal wage rate, w, suggests that workers will be better off. Is this right?

c. How do your results relate to the concept of the neutrality of money?

4. Economists who subscribe to the quantity theory of money believe that changes in the price level, P, are primarily the result of changes in the nominal quantity of money, M. Can this conclusion be based solely on theoretical reasoning?

5. Explain why a favorable shock to the production function tends to reduce the price level, P. How could the monetary authority prevent this fall in P?

6. Explain why it is important to distinguish between shifts in the nominal quantity of money, M, and shifts in the nominal demand for money, M^d. What association would we expect between the price level, P, and real GDP, Y, for periods in which both types of monetary shifts occurred?

7. What is the meaning of the term "endogenous money"? Under what circumstances would endogenous money generate a positive association between nominal money, M, and real GDP, Y?

B. Problems for discussion

8. Effects of other variables on the demand for money Assume given values of real GDP, Y; population; the nominal interest rate, i; and real transaction costs. If these variables are given, would you say that the following statements about the real demand for money are true, false, or uncertain?

a. Agricultural societies have lower real money demand than industrial societies.

b. Dictatorships have higher real money demand than democracies.

c. Countries with a larger fraction of persons who are elderly have higher real money demand.

d. Countries with a higher literacy rate have lower real money demand.

For empirical evidence on these effects, see the study by Lawrence Kenny (1991).

9. Transaction frequency and the demand for money Suppose that a household's consumption expenditure is $60,000 per year and is financed by monthly withdrawals from a savings account.

a. Show on a graph the pattern of the household's money holding over a year. What is the average money balance? Should we identify this average balance with the quantity of money demanded in our model?

b. Suppose now that the frequency of withdrawals from the savings account rises to two per month. What happens to the average money balance?

c. Return to question a, but assume now that consumption expenditure is $120,000 per year. If withdrawals from the savings account are still made monthly, what is the average money balance? How does this average compare to the one in question a? Is it optimal for the frequency of withdrawals to remain the same when consumption expenditure increases? Explain.

10. Velocity of money
The velocity of money is the ratio of the dollar volume of transactions—say, nominal GDP—divided by the nominal quantity of money. How is the velocity of money affected by

a. an increase in the nominal interest rate, i?

b. an increase in real GDP, Y, caused by a rise in per capita real GDP with population held constant?

c. an increase in real GDP, Y, caused by a rise in population with per capita real GDP held constant?

d. an increase in the price level, P?

e. Why might nominal GDP not be the correct measure of transactions?

f. What do you predict happens to the velocity of money as an economy develops?

11. The payments period and the demand for money
Suppose that a worker has an annual income of $60,000. Assume that the worker receives wage payments twice per month. The worker keeps all of these payments in money, does not use any alternative financial assets, and pays for consumption expenditure of $60,000 per year from money holdings.

a. What is the worker's average money balance?

b. What would the average money balance be if the worker were paid monthly, rather than twice per month?

c. What is the general relation between the payments period and the demand for money?

d. How do the results change if the worker puts part of his or her monthly wage payments into a savings account and then makes withdrawals as needed from this account?

12. Shopping trips and the demand for money
Assume again the conditions in the first part of question 11, with a worker paid once per month.

However, instead of making consumption expenditure as a uniform flow, the worker (or the worker's spouse) makes periodic shopping trips. During each trip, enough goods (groceries, for example) are bought to last until the next trip.

a. If the worker shops four times per month, what is the average money balance? Why is the answer different from that for part a of question 11?

b. What happens if the worker shops only twice per month?

c. What is the general relation between the frequency of shopping trips and the demand for money?

d. Suppose that the cost of a shopping trip rises, perhaps because of an increase in the price of gasoline. What would happen to the frequency of shopping trips? What would happen to the demand for money?

13. Transaction costs and households' budget constraints
In our model, we neglected the resources that households use up in transaction costs. Suppose that these costs take the form of purchases of goods and services (such as fees paid to banks or brokers). Assume that real transaction costs decline because of the expansion of ATM machines.

a. How does this change show up in households' budget constraints?

b. What is the income effect on consumption and leisure?

c. Suppose that transaction costs represent the time required to go to a bank, rather than a purchase of goods and services. Is there a change in the results for questions a and b?

14. A currency reform
Suppose that the government replaces the existing monetary unit with a new one. For example, the United States might shift from the old dollar to the Reagan dollar, defined to equal 10 old dollars. People would be able to exchange their old currency for the new currency at the ratio of 10 to 1. Also, any contracts that were written in terms of old dollars are reinterpreted in Reagan dollars at the ratio 10 to 1.

a. What happens to the price level, P, and the interest rate, i?

b. What happens to real GDP, Y; consumption, C; and labor, L?

c. Do the results exhibit the neutrality of money?

15. Denominations of currency
Consider how people divide their holdings of currency between large bills (say, $100 bills) versus

small ones. How would the dollar fraction of currency held in large bills depend on the following:

a. the price level, P?

b. real per capita GDP?

c. population?

d. incentives to avoid records of payments—for example, for tax evasion or to disguise illegal activities, such as the drug trade?

e. increased holdings of U.S. currency in foreign countries?

Given these results, the U.S. data on currency denominations are not so easy to explain. The fraction of the dollar value of currency (including coins) held in denominations of $100 and higher stayed nearly constant—between 20% and 22%—from 1944 to 1970. Then the fraction rose steadily to reach 72% at the end of 2005. What do you think explains these patterns?

Inflation, Money Growth, and Interest Rates

I n Chapter 10, we studied the determination of the price level, P. Now we will consider inflation, by which we mean a continuing upward movement in P. Our previous analysis suggests possible sources of inflation. Start with the equality between the nominal quantity of money supplied, M^s, and the nominal quantity demanded:

(10.5)
$$M^s = P \cdot L\,(Y, i)$$

nominal quantity of money supplied = nominal quantity of money demanded

We assume again that M^s is set exogenously by the monetary authority to equal a given quantity M. Therefore, we can write equation (10.5) as

(11.1)
$$M = P \cdot L\,(Y, i)$$

nominal quantity of money = nominal quantity of money demanded

We can divide by the price level, P, to express the equation in real terms:

(11.2)
$$M/P = L\,(Y, i)$$

real quantity of money = real quantity of money demanded

Suppose that the real quantity of money demanded, L(Y, i), decreases. The decrease in L(Y, i) could reflect a financial innovation, such as increased use of credit cards, or a reduction in real gross domestic product (real GDP), Y. Since L(Y, i) falls on the right-hand side of equation (11.2), M/P has to fall on the left-hand side. For given M, a fall in M/P requires P to increase. Therefore, it seems that declines in the real quantity of money demanded could be sources of inflation.

Notice, however, that each decrease in the real quantity of money demanded, L(Y, i), creates a single increase in P, rather than a continuing series of increases in P. To generate inflation along these lines, we would need a succession of reductions in L(Y, i). Although theoretically possible, this pattern is not realistic. Most countries experience long-term increases in real GDP, Y, which continually raise L(Y, i) on the right-hand side of equation (11.2). Therefore, M/P trends upward on the left-hand side of the equation, and P would trend downward if M did not change. Thus, we cannot explain inflation this way.

Look again at equation (11.2). Since we are ruling out a continuing series of decreases in the real quantity of money demanded as the cause of inflation, we are left with only one other possible explanation. The nominal quantity of money, M, must continually increase in order for P to rise continually. Our analysis from Chapter 10 already noted a link between increases in the nominal quantity of money, M, and expansions of the price level, P. Empirically, it is clear that M—measured as currency or as broader aggregates such as M1—typically grows over time. Moreover, the **money growth rate**—the rate at which M is increasing—varies substantially across countries and over time. Therefore, variations in money growth rates are good candidates for explaining inflation. To assess this linkage, we begin by considering international data on inflation and money growth.

Cross-Country Data on Inflation and Money Growth

Table 11.1 shows inflation rates and money growth rates for 82 countries from 1960 to 2000. We measure the price level, P, by the consumer price index (CPI). We use the CPI, rather than the GDP deflator, because of data availability. However, results with the GDP deflator are similar for countries that have these data.

Table 11.1 *Inflation Rates and Money Growth Rates for 82 Countries*

| Country | 1960–2000 | | | | 1980–2000 |
	Inflation Rate (1)	Growth Rate of Currency (2)	Growth Rate of Real Currency (3)	Growth Rate of Real GDP (4)	Inflation Rate (5)
Congo (Kinshasa)	0.831	0.820	−0.011	−0.005	1.456
Brazil	0.818	0.844	0.026	0.049	1.292
Argentina	0.700	0.695	−0.005	0.025	0.911
Peru	0.535	0.528	−0.007	0.033	0.893
Uruguay	0.407	0.390	−0.017	0.019	0.388
Bolivia	0.371	0.391	0.020	0.026	0.629
Chile	0.343	0.402	0.059	0.041	0.137
Turkey	0.313	0.340	0.027	0.045	0.471
Israel	0.285	0.323	0.038	0.055	0.370
Ghana	0.269	0.263	−0.006	0.033	0.293
Sierra Leone	0.248	0.227	−0.020	0.016	0.453
Indonesia	0.228	0.303	0.075	0.060	0.104
Mexico	0.212	0.251	0.039	0.045	0.335
Ecuador	0.195	0.244	0.050	0.040	0.314
Iceland	0.186	0.194	0.008	0.039	0.173
Tanzania	0.182	0.196	0.015	0.029	0.224
Colombia	0.174	0.212	0.038	0.042	0.199
Venezuela	0.165	0.180	0.015	0.024	0.284
Nigeria	0.157	0.190	0.033	0.019	0.223
Jamaica	0.143	0.177	0.034	0.019	0.180
Iran	0.130	0.179	0.049	0.047	0.192
Costa Rica	0.125	0.165	0.039	0.043	0.188
Paraguay	0.119	0.168	0.048	0.044	0.161

Table 11.1 *(Continued)*

Madagascar	0.117	0.131	0.014	0.018	0.158
Algeria	0.110	0.155	0.045	0.040	0.128
Kenya	0.110	0.138	0.028	0.041	0.128
Haiti	0.107	0.122	0.015	0.048	0.126
Dominican Rep.	0.106	0.144	0.037	0.052	0.153
Greece	0.104	0.141	0.037	0.037	0.131
Portugal	0.103	0.115	0.012	0.042	0.103
Philippines	0.099	0.133	0.034	0.039	0.102
Burundi	0.096	0.103	0.007	0.017	0.106
Syria	0.093	0.150	0.056	0.058	0.128
South Korea	0.091	0.177	0.086	0.075	0.055
Egypt	0.091	0.129	0.038	0.049	0.121
El Salvador	0.090	0.095	0.004	0.030	0.127
Rwanda	0.089	0.097	0.009	0.033	0.088
South Africa	0.088	0.117	0.030	0.033	0.111
Gambia	0.086	0.120	0.034	0.043	0.101
Honduras	0.086	0.122	0.036	0.035	0.121
Guatemala	0.085	0.119	0.035	0.039	0.120
Spain	0.082	0.122	0.040	0.041	0.064
Nepal	0.081	0.148	0.067	0.040	0.090
Mauritius	0.080	0.116	0.035	0.044	0.072
Sri Lanka	0.080	0.116	0.036	0.039	0.104
Trinidad	0.078	0.091	0.013	0.034	0.079
India	0.077	0.116	0.039	0.048	0.086
Italy	0.076	0.100	0.023	0.030	0.064
Pakistan	0.076	0.115	0.039	0.056	0.078
Cameroon	0.073	0.086	0.013	0.035	0.064
Fiji	0.071	0.100	0.029	0.034	0.052
Barbados	0.070	0.096	0.026	0.043	0.041
Jordan	0.070	0.092	0.022	0.052	0.052
New Zealand	0.069	0.063	−0.005	0.024	0.060
Ireland	0.068	0.101	0.033	0.048	0.050
Ivory Coast	0.066	0.093	0.027	0.039	0.054
United Kingdom	0.065	0.061	0.005	0.024	0.047
Gabon	0.062	0.097	0.035	0.049	0.047
Senegal	0.061	0.085	0.025	0.027	0.048
Togo	0.060	0.103	0.043	0.018	0.050
Ethiopia	0.060	0.083	0.023	0.029	0.055
Finland	0.060	0.088	0.029	0.033	0.042
Denmark	0.057	0.065	0.008	0.026	0.039
Sweden	0.056	0.065	0.009	0.025	0.048
Australia	0.056	0.086	0.031	0.037	0.050

(continued)

Table 11.1 *(Continued)*

| Country | 1960–2000 | | | | 1980–2000 |
	Inflation Rate (1)	Growth Rate of Currency (2)	Growth Rate of Real Currency (3)	Growth Rate of Real GDP (4)	Inflation Rate (5)
Norway	0.055	0.061	0.006	0.035	0.048
Morocco	0.053	0.103	0.050	0.049	0.054
France	0.052	0.052	0.000	0.033	0.039
Niger	0.051	0.063	0.011	0.013	0.030
Thailand	0.051	0.105	0.055	0.067	0.044
Canada	0.045	0.075	0.029	0.037	0.039
Cyprus	0.044	0.098	0.053	0.054	0.046
United States	0.044	0.074	0.030	0.035	0.037
Japan	0.043	0.101	0.058	0.050	0.014
Belgium	0.041	0.037	0.004	0.031	0.032
Netherlands	0.040	0.052	0.012	0.032	0.024
Luxembourg	0.039	0.093	0.054	0.042	0.032
Austria	0.038	0.058	0.020	0.033	0.029
Switzerland	0.034	0.041	0.007	0.022	0.026
Malaysia	0.033	0.087	0.054	0.065	0.033
Germany	0.032	0.065	0.033	0.022	0.024
Singapore	0.032	0.098	0.066	0.081	0.023

Notes: Countries are listed in descending order of the inflation rate for 1960–2000. Countries included are those with data from at least the early 1960s through the late 1990s. In some cases, the starting date is a few years after 1960 and the ending date is a few years before 2000. The inflation rate is based on consumer price indexes. Data are from International Monetary Fund, *International Financial Statistics.*

The inflation rate, shown in column 1 of Table 11.1, is the annual growth rate of the price level, P, from 1960 to 2000. The countries appear in descending order of the inflation rate. Column 2 shows the growth rate of nominal money, M, defined as currency. Column 3 shows the difference between the growth rate of currency and the inflation rate. This difference tells us the growth rate of real currency—that is, of M/P. Column 4 has the growth rate of real GDP. Finally, column 5 shows the inflation rate for a more recent period, 1980 to 2000. Here are some highlights from the table:

- The inflation rate was greater than zero for all countries from 1960 to 2000 (column 1) and from 1980 to 2000 (column 5). That is, all countries had some degree of inflation. Falling prices—called **deflation**—did not apply to any country, at least in terms of the

overall experience since 1960 or 1980. The lowest inflation rate was 1.4% per year, for Japan from 1980 to 2000. From 2000 to 2006, Japan did experience deflation—the rate of change of prices was −0.2% per year.

- The growth rate of nominal currency (column 2) was greater than zero for all countries from 1960 to 2000. (The same pattern holds from 1980 to 2000, not shown in the table.)

- The median inflation rate from 1960 to 2000 was 8.3% per year, with 30 countries exceeding 10%. For the growth rate of nominal currency, the median was 11.6% per year, with 50 above 10%.

- There is a broad cross-sectional range for the inflation rates and the growth rates of money. The inflation rates varied from 83% for Congo (Kinshasa) and 82% for Brazil to 3.2% for Singapore and

Germany. The growth rates of currency varied from 84% for Brazil and 82% for Congo (Kinshasa) to 3.7% for Belgium and 4.1% for Switzerland.

- In most countries, the growth rate of nominal currency, M, exceeded the growth rate of prices, P (the inflation rate). Therefore, the growth rate of real money balances, M/P, shown in column 3, was greater than zero in most countries. The median growth rate of real currency from 1960 to 2000 was 3.0% per year.

- A comparison of column 1 with column 5 shows the tendency for a country that has a high inflation rate in one period to have a high inflation rate in another period. For the 82 countries, the correlation of the inflation rate from 1960 to 1980 (not shown in the table) with that from 1980 to 2000 was 0.58. The corresponding correlation for growth rates of nominal currency was 0.54. Some countries did manage to reduce the inflation rate from the first half to the second half of the sample. For example, Chile went from an inflation rate of 56% per year from 1960 to 1980 to 14% from 1980 to 2000, and Indonesia went from 34% per year from 1960 to 1980 to 10% from 1980 to 2000.

- To understand inflation, the most important observation from the cross-country data is the strong positive association between the inflation rate and the growth rate of nominal currency. Figure 11.1 displays this relationship from 1960 to 2000. The vertical axis plots a country's inflation rate (column 1 of the table), and the horizontal axis plots the growth rate of currency (column 2). The graph shows that a country with a lot of inflation also had a high money growth rate; the correlation between the two variables is remarkably high, 0.99. The slope is close to one, so that an increase in the growth rate of nominal currency by 1% per year is associated with an increase in the inflation rate by around 1% per year. This strong association does not, however, tell us the direction of causation between inflation and money growth. That is, we cannot say whether a country had a high inflation rate because it had a high money growth rate, or vice versa. However, we can be sure that a country cannot have a high inflation rate over 40 years unless it also has a high money growth rate.

One lesson from the cross-country data is that, to understand inflation, we have to include money growth as a central part of the analysis. That is, we have to take seriously Milton Friedman's (1968b, p. 29) famous dictum: "Inflation is always and everywhere a monetary phenomenon." We will now extend our equilibrium business-cycle model to allow for inflation and money growth.

Inflation and Interest Rates

e now begin to incorporate inflation into our equilibrium business-cycle model. We will start by considering actual and expected inflation rates.

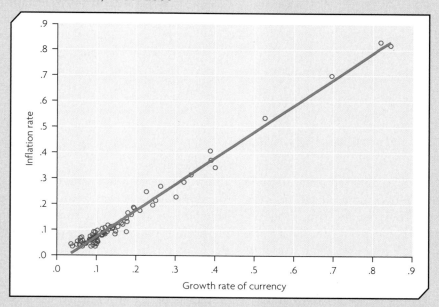

Figure 11.1 *Inflation Rate and Growth Rate of Nominal Currency for 82 Countries, 1960–2000*

This graph uses the data from Table 11.1. The vertical axis plots the inflation rate from 1960 to 2000, based on consumer price indexes. The horizontal axis plots the growth rate of nominal currency from 1960 to 2000. The two variables have a strong positive association—the correlation is 0.99. The slope of the relation is close to one; that is, an increase in the growth rate of nominal currency by 1% per year is associated with an increase in the inflation rate by about 1% per year.

Actual and Expected Inflation

Let the price level in year 1 be P_1 and that in year 2 be P_2. The change in the price level from year 1 to year 2 is $\Delta P_1 = P_2 - P_1$. Let π be the inflation rate. The inflation rate from year 1 to year 2, π_1, is the ratio of the change in the price level to the initial price level:

(11.3)
$$\pi_1 = (P_2 - P_1)/P_1$$
$$\pi_1 = \Delta P_1/P_1$$

For example, if $P_1 = 100$ and $P_2 = 105$, the inflation rate from year 1 to year 2 is

$$\pi_1 = (105 - 100)/100$$
$$= 0.05 \text{ or } 5\% \text{ per year}$$

Table 11.1 showed that inflation rates, π, are typically greater than zero. Therefore, we usually consider cases where prices are rising, so that $P_2 > P_1$ and, hence, $\pi_1 > 0$. We can, however, study falling prices, where $P_2 < P_1$ and, hence, $\pi_1 < 0$. These cases are called *deflations*. Economists have become more interested in deflations because the recent experiences of a few countries, notably Japan, suggest that deflations may become empirically relevant in the future.

We can rearrange equation (11.3) to solve for year 2's price level, P_2. First, multiply through by P_1 to get

$$\pi_1 \bullet P_1 = P_2 - P_1$$

Then add P_1 to both sides, combine the two terms that have P_1 on the left, and swap the left- and right-hand sides to get

(11.4)
$$P_2 = (1 + \pi_1) \bullet P_1$$

Over one year, the price level rises by the factor $1 + \pi_1$—if $P_1 = 100$ and $\pi_1 = 0.05$,

$$P_2 = (1.05) \bullet 100 = 105$$

In making choices, such as whether to consume this year or next year, households want to know how prices will change over time. Since the future is unknown, households have to form forecasts or **expectations of inflation**. Denote by π_1^e the expectation of the inflation rate π_1. If households know year 1's price level, P_1, equation (11.3) shows that the prediction for π_1 corresponds to a forecast of next year's price level, P_2.

Since future price levels are unknown, forecasts of inflation will be imperfect. Therefore, the actual inflation rate, π_1, will usually deviate from its expectation, π_1^e,

and the forecast error—or **unexpected inflation**—will be nonzero. Sometimes unexpected inflation is greater than zero and sometimes it is less than zero. Although these errors are unavoidable, households try to keep the errors as small as possible. Therefore, they use available information on past inflation and other variables to avoid systematic mistakes. Expectations formed this way are called **rational expectations**.[1] This rationality implies that unexpected inflation would not exhibit a systematic pattern of errors over time. For example, if unexpected inflation is greater than zero this year, this mistake will be factored into the calculation for next year.

Real and Nominal Interest Rates

In previous chapters, we assumed that the inflation rate was zero. Therefore, we did not have to distinguish between the *real interest rate* and the *nominal interest rate*. Now we make this distinction when the inflation rate is not zero.

Let i_1 be the interest rate on bonds in year 1. Suppose, for example, that $i_1 = 0.05$, or 5%, per year. If a household holds $1,000 of bonds in year 1, how much assets would the household have in year 2? First, the household still has the principal of $1,000. Second, the

---

[1] The idea of rational expectations comes from John Muth (1961). For applications to macroeconomics, see Robert Lucas (1977).

household has interest income equal to $1,000 \bullet 0.05 =$ $50. Therefore, the total of assets in year 2 is

$$principal\ (\$1,000) + interest\ (\$50) =$$
$$assets\ in\ year\ 2(\$1,000 + \$50)$$
$$= \$1,050$$

Now we generalize to allow for any interest rate, i_1. The principal carried over to year 2 is still $1,000. The interest income equals $1,000 \bullet i_1$. Therefore, we have

$$principal\ (\$1,000) + interest\ (\$1,000 \bullet i_1) =$$
$$assets\ in\ year\ 2(\$1,000 + \$1,000 \bullet i_1)$$
$$= \$1,000 \bullet (1 + i_1)$$

Thus, the dollar value of assets held as bonds rises over the year by the factor $1 + i_1$. The interest rate i_1 is the dollar or **nominal interest rate** because i_1 determines the change over time in the nominal value of assets held as bonds.

We have learned how the household's nominal assets change over time. However, the household does not care about the nominal value of assets. What it cares about are the goods that can be bought with these assets—that is, the real value of assets. Thus, we have to figure out what happens over time to the real value of assets.

Suppose that the inflation rate is $\pi_1 = 0.01$, or 1%, per year, as shown in row 1 of Table 11.2. Equation (11.4) shows that the price level rises over one year by the factor $1 + \pi_1$. Thus, the price level increases from $P_1 = 100$ in year 1 to $P_2 = 100 \bullet (1.01) = 101$ in year 2. These values appear in row 2 of the table. If the nominal interest rate is $i_1 = 0.05$, or 5%, per year, as in row 3

of Table 11.2, nominal assets still grow from $1,000 in year 1 to $1,050 in year 2, as shown in row 4.

What happens to real assets? In year 1, real assets are

$$year\ 1\ real\ assets = 1,000/100 = 10\ goods$$

In year 2, real assets are

$$year\ 2\ real\ assets = 1,050/101 = 10.4\ goods$$

(We rounded off the result to one digit to get 10.4 as an approximation.) These values appear in row 5 of Table 11.2.

Real assets rose by the proportion

$$(10.4 - 10)/10$$
$$= 0.4/10$$
$$= 0.04$$

Define the **real interest rate** as the rate at which the real value of assets held as bonds changes over time. Therefore, as shown in row 6, the real interest rate in this example is 0.04, or 4%, per year. Notice that the real interest rate, 4%, falls short of the nominal interest rate, 5%, by the inflation rate, 1%.

Now we generalize to allow for any nominal interest rate, i_1, and inflation rate, π_1. Since the nominal interest rate is i_1, dollar assets rise by the factor $1 + i_1$:

dollar assets in year 2 = (dollar assets in year 1) $\bullet$ *(1 + i$_1$)*

Since the inflation rate is π_1, the price level rises by the factor $1 + \pi_1$ (see equation [11.4]):

$$P_2 = P_1 \bullet (1 + \pi_1)$$

Table 11.2 *Nominal and Real Interest Rates*

		Year 1	Year 2
(1)	Inflation rate	0.01	
(2)	Price level	100	101
(3)	Nominal interest rate	0.05	
(4)	Nominal assets	1000	1050
(5)	Real assets	10	10.4
(6)	Real interest rate	0.04	

Note: Lines 1 and 2 show the effect of the inflation rate on the price level. Lines 3 and 4 show the effect of the nominal interest rate on the change over time in the nominal value of assets. Lines 5 and 6 show the effects of the nominal interest rate and the inflation rate on the change over time in the real value of assets. The change in the real value of assets depends on the real interest rate, which equals the difference between the nominal interest rate and the inflation rate.

Since real assets are the ratio of dollar assets to the price level, we can get an expression for real assets by dividing the first equation by the second one:

$$\frac{dollar\ assets\ in\ year\ 2}{P_2} = \left(\frac{dollar\ assets\ in\ year\ 1}{P_1}\right) \bullet \frac{(1 + i_1)}{(1 + \pi_1)}$$

$$real\ assets\ in\ year\ 2 = (real\ assets\ in\ year\ 1) \bullet (1 + i_1)/(1 + \pi_1)$$

Thus, real assets rise by the factor $(1 + i_1)/(1 + \pi_1)$.

Since the real interest rate, denoted by r_1, is the rate at which assets held as bonds change in real value, we have

(11.5) $\qquad (1 + r_1) = (1 + i_1)/(1 + \pi_1)$

For the example in Table 11.2, we had

$$1.04 \approx 1.05/1.01$$

so that the real interest rate was $r_1 \approx 0.04$.

In the general case, we can get a useful formula for the real interest rate, r_1, if we manipulate equation (11.5). Multiply through on both sides by $1 + \pi_1$ to get

$$(1 + r_1) \bullet (1 + \pi_1) = 1 + i_1$$

If we multiply out the two terms on the left-hand side, we get

$$1 + r_1 + \pi_1 + r_1 \bullet \pi_1 = 1 + i_1$$

If we cancel the "1" on each side and place all terms except for r_1 on the right-hand side, we get

$$r_1 = i_1 - \pi_1 - r_1 \bullet \pi_1$$

The right-hand side has the cross term, $r_1 \bullet \pi_1$, which tends to be small; for example, if $r_1 = 0.04$ and $\pi_1 = 0.01$, the term is 0.0004. In fact, this cross term appears only because we allowed interest rates and inflation rates to be compounded just once per year. A more accurate procedure would be to compound these rates continuously. In that case, the cross term disappears, and we get the simpler formula for the real interest rate:

> Key equation:
>
> *real interest rate =*
> *normal interest rate − inflation rate*
>
> **(11.6)** $\qquad r_1 = i_1 - \pi_1$

Henceforth, we use equation (11.6) to compute the real interest rate.

The Real Interest Rate and Intertemporal Substitution

We discussed intertemporal-substitution effects on consumption in Chapter 7. A higher interest rate, i_1, motivated the household to reduce year 1's consumption, C_1, compared to year 2's, C_2. When the inflation rate, π_1, is not zero, it is the real interest rate, r_1, rather than the nominal rate, i_1, that matters for intertemporal substitution.

To see why, assume that i_1 is 5% per year and π_1 is 2% per year, so that r_1 is 3% per year. Suppose that the household reduces C_1 by one unit and thereby raises real assets held as bonds or capital by one unit. These extra real assets become 1.03 additional real assets in year 2 (because r_1 is 3%). Therefore, the household can raise C_2 by 1.03 units. Thus, one unit less of C_1 can be transformed into 1.03 units more of C_2. If r_1 rises, the incentive to defer consumption increases, and the household reduces C_1 and raises C_2.

The nominal interest rate, i_1, is not the right variable for intertemporal substitution. If i_1 is 5% per year, the household can reduce year 1's nominal spending on C_1 by \$1.00 and raise year 2's nominal spending on C_2 by \$1.05. However, the extra \$1.05 of spending in year 2 buys only 1.03 additional units of goods (if the inflation rate is $\pi_1 = 2\%$ per year). Thus, the correct variable for intertemporal substitution is the real interest rate, $r_1 = 3\%$ per year. The same conclusion holds for intertemporal-substitution effects on labor supply: The real interest rate, r_1, matters.

Actual and Expected Real Interest Rates

When we refer to bonds, we usually have in mind assets such as U.S. Treasury bills that specify in advance the nominal interest rate, i. For example, a newly issued three-month U.S. Treasury bill (a T-bill) guarantees the nominal interest rate when held for three months. The real interest rate on the T-bill depends on the inflation rate over the three months.

As an example, during year t, the real interest rate on a 3-month T-bill is

(11.7) $\qquad r_t = i_t - \pi_t$

We can think of i_t as the nominal interest rate on a three-month T-bill issued on January 1 of year t. The rate i_t is expressed at an annual rate, such as 0.02, or 2%, per year. The variable π_t is the inflation rate, also expressed at an annual rate, from January to April. The problem is that this inflation rate is unknown in January, when the household buys the T-bill. The real interest rate, r_t, becomes known only later, when π_t is observed.

Suppose that, in January, households expect the inflation rate from January to April to be π_t^e. This expected inflation rate determines the **expected real interest rate**, r_t^e, on the T-bill from equation (11.7):

(11.8)
$$r_t^e = i_t - \pi_t^e$$
expected real interest rate =
nominal interest rate − expected inflation rate

For example, if $i_t = 0.03$ per year and $\pi_t^e = 0.01$ per year, $r_t^e = 0.02$ per year. Formally, the expected real interest rate is the expectation, formed at the beginning of year t, of the real interest rate, r_t, over a period such as the next three months.

When households choose today's consumption and labor supply, they know the expected real interest rate, r_t^e, not the actual rate, r_t. Thus, intertemporal-substitution effects depend on r_t^e, which we would like to measure. To do so, we have to calculate the expected inflation rate, π_t^e.

Measuring Expected Inflation
Economists have used three methods to measure the expected inflation rate:

1. Ask a sample of people about their expectations.
2. Use the hypothesis of rational expectations, which says that expectations correspond to optimal forecasts, given the available information. Then use statistical techniques to gauge these optimal forecasts.
3. Use market data to infer expectations of inflation.

The main shortcoming of the first approach is that the sample may not be representative of the whole economy. Also, economists have better theories of how households take actions than of how they answer survey questions. Nevertheless, surveys can be useful, and we discuss applications to expected inflation in the next section.

The second approach, based on rational expectations, has produced both successes and failures. One challenge is to figure out what information households possess when they form expectations. Another issue is the choice among statistical models to generate forecasts of inflation.

The third approach has become especially useful since the governments of many advanced countries

began in the 1980s and 1990s to issue **indexed bonds**. Unlike more familiar nominal bonds, which specify the nominal interest rate, indexed bonds prescribe the real interest rate. For example, a 10-year indexed bond adjusts nominal payouts of interest and principal in response to inflation to ensure the promised real rate of return over 10 years. We discuss later how to use these data to infer expected inflation rates, π_t^e.

U.S. Expected Inflation and Interest Rates Since World War II
A commonly used survey measure of expected inflation is the one initiated in 1946 by Joseph Livingston, a Philadelphia journalist. The survey asks around 50 economists for their forecasts of the CPI 6 and 12 months in the future.[2] These forecasts allow us to construct expected inflation rates. The 6-month-ahead forecasts of inflation are shown as the red graph in Figure 11.2. The figure also shows as the blue graph the actual inflation rate over the previous 12 months. These inflation rates were known to the survey respondents when they made their forecasts.

Figure 11.2 shows that actual and expected inflation rates tended to move together from 1954 to 2006. Inflation rates were low from the mid-1950s to the mid-1960s, rose until the start of the 1980s, then fell sharply in the early 1980s. Inflation rates were low and fairly stable following the mid-1980s. In June 2006, the expected inflation rate for the next six months was 2.2%.

Figure 11.3 shows as the blue graph the nominal interest rate, i_t, on three-month T-bills. The red graph is the expected real interest rate, r_t^e, calculated by subtracting the Livingston expected inflation rate, π_t^e, shown in Figure 11.2, from i_t:

(11.8)
$$r_t^e = i_t - \pi_t^e$$

The nominal interest rate, i_t, moved upward from the mid-1950s to the early 1980s. However, because the expected inflation rate, π_t^e, rose in a similar way, the expected real interest rate, r_t^e, did not have this upward trend. This tendency for i_t and π_t^e to move together is a typical long-run pattern. Therefore, we will want to explain this pattern with our model.

The expected real interest rate, r_t^e, was fairly stable at 2–3% from the mid-1950s until the early 1970s. Then r_t^e fell to near zero for much of the 1970s, before rising to around 4% in the 1980s. The rate r_t^e was again near zero in 1992–93, rose back to 3–4% for the rest of the 1990s, fell to near zero from mid-2001 through 2004, then rose to 2.4% in mid 2006.

---

[2] For a discussion of the Livingston survey, see John Carlson (1977).

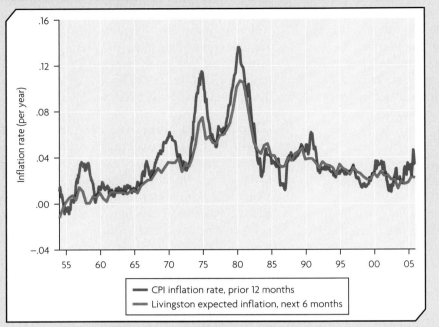

Figure 11.2 *Actual and Expected Inflation Rates in the United States*

Legend:
- CPI inflation rate, prior 12 months
- Livingston expected inflation, next 6 months

The blue graph shows the inflation rate over the prior 12 months, computed from the consumer price index (CPI). The red graph shows the expected CPI inflation rate. These expectations, formed six to eight months in advance, are from the Livingston survey, available from the Federal Reserve Bank of Philadelphia.

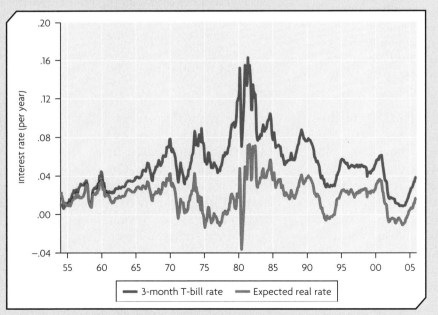

Figure 11.3 *Nominal and Expected Real Interest Rates in the United States*

Legend:
- 3-month T-bill rate
- Expected real rate

The three-month U.S. Treasury bill rate, shown as the blue graph, is a nominal interest rate. We compute the expected real interest rate by subtracting the expected CPI inflation rate given by the Livingston survey measure shown in Figure 11.2. The resulting expected real interest rate is the red graph.

Indexed Bonds, Real Interest Rates, and Expected Inflation Rates More reliable measures of real interest rates and expected inflation rates became available in the 1980s and 1990s from data on indexed government bonds, which adjust nominal payouts of interest and principal for changes in consumer-price indexes. These bonds guarantee the real interest rate over the maturity of each issue. The U.K. government first issued these types of bonds in 1981. Subsequently, indexed bonds were issued by the governments of Australia (1985), Canada (1991), Iceland (1992), New Zealand (1995), Israel (1995), the United States (1997), Sweden (1997), and France (1998).[3]

Since the real interest rates on indexed bonds are guaranteed, the expected real interest rate equals the actual rate. Figure 11.4 shows the real interest rate since 1997 for U.S. indexed bonds of 10-year maturity (the red graph), since 1998 for 30-year maturity (the green graph), and since 2001 for 5-year maturity (the blue graph). For the 10-year bonds, the real interest rate from 1997 to 2000 ranged from 3.3% to 4.3%, then fell to less than 2%. The

---

[3] The data are available from Global Financial Data (www.globalfinancialdata.com).

rate rose from 1.7% in mid-2005 to 2.4% in July 2006. This pattern is similar to that shown for the estimated expected real interest rate on three-month T-bills in Figure 11.3.

We will now show how to use the indexed-bonds data to measure the expected inflation rate. The basic principle that we use is that the prospective real returns on nominal bonds must be close to the guaranteed real returns on indexed bonds—otherwise, households would be unwilling to hold both types of bonds. We can use Figure 11.4 to get a time series on real interest rates, r_t, for indexed bonds of varying maturity. We can use data on U.S. Treasury nominal bonds to measure the nominal interest rate, i_t, for the same maturities. Remember that the expected real interest rate on nominal bonds is given from equation (11.8) by

$$r_t^e(\text{on nominal bonds}) = i_t(\text{on nominal bonds}) - \pi_t^e$$

If the expected real interest rate on nominal bonds, r_t^e, equals the guaranteed real rate, r_t, on indexed bonds,[4] we can substitute r_t on the indexed bonds for r_t^e on the nominal bonds to get

$$r_t(\text{on indexed bonds}) = i_t(\text{on nominal bonds}) - \pi_t^e$$

We can then rearrange terms to get the expected inflation rate, π_t^e, on the left-hand side:

(11.9) $\pi_t^e = i_t(\text{on nominal bonds})$
$- r_t(\text{on indexed bonds})$

Thus, we can calculate π_t^e from data on the interest rates on the right-hand side.

Figure 11.5 shows the expected inflation rate, π_t^e, computed from equation (11.9), for bonds of 10-year maturity (the red graph), 30-year maturity (the green graph), and 5-year maturity (the blue graph). In 2006, π_t^e

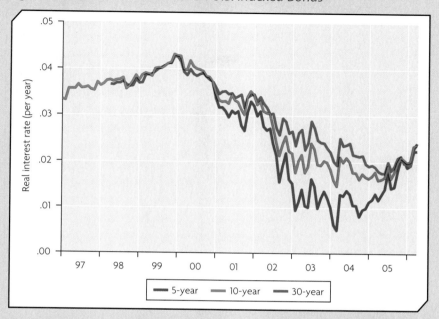

Figure 11.4 *Real Interest Rates on U.S. Indexed Bonds*

The graphs show the real interest rate on inflation-protected U.S. Treasury bonds (indexed bonds). The blue graph is for 5-year maturity, the red graph for 10-year maturity, and the green graph for 30-year maturity. Data are from Global Financial Data (www.globalfinancialdata.com).

was between 2% and 3%. These measures of π_t^e match up reasonably well with the 6-month-ahead expected inflation rate from the Livingston survey, shown by the red graph in Figure 11.2. The values in Figure 11.5 are more variable—and probably more accurate—than the Livingston numbers. However, the Livingston survey has the advantage of being available since the late 1940s.

Interest Rates on Money

Our analysis of nominal and real interest rates applies to money (currency), once we recognize that the nominal interest rate on money is zero. The real interest rate on money is

real interest rate on money =
nominal interest rate on money − π_t

real interest rate on money = $-\pi_t$

Thus, if π_t is greater than zero, the real interest rate on money is less than zero; the real value of money erodes over timxe because of increases in the price level.

[4] Uncertainty about the real interest rate on nominal bonds means that the expected real interest rate on these bonds could differ from the guaranteed real interest rate on indexed bonds. Nevertheless, equation (11.9) provides a reasonable approximation to the expected inflation rate, π_t^e.

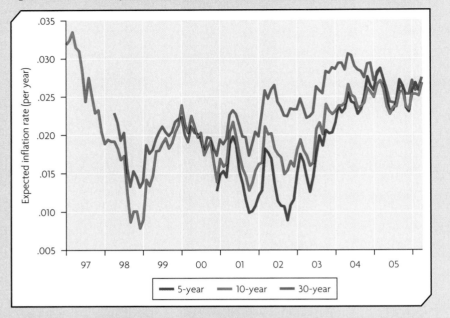

Figure 11.5 *U.S. Expected Inflation Rates, Based on Indexed Bond Yields*

We compute expected CPI inflation rates by taking the nominal interest rate on nominal U.S. Treasury bonds and subtracting the real interest rate on indexed U.S. Treasury bonds (from Figure 11.4). See equation (11.9). The blue graph is based on 5-year bonds, the red graph on 10-year bonds, and the green graph on 30-year bonds. Thus, the graphs measure expected CPI inflation rates over 5 years, 10 years, and 30 years, respectively.

Inflation in the Equilibrium Business-Cycle Model

We now extend the equilibrium business-cycle model to allow for inflation. In making this extension, we have two major objectives. First, we want to see how inflation affects our conclusions about the determination of real variables, including real GDP, consumption and investment, quantities of labor and capital services, the real wage rate, and the real rental price. The real interest rate is another real variable that can be added to this list. Second, we want to understand the causes of inflation.

In the rest of this chapter, we study fully anticipated inflation, so that the inflation rate, π_t, equals the expected rate, π_t^e. This analysis applies to long-lasting changes in inflation, because households would adjust to a changed inflation environment and, therefore, factor these changes into their expectations. When the actual inflation rate equals the expected inflation rate,

the real interest rate, r_t, equals the expected real interest rate, r_t^e. Chapter 15 considers unexpected inflation.

The cross-country data suggest that inflation is closely related to money growth. Therefore, we now extend the equilibrium business-cycle model to allow for money growth. In the simplest setting, the government prints new currency and gives it to people. According to an imaginary story by Milton Friedman (1969, pp. 4–5), public officials stuff a helicopter full of paper money and fly around, dropping money randomly over the countryside. When people pick up the money, they receive a **transfer payment** from the government. Although the story is unrealistic, it provides a simple device for introducing new money into the economy. The important assumption is that the payments are **lump-sum transfers**, meaning that the amount received is independent of how much the household consumes and works, how much money the household holds, and so on. Therefore, we do not have to analyze how people adjust their behavior to attract more transfers. We will find that more realistic forms of money creation yield similar results.

Now we will consider various ways in which inflation affects real variables in the equilibrium business-cycle model.

Intertemporal-Substitution Effects

For a given nominal interest rate, i_t, a change in the inflation rate, π_t, affects the real interest rate, $r_t = i_t - \pi_t$. Moreover, we are assuming that the expected inflation rate, π_t^e, equals the actual rate, π_t, so that the expected real interest rate, r_t^e, equals the actual rate, r_t. We know that the expected real interest rate, r_t^e, has intertemporal-substitution effects on consumption and labor supply. Therefore, for given i, a change in π_t will have these intertemporal-substitution effects.

Bonds and Capital

Households still hold two forms of earning assets: bonds and ownership of capital. We know from Chapter 9 that the rates of return on these two assets have to be equal; otherwise, households would be unwilling to hold both types. Therefore, when the inflation rate, π, was zero, we got the condition:

(9.5) $$i = (R/P) \bullet \kappa - \delta(\kappa)$$

rate of return on bonds =
rate of return from owning capital

The rate of return on capital on the right-hand side, $(R/P) \bullet \kappa - \delta(\kappa)$, depends on the real rental price, R/P, the utilization rate for capital, κ, and the depreciation rate, $\delta(\kappa)$.

When the inflation rate, π, is nonzero, the expression $(R/P) \bullet \kappa - \delta(\kappa)$ on the right-hand side of equation (9.5) still gives the real rate of return from owning capital. (All parts of this expression are in real terms.) However, we have to modify the left-hand side of equation (9.5) to replace the nominal interest rate on bonds, i, by the real rate, r, to get

> Key equation (equality of real rates of return):
>
> **[11.10]** $$r = (R/P) \bullet \kappa - \delta(\kappa)$$
> *real rate of return on bonds =*
> *real rate of return from owning capital*

Interest Rates and the Demand for Money

In Chapter 10, we discussed how the demand for money came from balancing transaction costs and asset income. By incurring more transaction costs, the household could hold less real money balances, M/P, and thereby more real earning assets, $(B/P + K)$. The nominal interest rate on earning assets was i, whereas that on money was zero. Therefore, i determined how much interest income was lost by holding money rather than earning assets. An increase in i made the potential loss of interest income more significant and, therefore, motivated households to incur more transaction costs to reduce M/P.

This analysis still applies when the inflation rate, π, differs from zero. The real interest rate on earning assets

is $r = i - \pi$, and the real interest rate on money is $-\pi$. The difference between the two real interest rates is

$$(i - \pi) - (-\pi)$$
$$= i$$

Therefore, the nominal interest rate, i, still determines the cost of holding money rather than earning assets. We can therefore still describe real money demand by the function used in Chapter 10:

[10.2] $$M^d/P = L(Y, i)$$

Notice an important point: *It is the real interest rate, r, that has intertemporal-substitution effects on consumption and labor supply. However, it is the nominal interest, i, that influences the real demand for money, M^d/P.*

Inflation and the Real Economy

We found in Chapter 10 that a change in the nominal quantity of money, M, was neutral. A doubling of M led to a doubling of the price level, P, and to no changes in real variables, such as real GDP. If we allow M to grow over time, we will find that P also grows. That is, money growth creates inflation—the inflation rate, π, will be greater than zero. We study in this section the effects of money growth and inflation on real GDP and other real variables.

Figure 9.5 in Chapter 9 analyzed the demand and supply of capital services, $(\kappa K)^d$ and $(\kappa K)^s$, where κ is the capital utilization rate and K is the capital stock. Figure 11.6 shows these demand and supply curves. A change in π does not shift $(\kappa K)^d$, because π does not affect the marginal product of capital services, MPK. (The demand, $[\kappa K]^d$, does not shift if labor input, L, is unchanged, as we will soon verify.) A change in π does not shift $(\kappa K)^s$, because K is fixed in the short run and π does not alter the optimal κ (for a given real rental price, R/P). Since the demand and supply curves do not shift, a change in π does not affect the market-clearing real rental price, $(R/P)^*$, and quantity of capital services, $(\kappa K)^*$.

Figure 8.15 in Chapter 8 analyzed the demand and supply of labor, L^d and L^s. Figure 11.7 shows these demand and supply curves. A change in π does not shift L^d, because π does not affect the marginal product of labor, MPL. However, L^s would shift if a change in π had an income effect. We assume that this income effect is small enough to ignore. In that case, a change in π does not shift L^s and, therefore, does not affect the market-clearing real wage rate, $(w/P)^*$, and quantity of labor input, L^*.

Why might a change in the inflation rate, π, have an income effect? The reason is that π will turn out to affect real money balances, M/P, and the transaction costs associated with money management. However, in normal times, these income effects are minor, and we can ignore them as a reasonable approximation. In this case, we are okay with our assumption in Figure 11.7 that a change in π does not shift the labor supply curve,

L^s. We then conclude that a change in π does not influence labor and capital input, L and κK; the real wage rate, w/P; and the real rental price, R/P.

Real GDP, Y, is determined by the production function from Chapter 9:

(9.1) $$Y = A \bullet F(\kappa K, L)$$

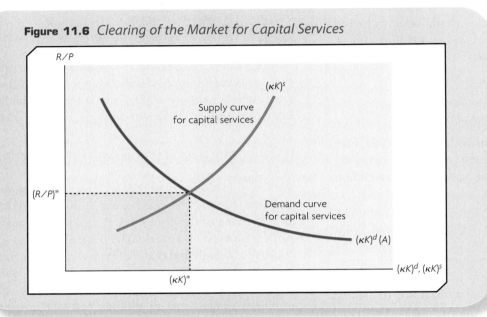

Figure 11.6 *Clearing of the Market for Capital Services*

A change in the inflation rate, π, does not shift the demand or supply curve for capital services. Therefore, $(R/P)^*$ and $(\kappa K)^*$ do not change.

We know that a change in the inflation rate, π, does not affect the inputs of capital services and labor, κK and L. Since the technology level, A, is fixed, we conclude that a change in π does not influence real GDP, Y.

The real rental price, R/P, and the capital utilization rate, κ, determine the real rate of return from owning capital, $(R/P) \bullet \kappa - \delta(\kappa)$, and therefore the real interest rate, r, from the formula worked out before:

(11.10) $$r = R/P) \bullet \kappa - \delta(\kappa).$$

Since R/P and κ are unchanged, we find that a change in the inflation rate, π, does not affect the real interest rate, r.

Finally, we can use our analysis from Chapters 8 and 9 to study the division of real GDP, Y, between consumption, C, and gross investment, I. If we continue to ignore income effects from inflation, π, we know that C does not change. (No substitution effects arise, because the real interest rate, r, and the real wage rate, w/P, are

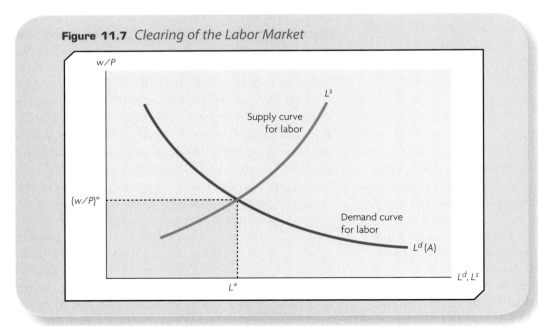

Figure 11.7 *Clearing of the Labor Market*

A change in the inflation rate, π, does not shift the demand or supply curve for labor. Therefore, $(w/P)^*$ and L^* do not change.

unchanged.) Since Y is fixed, we conclude that I does not change. Therefore, we can add C and I to the list of unchanged real variables.

We have found that—as an approximation when we ignore income effects—the time paths of money growth and inflation do not affect a group of real variables. This group comprises real GDP, Y; inputs of labor and capital services, L and κK; consumption and investment, C and I; the real wage rate, w/P; the real rental price, R/P; and the real interest rate, r. Therefore, our earlier results on the neutrality of money—which referred to a one-time change in the nominal quantity, M—apply, as an approximation, to the entire path of money growth. The approximate independence of real variables from money growth is an important result. Moreover, this independence simplifies our next topic—the linkages among money growth, inflation, and the nominal interest rate.

Money Growth, Inflation, and the Nominal Interest Rate

Our objective in this section is to analyze how the time path of the nominal quantity of money, M_t, determines the time path of the price level, P_t, and, hence, the inflation rate, π_t. We use the setting from Chapter 10 in which the monetary authority exogenously sets M_t each year. We know from the previous section that the time paths of real GDP, Y_t, and the real interest rate, r_t, will—as an approximation—be independent of money growth and inflation. To simplify further, we also assume for now that Y_t and r_t are constant over time.

Let M_t be the nominal quantity of money in year t and ΔM_t the change in this quantity from year t to year $t + 1$:

$$\Delta M_t = M_{t+1} - M_t$$

The growth rate of money from year t to year $t + 1$, denoted by μ_t, is the ratio of the change in money to the quantity of money:

[11.11]
$$\mu_t = \Delta M_t / M_t$$

For example, if $M_t = 100$ and $\Delta M_t = 5$, the growth rate of money is

$$\mu_t = 5/100$$
$$= 0.05, \text{ or } 5\%, \text{ per year}$$

If we multiply through equation (11.11) by M_t, we get

$$\mu_t M_t = M_{t+1} - M_t$$

If we move M_t from the right-hand side to the left-hand side, combine the terms involving M_t, and then switch the right- and left-hand sides, we get

[11.12]
$$M_{t+1} = (1 + \mu_t) \bullet M_t$$

Thus, the nominal quantity of money rises from year t to year $t + 1$ by the factor $1 + \mu_t$. For example, if $M_t = 100$ and $\mu_t = 0.05$, $M_{t+1} = 1.05 \bullet 100 = 105$.

Now we consider inflation. The inflation rate, π_t, for year t is

$$\pi_t = \Delta P_t / P_t$$
$$= (P_{t+1} - P_t)/P_t$$

If we multiply through by P_t, we get

$$\pi_t P_t = P_{t+1} - P_t$$

If we move P_t from the right-hand side to the left-hand side, combine the terms involving P_t, and then switch the right- and left-hand sides, we get

[11.13]
$$P_{t+1} = (1 + \pi_t) \bullet P_t$$

Thus, the price level rises from year t to year $t + 1$ by the factor $1 + \pi_t$. For example, if $P_t = 100$ and $\pi_t = 0.05$, $P_{t+1} = 1.05 \bullet 100 = 105$.

We now link inflation to money growth. Suppose that the growth rate of money is the constant $\mu_t = \mu$. In Chapter 10, we found that a once-and-for-all increase in the nominal quantity of money, M, raised the price level, P, in the same proportion. By analogy to this result, we now make a key conjecture: *When M_t grows steadily at the rate, μ, the price level, P_t, will also grow steadily at the rate μ. That is, the inflation rate, π_t, will be the constant $\pi = \mu$.* As we move through the steps of our analysis, we will verify that this conjecture is correct.

If the inflation rate, π, equals the money growth rate, μ, the level of real money balances, M_t/P_t, does not change over time. In Chapter 10, we used the equilibrium condition that the quantity of money supplied equaled the quantity demanded. We use the same condition here, but we have to ensure that this condition holds for every year t. Since real money balances, M_t/P_t, do not change over time, equilibrium requires that:

- The real quantity of money demanded, $L(Y, i)$, does not vary over time.
- The level of real money demanded, $L(Y, i)$, equals the unchanging level of real money balances, M_t/P_t.

The first condition is easy to satisfy, because we assumed that real GDP, Y, is fixed. Therefore, we require only that the nominal interest rate, i, be unchanging. Recall that i is the sum of the real interest rate, r, and the inflation rate, π. Moreover, our conjecture is that π equals the money growth rate, μ. Therefore, we have

(11.14)
$$i = r + \pi$$
$$i = r + \mu$$

Since we assumed that r and π are fixed, i is unchanging. Since Y and i are fixed, we have verified that the real quantity of money demanded, $L(Y, i)$, is unchanging.

Now we have to ensure that the level of real money demanded, $L(Y, i)$, equals the level of real money balances, M_t/P_t, in each year. Note that $L(Y, i)$ and M_t/P_t are both fixed over time. Therefore, if the levels of the two variables are equal in the current year, year 1, they will remain equal in every future year. Thus, the final equilibrium condition is that year 1's real quantity of money, M_1/P_1, equals the real quantity demanded, $L(Y, i)$:

(11.15)
$$M_1/P_1 = L(Y, i)$$

This condition is just like the ones we studied in Chapter 10. The key insight there was that, in equilibrium, the price level, P_1, adjusted so that the real quantity of money, M_1/P_1 on the left-hand side of equation (11.16), equaled the real quantity demanded, $L(Y, i)$, on the right-hand side. We can rearrange the terms to solve out for the equilibrium price level, P_1:

Key equation (determination of price level):

(11.16)
$$P_1 = M_1/L(Y, i)$$

*price level = nominal quantity of money/
real quantity of money demanded*

We know everything on the right-hand side of equation (11.16) because the nominal quantity of money, M_1, is given, and Y and i are known. In particular, equation (11.14) implies $i = r + \mu$. Thus, equation (11.16) determines year 1's price level, P_1.

After year 1, the nominal quantity of money, M_t, and the price level, P_t, grow at the same rate, μ. Therefore, real money balances, M_t/P_t, do not change. Hence, for any year t, M_t/P_t equals M_1/P_1, which appears on the left-hand side of equation (11.15). The right-hand side of this equation, $L(Y, i)$, does not vary over time. We conclude that real money balances, M_t/P_t, equal the real quantity demanded, $L(Y, i)$, in every year t.

Notice that the solution verifies our conjecture that the inflation rate, π_t, is the constant $\pi = \mu$. The full set of results is as follows:

- The inflation rate, π, equals the unchanging growth rate of money, μ.
- Real money balances, M_t/P_t, are fixed over time.
- The nominal interest rate, i, equals $r + \mu$, where r is the unchanging real interest rate, determined as in the equilibrium business-cycle model of Chapter 9.
- The real quantity of money demanded, $L(Y, i)$, is fixed over time, where Y is the unchanging real GDP, determined as in Chapter 9.
- Year 1's price level, P_1, is determined from equation (11.16) to equate year 1's real money balances, M_1/P_1, to the real quantity demanded, $L(Y, i)$.

A Trend in the Real Demand for Money

A simplifying assumption in the previous section was that the real quantity of money demanded, $L(Y, i)$, did not change over time. This assumption is unrealistic, particularly because growth of real GDP, Y, generates growth of $L(Y, i)$. We show in this section how to extend our results to allow for changes over time in $L(Y, i)$.

Assume that the real quantity of money demanded, $L(Y, i)$, grows steadily at the constant rate γ. This growth might reflect long-term growth of real GDP, Y; for example, in the steady state of the Solow model with technological progress from Chapter 5, Y grows at a constant rate. In equilibrium, the growth rate of real money balances, M_t/P_t, has to equal the growth rate, γ, of the real quantity demanded. To use this condition, we have to recalculate the rate at which real money balances, M_t/P_t, are growing.

We still assume that the nominal quantity of money, M_t, grows at the constant rate μ. The inflation rate, π, will turn out to be constant but less than μ if the growth rate of real money demanded, γ, is greater than zero. The reason that π is less than μ is that the rising real money demanded holds down the inflation rate. This result accords with our finding from Chapter 10 that a one-time increase in real money demand reduces the price level.

Real money balances, M_t/P_t, increase because of growth in the numerator, M_t, at the rate μ, but decrease because of growth in the denominator, P_t, at the rate π. We can show with a little algebra that the growth rate of M_t/P_t is given by

(11.17)   *growth rate of $M_t/P_t = \mu - \pi$*

*growth rate of real money balances =
growth rate of nominal money − inflation rate*

Thus, if μ is greater than π, M_t/P_t rises over time.

The equilibrium condition is again that real money balances, M_t/P_t, equal the real quantity of money demanded, $L(Y, i)$, each year. Thus, if $L(Y, i)$ grows at rate γ, M_t/P_t must also grow at rate γ. If we substitute this result for the left-hand side of equation (11.17), we get

$$\gamma = \mu - \pi$$

Therefore, if we rearrange terms, the inflation rate is

(11.18) $$\pi = \mu - \gamma$$

Thus, if γ is greater than zero, π is less than μ. However, an increase in μ by 1% per year still leads, for given γ, to a rise in π by 1% per year. Hence, as in Figure 11.1, variations in money growth rates across countries can still account for differences in inflation rates.

The new result from equation (11.18) is that variations in the growth rate, γ, of the real quantity of money demanded affect the relationship between the growth rates of money, μ, and prices, π. A higher γ raises $\mu - \pi$ and, therefore, increases the growth rate of real money balances, M_t/P_t.

Figure 11.8 uses information for 82 countries from Table 11.1 to check our prediction for the growth rate of real money balances. We assume that growth of real GDP is the main source of growth in the real quantity of money demanded. Thus, the horizontal axis plots the growth rate of real GDP, from column 4 of the table. The vertical axis plots the growth rate of real currency, from column 3. The graph shows that a higher growth rate of real GDP matches up with a higher growth rate of real currency. The correlation between the two variables is high: 0.72. The slope of the relation is close to one; that is, if the growth rate of real GDP is higher by 1% per year, the growth

rate of real currency is higher by about 1% per year. Therefore, if the real GDP growth rate is higher by 1% per year, the inflation rate, π, is lower by 1% per year for a given money growth rate, μ.

A Shift in the Money Growth Rate

In this section, we study the effects from a change in the money growth rate, μ, on the inflation rate, π, and the nominal interest rate, i. To simplify, return to the setting with no trend in the real quantity of money demanded, $L(Y, i)$. In particular, real GDP, Y, is fixed. Suppose that the nominal quantity of money, M_t, has been growing for a long time at the constant rate μ. Thus, M_t is given by the red line on the left-hand side of Figure 11.9. Since the graph uses a proportionate scale, the slope of the line equals μ.

Suppose that households initially expect the monetary authority to keep the nominal quantity of money, M_t, growing forever at the rate μ. In this case, our previous analysis applies, and the inflation rate is the constant $\pi = \mu$. We show the price level, P_t, as the blue line on the left-hand side of Figure 11.9. The slope of this

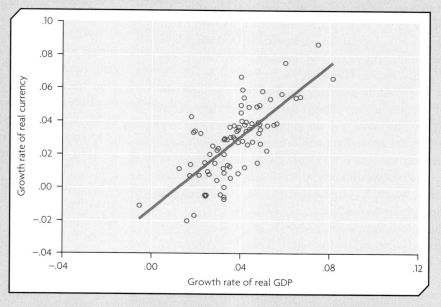

Figure 11.8 *Growth Rate of Real Currency and Growth Rate of Real GDP for 82 Countries, 1960–2000*

This graph uses the data from Table 11.1. The horizontal axis has the growth rate of real GDP from 1960 to 2000. The vertical axis has the growth rate of real currency (nominal currency divided by the CPI) from 1960 to 2000. The two variables have a correlation of 0.72. The slope is close to one; that is, an increase in the growth rate of real GDP by 1% per year is associated with an increase in the growth rate of real currency by about 1% per year.

Figure 11.9 Effect of an Increase in the Money Growth Rate on the Price Level

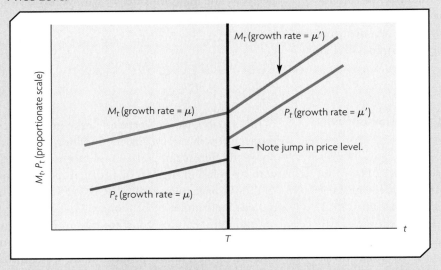

The red line shows that the nominal quantity of money, M_t, grows at the constant rate μ before year T. After year T, M_t grows along the brown line at the higher rate μ'. The blue line shows that the price level, P_t, grows at the same rate as money, μ, before year T. After year T, P_t grows along the green line at the same rate as money, μ'. The price level, P_t, jumps upward during year T. This jump reduces real money balances, M_t/P_t, from the level prevailing before year T to that prevailing after year T.

line equals the inflation rate, $\pi = \mu$, which equals the slope of the red line.

Now suppose that the monetary authority raises the money growth rate from μ to μ' in year T. The right-hand side of Figure 11.9 shows that the nominal quantity of money, M_t, follows the brown line after year T. This line has slope μ' and is steeper than the red line. We assume that the change in the money growth rate in year T is a surprise. However, once the change occurs, we assume that households expect the new growth rate of money, μ', to prevail forever. Therefore, after year T, the economy is in the same situation as before, except that the money growth rate is μ', rather than μ, and the inflation rate is $\pi' = \mu'$. The right-hand side of Figure 11.9 shows that the price level, P_t, follows the green line, which has the slope $\pi' = \mu'$, which equals the slope of the brown line.

The inflation rate after year T, π', is greater than the inflation rate, π, before year T. Therefore, the green line in Figure 11.9 is steeper than the blue line. Notice an important complication in the graph of P_t. The blue line does not intersect the green line. Instead, *the figure shows an upward jump in the price level in year T*. To see why, we have to consider the real quantity of money demanded.

Before year T, the nominal interest rate, i, is given by $i = r + \pi$, where r is the real interest rate and π is the inflation rate. Since $\pi = \mu$, we have

(11.19) $i = r + \mu$

Recall that a change in the money growth rate does not change the real interest rate, which remains at r. Therefore, the nominal interest rate after year T will be $i' = r + \pi'$, where π' is the inflation rate after year T. If we substitute μ' for π', we have

(11.20) $i' = r + \mu'$

If we subtract equation (11.19) from equation (11.20), we can calculate the increase in the nominal interest rate:

(11.21) $$i' - i = \mu' - \mu$$

increase in nominal interest rate =
increase in money growth rate

A key property of the demand for money, $L(Y, i)$, is that a rise in the nominal interest rate, i, lowers the real quantity of money demanded. Therefore, $L(Y, i)$ must be lower after year T than before. We still have the equilibrium condition that the real quantity of money, M_t/P_t, always equals $L(Y, i)$. Therefore, the real quantity of money, M_t/P_t, must be lower after year T.

The left-hand side of Figure 11.9 shows that, before year T, the nominal quantity of money, M_t, grows at the same rate, μ, as the price level, P_t. Therefore, the real quantity of money, M_t/P_t, is constant. The right-hand side shows that, after year T, M_t grows at the same rate, μ', as P_t. Hence, M_t/P_t is again constant. We therefore have three facts:

- M_t/P_t is constant before year T.
- M_t/P_t is constant after year T.
- M_t/P_t after year T is lower than that before year T (because of the rise in the nominal interest rate from i to i').

The way to reconcile these facts is that the price level, P_t, has to jump upward during year T, as shown in Figure 11.9. This rise in P_t lowers real money balances, M_t/P_t, from the level prevailing before year T to that prevailing after year T.

One way to think about the jump in the price level is that the inflation rate is exceptionally high during year T. Specifically, when the money growth rate rises in year T from μ to μ', the inflation rate, π_t, rises above μ' in the short run. The excess of π_t over μ' means that the price level, P_t, rises at a faster rate than the nominal quantity of money, M_t, so that real money balances, M_t/P_t, decline.

In the case shown in Figure 11.9, the interval of exceptionally high inflation is concentrated in a short period, essentially an instant of time. Thus, the transition from relatively low inflation, $\pi = \mu$, to relatively high inflation, $\pi' = \mu'$, takes place overnight. The more general result is that real money balances, M_t/P_t, decrease during a transition interval, because the higher nominal interest rate reduces the real quantity of money demanded. During the transition, the inflation rate, π_t, exceeds the money growth rate, μ_t. The exact nature of the transition depends on the details of the model—it is not necessarily limited to a single year or an instant of time.

In one modification of the model, households adjust their real quantity of money demanded downward only gradually in response to an increase in the nominal interest rate, i_t. This gradual adjustment makes sense if households have to change their underlying cash-management plans to hold lower real money balances. In this case, the transition to a lower real money balance, M_t/P_t, is stretched out. As the real quantity of money demanded falls gradually, M_t/P_t also decreases gradually. The period of falling M_t/P_t corresponds to an extended transition in which the inflation rate, π_t, exceeds the growth rate of money, μ_t.

As another example, households may know in advance that the monetary authority is planning to shift from relatively low money growth, μ, to relatively high money growth, μ'. Households may expect, before year T, that money growth and inflation will be higher from year T onward. In this case, some of the unusually high short-run inflation occurs *before* year T. That is, the expectation of higher inflation in the future leads to higher inflation today—before the rise in the money growth rate occurs. The higher short-run inflation arises because the anticipated future inflation decreases the real quantity of money demanded before year T.

Expectations about future changes in money growth rates and inflation have sometimes been at the center of political campaigns. For example, in the 1890s, William Jennings Bryan campaigned for the U.S. presidency on a program of easy money. In essence, he advocated a higher growth rate of money, μ, based on free coinage of silver as a supplement to the monetary role of gold. Bryan's defeat probably lowered expectations of future money growth rates and inflation.

As another example, in 1980, Ronald Reagan campaigned for the U.S. presidency partly on the promise of getting tough on inflation, which was then high. Reagan's defeat of Jimmy Carter likely lowered expectations of future money growth rates and inflation.

Another case is the post–World War I German *hyperinflation*, examined in the box entitled "Money and Prices During the German Hyperinflation." The end of the hyperinflation occurred in November 1923. However, people anticipated prior to November that a monetary reform was coming and that this reform would entail lower money growth rates, μ, and inflation rates, π. Empirical studies show that this anticipation reduced π before November 1923, even though the reduction in μ had not yet occurred.[5]

Government Revenue from Printing Money

We have assumed, thus far, that the monetary authority prints new money (currency) and gives it to households as transfer payments. More realistically, governments get **revenue from printing money** and can use this revenue to pay for a variety of expenditures. Governments do not usually use this revenue to finance Milton Friedman's imaginary helicopter drops of cash!

The government's nominal revenue from printing money between years t and $t + 1$ equals the change in the nominal quantity of money:

nominal revenue from printing money $= M_{t+1} - M_t$
$$= \Delta M_t$$

To calculate the real value of revenue, divide ΔM_t by P_{t+1}, the price level for year $t + 1$:

real revenue from printing money $= \Delta M_t/P_{t+1}$

---

[5] See Robert Flood and Peter Garber (1980) and Laura Lahaye (1985).

We want to relate this real revenue to the money growth rate, μ_t, which is given by

(11.9) $$\mu_t = \Delta M_t / M_t$$

We can use equation (11.9) to substitute $\mu_t \cdot M_t$ for ΔM_t in the formula for real revenue:

real revenue from printing money $= \mu_t \cdot (M_t / P_{t+1})$

The term on the far right-hand side, M_t / P_{t+1}, is approximately the level of real money balances, M_t / P_t. Therefore, the real revenue from printing money is

(11.22) *real revenue from printing money* $\approx$
$$\mu_t \cdot (M_t / P_t)$$
$= (money\ growth\ rate) \cdot$
(level of real money balances)

We know that a higher money growth rate, μ, leads to a higher inflation rate, π, and a higher nominal interest rate, i. We also know that the higher i reduces the real quantity of money demanded, $L(Y, i)$, and, therefore, lowers real money balances, M/P_t. Thus, an increase in μ_t has two opposing effects on the real revenue from printing money in equation (11.22): The rise in μ_t raises real revenue, but the decrease in M/P_t reduces real revenue. The net effect depends on how much $L(Y, i)$ falls in response to a rise in i.

As an example, suppose that real money balances, M/P_t, were initially equal to 100, and that μ_t then doubled from 5% to 10% per year. The real revenue from printing money would rise on net unless M/P_t fell below 50—that is, by more than 50%. More generally, the real revenue rises unless the decrease in the quantity of real money demanded is proportionately larger than the increase in the money growth rate. This condition holds empirically except for the most extreme cases. For example, during the German hyperinflation, considered in the box entitled "Money and Prices During

the German Hyperinflation," the condition was violated only when μ_t approached 100% per month between July and August 1923. Until then, the government extracted more real revenue by printing money at a faster rate.

In normal times for most countries, the government obtains only a small portion of its revenue from printing money. In 2005, the Federal Reserve obtained $24 billion from this source. This amount constituted 1.1% of total federal receipts and 0.2% of GDP. These figures are typical for most developed countries.

In a few high-inflation countries, the revenue from printing money became much more important. For example, in Argentina from 1960 to 1975, money creation accounted for nearly half of government revenue and about 6% of GDP. Some other countries in which the revenue from printing money was important were Chile (5% of GDP from 1960 to 1977), Libya (3% of GDP from 1960 to 1977), and Brazil (3% of GDP from 1960 to 1978).

John Maynard Keynes (1923, p. 41) observed that money creation became the main source of government receipts during the German and Russian hyperinflations after World War I: "A Government can live for a long time, even the German Government or the Russian Government, by printing paper money. That is to say, it can by this means secure the command over real resources—resources just as real as those obtained by taxation." In some hyperinflations, the revenue approached 10% of GDP, which seems to be about the maximum attainable from printing money. In Germany, from 1920 to 1923, a close connection existed between real government spending and the money growth rate.[6] Much of this spending went toward reparations payments to the victors in World War I. Therefore, the reduction in these payments after November 1923 was a major factor in ending the German hyperinflation.

---

[6] See Zvi Hercowitz (1981) for a detailed analysis.

bythenumbers

Money and Prices During the German Hyperinflation

A **hyperinflation** is a sustained period of super-high inflation rates. The post–World War I German hyperinflation provides a great laboratory experiment for studying the interplay between money growth rates and inflation.[7] From 1920 to 1923, inflation rates ranged from near zero to over 500% per month! Despite the extreme inflation, comparatively small changes occurred in real GDP.

When inflation rates are volatile, as in post–World War I Germany, it is impossible to predict accurately the real interest rate on loans that prescribe nominal interest rates. Therefore, this type of lending tends to disappear. For this reason, we have no good measures of the nominal interest rate during the German hyperinflation, and the best measure of the cost of holding money is the expected inflation rate, π_t^e. This rate determined how much income people lost by holding money rather than consuming or holding a durable good that maintained its real value over time. Empirical studies have estimated π_t^e by assuming that it adjusted gradually to changes in the actual inflation rate, π_t.

Table 11.3 shows the money growth rate, μ_t (based on currency in circulation); the inflation rate, π_t; and real money balances, M_t/P_t, in Germany from 1920 to 1925. In most cases, the table shows μ_t and π_t over six-month intervals. The level of M_t/P_t pertains to the ends of these intervals.

Hulton Archive/Getty Images

At the beginning of 1920, the money growth rate, μ_t, and the inflation rate, π_t, were already at 6% per month. Then μ_t declined in early 1921 to less than 1% per month. As our model predicts, π_t fell by more than μ_t, so that real money balances, M_t/P_t, rose by about 20% from early 1920 to early 1921.

From late 1921 through the end of 1922, the money growth rate, μ_t, rose to 30% per month. Since the inflation rate, π_t, exceeded μ_t, real money balances, M_t/P_t, fell to 25% of the early-1920 level by the end of 1922. From the end of 1922 through mid-1923, the money growth rate, μ_t, was extremely high but no longer trending upward—it averaged around 40% per month. Since the inflation rate, π_t, was also about 40% per month, real money balances, M_t/P_t, remained at 25% of the early-1920 level. However, in late 1923, the hyperinflation built to its climax, with μ_t reaching 300–600% per month in October and November. Since π_t exceeded μ_t, M_t/P_t fell to its low point in October of about 3% of the 1920 level.

A monetary reform occurred in November 1923. The reform included a new type of currency, a promise not to print new money beyond a specified limit to finance government expenditures, reductions in real government spending, reform of the tax system, and a commitment to back the value of the new currency by gold.[8] These changes led to sharp cutbacks in the money growth rate, μ_t, and the inflation rate, π_t, after December 1923. During 1924, μ_t averaged 5% per month, and π_t was less than 1% per month. The excess of μ_t over π_t allowed for the rebuilding of real money balances, M_t/P_t, which increased from 3% of the early-1920 level in October 1923 to 56% of that level by December 1924. Although π_t remained low for the rest of the 1920s, M_t/P_t did not reattain its early-1920 level. Perhaps this gap reflected a long-lasting negative influence of the hyperinflation on the real demand for money.

---

[7] This episode has fascinated many economists, starting with the classic study by Costantino Bresciani-Turroni (1937). Phillip Cagan (1956) studied the German hyperinflation along with six others: Austria, Hungary, Poland, and Russia after World War I, and Greece and Hungary after World War II. The Hungarian experience after World War II seems to be the all-time record: the price level rose by a factor of 3×10^{25} from July 1945 to August 1946. See William Bomberger and Gail Makinen (1983).

[8] For discussions of the reform, see Bresciani-Turroni (1937), Thomas Sargent (1982), and Peter Garber (1982). Sargent's analysis stresses the rapidity with which inflations can be ended once the government makes a credible commitment to limit money creation.

Table 11.3   *Money Growth and Inflation During the German Hyperinflation*

Period	μ_t	π_t	M_t/P_t (end of period)
2/20–6/20	5.7	6.0	1.01
6/20–12/20	3.0	1.1	1.13
12/20–6/21	0.8	0.1	1.18
6/21–12/21	5.5	8.4	0.99
12/21–6/22	6.5	12.8	0.68
6/22–12/22	29.4	46.7	0.24
12/22–6/23	40.0	40.0	0.24
6/23–10/23	233	286	0.03
Reform Period			
12/23–6/24	5.9	−0.6	0.44
6/24–12/24	5.3	1.4	0.56
12/24–6/25	2.0	1.6	0.57
6/25–12/25	1.2	0.4	0.60

Source: Sonderhefte zür Wirtschaft und Statistik, Berlin, 1929.

Note: The nominal quantity of money, M_t, is an estimate of the total circulation of currency. Until late 1923, the figures refer to total legal tender, most of which constituted notes issued by the Reichsbank. Later, the data include issues of the Rentenbank, private bank notes, and various "emergency moneys." Unofficial emergency currencies, as well as circulating foreign currencies, are not counted. The numbers are normalized so that M_t in 1913 is set to 1.0. The price level, P_t, is an index of the cost of living, based on 1913 = 1.0. Column 1 shows the period for the data. Column 2, in percent per month, is the money growth rate, μ_t, over the period shown. Column 3, also in percent per month, is the inflation rate, π_t, over the period shown. Column 4 is the level of real money balances, M_t/P_t, at the end of each period. Since the value of M_t/P_t for 1913 is 1.0, the values shown for M_t/P_t are relative to the level in 1913.

Questions and Problems

A. Review questions

1. Which of the following statements is correct?

a. A constant rate of increase in the price level, P, will lead to a continuous rise in the nominal interest rate, i.

b. A continuous increase in the inflation rate, π, will lead to a continuous rise in the nominal interest rate, i.

2. Define the real interest rate, r. Why does it differ from the nominal interest rate, i, in the presence of inflation?

3. Why does the actual real interest rate, r, generally differ from the expected real interest rate, r_t^e? How does this relation depend on whether bonds prescribe the nominal or real interest rate?

4. What is the Livingston survey of inflationary expectations? What are the pluses and minuses of using this type of information to measure the expected inflation rate, π_t^e?

5. Why does the real interest rate, not the nominal interest rate, have intertemporal-substitution effects on consumption and saving? Does the same result apply for intertemporal substitution of labor supply?

B. Problems for discussion

6. Money growth and inflation
Suppose that the money-demand function takes the form

$$M^d/P = L(Y, i) = Y \bullet \psi(i)$$

That is, for a given nominal interest rate, i, a doubling of real GDP, Y, doubles the real quantity of money demanded, M^d/P.

a. Consider the relation across countries between the growth rate of money (currency), μ, and the inflation rate, π, as shown in Figure 11.1. How does the growth rate of real GDP, $\Delta Y/Y$, affect the relationship between μ and π?

b. What is the relation between μ and π for a country in which the nominal interest rate, i, has increased?

c. Suppose that the expected real interest rate, r_t^e, is given. What is the relation between μ and π for a country in which the expected inflation rate, π_t^e, has increased?

7. Statistical relations between money growth and inflation
Students who have studied econometrics and have access to a statistical package can do the following exercise.

a. Use the data in Table 11.1 to run a regression of the inflation rate, π, on a constant and the growth rate of money (currency), μ. What is the estimated coefficient on μ, and how should we interpret it? What is the meaning of the constant term?

b. Run a regression of the growth rate of real money balances, $\mu - \pi$, on the growth rate of real GDP, $\Delta Y/Y$, and a constant. What is the estimated coefficient on $\Delta Y/Y$, and how should we interpret it?

c. Suppose that we add the variable $\Delta Y/Y$ to the regression run in question a. What is the estimated coefficient on $\Delta Y/Y$, and how should we interpret it?

8. Effects on the nominal interest rate
What are the effects on the price level, P, and the nominal interest rate, i, from the following events?

a. A once-and-for-all increase in the nominal quantity of money, M

b. A once-and-for-all increase in the money growth rate, μ

c. A credible announcement that the money growth rate, μ, will rise beginning one year in the future

9. Seasonal variations in money
Suppose that the real quantity of money demanded is relatively high in the fourth quarter of each year and relatively low in the first quarter. Assume that there is no seasonal pattern in real interest rates.

a. Suppose that there were no seasonal pattern in the nominal quantity of money, M. What would the seasonal pattern be for the price level, P; the inflation rate, π; and the nominal interest rate, i?

b. What seasonal behavior for the nominal quantity of money, M, would eliminate the seasonal variations in P, π, and i?

10. Interest-rate targeting
Suppose that the monetary authority wants to keep the nominal interest rate, i, constant. Assume that the real interest rate, r, is fixed. However, the real demand for money, M^d/P, shifts around a great deal.

a. How should the monetary authority vary the nominal quantity of money, M, if the real demand for money, M^d/P, increases temporarily? What if the real demand increases permanently?

b. How does the price level, P, behave in your answers to question a? What should the monetary authority do if it wants to dampen fluctuations of P, as well as maintain a constant nominal interest rate, i?

11. Money growth and government revenue
Can the government always increase its real revenue from printing money by raising the money growth rate, μ? How does the answer depend on the responsiveness of real money demand, M^d/P, to the nominal interest rate, i?

12. Prepayment of mortgages and callability of bonds
Mortgages typically allow the borrower to make early payments ("prepayments") of principal. Sometimes the mortgage contract specifies a prepayment penalty, and sometimes there is no penalty. Similarly, long-term bonds (though typically not those issued by the U.S. government) sometimes allow the issuer to prepay the principal after a prescribed date, with a specified penalty. When the bond issuer exercises this option to prepay, he or she is said to "call" the bond. Bonds that allow this prepayment are said to be "callable" or to have a "call provision."

a. When would a borrower want to prepay (or call) his or her mortgage or bond? Would we see more prepayments when the nominal interest rate, i, unexpectedly increased or decreased?

b. From the late 1970s until 1982, banks and savings and loan associations were eager for customers to prepay their mortgages. Why was this the case? Later on, customers wanted to prepay. Why did they want to do so?

c. Suppose that the year-to-year fluctuations in nominal interest rates become larger. (These fluctuations—or volatility—were particularly great from the mid-1970s through the early 1980s.) From the standpoint of a borrower, how does this change affect the value of having a prepayment option—that is, callability—in his or her mortgage or bond?

13. Rational expectations and measures of expected inflation
How would the hypothesis of rational expectations help us to measure the expected inflation rate, π_t^e? What seem to be the pluses and minuses of this approach?

14. Indexed bonds

a. Consider a one-year nominal bond that costs $1,000. After one year, the bond pays the principal of $1,000 plus an interest payment of $50. What is the one-year nominal interest rate on the bond? What are the actual and expected one-year real interest rates on the bond? Why is the nominal interest rate known but the real rate uncertain?

b. Consider now a one-year indexed bond (such as the U.S. Treasury's TIPS, Treasury Inflation-Protected Securities). Suppose that the bond costs $1,000. One year later, the nominal principal of the bond is adjusted to be $1,000 • $(1 + \pi)$, where π is the actual inflation rate over the year. Then the bond pays off the adjusted principal of $1,000 • $(1 + \pi)$ plus an interest payment of, say, 3% of the adjusted principal. What is the one-year real interest rate on the indexed bond? What are the actual and expected one-year nominal interest rates on the bond? Why is the real rate known but the nominal rate uncertain?

c. Can you think of other ways to design indexed bonds? Are the nominal and real interest rates both uncertain in some cases?

15. A case of counterfeiting
In 1925, a group of swindlers induced the Waterlow Company, a British manufacturer of bank notes, to print and deliver to them 3 million pounds' worth of Portuguese currency (escudos). Since the company also printed the legitimate notes for the Bank of Portugal, the counterfeit notes were indistinguishable from the real thing (except that the serial numbers were duplicates of those from a previous series of legitimate notes). Before the fraud was discovered, 1 million pounds' worth of the fraudulent notes had been introduced into circulation in Portugal. After the scheme unraveled (because someone noticed the duplication of serial numbers), the Bank of Portugal made good on the fraudulent notes by exchanging them for newly printed, valid notes. The Bank subsequently sued the Waterlow Company for damages. The company was found liable, but the key question was the amount of damages. The Bank argued that the damages were 1 million pounds (less funds collected from the swindlers). The other side contended that the Bank suffered only negligible real costs in having to issue an additional 1 million pounds' worth of money to redeem the fraudulent notes. (Note that the currency was purely a paper issue, with no convertibility into gold or anything else.) Thus, the argument was that the only true costs to the Bank were the expenses for paper and printing. Which side do you think was correct? (The House of Lords determined in 1932 that 1 million pounds was the correct measure. For discussions of this fascinating episode in monetary economics, see Ralph Hawtrey [1932] and Murray Bloom [1966].)

Government Expenditure

p to now, the government had very limited functions in our model. We considered only lump-sum transfers financed by money creation. Now we will allow for the government's purchases of goods and services. In the national accounts, these purchases are called government consumption and investment.[1] We assume in this chapter that government expenditures are financed by lump-sum taxes, *which are analogous to the lump-sum transfers that we considered before. We also continue to assume that the transfers are lump sum. In Chapter 13, we will allow for more realistic systems of taxes and transfers. It is useful to start with data on government expenditure for the United States and other countries.*

Data on Government Expenditure

overnment expenditure is the dollar amount spent at all levels of government for purchases of goods and services, transfer payments (amounts given to households and businesses), and interest payments. (We defer a discussion of interest payments until Chapter 14.) Figure 12.1 shows government expenditure as a ratio to gross domestic product (GDP) in the United States from 1929 to 2005. Excluding the wartime experiences, government expenditure went from 9.5% of GDP in 1929 to 18% in 1940, 21% in 1950, 26% in 1960, 30% in 1970, 32% in 1980,

34% in 1990, 30% in 2000, and 33% in 2005. Thus, after trending upward through the early 1980s, the ratio of government expenditure to GDP has remained close to one-third.

Figure 12.1 shows that in 1929, before the Great Depression and World War II, government expenditure was primarily for purchases of goods and services. However, over time, government expenditure shifted in a relative sense away from purchases and toward the second main component, transfer payments. In 2005, out of the 33% of GDP represented by total government expenditure, 17% of GDP went for purchases and 13% went for transfers. (The other 3% went for interest payments.)

Figure 12.2 shows the breakdown of government purchases into federal, state, and local parts, and also shows separately the federal purchases for

---

[1] The difference between government consumption and investment and government purchases is that the former category includes the implicit rental income on the government's capital stock. In practice, in the national accounts, this rental income is assumed to equal the estimated depreciation of government capital. In the model, the government owns no capital. Hence, depreciation of the government's capital stock is zero, and government investment is also zero. Therefore, in the model, government purchases are the same as government consumption.

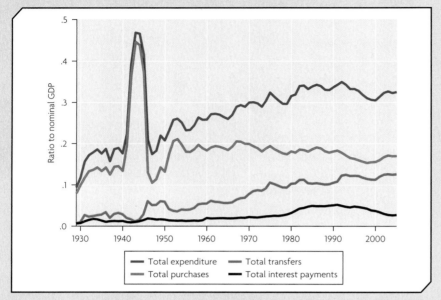

Figure 12.1 *Total Government Expenditure, Purchases, Transfers, and Interest Payments*

The graphs refer to total government and show ratios of each nominal expenditure component to nominal GDP. Purchases of goods and services are the outlays for consumption and investment. In the national accounts, purchases equal government consumption and investment less depreciation of public capital stocks. Total transfers exclude grants-in-aid from the federal government to state and local governments but include subsidies. Interest payments are the total paid (with no netting out of interest receipts by government). Total expenditure also includes relatively small amounts for capital transfer payments and net purchases of nonproduced assets.

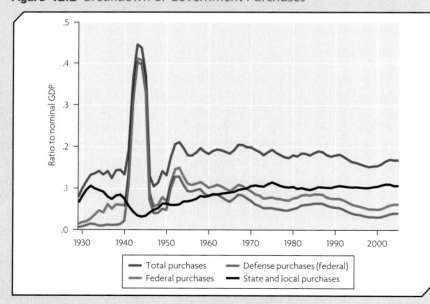

Figure 12.2 *Breakdown of Government Purchases*

The graphs show the ratio of each nominal government expenditure component to nominal GDP. Total purchases are broken down into those by the federal government, and those by state and local governments. The part of federal purchases spent on defense is shown separately.

defense. Except during the Great Depression from 1933 to 1940, the main part of federal purchases went for defense. Defense purchases were 8% of GDP in 1960 but fell to a low point of 4.8% in 1979, before rising during the defense buildup of the Reagan administration to 6.5% in 1986. Then the ratio fell steadily, probably because of the "peace dividend" associated with the end of the cold war, to 3.2% in 2000. Subsequently, the defense ratio turned upward again, reaching 4.2% in 2005. The graph also shows the peaks in the ratio of defense purchases to GDP during wartime: 40% of GDP in 1944 (World War II); 13% in 1952–53 (Korean War), 8.5% in 1967–68 (Vietnam War), and 4.2% in 2004–05 (Iraq war).

Purchases by state and local governments were 6.6% of GDP in 1929 and 6.3% in 1950, rose to a peak of 11.5% in 1975, then remained fairly stable and equaled 10.7% in 2005. About half of the increase in the ratio up to 1975 reflected growth in purchases for education, which went from 2.4% of GDP in 1952 to 5.6% in 1975. Thereafter, the ratio of state and local purchases for education to GDP was fairly stable and equaled 5.1% in 2004.

Figure 12.3 shows the rising path of government transfer payments as a ratio to GDP.[2] The ratio was 0.8% in 1929 and rose fairly steadily thereafter, reaching 12.6% in 2005. At the federal level, the largest expansions were in the main **Social Security** program—which covers payments for old age, survivors, and disability insurance (OASDI)—and Medicare—which pays for medical expenses of the elderly. Figure 12.4 shows that the ratio of OASDI expenditure to GDP went from zero in 1940 to 4.3% in 1980, then stayed roughly constant through 2004. The figure also shows that the ratio of Medicare spending to GDP went from zero in 1965 to 2.6% in 2004, and no end to this growth is apparent.

State and local transfers include welfare payments for family assistance. However, the main increase in state and local transfers has been in Medicaid, which pays for health outlays by poor persons. Figure 12.4 shows that the ratio of these expenditures to GDP went from zero in 1958 to 2.5% in 2004, about the same as Medicare, but Medicaid was growing even faster than Medicare. In 2004, the combination of the three main

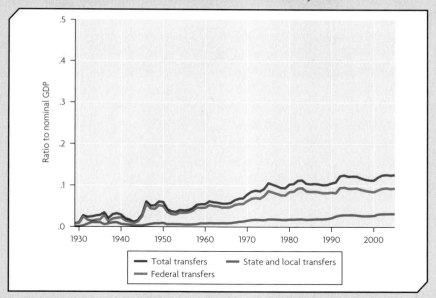

Figure 12.3 *Breakdown of Government Transfer Payments*

The graphs show the ratio of each nominal government expenditure component to nominal GDP. Transfer payments include subsidies. Total and federal transfers exclude grants-in-aid from the federal government to state and local governments.

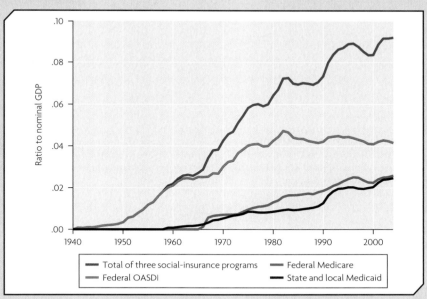

Figure 12.4 *Transfer Payments for Social Security, Medicare, and Medicaid*

The red graph is the ratio to GDP of federal transfers for the main Social Security program, OASDI (old age, survivors, and disability insurance). The green graph is for federal transfers for Medicare, the health program for elderly people. The black graph is for state and local transfers for Medicaid, the health program for poor people. The blue graph is the ratio to GDP for the sum of the three social-insurance programs.

---

[2] The transfers shown in Figure 12.3 include subsidies but exclude payments from the federal government to state and local governments (called federal grants-in-aid).

Table 12.1 *General Government Expenditure as a Ratio to GDP in a Sample of Countries, 2000–2002*

Country	Spending Ratio	Country	Spending Ratio
Australia	0.33	Latvia	0.39
Austria	0.50	Lithuania	0.32
Azerbaijan	0.23	Luxembourg	0.41
Belgium	0.47	Malaysia	0.27
Bolivia	0.37	Moldova	0.24
Botswana	0.42	Netherlands	0.42
Brazil	0.37	New Zealand	0.38
Bulgaria	0.41	Norway	0.42
Canada	0.38	Panama	0.28
Chile	0.23	Peru	0.29
Croatia	0.51	Russia	0.16
Czech Rep.	0.32	Singapore	0.18
Denmark	0.52	Slovakia	0.39
Ecuador	0.25	Slovenia	0.42
Egypt	0.26	South Korea	0.24
Estonia	0.37	Spain	0.38
Finland	0.44	Sweden	0.53
France	0.49	Switzerland	0.38
Germany	0.47	Taiwan	0.25
Greece	0.47	Thailand	0.18
Hong Kong	0.13	Trinidad	0.32
Hungary	0.53	Ukraine	0.26
Ireland	0.30	United Kingdom	0.38
Italy	0.46	United States	0.32
Japan	0.37	Venezuela	0.23
Kazakhstan	0.22		

Note: The table shows the ratio of general government expenditure to GDP, averaged for 2000–02. Countries are included only when data are available for general government expenditure, which includes spending at all levels of government for purchases of goods and services, transfers, and interest payments. Data for countries other than the United States are from Economist Intelligence Unit, *EIU Country Data* (www.eiu.com).

social-insurance programs—OASDI, Medicare, and Medicaid—represented 9.2% of GDP.

Table 12.1 shows ratios of total government expenditure to GDP for 51 countries for 2000–02. The countries listed are those for which data are available on a broad concept of government expenditure. This concept includes expenditure by all levels of government for purchases, transfers, and interest payments. The ratios shown range from 13% at the low end for Hong Kong to 53% at the high end for Hungary and Sweden. The median, or middle, position is 37%, and the United States, at 32%, is somewhat below the median.

The Government's Budget Constraint

ow we extend our equilibrium business-cycle model to allow for government purchases of goods and services and transfer payments. Let G_t represent government purchases in real terms for year t. In our previous analysis, we considered two forms of private real spending on goods and services: consumption, C_t, and gross investment, I_t. The total of the three terms, $C_t + I_t + G_t$, is the aggregate real spending on goods and services in year t. Let V_t represent the government's real expenditure on transfers. Unlike G_t, real transfers, V_t, are not spending on goods and services. A transfer just represents the government's shuffling income around, taking from one group of people (through taxes) and giving to another (through transfers).

In Chapter 11, the government's only revenue came from printing money. The real value of this revenue for year t is $(M_t - M_{t-1})/P_t$, where M_t is the nominal quantity of money in year t, and M_{t-1} is the quantity one year earlier. In the United States, the revenue from printing money accrues directly to the central bank, which is the Federal Reserve (or "Fed"). The Fed turns over most of its revenue to the U.S. Treasury. In the model, we consolidate the central bank with the government.

Now we assume that the government also levies taxes on households. These taxes might apply to businesses, but remember that the households own and run the businesses. Let T_t be the total real taxes collected by the government in year t.

The **government's budget constraint** says that its total uses of funds must equal its total sources of funds. The uses are for purchases of goods and services and transfer payments. The sources are taxes and money creation. Therefore, we can write the government's budget constraint in real terms for year t as

> Key equation (government budget constraint):
>
> *total uses of funds = total sources of funds*
>
> **(12.1)** $\qquad G_t + V_t = T_t + (M_t - M_{t-1})/P_t$
>
> *real purchases + real transfers =*
> *real taxes + real revenue from money creation*

Note that we have not introduced public debt in the model. Therefore, the government's uses of funds on the left-hand side do not include interest payments, and the government's sources of funds on the right-hand side do not include the proceeds from issue of public debt. We will make the extensions to include interest payments and public-debt issue in Chapter 14.

We mentioned in Chapter 11 that the real revenue from printing money, $(M_t - M_{t-1})/P_t$, is normally a minor part of overall government revenue. We shall find it convenient to ignore the revenue from printing money, and we can do this by returning to the case in which the nominal quantity of money, M_t, is constant. In this case, we can substitute $M_t - M_{t-1} = 0$ in equation (12.1) to get

(12.2) $\qquad G_t + V_t = T_t$
real purchases + real transfers = real taxes

In Chapter 11, transfer payments took the form of helicopter drops of cash that households picked up. The important assumption was that these transfers were lump sum—the amount the household received did not depend on the household's income, money holdings, and so on. We continue to assume that the real transfers, V_t, are lump sum. That is, the household's transfers do not depend on its decisions.

We also assume **lump-sum taxes** in this chapter. That is, the real taxes, T_t, that the household pays are independent of its income, consumption, and so on. This assumption is unrealistic. In the real world, elaborate tax laws specify how a household's taxes depend on its income, consumption, and so on. There are many things a household can do—including hiring accountants, working less, underreporting income, and exploiting tax loopholes—to lower its taxes. These possibilities imply substitution effects from the tax system on labor supply, consumption, and even the number of children. Although we want to study these substitution effects, we shall find it convenient to ignore them provisionally to isolate the effects from government expenditure. That is why we assume lump-sum taxes in this chapter. In Chapter 13, we will allow for substitution effects from realistic types of taxes. That analysis also brings in substitution effects from transfer programs.

Public Production

e assume that the government uses its real purchases of goods and services, G_t, to provide services to households and businesses, and that

the government delivers these services free of charge to the users. In most countries, public services include national defense, enforcement of laws and private contracts, police and fire protection, elementary and secondary schooling and some portions of higher education, parts of health services, highways, parks, and so on. The range of governmental activities has expanded over time, although this range varies from one country or locality to another.

We could model public services as the output from the government's production function. The inputs to this function would be the government-owned stock of capital, labor services from public employees, and materials that the government buys from the private sector. To simplify, we ignore government production and assume instead that the government buys final goods and services from private producers. That is, the government's purchases, G_t, add to the demand for goods and services by private consumers, C_t, and investors, I_t.

In effect, we are assuming that the government subcontracts all of its production to the private sector. In this setup, public investment, publicly owned capital, and government employment are zero. Ultimately, we would get different answers by allowing for public production only if the government's production function—that is, its technology and management capability—differed from that of the private sector. Otherwise, it would not matter whether the government buys final goods and services, as we assume, or, instead, buys capital and labor inputs to produce things itself.

Public Services

We have to take a position on the uses of the services that the government provides. One possibility is that these services yield utility for households. Examples are parks, libraries, school lunch programs, subsidized health care and transportation, and the entertaining parts of the space program. These public services may substitute for private consumption. For example, if the government buys a student's lunch at school, the student does not have to buy his or her own lunch.

Another possibility is that public services are inputs to private production. Examples include the provision and enforcement of laws and contracts, aspects of national defense, government-sponsored research and

development programs, the technologically valuable parts of the space program, fire and police services, and regulatory activities. In some cases, public services substitute for private inputs of labor and capital services. For example, the government's police services may substitute for guards hired by a private company. In other cases—including infrastructure activities such as the provision of a legal system, national defense, and perhaps transportation facilities—the public services are likely to raise the marginal products of private inputs.

We shall find it convenient to begin with the hypothetical case in which public services have zero effect on utility and production. This setup is akin to assuming that the government buys goods and services and then throws them into the ocean. We will consider later how the conclusions change if we allow public services to be useful.

The Household's Budget Constraint

The government's taxes and transfers affect each household's budget constraint. To see how, start with the household budget constraint from Chapter 8:

(8.6)

$$C + (1/P) \cdot \Delta B + \Delta K = (w/P) \cdot L^s + i \cdot (B/P + K)$$

consumption + real saving = real income

The analysis in Chapter 8 neglected inflation; that is, the price level, P_t, was constant over time. We simplify by returning to this case. Note that our assumption of a constant P_t is consistent with our assumption of a constant nominal quantity of money, M_t. Neither of these unrealistic assumptions affects our analysis of government purchases.

The right-hand side of equation (8.6) includes real asset income, $i \bullet (B/P + K)$, which depends on the nominal interest rate, i. However, since we are assuming that the inflation rate, π, is zero, the real interest rate, r, equals the nominal rate, i. We shall find it useful to replace i by r, because then the analysis will be valid when we allow π to be nonzero. If we apply equation (8.6) to year t and replace i by r, we get

(12.3)
$$C_t + (1/P) \bullet \Delta B_t + \Delta K_t =$$
$$(w/P)_t \bullet L_t^s + r_{t-1} \bullet (B_{t-1}/P + K_{t-1})$$
consumption + real saving = real income,

where $\Delta B_t = B_t - B_{t-1}$ and $\Delta K_t = K_t - K_{t-1}$.

The existence of the government leads to two modifications of the household's budget constraint in equation (12.3). First, year t's real taxes, T_t, subtract from real income on the right-hand side. One unit more of real taxes means one unit less of **real disposable income**, which is the real income available after taxes. Second, year t's real transfers, V_t, add to real income on the right-hand side. Therefore, the household's budget constraint becomes

(12.4)
$$C_t + (1/P) \bullet \Delta B_t + \Delta K_t =$$
$$(w/P)_t \bullet L_t^s + r_{t-1} \bullet (B_{t-1}/P + K_{t-1}) + \boxed{V_t - T_t}$$
consumption + real saving =
real disposable income

The new term on the right-hand side, shaded in yellow, is the difference between real transfers and real taxes, $V_t - T_t$.

We showed in Chapters 7 and 8 how to extend the household's one-year budget constraint to many years. The result, when we modify equation (8.7) to replace the nominal interest rate, i_t, by the real interest rate, r_t, is

(12.5)
$$C_1 + C_2/(1 + r_1) + C_3/[(1 + r_1) \bullet$$
$$(1 + r_2)] + \cdots = (1 + r_0) \bullet (B_0/P + K_0)$$
$$+ (w/P)_1 \bullet L_1^s + (w/P)_2 \bullet L_2^s/(1 + r_1)$$
$$+ (w/P)_3 \bullet L_3^s/[(1 + r_1) \bullet (1 + r_2)] + \cdots$$

present value of consumption =
value of initial assets + present value of wage incomes

When we allow for taxes and transfers, as we did in going from equation (12.3) to equation (12.4), we get

an extension to the multiyear budget constraint from equation (12.5). The extended version is

> **Key equation (multiyear household budget constraint with transfers and taxes):**
>
> **(12.6)**
> $$C_1 + C_2/(1 + r_1) + \cdots =$$
> $$(1 + r_0) \bullet (B_0/P + K_0) + (w/P)_1 \bullet L_1^s$$
> $$+ (w/P)_2 \bullet L_2^s/(1 + r_1) + \cdots$$
> $$\boxed{+ (V_1 - T_1) + (V_2 - T_2)/(1 + r_1) +}$$
> $$\boxed{(V_3 - T_3)/[(1 + r_1) \bullet (1 + r_2)] + \cdots}$$
>
> *present value of consumption =*
> *value of initial assets + present value of wage*
> *incomes + present value of transfers net of taxes*

The new term on the right-hand side, shaded in yellow, is the present value of real transfers net of real taxes,

(12.7)
$$(V_1 - T_1) + (V_2 - T_2)/(1 + r_1)$$
$$+ (V_3 - T_3)/[(1 + r_1) \bullet (1 + r_2)] + \cdots =$$
present value of real transfers net of real taxes

A lower present value of real transfers net of real taxes lowers the overall sources of funds for the household. Our analysis from Chapter 7 predicts that the household would react just as it would to any other loss of income. In particular, the income effects predict reductions in consumption, C_t, and leisure in each year. The decrease in leisure implies an increase in labor supply, L_t^s, in each year.

Our analysis from Chapter 7 tells us that the strength of the income effect depends on whether a change in real transfers net of real taxes is temporary or permanent. For a temporary change, we can consider a decrease in real transfers net of real taxes for year 1, $V_1 - T_1$, while holding fixed the terms $V_t - T_t$ for other years t. In this case, the present value of real transfers net of real taxes falls in equation (12.7), but by only a small amount. Therefore, we predict small decreases in C_t and small increases in L_t^s for each year. In contrast, if the decline in $V_t - T_t$ applies for all years t, the present value of real transfers net of real taxes falls in equation (12.7) by a large amount. Therefore, we predict large decreases in C_t and large increases in L_t^s for each year.

Permanent Changes in Government Purchases

We now turn our attention to government purchases. We begin by considering the economic effects from a permanent change in government purchases. Recall that Figure 12.2 showed the U.S. data on government purchases, expressed as a ratio to GDP. The present analysis does not apply to large temporary changes, such as the surges in defense purchases during World War II and the Korean War. The analysis does apply to most other variations in government purchases; empirically, most changes in the ratio of government purchases to GDP have been long lasting.

A Permanent Change in Government Purchases: Theory

Suppose that government purchases, G_t, rise by one unit each year. Since we are considering the same change each year, we can simplify by dropping the year subscript, t. In this case, the government's budget constraint from equation (12.2) is

$$G + V = T$$

Therefore, we can rearrange the terms to get a formula for real transfers net of real taxes:

(12.8) $$V - T = -G$$

If G rises by one unit each year, $V - T$ falls by one unit each year. Hence, the typical household's disposable real income falls by one unit each year. The income effects predict, accordingly, a decrease in each year's consumption, C, and an increase in each year's labor supply, L^s.

We can get the main results by ignoring for now the changes in labor supply, L^s. That is, we assume that each year's L^s equals a constant, L. We reconsider this assumption in Chapter 13, where we allow also for the substitution effects from realistic forms of taxes.

Consider the income effect on consumption, C. Since the typical household has one less unit of real disposable income each year, we predict that the decrease in C each year will be roughly by one unit. This prediction follows from the result in Chapter 7 that the propensity to consume out of a permanent change in income would be close to one.

Now let's consider how the increase in government purchases affects the demand and supply of capital services and real GDP. Recall that real GDP, Y, is given by the production function from Chapter 9:

(9.1) $$Y = A \cdot F(\kappa K, L)$$

This formulation allows for a variable capital utilization rate, κ, so that κK is the quantity of capital services. We are assuming that the capital stock, K, is fixed in the short run. We are also assuming that the technology level, A, and the quantity of labor input, L, are fixed.

As in Chapter 9, the quantity of capital services demanded, $(\kappa K)^d$, comes from the equation of the marginal product of capital services, MPK, to the real rental price, R/P. This condition determined a downward-sloping demand curve for capital services, as shown in Figure 9.5. We reproduce this demand curve as the red graph in Figure 12.4.

Since the capital stock, K, is given, the quantity of capital services supplied, $(\kappa K)^s$, varies only because of changes in the capital utilization rate, κ. As in Figure 9.5 in Chapter 9, the chosen κ and, hence, the quantity of capital services supplied, $(\kappa K)^s$, is an upward-sloping function of the real rental price, R/P. We show this supply curve as the blue graph in Figure 12.5.

The important observation is that an increase in government purchases, G, does not shift the curves for the demand or supply of capital services. The demand curve does not shift because the rise in G does not affect the MPK (for a given input of capital services, κK). The supply curve does not shift because, first, K is given, and, second, the change in G does not affect the choice of the capital utilization rate, κ (as worked out in Figure 9.3 in Chapter 9). Because the demand and supply curves do not shift in Figure 12.5, we conclude that the market-clearing real rental price, $(R/P)^*$, and quantity of capital services, $(\kappa K)^*$, do not change.

Real GDP, Y, is given from the production function in equation (9.1) as $Y = A \cdot F(\kappa K, L)$. We found that the quantity of capital services, κK, is unchanged, and we assumed that the technology level, A, and the quantity of labor input, L, are fixed. Therefore, Y is unchanged. Thus, *we have the important conclusion that a permanent increase in government purchases does not affect real GDP.*

Consider the real interest rate, r. We know from Chapter 11 that r is given by

(11.8) $$r = (R/P) \cdot \kappa - \delta(\kappa)$$

real rate of return on bonds =
real rate of return from owning capital

where R/P is the real rental price and κ is the capital utilization rate. The term $(R/P) \bullet \kappa$ is the real rental income per unit of capital. We have found that a permanent increase in government purchases, G, does not affect R/P or κ. Therefore, equation (11.8) implies that the real interest rate, r, does not change. Thus, we have another important result: *A permanent increase in government purchases does not affect the real interest rate.*

Now we turn to the labor market. As in Chapters 6 and 8, the quantity of labor demanded, L^d, comes from the equation of the marginal product of labor, MPL, to the real wage rate, w/P. This condition determines a downward-sloping demand curve for labor, as shown in Figures 6.4 and 8.6. We reproduce this demand curve as the red graph in Figure 12.6.

We discussed in Chapter 8 how an increase in the real wage rate, w/P, motivates households to increase the quantity of labor supplied, L^s. However, we are assuming for now that labor supply, L^s, is a constant, L. Therefore,

Figure 12.6 shows L^s as a vertical line at L. We assume that the increase in government purchases, G, does not change L.

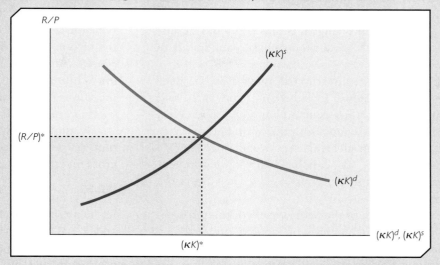

Figure 12.5 *Clearing of the Market for Capital Services*

This construction comes from Figure 9.5. The demand curve for capital services, $(\kappa K)^d$, comes from the equation of the marginal product of capital services, MPK, to the real rental price, R/P. When R/P rises, the quantity of capital services demanded falls. The supply of capital services, $(\kappa K)^s$, applies for a given capital stock, K. If R/P rises, owners of capital raise the capital utilization rate, κ. Therefore, the quantity of capital services supplied rises. The market clears where the quantity of capital services supplied equals the quantity demanded. At this point, R/P equals $(R/P)^*$ on the vertical axis, and κK equals $(\kappa K)^*$ on the horizontal axis.

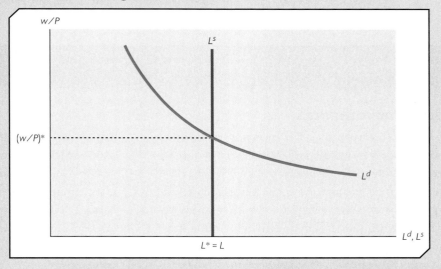

Figure 12.6 *Clearing of the Labor Market*

This construction comes from Figure 8.6. The demand curve for labor, L^d, shown in red, comes from the equation of the marginal product of labor, MPL, to the real wage rate, w/P. When w/P rises, the quantity of labor demanded falls. We assume here that labor supply, L^s, shown in blue, equals the constant L. The market clears where $w/P = (w/P^*)$ on the vertical axis, so that the quantity of labor demanded equals L.

The permanent increase in government purchases, G, does not shift the labor-demand curve, L^d, in Figure 12.6. The reason is that the rise in G does not affect the MPL (for given input of labor, L). To get this answer, we use the result from Figure 12.5 that the quantity of capital services, κK, is unchanged. If capital services had changed, the MPL would be different (at a given L), and the L^d curve would shift in Figure 12.6.

The increase in government purchases, G, does not shift labor supply, L^s, which is fixed at L, and does not shift the labor-demand curve, L^d. Therefore, the increase in G changes nothing in Figure 12.6. Hence, the market-clearing real wage rate, $(w/P)^*$, does not change. We conclude that *a permanent increase in government purchases does not affect the real wage rate*.

Now we return to the behavior of consumption, C. We know from our analysis of income effects that a permanent rise in government purchases, G, by one unit reduces C in each year by roughly one unit. To find the full effect on current consumption, we have to consider whether any substitution effects apply. The intertemporal-substitution effect depends on the real interest rate, r. Since r does not change, the intertemporal-substitution effect does not operate. Another substitution effect involves consumption and leisure, but we have assumed that the quantity of labor and, hence, quantity of leisure, is fixed. In any event, this substitution

effect depends on the real wage rate, w/P, which does not change.

Since no substitution effects arise, we can determine the change in current consumption, C, solely from the income effect. As already noted, the income effect causes C to decline by roughly one unit. Therefore, *our prediction is that a permanent increase in government purchases by one unit causes consumption to decrease by about one unit*.

To find the response of gross investment, I, recall that real GDP, Y, equals the sum of consumption, C, gross investment, I, and government purchases, G:

(12.9) $$Y = C + I + G$$

In the present case, Y is unchanged, G rises by one unit, and C falls by one unit. Therefore, equation (12.9) tells us that the changes in C and G fully offset each other and, thereby, allow I to remain unchanged. We conclude that *a permanent increase in government purchases does not affect gross investment*.

To sum up, we predict that a permanent increase in government purchases, G, reduces consumption, C, roughly one to one. The variables that do not change include real GDP, Y; gross investment, I; the quantity of capital services, κK; the real rental price, R/P; the real interest rate, r; and the real wage rate, w/P.

Extending the Model

Useful Public Services

We did not consider that the government may use its purchases, G, to provide useful public services. We study here the case in which these services provide utility for households. As examples, the government might provide free or subsidized school lunches or transportation, or concerts in the park. We assume that these publicly provided services combine with private consumer expenditure to determine overall household utility. For example, utility depends on transportation, one part of which is provided by the government.

Suppose that each household views a unit of government purchases, G, as equivalent in utility to λ units of private consumption, C. We assume that $\lambda \geq 0$ applies. Differences of opinion about the size of λ are at the heart of debates about the desirable size of government. The case

$\lambda = 1$ means that a unit of G is equivalent in utility to a unit of C. The case $\lambda < 1$ means that a unit of resources that goes through the government provides less utility than a unit of private consumer spending. This case might apply because the lack of market incentives makes government operations relatively inefficient. We could instead have $\lambda > 1$ if there are scale benefits in the provision of public goods.

Recall from equation (12.4) that the household budget constraint, when written without year subscripts, is

$$C + (1/P) \cdot \Delta B + \Delta K =$$
$$(w/P) \cdot L^s + r \cdot (B/P + K) + V - T$$
$$\textit{consumption} + \textit{real saving} = \textit{real disposable income}$$

We can add λG to each side of the equation to get

(12.10)
$$(C + \lambda G) + (1/P) \cdot \Delta B + \Delta K = (w/P) \cdot L^s + r \cdot (B/P + K) + V - T + \lambda G$$
effective consumption + real saving = effective real disposable income

The two new terms are shaded in yellow. This specification is useful because $C + \lambda G$ on the left-hand side can be thought of as *effective consumption*: the sum of private consumption, C, and the utility received from public services, λG. The new term on the right-hand side, λG, is the implicit value of the free or subsidized public services. Thus, we can think of the right-hand side as *effective real disposable income*, the sum of real disposable income and the implicit value of public services, λG.

Consider the case in which government purchases, G, rise by one unit each year. The government's budget constraint in equation (12.8) says that the difference between real transfers and real taxes, $V - T$, falls by one unit each year. Therefore, an increase in G by one unit changes the combination of the last three terms on the right-hand side of equation (12.10) by

$$\Delta(V - T + \lambda G) = \Delta(V - T) + \Delta(\lambda G)$$
$$= -1 + \lambda$$

where we used the conditions $\lambda(V - T) = -1$ and $\Delta(\lambda G) = \lambda$. Thus, the change in effective real disposable income depends on whether λ is less than, equal to, or greater than 1. If $\lambda < 1$, effective real disposable income declines by $1 - \lambda$ units when G rises by one unit, but if $\lambda > 1$, effective real disposable income rises by $\lambda - 1$ units when G increases by one unit. In the main text, we assumed $\lambda = 0$, so that effective real disposable income fell by one unit when G rose by one unit.

To fix ideas, consider the case in which $\lambda < 1$. (However, the analysis also applies if $\lambda = 1$ or $\lambda > 1$.) Since effective real disposable income falls by $1 - \lambda$ units each year, we predict that the household's effective consumption, $C + \lambda G$, would fall by about $1 - \lambda$ units each year. That is, the change in effective consumption will be close to the change in effective real disposable income. To determine the change in C, use the condition

$$\Delta(C + \lambda G) = -1 + \lambda$$

If we separate out the two changes on the left-hand side, we get

$$\Delta C + \lambda \cdot \Delta G = -1 + \lambda$$

If we substitute $\Delta G = 1$ and cancel out λ on each side, we get

$$\Delta C = -1$$

The result $\Delta C = -1$ means that a permanent increase in G by one unit crowds out private consumption, C, by one unit. We have found that this result holds for any value of λ. It works for the case in the main text in which public services are useless ($\lambda = 0$), when a unit of public services provides less utility than a unit of private consumption ($0 < \lambda < 1$), when public and private services are viewed equally ($\lambda = 1$), and when public services are valued more highly ($\lambda > 1$). The only difference among the cases—but an important difference—is that the higher λ, the happier households are when the government expands G.

The Cyclical Behavior of Government Purchases

One prediction from the equilibrium business-cycle model is that long-lasting changes in real government purchases would not have much impact on real GDP. We mentioned that most changes in U.S. real government purchases fit the assumption of being long lasting. The main contrary examples come from military purchases during wartime. If we look at U.S. data from 1955 to 2006, after the end of the Korean War, the variations in war-related government purchases were relatively minor. Therefore, the model predicts that the fluctuations in real government purchases from 1955 to 2006 should bear little relation to the fluctuations in real GDP.

To test this proposition, Figure 12.7 uses our standard approach of comparing the cyclical part of a variable—in this case, real government purchases—with the cyclical

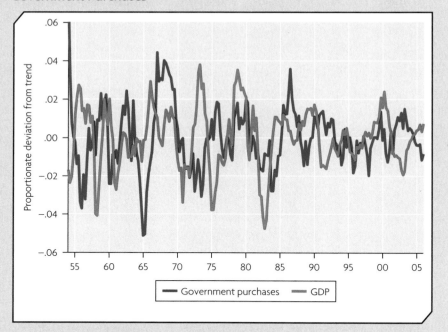

Figure 12.7 *Cyclical Behavior of U.S. Real GDP and Government Purchases*

The red graph is the deviation of real GDP from its trend. The blue graph is the deviation of real government purchases from its trend. (We measure government purchases by the national-accounts data on government consumption and investment—this concept adds to government purchases the estimated depreciation of government capital stocks.) The deviations are measured in a proportionate sense. The data on GDP and government purchases are quarterly and seasonally adjusted. Government purchases are about as variable as GDP but have little cyclical pattern. The correlation of the cyclical part of real government purchases with the cyclical part of real GDP was −0.01.

part of real GDP. The variability of real government purchases from 1955 to 2006 is similar to that of real GDP. However, the cyclical parts of the two variables were virtually unrelated—the correlation was −0.01. This result provides support for our equilibrium business-cycle model. Note also that the pattern for government purchases is very different from the ones we found for consumer expenditure and investment (Figures 8.9 and 8.10), each of which was strongly procyclical.

Temporary Changes in Government Purchases

ow we will analyze temporary changes in real government purchases. We begin by extending the equilibrium business-cycle model to include temporary variations in government purchases. Then we apply the extended model to wartime experiences.

A Temporary Change in Government Purchases: Theory

Assume now that year 1's real government purchases, G_1, rise by one unit, while those for other years, G_t, do not change. That is, everyone expects that G_t in future years will return to the original level. We can think of this case as representing a war that begins at the start of year 1 and is expected to last one year. Of course, this description is a simplification, intended to capture the main features of temporarily high government purchases. In reality, the durations of wars vary, and the interval of heightened government purchases might be greater or less than one year.

The government's budget constraint from equation (12.8) implies for year t:

(12.11)
$$V_t - T_t = -G_t$$

Therefore, in year 1, the net of real transfers over real taxes, $V_1 - T_1$, falls by one unit, and households have one unit less of real disposable income. In subsequent years, $V_t - T_t$ and, hence, real disposable incomes return to their original levels. Thus, the difference from a permanent rise in government purchases is that the expected real disposable income in future years is unchanged. Our analysis from Chapter 7 predicts that households would spread their reduced disposable income in year 1 over reduced consumption, C_t, in all years t. Therefore, the effect on year 1's consumption, C_1, will be relatively small. The propensity to consume out of a temporary change in income is greater than zero but much less than one.

Now, to simplify the notation, we again drop the time subscripts, with each variable implicitly applying to the current year, year 1. Much of the analysis of a temporary change in government purchases is the same as that worked out for a permanent change. As before, we ignore any changes in labor supply, so that $L^s = L$. In Figure 12.5, the change in government purchases still does not affect the MPK (for a given quantity of capital services, κK) and, therefore, does not shift the demand curve for capital services, $(\kappa K)^d$. The change in government purchases also does not affect the way that suppliers of capital services choose their utilization rate, κ (for a given real rental price, R/P). Therefore, with a fixed stock of capital, K, the supply curve for capital services, $(\kappa K)^s$, does not shift. Since neither curve shifts in Figure 12.5, we conclude, as before, that the real rental price, R/P, and the quantity of capital services, κK, do not change.

Since capital services, κK, do not change and labor is fixed at L, we know from the production function,

(9.1)
$$Y = A \bullet F(\kappa K, L)$$

that real GDP, Y, does not change. Since the real rental price, R/P, and the capital utilization rate, κ, do not change, we also have that the real interest rate, r, stays the same. This result follows from the formula:

(11.8)
$$r = (R/P) \bullet \kappa - \delta(\kappa)$$

real rate of return on bonds =
real rate of return from owning capital

In Figure 12.6, the change in government purchases still does not affect the MPL (for a given labor input, L) and, therefore, does not shift the labor demand curve, L^d. Since labor supply, L^s, is fixed at L, the change in government purchases also does not shift the labor-supply curve. Since neither curve shifts, the real wage rate, w/P, does not change.

New results come when we consider consumption and investment. Consider again the expression for real GDP:

(12.9)
$$Y = C + I + G$$

Real GDP, Y, is unchanged; real government purchases, G, are higher in year 1 by one unit; and consumption, C, is lower, but by much less than one unit. Consequently, equation (12.9) implies that gross investment, I, must fall. In fact, since the decrease in C is relatively small, the decline in I is large. That is, year 1's extra G comes mainly at the expense of I, rather than C. In contrast, when the change in G was permanent, we predicted that most or all of the extra G came at the expense of C.

Government Purchases and Real GDP During Wartime: Empirical

We will now evaluate the equilibrium business-cycle model's predictions for the effects of a temporary change in real government purchases. We test the model by studying the response of the economy to the temporary changes in government purchases that have accompanied U.S. wars.

Table 12.2 covers World War I, World War II, the Korean War, and the Vietnam War. We can measure the temporary part of real defense purchases by the difference between actual purchases and an estimated trend. The trend is calculated in our usual manner by fitting a line through the historical data. We focus on the peaks of wartime purchases: 1918, 1943–44, 1952–53, and 1967–68. The values of temporary real purchases, in 1996 dollars, were $84 billion, or 16% of trend real GDP, in 1918; $537 billion, or 44% of trend real GDP, in 1943–44; $56 billion, or 3% of trend real GDP, in 1952–53; and $46 billion, or 1.4% of trend real GDP, in 1967–68. Based on these numbers, we can be confident that wartime purchases, and possibly other effects from war, were the major influences on the economy during World Wars I and II. That is, we do not have to worry about holding constant other factors. Wartime purchases would also be a major influence during the Korean War, though not necessarily the dominant force. In the Vietnam War, the temporary military purchases of only 1.4% of real GDP were unlikely to be the overriding factor; other disturbances were likely of comparable or greater significance.

Table 12.2 *U.S. Wartime Spending, Real GDP, and Employment*

I: Real GDP and Components. Each entry is the deviation from trend in billions of 1996 dollars. Values in parentheses are percentage of own trend.

			Wartime Years	
	1918 (WW I)	**1943–44 (WW II)**	**1952–53 (Korea)**	**1967–68 (Vietnam)**
Category of GDP:				
Defense purchases	84 (679)	537 (317)	56 (25)	46 (15)
% of trend real GDP	16	44	3	1
Real GDP	42 (8)	433 (36)	49 (3)	81 (2)
Consumption	–21 (–5)	–1 (0)	0 (0)	31 (1)
Gross investment	–21 (–28)	–58 (–51)	0 (0)	5 (1)
Nondefense government	0 (0)	–20 (–19)	5 (3)	5 (1)
Net exports	0	–23	–11	–5

II: Employment. Each entry is the deviation from trend in millions. Values in parentheses are percentage of own trend.

Category of employment:				
Total employment	3.0 (8)	9.1 (17)	0.9 (1)	1.0 (1)
Civilian employment	0.5 (1)	1.5 (3)	0.2 (0)	0.4 (1)
Military personnel	2.5 (566)	7.7 (296)	0.7 (24)	0.6 (19)

Notes: In part I, each cell shows the deviation of a real expenditure component from its estimated trend in billions of 1996 dollars per year. The values in parentheses express the deviations as a percentage of the trend. For example, as an average for 1943 and 1944, defense purchases were $537 billion or 317% above trend, real GDP was $433 billion or 36% above trend, and so on. Each real expenditure component is the nominal value divided by the deflator for the GDP. (The trend for real GDP was constrained to equal the sum of the trends estimated for the components of GDP.) In part II, total employment is the sum of civilian employment and military personnel. Each entry shows the deviation of a component of employment from its own trend in millions. For example, as an average for 1943 and 1944, total employment was 9.1 million or 17% above its own trend, civilian employment was 1.5 million or 3% above its own trend, and military personnel was 7.7 million or 296% above its own trend. (The trend for total employment was constrained to equal the sum of the trends estimated for its two parts, civilian employment and military personnel.) Data for the last three wars are from Bureau of Economic Analysis (www.bea.gov). Data for 1918 are from John Kendrick (1961), Christina Romer (1988), and U.S. Department of Commerce (1975).

Other U.S. wartime experiences since 1869—the period with reliable national-accounts data—were of lesser magnitude, as gauged by the ratio of temporary defense purchases to GDP. The next largest ratios were 0.6% during the Spanish-American War in 1898 and 0.5% for the Afghanistan-Iraq conflicts in 2002–03. The ratio was 0.6% at the peak of the Reagan defense buildup in 1987. However, these defense purchases were not associated with a war and were probably not viewed as temporary. The ratio equaled 0.2% during the Gulf War in 1991.

Unfortunately, the lack of data prevents our studying some earlier large U.S. wars, notably the Civil War and the Revolutionary War. These wars, fought on U.S. soil, featured important negative effects on real GDP from the destruction of domestic capital stock. The loss of life was also substantial during the Civil War. Wartime destruction of domestic capital stock has not been important in the United States since the Civil War but was highly significant for many other countries during World Wars I and II.

To illustrate the main results, we focus in Table 12.2 on World War II and the Korean War. In each case, real GDP was above its trend, but by less than the excess of real defense purchases from its trend. For example, in 1943–44, the excess for real defense purchases of $537 billion was matched by an excess for real GDP of $433 billion. For 1952–53, the numbers were $56 billion and $49 billion, respectively.

EXTENDING THE MODEL

Effects on the Term Structure of Interest Rates

We found that a temporary increase in government purchases, G, did not affect the real interest rate, r. We also found that investment, I, declined. For example, I would be depressed during a war, which might last several years. Over time, the decline in investment means that the stock of capital, K, will be lower than it otherwise would have been—in particular, K will be lower at the end of the war. The decrease in K reduces the supply of capital services and leads, thereby, to an increase in the market-clearing real rental price, R/P. The rise in R/P leads to an increase in r, in accordance with equation (11.8), $r = (R/P) \cdot \kappa - \delta(\kappa)$. Hence, although the current real interest rate does not change, future real interest rates rise.

In our model, the real interest rate, r, is a short-term real rate. In the real world, bonds are traded with varying maturities. For example, if we think about the indexed U.S. Treasury bonds that we studied in Chapter 11, a one-year bond might pay the real rate of return $r(1)$, a five-year bond the real rate of return $r(5)$, and so on. The **term structure of real interest rates** is the relation between the real rate of return, $r(j)$, and the maturity, j. If $r(j)$ increases with j, the term structure is upward sloping; otherwise, it is flat or downward sloping.

If we consider, say, a five-year horizon, an individual can hold to maturity a five-year indexed U.S. government bond or can instead hold a sequence of five one-year indexed bonds. In the first case, the real rate of return is $r(5)$. In the second, the real rate of return is an average of the five one-year returns, $r(1)$. Competition in the financial markets will work to equate the anticipated rates of return from the two options. Hence, $r(5)$ will be an average of the $r(1)$s expected to prevail over the next five years.

In the case of a temporary increase in government purchases, short-term real interest rates, such as $r(1)$, did not change initially. However, anticipated future values of $r(1)$ increased. Therefore, the average of the $r(1)$s expected to prevail over the next five years rose. Since $r(5)$ equals the average of the expected $r(1)$s, it follows that $r(5)$ rises immediately when government purchases increase. In other words, the model predicts an effect on the term structure of real interest rates. Short-term rates do not change immediately, but longer-term rates increase. Hence, the term structure becomes more upward sloping.

Since real GDP was up by less than defense purchases, the other components of GDP had to be below trend overall. In 1943–44, the shortfalls from trend were $58 billion in gross investment and $20 billion in nondefense forms of government consumption and investment. Consumption was about equal to trend, and net exports of goods and services were $23 billion below trend. (We will study net exports in Chapter 17.) In 1952–53, gross investment and consumption were each about equal to trend, nondefense government consumption was $5 billion above trend, and net exports were $11 billion below trend.

Consider how the equilibrium business-cycle model relates to these wartime observations. The main discrepancy is that the model predicted no change in real GDP,

whereas the data reveal substantial increases in real GDP. The data also show that the rises in real GDP are by less than the increases in government purchases. That is, aside from military purchases, the totals of the other components of real GDP are down during wartime. The model accords with this pattern. However, the components of real GDP other than military purchases do not fall nearly as much as predicted by the model.

Wartime Effects on the Economy

The main failing of the model—and quite a striking one—is its prediction that real GDP would be unchanged during wartime. The source of this prediction is our assumption that labor input, L, is fixed. Therefore, it is worthwhile to reconsider this assumption. We begin by looking at the data on employment during wartime.

Employment During Wartime

We can illustrate the main pattern from World War II. The number of persons in the military soared—in 1943–44, military personnel reached 7.7 million persons above its estimated trend. But surprisingly, civilian employment also increased, rising by 1.5 million or 3% above its estimated trend. Putting the two parts together, total employment—civilian plus military—was 9.1 million or 17% above trend. The basic pattern is that the military took in a significant number of persons—primarily by the military draft in the wars up to Vietnam—and total employment expanded a little more. To do better with our predictions, we have to explain why the total quantity of labor supplied increased so much.

Effects of War on Labor Supply

At this point, there is no settled view among economists about the best way to understand labor supply during wartime. Thus, we consider a number of possibilities and will not be able to reach a definitive explanation. Here are some ideas that have been advanced.

- A large expansion of real government purchases, G, means that households have less real disposable income. The negative income effect predicts reductions in consumption and leisure and, hence, an increase in labor supply, L^s. Several considerations influence the size of the income effect. For one thing, we have stressed that the increase in G is likely to be temporary, at least if the wars are expected to last no more than a few years and if no major destruction of capital stock and population is anticipated.[3] This consideration makes the income effects on consumption and leisure relatively small. On the other hand, military outlays would not substitute for private consumption in the provision of utility—that is, the parameter λ introduced in the section entitled "Useful Public Services" would be zero. This consideration makes the income effects large in comparison with those from nonmilitary government purchases. Overall, the income effect predicts an increase in labor supply, L^s. The problem, however, is that the same argument predicts a decrease in consumption, C. This prediction conflicts with the finding in Table 12.2 that C did not decrease much during the wars.

- Casey Mulligan (1998) argues that labor supply, L^s, increases during wartime because of patriotism. That is, for a given real wage rate, w/P, and for given total real income, people are willing to work more as part of the war effort. The attraction of this argument is that it does not rely on a negative income effect and can, therefore, explain why consumption does not fall much during wartime. However, it may be that the effect of patriotism is more important during a popular war, such as World War II, than in other conflicts.

- From the standpoint of families, we want to understand how the military draft's forced removal of many men would influence the labor supply of those not drafted, especially women. One part of this analysis involves married couples, with the man drafted into the military. In these cases, the postponement of having children would be an important part of the story. Thus, women might participate more in the labor force as a temporary alternative to raising a family or having a larger family. Another consideration involves the postponement of marriage. Through this channel, the military draft would affect the labor supply of single women. That is, women who would otherwise have married and had children found market work to be an attractive, temporary alternative.

The upshot of these arguments is that wartime likely entails an increase in labor supply, L^s. Thus, we now assume that the occurrence of a war shifts the labor-supply curve, L^s, as shown in Figure 12.8. Unlike in Figure 12.6, we now allow for a positive effect of the real wage rate, w/P, on L^s. Thus, before the war, the labor-supply curve, shown in blue, slopes upward versus w/P. The war shifts the curve rightward to the green one, denoted $(L^s)'$. At any w/P, the quantity of labor supplied is larger along the green curve than along the blue one.

The labor-demand curve, denoted by L^d and shown in red in Figure 12.8, slopes downward versus w/P. This curve is the same as the one in Figure 12.6. We still assume that the occurrence of a war does not shift the labor-demand curve (because the change in government purchases, G, does not affect the MPL).

Before the war, the labor-market clears at the quantity of labor, L^*, and real wage rate, $(w/P)^*$, shown in Figure 12.8. During the war, the quantity of labor rises to $(L^*)'$ on the horizontal axis, and the real wage rate falls to $[(w/P)^*]'$ on the vertical axis. Thus, when we

---

[3] In terms of destruction of human life, the highest U.S. casualty rates in relation to the population were during the Civil War, when roughly 500,000 people died. U.S. war-related deaths during World Wars I and II were 117,000 and 405,000, respectively, well below 1% of the total labor force. Casualties for the Korean and Vietnam Wars were much smaller. For many countries during World Wars I and II, casualty rates were far higher than anything ever experienced by the United States.

allow for an increase in labor supply, the model can explain a rise in total employment, as observed in Table 12.2. A new prediction is that the occurrence of war lowers the real wage rate, w/P.

Effects of War on the Real Wage Rate

We now consider the prediction from Figure 12.8 that a war reduces the real wage rate, w/P. This proposition receives a mixed verdict from the main U.S. wartime experiences. If we compute the average percentage deviation of the real wage rate from its trend during the years of the main wars, we get the following:[4]

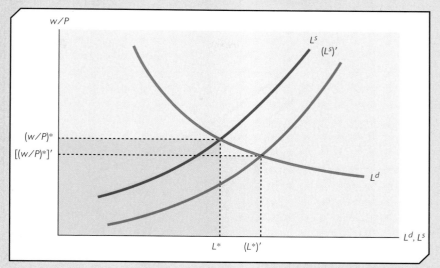

Figure 12.8 *Effect of a Wartime Increase in Labor Supply on the Labor Market*

The downward-sloping labor-demand curve, L^d, shown in red, comes from Figure 12.6. We now allow the real wage rate, w/P, to have a positive effect on labor supply, L^s, shown by the blue curve. We assume that the occurrence of a war shifts the labor-supply curve rightward from L^s to $(L^s)'$, shown in green. The quantity of labor input rises from L^* to $(L^*)'$ on the horizontal axis, and the real wage rate falls from $(w/P)^*$ to $[(w/P)^*]'$ on the vertical axis.

- World War I (1917–18): −4.0%
- World War II (1942–45): +3.1%
- Korean War (1951–53): 0.0%

Thus, the predicted negative effect on w/P shows up only for World War I. The excess of w/P from trend during World War II conflicts with our prediction. For the Korean War, w/P deviates negligibly from its trend.

A further analysis suggests that the model might be doing better than these numbers indicate. Price controls and rationing of goods were imposed during World War II and, to a lesser extent, during the Korean War. Consequently, the reported price level, P, understated the true price level—typically, households could not buy additional goods just by paying the stated price. For example, to buy more goods, a household might have to pay the black-market price, which exceeded the stated price at a time of price controls and rationing. Since P was understated, the measured real wage rate, w/P, overstated the true real wage rate. That is, because of rationing, households could not buy w/P additional goods with an additional hour of labor. In principle, we could

adjust P upward (by an unknown amount) to calculate the true price level, which is the amount that a household would actually have to pay on the black market to buy more goods. The upward adjustment in P means that the adjusted real wage rate would be lower than the measured one during World War II and the Korean War. With this amendment, the model would work better, because the adjusted real wage rate may have fallen below trend during World War II and the Korean War.

Effects of War on the Rental Market

We learned from Figure 12.8 that a wartime increase in labor supply, L^s, led to an increase in labor input, L. This change affects the rental market, because the rise in L tends to increase the MPK (for a given quantity of capital services, κK).

In the prewar environment, the demand for capital services, $(\kappa K)^d$, slopes downward versus the real rental price, R/P, as shown by the blue curve in Figure 12.9. The war shifts this demand rightward to the curve $[(\kappa K)^d]'$, shown in green. The demand curve shifts right because the higher quantity of labor, L, raises the MPK for a given quantity of capital services, κK. We still have

---

[4] The nominal wage rate is the average hourly earnings of production workers in manufacturing. The real wage rate is the nominal wage rate divided by the GDP deflator. The trend for the real wage rate is calculated in our usual manner. The results for the Korean War come from quarterly data since 1947. The results for World Wars I and II come from annual data since 1889.

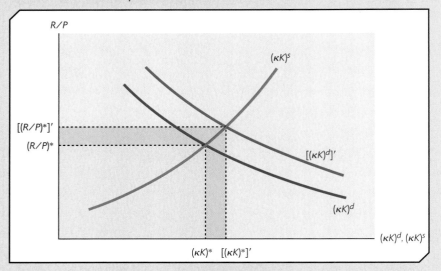

Figure 12.9 *Effect of a Wartime Increase in Labor Input on the Market for Capital Services*

The increase in employment from $L*$ to $(L*)'$, shown in Figure 12.8, raises the MPK (for a given quantity of capital services, κK). Therefore, the demand curve for capital services shifts rightward, from $(\kappa K)^d$, shown in blue, to $[(\kappa K)^d]'$, shown in green. The market-clearing real rental price of capital rises from $(R/P)*$ to $[(R/P)*]'$ on the vertical axis. The quantity of capital services expands from $(\kappa K)*$ to $[(\kappa K)*]'$ on the horizontal axis. This increase in capital services corresponds, for a given capital stock, K, to a rise in the capital utilization rate, κ.

that the war does not shift the supply curve for capital services, $(\kappa K)^s$, shown in red.

We see from Figure 12.9 that the real rental price, R/P, and the quantity of capital services, κK, increase. For a given capital stock, K, the rise in κK corresponds to an increase in the capital utilization rate, κ. Recall that the real interest rate is given by

[11.8] $$r = (R/P) \bullet \kappa - \delta(\kappa)$$

The increases in R/P and κ imply that r increases. Therefore, we have two new predictions about wartime. The capital utilization rate, κ, and the real interest rate, r, increase.

We looked before at data on capacity utilization rates. These numbers show that the utilization rate, κ, rose significantly above trend during the Korean

War—the average for 1952–53 was 0.025. These data are unavailable before 1948, but another series reveals a sharp rise in capital utilization rates in manufacturing during World War II.[5] Thus, the model's prediction for higher capital utilization during wartime accords with the facts.

The predictions for higher real interest rates during wartime conflict with the U.S. data. During the Korean War (1951–53), the real interest rate on three-month U.S. Treasury bills was, on average, about equal to its trend value. During World War II (1942–45), the nominal three-month T-bill rates were extremely low—less than 1%—and inflation rates averaged 5%. Therefore, real interest rates were negative.[6] In World War I, short-term nominal interest rates rose from 3% in 1916 to 6% in 1918, but the inflation rate soared to as high as 16%. Hence, real interest rates were again negative.

The occurrences of extremely low real interest rates during wartime are not well understood. One promising idea for explaining this puzzle involves the different amounts of uncertainty in the returns on alternative forms of assets. Wartime likely raises the perceived probability of global disaster and tends, thereby, to raise the demand for comparatively safe assets, such as government bills. This heightened demand might explain why the real interest rate paid on such assets is relatively low during wartime.

---

[5] This series, constructed by the Federal Reserve and the Bureau of Economic Analysis, is for manufacturing production per unit of installed equipment. These data start in 1925 and are therefore unavailable for World War I.

[6] The 5% average inflation rate is based on the reported consumer price index. Because of price controls, the true inflation rates were probably higher during the war, so that the true real interest rates were even more negative than the measured ones.

Questions and Problems

A. Review questions

1. What are the economic differences between the government's purchases of goods and services and the government's transfer payments?

2. Derive the households' multiyear budget constraint in equation (12.6). Explain how real transfers and real taxes enter into this equation.

B. Problems for discussion

3. Government consumption in the national accounts
   The national accounts treat all government purchases of goods and services, G, as part of real GDP. But suppose that the public services derived from government purchases are an input to private production, say

   $$Y = F(\kappa K, L, G)$$

   In this case, public services are an intermediate product—a good that enters into a later stage of production. Hence, we ought not to include these services twice in real GDP—once when the government buys them and again when the services contribute to private production.

   a. Suppose that businesses initially hire private guards. Subsequently, the government provides free police protection, which substitutes for the private guards. Assume that the private guards and public police are equally efficient and receive the same wage rates. How does the switch from private to public protection affect measured real GDP?

   b. How would you change the national accounts to get a more accurate treatment of government purchases of goods and services? Is your proposal practical? (These issues are discussed by Simon Kuznets, 1948, pp. 156–57, and Richard Musgrave, 1959, pp. 186–88.)

4. Public ownership of capital and the national accounts
   Until the revision of 1996, the U.S. national accounts included in GDP the government's purchases of goods and services but took no account of the flow of services on government-owned capital. The accounts also did not subtract depreciation of this capital to calculate net domestic product.

   a. In the pre-1996 system, what happened to GDP if the government gave its capital to a private business and then bought the final goods from that business?

   b. In the current system of national accounts, the GDP includes an estimate of the flow of implicit rental income generated by public capital. However, this income flow is assumed to equal the estimated depreciation of the public capital. Redo question a in the context of this system.

5. A prospective change in government purchases
   Suppose that people learn in the current year that government purchases, G_t, will increase in some future year. Current government purchases, G_1, do not change.

   a. What happens in the current year to real GDP, Y; consumption, C; and investment, I?

   b. Can you think of some real-world cases to which this question applies?

6. The price level during the Korean War
   In 1949, the inflation rate was negative. With the start of the Korean War, the price level (GDP deflator) rose at an annual rate of 10% from the second quarter of 1950 to the first quarter of 1951. In contrast, the inflation rate was only around 2% from the first quarter of 1951 to the first quarter of 1953. The table shows—for various periods—the inflation rate, π; the growth rates, μ, of currency and the M1 monetary aggregate; and the growth rate of real government purchases, $\Delta G/G$. Can we use these data to explain the surge of the price level at the start of the Korean War, followed by a moderate inflation rate?

   (This question does not have a definite answer. However, a significant fact is that price controls were stringent during World War II. People may have expected a return to these controls when the Korean War started in June 1950. The controls implemented beginning in December 1950 were more moderate than those applied during World War II.)

Period	Inflation Rate (π)	M1 Growth Rate (μ)	Currency Growth Rate (μ)	Growth Rate of G
	(all figures in percent per year)			
1949.1 to 1950.2	−1.2	1.8	−1.6	2.5
Start of War				
1950.2 to 1951.1	10.2	4.0	−0.5	19.3
1951.1 to 1952.1	1.7	5.3	4.7	32.0
1952.1 to 1953.1	2.2	3.2	4.5	9.4

7. The role of public services

We studied in the section entitled "Useful Public Services" the role of public services in providing utility to households. We assumed that each unit of government purchases, G, was equivalent to λ units of private consumption, C, in terms of household utility.

a. Consider various categories of government expenditure, such as military spending, police, highways, public transit, and research and development. How do you think the coefficient λ varies across these categories?

b. Suppose that G rises permanently by one unit. What are the responses of real GDP, Y; consumption, C; and investment, I? How do the results depend on the size of the coefficient λ?

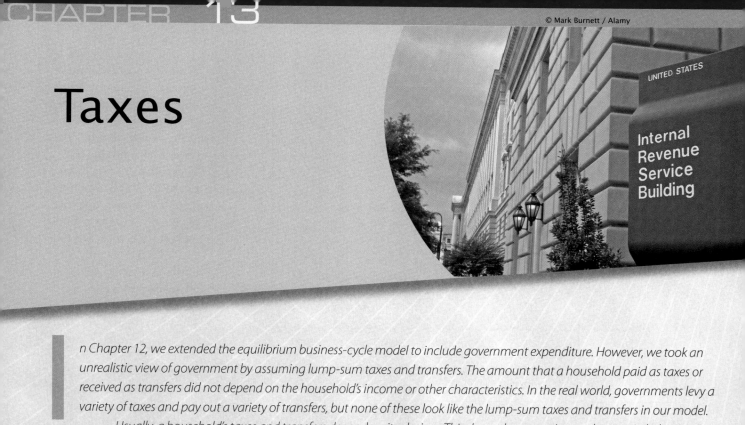

CHAPTER 13

Taxes

UNITED STATES

Internal
Revenue
Service
Building

I n Chapter 12, we extended the equilibrium business-cycle model to include government expenditure. However, we took an unrealistic view of government by assuming lump-sum taxes and transfers. The amount that a household paid as taxes or received as transfers did not depend on the household's income or other characteristics. In the real world, governments levy a variety of taxes and pay out a variety of transfers, but none of these look like the lump-sum taxes and transfers in our model.

Usually, a household's taxes and transfers depend on its choices. This dependence motivates changes in behavior. For example, taxes on labor income discourage households from working and earning income. Transfers to the unemployed motivate people not to be employed. Taxes on asset income discourage saving. Overall, the systems of taxes and transfers create substitution effects that influence labor supply, production, consumption, and investment. In this section, we extend the equilibrium business-cycle model to incorporate some of these effects. However, before we extend the theory, it is useful to have an overview of taxes in the United States.

Taxes in the United States

T he blue graph in Figure 13.1 shows the ratio of total government revenue to gross domestic product (GDP) from 1929 to 2005. The red graph shows the part for the federal government, and the green graph shows the part for state and local governments. (This construction does not count federal grants-in-aid, which are transfers from the federal to state and local governments, as revenue of the total or state and local governments.)

Total government revenue advanced from 10% of GDP in 1929 to 29% in 1981, remained close to 30%

through the mid-1990s, rose to a peak of 32% in 2000, and then fell to 28% in 2005. Until the New Deal programs in the second half of the 1930s, state and local revenue constituted the bulk of the total—for example, 76% in 1935. Just before the United States entered World War II, in 1940, state and local revenue was still over half of total revenue. However, since the start of World War II, federal revenue has been the dominant part of the total.

The ratio of federal revenue to GDP has been reasonably stable since the end of World War II. The ratio was 18% in 1946 and 19% in 1994. However, the ratio rose during the boom of the late 1990s to reach 21% in 2000, before falling to 17–18% in 2002–05. In contrast to the federal government, the ratio of state and local revenue to GDP rose steadily, from 5% in 1946 to 10% in 1970 and then remained fairly stable.

Figure 13.1 Government Revenue

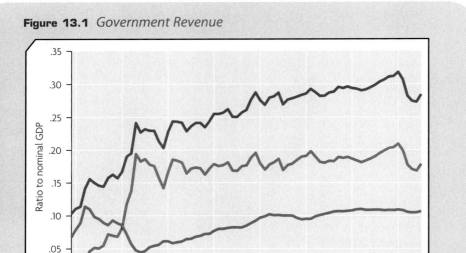

The blue graph shows total government revenue as a ratio to GDP. (Total government revenue excludes federal grants-in-aid, which are transfers from the federal government to state and local governments.) The red graph is for federal revenue, and the green graph is for state and local revenue (exclusive of federal grants-in-aid).

Figure 13.2 Breakdown of Federal Government Revenue

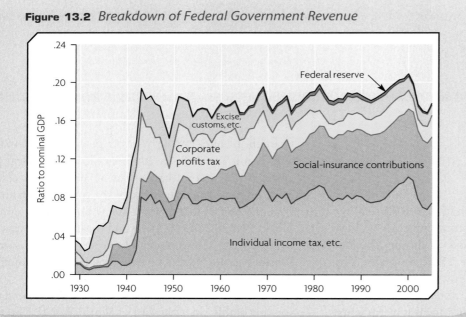

The figure shows federal government revenue, in five categories, as ratios to GDP. The categories are individual income taxes, and so forth (including estate taxes and personal nontax payments); contributions for social insurance (including payments by employers and employees for pension funds, Medicare, and unemployment insurance premiums); corporate profits taxes; excise taxes, customs duties, and so forth (including taxes on petroleum products, alcohol, and tobacco, and nontax payments, such as deposit-insurance premiums); and the Federal Reserve's transfers to the U.S. Treasury (treated in the national accounts as a part of corporate profits taxes).

Figure 13.2 gives a breakdown of federal tax revenue by major type. Individual income taxes began in 1913, except for some levies around the Civil War and in 1895. These taxes (including relatively small amounts from the estate tax and personal nontax payments) were only around 1% of GDP from 1929 until the sharp increases in levies beginning in 1942 because of World War II. The ratio to GDP reached 8% in 1943–45. Since the end of World War II, excluding 1949–50, the ratio remained between 7% and 9% until rising to 10% in 2000; then the ratio fell to 7% in 2003–05. The surge in this ratio in the 1990s reflected mainly the increased incomes and taxes of high-income persons—capital gains taxes paid on soaring stock market prices were part of the story. The fall in the ratio after 2000 reflected partly the recession of 2001–02 and partly the income tax cuts in 2001 and 2003.

The next component—contributions for social insurance funds—was essentially zero in 1929. However, social insurance revenue rose steadily following the advent of the unemployment insurance program in 1936 and the main Social Security program in 1937. The ratio of federal social insurance revenue to GDP reached

7% in the late 1980s. Since then, the ratio has changed little. In 2003–05, the revenue from federal social insurance contributions nearly equaled the receipts from the federal individual income tax.

Corporate profits taxes began in 1909. The ratio of these taxes to GDP rose from 1% in 1929 to 7% during World War II. After falling to 4% in 1946, the ratio rose again, to 6%, during the Korean War in 1951. Since then, the ratio of corporate profits taxes to GDP has fluctuated around a declining trend and was only 1–2% of GDP between 1980 and 2005.

The category that includes excise taxes and customs duties was the major source of federal revenue before World War I and still comprised about 60% of federal revenue in the early 1930s. As a ratio to GDP, this category was around 3% from 1933 to 1958 but has since declined steadily, to reach only 1% in 2005.

Finally, we have the payments from the Federal Reserve to the U.S. Treasury—these payments represent the government's revenue from printing money. This component of federal revenue is relatively minor—it peaked at 0.5% of GDP in 1982 and accounted for only 0.2% of GDP in 2002–05.

Figure 13.3 gives a breakdown of revenue for state and local governments. Property taxes were traditionally the largest component but declined in relative importance during World War II. The ratio to GDP has been close to 3% since 1949. Sales taxes rose from 1% of GDP in the early 1930s to 3% in 1970 and have since remained roughly stable. More recently, state and local governments have turned to individual income taxes. This category rose from less than 1% of GDP in 1965 to over 2% since 1987. The other form of state and local revenue that rose in relative importance is federal grants-in-aid, which are transfers from the federal government to state and local governments. These transfers go primarily for welfare,

medical care, transportation, education, housing, and training programs. As a share of GDP, federal grants-in-aid climbed from less than 1% of GDP in 1964 to 3% in 2002–05.

Types of Taxes

Some taxes fall on forms of income: individual income taxes, corporate profits taxes, and contributions for Social Security and Medicare. The social insurance contributions are collected from a payroll tax on wage earnings. Other taxes are based on expenditures: sales taxes, excise taxes, and customs duties. Many countries outside the United States use value-added taxes (VAT), which are like sales taxes but are assessed at various stages of production. Still other forms of taxes are based on ownership of property and are, therefore, forms of wealth taxes. An important point is that, for all of these taxes, the amount that a household or business pays depends on its economic activity. None of these taxes look like the lump-sum taxes in our model.

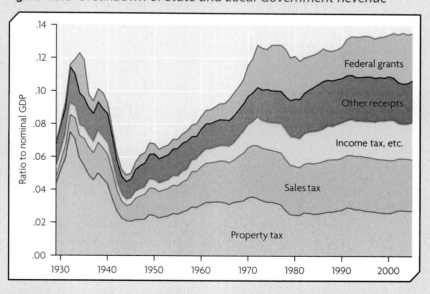

Figure 13.3 *Breakdown of State and Local Government Revenue*

The figure shows state and local government revenue, in five categories, as ratios to nominal GDP. The categories are: property taxes; sales taxes; individual income taxes and so forth (including estate taxes and personal nontax payments); other receipts (corporate profits taxes, social insurance contributions, and miscellaneous fees and taxes); and federal grants-in-aid (transfers from the federal government to state and local governments). The black graph is for total state and local revenue exclusive of federal grants-in-aid. This graph corresponds to the green graph in Figure 13.1.

Since the bulk of federal revenue comes from taxes that fall on income, it is worthwhile to incorporate income taxes into our equilibrium business-cycle model. A key point is the distinction between the **marginal tax rate** and the **average tax rate**. The marginal tax rate is the additional tax paid on an additional dollar of income. The average tax rate is the ratio of total taxes paid to total income. The marginal tax rate will turn out to have substitution effects that influence the behavior of households and businesses. The average tax rate will determine the government's revenue, which equals the average tax rate multiplied by income.

An important property of the U.S. federal individual income tax is that the marginal tax rate rises with income. Table 13.1 illustrates the nature of marginal and average income tax rates with numbers that approximate the U.S. individual income tax system in 2005. The first $22,800 of income is tax-exempt, corresponding to the standard deduction of $10,000 and personal exemptions of $12,800 for a family of four. Income in excess of $22,800 is taxed at a 10% rate. Therefore, at an income of $22,800, the marginal income tax rate becomes 10%. However, the average income tax rate is still zero, because no taxes have yet been paid. At an income of $37,400, taxes reach $1,460, so that the average tax rate is 4% (1,460/37,400). At this point, the marginal income tax rate rises to 15% for the next $44,800 of income. Therefore, at $82,200, the taxes paid are $8,180, and the average tax rate is 10%. Then the marginal income tax rate rises to 25% for the next $60,550 of income, and so on. Notice that all income above $349,250 is taxed at a marginal rate of 35%.

That is, the marginal income tax rate does not rise with income once income exceeds $349,250.

Table 13.1 illustrates two points about the U.S. federal income tax. First, the marginal income tax rate rises with income until income reaches $349,250. That is why the system is said to have a **graduated-rate tax** structure (sometimes called a progressive-rate structure). However, after $349,250, the marginal tax rate schedule is *flat*, rather than graduated. Second, the marginal income tax rate is always higher than the average tax rate. That is because the average tax rate incorporates the low taxes paid on early portions of income, including the zero tax paid on the first $22,800 of income. However, as income becomes very high—for example, above the $1 million shown in the table—the average tax rate approaches the top marginal tax rate of 35%.

Table 13.1 is a great simplification of the complex individual income tax system that prevails in the United States. For example, the calculations ignore many legal actions that reduce a household's taxes. These actions include itemized deductions (for mortgage interest payments, charitable contributions, state and local income taxes, and other items) and various credits and adjustments (such as the earned-income tax credit, child-care credit, and contributions to pension funds). Some fringe benefits paid by employers, notably for health insurance and pensions, also escape or defer taxation.

Higher-income taxpayers are better able to deal with the complexity of the income tax and also benefit more from some of the available deductions. For these reasons, economists have sometimes questioned whether the individual income tax is as graduated as the tax-rate

Table 13.1 The U.S. Graduated-Rate Income Tax in 2005

Income Level ($)	Taxes ($)	Marginal Tax Rate	Average Tax Rate
0	0	0	0
22,800	0	0.10	0
37,400	1460	0.15	0.04
82,200	8180	0.25	0.10
142,750	23,318	0.28	0.16
205,600	40,916	0.33	0.20
349,250	88,320	0.35	0.25
1,000,000	316,082	0.35	0.32

Note: This table applies to a family of four that takes the standard deduction in 2005 in the United States. The income tax rate is zero for the first $22,800 of income, 0.10 for the next $14,600 of income, 0.15 for the next $44,800 of income, 0.25 for the next $60,550 of income, 0.28 for the next $62,850 of income, 0.33 for the next $143,650 of income, and 0.35 on all additional income.

Table 13.2 *Percentages of Total U.S. Individual Income Taxes Paid by Top Taxpayers*

Year	Range of Tax Returns, Based on Taxes Paid				
	Top 1%	Top 5%	Top 10%	Top 25%	Top 50%
1970	16.7	31.4	41.8	62.2	83.0
	[7.4]	[18.3]	[28.0]	[49.4]	[74.7]
1980	17.4	33.7	45.0	66.6	87.0
	[7.8]	[19.2]	[29.1]	[51.4]	[76.7]
1990	25.1	43.6	55.4	77.0	94.2
	[14.0]	[27.6]	[38.8]	[62.1]	[85.0]
2000	37.4	56.5	67.3	84.0	96.1
	[20.8]	[35.3]	[46.0]	[67.2]	[87.0]

Note: The first number in each cell is the percentage of total taxes paid by the indicated range of tax returns. The number in brackets is the share of adjusted gross income represented by this group of tax returns.

Source: R. Glenn Hubbard (2002, p. 3).

structure suggests. However, Table 13.2 shows that the individual income tax is, in fact, progressive, in the sense that upper-income persons pay a high share of taxes. The entries in the table show values of the shares of total individual income taxes, from 1970 to 2000, paid by the top 1%, 5%, 10%, 25%, and 50% of tax returns. In 1970, the highest 1% of tax returns, ranked by taxes paid, accounted for 17% of taxes. The top 50% of the returns paid 83% of the taxes. By 2000, this pattern became more pronounced—the top 1% of returns accounted for 37% of taxes, whereas the top 50% accounted for 96%. In other words, the bottom half of tax returns, ranked by taxes paid, accounted for only 4% of taxes.

The numbers in brackets in Table 13.2 show the percentages of **adjusted gross income**—a broad concept of income shown on income tax forms—reported by the corresponding tax returns. For example, in 1970, the top 1% of returns ranked by taxes paid received 7% of the adjusted gross income. However, this group paid 17% of the taxes. The excess of the share of taxes paid over the share of income received for upper-income taxpayers is a reasonable measure of the progressivity of the income tax. By 2000, the top 1% had a higher share of income, 21%—but this group paid 37% of the taxes. The table provides similar information for other taxpayer groups. For example, in 2000, the top 50% of returns ranked by taxes paid received 87% of the adjusted gross income while paying 96% of the taxes.

Another important form of income tax in the United States is the levy on wage earnings and self-employment

© Rohit Seth/Fotolia

income to finance Social Security and Medicare. Although the government calls these levies a contribution, they are more like taxes because the benefits that individuals get do not depend very much on the amount that an individual pays. In the case of Social Security, the benefits do depend somewhat on the amounts paid over one's lifetime. Hence, the payments are partly a tax and partly a contribution.

The tax for Social Security and Medicare is much simpler than the individual income tax. In 2006, covered employees paid 6.2% of earnings up to an earnings ceiling

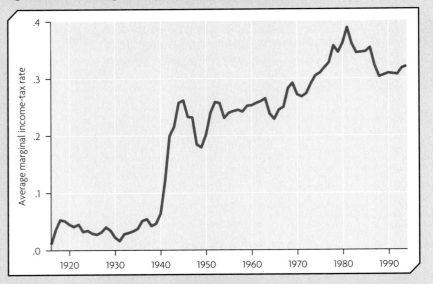

Figure 13.4 *Average Marginal Income Tax Rate, 1916–1994*

The graph shows the average across taxpayers of the marginal income tax rate from the federal individual income tax and Social Security. The average weights by adjusted gross income. This variable was constructed in Robert Barro and Chaipat Sahasakul (1983, 1986) and has been updated to 1994 in unpublished research by Casey Mulligan.

limitations, the measure does not include state and local income taxes.

Figure 13.4 shows that the average marginal income tax rate was very low in the pre-World War II years; individual income taxes covered a small minority of the population, and Social Security taxes were not yet significant. The tax rate rose dramatically to 26% at the end of World War II in 1945. Then the rate fell to 18% in 1949 before increasing back to 26% during the Korean War in 1952–53. From then until the early 1960s, the rate remained between 24% and 26%. Then the rate fell to 23%

of $94,200 to finance the old age, survivors, and disability program (OASDI) and 1.45% of all earnings to finance Medicare. Employers paid an equal amount. Thus, the combined marginal income tax rate was 15.3% for labor earnings between $0 and $94,200, and 2.9% thereafter.

Notice that, for incomes between $0 and $94,200, the average tax rate equals the marginal tax rate. This property applies to a **flat-rate tax** system. However, at $94,200, the system has a single, sharp reduction in the marginal tax rate to 2.9%. As income rises above $94,200, the average tax rate falls gradually from 15.3% to 2.9%. Therefore, in this range, the marginal tax rate is *less* than the average tax rate. This pattern is the opposite of the one that applies to the individual income tax.

Empirically, it is difficult to measure marginal income tax rates, because these rates differ across persons and types of income. Some studies have, however, computed the average of marginal income tax rates across all taxpayers. The blue graph in Figure 13.4 gives an estimate of this average marginal income tax rate in the United States.[1] The measure considers the two most important forms of income taxes: the federal individual income tax and Social Security taxes. These two levies accounted for 80% of federal revenue in 2005. Because of data

in 1965 because of the Kennedy-Johnson income tax cuts. The rate then rose gradually to its peak of 39% in 1981. Subsequently, the rate fell, because of the Reagan tax cuts of 1981 and 1986, to reach 30% in 1988. The rate then rose to 31% in 1990 and 32% in 1994, because of the tax rate increases under the first President Bush and Clinton. However, these increases in average marginal income tax rates were much smaller than those from 1965 to 1981. Unfortunately, these data have not been updated beyond 1994.

Taxes in the Model

To incorporate tax rates into the equilibrium business-cycle model, start with the household budget constraint from equation (12.4). When written without year subscripts, the budget constraint is

(13.1)
$$C + (1/P) \cdot \Delta B + \Delta K = (w/P) \cdot L^s + r \cdot (B/P + K) + V - T$$

consumption + real saving = real disposable income

---

[1] The construction weights households by their adjusted gross incomes. That is, higher-income households count more in the calculation of the average.

Up to now, we regarded real transfers, V, and real taxes, T, as lump sum. Therefore, the household's real transfers net of real taxes, $V - T$, did not depend on the household's characteristics, including its income and consumption. Now we allow a household's real taxes, T, to depend on some of its characteristics. Analogous considerations enter into an analysis of real transfers, V.

The various taxes that exist in the United States and other countries can be represented as levies on the terms that appear on the two sides of equation (13.1). Sales, excise, and value-added taxes depend on consumption, C. Labor-income taxes—for example, from the individual income tax and the Social Security payroll tax—depend on real labor income, $(w/P) \cdot L^s$. Taxes on asset income, a part of the individual income tax, depend on real asset income, $r \cdot (B/P + K)$.[2] In the real world, the income base for this tax includes interest, dividends, and capital gains.[3]

We will now assess the economic effects from taxation. In order to affect real GDP, a tax has to influence the quantities of one of the factors of production: labor or capital services. Therefore, the various taxes can be broken down into whether they affect labor or capital services, or both. We get the main results by considering two types of taxes—one that depends on labor income and another that depends on asset income.

A Tax on Labor Income

We start with a tax on labor income, such as the individual income tax or the payroll tax that finances Social Security. Let τ_w be the marginal tax rate on labor income. To simplify, we do not allow for a graduated-rate structure for τ_w, as in the U.S. individual income tax system. Rather, we assume that τ_w is the same at all levels of income. Our main results will apply to the real world if we think of τ_w as the average of the marginal income tax rates across households.

We assume that the marginal income-tax rate, τ_w, does not change over time—at least, households do not anticipate that future tax rates will differ from the current rate. Anticipated differences between today's tax rate and future tax rates would motivate households to work more in years with relatively low tax rates and less in years with relatively high tax rates. That is, anticipated changes in τ_w over time have intertemporal-substitution effects on labor supply. Since we treat τ_w as unchanging, we are ignoring these intertemporal-substitution effects.

Households may be eligible for deductions and credits that reduce the amount of taxes paid. These deductions create a gap between the average and marginal income tax rates; the average rate is less than the marginal rate because of the deductions. If the deductions are the same for everyone, the average tax rate will be lower for low-income households than for high-income households (as in the U.S. data). (Recall our assumption that the marginal tax rate, τ_w, is the same for all households.) In some cases, a household's tax payment would be negative, amounting to a transfer from the government. In the U.S. system, these negative taxes arise because of "refundable" tax credits, which are credits that not only reduce taxes but also allow for cash payments when the computed taxes are less than zero. The most important of these refundable credits is the earned-income tax credit (EITC).

The real taxes paid by a household equal the average tax rate multiplied by labor income. The average tax rate depends on the marginal income-tax rate, τ_w, and on the available deductions. If we hold constant the structure of deductions, a higher τ_w implies a higher average tax rate. Therefore, for given deductions, a higher τ_w will generate more tax revenue for the government unless the amount of labor income falls sharply.

To assess the economic effects from a tax on labor income, we have to extend our analysis of household labor supply. The key force is the substitution effect between leisure and consumption. Without taxation of labor income, this substitution effect depended on the real wage rate, w/P. If a household raised the quantity of labor supplied, L^s, by one unit of time, it raised real labor income, $(w/P) \cdot L^s$, by w/P units. This extra income enabled the household to increase consumption by w/P units. At the same time, the rise in L^s by one unit of time meant that leisure time fell by one unit. Therefore, the household could substitute w/P units of consumption for one unit of leisure time. If w/P rose, this deal became more favorable. Hence, we predicted

---

[2] U.S. taxes are levied on nominal interest payments, $i \cdot (B/P)$, which are computed from the nominal interest rate, i, rather than the real rate, r. This treatment of interest income leads to an effect of the inflation rate, π, on real taxes. Another real-world complication is that parts of household interest expenses are allowed as deductions from income for tax purposes. In the United States, the deduction applies to itemized deductions for interest on home mortgages and debt used to purchase financial assets.

[3] To consider a tax on corporate profit, we could reintroduce real business profit, Π, as a form of household income. We dropped Π before because it equaled zero in equilibrium. However, in most tax systems, the definition of profit differs from the one in our model. The most important difference is that our definition includes the real rental payments to capital, $(R/P) \cdot K$, as a negative item. In the real world, only parts of this rental income—depreciation and interest expenses—are allowed as deductions from income in the computation of corporate profits taxes. With this real-world definition of profit, the corporate profits tax amounts to another levy on the income from capital. Since the income from capital is also taxed at the household level, the corporate profits tax is often described appropriately as **double taxation** of income from capital.

that the household would raise the quantity of labor supplied, enjoy less leisure time, and consume more.

The new consideration is that an extra unit of labor income is taxed at the marginal income tax rate, τ_w. If the household raises the quantity of labor supplied, L^s, by one unit of time, it again raises pretax real labor income, $(w/P) \cdot L^s$, by w/P units. This extra income enters as the yellow shaded term on the right-hand side of the budget constraint in equation (13.1):

(13.1) $$C + (1/P) \cdot \Delta B + \Delta K = (w/P) \cdot L^s + r \cdot (B/P + K) + V - T$$

The additional labor income raises the household's real taxes, T, by τ_w units. These taxes also appear on the right-hand side of the equation—the pink shaded term—but with a negative sign. Overall, the right-hand side of the equation rises by $(1 - \tau_w) \cdot (w/P)$ units. That is, after-tax real labor income rises by this amount. We also see from the equation that the household can use this additional after-tax real income to increase consumption, C—the blue shaded term on the left-hand side—by $(1 - \tau_w) \cdot (w/P)$ units.

We found that, by working one more unit of time, the household can raise consumption, C, by $(1 - \tau_w) \cdot (w/P)$ units. The increase in work by one unit of time still means that leisure time falls by one unit. Therefore, households can substitute $(1 - \tau_w) \cdot (w/P)$ units of C for one unit of leisure time. Another way to say this is that, with a labor income tax, the substitution effect on labor supply depends on the **after-tax real wage rate**, $(1 - \tau_w) \cdot (w/P)$, rather than the pretax real wage rate, w/P. If the marginal tax rate, τ_w, rises, for a given w/P, $(1 - \tau_w) \cdot (w/P)$ falls. Hence, we predict that the household would reduce the quantity of labor supplied, take more leisure time, and consume less.

We stressed before that labor supply depends also on income effects. We predicted that more household income would lead to more consumption and more leisure—hence, less work. What income effects arise when the marginal income tax rate, τ_w, increases? Equation (13.1) shows that a household's real income on the right-hand side depends on real transfers net of real taxes, $V - T$. Recall also from Chapter 12 that the government's budget constraint requires

(12.8) $$V - T = -G$$

Therefore, if government purchases, G, are unchanged, equation (12.8) implies that real transfers net of real taxes, $V - T$, must also be unchanged. Hence, for given G, we do not get any changes in household real income

through the term $V - T$. In other words, if G is fixed, there are no income effects from a change in τ_w.

We need to explore this result further, because it seems that a rise in the marginal income-tax rate, τ_w, should have a negative income effect. The results depend on what else changes when the marginal income tax rate, τ_w, rises. One possibility is that the government adjusts other features of the tax system to keep the total real taxes collected, T, unchanged. For example, marginal income tax rates, τ_w, might rise in the individual income tax, but deductions also rise to keep T fixed. Another possibility is that the government shifts away from collecting revenue through a tax that has a relatively low marginal income tax rate—for example, the Social Security payroll tax—toward one that has a relatively high marginal rate—such as the individual income tax. Shifts of this kind raise the marginal tax rate on labor income, τ_w, for a given total of real taxes collected, T.

Another possibility is that real tax revenue, T, rises along with the increase in τ_w, and all the extra revenue pays for added real transfers, V. In that case, the term $V - T$ is again unchanged, and there is still no income effect.

Finally, we could have that real tax revenue, T, rises along with the increase in τ_w, and the extra revenue pays for added government purchases, G. In this case, the economic effects combine two forces: the rise in τ_w, which we are now studying, and the rise in G, which we considered in Chapter 12. Recall that the rise in G did have a negative income effect. To keep things straight, it is best to analyze the effects from τ_w and G separately. We are now assessing the effects from an increase in τ_w for given G. In this case, there are no income effects on labor supply. We can therefore be confident that, for a given real wage rate, w/P, a rise in τ_w reduces the quantity of labor supplied, L^s, through the substitution effect from a lower after-tax real wage rate, $(1 - \tau_w) \cdot (w/P)$.

Figure 13.5 shows the effects on the labor market from an increase in the marginal tax rate on labor income, τ_w. We use the construction from Figure 8.15 in Chapter 8. We plot the pretax real wage rate, w/P, on the vertical axis. As before, a lower w/P raises the quantity of labor demanded, L^d, along the red curve. Unlike in Chapter 12, we also allow for a positive effect of w/P on the quantity of labor supplied, L^s, along the blue curve. This positive slope applies if the substitution effect from a higher w/P dominates the income effect.

For a given pretax real wage rate, w/P, a higher τ_w implies a lower after-tax real wage rate, $(1 - \tau_w) \cdot (w/P)$. Therefore, in Figure 13.5, a rise in τ_w shifts the labor supply curve left from the blue one labeled L^s to the green one labeled $(L^s)'$. This decrease in labor supply reflects the substitution effect from the higher labor-income tax rate, τ_w.

The tax on labor income does not affect the labor demand curve, L^d, in Figure 13.5. The reason is that businesses (run by households) still maximize profit by equating the marginal product of labor, MPL, to the real wage rate, w/P. For a given w/P, the labor-income tax rate, τ_w, does not affect the profit-maximizing choice of the quantity of labor input, L^d.

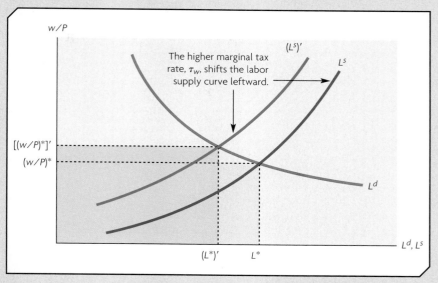

Figure 13.5 *Effect of an Increase in the Labor-Income Tax Rate on the Labor Market*

The higher marginal tax rate, τ_w, shifts the labor supply curve leftward.

The downward-sloping labor demand curve, L^d, shown in red, comes from Figure 8.15. The upward-sloping labor supply curve, L^s, shown in blue, also comes from Figure 8.15. An increase in the marginal tax rate on labor income, τ_w, shifts the labor supply curve leftward to the green one, $(L^s)'$. Consequently, the market-clearing, before-tax real wage rate rises from $(w/P)^*$ to $[(w/P)^*]'$ on the vertical axis. The market-clearing quantity of labor input falls from L^* to $(L^*)'$ on the horizontal axis.

We can see from Figure 13.5 that the market-clearing real wage rate rises from $(w/P)^*$ to $[(w/P)^*]'$ on the vertical axis. The market-clearing quantity of labor declines from L^* to $(L^*)'$ on the horizontal axis.

We also know that the after-tax real wage rate, $(1 - \tau_w) \bullet (w/P)$, must fall overall. That is, the rise in w/P less than fully compensates for the decrease in $1 - \tau_w$ due to the rise in τ_w. To see why, note from Figure 13.5 that L is lower (because the labor demand curve does not shift, and the labor supply curve shifts to the left). However, for L to be lower, the quantity of labor supplied, L^s, must be lower. The only way that L^s falls is that $(1 - \tau_w) \bullet (w/P)$ declines.

We found from our analysis of the labor market that a higher marginal tax rate on labor income, τ_w, lowers the quantity of labor input, L. This effect will spill over to the market for capital services because the reduction in L tends to reduce the marginal product of capital services, MPK.

Figure 13.6 shows the effects on the market for capital services. As in Figure 12.5, we plot the real rental price, R/P, on the vertical axis. The reduction in labor input, L, reduces the MPK (at a given quantity

of capital services, κK). The demand for capital services decreases accordingly from the blue curve, labeled $(\kappa K)^d$, to the green one, labeled $[(\kappa K)^d]'$. The supply curve for capital services, $(\kappa K)^s$, shown in red, does not shift. That is, the stock of capital, K, is given, and, for a given real rental price, R/P, suppliers of capital services have no reason to change the capital utilization rate, κ.

Figure 13.6 shows that the market-clearing real rental price falls from $(R/P)^*$ to $[(R/P)^*]'$ on the vertical axis. The quantity of capital services falls, because of a decrease in the utilization rate, κ, from $(\kappa K)^*$ to $[(\kappa K)^*]'$ on the horizontal axis. Thus, although the tax rate on labor income, τ_w, does not directly affect the market for capital services, it has an indirect effect on this market. By reducing labor input, L, and thereby decreasing the MPK, an increase in τ_w reduces the quantity of capital services, κ.[4]

Recall that real GDP, Y, is given by the production function from Chapter 9:

(9.1) $$Y = A \bullet F(\kappa K, L)$$

In the present case, the technology level, A, does not change. However, we found that a rise in the labor-income

---

[4] The decrease in κK lowers the MPL, and leads thereby to a leftward shift in the labor demand curve, L^d, in Figure 13.5. This shift leads to a further decrease in L.

Figure 13.6 Effect of an Increase in the Labor-Income Tax Rate on the Market for Capital Services

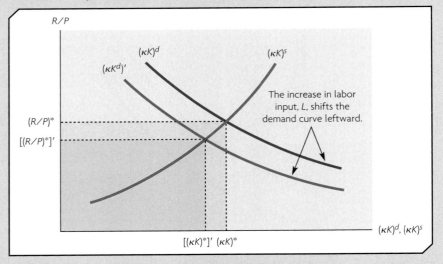

This construction comes from Figure 12.5. The reduction in employment from L^* to $(L^*)'$, shown in Figure 13.5, reduces the marginal product of capital services, MPK (at a given quantity of capital services, κK). Therefore, the demand curve for capital services shifts leftward, from $(\kappa K)^d$, shown in blue, to $[(\kappa K)d]'$, shown in green. The supply curve for capital services, $(\kappa K)^s$, shown in red, does not shift. Consequently, the market-clearing real rental price of capital falls from $(R/P)^*$ to $[(R/P)^*]'$ on the vertical axis. The quantity of capital services declines from $(\kappa K)^*$ to $[(\kappa K)^*]'$ on the horizontal axis. This decrease in capital services corresponds, for a given capital stock, K, to a reduction in the capital utilization rate, κ.

tax rate, τ_w, reduced the quantities of labor, L, and capital services, κK. Therefore, Y declines.[5] Thus, our conclusion is that a higher marginal tax rate on labor income, τ_w, leads to a reduction in overall market activity, as gauged by real GDP, Y.

A Tax on Asset Income

Now we will consider a tax on asset income. Go back to the household's budget constraint:

(13.1)
$$C + (1/P) \cdot \Delta B + \Delta K = (w/P) \cdot L^s + r \cdot (B/P + K) + V - T$$

Suppose now that real taxes, T, depend on a household's real asset income, $r \cdot (B/P + K)$, the term shaded in yellow. Note that this part of income equals the real interest payments on bonds, $r \cdot (B/P)$, plus the return

on ownership of capital, rK. The term rK equals the net real rental payments on capital, $[(R/P) \cdot \kappa - \delta(\kappa)] \cdot K$, because of the condition from Chapter 11 that the real rates of return on bonds and capital are the same:

(11.8)
$$r = (R/P) \cdot \kappa - \delta(\kappa)$$
real rate of return on bonds = real rate of return from owning capital

Let τ_r be the marginal tax rate on asset income. We assume that all forms of asset income are taxed at the same rate. In reality, tax systems treat differently various forms of asset income, which include interest, dividends, capital gains, and parts of self-employment income. However, the simplifying assumption that all forms of asset income are treated the same will give us the main effects from taxation of asset income. Since the tax rate, τ_r, is the same for interest income as for income on ownership of capital, the equality between the two rates of return still holds in equation (11.8).

We know that the real interest rate, r, has an intertemporal-substitution effect on consumption. A reduction in year 1's consumption, C_1, by one unit allowed the household to raise year 2's consumption, C_2, by $1 + r$ units. Therefore, an increase in r motivated the household to lower C_1 compared to C_2. The difference now is that the additional r units of asset income in year 2 are taxed at the rate τ_r. This taxation means that the added r units of income are offset by an added $\tau_r \cdot r$ units of taxes; that is, the pink shaded term, T, in equation (13.1) rises by $\tau_r \cdot r$. Thus, if the

---

[5] We can work out how the decrease in real GDP, Y, divides up between consumption, C, and gross investment, I. We know from Chapter 7 that a fall in Y by one unit corresponds to a decrease in real household income by one unit. Since the decrease in income is long lasting, we predict that the propensity to consume would be close to one. Hence, C would fall by roughly one unit. However, the decrease in R/P implies a fall in the real interest rate, r. This change has an intertemporal-substitution effect, which raises current consumption compared to future consumption. This effect offsets the decrease in C by one unit. Hence, we find that current consumption would decrease overall by less than Y. Since $Y = C + I + G$ and G is fixed, I must decline.

EXTENDING THE MODEL

A Consumption Tax

We show here that a consumption tax has the same effects as the labor income tax that we studied in the main text. Suppose that real labor income, $(w/P) \cdot L^s$, is untaxed, but an increase in consumption, C, by one unit raises each household's real taxes, T, by τ_c units. This tax could be a sales tax, an excise tax, or a value-added tax. We assume that the consumption tax is proportional to C, so that the marginal tax rate, τ_c, equals the average tax rate. We also assume that τ_c is the same for all households and does not vary over time.

If a household works one more unit of time, it again gets w/P additional units of real labor income. Our assumption now is that this additional labor income is untaxed. Suppose that the household raises consumption by ΔC units. This change raises consumption taxes by $\tau_c \cdot \Delta C$. Therefore, the extra income of w/P units must cover the added consumption, ΔC, plus the added taxes, $\tau_c \cdot \Delta C$:

$$w/P = \Delta C + \tau_c \cdot \Delta C$$
$$w/P = \Delta C \cdot (1 + \tau_c)$$

If we divide through by $1 + \tau_c$, we can solve out for the additional consumption:

(13.2) $\qquad \Delta C = (w/P)/(1 + \tau_c)$

Hence, for each unit more of labor—and, therefore, each unit less of leisure time—a household gets $(w/P)/(1 + \tau_c)$ units more of consumption. For example, if $\tau_c = 0.10$, the household gets about $0.9 \cdot (w/P)$ extra units of consumption. The important point is that the higher the τ_c, the worse the deal. Therefore, if τ_c rises, we predict that the household would work less, enjoy more leisure time, and consume less.

With a labor income tax at the marginal rate τ_w, a household's labor supply, L^s, depended on the after-tax real wage rate, $(1 - \tau_w) \cdot (w/P)$. With a consumption tax at the marginal rate τ_c, equation (13.2) shows that the after-tax real wage rate—in terms of the extra consumption that can be bought with an additional unit of labor—is $(w/P)/(1 + \tau_c)$. Therefore, L^s depends on $(w/P)/(1 + \tau_c)$. Thus, increases in τ_w and τ_c have analogous negative effects on L^s. The conclusion is that consumption taxation has the same economic effects that we found for labor income taxation.

The results are different if tax rates vary over time. If the consumption tax rate, τ_c, varies predictably, households would consume a lot in years when τ_c is relatively low. In contrast, if the labor income tax rate, τ_w, varies predictably, households would work a lot when τ_w was relatively low.

household reduces C_1 by one unit, it can raise C_2 by the amount

$$\Delta C_2 = 1 + r - \tau_r \bullet r$$
$$\Delta C_2 = 1 + (1 - \tau_r) \bullet r$$

What matters, therefore, for the choice between C_1 and C_2 is the **after-tax real interest rate**, $(1 - \tau_r) \bullet r$. If τ_r rises, for given r, $(1 - \tau_r) \bullet r$ declines. Therefore, the household has less incentive to defer consumption, and it reacts by increasing C_1 compared to C_2. For given real income in year 1, an increase in τ_r motivates the household to consume more and save less in year 1.

If we multiply both sides of equation (11.8) by $(1 - \tau_r)$, we can relate the after-tax real interest rate to the after-tax return on ownership of capital:

(13.3) $\quad (1 - \tau_r) \bullet r = (1 - \tau_r) \bullet [(R/P) \bullet \kappa - \delta(\kappa)]$

after-tax real interest rate =
after-tax rate of return on ownership of capital

Thus, we can calculate $(1 - \tau_r) \bullet r$ if we know—on the right-hand side of equation (13.3)—the real rental price, R/P, and the capital utilization rate, κ. These values are determined, as before, by the clearing of the market for capital services.

Refer back to Figure 13.6, which considered the demand for and supply of capital services. The marginal tax rate on asset income, τ_r, does not affect the demand curve for capital services, $(\kappa K)^d$, which is shown in blue. Since business profit, Π, is not taxed, this curve still comes from equating the MPK to R/P.[6] Therefore, a change in τ_r does not shift the demand curve, $(\kappa K)^d$.

In Chapter 9, we worked out the supply curve for capital services, $(\kappa K)^s$. For a given stock of capital, K, owners of capital chose the utilization rate, κ, to maximize the net rental income:

$$[(R/P) \bullet \kappa - \delta(\kappa)] \bullet K$$

We assumed that a higher κ resulted in a higher depreciation rate, as represented by the function $\delta(\kappa)$. From this formulation, we found that an increase in the real rental price, R/P, raised the utilization rate, κ, and thereby increased the quantity of capital services supplied, $(\kappa K)^s$. That is why the curve $(\kappa K)^s$, shown in red in Figure 13.6, slopes upward.

With a tax on income from capital at the rate τ_r, owners of capital would seek to maximize their after-tax net rental income, given by

$$(1 - \tau_r) \bullet [(R/P) \bullet \kappa - \delta(\kappa)] \bullet K$$

For any τ_r, this maximization is equivalent to the maximization of $[(R/P) \bullet \kappa - \delta(\kappa)] \bullet K$—that is, the same expression as before. Therefore, for a given real rental price, R/P, the chosen utilization rate, κ, does not depend on the tax rate, τ_r. Since the capital stock, K, is fixed, and τ_r does not affect κ, we conclude that τ_r does not affect the supply of capital services, $(\kappa K)^s$. Therefore, a change in τ_r does not shift the supply curve, $(\kappa K)^s$, in Figure 13.6.

Since a change in τ_r does not affect the demand and supply curves in Figure 13.6, it does not affect the market-clearing real rental price, $(R/P)^*$, and the quantity of capital services, $(\kappa K)^*$. That is, the capital stock, K, is fixed, and the capital utilization rate, κ, does not change.

Since the quantity of capital services, κK, does not change, there is no effect on the demand curve for labor, L^d, shown in red in Figure 13.5. The supply curve for labor, L^s, shown in blue, also does not shift. Therefore, the market-clearing real wage rate, $(w/P)^*$, and the quantity of labor, L^*, do not change. Since κK and L are the same, we have from the production function, $Y = A \bullet F(\kappa K, L)$, that real GDP, Y, does not change. Thus, our conclusion is that a change in the marginal tax rate on asset income, τ_r, does not affect real GDP. We should stress, however, that this result applies in the short run, when the stock of capital, K, is given.

Since the real rental price, R/P, and the capital utilization rate, κ, are unchanged, the pretax rate of return on ownership of capital, $(R/P) \bullet \kappa - \delta(\kappa)$, does not change. But then, the increase in τ_r implies that the after-tax rate of return, $(1 - \tau_r) \bullet [(R/P) \bullet \kappa - \delta(\kappa)]$, falls. Equation (13.3) tells us that the after-tax real interest rate, $(1 - \tau_r) \bullet r$, equals the after-tax rate of return on ownership of capital:

(13.3) $\quad (1 - \tau_r) \bullet r = (1 - \tau_r) \bullet [(R/P) \bullet \kappa - \delta(\kappa)]$

Therefore, the increase in τ_r lowers the after-tax real interest rate, $(1 - \tau_r) \bullet r$.

We know that a decrease in $(1 - \tau_r) \bullet r$ has intertemporal-substitution effects on consumption. The household raises year 1's consumption, C_1, compared to year 2's, C_2. Hence, for given real income in year 1, the household consumes more and saves less in year 1. Recall, however, that year 1's real GDP, Y_1, does not change, and that $Y_1 = C_1 + I_1 + G_1$. We are assuming that government purchases, G_1, are unchanged. Therefore, the increase in C_1 must correspond to an equal-sized reduction in year 1's gross investment, I_1. Thus, the key result is that a higher tax rate, τ_r, on asset income leads to higher C_1 and lower I_1.

In the long run, the reduction in gross investment, I, means that the stock of capital, K, is smaller than it otherwise would have been. This reduced K will lead to a lower real GDP, Y. Therefore, although an increase in the tax rate on asset income, τ_r, does not affect real GDP in the short run, it decreases real GDP in the long run.[7]

---

[6] A tax on business profit tends to affect the demand for capital services. For example, in the system of corporate profits taxation described in footnote 3, an increase in the tax rate on corporate profits would reduce this demand.

[7] A tax on asset income is equivalent to a consumption tax that taxes future consumption more heavily than current consumption. Most economists agree that the economy does better if the government raises a given total of revenue through a consumption tax that is uniform over time, rather than time varying. Therefore, from the standpoint of optimal taxation, a constant tax rate on consumption, τ_c, tends to be preferred to a tax on asset income, τ_r (which is equivalent to a time-varying consumption tax).

An Increase in Government Purchases Financed by a Labor Income Tax

In Chapter 12, we studied the effects from a permanent increase in government purchases, G. We assumed, unrealistically, that the increase in G was financed by lump-sum taxes. Our finding was that an increase in G by one unit left real GDP, Y, unchanged and reduced consumption, C, by about one unit. Hence, gross investment, I, was unchanged. Also unchanged were the real wage rate, w/P, the real rental price, R/P, and the real interest rate, r.

These results depended on the assumption that the quantity of labor supplied, L^s, was fixed. Now we reconsider this assumption while also allowing the additional government purchases, G, to be financed by a tax on real labor income, $(w/P) \bullet L$. In particular, we assume that an increase in the marginal income tax rate on labor income, τ_w, accompanies the permanent rise in G.

We will get different results from those in Chapter 12 if the combination of permanently increased government purchases, G, and the higher marginal income tax rate, τ_w, affects the quantity of labor supplied, L^s. Therefore, we have to consider the various forces that affect L^s.

- We observed from the government's budget constraint in Chapter 12 that an increase by one unit in each year's government purchases, G, required real taxes less real transfers, $T - V$, to rise by one unit in each year. Therefore, the household has one unit less of real disposable income each year. In response to the negative income effect, the household would raise the quantity of labor supplied, L^s, each year.

- In the box on useful public services in Chapter 12, we assumed that government purchases, G, provided public services that yield utility for households. We assumed that each unit of G was equivalent, in terms of utility, to λ units of consumption, C, where λ is greater than zero. When we include the service value of government purchases in the household's effective disposable income, we get that an increase in G by one unit raises effective disposable income by λ units. (See equation [12.10] in Chapter 12.) The combination of this effect with the rise in real taxes less real transfers, $T - V$, by one unit implies that the household's effective disposable income falls by $1 - \lambda$ units. If λ is less than one, we still get that effective disposable income falls when G rises. Therefore, the negative income effect still predicts that the quantity of labor supplied, L^s, rises each year. However, the higher λ, the weaker is this effect.

- We found in this chapter that the substitution effect from a higher marginal tax rate, τ_w, on labor income reduces the quantity of labor supplied, L^s. Figure 13.5 shows this effect. Recall that this analysis ignored any income effects.

We see that the overall effect from a rise in government purchases, G, on the quantity of labor supplied, L^s, depends on the offsetting influences from an income effect and a substitution effect. The income effect predicts that L^s would rise. The substitution effect predicts that L^s would fall. The overall effect on L^s is uncertain.

Empirically, the overall effect from permanently increased government purchases, G, on the quantity of labor supplied, L^s, seems to be small. This interpretation is consistent with the finding in Figure 12.7 that, from 1955 to 2006, the fluctuations in government purchases bore little relation to the fluctuations in real GDP. We found substantial effects on real GDP only when we looked at the temporary increases in G during major wars, notably World Wars I and II and the Korean War. Thus, in the end, our assumption in Chapter 12 that the quantity of labor supplied was fixed during nonwar periods may have been satisfactory. In particular, this assumption led to the reasonable conclusion that permanently higher government purchases had little effect on real GDP.

Transfer Payments

We assumed, thus far, that real transfer payments, V, were lump sum. But, as with taxes, transfers are not lump sum in the real world. Rather, most transfer programs relate an individual's payments to the individual's characteristics. For example, welfare programs give money or services such as health care to poor persons and then reduce or eliminate the transfers if a person's income rises. Similarly, to qualify for unemployment insurance, a recipient must not be working. Until recently, the U.S. Social Security program reduced the pension payments to an elderly person if that person received labor income above a specified amount. However, the law now allows a person of normal retirement age or older to earn income without triggering reductions in Social Security payments.

The point is that an income-tested transfer program—one that reduces transfers when labor income rises—effectively imposes a positive marginal income

BACK TO REALITY

The Laffer Curve

A permanent increase in government purchases, G, requires a permanent increase in real taxes, T. We assumed in the previous section that a rise in T went along with an increase in the marginal income tax rate, τ_w, on labor income. We can think of the higher τ_w as taking the form of increases in marginal tax rates at all levels of labor income in the individual income tax. We explore here the relation between T and τ_w. This relation is called a [...] curve, named after the economist Arthur Laffer.[8]

The real taxes, T, collected from a tax on labor income can be written as

$$T = \left[\frac{T}{(w/P) \cdot L}\right] \cdot (w/P) \cdot L$$

real taxes = (average tax rate) • (real tax base)

The real tax base for a labor income tax is real labor income, $(w/P) \cdot L$. The average tax rate is the ratio of T to $(w/P) \cdot L$.

For given deductions and other features of the tax system, a higher marginal income tax rate, τ_w, goes along with a higher average tax rate. Thus, the overall response of real taxes collected, T, to an increase in τ_w depends on the reaction of the tax base, $(w/P) \cdot L$, to an increase in τ_w. In the example discussed in the previous section, $(w/P) \cdot L$ did not change much when τ_w increased, accompanied by a permanent rise in government purchases, G. The reason was that the substitution effect from a higher τ_w—which lowered labor supply—was roughly offset by the income effect from a higher G—which raised labor supply.

The key idea behind the Laffer curve is that the substitution effect from a higher marginal tax rate, τ_w, becomes stronger as τ_w rises. Therefore, for high enough τ_w, the response of $(w/P) \cdot L$ to a further increase in τ_w becomes negative (because the substitution effect on labor supply more than offsets the income effect). Moreover, the substitution effect eventually becomes so strong that T falls when τ_w rises.

To understand the argument about substitution effects, start with a zero tax rate, τ_w. If τ_w is zero at all levels of income, the real taxes collected, T, are also zero. Therefore, the Laffer curve, shown in Figure 13.7, begins at the origin. If τ_w rises above zero, T becomes positive. Therefore, the Laffer curve has a positive slope when τ_w is small.

The substitution effect of τ_w on labor supply works through the after-tax real wage rate, $(1 - \tau_w) \cdot (w/P)$. Think about the term $1 - \tau_w$. If $\tau_w = 0$, an increase in τ_w by, say, 0.1 has a relatively small proportionate effect on $1 - \tau_w$. This term falls from 1.0 to 0.9, or by 10%. However, if $\tau_w = 0.5$, an increase in τ_w by 0.1 decreases $1 - \tau_w$ from 0.5 to 0.4, or by 20%. When $\tau_w = 0.8$, the corresponding decrease is 50% (from 0.2 to 0.1), and when $\tau_w = 0.9$, it is 100% (from 0.1 to 0). This arithmetic suggests that the strength of the substitution effect of τ_w on labor supply becomes greater as τ_w increases. Therefore, the quantity of labor supplied, L^s, would fall eventually as τ_w rose higher and higher. Eventually, this effect means that the tax base, $(w/P) \cdot L$, would fall enough to more than offset the rise in the average tax rate. At that point, real taxes, T, would decline with a further rise in τ_w.

The graph in Figure 13.7 reflects this discussion. The slope of the relation between real taxes, T, and the marginal tax rate, τ_w, is positive at the origin but becomes flatter as τ_w rises. Eventually, T reaches a peak, when τ_w attains the value denoted $(\tau_w)^*$ on the horizontal axis. For still higher marginal tax rates, T falls as τ_w rises. The graph assumes that, at a tax rate of 100%, real labor income, $(w/P) \cdot L$—at least the part reported to the tax authorities—declines to zero, so that T is zero.

In 1980, when Ronald Reagan was elected U.S. president, some advocates of "supply-side economics" used a picture like the one shown in Figure 13.7 to argue for an across-the-board cut in U.S. income tax rates. These economists contended that the average marginal tax rate on income (which we estimated in Figure 13.4) exceeded $(\tau_w)^*$, so that a general cut in tax rates would yield larger real tax revenue, T. However, there is no evidence that the United States has ever reached high enough average marginal tax rates for this result to apply.

Lawrence Lindsey (1987) estimated the effect of the Reagan tax cuts from 1982 to 1984 on the tax payments made by taxpayers in various income groups. He found that the reductions in tax rates lowered tax collections overall and for taxpayers with middle and low incomes. However,

---

[8] For a discussion of the Laffer curve, see Don Fullerton (1982).

among taxpayers with the highest incomes (adjusted gross incomes above $200,000), the increase of reported taxable incomes was so great that it more than offset the decrease in tax rates. Lindsey estimated that the tax-rate cuts raised collections in this group by 3% in 1982, 9% in 1983, and 23% in 1984. Therefore, although U.S. taxpayers as a whole were not on the falling portion of the Laffer curve in Figure 13.7, the taxpayers with the highest incomes appeared to be in this range.

A study by Charles Stuart (1981) estimated that the maximum of real tax revenue occurred in Sweden at an average marginal tax rate of 70%. That is, he estimated

$(\tau_w)^*$ in Figure 13.7 to be about 70%. The actual average marginal tax rate in Sweden reached 70% in the early 1970s and rose subsequently to about 80%. (These estimates of marginal tax rates include consumption taxes as well as income taxes.) Therefore, Sweden was operating on the falling portion of the Laffer curve during the 1970s. A similar study by A. Van Ravestein and H. Vijlbrief (1988) estimated that $(\tau_w)^*$ was also about 70% in the Netherlands. They found that the actual marginal tax rate in the Netherlands reached 67% in 1985—close to, but not quite as high as, the estimated $(\tau_w)^*$.

tax rate on labor income. An increase in the scale of a transfer program—for example, an expansion of the welfare system—raises the marginal income tax rate, τ_w, implied by the program. Therefore, to analyze the economic effects from increased real transfers, V, we have to take account of this increase in τ_w.

Suppose that the government increases real transfers, V, and finances these expenditures with increased real taxes, T, collected by a tax on labor income. In this case, marginal income tax rates, τ_w, rise for two reasons. First, the rise in T goes along with a higher τ_w for households that pay individual income taxes. Second, for households that are receiving transfers—such as poor welfare recipients—the expansion of the transfer program raises the implicit marginal income tax rate, τ_w, because of the

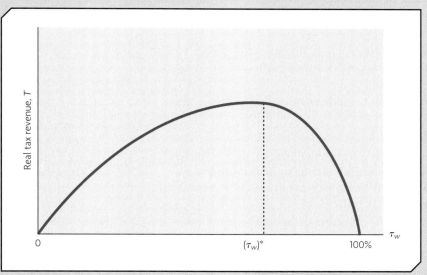

Figure 13.7 *The Relation Between Real Tax Revenue and the Marginal Income Tax Rate (a Laffer Curve)*

The horizontal axis shows the marginal tax rate on labor income, τ_w. The vertical axis has real tax revenue, T. Starting from zero, an increase in τ_w raises T. However, as τ_w rises, the slope gets less steep. Eventually, T reaches its peak when τ_w reaches $(\tau_w)^*$ on the horizontal axis. Beyond that point, T falls as τ_w rises toward 100%.

income testing for benefits. In other words, we get an increase in τ_w from both sides. We therefore predict even stronger effects of the sort analyzed in Figures 13.5 and 13.6. In particular, labor input, L, capital services, κK, and real GDP, Y, tend to decline.

Questions and Problems

A. Review questions

1. Distinguish between the average tax rate and the marginal tax rate. Must the two be equal for a flat-rate tax?

2. Could an increase in the tax rate on labor income reduce real tax revenue? How does the answer depend on the responsiveness of labor supply to the after-tax real wage rate?

3. What is the income effect from a rise in the tax rate on labor income, τ_w? Why did we assume no income effect in part of our analysis?

B. Problems for discussion

4. The flat-rate tax
    Some U.S. economists advocate shifting from the graduated individual income tax to a flat-rate tax. Under the new system, there would be few deductions from taxable income, and the marginal tax rate would be constant. Because of the elimination of the deductions, the average marginal tax rate would be lower than that under the current system.

a. What are the economic effects from a shift to a flat-rate tax on labor income?

b. How does the proposed flat-rate tax compare with the present Social Security payroll tax?

5. A consumption tax
    Suppose that consumption is taxed in each year at the constant rate τ_c.

a. What is the household budget constraint?

b. What are the effects of an increase in τ_c on the labor market? How do the results compare with those shown for an increase in the tax rate on labor income, τ_w, in Figure 13.5?

c. What are the effects of an increase in τ_c on the market for capital services? How do the results compare with those shown for an increase in the tax rate on labor income, τ_w, in Figure 13.6?

d. Suppose now that τ_c falls in year 1 but does not change in future years. How does this change affect the choice of consumption over time? How would the effects resemble those from an increase in the tax rate on asset income, τ_r? In what ways do the effects differ from those from a change in the tax rate on asset income, τ_r?

6. The U.S. income tax cuts of 2001 and 2003
    Summarize the U.S. income tax reforms of 2001 and 2003, as discussed in the 2005 *Economic Report of*

the President (available at www.whitehouse.gov/cea). What macroeconomic effects would you predict from these tax changes?

7. Effects of inflation on a graduated-rate income tax
    In 1985, before the tax simplification of 1986, the individual income-tax system in the United States had many different tax-rate brackets. A married couple paid individual income tax on labor income in accordance with the following table:

Range of Taxable Income ($)	Marginal Income Tax Rate (%)
3,540–5,719	11
5,720–7,919	12
7,920–12,389	13
12,390–16,649	16
16,650–21,019	18
21,020–25,599	22
25,600–31,119	25
31,120–36,629	28
36,630–47,669	33
47,670–62,449	38
62,450–89,089	42
89,090–113,859	45
113,860–169,019	49
169,020–	50

a. Suppose that each person's real income stays constant over time, so that inflation steadily raises each person's nominal income. If the tax schedule shown in the table had remained unchanged, what would have happened over time to each couple's marginal income tax rate?

b. Assume now that the dollar bracket limits shown in the left column of the table are adjusted proportionately (or "indexed") over time for changes in the price level. That is, if the price level rises by 5%, each dollar amount rises by 5%. What, then, is the effect of inflation on each couple's marginal income tax rate? (This indexing provision applies in the United States since 1985.)

8. Inflation and taxes on asset income
    Suppose that the tax rate on asset income is τ_r. Suppose (as is true in the United States) that the tax is levied on nominal interest income. Assume (as is not entirely accurate) that the tax applies to the real returns on capital.

a. What is the after-tax real interest rate on bonds? Consider a permanent, unanticipated increase in the money growth rate from μ' to μ, as studied in Chapter 11. Assume that τ_r does not change.

b. What is the effect on the inflation rate, π?

c. What is the effect on the after-tax real return on capital?

d. What is the effect on the after-tax real interest rate on bonds? What happens to the nominal interest rate, i? Does it move one-for-one with π?

9. Effects of transfer programs on labor supply
    Discuss the effects on labor supply from the following governmental transfer programs:

a. The food stamp program, which provides subsidized coupons for purchases of food. The allowable subsidies vary inversely with family income.

b. A negative income tax, such as the EITC. This program provides cash transfers to poor persons.

In the EITC, the amount transferred initially rises with labor income. Then, subsequently, the amount paid falls with labor income.

c. Unemployment insurance, which gives cash payments over a specified interval to persons who have lost jobs and are looking for work. In the United States, the benefits typically last as long as six months; many European countries have longer periods of eligibility.

d. Retirement benefits paid under Social Security. What is the consequence of the income-test provision? Before 1972, this test specified that an increase by $2 in labor income caused a reduction of $1 in retirement benefits. Since 2000, the test applies only to retirees below normal retirement age (currently, ages 66–67) and has two ranges: one where $2 of income reduce benefits by $1, and a second where $3 of income reduce benefits by $1.

CHAPTER 14

© Norman Chan/Fotolia

Public Debt

O ne of the most controversial economic issues is the government's budget deficit. *The news media suggest that the economy suffers greatly when the government runs a budget deficit. The most important task in this chapter will be to evaluate this view. As we shall see, the conclusions from the equilibrium business-cycle model depart substantially from those in the newspapers.*

A **budget deficit** *occurs when the government's tax revenue falls short of its expenditure. The government finances this shortfall by issuing interest-bearing government bonds—***public debt***. When the budget deficit is greater than zero, the quantity of public debt increases over time.*

We consider first the history of the public debt in the United States and the United Kingdom. With these facts as a background, we extend the equilibrium business-cycle model to allow for public debt. We use the model to assess the effects of budget deficits and public debt on economic variables, including real GDP, saving, investment, and the real interest rate.

The History of U.S. and U.K. Public Debt

T able 14.1 shows the history of the public debt in the United States and the United Kingdom. The table shows the nominal quantity of interest-bearing debt and the ratio of this debt to nominal GDP (gross national product, GNP, in earlier years).[1] Figure 14.1 shows the debt-GDP ratio for the United States from 1790 to 2005, and Figure 14.2 shows the ratio for the United Kingdom from 1700 to 2005.

For the United States, the major peaks in the ratio of public debt to GDP reflected the financing of wartime expenditures. The starting value, 0.33 in 1790, came from the Revolutionary War. A key decision at that time, advocated by Treasury Secretary Alexander Hamilton, was that the central government would honor all of the war debt, including the parts issued by individual colonies. The debt-GDP ratio reached 0.28 in 1866 after the Civil War (not including the Confederate debt, which was repudiated), 0.31 in 1919 after World War I, and 1.09 in 1946 after World War II. Another major influence is the business cycle. In recessions, the debt-GDP ratio typically rose, partly because of a drop in GDP and partly because of an increase in debt.

---

[1] The U.S. figures are net of holdings of public debt by U.S. government agencies and trust funds and the Federal Reserve. For example, in December 2005, of the $8.14 trillion of public debt securities, $2.70 trillion was held by agencies and trust funds and $0.74 trillion by the Federal Reserve, so that $4.71 trillion was held by the public. For the United Kingdom, the debt figures are the gross sterling debt of the central government. Net numbers are unavailable for the long-term history. In March 2004, the gross sterling debt of £428 billion corresponded to a public sector net debt of £376 billion.

Table 14.1 *Public Debt in the United States and the United Kingdom*

Year	U.S. Debt ($ billion)	U.S. Debt–GDP Ratio	U.K. Debt (£ billion)	U.K. Debt–GDP Ratio
1700	—	—	0.014	0.20
1710	—	—	0.030	0.31
1720	—	—	0.039	0.49
1730	—	—	0.037	0.49
1740	—	—	0.033	0.40
1750	—	—	0.059	0.68
1760	—	—	0.083	0.79
1770	—	—	0.106	1.01
1780	—	—	0.135	1.01
1790	0.075	0.33	0.179	1.05
1800	0.083	0.20	0.304	0.79
1810	0.048	0.082	0.436	0.96
1820	0.090	0.12	0.568	1.37
1830	0.039	0.038	0.544	1.12
1840	0.005	0.003	0.562	1.01
1850	0.063	0.029	0.557	0.94
1860	0.065	0.017	0.589	0.69
1870	2.04	0.28	0.593	0.51
1880	1.71	0.15	0.591	0.43
1890	0.711	0.054	0.578	0.37
1900	1.02	0.054	0.628	0.31
1910	0.913	0.028	0.665	0.28
1920	23.3	0.26	7.62	1.22
1930	14.8	0.16	7.58	1.55
1940	42.8	0.42	10.5	1.37
1950	219	0.74	26.1	1.77
1960	237	0.44	28.4	1.09
1970	283	0.27	33.4	0.64
1980	712	0.25	113	0.49
1990	2412	0.42	190	0.35
2000	3438	0.35	369	0.39
2005	4601	0.37	473	0.41

Note: For the United States, the public debt in billions of dollars is the amount of privately held, interest-bearing debt of the U.S. federal government at nominal par value. The figures are net of holdings by the Federal Reserve and U.S. government agencies and trust funds. (They include holdings by government-sponsored agencies and by state and local governments.) For the sources, see Barro (1978, Table 1). Values since 1939 are from the U.S. Treasury Department. The debt is expressed as a ratio to nominal GDP or GNP. The data on real GDP or GNP are described in Figure 1.1 of Chapter 1. Before 1869, nominal GNP is estimated by multiplying real GNP by a price index based on wholesale prices from Warren and Pearson (1933, Table 1).

For the United Kingdom, the public debt since 1917 is the central government's gross sterling debt in billions of pounds at nominal par value. Before 1917, the figures are the cumulation of the central government's budget deficit, starting from a benchmark stock of public debt in 1700. For discussions of the data, see Barro (1987). The underlying data are from Central Statistical Office, *Annual Abstract of Statistics,* various issues; Mitchell and Deane (1962); and Mitchell and Jones (1971). Data on nominal GDP or GNP are from the preceding and also from Feinstein (1972) and Deane and Cole (1969). Before 1830, nominal GNP is estimated from rough estimates of real GNP multiplied by a price index based on wholesale prices.

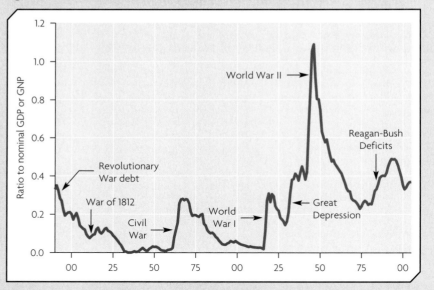

Figure 14.1 *Ratio of U.S. Public Debt to GDP, 1790–2005*

The graph shows the ratio of U.S. nominal public debt to nominal GDP (GNP before 1929), using the numbers described in Table 14.1.

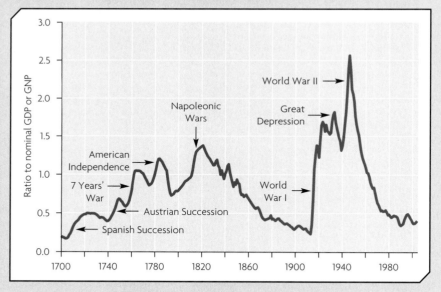

Figure 14.2 *Ratio of U.K. Public Debt to GDP, 1700–2004*

The graph shows the ratio of U.K. nominal public debt to nominal GDP or GNP, using the numbers described in Table 14.1.

ratio fell from 1.09 in 1946 to 0.23 in 1974. An exception to the usual pattern was 1983 to 1993, when the debt-GDP ratio rose from 0.32 to 0.49, despite the absence of war or substantial recession. However, the ratio declined to 0.33 in 2001, before rising—partly because of the 2001–02 recession—to 0.37 in 2005.

For the United Kingdom, the major peaks in the debt-GDP ratio were again associated with wartime: 0.50 after the Wars of Spanish and Austrian Succession in 1722, 1.1 at the end of the Seven Years' War in 1764, 1.2 after the War of American Independence in 1785, 1.3 after the Napoleonic Wars in 1816, 1.4 at the end of World War I in 1919, and 2.6 after World War II in 1946. The high points for U.K. debt in relation to GDP were more than twice as great as those for the United States. It is worth noting that the U.K. public debt constituted more than 100% of GDP in the 1760s—large amounts of public debt are not a modern invention!

Some researchers argue that Britain gained credibility in public-debt

A dramatic example is the Great Depression, during which the debt-GDP ratio increased from 0.14 in 1929 to 0.38 in 1933.

During peacetime, nonrecession years, the ratio of public debt to GDP typically declined. For example, the

management with the expanded role of parliament after the Glorious Revolution of 1688 (see Douglas North and Barry Weingast [1989] and Thomas Sargent and Francois Velde [1995]). The availability of debt finance may have given Britain a great advantage over France in the fighting of numerous wars up to the Napoleonic conflicts that ended in 1815.

Recessions raised the U.K. debt-GDP ratio—for example, from 1920 to 1923 and 1929 to 1933. Periods with neither war nor recession typically featured declining debt-GDP ratios. For example, the ratio declined from 2.57 in 1946 to 0.35 in 1990.

Characteristics of Government Bonds

 e will now expand the equilibrium business-cycle model to allow the government to issue interest-bearing bonds. We assume that government bonds pay interest and principal in the same way as private bonds. We still assume that all bonds have very short maturity[2] and that bonds specify nominal amounts of principal and interest. That is, we do not consider indexed bonds, which we discussed in Chapter 11.[3]

To simplify our analysis, we assume that bondholders (households in our model) regard government bonds as equivalent to private bonds. Specifically, we do not allow for the possibility that private bonds are riskier than government bonds in terms of the probability of default. Given our assumption, households would hold the two kinds of bonds only if they paid the same nominal interest rate, i. Therefore, our model has only one nominal interest rate, i, paid on all bonds. This result accords reasonably well with U.S. data if we interpret private bonds as prime corporate obligations. For example, the market yield on three-month maturity U.S. Treasury bills averaged 4.7% between 1947 and 2006, while that on three-month maturity commercial paper (short-term debt issued by the most creditworthy businesses) averaged 5.3%.

Denote by B_t^g the nominal amount of government bonds outstanding at the end of year t. We still use the symbol B_t for private bonds (issued by households in our model). Thus, the household's total holding of bonds at the end of year t is

$$total\ bond\ holdings = B_t + B_t^g$$
$$total\ bond\ holdings = private\ bonds + government\ bonds$$

The quantity of private bonds held by all households is still zero, because the positive amount held by one household must correspond to the debt of another household. Therefore, $B_t = 0$ still holds in the aggregate. This result means that the total quantity of bonds held by all households equals the public debt, B_t^g:

$$total\ bond\ holdings\ of\ all\ households = B_t^g$$

We usually think of the government as a net debtor to the private sector, so that B_t^g is greater than zero. However, the government could be a creditor, in which case B_t^g would be less than zero. The last time this became a serious possibility for the United States was in 1834–36, when the public debt came close to zero; see Figure 14.1.

Budget Constraints and Budget Deficits

T o consider budget deficits and public debt, we have to see how they fit into the government's budget constraint. We begin by extending the government's budget constraint.

The Government's Budget Constraint

We introduced the government's budget constraint for year t in Chapter 12:

(12.1) $G_t + V_t = T_t + (M_t - M_{t-1})/P_t$
real purchases + real transfers = real taxes + real revenue from money creation

The first new term we have to add is the government's interest payments, which are $i_{t-1} \cdot B_{t-1}^g$ in nominal units. The real value of these interest payments, $i_{t-1} \cdot (B_{t-1}^g/P_t)$, adds to the government's expenditure or uses of funds on the left-hand side of equation (12.1).

---

[2] In the United States, the average maturity of marketable, interest-bearing U.S. government bonds held by the public was around 9 years in 1946. This maturity declined to a low point of 2½ years in 1976. During most of this period, the U.S. Treasury was prohibited from issuing long-term bonds at interest rates that would have made them marketable. With the ending of this restriction, the average maturity rose to about 6 years in 1990. In 2005, the average maturity was around 5 years. For the United Kingdom, in 2003, 36% of marketable government bonds had a maturity of up to 5 years, 35% were between 5 and 15 years, and 29% were greater than 15 years.

[3] In 2005, indexed bonds constituted 7% of the total of U.S. government bonds held by the public. For the United Kingdom in 2004, indexed bonds were much more important—18% of the outstanding gross sterling debt of the central government.

The second new term is the debt issue during year t. The dollar amount of this debt issue is $B_t^g - B_{t-1}^g$. Note that the reissue of bonds as they come due is not a net source of funds for the government. What matters is the difference between the stock outstanding at the end of the year, B_t^g, and the amount outstanding at the end of the previous year, B_{t-1}^g. The real value of the debt issue, $(B_t^g - B_{t-1}^g)/P_t$, adds to the government's sources of funds on the right-hand side of equation (12.1).

When we introduce the two new terms into equation (12.1), we get an expanded version of the government budget constraint:

Key equation (expanded government budget constraint):

(14.1)
$$G_t + V_t + i_{t-1} \cdot (B_{t-1}^g/P_t)$$
$$= T_t + (B_t^g - B_{t-1}^g)/P_t + (M_t - M_{t-1})/P_t$$

real purchases + real transfers
+ real interest payments
= real taxes + real debt issue
+ real revenue from money creation

The two new terms are the real interest payments, $i_{t-1} \cdot (B_{t-1}^g/P_t)$, on the left-hand side, and the real debt issue, $(B_t^g - B_{t-1}^g)/P_t$, on the right-hand side.

To analyze budget deficits, we will find it convenient to reintroduce two simplifying assumptions from Chapters 12 and 13. Assume, first, that the nominal quantity of money, M_t, equals a constant, M. In this case, the revenue from money creation, $(M_t - M_{t-1})/P_t$, is zero on the right-hand side of equation (14.1). Second, ignore inflation, so that the price level, P_t, equals the constant P. In this case, the nominal interest rate, i_t, equals the real interest rate, r_t. These assumptions simplify the analysis without affecting our main conclusions about public debt and budget deficits.

When nominal money, M_t, and the price level, P_t, do not change over time, the government's budget constraint simplifies from equation (14.1) to

(14.2) $G_t + V_t + r_{t-1} \cdot (B_{t-1}^g/P) = T_t + (B_t^g - B_{t-1}^g)/P$

Starting from equation (14.1), we replaced P_t by P and i_{t-1} by r_{t-1}, and we eliminated the term $(M_t - M_{t-1})/P_t$.

The Budget Deficit

To define and calculate the government's budget deficit, it is helpful to think about how much the government saves or dissaves. We define real saving for the government

in the same way as for a household. If the government saves, its net real assets rise, and if the government dissaves, its net real assets fall. To use these ideas, we have to define the government's net real assets.

The real public debt, B_t^g/P, is a liability of the government. When B_t^g/P rises, the government owes more and, as a result, has more liabilities and fewer net real assets. Therefore, an increase in the real public debt, $(B_t^g - B_{t-1}^g)/P$, signifies that the government is saving less or dissaving more in real terms.

If the government owned capital, its net real assets would include this capital. In that case, an increase in government-owned capital stock—called net **public investment**—would mean that the government had more net real assets. Thus, an increase in net public investment means that the government is saving more or dissaving less in real terms. However, in our model, the government does not own capital, and net public investment is zero.

Since the money stock is constant and the government owns no capital, the government's real saving or dissaving equals the negative of the change in the real public debt. If the real public debt increases, the government's real saving is less than zero, and the government is dissaving. If the real public debt decreases, the government's real saving is greater than zero. Therefore, we have

(14.3) *real government saving* $= -(B_t^g - B_{t-1}^g)/P$

We can rearrange the government's budget constraint in equation (14.2) to relate real government saving, $(B_t^g - B_{t-1}^g)/P$, to real expenditure and taxes:

(14.4) $-(B_t^g - B_{t-1}^g)/P = T_t - [G_t + V_t + r_{t-1} \cdot (B_{t-1}^g/P)]$
real government saving =
real taxes − real government expenditure

Note that real government expenditure is the sum of real purchases, G_t, real transfers, V_t, and real interest payments, $r_{t-1} \cdot (B_{t-1}^g/P)$. When real taxes are greater than real government expenditure, real government saving is greater than zero, and the real public debt falls over time.

If the right-hand side of equation (14.4) is greater than zero, the government's revenue exceeds its expenditure, and the government has a **budget surplus**. Thus, the real surplus is the same as the government's real saving. Conversely, if the right-hand side is less than zero, the government has a budget deficit. The real deficit is the same as the government's real dissaving. If the right-hand side of equation (14.4) is zero, the government has a **balanced budget**, and the government's real saving is zero.

Figure 14.3 shows real budget deficits for the U.S. federal government from 1954 to 2005. To calculate real budget deficits, we first compute the stock of real public debt at the end of each year by dividing the nominal debt (the concept shown in the first column of Table 14.1) by the GDP deflator. Then the real budget deficit is the change over the year in the stock of real public debt.

If the price level, P_t, is constant, as we have been assuming, our method for calculating real budget deficits corresponds to standard calculations in the national-income accounts. If the inflation rate, π_t, is nonzero, so that P_t varies over time,

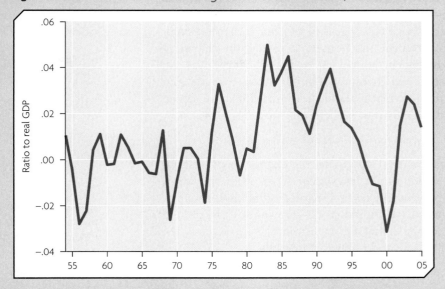

Figure 14.3 *Ratio of U.S. Real Budget Deficit to Real GDP, 1954–2005*

The graph shows the ratio of the real budget deficit to real GDP from 1954 to 2005. To compute the real budget deficit, we start by calculating the stock of real public debt at the end of each year as the ratio of the nominal debt to the GDP deflator. The real budget deficit is the change during the year of the stock of real public debt.

our approach still gives correct measures of real budget deficits, but national-accounts data have shortcomings. However, the discrepancy is small since the mid-1980s, because π_t has been low.[4]

Figure 14.3 shows that the highest ratios of the real budget deficit to real GDP were around 4% in 1983–86 and again in 1992. These deficits correspond in Figure 14.1 to the rising debt-GDP ratios associated with the budget deficits during the Reagan and first Bush administrations. The rest of the 1990s showed a steady movement toward budget surplus, culminating in the peak ratio above 3% in magnitude in 2000. Then the federal government moved back to a real budget deficit, reaching 2.7% of real GDP in 2003 but then falling to 1.4% in 2005.

Public Saving, Private Saving, and National Saving

To assess the economic effects of budget deficits, it is useful to organize our discussion around three concepts of saving: government (or public) saving, household (or

private) saving, and national (or total) saving. Real government saving is given from equation (14.3):

(14.3) *real government saving* $= -(B_t^g - B_{t-1}^g)/P$

If the government runs a real budget deficit, so that $(B_t^g - B_{t-1}^g)/P$ is greater than zero, real government saving is less than zero. Recall that, if the government owned capital, the change in this capital stock would add to government saving.

We know from Chapter 6 that the household's real saving equals the change in the household's real assets. In our previous analysis, these real assets consisted of private bonds, B_t/P_t; money, M_t/P_t; and capital, K_t. Now we have to add real assets held as government bonds, B_t^g/P_t. The economy-wide total of private bonds, B_t, still equals zero. Therefore, when we add up over all households, the change in these bonds equals zero. Also, we are assuming that M_t and P_t do not change over time. Therefore, the economy-wide total of household real saving equals the change in the capital stock plus the change in real government bonds:

(14.5) *real household saving (economy-wide)*
$$= K_t - K_{t-1} + (B_t^g - B_{t-1}^g)/P$$

---

[4] We want the real budget deficit to equal the change in real government bonds. To get this result, it turns out that real interest payments have to be computed using the real interest rate, that is, as $r_{t-1} \cdot (B_{t-1}^g/P)$, which is the term in equation (14.4). However, the national accounts use the nominal interest rate, so that the term for real interest payments is $i_{t-1} \cdot (B_{t-1}^g/P)$. To put it another way, the national accounts fail to consider that a positive inflation rate, π_{t-1}, reduces the real value of the nominal government bonds outstanding. To correct for this omission, one has to subtract the term $\pi_{t-1} \cdot (B_{t-1}^g/P)$ from the real budget deficit computed from the national accounts. This adjustment is equivalent to using the real interest rate, r_{t-1}, rather than the nominal rate, i_{t-1}, to calculate real interest payments.

The sum of real government saving and economy-wide real household saving equals real **national saving**—the saving of the whole nation. We can see from equations (14.3) and (14.5) that, when we combine government and household saving, the change in real government bonds, $(B_t^g - B_{t-1}^g)/P$ cancels out. An increase in real government bonds means that the government is saving less and that households are saving correspondingly more. Therefore, we get

(14.6)   *real national saving* $= K_t - K_{t-1}$

Real national saving equals the change in the capital stock, which is net investment. This result still holds if the government owns capital. In that case, K_t is the economy's total capital stock—the sum of private and public capital—and net investment, $K_t - K_{t-1}$, is the sum of private and public net investment.

Public Debt and Households' Budget Constraints

 e found in Chapter 12 that the household's multi-year budget constraint included the present value of real transfers net of real taxes, $V_t - T_t$:

(12.6) $C_1 + C_2/(1 + r_1) + \cdots = (1 + r_0) \cdot (B_0/P + K_0)$
$+ (w/P)_1 \cdot L_1^s + (w/P)_2 \cdot L_2^s/(1 + r_1) + \cdots$
$+ (V_1 - T_1) + (V_2 - T_2)/(1 + r_1)$
$+ (V_3 - T_3)/[(1 + r_1) \cdot (1 + r_2)] + \cdots$

present value of consumption = value of initial assets
+ present value of wage incomes
+ present value of transfers net of taxes

Now we have to modify equation (12.6) to include the household's initial holdings of real government bonds, B_0^g/P. When we make this change, the multiyear household budget constraint becomes

(14.7) $C_1 + C_2/(1 + r_1) + \cdots = (1 + r_0) \cdot (B_0/P$
$+ B_0^g/P + K_0) + (w/P)_1 \cdot L_1^s + (w/P)_2 \cdot L_2^s/$
$(1 + r_1) + \cdots + (V_1 - T_1) + (V_2 - T_2)/(1 + r_1)$
$+ (V_3 - T_3)/[(1 + r_1) \cdot (1 + r_2)] + \cdots$

Any income effects on households from the government's budget have to involve either the initial real government bonds, B_0^g/P, or the present value of real

transfers net of real taxes, $(V_1 - T_1) + (V_2 - T_2)/(1 + r_1) + (V_3 - T_3)/[(1 + r_1) \cdot (1 + r_2)] + \cdots$. To illustrate the results, it is convenient to begin with some simplifying assumptions.

A Simple Case of Ricardian Equivalence

Start with some unrealistic assumptions, which can then be relaxed:

- The real interest rate, r_t, is the same each year: $r_0 = r_1 = r_2 = \cdots = r$.
- As already assumed, the money stock, M_t, and the price level, P_t, do not change over time. With a zero inflation rate, π, the real interest rate, r, equals the nominal rate, i.
- Real transfers, V_t, are zero each year.
- The government starts with no debt, so that $B_0^g/P = 0$.
- Finally, the most important assumption: *the government has a given time path of purchases, G_t. We are not* assuming here that G_t is unchanging over time. Rather, we are assuming that, whatever complicated path G_t takes, this whole path stays the same when we consider different choices of budget deficits or different starting levels of public debt.

Since real transfers, V_t, are zero each year, the government's budget constraint for year t simplifies from equation (14.2) to

(14.8) $G_t + r \cdot (B_{t-1}^g/P) = T_t + (B_t^g - B_{t-1}^g)/P$

Since the government starts with zero debt, we have $B_0^g/P = 0$. Therefore, in year 1, the government's real interest payments, $r \cdot (B_0^g/P)$, are zero, and the budget constraint is

(14.9) $G_1 = T_1 + B_1^g/P$

government purchases in year 1 =
real taxed in year 1 + real debt at end of year 1

Suppose, to begin, that the government balances its budget each year. Then, in year 1, real purchases, G_1, equal real taxes, T_1. In that case, equation (14.9) implies that the real public debt remains at zero at the end of year 1; that is, $B_1^g/P = 1$. Continuing on, if the government balances its budget every year, the real public debt, B_t^g/P, is zero in every year t.

What happens if, instead of balancing its budget in year 1, the government runs a real budget deficit of one unit? Since we are assuming that the path of government purchases stays the same, year 1's real purchases, G_1, do not change. Therefore, the deficit must come from a cut in real taxes, T_1, by one unit. Equation (14.9) implies that the real deficit of one unit requires the government to issue one unit of real public debt at the end of year 1, so that $B_1^g/P = 1$.

Assume that the government decides to restore the public debt to zero from year 2 onward, so that $B_2^g/P = B_3^g/P = \cdots = 0$. We have to figure out what this policy requires for year 2's real taxes, T_2. To calculate T_2, we use the government's budget constraint for year 2. This constraint is given from equation (14.8) as

(14.10) $G_2 + r \bullet (B_1^g/P) = T_2 + (B_2^g - B_1^g)/P$

government purchases in year 2 + real interest payments in year 2 = real taxes in year 2 + real budget deficit in year 2

If we substitute $B_1^g/P = 1$ and $B_2^g/P = 0$ in equation (14.10), the constraint simplifies to

$$G_2 + r = T_2 - 1$$

Therefore, we can rearrange the terms to calculate real taxes for year 2:

$$T_2 = G_2 + 1 + r$$

This equation says that the government must raise real taxes in year 2, T_2, above year 2's government purchases, G_2, to pay the principal and interest, $1 + r$, on the one unit of debt, B_1^g/P, issued in year 1. (Recall our assumption that G_2 does not change.)

Putting the results together, year 1's real taxes, T_1, fall by one unit, and year 2's real taxes, T_2, rise by $1 + r$ units. How do these changes affect the total present value of real taxes paid by households? Recall the household's multiyear budget constraint:

(14.7) $C_1 + C_2/(1 + r_1) + \cdots = (1 + r_0) \bullet (B_0/P + B_0^g/P + K_0) + (w/P)_1 \bullet L_1^s + (w/P)_2 \bullet L_2^s/(1 + r_1) + \cdots + (V_1 - T_1) + (V_2 - T_2)/(1 + r_1) + (V_3 - T_3)/[(1 + r_1) \bullet (1 + r_2)] + \cdots$

According to this equation, we have to divide year 2's real taxes, T_2, by the discount factor, $1 + r$, to compute a present value. Therefore, the overall effect of the changes in T_1 and T_2 on the present value of real taxes is given by

decrease in year 1's real taxes
+ present value of increase in year 2's taxes
$$= -1 + (1 + r)/(1 + r)$$
$$= -1 + 1$$
$$= 0$$

Hence, households experience no net change in the present value of real taxes when the government runs a budget deficit in year 1 and pays off the debt with the necessary budget surplus in year 2.

In our simple example, the government's budget deficit does not affect the present value of real taxes. Moreover, we are assuming that real transfers, V_t, are zero in each period. Therefore, the budget deficit does not affect the present value of real transfers net of real taxes on the right-hand side of equation (14.7). We conclude that the budget deficit has no income effects on households.

We can interpret the result as follows. Households receive one unit extra of real disposable income in year 1 because of the cut in year 1's real taxes, T_1, by one unit. However, households also have $1 + r$ units less of real disposable income in year 2 because of the rise in year 2's real taxes, T_2, by $1 + r$ units. If households use the extra unit of real disposable income in year 1 to buy an extra unit of bonds, they will have just enough additional funds—$1 + r$ units—to pay the extra real taxes in year 2. Thus, the tax cut in year 1 provides enough resources, but no more, for households to pay the higher taxes in year 2. That is why there is no income effect. Nothing is left over to raise consumption or reduce labor supply in any year.

We can view the results as saying that households view real taxes in year 1, T_1, as equivalent to a real budget deficit in year 1, $(B_1^g - B_0^g)/P$. If the government replaces a unit of real taxes with a unit of real budget deficit, households know that the present value of next year's real taxes will rise by one unit. Thus, the real budget deficit is the same as a real tax in terms of the overall present value of real taxes. This finding is the simplest version of the **Ricardian equivalence theorem** on the public debt. (The theorem is named after the famous British economist David Ricardo, who first expressed the idea in the early 1800s.[5])

We can interpret the results in terms of saving. The real budget deficit of one unit in year 1 means that real government saving is minus one unit. Since households do not change consumption, they place the entire extra unit of year 1's real disposable income into bonds. Therefore, real household saving in year 1 rises by one unit. Thus, the extra real household saving exactly offsets the government's real dissaving. The sum of household and government real saving—real national saving—does not change. Thus, another way to express the result is that a budget deficit does not affect real national saving.

---

[5] For discussions, see David Ricardo (1846), James Buchanan (1958, pp. 43–46, 114–122), and Robert Barro (1989). Gerald O'Driscoll (1977) points out Ricardo's doubts about the empirical validity of his own theorem.

Another Case of Ricardian Equivalence

Our basic result was that a deficit-financed cut in year 1's real taxes by one unit led to an increase by one unit in the present value of future real taxes. In our simple example, all of the higher future taxes appeared in year 2. More generally, some of the increases in real taxes would show up in later years.

To get a more general result, we can drop the assumption that the government runs enough of a budget surplus in year 2 to pay off all the bonds issued in year 1. Assume, as before, that the government issues one unit of real debt, B_1^g/P, at the end of year 1. Recall that the government's budget constraint for year 2 is

(14.10) $\quad G_2 + r \bullet (B_1^g/P) = T_2 + (B_2^g - B_1^g)/P$

Suppose now that, in year 2, the government does not pay off the one unit of debt, B_1^g/P, issued in year 1.

Assume instead that the government carries the principal of this debt, one unit, over to year 3, so that

$$B_2^g/P = B_1^g/P = 1$$

If we substitute $B_1^g/P = 1$ and $B_2^g/P = 1$ into equation (14.10), we get

$$G_2 + r = T_2$$

Therefore, year 2's real taxes, T_2, cover the interest payment, r, but not the principal, 1, for the real debt, B_1^g/P, issued in year 1. In other words, the government balances its budget in year 2: Real taxes equal real purchases plus real interest payments.

If the government again balances its budget in year 3, we find by the same reasoning that year 3's real taxes, T_3, cover the interest payment, r, on the one unit of real debt. Similarly, if the government balances its budget every year, real taxes, T, cover year 3's interest payment, r. The time profile for the changes in real taxes is

- year 1: T_1 falls by 1
- year 2: T_2 rises by r
- year 3: T_3 rises by r

and so on. Hence, T_t increases by r units in each year after the first.

Think about the sequence of higher real taxes by r units each year. What quantity of real bonds would households need at the end of year 1 to pay these extra taxes? If households hold one more unit of real bonds, the real interest income in year 2 would be r, and this income could pay year 2's additional taxes. Then, if the principal of the bond—one unit—were held over to year 3, the real interest income of r could pay year 3's added taxes. Continuing this way, we find that the real interest income each year would allow households to meet their extra real taxes every year.

What, then, is the present value of the increase in real taxes by r units starting in year 2? This present value must be the same as the one extra unit of real bonds in year 1 needed to pay the additional real taxes in each subsequent year. But, obviously, the present value of one unit of real bonds in year 1 is one unit. Therefore, the present value of the additional future real taxes is one.[6]

---

[6] We can verify this answer by summing the present values:

$$\frac{r}{1+r} + \frac{r}{(1+r)^2} + \frac{r}{(1+r)^3} + \cdots = \left(\frac{r}{1+r}\right) \bullet \left[1 + \left(\frac{1}{1+r}\right) + \left(\frac{1}{1+r}\right)^2 + \cdots\right]$$

The infinite sum inside the brackets has the form of the geometric series $1 + x + x^2 + \cdots$, which equals $1/(1-x)$ if x is less than one in magnitude. In our case, $x = 1/(1+r)$. Therefore, we have

$$\frac{r}{1+r} + \frac{r}{(1+r)^2} + \frac{r}{(1+r)^3} + \cdots = \left(\frac{r}{1+r}\right) \bullet \left[\frac{1}{1 - \left(\frac{1}{1+r}\right)}\right]$$

$$= \left(\frac{r}{1+r}\right) \bullet \left(\frac{1+r}{1+r-1}\right)$$

$$= \left(\frac{r}{1+r}\right) \bullet \left(\frac{1+r}{r}\right)$$

$$= 1$$

Given the results about the present value of the higher future real taxes, the overall change in the present value of real taxes comes from combining two terms:

- −1: real tax cut in year 1
- +1: present value of real tax increases in future years

Since the sum of the two terms is zero, we conclude, as in our first example, that a deficit-financed cut in year 1's real taxes, T_1, leads to no change in the overall present value of real taxes. Therefore, we find again that the deficit-financed tax cut in year 1 has no income effects on households.

Ricardian Equivalence More Generally

We now have two examples in which a deficit-financed tax cut does not affect the present value of real taxes paid by households. To get this answer, we made a number of unrealistic assumptions. However, the result still holds if we relax most of these assumptions.

We can allow the initial real public debt, B_0^g/P, to be greater than zero. Notice that B_0^g/P enters as a part of households' sources of funds on the right-hand side of the multiyear budget constraint:

(14.7) $$C_1 + C_2/(1 + r_1) + \cdots = (1 + r_0) \bullet (B_0/P + B_0^g/P + K_0) + (w/P)_1 \bullet L_1^s + (w/P)_2 \bullet L_2^s/(1 + r_1) + \cdots + (V_1 - T_1) + (V_2 - T_2)/(1 + r_1) + (V_3 - T_3)/[(1 + r_1) \bullet (1 + r_2)] + \cdots$$

However, if the time path of government purchases, G_t, is given (and if real transfers, V_t, are zero), we can show that a higher B_0^g/P requires the government to collect a correspondingly higher present value of real taxes, T_t, to finance the debt. This higher present value of real taxes exactly offsets the higher B_0^g/P on the right-hand side of equation (14.7). Thus, we still have no income effects on households.

If we allow real transfers, V_t, to be greater than zero, we find that a deficit-financed tax cut does not affect the present value of real transfers net of real taxes, $V_t - T_t$, on the right-hand side of equation (14.7). Hence, there are again no income effects on households.

We can allow for variations in the money stock, M_t, and the price level, P_t. In this case, the new feature is that the revenue from money creation—often called the inflation tax—should be viewed as another form of tax. That is, real taxes, T_t, have to be broadened to include the inflation tax. With this extension, we still find that a deficit-financed tax cut does not affect the present value of real taxes paid by households.

We can allow for tax cuts and budget deficits in future years, not just for year 1. These deficits will require higher real taxes in years further into the future. In each case, the higher present value of real taxes exactly offsets the present value of the tax cut. Therefore, we still get no effect on the present value of real taxes paid by households. This conclusion holds for any time pattern of budget deficits and tax cuts.

What if the government has a deficit-financed tax cut and finances the extra public debt forever by issuing new debt? In this case, it seems that future real taxes would never increase. However, this form of financing requires an explosive path for the public debt—it amounts to a form of chain letter or pyramid scheme in which the real debt rises at a rate that is ultimately unsustainable. Our assumption is that the government cannot carry out these types of chain letters.

In all of these cases, we find that the income effects are nil. The reason we keep getting this result is that we have held fixed the time path of real government purchases, G_t. These purchases have to be paid for at some point with real taxes, T_t. By varying its budget deficits, the government can change the timing of taxes. However, the government cannot escape levying the taxes sometime; this conclusion is an example of the economic adage that there is no free lunch. If the government wants to change the present value of real taxes, it has to change the present value of its purchases, G_t. That is why the assumption of a fixed path of G_t is the really important assumption.

Economic Effects of a Budget Deficit

What happens in the equilibrium business-cycle model when the government cuts year 1's real taxes, T_1, and runs a budget deficit? Economists often refer to this type of change as a stimulative **fiscal policy**. We know, if the path of government purchases, G_t, does not change, that the budget deficit has no income effects on households' choices of consumption and labor supply. Today's real tax cut is matched by a higher present value of future real taxes. There may, however, be substitution effects from the tax changes. These effects, which we explored in Chapter 13, depend on the forms of the taxes that are cut today and raised in the future. We begin by assuming that taxes are lump sum, as in Chapter 12. Although this case is unrealistic, it does correspond to the one usually examined in macroeconomic textbooks. We will consider more realistic types of taxes in later sections.

Lump-Sum Taxes

Suppose that the cut in year 1's real taxes, T_1, and the increases in future real taxes, T_t, all involve lump-sum taxes. The important feature of these taxes is that they have no substitution effects on consumption and labor supply. Recall that the budget deficit also has no income effects on consumption and labor supply. We conclude that, for a given real interest rate, r, and real wage rate, w/P, a deficit-financed tax cut would not affect consumption, C, and labor supply, L^s. (For convenience, we now omit the time subscripts on variables.)

A deficit-financed tax cut does not affect the marginal products of labor and capital, MPL and MPK. Therefore, the deficit does not shift the demand curve for labor (shown in Figure 13.5) or the demand curve for capital services (shown in Figure 13.6). Since the supply curve for labor does not shift, we find that the market-clearing real wage rate, $(w/P)^*$, and quantity of labor, L^*, are unchanged (Figure 13.5). Since the supply curve for capital services does not shift, we find that the market-clearing real rental price, $(R/P)^*$, and quantity of capital services, $(\kappa K)^*$, are unchanged (Figure 13.6). The fixity of R/P implies that the real interest rate, r, does not change.

Since the quantities of labor, L, and capital services, κK, do not change, we know from the production function, $Y = A \cdot F(\kappa K, L)$, that real GDP, Y, must be the same. The real GDP goes, as usual, for consumption, gross investment, and government purchases:

$$Y = C + I + G$$

We just found that Y stayed the same. Recall that one of our assumptions is that government purchases, G, do not change. We also know that C is unchanged, because no income or substitution effects motivate households to change C. Therefore, we must have that gross investment, I, stays the same. This result tells us that today's budget deficit will not affect future capital stocks.

We can look at the results in terms of saving. Since the budget deficit has no income or substitution effects, households do not change consumption, C. However, a cut in year 1's real taxes by one unit raises households'

real disposable income by one unit. Since C is the same, households must raise year 1's real saving by one unit. Therefore, the households willingly absorb the one unit of extra bonds issued by the government to cover its budget deficit. Or, as we put it before, the increase by one unit in real household saving fully offsets the reduction by one unit in real government saving. This offset means that real national saving in year 1 does not change.

We have found in our equilibrium business-cycle model that a deficit-financed tax cut does not stimulate the economy. In particular, real GDP, Y; gross investment, I; and the real interest rate, r, do not change. Since these results are controversial and important, we shall want to see how modifications of the model change the conclusions. We begin by assuming more realistic forms of taxes.

Labor Income Taxes

Suppose that, instead of lump-sum taxes, the government levies taxes on labor income. As in Chapter 13, let τ_w be the marginal tax rate on labor income. Consider again a reduction in year 1's real taxes, T_1, financed by a budget deficit. We assume that the fall in T_1 is accompanied by a decline in the marginal income tax rate, $(\tau_w)_1$.

Since the path of government purchases, G_t, does not change, year 1's real deficit will require real taxes, T_t, to rise in future years. To keep things simple, while still bringing out the main results, assume that year 2's real taxes, T_2, rise by enough to pay off the extra real debt issued in year 1. Thus, real taxes do not change beyond year 2. We assume that the rise in T_2 goes along with an increase in year 2's marginal income tax rate, $(\tau_w)_2$.

The changes in marginal income tax rates, $(\tau_w)_1$ and $(\tau_w)_2$, affect the labor market in years 1 and 2. Figure 14.4 shows the effects for year 1. (The construction is the same as in Figure 13.5, except that we now consider a decrease, rather than an increase, in τ_w.) Figure 14.4 shows that the cut in $(\tau_w)_1$ raises labor supply in year 1. This increase in labor supply leads, when the labor market clears, to a higher quantity of labor, $(L_1)'$. The higher labor input leads to a rise in year 1's real GDP, Y_1.[7]

The effects for year 2, shown in Figure 14.5, are the reverse. The increase in $(\tau_w)_2$ lowers labor supply in year 2. This decrease in labor supply leads, when the labor market clears, to a lower quantity of labor, $(L_2)'$. The reduced labor input leads to a decrease in year 2's real GDP, Y_2.

---

[7] An additional effect is that the increase in L_1 tends to raise year 1's MPK. This change leads to an increase in year 1's capital utilization rate, κ_1, and, hence, to a rise in capital services, $(\kappa k)_1$. The increase in $(\kappa k)_1$ contributes to the rise in real GDP, Y_1.

Our main finding is that a budget deficit allows the government to change the timing of labor-income tax rates and thereby alter the timing of labor input and production. Specifically, a budget deficit that finances a cut in year 1's tax rate on labor income motivates a rearrangement of the time pattern of work and production—toward the present (year 1) and away from the future (year 2).

Asset Income Taxes

The effects of a budget deficit depend on the types of taxes that change. To illustrate, consider another form of tax studied in Chapter 13—a tax on asset income at the rate τ_r. Assume now that year 1's budget deficit finances a cut in taxes on asset income, thereby resulting in a decrease in year 1's asset-income tax rate, $(\tau_r)_1$. Future taxes must again increase. We assume that only the tax rate, $(\tau_r)_2$, on year 2's asset income rises.

The results in Chapter 13 tell us that a cut in year 1's tax rate on asset income, $(\tau_r)_1$, raises year 1's after-tax real interest rate, $[1 - (\tau_r)_1] \bullet r_1$. In response, households save more and consume less. The increase

Figure 14.4 *Effect of a Decrease in Year 1's Labor-Income Tax Rate on the Labor Market*

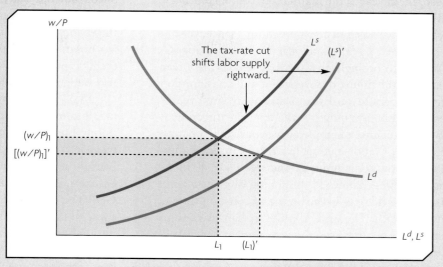

The downward-sloping labor demand curve, L^d, shown in red, comes from Figure 13.5. The upward-sloping labor supply curve, L^s, shown in blue, also comes from Figure 13.5. A decrease in year 1's marginal tax rate on labor income, $(\tau_w)_1$, shifts the labor supply curve rightward to the green one, $(L^s)'$. Consequently, year 1's market-clearing, before-tax real wage rate falls from $(w/P)_1$ to $[(w/P)_1]'$ on the vertical axis. The market-clearing quantity of labor rises from L_1 to $(L_1)'$ on the horizontal axis.

Figure 14.5 *Effect of an Increase in Year 2's Labor-Income Tax Rate on the Labor Market*

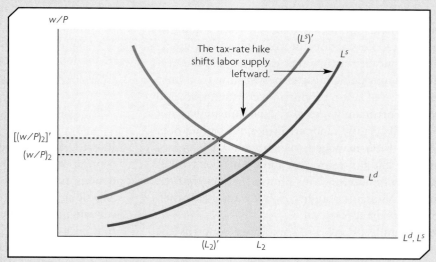

The downward-sloping labor demand curve, L^d, shown in red, comes from Figure 13.5. The upward-sloping labor supply curve, L^s, shown in blue, also comes from Figure 13.5. An increase in year 2's marginal tax rate on labor income, $(\tau_w)_2$, shifts the labor supply curve leftward to the green one, $(L^s)'$. Consequently, the market-clearing, before-tax real wage rate rises from $(w/P)_2$ to $[(w/P)_2]'$ on the vertical axis. The market-clearing quantity of labor falls from L_2 to $(L_2)'$ on the horizontal axis.

in saving leads to a rise in year 1's gross investment, I_1. Therefore, for given real GDP, Y_1, year 1's consumption, C_1, must fall. In year 2, the tax rate on asset income, $(\tau_r)_2$, rises. The effects are in the opposite direction from year 1: Households save less and consume more. Hence, year 2's gross investment, I_2, falls, and year 2's consumption, C_2, rises. We see, accordingly, that the main effects are a rearrangement of the timing of investment and consumption. Investment moves toward year 1 and away from year 2, whereas consumption moves in the opposite direction.

In our previous example, we found that changes in the timing of labor-income tax rates caused changes in the timing of labor input, L, and real GDP, Y. In the present example, changes in the timing of asset-income tax rates cause changes in the timing of consumption, C, and investment, I. The general point is that, by running budget deficits or surpluses, the government can change the timing of various tax rates. Thereby, the government can induce changes in the timing of various aspects of economic activity: L, Y, C, and I. In the next section, we consider whether it is a good idea for the government to induce these variations in the timing of economic activity.

The Timing of Taxes and Tax-Rate Smoothing

We have found that budget deficits and surpluses allow the government to change the timing of tax rates. However, it would not be a good idea for the government randomly to make tax rates high in some years and low in others. These fluctuations in tax rates cause unnecessary economic distortions, because they give households the wrong signals in determining how to choose the time pattern of labor, production, consumption, and investment. Fortunately, the U.S. government has not behaved in this erratic manner; rather, the public debt has typically been managed to maintain a pattern of reasonably stable tax rates over time. This behavior is called **tax-rate smoothing**. This phrase signifies that the government maintains stability in tax rates even when economic disturbances occur.

One example of tax-rate smoothing concerns the response of income tax rates to economic fluctuations. Real government expenditures typically do not rise as much in proportion as real GDP does during booms, or fall as much during recessions. In fact, some real transfers, such as unemployment compensation and family assistance, tend to fall in real terms during booms and rise during recessions. Therefore, to maintain a balanced budget, the government would have to cut tax rates when the economy booms and raise them when the economy contracts. Instead of cutting tax rates during booms and raising them during recessions, governments typically run real budget surpluses in booms and real budget deficits in recessions.

Many tax systems, such as the U.S. individual income tax, automatically collect more taxes as a ratio to GDP during booms and fewer taxes as a ratio to GDP during recessions. This tendency operates for a given tax law because a boom pushes taxpayers into higher tax-rate brackets, and because deductions do not rise along with GDP. The opposite forces operate during a recession. Because of the automatic tendency to run budget surpluses during booms and deficits during recessions, economists sometimes estimate what the budget deficit would have been if the economy had been operating at a level of "full capacity" or "full employment." For discussions of the full-employment deficit, see E. Cary Brown (1956) and Council of Economic Advisers, *Economic Report of the President* (U.S. President, 1962, pp. 78–82).

As another example, during wartime, government purchases rise substantially above normal. To maintain a balanced budget, tax rates would have to be abnormally high during wars. To avoid these unusually high wartime tax rates, governments tend to run real budget deficits during wars. In this way, the necessary increases in tax rates are spread roughly evenly over time. Tax rates rise somewhat during wartime but also increase afterward to finance the public debt built up during the war. This wartime deficit financing explains much of the long-term evolution of the U.S. and U.K. public debts, as shown in Figures 14.1 and 14.2.

Strategic Budget Deficits

In the U.S. history shown in Figure 14.1, the major exception to tax-rate smoothing concerns the real budget deficits run during the Reagan and first Bush administrations after the end of the 1982–83 recession. For the remainder of the 1980s, and continuing through the first part of the 1990s, the real deficits raised the ratio of public debt to GDP, despite the absence of war or significant recession.[8] The debt-GDP ratio increased from 0.32 in 1983 to 0.40 at the end of Reagan's second term in 1988, then continued upward to reach 0.49 in 1993, early in the Clinton administration.

---

[8] The 1990–91 recession was mild and would not have exerted a major effect on the debt-GDP ratio.

One interpretation offered for these budget deficits is that Reagan wanted to halt the upward trend in the ratio of total government expenditure to GDP, as shown in Figure 12.1 of Chapter 12. This ratio had been trending upward from the late 1940s through the early 1980s. Reagan apparently wanted to curb the growth of both federal spending and taxes. However, he was more successful initially at cutting taxes than cutting spending; hence, the government ran real budget deficits. Some economists have argued that these deficits, and the consequent buildup of public debt, created political pressure on the U.S. Congress to curtail the growth of federal spending. Therefore, in the longer run, Reagan may have been successful in forcing the ratio of total government expenditure to GDP to be smaller than it otherwise would have been. In any event, it is clear from Figure 12.1 that the upward trend in the ratio of government expenditure to GDP stopped in the early 1980s.

This view of the Reagan–Bush budget deficits after 1983 gave rise to a new theory called **strategic budget deficits**.[9] The word "strategic" is used because the models involve political strategies analogous to those analyzed in game theory. To get the basic idea, suppose that an administration—perhaps the Reagan administration—is currently in power and favors a small government. Assume that this administration believes that it will be followed eventually by an administration that favors a large government (perhaps the Clinton administration, which came to power in 1993). How can the Reagan administration influence future government officials of a different political persuasion to choose relatively low levels of real purchases and transfers? One answer is to run a budget deficit that will leave behind a high ratio of public debt to GDP. The financing of this large public debt makes it politically difficult for the future government to select high levels of purchases and transfers. Arguably, this is what happened in the 1990s. In this sense, the Reagan–Bush strategic budget deficits may have worked.

BACK TO REALITY

"Unpleasant Monetarist Arithmetic"

Thomas Sargent and Neil Wallace (1981) analyzed effects from changes in the timing of the inflation tax—that is, the government's revenue from printing money. Their analysis applies especially to countries such as Argentina and Brazil, which have often relied heavily on the printing press for government revenue.

Suppose that the government cuts the current money growth rate in an attempt to reduce inflation. (See the discussion of money growth and inflation in Chapter 11.) Assume, however, that the government does not change its current or prospective real purchases and transfers. Assume also that the government does not change its current or prospective real taxes from the income tax or other forms of taxation. In this case, the decrease in current real revenue from printing money must correspond to an increase in the real public debt—that is, to a real budget deficit. As usual, the increased real public debt implies that the government's present value of future real revenue has to rise. However, if real taxes are fixed, the future real revenue has to come from future money creation. In other words, the government is changing the timing of the inflation tax, so that less is collected now and more later. The rise in future real revenue from money creation means that future money growth rates have to rise; that is, they have to be even higher than they were initially.

Because future money growth rates increase, today's reduction in money growth will be unsuccessful in the long run at reducing the inflation rate. The inflation rate will rise in the long run, along with the money growth rate. Moreover, if people anticipate the higher future inflation rate, the cut in the current money growth rate may not even reduce the inflation rate in the short run. The expectation of rising inflation rates tends to lower today's real quantity of money demanded and leads, thereby, to a rise in the inflation rate in the short run. Sargent and Wallace use this analysis to argue that a program to curb inflation by reducing money growth will be unsuccessful on its own. The program has to be part of a fiscal plan that cuts current or prospective real government expenditure or increases current or prospective real taxes.

[9] This theory was developed by Torsten Persson and Lars Svensson (1989) and by Alberto Alesina and Guido Tabellini (1990).

The Standard View of a Budget Deficit

Our equilibrium business-cycle model led to Ricardian equivalence, which implies that a deficit-finance tax cut does not affect real GDP and other macroeconomic variables. Many economists disagree with this proposition and predict, instead, that budget deficits raise real interest rates and reduce investment. Are there reasonable modifications of the equilibrium business-cycle model that generate these more standard predictions? We explore the necessary modifications in this section but do not settle the question of which theory of budget deficits is correct. In the end, the reader will have to weigh the theories and empirical evidence to decide which approach is most persuasive.

To bring out the main issues, we can simplify by returning to the assumption that taxes are lump sum. The key point in the equilibrium business-cycle model was that a deficit-financed tax cut had no income effects on households' choices. Since the income effect was nil, a deficit-financed cut in year 1's real taxes, T_1, did not change consumption, C_1. Consequently, households saved all of the increase in year 1's real disposable income. Since real GDP, Y_1, did not change (because the inputs of labor and capital services stayed the same), and since government purchases, G_1, were unchanged, gross investment, I_1, did not change.

The starting point for the standard analysis is that a deficit-financed tax cut makes households feel wealthier; hence, there is a positive income effect. We look first at how these income effects modify our conclusions about budget deficits. Then we consider arguments that economists have offered for why deficit-financed tax cuts make households feel wealthier.

Since a deficit-financed tax cut makes households feel wealthier, consumption, C_1, increases in the standard approach. Suppose, to keep things simple, that the quantity of labor supplied is fixed; that is, we ignore any income effects on labor supply. In this case, year 1's inputs of labor and capital services stay the same, and real GDP, Y_1, still does not change. Since C_1 increases, gross investment, I_1, has to decline for given government purchases, G_1. Thus, *a major new conclusion is that a budget deficit reduces investment.*

Another way to look at the results is that households respond to the increase in year 1's real disposable income partly with more consumption and partly with more saving. Most importantly, household saving no longer rises by the full amount of the tax cut. Thus, national saving falls, and this decrease corresponds to the reduction in gross investment, I_1.

The longer-run effects depend on whether the government pays off the extra real public debt in year 2 or, instead, allows the debt to remain permanently higher. For the first case, we assumed in one of our earlier scenarios that year 2's real taxes, T_2, rose by enough to pay off the extra public debt. In this case, the effects in year 2 reverse those in year 1; in particular, investment is high in year 2. After year 2, the level of real public debt equals its original value, and there are no long-term effects on the capital stock.

As an example of the second case, we assumed in another of our scenarios that real taxes in each year, T_t, rose only by enough to pay the added interest expense each year. In this case, the stock of real public debt is permanently higher, and the capital stock, K, is permanently lower than it otherwise would have been. Therefore, future levels of capital services, K, and, hence, real GDP, Y, will be lower than they would have been. Thus, additional real public debt contracts the economy in the long run.[10] These long-term negative effects on capital stock and real GDP are sometimes described as a **burden of the public debt**.[11]

In the standard approach, the smaller long-run stock of capital, K, implies a higher MPK (for a given labor input, L). This higher MPK leads to a higher real rental price, R/P, which implies a higher real interest rate, r. Therefore, a larger public debt leads, in the long run, to a higher r.

To reach the standard conclusions about the effects of budget deficits, we had to assume that a tax cut made households feel wealthier. We will now explore two of the more persuasive arguments for this assumption. The first one concerns the finiteness of life, and the second involves imperfections of credit markets.

Finite Lifetimes Suppose, again, that the government runs a budget deficit and cuts year 1's real taxes, T_1, by one unit. We know that the present value of the added future real taxes is one unit, the same as the

---

[10] We can also allow for a negative income effect on labor supply. That is, households work less if the tax cut makes them feel wealthier. In this case, labor input declines, and this change reinforces the tendency for real GDP to fall.

[11] For discussions, see the papers in the volume edited by James Ferguson (1964). Note especially the paper by Franco Modigliani, "Long-Run Implications of Alternative Fiscal Policies and the Burden of the National Debt."

© Jim Powell/Alamy

initial tax cut. Suppose, however, that some of the future taxes needed to finance the public debt show up in the distant future—after the death of the typical person alive in year 1. In that case, the present value of the future taxes paid during the lifetimes of people living in year 1 falls short of one unit. Hence, these people experience a reduction in the overall present value of their real taxes.

Why does a budget deficit make people feel wealthier when they have finite lifetimes? The decrease in the present value of real taxes for current generations coincides with an increase in the present value of real taxes for members of future generations. Individuals will be born with a liability for a portion of taxes to pay the interest and principal on the higher stock of real public debt. However, these people will not share in the benefits from the earlier tax cut. Present taxpayers would not feel wealthier if they counted fully the present value of the prospective taxes on descendants.

Budget deficits effectively enable members of current generations to die in a state of insolvency, where they leave debts—that is, public debts—for their descendants. Therefore, budget deficits make people feel wealthier if they view this governmental shifting of incomes across generations as desirable. However, most people already have opportunities for intergenerational transfers, which they have chosen to exercise to a desired extent. For example, parents make contributions to their children in the forms of educational investments, other expenses in the home, and bequests. In the other direction—and especially before the growth of Social Security programs—children provide support for their aged parents. To the extent that private transfers of this sort are operative, the government's budget deficit does not offer the typical person a new opportunity to extract funds from his or her descendants. Therefore, the predicted response to a rise in public debt would be to shift private transfers by the amount necessary to restore the balance of incomes across generations that was previously deemed optimal. In this case, even though people do not live forever, a budget deficit would not make the current generation of households feel wealthier.[12] Therefore, we return to the case where budget deficits have no income effects on households.

As a concrete example, assume that a married couple plans to leave a bequest with a present value of $50,000 to their children. Then suppose that the government runs a budget deficit, which cuts the present value of the couple's taxes by $1,000 but raises the present value of their children's taxes by $1,000. Our prediction is that the parents use the tax cut to raise the present value of their intergenerational transfers to the children to $51,000. The extra $1,000 provides the children with just enough resources to pay their higher taxes. Parents and children then end up with the same amounts of consumption that they enjoyed before the government ran its budget deficit.

One concern is that these kinds of calculations assume that each person possesses a lot of information and computational ability. More realistically, we should acknowledge that budget deficits make it harder for households to figure out exactly the future taxes that they or their descendants will bear. However, it is not obvious that this uncertainty would cause households systematically to underestimate the consequences of budget deficits for future taxes. In fact, the typical response to greater income uncertainty—caused, in this case, by uncertainty about future taxes—is to raise saving. This *precautionary saving* guards against a future

---

[12] For a discussion of the interplay between public debt and private intergenerational transfers, see Robert Barro (1974). A different view is that parents use bequests to control their children's behavior, rather than purely for altruistic reasons. For a discussion of this "strategic bequest theory," see B. Douglas Bernheim, Andrei Shleifer, and Lawrence Summers (1985).

that might be worse than anticipated. This behavior implies that private saving may increase by more than one unit when the budget deficit increases by one unit. That is, national saving might increase in response to a budget deficit—the opposite of the standard view.

Imperfect Credit Markets Thus far, we have assumed that the real interest rate, r, on private bonds equaled the rate on government bonds. Since households could issue private bonds, as well as hold them, our model assumes that households can borrow at the same real interest rate, r, as the government. In practice, credit markets are not this perfect. Many households that would like to borrow have to pay substantially higher real interest rates than the government. The borrowing rate is especially high if people borrow without collateral (such as a house or car).

When credit markets are imperfect, some households will calculate present values of future real taxes by using a real interest rate above the government's rate. We found before that a deficit-financed cut in year 1's real taxes by one unit led to an increase in the present value of future real taxes by one unit. However, we got this result when we calculated present values using the government's real interest rate, r. For households that face a higher real interest rate, the present value of the future real taxes will fall short of one unit.

To illustrate, suppose again that the government cuts year 1's real taxes by one unit and runs a budget deficit of one unit. Assume, as in one of our previous cases, that the government raises real taxes in year 2 by enough to pay the principal and interest on the one unit of new public debt. If the government's real interest rate is 2%, real taxes in year 2 rise by 1.02 units. To calculate the present value of these taxes, households would discount the 1.02 not by the government's interest rate but by the real interest rate paid by households. If households use a real interest rate of, say, 5%, the result is

present value of increase in year 2's real taxed
$$= 1.02/1.05$$
$$\approx 0.97$$

Thus, the overall change in the present value of real taxes paid by households is

change in present value of real taxes

$= $ *tax cut in year 1 + present value of increase in year 2's real taxes*

$= -1 + 0.97$

$= -0.03$

Hence, the tax cut by one unit in year 1 decreases the overall present value of real taxes by 0.03 units. The effect would be larger if the government delayed its repayment of public debt beyond year 2.

Suppose now that some households (or businesses) have good access to credit and therefore use a real interest rate equal to the government's rate to calculate present values of future real taxes. For these households, a deficit-financed tax cut still leaves unchanged the overall present value of real taxes. What happens if the economy consists partly of households that face the same real interest rate as the government and partly of households that face higher real interest rates? In this case, a deficit-financed tax cut leaves unchanged the present value of real taxes for the first group and reduces the present value for the second group. Thus, in the aggregate, the tax cut makes households feel wealthier.

Why does the imperfection of credit markets make households feel wealthier in the aggregate when the government runs a budget deficit? By running a deficit, the government effectively loans money to households—the loan is one unit if real taxes fall in year 1 by one unit. Then the government effectively collects on the loan in future years when it raises real taxes. The real interest rate charged on these loans is implicitly the rate paid by the government on its bonds. Households view this loan as a good deal if the government's real interest rate is less than the rate at which households can borrow directly. That is why the overall real present value of taxes falls for households that use a high real interest rate to calculate present values.

The implicit assumption is that the government's use of the tax system is an efficient way to lend money to some households. That is, the government is better than private institutions, such as banks, at lending funds (by cutting taxes) and then collecting on these loans in the future (by raising future taxes). If the government is really superior at this lending process, the economy will function more efficiently if the government provides more credit—that is, in our case, if the government runs a larger budget deficit. By operating more efficiently, we mean that the available resources will be better channeled toward higher-priority uses. These uses might be for year 1's consumption or investment by households that previously lacked good access to credit.

In the end, the imperfection of credit markets can provide a reason why budget deficits affect the economy. However, the results do not resemble those from the conventional analysis, in which a larger public debt leads in the long run to lower levels of the capital stock and real GDP. With imperfect credit markets, budget deficits matter if they improve the allocation of credit—that is, if they alleviate some of the imperfections in private credit markets. In other words, budget deficits matter, but in a desirable way. Therefore, we cannot use this reasoning to argue that budget deficits and public debt are burdens on the economy.

Social Security

Retirement benefits paid through social security programs are substantial in the United States and most other developed countries. Some economists, such as Martin Feldstein (1974), argue that these public pension programs reduce saving and investment. We can use our equilibrium business-cycle model to examine this idea.

The argument for an effect on saving applies when social security is not a **fully funded system**. In a funded setup, workers' payments accumulate in a trust fund, which later provides for retirement benefits. The alternative is a **pay-as-you-go system**, in which benefits to elderly persons are financed by taxes on the currently young. In this setup, people who are at or near retirement age when the program begins or expands receive benefits without paying a comparable present value of taxes. Correspondingly, members of later generations (including most readers of this book) pay taxes that exceed their expected benefits in present-value terms.

The U.S. system, like that of most countries, operates mainly on a pay-as-you-go basis.[13] Although the initial plan in 1935 envisioned an important role for the Social Security trust fund, the system evolved after 1939 primarily toward a pay-as-you-go operation. Retirees increasingly received benefits that exceeded their prior contributions in present-value terms.

Consider the economic effects of social security in a pay-as-you-go system. We focus here on income effects and neglect the types of substitution effects from taxes and transfers that we discussed in Chapter 13. The usual argument goes as follows. When a social security system starts or expands, elderly persons experience an increase in the present value of their social security benefits net of taxes. The increase in the present value of real transfers net of real taxes implies a positive income effect on the consumption of this group.

Young persons face higher taxes, offset by the prospect of higher retirement benefits. Thus, the present value of real transfers net of real taxes may fall for this group. However, the decline in this present value is not as large in magnitude as the increase for the currently old. Why? Because the currently young will be able to finance their future retirement benefits by levying taxes on members of yet unborn generations. Thus, the fall in consumption by the currently young tends to be smaller in size than the increase for the currently old. Hence, we predict an increase in current aggregate consumption. Or, to put it another way, total private saving declines. Since government saving does not change, national saving falls. The decline in national saving leads in the short run to a decrease in investment and, in the long run, to a reduced stock of capital.

This analysis of the economic effects of social security parallels our previous discussion of the conventional analysis of a budget deficit. In both cases, the increase in aggregate consumption arises only if people neglect the adverse effects on descendants. Specifically, an increase in the scale of a pay-as-you-go social security program means that the typical person's descendants will be born with a tax liability that exceeds their prospective retirement benefits in present-value terms. If persons currently alive took full account of these effects on descendants, the income effects from a social security program would be nil.

As in the case of a deficit-financed tax cut, more social security enables older persons to extract funds from their descendants. However, also as before, people value this change only if they give no transfers to their children and receive nothing from their children. Otherwise, people would respond to more social security by shifting private intergenerational transfers, rather than by consuming more. In the United States, for example, the growth of Social Security has strongly diminished the tendency of children to support their aged parents.

On an empirical level, there has been a great debate since the 1970s about the connection of social security to saving and investment. Martin Feldstein (1974) reported a dramatic negative effect of Social Security on capital accumulation in the United States. However, subsequent investigators argued that this conclusion was unwarranted.[14] The evidence for the United States and from a broad cross-section of countries does not yield convincing evidence that social security depresses saving and investment.

---

[13] Privatized arrangements, such as the main pension system in Chile, are fully funded but do not involve a government trust fund. For a discussion, see Jose Pinera (1996). The World Bank (1994) provides an overview of social security systems throughout the world.

[14] For a summary of the debate, see Louis Esposito (1978) and Dean Leimer and Selig Lesnoy (1982).

bythenumbers

Empirical Evidence on the Macroeconomic Effects of Budget Deficits

An important prediction from the conventional analysis is that real budget deficits raise consumption and reduce national saving and investment. Over time, the reduction in investment leads to a lower stock of capital. This smaller capital stock implies a higher marginal MPK, which leads to a higher real interest rate, r.

Many economists believe that budget deficits reduce national saving and investment and raise real interest rates. Nevertheless, this belief is not well supported by empirical evidence. For example, Charles Plosser (1982, 1987) and Paul Evans (1987a, 1987b) carried out statistical analyses of the effects of budget deficits on interest rates in the United States and other developed countries. Their main finding was that budget deficits had no significant effects on real or nominal interest rates.

Despite many empirical studies for the United States and other countries, it has proved difficult to reach definitive conclusions about the effects of budget deficits on consumption, national saving, and investment. One difficulty concerns the direction of causation. As discussed before, budget deficits often arise as responses to economic fluctuations and temporary government purchases, such as in wartime. Since consumption, national saving, and investment tend to vary as part of economic fluctuations and during wartime, it is hard to isolate the effects of budget deficits on these variables.

An empirical study by Chris Carroll and Lawrence Summers (1987) avoids some of these problems by comparing saving rates in the United States and Canada.

The private saving rates were similar in the two countries until the early 1970s but then diverged; for 1983–85 (the final years in their study), the Canadian rate was higher by six percentage points. After holding fixed the influences of macroeconomic variables and tax systems, Carroll and Summers concluded that budget deficits did not affect national saving. That is, the higher private saving rates in Canada were just offsets to higher budget deficits. This finding is consistent with Ricardian equivalence.

The Israeli experience from 1983 to 1987 comes close to providing a natural experiment for studying the interplay between budget deficits and saving. In 1983, the national saving rate of 13% corresponded to a private saving rate of 17% and a public saving rate of −4%. (This measure of public saving includes public investment.) In 1984, a dramatic rise in the budget deficit reduced the public saving rate to −11%. The interesting observation is that the private saving rate rose to 26%, so that the national saving rate changed little, actually rising from 13% to 15%. Then a stabilization program in 1985 eliminated the budget deficit, so that the public saving rate rose to 0% in 1985–86. The private saving rate declined dramatically at the same time—to 19% in 1985 and 14% in 1986. Therefore, the national saving rate remained relatively stable, going from 15% in 1984 to 18% in 1985 and 14% in 1986. Thus, the changes in private saving roughly offset the fluctuations in public saving and led to near stability in national saving. This experience therefore accords with Ricardian equivalence.

Open-Market Operations

The inclusion of public debt in the equilibrium business-cycle model allows us to analyze **open-market operations**. An open-market purchase occurs when the central bank, such as the Federal Reserve, buys bonds—typically government bonds—with newly created money. (In this context, money refers to high-powered money, which is the sum of currency in circulation and reserves held by depository institutions at the central bank.) An open-market sale occurs when the central bank sells bonds for money. These open-market operations are the main way that the Federal Reserve and most other central banks control the quantity of money. We want to know whether this realistic way of changing the quantity of money leads to results that differ from those of the unrealistic "helicopter drops" of money that we studied in Chapters 10 and 11.

Consider an open-market purchase, whereby the quantity of money, M, increases by \$1, and the stock of government bonds, B^g, decreases by \$1. Assume that no subsequent changes in the quantity of money occur; that is, we are considering a one-time increase in M.

Table 14.2 shows that an open-market purchase of government bonds amounts to a combination of two policies that we have already studied. Suppose, first, that the government prints an extra dollar of money, M, and uses the money to cut lump-sum taxes by \$1 or raise lump-sum transfers by \$1. For example, the government might have a helicopter drop of \$1 of money—the unrealistic story considered in Chapters 10 and 11. This change is labeled as policy 1 in the table. Suppose, next, that the government raises lump-sum taxes by \$1 or cuts lump-sum transfers by \$1 and uses the proceeds to pay off \$1 of government bonds, B^g. That is, the government raises taxes net of transfers and, thereby, runs a budget surplus. These changes are called policy 2 in the table. If we combine the two policies, we find that the quantity of money, M, rises by \$1, taxes and transfers are unchanged, and the quantity of government bonds, B^g, falls by \$1. Thus, we end up with an open-market purchase of government bonds, policy 3 in the table.

We know from Chapter 10 that policy 1—a one-time increase in the quantity of money, M, used to cut lump-sum taxes or raise lump-sum transfers—raises the price level, P, in the same proportion as the increase in M. We also know that there are no effects on real variables, including real GDP, Y, and the real interest rate, r. We know from our analysis in this chapter that policy 2—the budget surplus created by an increase in taxes net of transfers—does not affect the same group of real variables. The budget surplus also does not affect the price level, P, because the nominal quantity of money, M, does not change. Therefore, the overall effect from policy 3—the open-market purchase of government bonds—is that P rises in the same proportion as M, and the group of real variables does not change. That is, an open-market purchase has the same effects as the unrealistic helicopter drop of money considered in Chapters 10 and 11. We conclude that this unrealistic story gave us a reasonable and simple way to assess the linkages between money and the price level.

Table 14.2 *Open-Market Purchases of Government Bonds*

Change in Government Policy	Change in Money, M	Government Bonds, B^g	Change in Taxes, T
1. Print more money and reduce taxes.	+\$1	0	−\$1
2. Raise taxes and reduce public debt.	0	−\$1	+\$1
3. Open-market purchase of government bonds.	+\$1	−\$1	0

Note: Policy 3—an open-market purchase of government bonds—amounts to a combination of policies 1 and 2, which we have already studied.

Questions and Problems

A. Review questions

1. Under what circumstances is an open-market operation neutral?

2. Suppose that the government announces a reduction in next year's tax rate on labor income. What intertemporal-substitution effect will this announcement have on the current quantity of labor supplied?

3. Briefly compare the conventional view of government debt and the Ricardian view. What are the main differences in the assumptions and the conclusions?

B. Problems for discussion

4. **The income effect from a budget deficit**
Suppose that, in year 1, the government cuts current, lump-sum taxes and runs a budget deficit. Assume that the real public debt remains constant in future years. Also, no changes occur in government purchases of goods and services, G, or in real transfers, V. Analyze the income effect from the government's tax cut. How does this effect depend on the following:

a. finite lifetimes?

b. the existence of childless persons?

c. uncertainty about who will pay future taxes?

d. the possibility that the government will print more money in the future rather than levying future taxes?

e. the imperfection of private credit markets?

5. **Phased-in tax cuts**
President Reagan's initial proposal in 1981 for cutting U.S. individual income tax rates involved a 23% overall reduction in rates. The full cut was to be phased in over a three-year period ending in 1983. The plan also involved gradual reductions in government expenditure expressed as a ratio to GDP.

Consider an alternative plan that would have yielded the same present value of real tax revenue but that implemented the entire cut in tax rates in 1981. Assume that real government expenditure is the same as under Reagan's plan. Compare this plan with Reagan's with respect to the effects on labor and real GDP over the period 1981–83.

Similarly, the Bush tax cut of 2001 scheduled decreases in marginal income tax rates from 2001 to 2006. The 2003 law advanced the scheduled tax-rate cuts to 2003. How does your analysis of the Reagan tax plan apply to the 2001 and 2003 tax cuts?

6. **Social security and the capital stock**
Suppose that the government introduces a new Social Security program, which will make payments to covered persons when they retire.

a. What long-run effects do you predict on the capital stock, K?

b. How does your answer to question a depend on whether the Social Security program is fully funded or pay-as-you-go? (In a funded scheme, workers pay into a trust fund, which is then used to pay benefits. A pay-as-you-go system taxes current workers to pay benefits for current retirees.)

CHAPTER 15

Alan Schein Photography/Corbis

Money and Business Cycles I: The Price-Misperceptions Model

Thus far, our macroeconomic model has stressed real factors, such as shifts in technology, as sources of business fluctuations. The government can affect real variables by changing its purchases of goods and services and its tax rates, but there is little evidence that these fiscal actions have been major sources of economic fluctuations in the United States. Many economists believe that **monetary shocks**—created mainly by the monetary authority—have been a principal cause of these fluctuations in the U.S. and other economies. In this chapter, we begin our analysis of monetary effects by studying the price-misperceptions model.

Effects of Money in the Equilibrium Business-Cycle Model

e should start by recalling our results on the interactions between nominal and real variables in the equilibrium business-cycle model. One result from Chapter 10 is that a one-time change in the nominal quantity of money, M—interpreted in our model as currency—is neutral. This change leads to responses in the same proportion of nominal variables, such as the price level, P, and the nominal wage rate, w. Real variables, including real GDP, Y, employment, L, and the real interest rate, r, do not change.

We found in Chapter 11 that persisting changes in the nominal quantity of money affect the inflation rate, π, and thereby the nominal interest rate, i. A change in i affects the real quantity of money demanded, L(Y, i),

and thereby influences the quantity of real money, M/P. These changes have real effects, because increases in π and i induce people to spend more time and other resources to economize on real money holdings, M/P. Higher inflation leads to more resources expended on transaction costs. If we broadened the model to include costs of changing prices, we would find that higher inflation raises these costs as well. However, transactions costs and costs of changing prices are not important enough in normal times to have significant effects on real GDP.

Although money is neutral, at least as an approximation, we were able to use the model in Chapter 10 to derive implications for the empirical association between real and nominal variables. In our equilibrium business-cycle model, technology shocks affect real GDP, Y, and the nominal interest rate, i, and thereby influence the real quantity of money demanded, L(Y, i). Typically, this real quantity demanded will be high in booms and low in recessions (because the effect from Y dominates that from i). If the nominal quantity of money, M, does not respond to changes in the real quantity demanded, the price level, P, will move in the direction opposite to the change in $L(Y, i)$. Therefore, the model predicts that P would be countercyclical—low in booms and high in recessions. This prediction accords with U.S. data from 1954 to 2006. (See Figure 10.4 in Chapter 10.)

If the monetary authority wants to stabilize the price level, P, it should adjust the nominal quantity of money, M, to balance the changes in the real quantity demanded, $L(Y, i)$. In this case, M will be procyclical. The U.S. data from 1954 to 2006 show a weak procyclical pattern in currency. However, the procyclical pattern is stronger for broader monetary aggregates, such as M1 and M2.

The Price-Misperceptions Model

Empirical evidence suggests that money is not as neutral as predicted by our equilibrium business-cycle model. The **price-misperceptions model** provides a possible explanation for the non-neutrality of money.[1] In this model, households sometimes misinterpret changes in nominal prices and wage rates as changes in relative prices and real wage rates. Therefore, monetary shocks—which affect nominal prices and wage rates—end up affecting real variables, such as real GDP and employment.

A Model with Non-Neutral Effects of Money

The model retains most of the features of our equilibrium business-cycle model. We still maintain the microeconomic foundations that underlie the supply and demand functions for labor and capital services. We continue to assume that prices—prices of goods, wage rates, and rental prices—adjust rapidly to clear markets. However, the important difference from before is that households have *incomplete current information* about prices in the economy. For example, a worker may know his or her current nominal wage rate and the prices of goods purchased recently. But the worker has less accurate information about wage rates available on other jobs, prices of goods encountered in the distant past or not at all, and so on.

The price-misperceptions model usually focuses on the labor market. We analyzed this market in Figure 8.15 in Chapter 8; Figure 15.1 reproduces the main parts of this analysis. Recall that an increase in the real wage rate, w/P, lowers the quantity of labor demanded, L^d. This demand comes from producers (households that own and run businesses) who pay the nominal wage rate, w, to workers and receive the price level, P, on sales of goods.

An increase in the real wage rate, w/P, makes work more attractive to households. Therefore, Figure 15.1 shows that a rise in w/P raises the quantity of labor supplied, L^s. More precisely, we found in Chapter 8

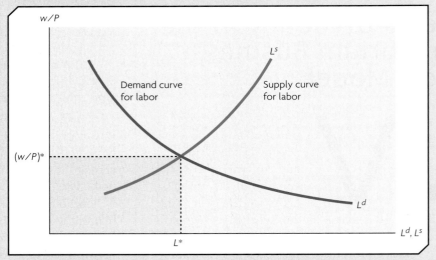

Figure 15.1 *Clearing of the Labor Market*

This figure reproduces our analysis of the labor market from Figure 8.15 in Chapter 8. A reduction in the real wage rate, w/P, raises the quantity of labor demanded, L^d. An increase in w/P raises the quantity of labor supplied, L^s. The market clears when the real wage rate is $(w/P)^*$ on the vertical axis and the quantity of labor is L^* on the horizontal axis.

[1] This model originated from Milton Friedman (1968c) and Edmund Phelps (1970). Later contributions were made by Robert Lucas—see his papers collected in Lucas (1981). For a survey of the main research through the 1970s, see Ben McCallum (1979).

that the slope of the labor supply curve depends on the balancing between a substitution effect and an income effect. The substitution effect from a higher w/P motivates less leisure time—hence, more work—and more consumption. The income effect from a higher w/P motivates more leisure time—hence, less work—and more consumption. Thus, the labor supply curve has a positive slope, as shown in Figure 15.1, if the substitution effect dominates the income effect.

Now we will allow for incomplete current information about prices across the economy. Consider the effect of the real wage rate, w/P, on the quantity of labor demanded, L^d. The demanders of labor are the employers. We can reasonably assume that an employer has accurate current information about the nominal wage rate, w, paid to his or her employees. With respect to the price level, P, the price that matters is the one attached to the employer's own product. That is, the employer compares the nominal cost of labor, given by w, with the nominal amount, P, received on sales of the employer's good or service.[2] We can reasonably assume that the employer has accurate current information about prices of his or her own products. Therefore, the real wage rate that determines the quantity of labor demanded, L^d, is the actual value, w/P. Hence, we do not have to modify the labor-demand curve drawn in Figure 15.1.

Consider now the real wage rate that matters for labor supply, L^s. The suppliers of labor are the workers. For a worker, the relevant nominal wage rate, w, is the amount received from the employer. We can again reasonably assume that a worker has accurate current information about his or her own w. However, for the price level, P, the relevant variable is the price of a market basket of goods. These goods will be purchased from many locations at various times. Therefore, a worker will typically lack good current information about some of these prices. To bring in this effect, we denote by P^e the price that a worker expects to pay for a market basket of goods. The real wage rate that determines the quantity of labor supplied, L^s, is the ratio of w to this expected price—that is, w/P^e.

Consider again the effects from an increase in the nominal quantity of money, M. In Chapter 10, we found that the nominal wage rate, w, and the price level, P, rose in the same proportion as the increase in M. In particular, in Figure 15.1, an increase in M does not change the market-clearing real wage rate, $(w/P)^*$,

and the market-clearing quantity of labor input, L^*. The constancy of $(w/P)^*$ and L^* accords with the result from Chapter 10 that a change in M is neutral; that is, does not affect any real variables.

Consider, however, what happens when workers do not understand that an increase in the nominal wage rate, w, stems from a monetary expansion that inflates all nominal values, including the price level, P. Each worker may think instead that the rise in w constitutes an increase in his or her real wage rate, w/P. The **perceived real wage rate** is the ratio of w to the expected price level, P^e. This ratio, w/P^e, rises if the expected price level, P^e, increases proportionately by less than w. If w/P^e increases, the worker increases the quantity of labor supplied, L^s.

As an example, suppose that the nominal wage rate, w, is initially \$10 per hour, and the price level is $P = 1$. Thus, the real wage rate, w/P, is initially 10 units of goods per hour worked. Assume that w doubles to \$20 per hour. As a worker, how would you respond to this change? If P is still 1, w/P has gone up to 20 units of goods per hour worked, and it is attractive to work more hours. However, if P also doubles, so that $P = 2$, the real wage rate, w/P, is still 10 units of goods per hour worked. In this case, you have no reason to work more.

If the worker does not immediately observe the actual price level, P, the assessment of the higher nominal wage rate, w, depends on the change in the expected price level, P^e. If P^e starts at 1 and then rises to less than 2, the perceived real wage rate, w/P^e, goes up, and the worker will supply more labor. If P^e rises to 2—that is, if the worker regards the higher w as just a sign of general inflation—w/P^e does not change, and labor supply stays the same.

To analyze the new effect graphically, we can use the revised version of Figure 15.1 shown in Figure 15.2. The labor demand curve, L^d, is the same as before, because employers determine their quantity of labor demanded in accordance with the actual real wage rate, w/P.

The labor supply curves in Figure 15.2 are different from before, because the perceived real wage rate, w/P^e, determines the quantity of labor supplied. To understand the new labor supply curves, we can use the condition.

(15.1) $\qquad w/P^e = (w/P) \bullet (P/P^e)$

This equation implies that, for a given actual real wage rate, w/P, an increase in P/P^e raises the perceived real wage rate, w/P^e. In other words, if workers are

<hr>

[2] The employer cares also about the prices of other inputs to production, including the nominal rental price, **R**, paid for capital services. In a more general model, another important input price would be for energy. We are assuming that the employer knows the values of all these input prices.

underestimating the price level—so that $P^e < P$—they must be overestimating their real wage rate—that is, $w/P^e < w/P$.

To see how price misperceptions affect the labor market, assume that, initially, $P^e = P$ holds, so that $w/P^e = w/P$. The first labor supply curve, denoted by L^s and shown in green in Figure 15.2, applies in this situation. As usual, along this curve, an increase in w/P raises the quantity of labor supplied, L^s.

Suppose, as in Chapter 10, that an increase in the nominal quantity of money, M, raises the price level, P. If the rise in P is only partly perceived by households, P^e increases proportionately by less than P. Consequently, P/P^e goes up, and equation (15.1) implies that w/P^e rises for a given w/P. Therefore, at any given w/P, the quantity of labor supplied is greater than before. We show this result in Figure 15.2 with the new labor supply curve, denoted by $(L^s)'$ and shown in red. This curve lies to the right of the original one, L^s. *Because of price misperceptions, the increase in P raises the quantity of labor supplied at a given w/P.*[3]

In the initial situation, where $P = P^e$, the labor market clears in Figure 15.2 at the real wage rate $(w/P)^*$ and the quantity of labor input L^*. With an unperceived rise

in the price level, the market clears at the lower real wage rate, $[(w/P)^*]'$, and the higher labor input, $(L^*)'$. Thus, an increase in the nominal quantity of money, M, that creates an unperceived rise in the price level affects the real economy and is, therefore, non-neutral. Specifically, an increase in M raises the quantity of labor input, L.

The rise in labor input, L, will lead to an expansion of production. That is, real GDP, Y, increases in accordance with the production function:

(15.2) $$Y = A \bullet F(\kappa K, L)$$

where κK is the quantity of capital services (the product of the capital utilization rate, κ, and the stock of capital, K). For given κK, the rise in L implies an increase in Y.

As usual, we assume that the quantity of capital, K, is fixed in the short run. However, in the price-misperceptions model, the increase in money, M, tends to raise the capital utilization rate, κ. The rise in labor input, L, tends to increase the marginal product of capital services, MPK. A higher MPK causes an increase in the demand for capital services. As in Chapter 9, this increase in demand raises the real rental price, R/P, and the quantity of capital services, κK (by raising κ). This expansion of κK reinforces the increase of real GDP, Y, in equation (15.2).

Money Is Neutral in the Long Run

The difference between the long run and the short run in the price-misperceptions model is that the expected price level, P^e, adjusts toward the actual price level, P, in the long run. An increase in the nominal quantity of money, M, raised labor input, L, in the short run in

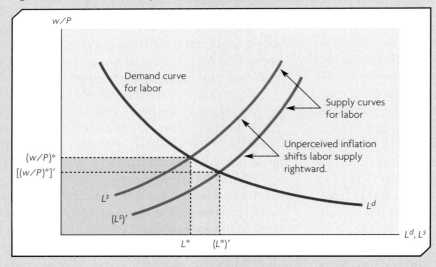

Figure 15.2 *Effect of Unperceived Inflation on the Labor Market*

Demand curve for labor

Supply curves for labor

Unperceived inflation shifts labor supply rightward.

$(w/P)^*$

$[(w/P)^*]'$

L^s

$(L^s)'$

L^d

L^d, L^s

L^* $(L^*)'$

w/P

A rise in P/P^e for suppliers of labor (employees) raises w/P^e for a given w/P. Therefore, the labor supply curve shifts rightward, from L^s to $(L^s)'$. We conclude that unperceived inflation raises labor input—from L^* to $(L^*)'$—and lowers the real wage rate—from $(w/P)^*$ to $[(w/P)^*]'$.

[3] An increase in the nominal quantity of money, M, might also raise the nominal wage rate, w, compared to the nominal wage rate, w^e, that workers expect to receive in future years. This effect arises if workers think that the change in w is temporary. An increase in w/w^e increases current labor supply, L^s, through an intertemporal-substitution effect. That is, workers work a lot when w is perceived to be temporarily high and work relatively little when w is perceived to be unusually low. This intertemporal-substitution effect reinforces the result that an increase in M leads to a higher quantity of labor supplied.

Figure 15.2; P^e rose by less than P, and, therefore, the labor supply curve shifted to the right. However, over time, households learn that they have underestimated the rise in P, and P^e increases accordingly. The rise in P^e reverses the shift in the labor supply curve shown in the figure. That is, w/P^e now decreases for a given w/P, and the labor supply curve shifts back to the left.

Eventually, when P^e rises as much as P, the labor supply curve in Figure 15.2 returns to its initial position, denoted by L^s and shown in green. Therefore, the real wage rate, w/P, and the quantity of labor input, L, return to their initial values, $(w/P)^*$ and L^*. We conclude that the effects of an increase in the nominal quantity of money, M, on these real variables are only temporary. In the long run, an increase in M leaves the real variables unchanged. In this situation, the price level, P, and the nominal wage rate, w, rise by the same proportion as the increase in M. We conclude that, in the long run, money is neutral, just as in Chapter 10.

Only Unperceived Inflation Affects Real Variables

One important conclusion from the price-misperceptions model is that only unperceived changes in the price level, P, affect labor input, L, and real GDP, Y. The nonneutral effects that we found in the short run depended on the increase in the ratio of actual to expected prices, P/P^e. This change made workers believe that the real wage rate, perceived to be w/P^e, had risen and led, accordingly, to the rightward shift in the labor supply curve shown in Figure 15.2.

Suppose, instead, that an increase in the nominal quantity of money, M, raises expected prices, P^e, in the short run by the same amount as actual prices, P. In this case, the monetary change will be neutral, just as we found for the long run. The reason is that, when $P^e = P$, workers understand that the increase in their nominal wage rate, w, is due to a general increase in the nominal quantity of money, M, and the price level, P, and not to a rise in their real wage rate, w/P.

Consider, as an example, the long-run inflation analyzed in Chapter 11. In this situation, the price level, P, rises over time. However, the anticipated part of this inflation—the part considered in Chapter 11—represents movements in P^e along with P. Therefore, in the price-misperceptions model, this anticipated inflation will not affect labor input, L, and real GDP, Y.

We get an analogous result for systematic monetary policy. Suppose that the monetary authority attempts to moderate economic fluctuations by printing a lot of money in response to recessions. In the price-misperceptions model, this policy will have the intended real effects only if the actual price level, P, rises systematically above its expected level, P^e, when the economy is weak. This kind of policy is difficult to engineer—at times of recession, the monetary authority would have to fool people regularly into thinking that the price level, P, is lower than it actually is. That is, the expectation, P^e, would have to lag systematically behind the change in P. This systematic deception is inconsistent with the notion of rational expectations introduced in Chapter 11.[4] If people form price-level expectations, P^e, rationally, these expectations will take into account easily recognizable patterns, such as a tendency for the nominal quantity of money, M, and the price level, P, to rise in response to recessions. This adjustment of expectations tends to eliminate the real effects of systematic monetary policy.[5] That is, we return to a situation in which changes in the nominal quantity of money, M, are neutral, even in the short run.

Aside from the difficulty in systematically fooling workers, there is the question of why the monetary authority would want to deceive workers in this manner. One possibility is that central bankers have unusual preferences; that is, they seek outcomes that differ from those that would be voluntarily chosen by well-informed households. However, we do not have to rely on central bankers having odd preferences. Under some circumstances, the economy might actually perform better if everyone could be tricked into working and producing more. To get this result, we have to assume that labor input, L, and, hence, real GDP, Y, are typically too low from a social perspective. Distortions in the economy, such as those from income taxation and welfare programs, can lead to this outcome. Under these conditions, the monetary authority might make everyone better off if it can fool all workers and producers into raising L and Y. Thus, the monetary authority may be motivated to raise P above P^e even if the authority has normal preferences. However, even given this basis for

---

[4] Abraham Lincoln's perspective may be relevant: "You may fool all of the people some of the time; you can even fool some of the people all of the time; but you cannot fool all of the people all of the time" (quoted in Alexander McClure, 1901, p. 124). Unfortunately, there is controversy about whether Lincoln actually made this famous statement.

[5] This finding is called the **irrelevance result for systematic monetary policy**. For the initial derivation, see Thomas Sargent and Neil Wallace (1975). Ben McCallum (1979) has an interesting discussion.

creating unperceived increases in the price level, there remains the issue of whether this deception is feasible as an ongoing policy.

In contrast to systematic policy, the monetary authority can surely create unperceived changes in the price level, P, by behaving erratically. By randomly printing lots of money, M, at some times and little money at other times, the monetary authority could generate volatility in the price level, P. In this circumstance, the ratio of actual to expected prices, P/P^e, would likely fluctuate a great deal. Sometimes P would be higher than P^e, and sometimes P would be lower than P^e. This volatility would cause fluctuations in labor input, L, and real GDP, Y. Therefore, an erratic monetary policy would have real effects and, hence, not be neutral. However, this kind of "monetary policy" would not tend to improve the workings of the economy.

Robert Lucas (1973) argued that the extent of the response to a monetary shock—that is, a change in the nominal quantity of money, M—depends on whether a country's monetary policy has a history of stability or volatility. In an unstable monetary setting, such as in many Latin American countries, households tend to view observed movements in nominal wage rates and prices, w and P, as reflections of general inflation. Consequently, monetary expansions do not usually fool workers into thinking that their real wage rate, w/P, has increased. Hence, in a Latin American type environment, monetary shocks tend to have small effects on labor input, L, and real GDP, Y.

In contrast, in a stable monetary setting—such as the United States and many other advanced economies since the mid 1980s—households are more likely to think that observed movements in nominal wage rates and prices, w and P, represent variations in real wage rates and relative prices. Consequently, monetary shocks tend to have significant effects on labor input, L, and real GDP, Y. A summary statement of the **Lucas hypothesis on monetary shocks** is that *the real effect of a given size monetary shock is larger, the more stable the underlying monetary environment.*

The Lucas hypothesis receives empirical support from cross-country studies for the post–World War II period.[6] First, it turns out that monetary shocks (measured by unanticipated changes in monetary aggregates) have a positive relation to real GDP in many countries. Second, as the theory predicts, the strength of this relation diminishes as a country's money growth rate and inflation rate become less predictable. Countries, such as the United States, that have reasonably stable money growth and inflation turn out to be the ones in which monetary shocks have a significantly positive relation to real GDP. For countries such as Argentina and Brazil, where money growth and inflation have fluctuated violently, there is virtually no connection between monetary shocks and real GDP.

Predictions for Economic Fluctuations

In our equilibrium business-cycle model, we imagined that economic fluctuations resulted from shocks to the technology level, A. Then we worked out the predicted cyclical patterns for a number of macroeconomic variables. The first row of Table 15.1 summarizes these predictions for five variables: the nominal quantity of money, M; the price level, P; the quantity of labor input, L; the real wage rate, w/P; and the average product of labor, Y/L. Recall that M is procyclical because of endogenous changes in the nominal quantity of money, as worked out in Chapter 10. The price level, P, is countercyclical for given M, as also discussed in Chapter 10. The procyclical patterns for L, w/P, and Y/L come from Chapters 8 and 9. The predicted patterns for these five variables accord with empirical observations, summarized in line 3 of Table 15.1. However, in the data, M and Y/L are only weakly procyclical.

Now we can use the price-misperceptions model to get alternative predictions of cyclical patterns for macroeconomic variables. In this analysis, we imagine that economic fluctuations result from monetary shocks—that is, exogenous variations in the nominal quantity of money, M.

In the price-misperceptions model, an increase in the nominal quantity of money, M, raises the price level, P, and the nominal wage rate, w. The increase in the ratio of P to the expected price level, P^e, shifts the labor supply curve rightward, as in Figure 15.2. This shift leads to a rise in labor input, L, and a decline in the real wage rate, w/P. The increase in L tends to raise the MPK. The increase in MPK increases the input of capital services, κK, by raising the capital-utilization rate, κ.

The production function is still given by

(15.2) $$Y = A \cdot F(\kappa K, L)$$

---

[6] See Robert Lucas (1973), Roger Kormendi and Phillip Meguire (1984), and Cliff Attfield and Nigel Duck (1983).

Table 15.1 *Cyclical Patterns of Macroeconomic Variables in Two Models*

	Nominal Quantity of Money, M	Price Level, P	Labor Input, L	Real Wage Rate, w/P	Average Product of Labor, Y/L
1. Equilibrium business-cycle model	procyclical	counter-cyclical	procyclical	procyclical	procyclical
2. Price-misperceptions model	procyclical	procyclical	procyclical	counter-cyclical	counter-cyclical
3. Empirical observations	procyclical (weak)	counter-cyclical	procyclical	procyclical	procyclical (weak)

Note: The cells show the cyclical pattern of five macroeconomic variables in three settings. First is the equilibrium business-cycle model with economic fluctuations driven by shocks to the technology level, A (described in Chapters 8–10). Second is the price-misperceptions model from this chapter, with economic fluctuations driven by shocks to the nominal quantity of money, M. Third is the empirical pattern from U.S. data.

The technology level, A, has not changed. Therefore, the rises in L and κK imply an increase in real GDP, Y. For a given production function and given κK, the rise in L encounters diminishing marginal product of labor, MPL. The average product of labor, Y/L, also tends to decline as L rises. Hence, we predict that a fall in Y/L accompanies the rise in Y.[7]

The second row of Table 15.1 summarizes the predictions from the price-misperceptions model for the five macroeconomic variables. The procyclical patterns for the nominal quantity of money, M, and labor input, L, are the same as those from the equilibrium business-cycle model and also conform to the data. Differences from the equilibrium business-cycle model show up for the price level, P, the real wage rate, w/P, and the average product of labor, Y/L. The price-misperceptions model predicts, counterfactually, that P will be procyclical, whereas w/P and Y/L will be countercyclical. These discrepancies suggest that monetary shocks, working through the channels isolated in the price-misperceptions model, cannot be the major source of economic fluctuations.

We can do better with a richer model that allows for both kinds of shocks—one to the technology level, A, and another to the nominal quantity of money, M. In this setting, the price level, P, would be countercyclical; and the real wage rate, w/P, and the average product of labor, Y/L, would be procyclical if the variations in A are usually the dominant source of economic fluctuations. However, monetary shocks also occur. Most importantly, this composite model predicts non-neutrality of money.

From the data, we know that nominal money, M, is weakly procyclical. (The procyclical pattern is more pronounced for broad monetary aggregates, such as M1 and M2, than for narrow aggregates, such as currency and the monetary base.) The equilibrium business-cycle model and the price-misperceptions model provide alternative explanations of this pattern. The equilibrium business-cycle model says that M is procyclical because the central bank wants to stabilize the price level, P. This objective makes M move *endogenously* in the same direction as the real quantity of money demanded, $L(Y, i)$, which tends to move in the same direction as real GDP, Y. The price-misperceptions model says that an exogenous, unanticipated increase in M raises P more than expected and, thereby, raises real GDP, Y.

Although the nominal quantity of money, M, is procyclical in both models, the directions of causation are opposite. In the equilibrium business-cycle model, the causation runs from real GDP, Y, to M. In other words, money is endogenous. In the price-misperceptions model, the causation runs from exogenous (and unanticipated) changes in M to Y. Thus, to sort out the two stories, we have to observe something more than a positive correlation between the cyclical parts of nominal

---

[7] The increase in κK offsets the decline in the MPL. However, the real wage rate, w/P, has to fall overall to raise the quantity of labor demanded. Therefore, the MPL—which equals w/P in equilibrium—has to decline overall. Typically, a lower average product of labor, Y/L, accompanies a fall in the MPL.

money and real GDP. This pattern accords with both models and, therefore, does not distinguish between them.

Empirical Evidence on the Real Effects of Monetary Shocks

Friedman and Schwartz's *Monetary History*   The classic study of the interplay between money and output is Milton Friedman and Anna J. Schwartz's (1963) analysis of U.S. monetary policy from 1867 to 1960. Their research considered, first, the historical sources of changes in the nominal quantity of money and, second, the interactions of these changes with variations in economic activity. Their main conclusions were (p. 676): "Throughout the near-century examined in detail we have found that:

1. Changes in the behavior of the money stock have been closely associated with changes in economic activity, money income, and prices.

2. The interrelation between monetary and economic change has been highly stable.

3. Monetary changes have often had an independent origin; they have not been simply a reflection of changes in economic activity."

The first two points are essentially a statement that nominal monetary aggregates are procyclical. We have also found this property, although the relation is not as strong or stable as Friedman and Schwartz suggested. The most important point, however, is their third one—the statement that the procyclical pattern for monetary aggregates cannot be explained entirely by endogenous money. Friedman and Schwartz made their third point by isolating historical episodes in which changes in the nominal quantity of money, M, resulted from largely exogenous factors. The factors included gold discoveries (important for monetary policy especially before 1914, when the United States was on the gold standard), changes in the structure of the Federal Reserve System and in commercial banking, and shifts in the leadership of the Federal Reserve. Overall, Friedman and Schwartz make a convincing case that exogenous changes in M have sometimes exerted significant influences on real economic activity. These findings support the price-misperceptions model.

Unanticipated Money Growth   In studies done during the late 1970s (summarized in Barro [1981]), I attempted to isolate the effects of monetary shocks on real economic activity by constructing measures of **unanticipated money growth**. The first step was to estimate anticipated money growth, which I did by using a set of explanatory values to determine the money growth rate that could have been predicted from historical patterns (using M1 as the definition of money). The variables I used included a measure of federal spending and an indicator of the business cycle (based on the unemployment rate). I then determined unanticipated money growth by taking the difference between the actual and anticipated values. I found that an increase in unanticipated money growth raised real GDP over periods of a year or more. In a related study, Ben Broadbent (1996) observed that the positive link between unanticipated money growth and real GDP worked through surprise movements in the price level, P. This channel is the one isolated in the price-misperceptions model.

The results for unanticipated money growth are analogous to our finding in Chapter 10 that the cyclical parts of nominal monetary aggregates are at least weakly procyclical. That is, unanticipated money growth is similar to the cyclical part of money growth. The problem is that a positive relation of unanticipated money growth or the cyclical part of money to real GDP does not convincingly isolate causation from nominal money, M, to real GDP, Y. Even if the changes in M precede the changes in Y—as some economists have found—we cannot be sure about the direction of causation. The monetary authority might be adjusting M in response to anticipated future changes in Y; that is, the movements in money may still be endogenous.

Romer and Romer on Federal Reserve Policy
In ongoing research inspired by the historical analysis of Friedman and Schwartz (1963), Christina Romer and David Romer (2003) attempt to isolate exogenous monetary shocks. They measure these shocks by looking at changes during meetings of the Federal Reserve's Federal Open Market Committee (FOMC) in the target for the federal funds rate. This rate is the overnight nominal interest rate, i, which the Fed monitors closely. In the short run, an increase in the federal funds rate goes along with a monetary contraction. This contraction typically shows up as reduced growth rates of monetary aggregates, such as currency, the monetary base, and M1.

Romer and Romer estimated the relationship of changes in the Fed's target for the federal funds rate to the Fed's forecasts of inflation and real GDP. Then they measured monetary shocks as the difference between the actual change in the funds rate target and the one predicted from their estimated relationship. They found that unanticipated increases in the federal funds rate tended to reduce real GDP, whereas unanticipated decreases tended to raise real GDP.

One important example of monetary contraction discussed by Romer and Romer took place during the tenure of Federal Reserve Chairman Paul Volcker, who became chair in 1979. In the fourth quarter of 1980 and the first quarter of 1981, the inflation rate calculated from the GDP deflator rose to over 10%. In spring 1981, Volcker committed to using monetary contraction to end inflation. As a consequence, the federal funds rate soared from the already high value of 15% in March to 20% in May. The growth rates of monetary aggregates fell sharply—the growth rate of M1 declined from around 10% to zero, and the growth rates of currency and the monetary base fell from 6–8% to 3–4%. Many economists believe that this shift to a contractionary monetary policy explains part of the recession in 1982–83. The shift was also successful in curbing inflation—the growth rate of the GDP deflator fell from 10% in the first quarter of 1981 to around 3% by the first quarter of 1983.

There are questions about how well the Volcker disinflation, as it is called, fits with the price-misperceptions model. If Volcker's commitment in 1981 to using monetary contraction was immediately fully credible and understood, the resulting cutbacks in money growth

and inflation would have been anticipated—at least as of 1981. Then the model would not explain the recession of 1982–83. However, to the extent that the program was either not immediately fully credible or not fully understood, the model might explain a decline in real GDP.

More broadly, the shortcoming of the Romer and Romer analysis is that it does not clearly isolate the exogenous parts of monetary policy. As with my constructs of unanticipated money growth, the new measures—essentially unanticipated movements in the federal funds rate—might pick up responses of monetary policy to past or anticipated future variations in real economic variables. Thus, the correlation of the constructed monetary policy shocks with real GDP may still reflect reverse effects of real economic activity on the monetary variables.

A Brief Overview
At this point, the empirical evidence suggests that positive monetary shocks tend to expand the real economy, whereas negative monetary shocks tend to contract the real economy. However, the evidence is not 100% conclusive, and we surely lack reliable estimates of the strength of this relationship.

Real Shocks

We now consider how price misperceptions affect our previous analysis of a shock to the technology level, A—the main disturbance assumed in the equilibrium business-cycle model. We know from Chapters 8 through 10 that an increase in A raises real GDP, Y, but lowers the price level, P, at least if the monetary authority holds constant the nominal quantity of money, M. Conversely, a decrease in A reduces Y and increases P.

In the equilibrium business-cycle model, we assumed that households had accurate current information about the price level, P. We now assume, as in the price-misperceptions model, that the expected price level, P^e, lags behind the actual price level, P. For example, in a boom, when P declines, P^e decreases by less than P. Hence, P/P^e falls—that is, workers overestimate P during a boom. This overestimate of P means that workers underestimate their real wage rate, w/P: The perceived real wage rate, w/P^e, falls below w/P. It follows that the quantity of labor supplied, L^s, decreases for a given w/P.

The effect of this price misperception on the L^s curve is analogous to that shown in Figure 15.2, except in the opposite direction. At any real wage rate, w/P, the quantity of labor supplied is now lower. We show this

BACK TO REALITY

Incomplete Information About Prices:
Is It Significant?

A key assumption in the price-misperceptions model is that households do not observe immediately the economy-wide price level, P. If households always knew the current P —perhaps because they looked regularly at a useful index, such as the CPI—they would not get confused about movements in real wage rates. In particular, the perceived price level, P^e, would stay close to the actual value, P. Therefore, the perceived real wage rate, w/P^e, would stay close to the actual value, w/P. But then the model predicts that monetary shocks would be close to neutral.

Households can, in fact, observe quickly an index of consumer prices—with a one-month lag for the CPI. Of course, most people do not bother to monitor this index on a regular basis. But, presumably, they ignore this information because, in stable economies, it is not very important to keep a close watch on the general price level.

One reason that available price indexes may not be so helpful is that each household cares about a different

market basket of goods, each of which differs from the basket used to construct the indexes. Then, in order to keep well informed about prices, households would have to take detailed samples from a variety of locations. Since this process is costly, households would sometimes make errors in their interpretations of the prices and wage rates that they see. However, this argument cannot explain why variations in the general price level would be important enough to generate major errors in labor supply decisions. After all, a relatively small investment—looking at published price indexes—would be sufficient to eliminate the mistakes caused by general inflations of nominal prices and wage rates.

The bottom line is that ignorance about the general price level may account for small and short-lived confusions about relative prices and real wage rates. However, it is unlikely that large and long-lasting confusions would arise. The costs of being misinformed—and, therefore, making incorrect decisions about labor supply—seem excessive relative to the costs of gathering the necessary information on the general price level.

This viewpoint suggests that monetary shocks in the context of the price-misperceptions model can account for only a small part of observed economic fluctuations. This conclusion reinforces our findings about the cyclical properties of some key macroeconomic variables, notably the price level, P, and the real wage rate, w/P. If monetary shocks and price-perception errors were of major importance, we would predict that P would be procyclical and w/P would be countercyclical. However, as noted in Table 15.1, the data show that P is countercyclical and w/P is procyclical.

© Susan Van Etten/Photo Edit

shift to L^s in Figure 15.3. The original curve, in green, is labeled $L^s(A)$ where A is the initial technology level. The new curve, in brown, is labeled $L^s(A')$, where A' is the higher technology level. The increase in the technology level from A to A' reduces the price level, P, and, therefore, shifts the L^s curve leftward.

An increase in the technology level also affects the labor demand curve, L^d, as we know from our analysis in Figure 8.15 in Chapter 8. The increase in the technology level from A to A' raises the MPL and thereby increases the quantity of labor demanded at any w/P.

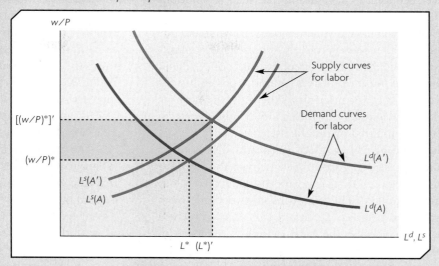

Figure 15.3 *Response of the Labor Market to a Technology Shock: Effects of Price Misperceptions*

The technology level, A rises from A to A'. The labor demand curves come from Figure 8.15. At any real wage rate, w/P, the quantity of labor demanded is higher along the red curve, $L^d(A')$, than along the blue one, $L^d(A)$. The increase in A also reduces the price level, P. Because of price misperceptions, the quantity of labor supplied falls at any w/P. Therefore, $L^s(A')$, in brown, lies to the left of the initial curve, $L^s(A)$, in green. The increase in L from L^* to $(L^*)'$, is less than it would have been if the L^s curve had not shifted. Therefore, price misperceptions lessen the response of L to a technology shock.

We show this shift to L^d in Figure 15.3 as the rightward movement from the blue curve to the red one. Keep in mind our assumption that employers know the real wage rate, w/P. Therefore, price misperceptions do not affect the L^d curves.

Figure 15.3 shows that the increase in the technology level, A, raises labor, L, and the real wage rate, w/P. These changes are in the same direction as those in Figure 8.15. The new effect in Figure 15.3 comes from the leftward shift of the labor supply curve, L^s. We see graphically that this shift means that L rises by less than it would have otherwise.[8] Therefore, price misperceptions weaken the effect of a change in the technology level, A on L—and, hence, on real GDP, Y.

These new effects from price misperceptions apply only in the short run, when the perceived price level, P^e, lags behind the actual price level, P. In Figure 15.3, as P^e adjusts downward toward the lower P, the labor supply curve shifts rightward, back toward its initial position. Hence, the real wage rate, w/P, and the quantity of labor input, L, tend toward the values, $(w/P)^*$ and L^*, that applied in the original version of our equilibrium business-cycle model (Figure 8.15).

If we combine the findings about real shocks with the earlier ones for monetary shocks, we get the following summary of results for the price-misperceptions model:

- Because of price misperceptions, unanticipated increases in the nominal quantity of money, M, raise real GDP, Y, and labor input, L, in the short run. Since money was neutral in the model without price misperceptions, we can also say that these misperceptions accentuate the real effects of monetary shocks.

- Price misperceptions lessen the short-run real effects of real shocks. A favorable shock to the technology level, A, still raises Y and L, but by less than before.

Rules Versus Discretion

e have found that unanticipated money shocks can affect the real economy in the short run. Given these results, it is not surprising that monetary

---

[8] Labor, L, still has to increase overall. If L declined, real GDP, Y, would fall. Then the price level, P, would increase, and the L^s curve would shift in the direction opposite to that assumed in Figure 15.3.

authorities would be tempted to exercise their power to create money shocks as a way to influence real variables. However, economists have found that such temptations can lead to bad economic outcomes. The reasons for the bad results involve the distinction between rules and discretion. Under a **monetary rule**, the central bank commits itself to a designated mode of conducting policy. Under discretion, the authority leaves open the possibility for surprises—that is, for monetary shocks. In this section, we seek to understand why the economy might perform better in a committed or rule-like setting.

The ongoing debate over rules and discretion is an exciting research topic that involves the application of strategic analysis—a part of game theory—to government policy.[9] The initial inspiration came from the distinction between perceived versus misperceived price-level changes in the kind of model explored in this chapter. In this model, the real economy reacts to a change in the nominal quantity of money, M, only when the change is unanticipated—in particular, only when the money shocks cause the price level, P, to deviate from its perceived level, P^e. Consequently, the monetary authority may be motivated to create price surprises as a way to affect real economic activity. However, under rational expectations, systematic surprises tend not to be attainable. Despite this difficulty, the temptation to act in a surprising manner remains, and this temptation can influence the equilibrium inflation rate, π. We will now work out a simple model of strategic interaction that determines π.

Suppose that the monetary authority can use its policy instruments—which could be open-market operations—to achieve a desired inflation rate, π. The authority seeks to raise real GDP, Y, and labor input, L, but can do so only by making π exceed the inflation rate that households expect, π^e. For given π^e, we assume that Y and L rise with π. The mechanism for this effect can be a link between misperceived price-level changes and labor supply, as in the model worked out before.

We assume that the monetary authority does not like inflation for its own sake. If π and π^e rise together, the economy experiences costs of inflation, perhaps due to transaction costs or costs of changing prices. Our assumption is that inflation and deflation are both costly; that is, costs of inflation are minimized when the price level is constant, so that $\pi = 0$. We also assume that, as π rises above zero, additional inflation becomes increasingly burdensome for the economy. More formally, the marginal cost of inflation rises with π.

For given inflationary expectations, π^e, the monetary authority faces a trade-off when considering whether to use its policy instruments to raise the inflation rate, π. An increase in π is beneficial because it raises the inflation surprise, $\pi - \pi^e$, and thereby expands real GDP, Y, and labor input, L. We assume that these increases in Y and L are attractive.[10] However, if π is already greater than zero, an increase in π is undesirable because it raises the costs of inflation.

The trade-off between the benefits and costs of inflation determines the inflation rate, denoted by $\hat{\pi}$, that the monetary authority selects. Typically, $\hat{\pi}$ will depend on the inflation rate, π^e, that households expect. As an example, if households expect zero inflation, $\pi^e = 0$, the authority might find it optimal to pick 5% inflation—$\hat{\pi} = 5$. If expected inflation rises—say, to $\pi^e = 5$—the authority might choose still higher inflation to keep ahead of expectations and, thereby, maintain a stimulus to real GDP and labor input. Thus, the policymaker might choose $\hat{\pi} = 8$. Typically, a higher π^e motivates a higher $\hat{\pi}$. However, as $\hat{\pi}$ rises, inflation may become increasingly burdensome for the economy. This consideration motivates the monetary authority not to react too strongly to a rise in π^e. Specifically, our assumption is that the response of $\hat{\pi}$ is always by less than the increase in π^e. For example, if π^e rises by five percentage points, from 0 to 5, $\hat{\pi}$ might increase by only three percentage points, from 5 to 8.

We show the graph of $\hat{\pi}$ versus π^e as the red line in Figure 15.4. The important properties of this line are: First, $\hat{\pi}$ is greater than 0 when $\pi^e = 0$; second, the slope of the line is greater than zero; and, third, the slope is less than one.

Consider how households form rational expectations of inflation in this model. A key assumption is that households understand the objective of the monetary authority. Each household recognizes that, if all households expect the inflation rate to be π^e along the horizontal axis, the authority will actually select the inflation rate $\hat{\pi}$ given on the vertical axis by the red line in Figure 15.4. For example, if all households expect zero inflation, $\pi^e = 0$, the authority would set $\hat{\pi} = 5$. But, then, zero cannot be a rational expectation of inflation; no sensible household would expect zero inflation. Similarly, if all households expect 5% inflation, $\pi^e = 5$, the authority would set

[9] The pioneering paper in this area—an important reason for their 2004 Nobel Prize in Economics—is by Finn Kydland and Edward Prescott (1977). Further developments are in Robert Barro and David Gordon (1983a, 1983b). Ken Rogoff (1989) has a useful survey of this literature.

[10] As discussed before, because of existing distortions in the economy, it may be socially desirable for the monetary authority to trick all households into working and producing more.

$\hat{\pi} = 8$. Thus, again, $\pi^e = 5$ is not a rational expectation. In this model, an expectation π^e will be rational only if the monetary authority is motivated to validate the belief—that is, to set $\hat{\pi} = \pi^e$. Thus, in Figure 15.4, the chosen $\hat{\pi}$ must lie along the blue, 45-degree line, which shows outcomes for which $\hat{\pi} = \pi^e$.

The equilibrium inflation rate, π^*, is given from the intersection of the two lines in Figure 15.4. The value π^* satisfies two conditions. First, if $\pi^e = \pi^*$ on the horizontal axis, the monetary authority selects the inflation rate $\hat{\pi} = \pi^*$ on the vertical axis, as given by the red line. That is, the authority is optimizing (by picking $\hat{\pi}$) for given inflationary expectations, π^e. Second, the expectation $\pi^e = \pi^*$ is rational because it gives the most accurate possible forecast of inflation.

In this model, households have **perfect foresight** about inflation; that is, the forecast error is zero in equilibrium. In richer versions of this type of model, inflationary expectations would still be optimal forecasts of inflation, but the forecast error would generally be nonzero. For example, we would have nonzero forecast errors if the monetary authority sometimes makes unavoidable and unpredictable mistakes by randomly setting π different from $\hat{\pi}$.

The unappealing aspect of the equilibrium in Figure 15.4 is that it entails a high inflation rate, π^*, without any of the benefits that come from surprisingly high inflation. That is, in equilibrium, expected inflation, π^e, equals π^*. Recall that, in the underlying model, money growth and inflation stimulate real GDP, Y, and labor input, L, only when the inflation rate, π, exceeds its expectation, π^e. Thus, in the equilibrium displayed in Figure 15.4, Y and L receive no stimulus from surprisingly high inflation.

The outcomes would be more favorable if actual and expected inflation were lower than those that arise in equilibrium; for example, if $\pi = \pi^e = 0$. In this case,

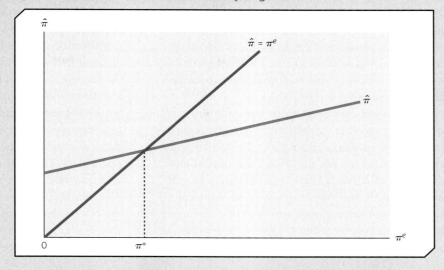

Figure 15.4 *Inflation in a Discretionary Regime*

The red line shows the policymaker's optimal choice of inflation, $\hat{\pi}$, as a function of households' expected rate of inflation, π^e. The blue, 45-degree line shows points where the chosen inflation rate, $\hat{\pi}$, equals the expected inflation rate, π^e. Under rational expectations, the pair ($\hat{\pi}, \pi^e$) must lie on the blue line. The value π^* is the equilibrium inflation rate in a discretionary regime. At π^*, the policymaker is optimizing for given expectations, and expectations are rational.

the inflation surprise, $\pi - \pi^e$, would again be zero, so that there would be no stimulus to real GDP, Y, and labor input, L. However, since π is low—specifically, zero—the economy would not suffer costs of inflation. Figure 15.4 makes clear, however, that $\pi = \pi^e = 0$ is not an equilibrium in the model. If the monetary authority managed to persuade households to expect zero inflation—so that $\pi^e = 0$ applied—the authority would actually opt for positive inflation. That is, if $\pi^e = 0$, $\hat{\pi}$ would be greater than zero along the red line in the figure. Knowing this, households would not set $\pi^e = 0$ in the first place, because they know that this expectation is irrational.

The high-inflation equilibrium in Figure 15.4, where $\pi = \pi^e = \pi^* > 0$, is often referred to as the outcome under **discretionary policy**. This equilibrium prevails if the monetary authority cannot or, at least, does not make commitments about future monetary actions. In contrast, an authority that makes such commitments is viewed as operating under an explicit or implicit **policy rule**. One simple form of rule commits the monetary authority to adjust its instruments to approximate **price stability**—that is, to set $\pi = 0$ in each period. Another rule has the authority target a positive but low inflation rate. In the present setting, the commitment to zero inflation—if feasible—is the best option for the monetary authority.

Figure 15.4 illustrates the tension in a rule that specifies zero (or, more generally, low) inflation. When

$\pi^e = 0$, the policymaker would like to renege on commitments by setting $\pi = \hat{\pi} > 0$ along the red line. But then the outcomes would tend toward the discretionary equilibrium shown at the high inflation rate, π^*. Thus, an important aspect of a rule is that the monetary authority be firmly committed to it. The authority has to ensure that it will not exploit an opportunity for surprisingly high inflation, ex post.

In some cases, a commitment to low inflation may not require a formal rule, which might even be embedded in a law. Instead, the authority may be able to build up a reputation for low inflation. Since a reputation for low inflation is valuable, a central banker may be able to convince households that he or she will not exploit short-run opportunities to create surprises by inflating at a rate higher than expected. These kinds of reputational equilibria are more likely to apply if the benefits from cheating (by creating surprisingly high inflation in the short run) are not too great, and if episodes of cheating generate a substantial loss of reputation.[11]

Over the last two decades, central banks in most advanced economies have become committed to low and stable inflation. In many countries, the commitments are reinforced by formal provisions stipulating that the central bank's objective is price stability. With increasing frequency, this objective is stated in terms of **inflation targeting**. In a regime of inflation targeting, the central bank commits to using its policy instruments, usually open-market operations, to attain a specified range of the inflation rate over a prescribed interval, such as a year. This commitment is reinforced by transparency about the central bank's objectives and procedures, including the regular publication of inflation reports. Table 15.2 lists 20 countries, beginning with New Zealand in 1989,

Table 15.2 *Countries with Central Banks that Adopted Formal Inflation Targeting*

Country	Date of Adoption of Inflation Targeting
New Zealand	1989
Canada	1991
United Kingdom	1992
Australia	1993
Finland	1993 (dropped in 1999 on adoption of the euro)
Sweden	1993
Spain	1995 (dropped in 1999 on adoption of the euro)
Czech Republic	1997
Israel	1997
Brazil	1999
Chile	1999
Poland	1999
Colombia	2000
South Africa	2000
South Korea	2000
Thailand	2000
Hungary	2001
Iceland	2001
Mexico	2001
Norway	2001

Note: The list shows countries in which the central banks have formal procedures in place for targeting the inflation rate. This list comes from Frederic Mishkin and Klaus Schmidt-Hebbel (2001) and Alina Carare and Mark Stone (2003).

---

[11] For further discussion, see Robert Barro and David Gordon (1983b).

that have adopted a formal regime of inflation targeting. In other countries, notably the United States, the European Monetary Union (euro area), and Japan, central banks have not adopted formal inflation targets but have established reputations for maintaining low and stable inflation. However, a formal inflation-targeting regime may eventually prove irresistible even to the United States, the European Monetary Union, and Japan. In any event, the evolution of central-bank policies since the 1980s has been increasingly toward commitments to low and stable inflation.

Strategic interactions analogous to those for monetary policy arise in many areas in which policymakers perceive benefits from surprising the public. As examples, debtor countries may surprise foreign creditors by defaulting on international debts, governments may surprise owners of domestic capital by assessing high tax rates on capital that is already in place (a so-called **capital levy**), tax collectors may surprise taxpayers by announcing tax amnesties, and governments may renege on patents after inventions have been made. In all of these cases, surprises are tempting after the fact. However, if people's expectations take account of these temptations, the equilibria tend to have undesirable properties: little foreign borrowing, low investment, poor tax compliance, and a small volume of inventions. To avoid these outcomes, governments are motivated to make commitments—sometimes involving laws and constitutional provisions—to resist temptations that arise after the fact. However, the credibility of these commitments is a major issue. Arguably, the degree of success of public institutions in resolving these commitment problems is a central feature that distinguishes prosperous countries from poor ones.

Questions and Problems

A. Review questions

1. Explain why it is reasonable to assume that individuals have imperfect information about prices throughout the economy. What are the costs of collecting and processing information about prices?

2. What is a relative price? Is the real wage rate, w/P, an example of a relative price?

3. Can there be unanticipated changes in the nominal quantity of money, M, even when people have rational expectations? If so, does a policymaker have the option of moderating economic fluctuations through surprise changes in M?

4. What do workers perceive about their real wage rate, w/P, when they see an increase in their nominal wage rate, w? Under what circumstances do workers make mistakes about their real wage rate?

B. Problems for discussion

5. Persisting effects on output
When expectations are rational, errors made in estimating the price level will not persist over time. How, then, can price-perception errors explain persistent excesses or shortfalls of real GDP from its trend?

6. The timing of money and output
Suppose that the data show that movements in nominal money are positively correlated with subsequent movements in real GDP. Does this finding demonstrate that money affects the real economy, rather than the reverse? If not, give some examples of endogenous money in which the movements of money precede those in real GDP.

7. Irrelevance results for monetary policy

a. Under what circumstances does systematic monetary policy not matter for economic fluctuations?

b. Does the result in question a mean that the unpredictable parts of money growth do not affect real GDP?

c. Does the result in question a generalize to the idea that the systematic parts of all government policies are irrelevant for real GDP? Consider, as examples, the following:

i. a policy of cutting labor-income tax rates during recessions

ii. a policy of raising government purchases of goods and services during recessions

iii. a policy of enhancing the generosity of unemployment insurance programs during recessions

8. The predictability of money growth
Suppose that the money growth rate becomes less predictable from year to year. What happens to the following:

a. the effect of a given size money shock on real GDP, Y?

b. the effect of a given size money shock on the price level, P?

9. Rules versus discretion
Assume that the monetary authority's preferred inflation rate is zero, but the authority also wants to reduce unemployment by making inflation surprisingly high.

a. Show how the equilibrium inflation rate can be high. Is the rate surprisingly high? Does the result depend on the authority's having the wrong objective or being incompetent?

b. Can the results improve if the policymaker has the power to bind him- or herself in advance to a specified inflation rate? If so, explain why this constraint (or rule) can improve matters.

c. Might the policymaker's reputation be a satisfactory alternative to a formal rule that dictates future policies?

d. Can you think of reasons, aside from reducing unemployment, why a policymaker might like surprisingly high inflation?

Money and Business Cycles II: Sticky Prices and Nominal Wage Rates

I n the previous chapter, we developed a model where monetary shocks were non-neutral because of misperceptions about prices. In this chapter, we explore other models that economists have developed to explain the non-neutrality of money. In these models, the price level and nominal wage rate are sticky: They do not adjust instantaneously to clear all the markets. The lack of market clearing is a significant departure from our previous models. In the equilibrium business-cycle model—and also in the price-misperceptions model—the price level and nominal wage rate adjusted rapidly to balance quantities of goods supplied and demanded in each market. That is, until now, we assumed that all markets cleared. Now we will relax this assumption.

John Maynard Keynes (1936), in his General Theory of Employment, Interest, and Money, stressed the importance of stickiness in nominal prices and wages. His emphasis was on the stickiness of nominal wage rates. He thought it was unrealistic to assume that nominal wage rates adjusted rapidly to ensure continual balance between the quantities of labor supplied and demanded. Modern Keynesian economists usually focus instead on stickiness of nominal goods prices. As we shall see, the reason for the new focus is that it leads to a better fit with some features of economic fluctuations. We begin our analysis by developing a model with sticky nominal goods prices.

The New Keynesian Model

T he usual explanation for **sticky prices**—nominal goods prices that do not react rapidly to changed circumstances—relies on two main ingredients. First, the typical producer actively sets the price of the good that he or she sells in the market. This price-setting behavior differs from our previous analysis, where each perfectly competitive producer (a household or business) took the price as given by the market. Second, when choosing the price to set, each producer takes into account a cost of changing prices. This cost is sometimes called a **menu cost**, analogous to the expense that a restaurant incurs when it alters the prices listed on its menu.

Our previous setting of perfect competition applies most naturally to large-scale organized markets on which standardized goods are traded. Examples are stock exchanges (on which financial claims are traded) and commodity exchanges (on which claims to goods such as oil or corn are traded). In these organized markets, each trader takes as given the market prices of goods. That is, in most circumstances, each participant is small enough to neglect the impact of his or her actions on the market price.

The situation is different for markets with small numbers of sellers and buyers. For example, the markets for automobiles or computers in the United States have relatively few producers. Moreover, the goods traded on these markets are not fully standardized. Each kind of automobile or computer has different features, some of which are distinguished by brand names. These kinds of markets have substantial competition, but not the perfect competition associated with price-taking behavior by all participants. Instead, each producer has some latitude in deciding what price to set. Economists call this environment **imperfect competition**.

In a perfectly competitive market, a producer who charges more than the market price would find that the quantity demanded would fall to zero. Conversely, a producer who asks less than the market price would find that the quantity demanded would soar toward infinity. In markets with imperfect competition, a decrease in a seller's price generates a finite increase in the quantity of goods demanded from that seller. Similarly, a rise in price leads to a finite reduction in the quantity demanded. Thus, each producer can make a meaningful choice of what price to charge. This perspective applies to many large companies, such as automobile producers, but also holds for small businesses, such as neighborhood grocery stores. One reason that a retail store, such as a grocery, has some latitude in setting its price is that its location is convenient for buyers who live nearby or are familiar with the store. For this reason, a small increase in price above that charged by other stores would not, at least immediately, drive the quantity demanded to zero.

Price Setting Under Imperfect Competition

In this section, we examine how a producer in an environment of imperfect competition chooses the price of his or her goods. In the following section, we will learn how the producer takes menu costs into account when determining how to adjust prices to changed circumstances—for example, in response to a monetary shock.

To illustrate the main points, we will find it convenient to work with a formal model. Let $P(j)$ be the price charged for a good by firm j. As in our previous models, we can think of each business as owned and run by one of the households in the economy. The quantity of firm j's goods demanded, $Y^d(j)$, depends on how high

$P(j)$ is compared to prices charged by other producers. For example, if firm k is a competitor—perhaps because it is the grocery store on the next block—then a cut in k's price, $P(k)$, reduces $Y^d(j)$.

Generally, the quantity demanded of firm j's goods, $Y^d(j)$, will be more sensitive to prices charged on similar goods in nearby locations than to prices offered on very different products or in faraway locations. However, the model would become unmanageable if we tried to keep track of all of these prices. We can get the main results by assuming that the customers of firm j compare the price, $P(j)$, with the average of the prices charged by other firms. If we let this average price be P, then $Y^d(j)$ depends on the price ratio, $P(j)/P$. An increase in $P(j)/P$ lowers $Y^d(j)$, and a decrease in $P(j)/P$ raises $Y^d(j)$.

The quantity of goods demanded at firm j, $Y^d(j)$, depends also on the incomes of persons who are current or potential customers of the firm. For example, if the real income in the whole economy increases, the demand, $Y^d(j)$, will rise for each firm j.

Now we move from the demand for firm j's goods to the production of these goods. The production function for firm j looks like the function we have used before:

(16.1) $$Y(j) = F[\kappa(j) \bullet K(j), L(j)]$$

where $\kappa(j) \bullet K(j)$ and $L(j)$ are the quantities of capital services and labor used by firm j. To keep things simple, we ignore changes in the capital utilization rate, $\kappa(j)$, and we assume that the capital stock, $K(j)$, is fixed in the short run. We are also neglecting inputs of intermediate goods, which are materials and products produced by other firms. Extensions to allow for variable capital utilization and intermediate inputs are useful but do not change the basic conclusions.

Suppose that the nominal wage rate, w, is the same for labor used by all the firms in the economy. In other words, we are thinking of labor as a standardized service that is traded in the overall economy under conditions of perfect competition. More specifically, when we consider sticky nominal prices, we will ignore the possibility of sticky nominal wage rates— w will adjust to balance the total quantities of labor supplied and demanded in the economy. This assumption about the labor market can be questioned and was surely not the environment envisioned by Keynes (1936) in his *General Theory*. We will allow later for *sticky nominal wage rates*.

We begin with a setup in which the nominal price charged by each firm, $P(j)$, is fully flexible. That is, it is convenient to construct our basic setup while first ignoring any menu costs for changing prices. Given the nominal wage rate, w, and the average nominal price, P, charged by competitors, each firm sets $P(j)$ at the level that maximizes its profit.

To determine the profit-maximizing price, $P(j)$, we begin by considering the nominal cost of producing an additional unit of goods—that is, the **marginal cost of production**. To relate this concept to our discussion of labor demand in Chapter 6, recall that the marginal product of labor, MPL, is the ratio of additional output, ΔY, to additional labor input, ΔL. Therefore, for firm j:

(16.2) $MPL(j) = \Delta Y(j)/\Delta L(j)$

If we rearrange this condition, we see that the added labor, $\Delta L(j)$, needed to raise output by $\Delta Y(j)$ units is

(16.3) $\Delta L(j) = \Delta Y(j)/MPL(j)$

The higher the $MPL(j)$, the lower the quantity of labor, $\Delta L(j)$, needed to raise output by the amount $\Delta Y(j)$. If we set $\Delta Y(j) = 1$, the labor needed to raise output by one unit is

$$\Delta L(j) = 1/MPL(j)$$

The nominal cost of each unit of labor is the nominal wage rate, w. Therefore, the added nominal cost of raising output by one unit is $w \bullet [1/MPL(j)]$. In other words, the nominal marginal cost of production for firm j is

(16.4)   *firm j's nominal marginal cost = $w/MPL(j)$*

= ratio of nominal wage rate to marginal product of labor

Thus, for given $MPL(j)$, a higher w means a higher nominal marginal cost.

Under perfect competition, profit maximization dictates that each firm's nominal marginal cost, given from equation (16.4) by $w/MPL(j)$, equal its price, $P(j)$.[1] However, under imperfect competition, each firm can set $P(j)$ above its nominal marginal cost. The ratio of $P(j)$ to the nominal marginal cost is called the **markup ratio**:

(16.5)   *firm j's markup ratio = $P(j)/$(firm j's nominal marginal cost)*

= $P(j)/[w/MPL(j)]$

where we used the formula for firm j's nominal marginal cost from equation (16.4). The markup ratio that a firm chooses depends on how sensitive a firm's product demand, $Y^d(j)$, is to $P(j)$. More market power—that is, less competition—tends to imply less sensitivity of demand to price and, therefore, motivates a higher markup ratio. If the sensitivity of demand becomes extremely high (because of greater competition), the markup ratio approaches one. That is, we get close to the perfectly competitive outcome in which $P(j)$ equals nominal marginal cost. In our analysis, we assume that each firm's markup ratio is a given constant.

We can rearrange the formula for the markup ratio to get an expression for each firm's price:

(16.6) $P(j) = $ *(firm j's markup ratio)* $\bullet$
(firm j's nominal marginal cost)

Therefore, for a given markup ratio, an increase in firm j's nominal marginal cost raises its price, $P(j)$, in the same proportion. For example, if nominal marginal cost doubles, $P(j)$ doubles. If we substitute the formula for nominal marginal cost from equation (16.4), we get

(16.7) $P(j) = $ *(markup ratio)* $\bullet [w/MPL(j)]$

Therefore, for a given markup ratio, an increase in the nominal wage rate, w, leads to a rise in the same proportion in the nominal price, $P(j)$. For example, a doubling of w causes all firms in the economy to double their nominal prices. Therefore, the average of these prices, P, also doubles.

In our model, we do not have to worry about the full array of individual prices, $P(j)$, that prevails in equilibrium. The important point is that, with imperfect competition, the profit-maximizing decisions of firms determine a distribution of the $P(j)$. For example, if we think about grocery stores, some of the stores will have relatively high $P(j)$, whereas others will have relatively low $P(j)$.

Each firm demands labor, and the total of these demands determines the economy-wide labor demand, L^d. As in our previous models, the equilibrium of the economy-wide labor market equates the aggregate quantity of labor demanded, L^d, to the aggregate quantity supplied, L^s. This condition determines the economy-wide real wage rate, w/P, as well as the total quantity of labor, L. Finally, if we know w/P and P, we can calculate the economy-wide nominal wage rate, w (by multiplying w/P by P).

---

[1] If we rearrange the terms, the condition is $MPL(j) = W/P(j)$. Aside from the index j, this equation is the same as the condition for profit maximization worked out in Chapter 6 under perfect competition.

Short-Run Responses to a Monetary Shock

Consider what happens when a monetary shock occurs. To be concrete, imagine that the nominal quantity of money, M, doubles. We found in Chapter 10 that this change in money was neutral. The price level, P, and the nominal wage rate, w, doubled. Real variables, including the quantity of real money balances, M/P, and the real wage rate, w/P, did not change.

With fully flexible prices and wages, money would still be neutral in the model that includes an array of imperfectly competitive firms. In this setting, each nominal price, $P(j)$, doubles when M doubles. Therefore, the average price, P, doubles, as in the model in Chapter 10. The economy-wide nominal wage rate, w, also doubles as before. These changes leave unchanged the real variables in the economy. The real variables now include not only the economy-wide real wage rate, w/P, but also the ratio of each firm's price to the average price, $P(j)/P$.

New results arise when we allow for stickiness in the nominal price, $P(j)$, set by each firm j. As mentioned before, these prices might change infrequently because of menu costs for changing prices. To illustrate the effects of price stickiness, we can consider the extreme case in which all the $P(j)$ are rigid in the short run. The average price, P, would then also be fixed. If P is constant and the nominal quantity of money, M, doubles, each household would have twice as much real money, M/P, as before. However, nothing has changed to motivate households to hold more money in real terms. Each household would therefore try to spend its excess money, partly by buying the goods produced by the various firms.[2] Each firm j would then experience an increase in the quantity demanded of its goods, $Y^d(j)$.

How does a business react when it sees an increase in demand, $Y^d(j)$, while its price, $P(j)$, is fixed (by assumption)? We noted before that, under imperfect competition, the markup ratio is greater than one. Since the price of goods sold, $P(j)$, is greater than nominal marginal cost, an expansion of production and sales, $Y(j)$, would raise firm j's profit. For example, if $Y(j)$ rose by one unit, the added nominal revenue would be $P(j)$, and the added nominal cost would be the nominal marginal cost, which is less than $P(j)$. Therefore, if $P(j)$ is fixed, a profit-maximizing firm would—over some range—meet an increase in demand by raising production, $Y(j)$.

To raise its production, $Y(j)$, firm j has to increase its quantity of labor input, $L(j)$. Therefore, the quantity of labor demanded, $L^d(j)$, rises by the amount[3]

[16.3] $$\Delta L^d(j) = \Delta Y(j)/MPL(j)$$

The important point is that, with a fixed price, $P(j)$, an increase in the nominal quantity of money, M, leads to an expansion of labor demand by each firm j.

How does an increase in the nominal quantity of money, M, affect the economy-wide labor market? Since each firm j increases its labor demand, $L^d(j)$, the aggregate quantity of labor demanded, L^d, rises at any given economy-wide real wage rate, w/P. We show this effect in Figure 16.1. The increase in the nominal quantity of money from its initial value, M, to the higher value, M', shifts labor demand rightward from the blue curve to the red curve.

We assume, as in Figure 8.15 in Chapter 8, that an increase in the real wage rate, w/P, raises the quantity of labor supplied, L^s. Thus, L^s is given by the upward-sloping green curve in Figure 16.1.

We see from Figure 16.1 that an increase in the nominal quantity of money from M to M' raises the market-clearing labor input from L^* to $(L^*)'$ on the horizontal axis. With the increase in labor input, each firm produces more goods in accordance with the production function:

[16.1] $$Y(j) = F[\kappa(j) \bullet K(j), L(j)]$$

Thus, real GDP, Y, increases.[4] We therefore have that a monetary expansion is non-neutral. An increase in the nominal quantity of money raises real GDP. Moreover, labor input, L, moves in a procyclical manner—it rises along with Y.

New Keynesian Predictions

Thus far, the predictions from the new Keynesian model are similar to those from the price-misperceptions model, considered in Chapter 15. That model also gave the result that a monetary expansion raised real GDP,

---

[2] Households might also buy interest-bearing assets—that is, bonds. In the end, we would get the same results if we allowed for this additional channel of effects.

[3] The expansion of $L(j)$ reduces the marginal product of labor, $MPL(j)$, and therefore raises the nominal marginal cost of production, given by equation (16.4). At a fixed price $P(j)$, a profit-maximizing firm would be willing to meet an increase in demand up to the point at which the nominal marginal cost rose to equal $P(j)$.

[4] We have not considered that the rise in real GDP, Y, increases the nominal quantity of money demanded, M^d. This change dampens the effect on Y from the expansion of the nominal quantity of money, M.

Y, and labor input, L. However, one difference between the two models concerns the real wage rate, w/P. In the price-misperceptions model, an expansion of L had to be accompanied by a fall in w/P in order to induce employers to use more labor input. Thus, that model predicted—counterfactually—that w/P would be counter-cyclical. We now dem-onstrate that the new Keynesian model does not have this problem.

Figure 16.1 shows that a monetary expan-sion increases the market-clearing real wage rate from $(w/P)^*$ to $[(w/P)^*]'$ on the vertical axis. There-fore, the model generates a procyclical pattern for

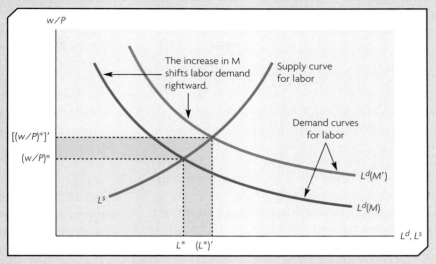

Figure 16.1 *Effect of a Monetary Expansion in the New Keynesian Model*

When the nominal quantity of money is M, the demand for labor, labeled $L^d(M)$, slopes downward versus the real wage rate, w/P, and is given by the blue curve. When the nominal quantity of money rises to M'—but the price level, P, is held fixed—the demand for labor, labeled $L^d(M')$ along the red curve, is larger at any given w/P. The supply of labor, L^s, in green, slopes upward versus w/P. The increase in the nominal quantity of money from M to M' raises the real wage rate from $(w/P)^*$ to $[(w/P)^*]'$ on the vertical axis and increases labor input from L^* to $(L^*)'$ on the horizontal axis.

w/P. Thus, the new Keynesian model correctly predicts that w/P will be procyclical. The reason that the model gets this result is that employers are willing to employ more labor, even though w/P is higher. The key point is that, under imperfect competition, the markup ratio is greater than one. The margin provided by this markup means that—at fixed prices of goods—firms can profit-ably use more labor to produce and sell more goods, even though the real cost of production has gone up (because w/P increased). The monetary expansion does cut into the markup ratios of firms. However, as long as the markup ratio remains above one, firms are willing to expand labor input and production.

As in the equilibrium business-cycle model studied in Chapter 8, the prediction for procyclical labor input, L, in the new Keynesian model depends on the upward slope of the labor supply curve, L^s, in Figure 16.1. That is, the analysis relies on the assumption that an increase in the real wage rate, w/P, motivates households to work more.

One respect in which the new Keynesian model works less well than the equilibrium business-cycle model concerns the average product of labor, Y/L. We found in Chapter 8 that Y/L was procyclical because of the direct effect of a change in the technology level, A,

on the production function. This prediction for procy-clical labor productivity accords with the U.S. evidence, discussed in Chapter 8.

In contrast, the new Keynesian model assumes that the technology level, A, is fixed. Therefore, we know from the production function that an increase in L tends to reduce the MPL and the average product of labor, Y/L. Hence, an expansion of L during an eco-nomic boom goes along with a reduction in the average product of labor, Y/L, whereas a decrease of L during a recession goes along with a rise in Y/L. Consequently, the new Keynesian model predicts, counterfactually, that Y/L would be countercyclical.

Keynesian economists have used the idea of **labor hoarding** to improve the model's predictions about labor productivity. Because of the costs of hiring and firing workers, employers are motivated to retain work-ers during temporary downturns. Therefore, businesses may "hoard labor" in recessions as a cost-effective way of having labor available for the next upturn. Although labor input, L, still falls during a recession, it falls by less than it would if not for the hoarded labor. More-over, during a recession, the "excess" labor may not actually produce much output. The workers may be exerting less than full effort on the job, or they may be performing maintenance tasks that do not show up in measured output.[5] In either case, measured output per worker, Y/L, would be relatively low in a recession. Thus, we may be able to use labor hoarding to explain why the observed average product of labor, Y/L, is procyclical.[6]

Price Adjustment in the Long Run

Our analysis of the new Keynesian model applies in the short run, when we do not allow for adjustments in the prices, $P(j)$, set by each firm j. In the longer run, the prices adjust, and these adjustments tend to undo the real effects from a change in the nominal quantity of money, M.

To study the longer run dynamics, go back to the formula for firm j's markup ratio:

(16.5) $\quad$ *firm j's markup ratio = $P(j)/$(firm j's nominal marginal cost)*

$$= P(j)/[w/MPL(j)]$$

We assumed, thus far, that $P(j)$ was fixed for each firm j. Therefore, the overall price level, P, was also fixed. We then got the result, in Figure 16.1, that an increase in the nominal quantity of money, M, raised the real wage rate, w/P, and the quantity of labor input, L. Since P is fixed, the increase in w/P must correspond to a rise in the nominal wage rate, w. We can see from equation (16.5) that, for fixed $P(j)$, the increase in w raises firm j's nominal marginal cost and, thereby, lowers its markup ratio. Moreover, the increase in $L(j)$ reduces the marginal product of labor, $MPL(j)$. Equation (16.5) shows that the fall in $MPL(j)$ further raises firm j's nominal marginal cost and, therefore, further decreases the markup ratio.

Suppose, as an example, that firm j's preferred (profit-maximizing) markup ratio is 1.2; that is, the firm likes to set its price, $P(j)$, 20% above its nominal marginal cost, $w/MPL(j)$. With $P(j)$ fixed, the increase in the nominal wage rate, w, and the decrease in the marginal product of labor, $MPL(j)$, cut into the markup ratio and lower it to, say, 1.1. Since the markup ratio is still above one, the firm meets the extra demand for its good at the fixed price, $P(j)$. However, the firm would still like to have a markup ratio of 1.2. Therefore, at

least eventually, the firm would restore this ratio by raising its price, $P(j)$.

When each firm j raises its price, $P(j)$, the overall price level, P, increases. Therefore, for a given nominal quantity of money, M, real money balances, M/P, decrease. This change reverses the initial effect, whereby M rose for fixed P, and, therefore, M/P increased. In Figure 16.1, the rightward shift in the labor demand curve came from the effect of the higher M/P on the demand for each firm's good, $Y^d(j)$. As P rises and M/P declines, the demand for each firm's good, $Y^d(j)$, comes back down. Hence, the labor demand curve shifts leftward, back toward its initial position. In the long run, P rises in the same proportion as M, and the labor demand curve is back where it started. Thus, in the long run, we get back to our familiar conclusion that a change in the nominal quantity of money, M, is neutral: there are no effects on real variables, including the real wage rate, w/P, labor input, L, and real GDP, Y.

Our conclusion is that the real effect of a monetary shock in the new Keynesian model is a short-run result that applies only as long as prices fail to adjust to their equilibrium levels. In this respect, the results are analogous to those from the price-misperceptions model from Chapter 15. In that context, the real effect of a monetary shock applied only in the short run as long as households failed to perceive fully the economy-wide changes in prices. Thus, a key issue for the price-misperceptions model was whether the slow adjustment of price expectations was quantitatively significant. In the new Keynesian model, the parallel issue is whether the slow adjustment of prices is quantitatively significant.

Recently available data, discussed in the box "Evidence on the Stickiness of Prices," give us a lot of information about the frequency of price adjustment at the microeconomic level. These data do reveal stickiness of some prices; that is, prices for some types of products often do not change for several months. However, a tentative conclusion from empirical research with these new data is that price stickiness is insufficient to explain a major part of economic fluctuations. Thus, this evidence suggests that the new Keynesian model, although useful, might not explain a large part of economic fluctuations.

---

[5] Jon Fay and James Medoff (1985) found from a survey of 168 manufacturing companies that the typical firm responded to a recession by assigning an additional 5% of its work hours to maintenance, overhaul of equipment, training, and other activities that do not show up in measured output. This reallocation of labor can help to explain why measured output per worker, Y/L, tends to be low during a recession.

[6] A richer version of the new Keynesian model has a different way of explaining why the average product of labor, Y/L, is procyclical. The new feature is that goods produced by firms serve not only as final products but also as intermediate inputs for other firms. A monetary expansion lowers markup ratios and, therefore, lowers the real cost of intermediate inputs. Consequently, firms use more of these intermediate inputs, and this increased use tends to raise the MPL and the average product of labor, Y/L. Therefore, Y/L can rise in a boom even though L increases.

bythenumbers

Evidence on the Stickiness of Prices

A study by Mark Bils and Peter Klenow (2004) quantified the stickiness in prices of goods and services contained in the U.S. consumer price index (CPI). Each month, the Bureau of Labor Statistics (BLS) collects prices on about 75,000 individual items. The flexibility of prices varies greatly, depending on the type of good or service. Some types saw price changes almost every month—these goods include gasoline, airline fares, and fresh produce. Others changed infrequently—including vending machines, newspapers, and taxi fares. Overall, from 1995 to 1997, 22% of the individual items had changes in prices from one month to the next. The median duration of prices was 4 to 5 months.[7]

Emi Nakamura and Jon Steinsson (2006) looked in more detail at the price data from 1988 to 2005 on the individual items comprising the CPI, as well as the producer price index (PPI). For the CPI, temporary price cuts during sales played a large role, for example, in goods such as apparel and furniture. The median duration of all prices was 4 to 5 months, as in Bils and Klenow, but the median duration of regular prices (with sales excluded) was much higher, 10 months. For the PPI, where sales were not important, the median duration of prices was 9 months. Nakamura and Steinsson found that about two-thirds of price changes (regular price changes in the CPI and all changes in the PPI) were price increases, whereas one-third were decreases. The average magnitude of individual price change was 8% for regular CPI changes and 7% for PPI changes.

Mikhail Golosov and Robert Lucas (2006) used the Bils and Klenow findings to estimate how important the stickiness of prices is for U.S. economic fluctuations. In the Golosov-Lucas model, one reason that firms want to change prices is individual shocks, which affect a specific firm's product demand or technology. For example, a rise in individual product demand motivates each firm to raise its relative price—$P(j)/P$—in the model that we worked out before. The second reason to change prices is an economy-wide monetary disturbance. For example, an increase in the nominal quantity of money, M, motivates each firm to raise its nominal price, $P(j)$.

Both types of price change incur a menu cost. Because of these costs of changing prices, an individual firm does not always adjust its price, $P(j)$, in response to an individual shock or a monetary disturbance. Suppose that $[P(j)]^*$ represents a firm's "ideal price," the price that would be chosen if menu costs were zero. Each firm will find it optimal to make a price change when $P(j)$ deviates substantially from $[P(j)]^*$. When a price change occurs, $P(j)$ will typically adjust by a substantial amount, for example, by the average of 7–8% upward or downward found by Nakamura and Steinsson.

Golosov and Lucas construct a model that has an array of individual firms, each of which has the same menu cost for changing its price. (An extension to allow for differences in menu costs turns out not to affect the main results.) A higher menu cost motivates less frequent price changes. Golosov and Lucas assume that the menu cost takes on a value that generates a frequency of price change in the model that equals the average frequency found in the data by Bils and Klenow. Thus, in the Golosov-Lucas model of the U.S. economy, individual firms adjust their prices, on average, every 4 to 5 months.

One finding in the model is that, for the U.S. economy, individual shocks are responsible for most of the price changes. That is, most prices change in response to shifts in individual demand or technology, rather

---

[7] Earlier studies of price stickiness include Dennis Carlton (1986), Steve Cecchetti (1986), Anil Kashyap (1995), and Alan Blinder et al. (1998). These studies concluded that price stickiness was more important than found by Bils and Klenow (2004). One reason is that the earlier studies looked only at a few products, such as newspapers and items listed in catalogs, which happen to have above-average price stickiness.

than economy-wide monetary shocks. The situation is different for an economy with high and variable inflation; Golosov and Lucas take Israel in the late 1970s and early 1980s as an example. In that high-inflation environment, most price changes occurred because of economy-wide monetary shocks.

In the Golosov-Lucas model, monetary shocks affect labor input and output, as in the new Keynesian model that we studied. However, it turns out, for the U.S. economy, that observed monetary fluctuations account for only a small fraction of the observed fluctuations in real GDP. Golosov and Lucas conclude that, although money is non-neutral, monetary shocks play a minor role in economic fluctuations.

© iStockphoto.com/Paul Hart

We can also use our analysis of price adjustment to see what the new Keynesian model predicts for the cyclical behavior of the price level, P. When the nominal quantity of money, M, rose, P responded relatively little at first. Therefore, the expansion of real GDP, Y, was accompanied by little change in P. As P gradually increased, Y declined but remained above its initial level. Eventually, P rose in the same proportion as M, and, at that point, Y returned to its initial level. The upshot of this discussion is that Y is relatively high when P is relatively low.

We can also do the analysis in reverse, where a decrease in the nominal quantity of money, M, leads to a temporary decrease of real GDP, Y. In that case, we get that Y tends to be relatively low (for example, just after the decrease in M) when P is relatively high.

Overall, the new Keynesian prediction is that the price level, P, tends to be relatively low during a boom—where real GDP, Y, is relatively high—and relatively high during a recession—where Y is relatively low. In other words, the model predicts that P is countercyclical. This prediction is the same as that in the equilibrium business-cycle model. As we saw in Chapter 10, the prediction for a countercyclical P accords with the U.S. data.

Comparing Predictions for Economic Fluctuations

Table 16.1 extends Table 15.1 from Chapter 15 to include the cyclical predictions for five macroeconomic variables from the new Keynesian model. We can use

Table 16.1 to compare these predictions with those from two alternative models—the equilibrium business-cycle model from Chapters 8 through 10 and the price-misperceptions model from Chapter 15—and with the empirical patterns in the U.S. data.

Table 16.1 shows that, unlike the price-misperceptions model, the new Keynesian model correctly predicts a procyclical pattern for the real wage rate, w/P, and a countercyclical pattern for the price level, P. The one respect in which the new Keynesian model differs from the equilibrium business-cycle model and also deviates from the empirical pattern is for the average product of labor, Y/L. The new Keynesian model errs by predicting a countercyclical pattern for Y/L, although the idea of labor hoarding might fix this problem.

Shocks to Aggregate Demand

Our discussion of the new Keynesian model focused on the economy's responses to an increase in the nominal quantity of money, M. A key part of the analysis was that each firm j experienced an increase in the demand for its goods, $Y^d(j)$, while its price, $P(j)$, was held fixed. The same results apply if $Y^d(j)$ rises for each firm j for reasons having nothing to do with money. The essential ingredient is an increase in the **aggregate demand** for goods.

One way for aggregate demand to rise is for households to shift exogenously away from current saving and toward current consumption, C. That is, households might become less thrifty for reasons not explained by

Table 16.1 *Cyclical Patterns of Macroeconomic Variables in Three Models*

	Nominal Quantity of Money, M	Price Level, P	Labor Input, L	Real Wage Rate, w/P	Average Product of Labor, Y/L
1. Equilibrium business-cycle model	procyclical	countercyclical	procyclical	procyclical	procyclical
2. Price-misperceptions model	procyclical	procyclical	procyclical	countercyclical	countercyclical
3. New Keynesian model	procyclical	countercyclical	procyclical	procyclical	countercyclical
4. Empirical observations	procyclical (weak)	countercyclical	procyclical	procyclical	procyclical (weak)

Note: This table extends Table 15.1 from Chapter 15. The cells show the cyclical patterns for five macroeconomic variables in four settings. First is the equilibrium business-cycle model, with economic fluctuations driven by shocks to the technology level, A (described in Chapters 8 through 10). Second is the price-misperceptions model from Chapter 15, with economic fluctuations driven by shocks to the nominal quantity of money, M. Third is the new Keynesian model from this chapter, with economic fluctuations driven by shocks to M. Fourth is the empirical pattern from U.S. data.

the model.[8] The increase in consumer demand means that the typical firm j sees an increase in the demand for its goods, $Y^d(j)$. If the price level, P, is fixed in the short run, we can again use the analysis from Figure 16.1 to show that aggregate labor input, L, increases. Therefore, the increase in the aggregate demand for goods leads to an increase in real GDP, Y.

Another possibility is that the government could boost the aggregate demand for goods by increasing its real purchases, G. This expansion would again raise the demand, $Y^d(j)$, seen by the typical firm. As before, if the price level, P, is held fixed, labor input, L, and real GDP, Y, tend to rise.

The new Keynesian model has the property that an increase in the aggregate demand for goods may end up increasing real GDP, Y, by even more than the initial expansion of demand. That is, there may be a **multiplier** in the model—the rise in Y may be a multiple greater than one of the rise in demand.

The reasoning is that, at a fixed price level, P, the initial rise in the aggregate demand for goods leads to an equal size increase in production, Y. This response applies if all firms have markup ratios significantly above one and are, therefore, willing to meet fully the extra demand at a fixed price. The expansion of Y leads to increases in real income, notably in real labor income, $(w/P) \cdot L$. This extra income motivates another increase in consumer demand, which adds to the demand for

each firm's goods, $Y^d(j)$. The further increase in production, Y, in response to the additional demand generates the multiplier.

The Keynesian multiplier is an interesting theoretical result. However, economists have not verified empirically the existence of a multiplier. For example, we found in Chapter 12 that it was difficult to document in the U.S. data even a positive effect from changes in government purchases, G, on real GDP, Y. The positive relation was clear only for the large temporary expansions of G during major wars. Moreover, even in these cases, the response of Y was less than the increase in G; that is, the multiplier was less than one.

Money and Nominal Interest Rates

In practice, central banks—such as the Federal Reserve—tend to express monetary policy as targets for short-term nominal interest rates, rather than monetary aggregates. In the United States, especially since the early 1980s, the Fed focuses on the **Federal Funds rate**—the overnight nominal interest rate in the **Federal Funds market**, which comprises financial institutions, such as commercial banks. Although monetary policy is not expressed in terms of

---

[8] The government might also stimulate consumer demand by cutting taxes. If households regard themselves as wealthier when taxes are cut—unlike the Ricardian case explored in Chapter 14—current consumer demand would increase.

monetary aggregates, the Fed's adjustments of nominal interest rates nevertheless translate into changes in these aggregates. For the rest of the discussion in this section, we refer to the Fed, although we can for most purposes think more generally about a central bank.

The Federal Reserve's Federal Open Market Committee (FOMC) meets eight or more times a year. At each meeting, the FOMC adopts a target for the Federal Funds rate. Then the FOMC instructs the Federal Reserve's New York trading desk to conduct open-market operations to achieve the desired target for the Funds rate. Recall from Chapter 14 that open-market operations are exchanges between the monetary base (currency in circulation plus reserves held by depository institutions at the Fed) and interest-bearing assets, principally U.S. Treasury securities. These securities correspond to the bonds in our model. In practice, the Fed holds mainly government bonds, but our analysis of open-market operations would be essentially the same if the Fed instead held private bonds. In an expansionary operation, the Fed creates a new monetary base to buy bonds. In a contractionary operation, the Fed sells bonds from its portfolio and uses the proceeds to reduce the monetary base.

The central idea is that, in the short run with sticky prices, open-market operations affect nominal interest rates—the Federal Funds rate in the United States and the nominal interest rate, i, in our model. We can think of the relation between money and nominal interest rates from our familiar equilibrium condition in Chapter 10 whereby the nominal quantity of money, M, equals the nominal quantity demanded, $P \cdot L(Y, i)$:

(16.8) $$M = P \cdot L(Y, i)$$

In our model, we have thought of M as nominal currency. Now we should broaden the concept of M to the monetary base, which is the monetary aggregate affected directly by the Fed's open-market operations. Through these operations, the Fed can control the quantity of monetary base on a day-by-day basis.

The equilibrium condition in equation (16.8) specifies a relationship between the nominal monetary base, M, and the determinants of the nominal quantity of money demanded: the price level, P; real GDP, Y; and the nominal interest rate, i. In the new Keynesian model, P is fixed in the short run. Thus, in the short run, if M increases, equilibrium requires some combination

of higher Y or lower i to raise the nominal quantity of money demanded by the same amount as the increase in M. For a given Y, equation (16.8) says that a higher M has to match up with a lower i.

In our previous analysis, we thought of an expansionary monetary shock as an increase in the nominal quantity of money, M. Now we can think of an expansionary monetary action as a decrease in the nominal interest rate, i.

If equation (16.8) were a fixed relationship, the Fed could operate equivalently by changing the nominal quantity of money, M, or the nominal interest rate, i. However, in practice, the real quantity of money demanded, $L(Y, i)$, tends to fluctuate a great deal.[9] These fluctuations make it nearly impossible for the Fed to designate in advance the precise time path for the monetary base or some other monetary aggregate needed to achieve a desired part for i. Such a designation would require knowledge about future quantities of real money demanded, $L(Y, i)$. Because this knowledge is unattainable, central banks tend not to conduct monetary policy by specifying the path of a nominal monetary aggregate. More specifically, central banks have rejected proposals, originally put forward by Milton Friedman (1960, pp. 90–93), to have a **constant-growth-rate rule** for a designated monetary aggregate; Friedman's preferred candidates were M1 or M2. Such rules for money growth require i (or P or Y) to respond to each variation in the real quantity of money demanded.

Because of the shortcomings in rules based on monetary aggregates, the Fed and other central banks tend to frame their policies in terms of targeted adjustments in nominal interest rates, i. By targeting i, the Fed is led automatically to carry out the volume of open-market operations needed to obtain the required changes in the monetary base, M. For example, if the Fed wants to lower i, it raises M (through open-market operations) until the desired nominal interest rate prevails in the bond market (or, more specifically, the Federal Funds market). From equation (16.8), we know that the necessary increase in M equals the rise in real money demanded, $L(Y, i)$, caused by the fall in i (for given P and Y). However, an important point is that the Fed does not have to know the exact specification for $L(Y, i)$. The Fed just keeps raising M until it sees the nominal interest rate that it wants.

---

[9] As an example, we noted in Chapter 10 that the real quantity of money demanded has a lot of seasonal variation. The Fed accommodates this seasonality by introducing an appropriate amount of seasonal variation in M. This seasonality in the monetary base avoids having seasonality in the nominal interest rate, i; in fact, the elimination of seasonal variations in nominal interest rates was one of the main reasons for the creation of the Federal Reserve in 1914. For discussions, see Truman Clark (1986) and Jeffrey Miron (1986).

As another exam-
ple, suppose that the
Fed does not want
the nominal interest
rate, i, to change, but
that the real quantity
of money demanded,
$L(Y, i)$, increases. If the
Fed kept M constant,
i would have to rise to
bring $L(Y, i)$ back down.
Instead, the Fed raises M
to balance the increase in
$L(Y, i)$. (This adjustment
is sometimes described
as an *accommodation* of
money demand.) More-
over, as in our previous
example, the Fed does
not have to know exactly
how $L(Y, i)$ changed.
The Fed just keeps rais-
ing M (through open-
market operations) until
the nominal interest rate

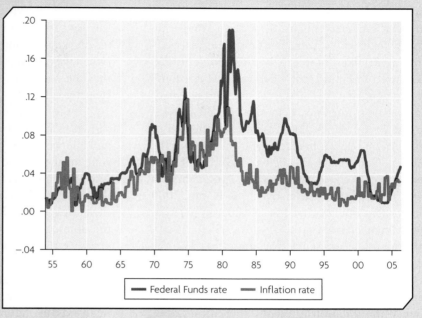

Figure 16.2 *The Federal Funds Rate and the Inflation Rate*

The blue line is the monthly Federal Funds rate, the short-term nominal interest rate monitored closely by the Federal Reserve. The red line is the inflation rate, calculated quarterly from the GDP deflator.

that prevails in the financial markets is the one that it wants—in this case, an unchanged i.

Since the early 1980s, the Federal Reserve has adjusted its target for the Federal Funds rate, i, to achieve a moderate and stable inflation rate, π. In recent years, the Fed apparently regarded an inflation rate of around 2% per year as acceptable, so that π above 2% was viewed as too high and π below 2% as too low. If π was greater than 2% for some time, the Fed tended to take contractionary action—raising i by means of contractionary open-market operations. Conversely, if π was below 2% for some time, the Fed tended to take expansionary action—lowering i by means of expansionary open-market operations.

Figure 16.2 shows the history of the Federal Funds rate and the inflation rate (calculated from the GDP deflator) from 1954 to 2006. One important obser-vation is that the Fed seems to have changed the way it sets the Funds rate in response to inflation. From 1972 to 1975, when the inflation rate rose sharply, the Funds rate increased only along with the inflation rate. Then, when the inflation rate came down after 1975, the Funds rate declined along with it. In contrast, in 1979–80, the rise in the inflation rate resulted in an even greater increase in the Funds rate, which soared to 20% in 1981. The Fed brought the Funds rate down

below 8% only after the inflation rate fell sharply in the early and mid-1980s.

The change in the Fed's monetary policy, whereby the Funds rate reacts strongly to inflation, was initiated by Paul Volcker, who was chair of the Fed from August 1979 until August 1987. His general procedures were continued by Alan Greenspan, who became chair in August 1987. In 2006, when Ben Bernanke was appointed to head the Fed, the expectation was that he would maintain the kinds of policies established by Volcker and Greenspan. This policy seems to have succeeded in maintaining low and stable inflation. As Figure 16.2 shows, the inflation rate since 1985 averaged a little over 2% and has fluctu-ated within a narrow range.

As we discussed in Chapter 15 and detailed in Table 15.2, since 1990, central banks in many countries have adopted formal inflation-targeting procedures. In these regimes, nominal interest rates react to changes in the inflation rate—higher inflation induces higher nominal interest rates, and lower inflation induces lower nominal interest rates. Thus, although the inflation-targeting central banks have more formal rules, the basic approach to monetary policy is similar to the one practiced since the early 1980s by the Federal Reserve. Greenspan was not a fan of formal rules, and he resisted moving the Fed in this direction. However, Bernanke is much more of a proponent of formal inflation targeting, and his appointment in 2006 increased the odds that the Fed would move in this direction.

Many of the movements in the Federal Funds rate during the Volcker and Greenspan eras were reactions to economic variables other than inflation. The Fed tended to raise the Funds rate when the real economy was strong, gauged especially by high employment growth and a low unemployment rate. An example is the steep rise in the Funds rate from 3% at the end of 1993 to 6% in mid-1995, in response to strength in the labor market. Conversely, the Fed reduced the Funds rate when the real economy was weak. An example is the cut in the Funds rate from over 6% in mid-2000 to the remarkably low level of 1% in 2003, in reaction to the weak labor market.

At this point, economists are confident that the response of monetary policy to inflation has been beneficial. That is, the success in curbing inflation derives from the policy of raising nominal interest rates sharply when the inflation rate rises and cutting rates sharply when the inflation rate falls. This policy can be expressed alternatively as having contractionary open-market operations when the inflation rate increases and expansionary open-market operations when the inflation rate decreases.

The benefits from the other parts of the Fed's monetary policy are less clear. That is, we do not know whether the economy has performed better or worse because the Fed has adjusted nominal interest rates in response to strength or weakness in the real economy, gauged particularly by the labor market.

The Keynesian Model—Sticky Nominal Wage Rates

s mentioned at the beginning of this chapter, the model in Keynes's (1936) *General Theory* relies on **sticky nominal wage rates**—that is, a failure of nominal wage rates to react rapidly to changed circumstances. To focus on the consequences of sticky nominal wage rates, we now simplify by assuming that prices of goods are perfectly flexible. Therefore, we can return to the model from previous chapters in which the suppliers and demanders of goods are perfect competitors. In this setting, the single nominal price, P, applies to all goods.

Keynes just assumed that the nominal wage rate, w, was sticky; that is, he assumed that w did not adjust rapidly to clear the labor market. Moreover, Keynes focused on a case in which w was higher than its market-clearing level. This assumption will imply (when we consider how the price level, P, is determined) that the real wage rate, w/P, will be above its market-clearing value.

In the Keynesian model, the labor market looks as shown in Figure 16.3. In this graph, the labor demand and supply curves are the same as those in our equilibrium business-cycle model (see Figure 8.15 in Chapter 8). Note that an increase in the real wage rate, w/P, lowers the quantity of labor demanded, L^d, but raises the quantity supplied, L^s. The only difference from before is that the nominal wage rate, w, is assumed not to adjust to generate the real wage rate, $(w/P)^*$, that balances the quantities of labor demanded and supplied. Instead, the prevailing real wage rate, $(w/P)'$, is greater than $(w/P)^*$.

At the real wage rate $(w/P)'$ shown on the vertical axis in Figure 16.3, the quantity of labor supplied is greater than the quantity demanded. Since the quantities supplied and demanded are unequal, we have to reconsider how the quantity of labor, L, is determined. We use the principle that L equals the smaller of the quantities demanded and supplied—in this case, the quantity demanded, L^d. Hence, $L = L'$ on the horizontal axis. Labor input cannot be higher than this amount, because some demander of labor would then be forced to employ more labor than the quantity desired at the given real wage rate, $(w/P)'$. In other words, we assume that the labor market respects the rule of **voluntary exchange**. No market participant can be forced to hire more labor than the amount desired—or to work more than the amount desired—at the prevailing real wage rate.

Notice in Figure 16.3 that the quantity of labor supplied, L^s, at the given real wage rate, $(w/P)'$, is greater than the quantity demanded, L^d, which equals the quantity of labor, L'. The usual assumption about markets is that the nominal wage rate, w, would decline in this situation. That is, the eager suppliers of labor would compete for jobs by bidding down w. However, this response is ruled out by assumption in the Keynesian model, at least in the short run. The excess of the quantity of labor supplied (at the given real wage rate, $[w/P]'$) over L' is called **involuntary unemployment**. This amount is shown in green in Figure 16.3. Involuntary unemployment is the difference between the quantity of labor that households would like at $(w/P)'$— the quantity supplied, L^s—and the quantity that they actually get, L'.

Suppose, now, that a monetary expansion raises the price level, P. If the nominal wage rate, w, does not change, the rise in P lowers the real wage rate, w/P. We assume in Figure 16.4 that the increase in P reduces the real wage rate on the vertical axis from $(w/P)'$ to $(w/P)'$. This fall in w/P raises the quantity of labor demanded, L^d, and, thereby, increases labor input on the horizontal axis from L' to L'. Hence, in the model with sticky nominal wage rates, a monetary expansion raises labor input, L. The increase in L leads through the production function to an expansion of real GDP, Y.

As long as the nominal wage rate, w, is fixed, monetary expansions reduce the real wage rate, w/P, and raise labor input, L, through the mechanism shown in Figure 16.4. This process can continue until w/P falls to its market-clearing value, $(w/P)^*$, on the vertical axis. At that point, L reaches its market-clearing level, L^*, on the horizontal axis.[10]

We see from Figure 16.4 that a monetary expansion raises labor input, L, and, thereby, real GDP, Y,

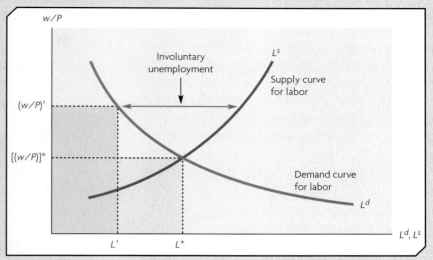

Figure 16.3 *The Labor Market in the Keynesian Model with Sticky Nominal Wage Rates*

In the Keynesian model, the nominal wage rate, w', is fixed above its market-clearing value, w^*. Consequently, the real wage rate, $(w/P)'$, will be greater than the market-clearing value, $(w/P)^*$, on the vertical axis. At $(w/P)'$, the quantity of labor supplied, along the L^s curve, exceeds the quantity demanded, along the L^d curve. On the horizontal axis, the quantity of labor, $L⊠$, equals the quantity demanded and is less than the market-clearing value, L^*.

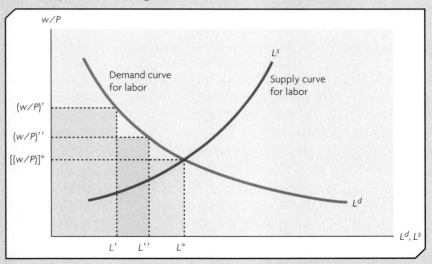

Figure 16.4 *Effect of Monetary Expansion in the Keynesian Model with Sticky Nominal Wage Rates*

In the Keynesian model, the nominal wage rate, w, is fixed above its market-clearing value, w^*. Therefore, on the vertical axis, the real wage rate, $(w/P)'$, is greater than the market-clearing value, $(w/P)^*$. On the horizontal axis, labor input, L', equals the quantity of labor demanded at $(w/P)'$. A monetary expansion raises the price level and, thereby, lowers the real wage rate to $(w/P)''$ on the vertical axis. On the horizontal axis, labor input rises to L'', the quantity of labor demanded at $(w/P)''$. A sufficient monetary expansion would raise L up to the market-clearing value, L^*.

[10] Further monetary expansion, with w still held fixed, would lower w/P below $(w/P)^*$. In this situation, the quantity of labor demanded, L^d, becomes larger than the quantity supplied, L^s. According to the principle of voluntary exchange, labor input, L, would then equal the quantity supplied, L^s. In this circumstance, reductions in w/P brought about by further monetary expansions would lower the quantity of labor supplied, L^s, and, thereby, reduce L. Thus, in the Keynesian model, too much monetary expansion would have adverse consequences.

BACK TO REALITY

Keynes, Friedman, and the Great Depression

John Maynard Keynes was a famous British economist who taught at Cambridge University. Important publications from 1919 to 1923 concerned German reparations payments and hyperinflation following World War I. His monumental work, *The General Theory of Employment, Interest, and Money*, appeared in 1936. This book worked out a new framework to provide remedies for economies caught up in the global depression of the 1930s. His model did not explain the origins of the Great Depression but did argue that market economies had a general tendency to experience persistently low aggregate output and persistently high unemployment rates. He argued that these poor aggregate outcomes could be improved by active fiscal policy—specifically, increases in government expenditure and cuts in taxes in response to a recession.

Although he discussed monetary policy, Keynes in *General Theory* deemphasized monetary shocks as a source of business fluctuations, and he downplayed monetary policy as an antirecession device. In contrast, particularly since the 1980s, new Keynesian economists have embraced activist monetary policy as a centerpiece of countercyclical policy.

Whatever the merits of Keynes's model in *General Theory*, there is no doubt about the extent of its intellectual influence. *General Theory* essentially established macroeconomics as a distinct field of economics. Moreover, the term *Keynesian economics* is one of the most widely used phrases in the economics literature. The term refers to models in which government intervention at the macroeconomic level can help to improve the functioning of poorly performing market economies. Keynesian models typically assume, at least implicitly, that private markets can be trusted for microeconomic decisions—for example, how much to work and consume and which goods to buy and produce. The market failures in these models relate

to aggregates, such as real GDP and overall employment. Correspondingly, the suggested government interventions are not microeconomic ones—such as controls on individual prices or detailed regulations of firms and households—but rather macroeconomic policies.

Milton Friedman, some of whose research we discussed in this and earlier chapters, was the only economist to rival Keynes for policy influence in the twentieth century. Friedman's main work appeared while he was at the University of Chicago; he is known as one of the pillars of the Chicago School of Economics. In contrast to Keynes, Friedman put the primary blame for the U.S. Depression from 1929 to 1933 on government failure, especially the Federal Reserve's monetary policy. The Fed did not respond aggressively enough to bank failures and the consequent sharp declines in broad monetary aggregates and the general price level. Documentation for this viewpoint is in *Monetary History*, written by Friedman and Schwartz (1963). This interpretation of events meant that the Great Depression posed no dilemma for Friedman's broad preference for small government, and he found in the Fed's failures to prevent deflation an argument in favor of monetary rules.

Even today, there is no full consensus among economists on the sources of the Great Depression. However, there is general agreement that the monetary collapse—an aspect deemphasized by Keynes—is a central part of the story. Many economists believe that the fall in monetary aggregates was particularly important because the accompanying deterioration of the financial sector led to collapses of credit and sharp increases in bankruptcies. The importance of the credit channel in explaining the size and duration of the Great Depression was stressed by the recently appointed chair of the Federal Reserve, Ben Bernanke, in his early research (Bernanke [1983]).

by lowering the real wage rate, w/P. The Keynesian model is similar to the new Keynesian model in predicting that nominal money, M, and labor, L, would be procyclical. However, unlike the new Keynesian model, the Keynesian model predicts that w/P would

be countercyclical—low when L and Y are high, and high when L and Y are low. We have stressed that w/P typically moves in a procyclical manner. Therefore, the Keynesian model has difficulty explaining the observed cyclical behavior of w/P. In this respect, the model has the same flaw as the price-misperceptions model from Chapter 15.

Keynes himself recognized that his model had problems with respect to its predictions about the cyclical behavior of the real wage rate, w/P. However, he did not come up with convincing solutions for this problem. One of the main motivations for the new Keynesian model—developed earlier in this chapter—is that it eliminates the counterfactual predictions for w/P. That is, as shown in Table 16.1, w/P is procyclical in the new Keynesian model. On the other hand, the new Keynesian model relies on sticky nominal prices, and many economists believe—like Keynes—that sticky nominal wage rates are more important in practice.

Long-Term Contracts and Sticky Nominal Wage Rates

For many workers, nominal wage rates are set for one or more years by the terms of agreements made with employers. These agreements are sometimes formal contracts between firms and labor unions. More commonly, firms and workers have implicit contracts that specify in advance the nominal wage rate over some period, often a

BACK TO REALITY

The Real Wage Rate During the New Deal

Typically, the real wage rate, w/P, is procyclical: high when the economy is doing well and low when the economy is doing badly. However, Harold Cole and Lee Ohanian (2004) find that w/P behaved in an unusual manner during President Franklin Roosevelt's New Deal period from 1934 to 1939. At that time, the economy was recovering from the Great Depression, which was at its worst in 1933. According to Figure 8.4 in Chapter 8, real GDP was 17% below trend in 1933. Thereafter, the economy grew rapidly (except during the 1937–38 recession) but at a pace that many economists regard as surprisingly slow. For example, real GDP was still 9% below trend in 1939.

Cole and Ohanian attribute much of the slow economic recovery from 1934 to 1939 to New Deal policies that limited competition in product markets and increased labor bargaining power. Notably, these policies raised nominal and real wage rates in manufacturing and other sectors covered by the National Industrial Recovery Act (in place for 1933–35 until it was declared unconstitutional) and the National Labor Relations Act (in effect from 1935 onward). For example, in manufacturing, the real wage rate, w/P, in 1939 was 20% higher, relative to trend, than in 1933.[11] Cole and Ohanian argue that the government's

policies for promoting an artificially high w/P and for restricting competition among businesses were harmful to the economy. Specifically, they estimate that the rate of economic growth from 1934 to 1939 would have been substantially higher if the New Deal policies had not been in place. Interestingly, Roosevelt came to the same conclusion in 1939, when he abandoned his efforts to limit competition in the economy.

© Photos 12/Alamy

---

[11] See Cole and Ohanian (2004, Table 2).

fiscal or calendar year. The existence of these agreements has been offered as a defense for the Keynesian assumption that the nominal wage rate, w, is sticky. The contracting approach has also been used to explain why some nominal prices are sticky, for example, the prices of intermediate goods sold to businesses by regular suppliers.

There are many good reasons why trading partners would specify in advance the wage rates or prices on which services and goods will be exchanged. This presetting of wage rates or prices can prevent one party from demanding "unreasonable" terms, ex post. That is, a wage or price agreement can alleviate what economists call the "hold-up problem." In the absence of a contract, an employer might, for example, lower the nominal wage rate after an employee has incurred substantial costs in moving to a job. Similarly, a supplier might raise the price for materials at a time when delays in a construction project are prohibitively expensive. Presetting the wage rate or price can avoid some of these problems.

Suppose that an employer and employee agree on a fixed nominal wage rate, w, for the next year.[12] A natural choice is to set w equal to the best estimate of the average market-clearing nominal wage rate, w^*, that will prevail over the year. Although the chosen w may be a rational expectation of w^*, unanticipated events lead to mistakes. For example, if the inflation rate, π, is surprisingly high, the average price level, P, during the year will be higher than anticipated. If nothing else changes in the economy, the market-clearing nominal wage rate, w^*, would rise along with P to maintain the market-clearing real wage rate, $(w/P)^*$. In this case, the agreed-upon nominal wage rate, w, will fall short of the average w^* for the year. Conversely, if π is surprisingly low, the fixed w will be greater than the average w^* for the year.

When the contract expires, the employer and employee agree on a new nominal wage rate, w, for the next year. This new w takes account of events during the current year, including the inflation rate, π. Thus, if expectations are rational, mistakes in the setting of w for this year—due perhaps to underestimation of inflation—tend not to be repeated the next year. The rationality of expectations implies also that deviations of w from w^* would not be systematically greater than or less than zero. Thus, the contracting perspective does not support the Keynesian emphasis on situations in which w is greater than w^*. In the contracting scenario, w greater than w^* and w less than w^* would each apply roughly half the time.

At any point in time, the economy has an array of existing labor contracts, each of which specifies a nominal wage rate, w, that likely deviates somewhat from the market-clearing value, w^*. Some of these agreements have w greater than w^*, and others have w less than w^*. However, aggregate shocks can create differences between the economy-wide averages of w and w^*. For example, unexpectedly low inflation tends to make w greater than w^* throughout the economy. Some macroeconomists have used this result to explain why a monetary contraction reduces employment and output. That is, the contracting approach has been used to fill a gap in the Keynesian model—explaining why the nominal wage rate, w, is sticky in the face of a monetary contraction.[13]

Unfortunately, this application of the contracting approach encounters logical problems. The Keynesian results emerge when the nominal wage rate, w, is fixed at too high a level *and* when the principle of voluntary exchange determines the quantity of labor, L. Suppose, for example, that w and, hence, w/P are too high, so that the quantity of labor supplied, L^s, is greater than the quantity demanded, L^d. In this case, voluntary exchange dictates that L equals the quantity demanded. This approach makes sense for an impersonal market. However, the idea is typically not applicable to a long-term contract, which is supposed to be the rationale for sticky nominal wage rates.

In an enduring relationship, in which explicit or implicit contracts arise, the trading parties do not have to change prices or wage rates at every instant to get the "right" behavior of quantities. Workers can, for example, agree in advance that they will work harder when there is more work to do—that is, when the demand for a firm's product is high—and work less hard when there is little work. Unlike in an impersonal auction market, these efficient adjustments in work and production can occur even if wage rates do not change from day to day.[14] The important point is that, in the context of labor contracts, stickiness of nominal wage rates does not necessarily cause errors in the determination of labor input and production.

---

[12] The contracting approach motivates the presetting of a real wage rate, w/P, rather than a nominal wage rate, w. Yet most labor agreements in advanced economies are not explicitly "indexed"; that is, they do not contain automatic adjustments of nominal wage rates for changes in the price level, P. Apparently, firms and workers find it convenient to specify agreements in terms of the standard nominal unit of account—such as the U.S. dollar—even though the future price level is uncertain. There is evidence, however, that higher and more variable inflation tends to generate shorter contracts and more frequent use of formal indexation of nominal wage rates.

[13] The original applications of the contracting approach to macroeconomics were by Donald Gordon (1974), Costas Azariadis (1975), and Martin Baily (1974). Applications to monetary shocks were made by Jo Anna Gray (1976), Stanley Fischer (1977), and John Taylor (1980).

[14] However, for large short-term increases in labor input, contracts often prescribe overtime premiums or other types of bonuses.

bythenumbers

Empirical Evidence on the Contracting Approach

A number of empirical studies provide evidence about the macroeconomic implications of the contracting approach. Shaghil Ahmed (1987) used a data set for 19 industries in Canada over the period 1961–74. He used these data because an earlier study by David Card (1980) calculated the extent of **indexation**—automatic adjustment of nominal wage rates for changes in the price level—in each industry's labor contracts. Indexation ranged from zero to nearly 100%. According to theories in which labor contracts are the basis for the Keynesian model, industries with little indexation should show substantial responses of real wage rates and, hence, of employment and output, to nominal shocks. Industries with a lot of indexation would be affected little by nominal disturbances.

Ahmed found that monetary shocks had positive effects on hours worked in most of the 19 industries. The important point for present purposes, however, is that the extent of an industry's response to these shocks bore no relation to the amount of indexation in the industry. Those with a lot of indexation were as likely as those with little indexation to respond to monetary shocks. This finding is damaging to theories that use long-term contracts as the basis for the Keynesian sticky-wage model.

Mark Bils (1989) studied labor contracts for 12 manufacturing industries in the United States. He reasoned that, if the signing of new contracts was important, we should observe unusual behavior of employment and real wage rates just after these signings. His results were mixed. Some industries, notably motor vehicles, showed substantial changes in employment just after the implementation of new labor agreements. Prior changes in employment tended to be reversed just after a new contract came into effect. These results, although applying only to a few industries, support the contracting approach. However, Bils did not find any corresponding changes in real wage rates after the new labor contracts were implemented. Since these changes in real wage

rates are central to the contracting approach, it is difficult to reconcile this part of Bils's findings with that approach.

A study by Giovanni Olivei and Silvana Tenreyro (2007) suggests that the contracting approach may be important for understanding the real effects of monetary policy. They first observed that a preponderance of firms set wage rates toward the end of each calendar year, with the changes taking effect in January of the next year. In the contracting approach, this timing means that monetary disturbances that occur toward the end of the calendar year would be undone within a few months by the changes of wage rates in the next annual adjustment. In contrast, monetary disturbances early in the calendar year would take up to 12 months to be undone by the next adjustment.

Using this conceptual framework, Olivei and Tenreyro investigate whether the response of real GDP to monetary shocks looks different depending on the quarter of the year in which the shock occurs. They measure the shocks by unusual movements in the Federal Funds rate. The unusual movements are those that cannot be explained by prior variations in real GDP, the GDP deflator, and commodity prices. The main finding, for the period 1966 to 2002, was that the response of real GDP to a Funds-rate shock is substantial when the shock takes place in the first or second quarter of the year. A decline in the interest rate by one-quarter of a percentage point is estimated to raise real GDP by 0.2% over the following two years. However, the response is smaller if the shock to the Funds rate occurs in the third or fourth quarter of the year. In that case, a decrease in the funds rate by one-quarter of a percentage point is estimated to raise real GDP by less than 0.1% over the following two years. Olivei and Tenreyro suggest that the difference in response arises because nominal wage rates tend to be sticky during the calendar year but flexible from the end of one calendar year to the beginning of the next.

To take a concrete example, suppose that inflation is sometimes lower than expected and sometimes higher. Rational firms and workers know that inflation—if not accompanied by real changes in the economy—does not alter the efficient levels of labor input and production. Therefore, it makes sense to agree on a contract that insulates the choices of labor input and production from the inflation rate. Over many years, when the effects of unanticipated inflation on real wage rates tend to average out, both parties to the contract would benefit from this provision. However, in an economic climate where inflation is high and unpredictable, firms and workers prefer either to index nominal wage rates to the price level or to renegotiate contracts more frequently.

An important lesson from the contracting approach is that stickiness of the nominal wage rate, w, need not lead to the unemployment and underproduction that appears in the Keynesian model. Within a long-term agreement, it is unnecessary for w to move all the time in order for the economy to approximate the market-clearing quantity of labor, L^*. Thus, instead of supporting the Keynesian perspective, the contracting analysis demonstrates that observed stickiness of nominal wage rates may not matter very much for the workings of the macroeconomy. This reasoning applies also to the sticky prices in the new Keynesian model if we try to explain this price stickiness not from literal menu costs but instead from contractual agreements—for example, between producers and their suppliers.

Questions and Problems

A. Review questions

1. What is involuntary unemployment?

2. Explain how an increase in the nominal quantity of money, M, reduces the nominal interest rate, i, in the new Keynesian model. Why does this effect not arise in the market-clearing model?

B. Problems for discussion

3. The new Keynesian model

a. What are the main differences between the new Keynesian model and the equilibrium business-cycle model?

b. Does a change in the nominal quantity of money, M, have real effects in the new Keynesian model? Is imperfect competition among producers sufficient to generate non-neutrality of money in this model?

c. How does the new Keynesian model explain sticky prices?

d. What does the new Keynesian model predict for the cyclical behavior of the real wage rate and the average product of labor? Are the results consistent with the data?

e. Are money-supply shocks the only kinds of shocks that have real effects in the new Keynesian model? What other shocks have real effects in this model?

f. What are the relative strengths of the new Keynesian and equilibrium business-cycle models?

4. The paradox of thrift
Suppose that households become thriftier in the sense that they decide to raise current saving and reduce current consumer demand.

a. In the new Keynesian model, what happens to real GDP, Y, and labor, L?

b. What happens to the amount of saving? If it decreases, there is said to be a *paradox of thrift*.

c. Can there be a paradox of thrift in the equilibrium business-cycle model?

5. The Keynesian multiplier
Explain why there can be a multiplier in the new Keynesian model. How is the size of the multiplier affected by the following:

a. adjustments of the price level, P?

b. the extent to which markup ratios exceed one?

c. reactions of the nominal quantity of money demanded, M^d, to real GDP, Y?
Can there be a multiplier in the equilibrium business-cycle model?

6. Perceived wealth in the new Keynesian model
Suppose that the U.S. president makes a speech and announces that we are all wealthier than we thought. If we all believe the president, what does the new Keynesian model predict for changes in real GDP, Y, and labor, L? Do we actually end up being "wealthier"? Contrast these predictions with those from the equilibrium business-cycle model.

7. Sticky-wage models
How does the model with sticky nominal wage rates differ from the new Keynesian model? What are the relative strengths of the two kinds of models? Why do you think that Keynes emphasized sticky nominal wages, rather than sticky prices?

absolute convergence The tendency of real per capita GDP in poor economies to grow faster than in rich ones, so that poor economies catch up over time to rich ones. The term "absolute" means that the convergence is not conditioned on other economic variables.

absolute form of PPP The version of purchasing-power parity that involves levels of exchange rates and prices.

acyclical Having no regular relation with the business cycle; that is, with detrended real GDP.

adjusted gross income Gross income less adjustments for tax purposes, such as business and moving expenses and deferred compensation through pension plans.

adjustment costs for investment Costs that have to be paid to change the quantity of capital (plant and equipment) used in production.

after-tax real interest rate The real interest rate calculated after netting out the real income tax paid on the interest earnings.

after-tax real wage rate The real wage rate calculated after netting out the real income tax paid on the wage income.

aggregate demand The total demand for goods and services in the forms of consumption, gross investment, and government purchases.

Ak model A growth model in which the production function is linear in capital; that is, $y = Ak$, where y is output per worker and k is capital per worker.

average product of capital The ratio of output (real GDP) to the capital stock.

average tax rate The ratio of taxes to a measure of income. See *marginal tax rate*.

balance of international payments The summary statement of a country's international trade in commodities, bonds, and international reserves.

balance on current account A zero current-account balance.

balanced budget Equality between the government's purchases, transfers, and interest payments and the government's tax revenue.

Balassa-Samuelson hypothesis Theory that, in poor countries, the prices of nontraded goods and services are low compared to prices of traded goods. Therefore, a market basket of goods and services tends to be less expensive in poor countries than in rich ones.

barter Direct exchange of one good for another, without the use of money. See *medium of exchange*.

bond A contract that gives the holder (lender) a claim to a specified stream of payments from the issuer (borrower).

bond market Market on which bonds are traded.

boom A period in which real GDP is high and rising.

Bretton Woods System A system of international payments established after World War II in which each country pegged the exchange rate between its own currency and the U.S. dollar. The United States exchanged dollars for gold at a fixed price ($35 per ounce), thus pegging the value of each country's currency to gold.

budget constraint An equation relating the sources of funds in a period, such as wage and asset income and initial assets, to the uses of funds in that period, such as consumption and end-of-period assets.

budget deficit Excess of the government's purchases, transfers, and interest payments over the government's tax revenue.

budget line A graph of the combinations of consumptions over two periods that satisfy the household's two-period budget constraint.

budget surplus Excess of the government's tax revenue over the government's purchases, transfers, and interest payments.

burden of the public debt The possible negative effect of the public debt on saving and investment and, hence, on the stock of capital available later.

business cycle Pattern of real GDP rising during a boom and falling during a recession.

capital levy Tax rate on capital when levied after investments have been made.

capital stock Stock of goods in the forms of plant and equipment, used as input to production.

capital utilization rate Rate at which stock of capital is used in production.

chain-weighted real GDP A method for constructing real GDP in which the relative-price weights continually adjust for the changing composition of production.

checkable deposits Deposits, issued by financial institutions, against which account holders can write checks.

closed economy An economy isolated from the rest of the world.

Cobb-Douglas production function This production function satisfies constant returns to scale.

commodity money Money that takes a physical form, such as gold and silver coins.

common currency A regime in which all countries use the same currency and quote prices in units of this currency.

conditional convergence The idea that real per capita GDP in poor countries grows faster than in rich countries, for given values of government policies, propensities to save money and have children, and other variables.

constant-growth-rate rule A rule for monetary policy in which a specified monetary aggregate grows at a constant rate.

constant returns to scale   The property of a production function that a proportionate increase in all inputs results in an equiproportionate increase in output.

consumer durables   Consumable commodities purchased by households that last for a long time. Examples are automobiles, furniture, and appliances.

consumer nondurables and services   Consumable commodities purchased by households that last for a short time.

consumer price index (CPI)   A weighted average of prices of consumer goods, measured relative to a base year.

convergence   The tendency of real per capita GDP in a poor economy to grow faster than in a rich one. Therefore, the poor economy's real per capita GDP tends to catch up over time to that in the rich economy.

copyright   Property right over the use of a book, trademark, or similar object.

countercyclical   Moving in the direction opposite to the business cycle; that is, to detrended real GDP.

CPI   See *consumer price index*.

currency   Non-interest-bearing paper money issued by the government.

currency union   A group of countries that use a common currency.

current-account balance   The value of goods and services produced by domestic residents (including the net factor income from abroad) plus net transfers from abroad, less the expenditure by domestic residents on goods and services. If the current-account balance is positive (negative), the current account is in surplus (deficit).

current-account deficit   A negative current-account balance.

current-account surplus   A positive current-account balance.

cyclical part of real GDP   The difference between real GDP and its trend.

deflation   A sustained decrease in the general price level over time. See *inflation*.

demand curve   A curve expressing the relation between the quantity demanded and the price of a good or service.

demand for money   The amount of money that households desire to hold, expressed as a function of real GDP, the nominal interest rate, transaction costs, and other variables.

depreciation   The wearing out of capital goods over time.

devaluation   An action by the central bank that raises the number of units of a country's currency that exchange for other currencies.

diffusion of technology   Spread of technology from one country or region to another.

diminishing average product of capital   Tendency for the average product of capital to fall as capital per worker rises.

diminishing marginal product of capital   Tendency for the marginal product of capital to fall as capital per worker rises.

diminishing marginal product of labor   Tendency for the marginal product of labor to fall as the quantity of labor rises, for given capital input.

discount factor   The relative value of a dollar in different periods of time; for example, between one year and the next. The nominal discount factor is one plus the nominal interest rate.

discounted   Use of the discount factor to express future income or expenditure in units comparable to current income or expenditure.

discouraged workers   Workers who leave the labor force following a period of unemployment.

discretionary policy   A setup in which government policy is not restricted by prior commitments.

disequilibrium   Absence of equilibrium in a market; lack of market clearing.

disposable personal income   Personal income less taxes.

double taxation   Taxation of something twice. For example, corporate profits are taxed at the corporate level and then taxed again at the household level when paid out as dividends.

duration of unemployment   The length of time that a spell of unemployment is expected to last. The duration of unemployment is inversely related to the job-finding rate.

economic fluctuations   Variations in real GDP during a business cycle.

economies of scale in cash management   The property of the demand for money that the desired average real money-holding increases less than proportionately with a rise in real GDP.

employment   The number of persons working at jobs in the market sector.

employment rate   The ratio of employment to the labor force.

endogenous growth theory   Long-run economic growth that is explained by the interactions within a model.

endogenous money   The automatic response of the quantity of money to changes in the economy. Money is endogenous under the gold standard and in regimes in which the monetary authority targets nominal interest rates or the price level.

endogenous variables   Variables determined by the model.

equilibrium   Condition that determines quantities and prices in a market. *Quantity supplied equals quantity demanded* is an example of an equilibrium condition.

equilibrium business-cycle model   A model of economic fluctuations that uses equilibrium conditions to determine how shocks affect real GDP and other macroeconomic variables. In our model, supply and demand functions accord with microeconomic foundations. Given these functions, the key equilibrium conditions are that markets have to clear.

exchange market   Market in which the currency of one country is traded for that of another country.

exchange rate   The number of units of a country's currency that trades for one unit of another currency, such as the U.S. dollar. See *nominal exchange rate*.

exogenous technological progress   Improvements of technology that are not explained within the model.

exogenous variables   Variables that are not explained within the model.

expectations of inflation   Forecast of the inflation rate.

expected real interest rate   The real interest rate that is expected to be earned (or paid) after adjusting the nominal interest rate by the expectation of inflation.

exports   Goods and services produced by the residents of the home country that are sold to foreigners.

Federal Funds market   The market for very short-term borrowing and lending between financial institutions, such as commercial banks.

Federal Funds rate   The interest rate on loans made in the Federal Funds market.

Federal Open-Market Committee (FOMC)   A committee of the Federal Reserve that has responsibility for open-market operations.

fiat money   Money, such as paper currency, that has value due to government fiat, rather than intrinsic value, such as gold.

finite horizon   Finite planning period used by households in determining consumption, saving, and labor supply. See *infinite horizon*.

fiscal policy   The choice of government spending, taxes, and borrowing to influence the level of aggregate economic activity.

fixed exchange rates   Systems in which countries peg the exchange rate between their currency and other currencies, such as the U.S. dollar. Examples of fixed-exchange rate regimes are the gold standard, the Bretton Woods System, and a currency union.

flat-rate tax   A kind of income tax in which the amount of tax is a constant fraction of taxable income. See *graduated-rate tax*.

flexible exchange rates   Systems of international payments, prevalent since the early 1970s, in which countries allow the exchange rates for their currencies to fluctuate so as to clear the exchange market.

flow variable   A variable, such as real GDP or consumption, expressed per unit of time, such as a year.

foreign direct investment   Purchases of capital goods by home-country residents in foreign countries.

fully funded system (for Social Security)   A system in which each individual's payments accumulate in a trust fund, and retirement benefits are paid out of the accumulated funds. See *Social Security; pay-as-you-go system*.

GDP   See *gross domestic product*.

GDP in constant dollars   Gross domestic product expressed in terms of dollars from a base year. See *real GDP*.

GDP in current dollars   Gross domestic product expressed in current dollars. See *nominal GDP*.

general equilibrium   Clearing of all markets at the same time.

general price level   The dollar price per unit of goods and services. The average price of all goods and services.

globalization   The increased tendency for production and other economic activities to be carried out on a worldwide basis.

GNP   See *gross national product*.

gold standard   A system of international payments under which countries agree to buy or sell gold for a fixed amount of their currencies. The high point of this system was from 1890 to 1914.

goods market   A market in which goods and services are exchanged for money.

governmental budget constraint   The equation showing the balance between the government's sources and uses of funds.

graduated-rate tax   A kind of income tax in which the marginal tax rate rises with taxable income. See *flat-rate tax*.

Great Depression   The worldwide decline in aggregate economic activity in the United States and many other countries from 1929 to 1933.

gross domestic product (GDP)   The market value of an economy's domestically produced goods and services over a specified period of time, such as a year.

gross investment   Purchases of capital goods with no adjustment for the depreciation of the existing capital goods.

gross national product (GNP)   The total market value of the goods and services produced by the residents of a country over a specified period of time; GNP equals gross domestic product plus the net factor income from abroad.

gross private domestic investment   Total private expenditure on capital goods, including business spending on plant and equipment, the net change in business inventories, and residential construction. This total contains no adjustment for depreciation.

gross state product (GSP)   Gross domestic product for an individual state.

growth accounting   A formula that relates growth of real GDP to the growth of inputs, capital and labor, and to technological change.

GSP   See *gross state product*.

help-wanted advertising   Media advertising for job openings; used as a proxy for job vacancies.

high-powered money   The total amount of Federal Reserve notes (currency) and non-interest-bearing deposits (reserves) held at the Fed by depository institutions; the monetary base.

household budget constraint in nominal terms   The equation showing the balance between a household's sources and uses of funds. In this case, the equation is in nominal terms.

household budget constraint in real terms   The equation showing the balance between a household's sources and uses of funds. In this case, the equation is in real terms.

human capital   Skills and training that are embodied in workers and add to productivity.

hyperinflation   A sustained period with an extraordinarily high inflation rate, such as in Germany after World War I.

imperfect competition   A competitive environment in which each business has some pricing power. See *perfect competition*.

implicit GDP deflator   The price index that relates the gross domestic product, measured in nominal terms, to real GDP.

imports   Goods and services produced in foreign countries that are purchased by the residents of the home country.

imputed rental income   Rental income on capital, such as owner-occupied housing, that is not explicitly paid and received.

income effect   The effect of higher income on choices such as consumption and labor supply.

indexation   A system of contracts, such as for labor, in which payments are revised upward or downward automatically for increases or decreases in the general price level, so as to keep the real value of payments independent of inflation.

indexed bonds   Bonds on which the nominal payments of interest and principal are automatically adjusted for inflation to ensure a contracted real interest rate.

inequality   Differences in levels of real income across persons in an economy or across economies.

infinite horizon   Planning period of indefinite (infinite) length used by households in determining consumption, saving, and labor supply. See *finite horizon*.

infinite-horizon budget constraint   Budget constraint for a household over an infinite horizon.

inflation rate   The percentage change in a price index between two periods of time, such as from one year to the next.

inflation targeting   A regime for monetary policy in which the central bank adjusts nominal interest rates to achieve a target inflation rate.

infrastructure capital   Capital, often publicly owned, in the form of transportation, communications, energy and water provision, and so on.

intellectual property rights   Ownership rights in discoveries and ideas.

interest-bearing assets   Assets, such as bonds, that pay interest.

interest rate   The ratio of the interest payment to the amount borrowed; the return to lending or the cost of borrowing.

interest-rate parity   Equalization of interest rates across countries, adjusting for prospective changes in exchange rates.

international reserves   Assets, such as U.S. dollars and gold, that are commonly used for international transactions and as stores of value by central banks and other financial institutions.

intertemporal-substitution effect   The effect on current consumption (leisure) when the cost of future consumption (leisure) changes relative to that of current consumption (leisure).

inventories   Stores of commodities held by businesses either for sale or for use in production.

involuntary unemployment   The inability of workers to obtain employment at the prevailing market wage; a feature of Keynesian models.

irrelevance result for systematic monetary policy   The theoretical finding that a systematic policy of changing the quantity of money in response to the state of the economy is predictable and therefore powerless to affect real variables.

job-finding rate   The rate at which workers move from unemployment or outside of the labor force to employment.

job-separation rate   The rate at which workers move from employment to unemployment or outside of the labor force.

labor force   The total number of employed workers plus the number of unemployed.

labor hoarding   The tendency of firms to retain their workers during a recession. Labor hoarding may explain the tendency for measured labor productivity to fall during recessions and rise during booms.

labor market   The market on which workers sell, and producers buy, labor services.

labor-force participation rate   The fraction of the population (sometimes the noninstitutional population) that participates in the labor market.

Laffer curve   A graph showing that tax revenues initially rise as the marginal income tax rate rises, but eventually reach a maximum and subsequently decline with further increases in the marginal tax rate.

law of one price   The condition that identical goods in different places must sell at the same dollar price.

legal tender   A characteristic of money, whereby its use as a medium of exchange is reinforced by government statute.

life-cycle model   The theory of the choices of consumption and leisure that are made when the planning horizon equals an individual's expected remaining lifetime. The theory predicts that an individual will build up savings during working years and exhaust them during retirement years.

Lucas hypothesis on monetary shocks   The hypothesis that the effect of a given-size money shock on real GDP is larger, the less volatile money growth is historically.

lump-sum tax   A tax paid by an individual to the government in which the amount paid does not depend on any characteristic of the individual, such as income or wealth.

lump-sum transfer   A transfer payment from the government to an individual in which the amount paid does not depend on any characteristic of the recipient, such as income or wealth.

M1   The monetary aggregate that comprises currency held by the public, checkable deposits, and travelers' checks. M1 comprises the assets that serve regularly as media of exchange.

M2   M1 plus household holdings of savings deposits, small time deposits, and retail money-market mutual funds.

marginal cost of production   The added nominal cost to a producer from raising output by one unit.

marginal product of capital (MPK)   The increase in output from an increase in capital services by one unit, while holding fixed the technology and the quantity of labor.

marginal product of labor (MPL)   The increase in output from an increase in labor by one unit, while holding fixed the technology and the quantity of capital services.

marginal tax rate   The fraction of an additional dollar of income that must be paid as tax. In a graduated-rate system, this tax rate rises with the level of income. See *average tax rate*.

market-clearing approach   The viewpoint that prices, such as the wage rate, rental price, and general price level, are determined to clear markets.

market-clearing conditions   Conditions that quantity supplied equal quantity demanded in a market.

markup ratio   In imperfect competition, the ratio of the price charged to the marginal cost of production.

maturity   The date at which a bond expires and its principal is repaid.

medium of exchange   A commodity or other item used as a means of payment; money.

menu cost   Cost that must be paid to adjust a nominal price or wage. New Keynesian models rely on these costs to rationalize the sluggish adjustment of prices.

microeconomic foundations   The microeconomic analysis of individual choices that underlies the macroeconomic model of the economy.

monetary aggregate   Total nominal quantity of a concept of money, such as the monetary base, M1, or M2.

monetary approach to the balance of payments   Analyses of the balance of international payments and exchange rates that stress the nominal quantity of money and the demand for money in each country.

monetary base   Another name for high-powered money.

monetary rule   A regular procedure for altering the nominal quantity of money in response to developments in the macro economy.

monetary shocks   Unanticipated changes in the nominal quantity of money.

money   The usual means of payment or medium of exchange in an economy. Money also serves as a store of value. Money may take the form of paper currency, commodities, or deposits at financial institutions.

money growth rate   The proportionate change per year in the nominal quantity of money.

MPK   See *marginal product of capital*.

MPL   See *marginal product of labor*.

multiplier   The change in aggregate output per unit of increase in real aggregate demand. In Keynesian models, the multiplier can be greater than one.

multiyear budget constraint   The budget constraint for a household over more than one year.

national income   The income earned from aggregate production. National income equals gross domestic product less depreciation, which equals net domestic product.

national-income accounting   The summary statement of gross domestic product and its components during a year.

national saving   Total saving carried out by the residents of a country; the sum of private and public saving.

natural unemployment rate   The average unemployment rate that prevails in an economy in the long run. The unemployment rate tends to adjust over time toward the natural unemployment rate.

NDP   See *net domestic product*.

neoclassical growth model   A model of economic growth that extended the Solow growth model to allow for household choices of saving rates.

net domestic product (NDP)   Gross domestic product less depreciation.

net exports   The difference between the value of exports and the value of imports.

net factor income from abroad   Net income earned by the residents of a country from claims on foreign assets and from labor supplied to foreign countries.

net foreign investment   The change in a country's net holdings of foreign assets.

net international investment position   The stock of foreign claims held by home residents (including the home government) net of the stock of home claims held by foreign residents (including foreign governments).

net investment   The change in the capital stock; gross investment less depreciation.

net private domestic investment   Gross private domestic investment less depreciation.

neutrality of money   The theoretical finding that once-and-for-all changes in the nominal quantity of money affect nominal variables, such as the general price level, but do not affect real variables, such as real GDP.

new Keynesian model   Models that attempt to explain the role of sticky prices and aggregate demand in the Keynesian framework. These models incorporate imperfect competition and allow for menu costs of changing prices.

nominal   Measured in current dollar magnitudes; valued at current dollar prices; unadjusted for changes in the general price level.

nominal exchange rate   The exchange rate between one currency and another. See *real exchange rate*.

nominal GDP   Gross domestic product expressed in current dollars.

nominal interest rate   The amount paid as interest per dollar borrowed for each period; the rate at which nominal assets held as bonds grow over time.

nominal rental price   The nominal amount paid per year for each unit of capital used in production.

nominal saving   The current dollar value of real saving, calculated by multiplying real saving by a price index.

nominal wage rate   The nominal amount paid per year for each unit of labor used in production.

nonrival good   A good used by one household that does not reduce the quantity available for other households. An idea is an example of a nonrival good.

nontradable goods   Goods and services, such as labor services and real estate, that do not enter readily into international trade.

open economy   An economy that conducts trade with the rest of the world.

open-market operations   The purchase or sale of government securities by the central bank in exchange for high-powered money.

patent   Property right over the use of an invention.

pay-as-you-go system (for Social Security)   A system in which benefits to retired persons are financed by taxes on the current working generation.

perceived real wage rate   The real wage rate as perceived by workers. In the price-misperceptions model, the perceived real wage rate is the ratio of the nominal wage rate to the expected price level.

perfect competition   Market setting in which each participant is sufficiently small to neglect any influence on the market price. A perfect competitor assumes that he or she can buy or sell any quantity desired at the market price.

perfect foresight   A situation in which expectations of inflation or of other variables are accurate, so that there are no forecast errors.

permanent income   Long-run average real income. The hypothetical amount of real income that, when received constantly throughout a household's planning horizon, has the same real present value as the actual flow of income.

personal consumption expenditure   Purchases of goods and services by households for use in consumption.

personal income   Income received directly by persons; national income adjusted for undistributed corporate profits, Social Security contributions, transfer payments, and some other items.

planning horizon   The number of years that enter into the household's plan for choosing consumption, saving, and labor supply.

policy rule   A rule or commitment for governmental actions with regard to money or other variables.

population growth   Increase over time in population.

poverty   An estimated level of real income required to pay for basic necessities of life.

PPI   See *producer price index*.

PPP   See *purchasing-power parity*.

present value   The value of future dollar expenses or receipts, expressed in terms of current-dollar equivalents.

price level   Dollar price of a market basket of goods and services.

price stability   Rough constancy over time in the price level.

price taker   A participant in a market who regards the market price as given. See *perfect competition*.

price-level targeting   A rule for monetary policy that dictates maintenance of price stability.

price-misperceptions model   A model of economic fluctuations in which some participants incorrectly perceive the general price level. Money is not neutral in this model.

principal of bond   The dollar amount borrowed, to be repaid at maturity.

procyclical   Moving in the same direction as the business cycle; that is, with detrended real GDP.

producer price index (PPI)   A weighted average of prices of raw materials and semifinished goods, measured relative to base-year prices.

production function   The relationship between the quantity of output and the quantities of inputs to production, such as labor and capital.

productivity   Output measured relative to quantities of inputs, such as labor.

productivity slowdown   A reduction in the rate of growth of output per worker, thought to have occurred in OECD countries after the early 1970s.

profit   The difference between revenue and costs for a firm.

propensity to consume   The response of real consumer expenditure to a rise in real income.

propensity to save   The response of real saving to a rise in real income.

public debt   The dollar stock of interest-bearing government bonds.

public investment   Investment by government in plant and equipment or in public infrastructure.

purchasing-power parity (PPP)   The condition that the exchange rate between the foreign and home currencies equals the ratio of prices of foreign goods to prices of home goods.

quantity theory of money   The theory that changes in the nominal quantity of money account for the bulk of long-run movements in the general price level. This theory usually assumes that money is neutral in the long run.

quota   A limitation on the quantity of goods that can be imported or exported.

Ramsey model   A form of the neoclassical growth model due to the economist Frank Ramsey.

rate of economic growth   Proportionate change per year in real GDP.

rational expectations   The viewpoint that individuals make forecasts or estimates of unknown variables, such as the general price level, in the best possible manner, utilizing all information currently available.

real business-cycle (RBC) model   A theory of economic fluctuations that relies on real disturbances rather than monetary shocks. The RBC model is a type of equilibrium business-cycle model.

real demand for money   A function that determines the quantity of real money demanded.

real disposable income   Income measured after taxes and in real terms.

real exchange rate   The exchange rate between the foreign and home currencies divided by the ratio of the foreign price level to the home price level.

real GDP   See *real gross domestic product*.

real GNP   See *real gross national product*.

real gross domestic product   The real value of the nominal gross domestic product.

real gross national product   The real value of the gross national product.

real interest rate   The nominal interest rate on a bond less the inflation rate. The rate at which the real value of dollar assets held as bonds grows over time.

real rental price   The real value of the nominal rental price.

real saving   The change in the real value of assets held by households or by the economy as a whole. The real value of nominal saving.

real terms   Measured in units of goods; valued at base-year prices; dollar magnitudes adjusted for inflation by deflating by a price index.

real wage rate   The real value of the nominal wage rate.

recession   A period of decline in real GDP. A shortfall of real GDP from trend.

relative form of PPP   The version of purchasing-power parity that involves changes in exchange rates and in the ratio of foreign to home prices.

rental market   A market in which capital services are bought and sold at the rental price.

rental price   The price charged per year for using a unit of capital.

research and development (R&D)   Expenditure dedicated to discovery of new goods and improved methods of production.

reservation real wage   The real wage rate that is just high enough to induce someone to accept a job.

revaluation   An increase in the value of a country's currency in terms of another currency, such as the U.S. dollar.

revenue from printing money   Revenue that the government obtains by printing paper currency.

Ricardian equivalence theorem   The theoretical finding that, for given government purchases, an increase in current taxes has the same effect on the economy as an equal increase in the government budget deficit.

risk premium   The higher rate of return required on risky assets, such as corporate stock, compared to safe assets.

rival good   A good that, if used by one person, cannot be used by another person.

saving   The change in a household's assets over a year. The difference between total income and consumption.

seasonally adjusted data   Adjustment of economic variables, such as real GDP, for normal seasonal variations.

shocks   Exogenous disturbances that affect the macro economy. A shift to the technology level is an example of a shock.

Social Security   Transfer payments made by the government to households to cover old age pensions, survivors' benefits, and disability insurance.

Solow growth model   A model of economic growth. Key elements are a production function with capital and labor inputs, the saving rate, the population growth rate, and the rate of technological progress.

Solow residual   we can use this equation to measure the growth rate of technology, $\Delta A/A$.

sources of funds   In a budget constraint for households or government, the sources of funds are initial assets and various types of income.

standard deviation   A measure of the variability of a variable. The standard deviation is the square root of the variance. The variance is the average squared deviation from the mean.

standard of living   Level of consumption that can be sustained, given a household's long-run income.

steady state   A long-run situation in which variables such as capital per worker and real GDP per worker are not changing.

steady-state growth   A long-run situation in which variables such as capital per worker and real GDP per worker are growing at a constant rate.

sterilization   An action by the central bank that prevents increases (decreases) in the amount of international reserves from increasing (decreasing) the nominal quantity of money in the country.

sticky nominal wage rates   Sluggish adjustment of the nominal wage rate to changed conditions in the labor market. A characteristic of the Keynesian model.

sticky prices   Sluggish adjustment of goods prices to changed conditions in the goods market. A characteristic of the new Keynesian model.

stock market   A market on which households trade shares of ownership in firms. The owners of stock receive the dividends paid out by firms.

stock variable   A variable, such as capital or money, expressed in units of goods or dollar value. Stock variables do not have a dimension per unit of time. See *flow variable*.

stores of value   Forms of holding assets, such as bonds, money, and ownership of capital.

strategic budget deficits   Manipulation of budget deficits to influence choices made by future governmental regimes.

subsistence level   Standard of living regarded as the minimal requirement for sustaining life.

supply curve   A curve expressing the relation between the quantity supplied and the price of a good or service.

surplus (deficit) on current account   A positive (negative) current-account balance.

tariff   Tax levied on international trade, usually on imports.

tax-rate smoothing   Fiscal policy aimed at maintaining stable tax rates over time.

technological progress   Inventions and improved knowledge about methods of production that generate continuing upward shifts of the production function.

technology level   The level of the production function. A higher technology level means that real GDP is higher for given inputs of capital and labor.

term structure of real interest rates   The relation of real interest rates to the maturity of bonds.

terms of trade   The price of a country's produced tradable goods expressed relative to the price of the world's produced tradable goods.

total hours worked   Total worker-hours per year; the product of employment and average hours worked per year for each worker.

trade balance   The difference between the value of exports of goods and services and the value of imports of goods and services.

transaction costs   Costs incurred in the process of making sales or purchases, such as brokerage fees or the value of the time required.

transfer payment   Transfers of funds from government to individuals, such as welfare payments.

transition path   In a growth model, such as the Solow model, the path from the initial position to the steady-state position.

trend real GDP   The smooth part of the time series on real GDP. We view this trend as reflecting long-run economic growth, rather than economic fluctuations.

twin deficits   Simultaneous appearance of budget and current-account deficits.

two-year budget constraint   The budget constraint for a household over two years.

unanticipated money growth   The difference between actual money growth and anticipated money growth.

unemployment   The number of persons in the labor force (and, therefore, classified as seeking work) without a job.

unemployment insurance   The government program of providing temporary benefits to workers who have lost their jobs and are currently unemployed.

unemployment rate   The ratio of unemployment to the labor force.

unexpected inflation   The difference between the actual inflation rate and the expected inflation rate; the forecast error made in predicting inflation.

user costs   Additional costs incurred while using capital goods; for example, the costs of electric power, security services, and so on.

uses of funds   In a budget constraint for households or government, the uses of funds are expenditures on goods and services and final values of assets.

utility   The level of happiness of a household, measured in units called utils. Utility increases with increases in either consumption or leisure. See *utility function*.

utility function   The relationship between the amount of utility obtained and the amounts of consumption and labor chosen by the household.

vacancies   The difference between the number of job openings at firms and the level of employment.

vacancy rate   The ratio of vacancies to the total number of jobs that firms want occupied.

value added   The increase in value of a product at various stages of production.

voluntary exchange   Voluntary sales and purchases made at going prices.

wage rate   The dollar amount paid and received on the labor market for each hour of labor services.

wholesale price index   Another name for the producer price index.

INDEX

capital (cont.)
  accumulation of, 79
  constant average product of capital, 78–79
  convergence, 60–68
  convergence and, 75–76
  demand for money, 174–179
  diminishing marginal product of capital, 36–37
  equilibrium business cycle model, 135–138
  government owned, 256
  growth accounting, 38–39
  growth rate, 42–45
  household budget constraint, 99
  income, growth and, 41–42
  inflation and, 203
  input, 149–155
  market clearing, 152–155
  ownership, risk premium, 101
  rental market, 94–95
  Solow Growth model, 39–45, 57–59
  taxes on, 244–246, 262
capital gains taxes, 236, 241–246
capital goods, 17–18
capital levy, 287
capital per worker
  convergence, 59–68, 70–72
  exogenous technological progress, 81–82
  steady state, 57–59
  technology and, 53–54
capital services
  demand and inflation, 203–205
  equilibrium business cycle model, 133
  government purchases, permanent, 222–226
  government purchases, temporary, 227–232
  market clearing, 103–109
  price misperception model, 274–283, 276
  rental market, 94–95, 181–182
  technology, 142
capital stock
  equilibrium business cycle model, 134–138
  government purchases, permanent, 222–226
  growth of, 41–42
  imperfect competition, 290–291
  production function, 35–37
  public debt and, 270
  rental market, 94–95
  taxes and, 246
  technology, 80–81
  wartime destruction of, 228
capital utilization rate
  government purchases, permanent, 222–226
  government purchases, temporary, 227–232
  imperfect competition, 290–291
  inflation and, 203–205
  overview, 149–155
  taxes and, 246

Card, David, 305
Caribbean countries, 95. See also individual country name
Carroll, Chris, 270
Carter, Jimmy, 209
Cass, David, 53
Central America, 95
central banks, 270–271, 299
CFA fanc, 95
chain-weighted consumer price index (CPI), 25
chain-weighted real GDP, 14–15
checkable deposits, 173
Chile, 192, 218, 286
China, 28–31, 32–34, 95, 174–175
clearing of capital services market, 107–108
Clinton, William, 264–265
closed economy, 18
Cobb-Douglas production function, 49–50
coffee market, example, 6–10
Cole, Harold, 303
Columbia, 192, 286
commodity exchange, 289
commodity money, 171. See also money
competition, 290
conditional convergence. See also convergence
  constant average product of capital, 78–79
  determinants of economic growth, 74–75
  endogenous growth theory, 83–87
  long-run growth, 77–78
  in practice, 73–77
  Solow Growth model, 64–68
  technology and, 79–82, 87
Congo, 28–31, 192
constant-growth-rate rule, 298
constant returns to scale, 37
consumer durable goods, 17
consumer nondurable goods, 17
consumer price index (CPI), 23–26, 25, 96, 192–195, 275, 282, 295–296
consumption
  anticipated income changes, 124
  deficit-financed tax cuts, 266–269
  demand for money, 175–179
  equilibrium business cycle model, 123–125, 137–138
  goods market, 93
  government expenditures and, 220–221
  government purchases, permanent, 222–226, 224–226
  government purchases, temporary, 226–232
  household budget constraint, 99–100
  inflation and, 196, 202–203
  interest rate and, 198, 199
  labor, variations in, 142–147
  markets and prices, 96–98
  matching fact and theory, 138–141
  over many years, 121–123, 127–128
  over two years, 114–121
  overview, 112–114
  personal, 17
  price misperception model, 275–283

Ricardian equivalence, 259
Social Security and, 269
Solow Growth model, 55
taxes and, 240–246, 263–264
technology, 141–142
consumption tax, 245
contraction, defined, 2
contracts, long term, 303–306
convergence
  conditional, in practice, 73–77
  rate of, 70–72
  Solow Growth model, 59–68
  technological progress, 81–82
copyright, 84–85
corporate profits taxes, 237
corruption, 77
Costa Rica, 192
cost of credit, 98
countercyclical variables, 138
CPI (consumer price index), 23–26, 96, 192–195, 275, 282, 295–296
credit markets, 97–98, 268–269
credits, taxes, 241
Croatia, 218
Cuba, 56
currency, 95–96, 171–179. See also money
customs duties, 237
cyclical behavior. See also equilibrium business cycle model
  government purchases, 225–226
  labor productivity, 147
  of money, 187
  patterns in models, 279
  of price, 184
  real GDP, 129–133
  variables, 138
Cyprus, 28–31, 30, 194
Czech Republic, 218, 286

D

debt relief, 76–77
deductions, tax, 241
defense spending, 216, 227–232
deficits, government, 255–258, 261–269
deflation, 194, 196
demand
  capital services, 106–108, 150–155, 203–205, 246
  for labor, 104–105
  market, example, 6–10
  for money, 100, 174–179, 203
  overview, 92–93
demand curves, 6–10
democracy, economic growth and, 75
Denmark, 174–175, 193, 218
depreciation
  capital services, supply of, 151–155
  capital stocks, growth rate, 41–42
  constant average product of capital, 78–79
  defined, 17
  equilibrium business cycle model, 137–138

Learning Outcomes

- You should have a basic understanding of the historical record of some of the major macroeconomic variables in the United States.

- You should understand the basic function of economic models.

- You should understand demand curves, supply curves and market clearing conditions.

Key Terms and Concepts

boom (p. 2)
business cycle (p. 2)
demand curve (p. 6)
disequilibrium (p. 10)
economic fluctuations (p. 2)
employment (p. 1)
endogenous variables (p. 5)
equilibrium (p. 9)
exchange rate (p. 1)
exogenous variables (p. 5)

general price level (p. 1)
gold standard (p. 5)
Great Depression (p. 3)
gross domestic product (GDP) (p. 1)
inflation rate (p. 4)
interest rate (p. 1)
microeconomic foundations (p. 6)
national-income accounting (p. 2)
new Keynesian model (p. 11)
perfect competition (p. 6)

price taker (p. 6)
real GDP (p. 2)
real gross domestic product (p. 2)
recession (p. 2)
rental price (p. 1)
supply curve (p. 8)
unemployment (p. 1)
unemployment rate (p. 3)
wage rate (p. 1)

Chapter Summary

• You should have a basic understanding of the historical record of some of the major macroeconomic variables in the United States.

The mean growth rate of the U.S. economy was 3.5% from 1870–2005. The year-to-year real GDP growth rates of the U.S. economy varied substantially around the mean of 3.5%. The mean unemployment rate of the U.S. economy from 1890 to 2005 was 6.3%, the median was 5.5%. The highest the U.S. unemployment rate reached was 22% in 1932.

• You should understand the basic function of economic models.

Economic models can take the form of equations, graphs and ideas. Economists create models that represent markets and behave as the markets do. Economist can make changes to those models and observe market may react. Models may contain endogenous variable that we want to explain by the use of exogenous variables.

• You should understand demand curves, supply curves and market clearing conditions.

Demand curves show the total quantity demanded at each possible price. The supply curve shows the total quantity supplied at each possible price. The market clearing price and quantity occurs at the intersection of the supply and demand curves and determines the equilibrium price and quantity. Subsequent changes in the supply or demand curves may result in a new equilibrium and according new equilibrium price and quantity.

Key Graphs

Figure 1.1 *U.S. Real GDP, 1869–2005*

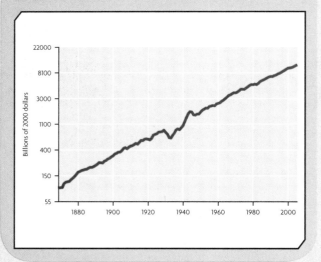

The graph shows the real gross domestic product (GDP) on a proportionate (logarithmic) scale. Data before 1929 are for real gross national product (GNP). The numbers are in billions of 2000 U.S. dollars.

Figure 1.4 *U.S. Price Level, 1869–2005*

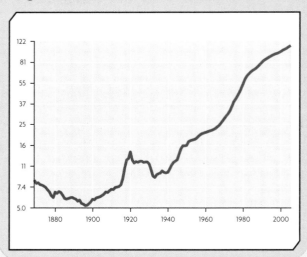

The graph shows the price defl ator for the GDP (GNP before 1929). The numbers are on a proportionate (logarithmic) scale, with the value for the year 2000 set at 100. The sources are those indicated for GDP in Figure 1.1.

Learning Outcomes

- You should be able to explain the difference between nominal and real variables and understand how the CPI is used to transform nominal variables in to real variables.

- You should be able to define GDP and understand it importance as a National Income Accounting tool and understand the shortcomings of GDP as a measurement of Welfare.

- You should identify the four components of the Expenditure approach to calculating GDP understanding that the exclusion of net exports allows analysis of a closed economy.

- You should distinguish between the CPI and GDP Deflator and reveal which one might overstate inflation.

Key Equations

$$(nominal\ GDP)/(implicit\ price\ level) = real\ GDP$$

If we rearrange the terms in the equation, we have

$$implicit\ price\ level = (nominal\ GDP)/(real\ GDP)$$

Worked Problems

Ques. 1

What are some of the shortcomings of real GDP from a welfare perspective? Do you have any practical suggestions for revising the computation of GDP to achieve a better measure of welfare?

Ans. 1

Official estimates of GDP do not measure welfare exactly, although higher GDP is highly correlated with widely accepted measures of welfare such as literacy, life expectancy, infant mortality rates and so forth. One of the reasons why GDP may underestimate the true change in welfare is because it fails to take into account non-market goods such as leisure. It also may fail to take into account changes in the quality of goods because these are not accurately captured in the implicit price deflator. On the other hand, GDP may overestimate changes welfare because it fails to take into the environmental impact of production. Clear cutting an old growth forest may simply convert a valuable non-market good to a less valuable market good, but the activity would tend to raise GDP. One way to take these effects into account is to incorporate the implicit value of nonmarket goods like leisure and environmental goods into a broader measure of welfare.

Key Terms and Concepts

chain-weighted real GDP (p. 14)
closed economy (p. 18)
consumer durables (p. 17)
consumer nondurables and services (p. 17)
consumer price index (CPI) (p. 23)
depreciation (p. 17)
disposable personal income (p. 21)
exports (p. 18)
flow variable (p. 12)
GDP in constant dollars (p. 14)

GDP in current dollars (p. 14)
gross national product (GNP) (p. 21)
gross private domestic investment (p. 17)
gross state product (GSP) (p. 23)
implicit GDP deflator (p. 15)
imports (p. 18)
imputed rental income (p. 12)
inventories (p. 17)
national income (p. 18)
net domestic product (NDP) (p. 18)
net exports (p. 18)

net factor income from abroad (p. 20)
net private domestic investment (p. 17)
nominal GDP (p. 12)
open economy (p. 18)
personal consumption expenditure (p. 17)
personal income (p. 21)
producer price index (PPI) (p. 23)
seasonally adjusted data (p. 23)
stock variable (p. 17)
value added (p. 19)
wholesale price index (p. 23)

reviewcard

Chapter Summary

• You should be able to explain the difference between nominal and real variables and understand how the CPI is used to transform nominal variables in to real variables.

Nominal Variables cannot be compared across years but rather have to be transformed by a price index like the CPI or GDP deflator into real variables for comparison.

• You should be able to define GDP and understand it importance as a National Income Accounting tool and understand the shortcomings of GDP as a measurement of Welfare.

GDP can be measured by any of the following three methods; Expenditure, Income and Production. Either of these methods for calculating GDP yield the same results and is the National Income Accounting Identity.

• You should identify the four components of the Expenditure approach to calculating GDP understanding that the exclusion of net exports allows analysis of a closed economy.

The Expenditure Approach to measuring GDP includes 4 components; personal consumption expenditure, gross private domestic investment, government purchases of goods and services and net exports. Economist analyzing a national economy closed to international trade would exclude net imports from the expenditure method for calculating GDP.

• You should distinguish between the CPI and GDP Deflator and reveal which one might overstate inflation.

The CPI is commonly used to gauge inflation. Economists think the CPI overstates inflation 0.4% annually and does not account for changes in product quality.

Key Graphs

Table 2.5 *Relations Between U.S. GDP and Income in 2005*

Category of Product or Income	Trillions of Dollars
Gross domestic product (GDP)	**12.49**
Plus: income receipts from rest of world	0.51
Less: income payments to rest of world	(0.47)
Equals: Gross national product (GNP)	**12.52**
Less: depreciation of capital stock	(1.57)
Equals: Net national product (NNP)	**10.95**
Less: statistical discrepancy	(0.04)
Equals: National income	**10.90**
Less: corporate profits, taxes on production, contributions for social insurance, net interest, business transfers, surplus of government enterprises	(3.64)
Plus: personal income receipts on assets, personal transfer payments	2.98
Equals: Personal income	**10.25**
Less: personal taxes	(1.21)
Equals: Disposable personal income	**9.04**

Source: Bureau of Economic Analysis (*http://www.bea.gov*).

Learning Outcomes

- You should understand the basic facts about U.S. and other country economic growth from 1960 to 2000.

- You should understand how a country's technology and factors of production determine it output of goods and services, measure by real GDP.

- You should be able to explain the growth rates of technology, capital and labor.

Key Equations

Key equation (production function):

(3.1) $\quad Y = A \cdot F(K, L)$

Key equation (growth-accounting formula):

(3.4) $\quad \Delta Y/Y = \Delta A/A + \alpha \cdot (\Delta K/K) + (1-\alpha) \cdot (\Delta L/L)$

Key equation (Solow growth model):

(3.16) $\quad \Delta K/K = s \cdot (y/k) - s\delta - n$

Worked Problems

$1 invested for 2 years at an interest rate I would be worth $1(1+i)$ at the end of the first year and $1(1+i)(1+i)=\$1(1+i)^2$ at the end of the second year. We can use this formula to compute the annual interest rate implied by bond which sells for P^B today and generates a payoff of $1000 two years from now:

$$P^B(1+i)^2 = \$1000 \quad \text{or} \quad (1+i)^2 = \$1000/P^B$$

Taking the square root of both sides and then subtracting 1 from each side yields:

$$i = (\$1000/P^B)^{1/2} - 1$$

Key Terms and Concepts

average product of capital (p. 42)
capital stock (p. 48)
constant returns to scale (p. 37)
diminishing average product
  of capital (p. 43)
diminishing marginal product
  of capital (p. 36)
diminishing marginal product
  of labor (p. 37)
gross investment (p. 41)
growth accounting (p. 48)

human capital (p. 36)
inequality (p. 32)
labor force (p. 36)
labor-force participation rate (p. 39)
marginal product of capital (MPK) (p. 36)
marginal product of labor (MPL) (p. 36)
neoclassical growth model (p. 40)
net investment (p. 41)
population growth (p. 42)
poverty (p. 29)
production function (p. 35)

productivity (p. 36)
productivity slowdown (p. 34)
Ramsey model (p. 40)
rate of economic growth (p. 27)
saving (p. 41)
Solow growth model (p. 39)
standard of living (p. 27)
steady state (p. 43)
technology level (p. 44)
transition path (p. 44)

Chapter Summary

• You should understand the basic facts about U.S. and other country economic growth.

The U.S. with a real GDP of $34,500 was the 2nd richest country in the world in 2000, 1st was Luxembourg. From 1869 to 2005 the U.S. real GDP per person grew at a rate of 2%. That means that in 2005 the real GDP per person was 16 times what it was in 1869. In 2005 typical U.S. families not only owned a comfortable home and had ample food supplies and clothes but also possessed television sets, automobilies, telephones, personal computers and internet access.

• You should understand how a country's technology and factors of production determine it output of goods and services, measured by real GDP.

The Solow Growth model assumes no unemployment, no government and a closed economy. The key to the Solow growth model is equation 3.16 with revels the growth rate of capital per worker. This growth rate per worker depends on the savings rate, s, the depreciation rate, δ. The population growth rate, n, the average product of capital y/k.

• You should be able to explain the growth rates of technology, capital and labor.

The growth rate of technology is directly proportion to the growth rate of real GDP. That is holding the growth rate of capital and labor constant, a 1% increase in the technology growth rate will yield a 1% increase in the growth rate of real GDP. The growth rate of capital is dependent on the economy's saving rate. The growth rate of labor is dependent on the population growth rate. In the U.S. the population growth rate has been about 1% per year.

Key Graphs

Figure 3.4 (a) World Income Distribution in 1970; (b) World Income Distribution in 2000

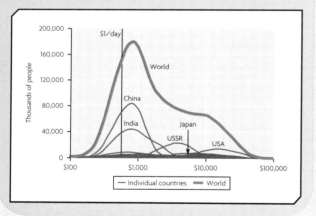

Figure 3.4a is for 1970 and Figure 3.4b is for 2000. In each case, the horizontal axis plots real income in 1985 U.S. dollars on a proportionate scale. For the upper curves in the two figures, the vertical axis shows the number of people in the world with each level of income. The vertical lines marked $1 show the annual real incomes that correspond to the standard poverty line of $1 per day ($570 per year in 1996 prices). The income distributions for a few large countries are shown separately. FSU is the former Soviet Union. (Nigeria is hidden beneath the Asian countries in Figure 3.4a.) The values shown on the upper curves for numbers of people in the world are the vertical sums of the numbers of people in all of the individual countries. However, only a few of the countries can be discerned in these graphs.

Figure 3.10 *Determination of the Growth Rate of Capital per Worker in the Solow Model*

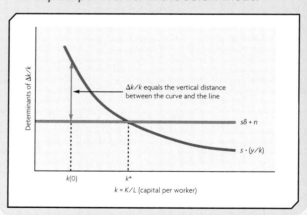

The technology level, A, is fixed. The vertical axis plots the two determinants of the growth rate of capital per worker, $\Delta k/k$, from the right-hand side of equation (3.16). $\Delta k/k$ equals the vertical distance between the negatively sloped $s \cdot (y/k)$ curve (in blue) and the horizontal line at $s\delta + n$ (in red). At the steady state, where $k = k^*$, the curve and line intersect, and $\Delta k/k = 0$. The initial capital per worker, $k(0)$, is assumed to be less than k^*. Therefore, when $k = k(0)$, $\Delta k/k$ is greater than zero and equal to the vertical distance shown by the green arrows.

Learning Outcomes

- You should understand how to show that changes in the key parameters of the solow model affect growth rates and the steady state level of income.

- You should understand the concept of absolute convergence.

- You should understand the concept of conditional convergence and the implications for developing countries.

Key Equations

Key equation (conditional convergence in the Solow model):

(4.9)
$$\Delta k/k = \varphi[k(0), k^*]$$
$$(-) \quad (+)$$

growth rate of capital per worker = function of initial and steady-state capital per worker

Worked Problems

Ques. 1

Variations in the saving rate

Suppose that the saving rate, s, can vary as an economy develops.

a. The equation for the growth rate of capital per worker, k, is given by

(4.1)
$$\Delta k/k = s \cdot (y/k) - s\delta - n$$

Is this equation still valid when s is not constant?

b. Suppose that s rises as an economy develops; that is, rich countries save at a higher rate than poor countries. How does this behavior affect the results about convergence?

c. Suppose, instead, that s falls as an economy develops; that is, rich countries save at a lower rate than poor countries. How does this behavior affect the results about convergence?

d. Which case seems more plausible—b. or c. above? Explain.

Ans. 1

a. Yes, the growth rate in capital at any given period will depend on the savings rate in that period. However, the idea that the economy approaches a steady state level of per-capita income cannot be assumed.

b. A pattern of rising savings rates would offset to some extent the effects of diminishing returns and depreciation on capital accumulation. The increase in the savings rate could cause the growth rate to increase over time. This would reduce the tendency toward convergence.

c. A tendency for savings rates to fall at higher levels of income would reinforce the effects of diminishing returns and capital depreciation on capital accumulation; this would increase the tendency toward convergence.

d. A small increase in the level of consumption in the present when someone is poor is likely to provide a higher rate of marginal utility than a similar increase when they are rich, due to diminishing marginal utility of consumption. Therefore, it may seem more likely that a poor person would save less than a wealthy person with similar preferences. This is the basis for the well known prediction that the marginal propensity to consume falls as income rises. However, this is complicated by the fact that the rate of return on savings should be higher when capital is relatively scarce; this would provide a relatively strong incentive to invest in capital poor countries. So for example, we observe that savings rates in China, which is still a relatively less developed country, are much higher than in the U.S.

Key Terms and Concepts

Chapter Summary

• You should understand how to show that changes in the key parameters of the Solow model affect growth rates and the steady state level of income.

Each of the parameters of the Solow Model can be manipulated and will affect growth rates and the steady state level of income. Changes in the accumulation of capital, savings rates, population growth rates or the labor force, and technology affect growth rates and the steady state level of income. The steady state level of output per worker is shown to increase as savings rates or technology increase. The steady state level of output per worker falls as the population or grows. Changes to the labor force can affect the growth rate because they change the capital labor ratio, but they do not affect the ultimate steady state level of output per worker.

• You should understand the concept of absolute convergence.

Since the rate of capital accumulation per worker is essentially determined by the current stock of capital per worker, lesser developed countries are predicted by the model to grow more quickly than developed countries.

• You should understand the concept of conditional convergence and the implications for developing countries.

Conditional Convergence asserts that the capital per worker will only generate faster growth rates if the values of the other parameters (savings, technology, population growth, etc.) are somewhat comparable. This implies that there is only conditional convergence. The empirical evidence presented in the chapter confirms this view. Data from more than 100 countries suggest that conditional convergence exists, but there is little evidence to confirm the existence of absolute convergence.

Key Graphs

Figure 4.1 *Effect of an Increase in the Saving Rate in the Solow Model*

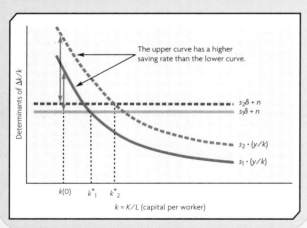

Figure 4.2 *Effect of an Increase in the Technology Level in the Solow Model*

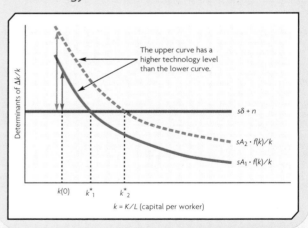

This graph comes from Figure 3.9. The curves for $s \cdot (y/k)$ are for the saving rates s_1 and s_2, where s_2 is greater than s_1. Similarly, the horizontal lines for $s\delta + n$ are for the saving rates s_1 and s_2. The growth rate of capital per worker, $\Delta k/k$, is higher at any k when the saving rate is higher. For example, at $k(0)$, when the saving rate is s_1, $\Delta k/k$ equals the vertical distance shown by the green arrows. When the saving rate is s_2, $\Delta k/k$ equals the vertical distance shown by the red arrows. In the steady state, $\Delta k/k$ is zero, regardless of the saving rate. The higher saving rate yields a higher steady-state capital per worker; that is, k_2^* is greater than k_1^*.

The upper curve has a higher technology level than the lower curve. This graph comes from Figure 3.9. The two curves for $s \cdot (y/k) = sA \cdot f(k)/k$ are for the technology levels A_1 and A_2, where A_2 is greater than A_1. The growth rate of capital per worker, $\Delta k/k$, is higher at any k when the technology level is higher. For example, at $k(0)$, when the technology level is A_1, $\Delta k/k$ equals the vertical distance shown by the blue arrows. When the technology level is A_2, $\Delta k/k$ equals the vertical distance shown by the red arrows. In the steady state, $\Delta k/k$ is zero, regardless of the technology level. The higher technology level yields a higher steady-state capital per worker; that is, k_2^* is greater than k_1^*.

Learning Outcomes

- You need to be aware of some important relevant variables that influence economic growth.
- You should understand the concept of constant average product of capital and what capital represents in the Solow model.
- You should understand how technological diffusion impacts economic growth.

Key Equations

Key equation (conditional convergence for real GDP per worker):

(5.1)
$$\Delta y/y = \varphi[y(0), y^*]$$
$$(-) \quad (+)$$

Key equation (growth rate of real GDP per worker with technical progress):

(5.9)
$$\Delta y/y = g + \alpha \cdot [sA \cdot f(k)/k - s\delta - n]$$

Key equation (steady-state growth rate with technological progress):

(5.12)
$$(\Delta y/y)^* = g/(1 - \alpha)$$

Worked Problems

Ques. 1

Problems for discussion

Convergence and the dispersion of income (difficult)

Consider a group of economies that satisfies absolute convergence; that is, poor economies tend to grow faster than rich ones.

a. Does this convergence property imply that a measure of the dispersion of income per person—or income inequality—across the economies will narrow over time? (This question relates to Galton's fallacy, an idea applied by Galton to the distribution of heights and other characteristics in a population. If a parent is taller than average, the child tends to be taller than average but shorter than the parent. That is, there is reversion to the mean, an effect that parallels the idea of absolute convergence. Does the presence of reversion to the mean imply that the distribution of heights across the population will narrow over time? The answer is no, but you are supposed to explain why.)

b. We found in Figure 4.11 that absolute convergence held for the U.S. states from 1880 to 2000. A measure of the dispersion of per capita income across the states declined for most of the period from 1880 to 1970 (except for the 1920s and 1930s). Dispersion did not change a great deal from 1970 to 2000. Can you relate these observations to your answer from question a.?

c. We found in Figure 4.9 that absolute convergence did not hold for a broad group of countries from 1960 to 2000. We did find in Figure 5.1 that conditional convergence held for these countries. A measure of the dispersion of per capita real GDP across these countries shows a mild, but persistent, increase from 1960 to 2000. How would you account for this pattern?

Ans. 1

a. The key to understanding Galton's fallacy is to recognize that some of the variation in height is due to chance. For the sake of clarity, let us take an example where height is entirely due to

chance: the height of the father has no predictive power on the height of the son. In particular, suppose that the height of the child can take on one of three values: short, tall or average, and that the probability of each outcome is exactly 1/3, regardless of the father's height. In this case, short fathers will have children who are, on average, taller than themselves. Tall fathers will have on average, children who are shorter than themselves. This may give the appearance of "height convergence"; but in fact the distribution of heights will remain unchanged: 1/3 of the population will be short, 1/3 will be tall, and 1/3 will be average.

Applying the logic outlined above to the case of rich and poor countries, we find that the appearance of convergence is possible even though incomes are not becoming more equal. At any particular point in time, the distribution of income per person will be determined to a certain extent by "chance"—that is, by events and circumstances not described in our growth model. These can have positive negative effects. If, over time, the good and bad effects balance out, then we would expect that wealthier countries have experienced "good luck" in the past and poorer countries have experienced "bad luck" over the same period. Since there is no systematic probability for either kind of luck to persist from period to period, the likelihood is for rich countries to grow more slowly as their luck "regresses to the mean". Likewise, poor countries will grow more quickly as their luck "regresses to the mean". Poor countries can grow more quickly than rich countries without changing the dispersion of income.

b. In part "a" to this question, we recognized that part of the growth rate of income per person is due to chance. But obviously, the theory of growth we learned in the text suggests that much of it can be predicted by specific factors- in particular, by the difference between current capital-worker ratio and its steady state value. It is reasonable to expect that during the earlier period (1880–1970) that some regions in the U.S. were closer to their steady state than others. Thus, much of the convergence could be attributed to the differences in the capital per worker that existed at that time. As the various regions developed, these differences diminished, and the apparent convergence in more recent times is due to random variations in growth rates between the states.

c. Conditional convergence implies that rich and poor countries with different steady states will not converge, but their will be groups of countries for which convergence will be observed. If technological change allows steady state growth, then each group would be expected to have a different steady state growth rate as seen in equation (5.12).

The next question is, why would the rate of technological change differ among groups of countries? The answer lies in the institutions that encourage innovation or adoption of new technology. Countries which are relatively open to trade have high education levels, and a well functioning legal and political system, including support for intellectual property rights.

Key Terms and Concepts

Ak model (p. 78)
copyright (p. 84)
diffusion of technology (p. 87)
endogenous growth theory (p. 80)
exogenous technological progress (p. 79)

infrastructure capital (p. 78)
intellectual property rights (p. 84)
non-rival good (p. 84)
patent (p. 84)
research and development (R&D) (p. 83)

rival good (p. 84)
steady-state growth (p. 80)
technological progress (p. 79)

Chapter Summary

• You need to be aware of some important relevant variables that influence economic growth.

Listed on page 98 of the text are variables thought to influence economic growth. The list includes savings rate, size of government, measures of investment in education and health and average rate of inflation. There are many other variables that likely influence growth for which data may or may not be available. Possible growth influencing variables for which data may or may not be available is maintenance of rule of law or sophistication of banking or financial markets.

• You should understand the concept of constant average product of capital and what capital represents in the Solow model. The assumption has been that the average product of capital is constant. It however makes more sense that that average product of capital declines as more units of machines and buildings are added without adding workers. Fewer workers to run more and more machines, average product of capital should decline.

Alternatively we could broaden the definition of capital to include human capital including education, on the job training and health. We could expand that further and include infrastructure capital such as interstates, pipelines and electric grids.

• You should understand how technological diffusion impacts economic growth.

For the world as a whole the only way to raise the technology level is for someone to discover something new. For an individual country it is possible to raise the technology level, A, by adapting someone else's innovation. Diffusion of technology is the imitation and adaption of one country's technology by another. Imitation and adaption is less expensive than invention. Technology diffusion is the main method by which low income countries raise their technology levels. This helps to explain convergence of poor countries toward rich countries but does not explain technological progress for the whole world.

Learning Outcomes

- You should be able to describe the economy's four markets in our macro model.
- You should understand the characteristics of the market for labor services and its equilibrium condition.
- You should understand the characteristics of the market for capital services and its equilibrium condition.

Key Equations

Key equation:

rate of return on bonds = rate of return on ownership of capital

(6.6) $$i = R/P - \delta$$

Key equation (household budget constraint in nominal terms):

(6.11) $$PC + \Delta B + P \cdot \Delta K = \Pi + wL + i \cdot (B + PK)$$

nominal consumption + nominal saving = nominal income

Key equation (household budget constraint in real terms):

(6.12) $$C + (1/P) \cdot \Delta B + \Delta K = \Pi/P + (W/P) \cdot L + i \cdot (B/P + K)$$

consumption + real saving = real income

Key equation (equilibrium interest rate):

(6.16) $$i = MPK \, (evaluated \, at \, K) - \delta$$

Worked Problems

Ques. 1

Discount bonds

The bonds in our model have a maturity close to zero; they just pay interest in accordance with the current interest rate, i, as a flow over time. We could consider, instead, a discount bond, such as a U.S. Treasury Bill. This type of asset has no explicit interest payments (called *coupons*) but pays a principal of, say, $1000 at a fixed date in the future. A Bill with one-year maturity pays off one year from the issue date, and similarly for three-month or six-month Bills. Let P^B be the price of a discount bond with one-year maturity and principal of $1000.

a. Is P^B greater than or less than $1000?
b. What is the one-year interest rate on these discount bonds?
c. If P^B rises, what happens to the interest rate on these bonds?
d. Suppose that, instead of paying $1000 in one year, the bond pays $1000 in two years. What is the interest rate per year on this two-year discount bond?

Ans. 1

a. The rate of interest on the bond will be given by the formula:
$$i = (principal - P^B)/P^B$$
A positive rate of interest requires that (principal $- P^B$) > 0 or $P^B < \$1000$. If not, the rate of return on the bond would be negative.

b. Using the formula given in part (6a) we have $i = (\$1000 - P^B)/P^B$

c. An increase in the purchase price reduces the rate of interest because it increases the size of the denominator while reducing the size of the numerator.

d. $1 invested for 2 years at an interest rate I would be worth $1(1 + i)$ at the end of the first year and $1(1 + i)(1 + i) = \$1(1 + i)^2$ at the end of the second year. We can use this formula to compute the annual interest rate implied by bond which sells for P^B today and generates a payoff of $1000 two years from now:
$$P^B(1 + i)^2 = \$1000 \quad or \quad (1 + i)^2 = \$1000/P^B$$
Taking the square root of both sides and then subtracting 1 from each side yields:
$$i = (\$1000/P^B)^{1/2} - 1$$

Key Terms and Concepts

bond (p. 97)
bond market (p. 95)
budget constraint (p. 98)
budget line (p. 102)
common currency (p. 95)
currency (p. 96)
currency union (p. 95)
goods market (p. 93)
household budget constraint
  in nominal terms (p. 102)
household budget constraint
  in real terms (p. 102)

labor market (p. 94)
market-clearing conditions (p. 93)
maturity (p. 97)
medium of exchange (p. 95)
money (p. 95)
nominal (p. 96)
nominal rental price (p. 97)
nominal saving (p. 101)
nominal wage rate (p. 96)
price level (p. 96)
principal (of bond) (p. 97)

profit (p. 98)
real rental price (p. 97)
real saving (p. 102)
real terms (p. 96)
real wage rate (p. 97)
rental market (p. 94)
risk premium (p. 101)
sources of funds (p. 98)
stock market (p. 93)
uses of funds (p. 98)

Chapter Summary

- You should be able to describe the economy's four markets in our macro model.
- The four markets in our model are the goods market, labor market, capital market, and bond market.
- An individual works on the productions of goods and receives income accordingly for the production of those goods sold in a **Goods Market**. That person then spends this income on the goods needed in their household. Households buy goods for *consumption* and to increase their stock of capital goods called *investment*.
- Households supply labor to the **Labor Market** and households as business managers demand labor from the Labor market.
- Households own the capital stock, *K*, as input to the production process. We think of the capital offered on the rental market as the supply of capital services, *Ks*.

- The Bond Market is the market where households borrow or lend money.
- You should understand the characteristics of the market for labor services and its equilibrium condition.
- In the market for labor services equilibrium occurs where the quantity of labor demanded, *Ld*, equals the quantity of labor supplied, *Ls*. This equality implies that the market clearing real wage rate *w/P* equals the marginal product of labor, *MPL*.
- You should understand the characteristics of the market for capital services and its equilibrium condition.
- In the market for capital services equilibrium occurs where the aggregate quantity of capital services, *Ks*, equates the aggregate quantity demanded of capital services, *Kd*. The market clearing real rental price, R/P equals the marginal product of capital, *MPK*.

Key Graphs

Figure 6.1 *An Example of Market Clearing: The Labor Market*

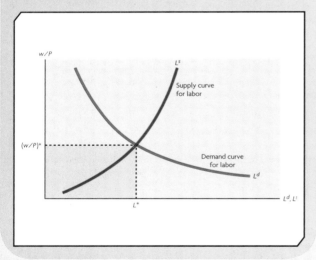

This figure gives a simple example of how a market—in this case, the labor market—clears. The labor-demand curve, L^d, slopes downward versus the real wage rate, *w/P*. The labor-supply curve, L^s, slopes upward versus *w/P*. Market clearing corresponds to the intersection of the two curves. The market-clearing real wage rate is $(w/P)^*$, and the market-clearing quantity of labor is L^*.

Figure 6.2 *The Household Budget Constraint*

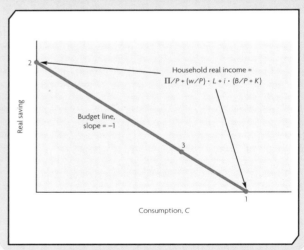

Households have a given total of real income, $\Pi/P + (w/P) \cdot L + i \cdot (B/P + K)$. This total must be divided between consumption, *C*, and real saving, $(1/P) \cdot \Delta B + \Delta K$. Thus, if real saving is zero, *C* equals the total of real income along the horizontal axis at point 1. If *C* is zero, real saving equals the total of real income along the vertical axis at point 2. The budget constraint in equation (6.12) allows the household to select any combination of consumption and real saving along the budget line, shown in red, such as point 3. The budget line has a slope of −1. Therefore, along this line, one unit less of consumption corresponds to one unit more of real saving.

Learning Outcomes

- You should understand the households' choices of consumption and saving and their implications.
- You should be able to analyze consumption choices in terms of income and intertemporal-substitution effects.
- You should understand the marginal propensity of consumption and savings regarding permanent and temporary changes in income.

Key Equations

Key equation (two-year household budget constraint):

(7.9) $C_1 + C_2/(1 + i_1) = (1 + i_0) \cdot (B_0/P + K_0) + (w/P)_1 \cdot L$
$$+ (w/P)_2 \cdot L/(1 + i_1) - (B_2/P + K_2)/(1 + i_1)$$

Key equation (multiyear budget constraint):

(7.12) $C_1 + C_2/(1 + i_1) + C_3/[(1 + i_1) \cdot (1 + i_2)] + \cdots$
$$= (1 + i_0) \cdot (B_0/P + K_0) + (w/P)_1 \cdot L$$
$$+ (w/P)_2 \cdot L/(1 + i_1) + (w/P)_3$$
$$\cdot L/[(1 + i_1) \cdot (1 + i_2)] + \cdots$$

present value of consumption = value of initial assets + present value of wage incomes

Key equation (aggregate form of household budget constraint):

(7.13) $$C + \Delta K = Y - \delta K$$

consumption + net investment = real GDP − depreciation = real net domestic product

Worked Problems

Ques. 1

Permanent income

The idea of permanent income is that consumption depends on a long-run average of income, rather than current income. Operationally, we can define permanent income as the hypothetical, constant income that has the same present value as a household's sources of funds on the right-hand side of the multiyear budget constraint:

(7.12) $C_1 + C_2/(1 + i_1) + C_3/[(1 + i_1) \cdot (1 + i_2)] + \cdots$
$$= (1 + i_0) \cdot (B_0/P + K_0) + (w/P)_1 \cdot L$$
$$+ (w/P)_2 \cdot L/(1 + i_1) + (w/P)_3$$
$$\cdot L/[(1 + i_1) \cdot (1 + i_2)] + \cdots$$

a. Use equation (7.12) to get a formula for permanent income, when evaluated in year 1.

b. What is the propensity to consume out of permanent income?

c. If consumption, C_t, for $t = 1, 2$, and so on is constant over time, what is the value of permanent income?

Ans. 1

a) In order to keep the notation somewhat manageable, we will make the simplifying assumption that interest rates are constant.

Then permanent income $= (1 + i)((B_0/P + K_0) + L^* \Sigma_{t=1}^{\tau}(w/P))/(1 + i)^t$

Where T represents the number of periods of earned income. Permanent income in this case, consists in the value of assets in period one plus the sum of the discounted real wages earned.

b) The permanent household budget constraint is given by:

$\Sigma_{t=1}^{\tau} C_t/(1 + i)^t = (1 + i)((B_0/P + K_0) + L^* \Sigma_{t=1}^{\tau}(w/P))_t/(1 + i)^t$, which implies a propensity to consume $= 1$. (permanent consumption $=$ permanent income)

c) Permanent income in that case is given by $C\Sigma_{t=1}^{\tau} 1/(1 + i)^t$, where C is the amount consumed in each period. (If the time horizon is very long, this number converges to C/i.) For example, if consumption is 10,000 per month and the interest rate is 1% per month, then permanent income over a period of 50 years (600 months) is approximately 10,000/.01 or $1,000,000.

Key Terms and Concepts

discount factor (p. 117)
discounted (p. 117)
finite horizon (p. 128)
income effects (p. 118)
infinite horizon (p. 128)
infinite-horizon budget constraint (p. 128)

intertemporal-substitution effect (p. 118)
life-cycle models (p. 128)
multiyear budget constraint (p. 121)
permanent income (p. 122)
planning horizon (p. 128)
present value (p. 117)

propensity to consume (p. 122)
propensity to save (p. 122)
two-year budget constraint (p. 116)
utility (p. 117)
utility function (p. 117)

review card

Chapter Summary

- You should understand the households' choices of consumption and saving and their implications.
- Households make decisions regarding use of income for consumption and saving. Savings increases assets and therefore consumption in the future. Savings reduces consumption in the current period and essentially moves that consumption to the future.
- You should be able to analyze consumption choices in terms of income and intertemporal-substitution effects.
- Higher initial assets, higher current real wage income, or higher future real wage income, raise consumption and lower saving due to the income effect.
- Higher interest rates now will reduce consumption now and increase saving. Households are essentially forgoing consumption now and increasing their saving now in exchange for

higher consumption in the future. This is the intertemporal-substitution effect.
- Alternatively, the higher interest rate will also increase current consumption due to an income effect. The overall effect of the higher interest rate on saving is ambiguous, the intertemporal-substitution effect increases saving and the income effect reduces saving.
- You should understand the propensity of consumption and saving regarding permanent and temporary changes in income.
- For a permanent change in wage income the propensity to consume is high and the propensity to save is low. If the change in wage income is temporary the propensity to consume is low and the propensity to save is high.

Key Graphs

Figure 7.1 *The Household Budget Constraint*

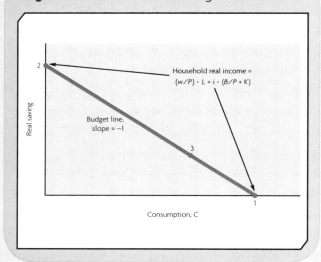

Households have a given total of real income, $(w/P) \cdot L + i \cdot (B/P + K)$. This total must be divided between consumption, C, and real saving, $(1/P) \Delta B + \Delta K$. Thus, if real saving is zero, C equals the total of real income along the horizontal axis at point 1. If C is zero, real saving equals the total of real income along the vertical axis at point 2. The budget constraint in equation (7.1) allows the household to select any combination of consumption and real saving along the budget line, shown in red, such as point 3. The budget line has a slope of -1. Along this line, one unit less of consumption corresponds to one unit more of real saving.

Figure 7.2 *Change in Real Assets in Year 1*

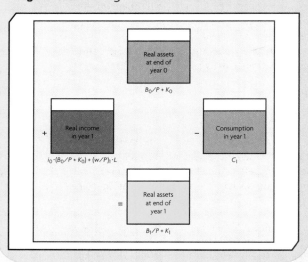

The red bin has the real assets at the end of year 0, $B_0/P + K_0$, the first term on the right-hand side of equation (7.4). The real income for year 1, $i_0 \cdot (B_0/P + K_0) + (w/P)_1 \cdot L$ in the blue bin, corresponds to the second term on the right-hand side of equation (7.4) and adds to the red bin. The consumption for year 1, C_1 in the green bin, corresponds to the third term on the right-hand side of equation (7.4) and subtracts from the red bin. The final result is the real assets at the end of year 1, $B_1/P + K_1$ in the yellow bin. This amount is the left-hand side of equation (7.4).

Learning Outcomes

- You should understand that shocks to the technology level, A, deliver a variety of real disturbances to the economy.
- You should understand the equilibrium business-cycle model explanation regarding fluctuations in consumption and investment.
- You should understand the cyclical behavior of labor in the equilibrium business-cycle model.

Key Equations

(8.6)

$$C + (1/P) \cdot \Delta B + \Delta K = (w/P) \cdot L^s + i \cdot (B/P + K)$$
$$\text{consumption} + \text{real saving} = \text{real income}$$

Worked Problems

Ques. 1

Shift in desired saving

Suppose that households change their preferences so that they wish to consume more and save less in the current year. That is, current consumption, C_1, rises for a given interest rate, and for given current and future income.

a. Use a variant of Figure 8.15 to determine the effects on the labor market. What happens to labor input, L, and the real wage rate, w/P?

b. Use a variant of Figure 8.8 to determine the effects on the market for capital services. What happens to the real rental price, R/P? What happens to the interest rate, i?

c. What happens to consumption, C, and investment, I? What happens over time to the stock of capital, K?

Ans. 1

A reduction in desired saving

a. Since the reduction in the desired savings rate has no effect on labor productivity, the demand for labor will not change. There will be no *direct* effects on labor supply. However, since the reduced savings rate will have the effect of increasing interest rates (see part 5b), the opportunity cost of current leisure will increase, and the labor supply curve will shift to the right (intertemporal substitution effect). This chain of events would cause real wages to fall and labor input to rise.

b. A decrease in savings rates would cause an excess supply of bonds in the market, which would raise interest rates. In the graph for capital services, In we will assume that the supply of capital is fixed in the current period. Later, in chapter 9, we will relax this assumption somewhat to allow for different capital utilization rates. The marginal product of capital is determined by the level of technology and the labor force. As we saw in part 5a, there might be a slight increase in labor input which would cause the MPK curve to shift to the right. This would result in higher real rental rates on capital services. This is consistent with the notion that in equilibrium, both interest rates and the real rental rate on capital must be equal.

c. Aggregate consumption increases, investment falls. The lower rate of investment will cause the capital stock to grow more slowly or even decrease over time. This is especially true if the intertemporal substitution effect described in 5a and 5b is too small to restore equilibrium in the asset markets. In that case, the additional labor does not increase MPK enough, and the only alternative is for the supply of capital to fall. This would require negative net investment.

Key Terms and Concepts

acyclical (p. 138)
countercyclical (p. 138)
cyclical part of real GDP (p. 130)
equilibrium business-cycle model (p. 133)

procyclical (p. 138)
real business-cycle model (p. 133)
shocks (p. 133)
standard deviation (p. 131)

total hours worked (p. 145)
trend real GDP (p. 129)

Chapter Summary

• You should understand that shocks to the technology level, A, deliver a variety of real disturbances to the economy.

In the equilibrium business-cycle model, if the technology level rises, the model predicts an economic boom. In that economic boom real GDP will rise, the MPL will rise and accordingly will the real wage rate, the MPK will rise and according will the real rental price of capital. The increase in the real wage rate and the real rental price of capital translate into an increase in household income. The increase in household income means an increase in consumption and saving. The equilibrium business-cycle model explains why the real wage rate, the real rental price of capital, consumption and investment are all procyclical. Conversely, during a recession, we will have a relatively low; real wage rate, real rental rate on capital, consumption and investment.

• You should understand the equilibrium business-cycle model explanation regarding fluctuations in consumption and investment.

Real consumer expenditure and real investment are procyclical. When changes in A are long lasting but not fully permanent consumption can fluctuate proportionally less than real GDP. This can be due to the intertemporal-substitution effect on consumption outweighing the income effect. Hence, net investment, rises by nearly as much or possibly more than real GDP. The model explains why investment fluctuates proportionately more than consumption.

• You should understand the cyclical behavior of labor in the equilibrium business-cycle model.

The equilibrium business-cycle model matches the procyclical behavior of employment and worker hours. When labor supply is variable, and a positive response of the labor supply to the real wage rate, the substitution effect from the real wage rate dominates the income effect and labor input contributes to the rise of real GDP in a boom and a decline of real GDP in a recession.

Key Graphs

Figure 8.8 *Effect of an Increase in the Technology Level on the Real Rental Price of Capital*

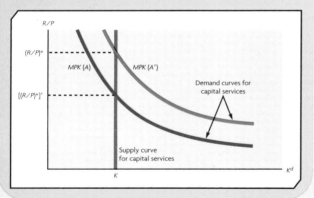

The supply of capital services is the given value K, shown on the horizontal axis. If the technology level is A, the schedule for the MPK is given by the blue curve, labeled $MPK (A)$. This curve gives the demand for capital services when the technology level is A. The market-clearing real rental price is $(R/P)^*$, shown on the vertical axis. The technology level A' is greater than A, as in Figure 8.7. Therefore, the schedule for the MPK is given by the red curve, labeled $MPK (A)$. This curve gives the demand for capital services when the technology level is A'. In this case, the market-clearing real rental price is $[(R/P)^*]'$, which is greater than $(R/P)^*$.

Figure 8.15 *Cyclical Behavior of U.S. Real GDP and Total Hours Worked*

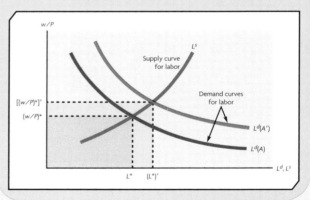

At the technology level A, the demand for labor, labeled $L^d (A)$ along the blue cuve, slopes downward versus the real wage rate, w/P. At the higher technology level, A', the demand for labor, labeled $L^d (A')$ along the red curve, is larger at any given w/P. These two curves are from Figure 8.5. The supply of labor, L^s, shown in green, slopes upward versus w/P because we assume that the substitution effect from a change in w/P dominates the income effect. The increase in the technology level from A to A' raises the real wage rate from $(w/P)^*$ to $[(w/P)^*]'$ on the vertical axis, and increases labor input from L^* to $(L^*)'$ on the horizontal axis.

Learning Outcomes

- You should understand the concept of capital services and how changes in capital services impact the production function in key equation 9.1

- You should understand the relationship between capacity utilization and the business cycle.

- You should understand the natural rate of unemployment.

- You should understand how economic fluctuations impact employment and unemployment.

Key Equations

Key equation (Production Function with variable capital utilization):

(9.1) $$Y = A \cdot F(\kappa K, L)$$

Key equation (rate of return on capital):

(9.4) $$\text{rate of return from owning capital} = (R/P) \cdot \kappa - \delta(\kappa)$$

Key equation (natural unemployment rate):

(9.7) $$u^n = \sigma/(\varphi + \sigma)$$

Worked Problems

Ques. 1

Cyclical behavior of the labor force

Figure 9.7 shows that the labor force is weakly procyclical. What pattern would you predict on theoretical grounds? (Hint: think first about people's incentives to leave the labor force—that is, to stop looking for work—during a recession. Are there also incentives for people to enter the labor force during a recession?)

Ans. 1

Unemployed persons not "actively seeking work" are not counted in the labor force. It may be that some of them are not seeking work until business conditions improve, that is, until the expected probability (and therefore, the net benefits) of the job search increase. In this case, the labor force would be pro-cyclical, and the unemployment rates would decrease during a recession not because people are finding jobs, but because they have stopped looking for them. These people are officially designated as "discouraged workers". When business conditions pick up and these "discouraged workers" begin actively looking for work again, their presence in the labor force would tend to push unemployment rates up again. On the other hand, if one person in a household loses a job or suffers a loss of income, another member of the household not currently in the labor force may decide to enter in an effort to maintain household income.

Key Terms and Concepts

capital utilization rate (p. 149)
discouraged workers (p. 163)
duration of unemployment (p. 160)
employment rate (p. 157)
help-wanted advertising (p. 157)

job-finding rate (p. 160)
job-separation rate (p. 162)
natural unemployment rate (p. 165)
reservation real wage (p. 160)
unemployment insurance (p. 159)

user costs (p. 153)
vacancies (p. 157)
vacancy rate (p. 151)

Chapter Summary

• You should understand the concept of capital services and how changes in capital services impact the production function in key equation 9.1.

The quantity of capital services , κK, is the product of capital stock, K, and κ, the capital utilization rate. As is indicated in the production function the level of capital stock is given. For a given K, κK, rises with the utilization rate κ. Increases in κ raise real GDP and Y for given level of A, K and L.

• You should understand the relationship between capacity utilization and the business cycle.

The capacity utilization rate is procyclical. During economic booms the rate is above the trend in real GDP and below the trend during recessions.

• You should understand the natural rate of unemployment.

Based on recent data, 2000–2006, the natural rate of unemployment in the U.S. is 5.7%. Natural implies that the economy tends toward this value automatically. While the economy is at this natural rate about 4 million people lose and find jobs each month.

• You should understand how economic fluctuations impact employment and unemployment.

Employment is procyclical while unemployment is countercyclical. In a boom job seekers are more likely to accept job offers because of the increase in the real wage rate. In a boom, the rate of job acceptance increases partly because the wage offers are better and partly because jobs are easier to find. Conversely, in a recession, the rate of job acceptance decreases because the real wage declines and positions are harder to find.

Key Graph

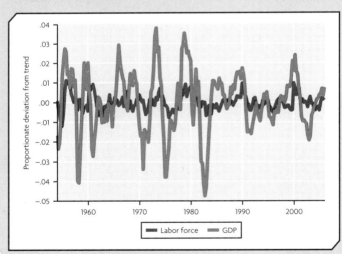

Figure 9.7 *Cyclical Behavior of U.S. Real GDP and the Labor Force*

The red graph is the deviation of real GDP from its trend. The blue graph is the deviation of the civilian labor force from its trend. The civilian labor force—the number of persons employed or seeking employment—comes from the BLS Household Survey (www.bls.gov). The data on real GDP and the labor force are quarterly and seasonally adjusted. (The underlying data on the labor force are monthly.) The labor force is weakly procyclical—it fluctuates weakly with real GDP and is less variable than real GDP.

Learning Outcomes

- You should understand the basic concepts of money.

- You should understand the components of the demand for money.

- You should understand the factors the influence the demand for money.

- You should understand the implications of a change in the nominal quantity of money.

Key Equations

Key equation (money-demand function):

(10.2) $$M^d = P \cdot L(Y, i)$$

Key equation (nominal quantity of money supplied equals nominal quantity demanded):

(10.5) $$M^s = P \cdot L(Y, i)$$

Key equation (endogenous determination of money):

(10.8) $$M = \bar{P} \cdot L(Y, i)$$

nominal quantity of money = price-level target · real quantity of money demanded

Worked Problems

Ques. 1

Velocity of money

The velocity of money is the ratio of the dollar volume of transactions—say, nominal GDP—divided by the nominal quantity of money. How is the velocity of money affected by

a. an increase in the nominal interest rate, I?
b. an increase in real GDP, Y caused by a rise in per capita real GDP with population held constant?
c. an increase in real GDP, Y caused by a rise in population with per capita real GDP held constant?
d. an increase in the price level, P?
e. Why might nominal GDP not be the correct measure of transactions?
f. What do you predict happens to the velocity of money as an economy develops?

Ans. 1

One way to approach these problems is to refer to an equation for velocity such as this: $V = Y/L$, where Y is real GDP and L is real money demand.

a. Higher values for i reduce real money demand; V increases.
b. An increase in Y leads to an increase in V.
c. Similar to (b); there will be an increase in V. The change in V in this case might be slightly less due to economies of scale in money management. In other words, people in part b would have larger real money balances. Economies of scale would reduce the transactions cost of shifting between money and other assets, and therefore the overall demand for money might be lower in part (b), which implies V would be slightly higher.
d. Since P does not change the demand for real money balances, there should be no change in velocity. (However, inflation would have an effect on money demand and velocity because it would reduce L).
e. Nominal GDP measures current income in dollars, but the desired volume of transactions depends on wealth as well as income.
f. As an economy develops, financial institutions become more sophisticated and convenient, portfolio management becomes more important and related transactions costs fall. All of this has the effect of reducing the real demand for money; Y and L increase over time, but L will grow more slowly; V increases.

Key Terms and Concepts

barter (p. 171)
checkable deposits (p. 173)
commodity money (p. 171)
demand for money (p. 171)
economies of scale in cash management (p. 177)
endogenous money (p. 185)
fiat money (p. 171)

general equilibrium (p. 180)
high-powered money (p. 172)
interest-bearing assets (p. 174)
legal tender (p. 172)
M1 (p. 173)
M2 (p. 173)
monetary aggregate (p. 172)

monetary base (p. 172)
neutrality of money (p. 182)
price-level targeting (p. 185)
quantity theory of money (p. 184)
real demand for money (p. 176)
stores of value (p. 174)
transaction costs (p. 175)

Chapter Summary

• You should understand the basic concepts of money.

The money referred to in this text is paper currency such as dollars. It may be called fiat money which means that it has no value other than that determined by the government. Commodity money, such as gold and silver coins, was used by earlier societies and was replaced by fiat money. Monetary aggregate is a broader yet definition of money and includes various financial assets in addition to money.

• You should understand the components of the demand for money.

We assume that the interest rate paid on money is zero. This implies that the rate of return on cash is zero. Nonetheless households hold cash to facilitate transactions. Households also hold cash as an asset.

• You should understand the factors the influence the demand for money.

At higher interest rates, i, households reduce holdings of Money, M. A doubling of the price level, P, will induce households to double their holdings of the nominal quantity of money, M. With a doubling of real GDP, households would double their holdings of nominal quantity of money, M.

• You should understand the implications of a change in the nominal quantity of money.

Money takes the form of currency and is given as, M, and is determined by the monetary authority, for example the Federal Reserve in the U.S. A doubling of the nominal quantity of money supplied, M^s, lead to a doubling of all of the nominal prices: the price level, P; the nominal wage rate, w; and the nominal rental price, R. There are no changes in real variables including real GDP and Y.

Key Graphs

Figure 10.1 *The Nominal Quantity of Money Supplied Equals the Nominal Quantity Demanded*

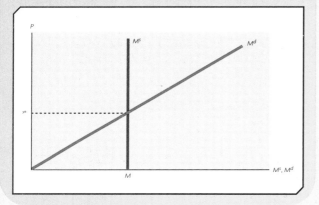

The nominal quantity of money demanded is given by $M^d = P \cdot L(Y, i)$ from equation (10.2). For a given real quantity of money demanded, $L(Y, i)$, M^d is proportional to the price level, P. Therefore, the nominal quantity demanded, M^d, is given by the upward-sloping red line, which starts from the origin. The nominal quantity of money supplied is the constant $M^s = M$, shown by the vertical blue line. The equilibrium condition $M^s = M^d$ holds when the price level is P^* on the vertical axis. Thus, P^* is the equilibrium value of P.

Figure 10.2 *An Increase in the Nominal Quantity of Money*

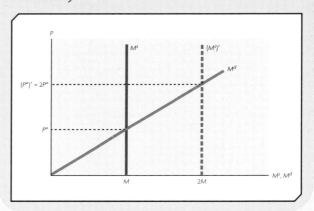

The nominal demand for money, M^d, shown by the red line, is the same as in Figure 10.1. The nominal quantity of money supplied, M^s, doubles from M (the vertical blue line) to $2M$ (the vertical green line). Therefore, the equilibrium price level doubles, on the vertical axis, from P^* to $(P^*)' = 2P^*$.

Learning Outcomes

- You should understand the relationship between money growth and inflation.

- You should understand the relationship between the nominal interest rate and inflation.

- You should understand how an increase in the money growth rate affects real variables.

Key Equations

Key equation:

real interest rate = nominal interest rate − inflation rate

[11.6] $$r_1 = i_1 - \pi_1$$

Key equation (equality of real rates of return):

[11.10] $$r = (R/P) \cdot \kappa - \delta(\kappa)$$

real rate of return on bonds = real rate of return from owning capital

Key equation (determination of price level):

[11.16] $$P_1 = M_1/L(Y, i)$$

price level = nominal quantity of money/real quantity of money demanded

Worked Problems

Ques. 1

Money growth and inflation

Suppose that the money-demand function takes the form

$$M^d/P = L(Y, i) = Y \cdot \psi(i)$$

That is, for a given nominal interest rate, i, a doubling of real GDP, Y, doubles the real quantity of money demanded, M^d/P.

a. Consider the relation across countries between the growth rate of money (currency), μ, and the inflation rate, π, as shown in Figure 11.1. How does the growth rate of real GDP, $\Delta Y/Y$, affect the relationship between μ and π?

b. What is the relation between μ and π for a country in which the nominal interest rate, i, has increased?

c. Suppose that the expected real interest rate, r_t^e, is given. What is the relation between μ and π for a country in which the expected inflation rate, π_t^e, has increased?

Ans. 1

a. A high rate of growth in real GDP weakens the link between m and p. If the real economy grows at about the same rate as the money supply, there is no reason to expect positive rates of inflation. Given the assumptions on money demand made in this problem, money demand will grow at the same rate as the money supply.

b. A rising nominal interest rate reduces the growth in the real demand for money. For a given growth rate in the supply of money, this would result in a higher rate of inflation.

c. Higher rates of expected inflation leads to higher nominal interest rates, reducing the demand for money and creating inflationary pressure in the economy. The expectation of inflation can create the inflation.

Key Terms and Concepts

deflation (p. 194)
expectations of inflation (p. 196)
expected real interest rate (p. 199)
hyperinflation (p. 211)
indexed bonds (p. 199)

lump-sum transfers (p. 202)
money growth rate (p. 192)
nominal interest rate (p. 197)
rational expectations (p. 196)

real interest rate (p. 197)
revenue from printing money (p. 209)
transfer payment (p. 202)
unexpected inflation (p. 196)

reviewcard

Chapter Summary

- You should understand the relationship between money growth and inflation.

According to the cross-country data, sustained inflation requires persistent money growth. Increasing the money growth rate by 1% per year is associated with an increase in the inflation rate by 1% per year. An increase in the growth rate of real GDP by 1% per year is associated with and increase by 1% per year in the growth rate of real money balances. A higher growth rate of real GDP lowers the inflation rate for a given growth rate of money.

- You should understand the relationship between the nominal interest rate and inflation.

The real rate of interest is equal to the nominal rate of interest less inflation. The real rate of interest can be less than zero.

Conventional nominal bonds specify in advance the nominal interest rate. Indexed bonds specify the real rate of interest.

- You should understand how an increase in the money growth rate affects real variables.

Intertemporal-substitution effects depend on the real interest rate. The demand for money depends on the nominal interest rate. In the equilibrium business-cycle model and increase in the money growth rate leads, one for one, to a higher inflation rate and higher nominal inflation rate. A change in the money growth rate does not affect real GDP, consumption, investment, the real wage rate, the real rental price of capital and the real interest rate. A higher money growth rate, however, does lead to lower real money balances and to greater revenue for the government.

Key Graphs

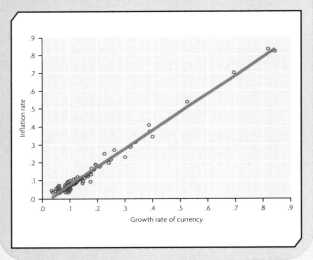

Figure 11.1 *Inflation Rate and Growth Rate of Nominal Currency for 82 Countries, 1960–2000*

This graph uses the data from Table 11.1. The vertical axis plots the inflation rate from 1960 to 2000, based on consumer price indexes. The horizontal axis plots the growth rate of nominal currency from 1960 to 2000. The two variables have a strong positive association—the correlation is 0.99. The slope of the relation is close to one; that is, an increase in the growth rate of nominal currency by 1% per year is associated with an increase in the inflation rate by about 1% per year.

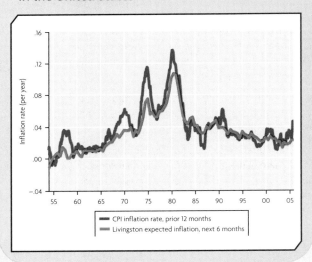

Figure 11.2 *Actual and Expected Inflation Rates in the United States*

The blue graph shows the inflation rate over the prior 12 months, computed from the consumer price index (CPI). The red graph shows the expected CPI inflation rate. These expectations, formed six to eight months in advance, are from the Livingston survey, available from the Federal Reserve Bank of Philadelphia.

Learning Outcomes

- You should be able to distinguish between public production and public services.

- You should understand the implications of a permanent change in government purchases.

- You should understand the implications of temporary changes in government purchases.

Key Equations

Key equation (government budget constraint):

$$total\ usees\ of\ funds = total\ sources\ of\ funds$$

(12.1) $$G_t + V_t = T_t + (M_t - M_t - M_{t-1})/P_t$$

real purchases + real transfers = real taxes + real revenue from money creation

Key equation (multiyear household budget constraint with transfers and taxes):

(12.6)
$$C_1 + C_2/(1 + r_1) + \ldots = (1 + r_0) \cdot (B_0/P + K_0) + (W/P)_1 \cdot L_1^s + (W/P)_2 \cdot L_2^s/(1 + r_1) + \ldots + (V_1 - T_1) + (V_2 - T_2)/(1 + r_1) + (V_3 - T_3)/[(1 + r_1) \cdot (1 + r_2)] + \ldots$$

present value of consumption = value of initial assests + present value of wage incomes + present value of transfers net of taxes

Worked Problems

Ques. 1

Public ownership of capital and the national accounts

Until the revision of 1996, the U.S. national accounts included in GDP the government's purchases of goods and services but took no account of the flow of services on government-owned capital. The accounts also did not subtract depreciation of this capital to calculate net domestic product.

a. In the pre-1996 system, what happened to GDP if the government gave its capital to a private business and then bought the final goods from that business?

b. In the current system of national accounts, the GDP includes an estimate of the flow of implicit rental income generated by public capital. However, this income flow is assumed to equal the estimated depreciation of the public capital. Redo question a. in the context of this system.

Ans. 1

a. Prior to the 1996 revisions, the services provided by the capital would have added nothing to GDP. If they were given to the private sector and purchased by the government, GDP would increase. For example if government built a marina for coast guard patrol boats, the services would not be counted as GDP. If the government gave the dock to a private owner and paid the private owner rental fees, the GDP would increase.

b. Under government ownership the implicit flow of services would be valued at the estimated depreciation rate of the dock. If they gave it to a private owner and rented it, then the GDP would increase by that amount. In this case, since the market value of the service is likely to be greater than the estimated depreciation rate, government ownership is still likely to understate the true GDP, though the bias will be reduced.

Key Terms and Concepts

government's budget constraint (p. 219)
lump-sum taxes (p. 219)

real disposable income (p. 221)
Social Security (p. 217)

term structure of real interest rates (p. 229)

Chapter Summary

• You should be able to distinguish between public production and public services.

Government uses it real purchases of goods and services, *G*, to provide services to households and businesses free of charge. These services can include national defense, enforcement of laws and private contracts, police protection and etc. Regarding public production we assume that the government purchases its goods and services through the private sector.

• You should understand the implications of a permanent change in government purchases.

A permanent increase in government purchases, *G*, will reduce consumption, *C*, roughly one to one. This permanent increase

in, *G*, does not impact the marginal productivity of capital and therefore does not change the amount of labor input in the economy leaving real GDP and *Y* unchanged.

• You should understand the implications of temporary changes in government purchases.

A temporary increase in government purchases, *G*, decreases consumption, *C*, by a relatively small amount and reduces gross investment, *I*, by a larger amount. The temporary increase in government expenditures comes mainly at the expense of gross investments, *I*, leaving real GDP and *Y* unchanged.

Key Graphs

Figure 12.1 *Total Government Expenditure, Purchases, Transfers, and Interest Payments*

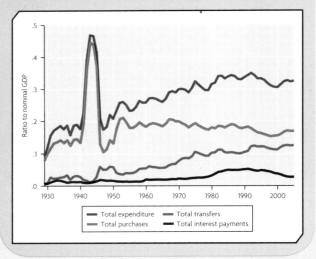

The graphs refer to total government and show ratios of each nominal expenditure component to nominal GDP. Purchases of goods and services are the outlays for consumption and investment. In the national accounts, purchases equal government consumption and investment less depreciation of public capital stocks. Total transfers exclude grants-in-aid from the federal government to state and local governments but include subsidies. Interest payments are the total paid (with no netting out of interest receipts by government). Total expenditure also includes relatively small amounts for capital transfer payments and net purchases of nonproduced assets.

Figure 12.7 *Cyclical Behavior of U.S. Real GDP and Government Purchases*

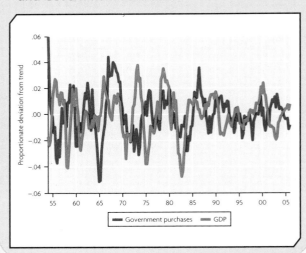

The red graph is the deviation of real GDP from its trend. The blue graph is the deviation of real government purchases from its trend. (We measure government purchases by the national-accounts data on government consumption and investment—this concept adds to government purchases the estimated depreciation of government capital stocks.) The deviations are measured in a proportionate sense. The data on GDP and government purchases are quarterly and seasonally adjusted. Government purchases are about as variable as GDP but have little cyclical pattern. The correlation of the cyclical part of real government purchases with the cyclical part of real GDP was −0.01.

Learning Outcomes

- You should understand the basic differences between various types of taxation.

- You should understand the implications of an increase in taxation of labor income.

- You should understand the implications of an increase in taxation on asset income.

- You should understand the overall effect on the labor supply of an increase in government purchases financed by a tax on labor income.

Worked Problems

Ques. 1

The flat-rate tax

Some U.S. economists advocate shifting from the graduated individual income tax to a flat-rate tax. Under the new system, there would be few deductions from taxable income, and the marginal tax rate would be constant. Because of the elimination of the deductions, the average marginal tax rate would be lower than that under the current system.

a. What are the economic effects from a shift to a flat-rate tax on labor income?

b. How does the proposed flat-rate tax compare with the present Social Security payroll tax?

Ans. 1

a. If the elimination of deductions permits government to reduce the marginal tax rate on labor income, then the substitution effect predicts an increase in labor income. More labor employed will make capital more productive and should result in an increase in capacity utilization rates. The net result would be to raise GDP, Y.

b. There are similarities. Currently, the payroll tax provides a constant marginal tax rate on labor income, just as the proposed flat tax would. However, social security taxes provide no exemption until income exceeds a particular level (approximately $90,000), after which the marginal tax rate falls to zero. Under this system, the average tax rate falls as incomes exceed the $90,000 mark. Under a flat tax, the exemption is applied to the first portion of earned income, so that the average rate increases with income. In other words, the social security tax is regressive in the average tax rate, but the flat tax is progressive.

Key Terms and Concepts

adjusted gross income (p. 239)
after-tax real interest rate (p. 245)
after-tax real wage rate (p. 242)

average tax rate (p. 238)
double taxation (p. 241)
flat-rate tax (p. 240)

graduated-rate tax (p. 238)
Laffer curve (p. 248)
marginal tax rate (p. 238)

Chapter Summary

- You should understand the basic differences between various types of taxation.

Some taxes fall on income like individual income tax and corporate profit taxes. Other forms of tax fall on wealth owners an example might be property tax.

- You should understand the implications of an increase in taxation of labor income.

An increase in the tax on labor income will reduce the supply of labor to the market thereby reducing the quantity of labor input leading to a reduction in the marginal product of capital services and ultimately reducing GDP and Y.

- You should understand the implications of an increase in taxation on asset income.

In the short run an increase in the marginal tax rate on asset income does not change the quantity of capital services, the demand for labor or the supply of labor. The market clearing wage rate does not change. Thus our conclusion is that a change in the marginal tax rate does not change GDP. However, in the long run, an increase in the marginal tax rate on assets will lower gross investment, I, resulting in a lower capital stock leading to lower GDP and Y.

- You should understand the overall effect on the labor supply of an increase in government purchases financed by a tax on labor income.

The overall effect depends on the offsetting influences of the income effect and substitution effect. The income effect predicts that the supply of labor would rise. The substitution effect predicts that the supply of labor would fall. The overall effect on labor is uncertain.

Key Graphs

Figure 13.5 *Effect of an Increase in the Labor-Income Tax Rate on the Labor Market*

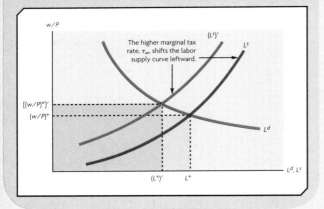

The downward-sloping labor demand curve, L^d, shown in red, comes from Figure 8.15. The upward-sloping labor supply curve, L^s, shown in blue, also comes from Figure 8.15. An increase in the marginal tax rate on labor income, τ_w, shifts the labor supply curve leftward to the green one, $(L^s)'$. Consequently, the market-clearing, before-tax real wage rate rises from $(w/P)^*$ to $[(w/P)^*]'$ on the vertical axis. The market-clearing quantity of labor input falls from L^* to $(L^*)'$ on the horizontal axis.

Figure 13.6 *Effect of an Increase in the Labor-Income Tax Rate on the Market for Capital Services*

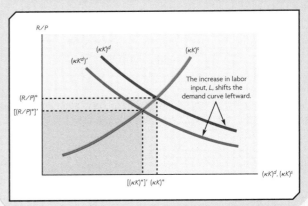

This construction comes from Figure 12.5. The reduction in employment from L^* to $(L^*)'$, shown in Figure 13.5, reduces the marginal product of capital services, MPK (at a given quantity of capital services, κK). Therefore, the demand curve for capital services shifts leftward, from $(\kappa K)^d$, shown in blue, to $[(\kappa K)d]'$, shown in green. The supply curve for capital services, $(\kappa K)^s$, shown in red, does not shift. Consequently, the market-clearing real rental price of capital falls from $(R/P)^*$ to $[(R/P)^*]'$ on the vertical axis. The quantity of capital services declines from $(\kappa K)^*$ to $[(\kappa K)^*]'$ on the horizontal axis. This decrease in capital services corresponds, for a given capital stock, K, to a reduction in the capital utilization rate, κ.

Learning Outcomes

- You should understand the relationships between deficits, public debt and government bonds

- You should be able to distinguish between public, private and national savings.

- You should understand the implications of the Ricardian Equivalence proposition

- You should understand the potential impacts various fiscal policy tax changes.

- You should understand open market operations and their purpose

Key Equations

Key equation (expanded government budget constraint):

(14.1)

$$G_t + V_t + i_{t-1} \cdot (B^g_{t-1}/P_t)$$
$$= T_t + (B^g_t - B^g_{t-1})/P_t + (M_t - M_{t-1})/P_t$$

real purchases + real transfers + real interest payments = real taxes + real debt issue + real revenue from money creation

Worked Problems

Ques. 1

The income effect from a budget deficit

Suppose that, in year 1, the government cuts current, lump-sum taxes and runs a budget deficit. Assume that the real public debt remains constant in future years. Also, no changes occur in government purchases of goods and services, G, or in real transfers, V. Analyze the income effect from the government's tax cut. How does this effect depend on the following:

a. finite lifetimes?
b. the existence of childless persons?
c. uncertainty about who will pay future taxes?
d. the possibility that the government will print more money in the future rather than levying future taxes?

Ans. 1

a. The tax cut allows individuals to shift the tax liability onto future generations *should they wish to do so*. In this case the income effect would increase current consumption and reduce investment. On the other hand, if people care about the the finances of the next generation, they will accumulate savings which will be left to their children (bequest motive) and the income effects will be eliminated.

b. If people don't have any children then they will be able to shift the burden of the debt onto other people's children. The bequest motive is weakened, and the income effect is larger than in the previous example.

c. Just as in case b, people may feel that "someone else" will be liable for the future taxes. In this case, a positive income effect is likely.

d. The increase in the stock of money will create inflation, which is a kind of tax. Therefore there is no change in the present value of household income and no income effect.

Key Terms and Concepts

balanced budget (p. 256)
budget deficit (p. 252)
budget surplus (p. 256)
burden of the public debt (p. 266)
fiscal policy (p. 261)

fully funded system (p. 269)
national saving (p. 258)
open-market operations (p. 270)
pay-as-you-go system (p. 269)
public debt (p. 252)

public investment (p. 256)
Ricardian equivalence theorem (p. 259)
strategic budget deficits (p. 265)
tax-rate smoothing (p. 264)

reviewcard

Chapter Summary

• You should understand the relationships between deficits, public debt, government bonds and budget surplus.

When a governments tax revenues fall short of expenditures the government runs a budget deficit. The accumulation of those deficits across years is the nations public debt. Governments issue government bonds as financial vehicles to borrow the money necessary to finance the public debt. When tax revenues are in excess of expenditures the government's budget is in surplus.

• You should be able to distinguish between public, private and national savings.

• You should understand the implications of the Ricardian Equivalence proposition.

The Ricardian Equivalence Proposition suggests that if governments replace a unit of real taxes with a unit of real budget deficit, give a tax cut this year by deficit spending, that households will realize that the present value of next years real taxes will rise by one unit. Implication is that the household increase

in real savings is offset by the government real increase in dissavings and their will be no change in national savings.

• You should understand the potential impacts various fiscal policy tax changes.

Fiscal policy changes in the form of tax cuts can come in various different forms. Lump sum tax cuts do not impact an real variables and does not stimulate the economy. Labor income tax cuts motivates a rearrangement of the time pattern of work and production. Changing the timing of asset income taxes causes changes in the timing of C and I.

• You should understand open market operations and their purpose.

Open market operations are conducted by the central bank and are intended to change the money supply and correspondingly interest rates. An open market purchase of government bonds results in an increase in the money supply and reduction in interest rates. An open market sale results in a decrease in the money supply and an increase in the interest rate.

Key Graphs

Figure 14.1 *Ratio of U.S. Public Debt to GDP, 1790–2005*

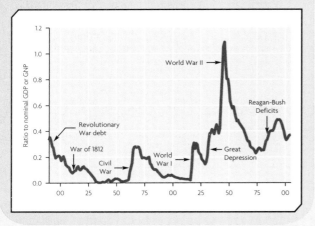

The graph shows the ratio of U.S. nominal public debt to nominal GDP (GNP before 1929), using the numbers described in Table 14.1.

Figure 14.3 *Ratio of U.S. Real Budget Deficit to Real GDP, 1954–2005*

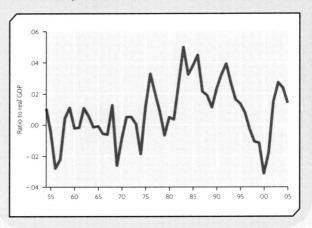

The graph shows the ratio of the real budget deficit to real GDP from 1954 to 2005. To compute the real budget deficit, we start by calculating the stock of real public debt at the end of each year as the ratio of the nominal debt to the GDP deflator. The real budget deficit is the change during the year of the stock of real public debt.

Learning Outcomes

- You should understand the possible explanation for the non-neutrality of money provided by the price-misperceptions model.

- You should understand the labor market response to a technology shock based on the price-misperceptions model.

- You should understand the consequences and implications of a central bank policy that strictly follows rules vs. a policy that allows for discretion.

Worked Problems

Ques. 1

Persisting effects on output

When expectations are rational, errors made in estimating the price level will not persist over time. How, then, can price-perception errors explain persistent excesses or shortfalls of real GDP from its trend?

Ans. 1

The model predicts that deviations from trend GDP will be temporary. Persistent effects on GDP can arise from other sources. For example, a shock that produces above trend GDP will generate an increase in income, some of which will be devoted to investment. The investment will raise the capital stock and increase future labor productivity. The result is a persistent increase in employment and output, even though labor supply curve has shifted back to its original position.

Ques. 2

The timing of money and output

Suppose that the data show that movements in nominal money are positively correlated with subsequent movements in real GDP. Does this finding demonstrate that money affects the real economy, rather than the reverse? If not, give some examples of endogenous money in which the movements of money precede those in real GDP.

Ans. 2

Correlation is not causation. It could be that the central bank is forecasting economic activity accurately, and adjusting the money supply to keep up with anticipated changes in money demand (recall that money demand increases as GDP increases). Even if the central bank does not actively manage the money supply, M1 would still increase prior to an investment boom because bank lending expands the volume of demand deposits. An investment boom could be associated with a technological change that increases productivity. In this case, the expansion in the money supply "accommodates" the expansion of real GDP rather than causing it.

Key Terms and Concepts

capital levy (p. 287)
discretionary policy (p. 285)
inflation targeting (p. 286)
irrelevance result for systematic
   monetary policy (p. 277)

Lucas hypothesis on monetary shocks
   (p. 278)
monetary rule (p. 284)
monetary shocks (p. 273)
perceived real wage rate (p. 275)

perfect foresight (p. 285)
policy rule (p. 285)
price stability (p. 285)
price-misperceptions model (p. 274)
unanticipated money growth (p. 280)

reviewcard

Chapter Summary

• You should understand the possible explanation for the non-neutrality of money provided by the price-misperceptions model.

The assumption is that money is neutral in the long run. However, in the price-misperceptions model, households with incomplete current information about prices, sometimes misinterpret changes in nominal prices and wages for changes in relative prices and real wages. Therefore monetary shocks which affect nominal prices and wages end up affecting real variables like real GDP and employment.

• You should understand the labor market response to a technology shock based on the price-misperceptions model.

Given a positive technology shock, the technology level, A, rises. This increase in technology leads to decline in the price level, P. Firms correctly interpret prices and increase their demand for labor. Workers overestimate P and underestimate

their real wage and subsequently reduce their supply of labor to the market. This is a short run event and once perceived price level catches up to the actual price level the labor supply curve shifts back to its equilibrium position.

• You should understand the consequences and implications of a central bank policy that strictly follows rules vs. a policy that allows for discretion.

We have found that unanticipated money supply shocks can affect the real economy in the short run. It is possible that the monetary authorities might be tempted to exercise their power to create monetary shocks to influence real variables. The belief of economists is that this behavior will lead to bad outcomes. Under a monetary rule, the central bank commits itself to a designated role of monetary policy. Under monetary discretion the central bank leaves open the possibility for surprises.

Key Graphs

Figure 15.2 *Effect of Unperceived Inflation on the Labor Market*

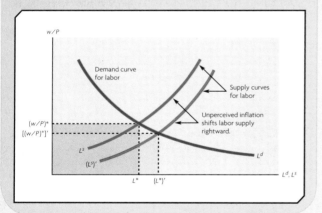

A rise in P/P^e for suppliers of labor (employees) raises w/P^e for a given w/P. Therefore, the labor supply curve shifts rightward, from L^s to $(L^s)'$. We conclude that unperceived inflation raises labor input—from L^* to $(L^*)'$—and lowers the real wage rate—from $(w/P)^*$ to $[(w/P)^*]'$.

Figure 15.3 *Response of the Labor Market to a Technology Shock: Effects of Price Misperceptions*

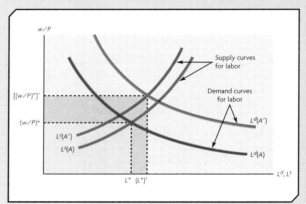

The technology level, A rises from A to A'. The labor demand curves come from Figure 8.15. At any real wage rate, w/P, the quantity of labor demanded is higher along the red curve, $L^d(A')$, than along the blue one, $L^d(A)$. The increase in A also reduces the price level, P. Because of price misperceptions, the quantity of labor supplied falls at any w/P. Therefore, $L^s(A')$, in brown, lies to the left of the initial curve, $L^s(A)$, in green. The increase in L from L^* to $(L^*)'$, is less than it would have been if the L^s curve had not shifted. Therefore, price misperceptions lessen the response of L to a technology shock.

Learning Outcomes

- You should understand the distinction between the "sticky wages" and "sticky price" variations in the Keynesian model.

- You should understand the impact on the labor market of stickiness in prices.

- You should understand the implications of the federal reserves' open market operations under "sticky wages" and "sticky price" variations in the Keynesian model.

Worked Problems

Ques. 1

The paradox of thrift

Suppose that households become thriftier in the sense that they decide to raise current saving and reduce current consumer demand.

a. In the new Keynesian model, what happens to real GDP, Y, and labor?

b. What happens to the amount of saving? If it decreases, there is said to be a *paradox of thrift*.

c. Can there be a paradox of thrift in the equilibrium business-cycle model?

Ans. 1

a. The reduction in aggregate demand reduces real output and employment.

b. In the one hand savings will increase relative to consumption, due to the higher savings rate. Although it is theoretically possible that savings could fall in the aggregate, this would require that real GDP falls by a multiple of the original change in consumption. If real wages and employment fall, then spending could drop further than originally planned, leading to further reductions in income and spending. The end result could be the *paradox of thrift* described in the chapter.

c. Because the equilibrium business cycle model is based on supply side factors, the idea that an increase in savings would lead to a reduction in real output doesn't apply. In this case, the increase in savings would simply result in higher rates of investment. Therefore, there is no multiple reduction in spending and income as in the Keynesian model.

Key Terms and Concepts

Chapter Summary

• You should understand the distinction between the "sticky wages" and "sticky price" models.

The original Keynesian model of recession and unemployment was based on **"sticky wages"**. This produced countercyclical movements in the real wage and procyclical movements in the price level, just as the monetary misperceptions model. Empirical evidence since 1950 contradicts the "sticky wages" model. Economists working in the Keynesian tradition developed a **"sticky price"** model that predicts a procyclical real wage. The key assumption of the theory is that of **imperfect competition** in which firms establish prices using the **markup ratio**.

• You should understand the impact on the labor market of stickiness in prices.

Under conditions of imperfect competition firms may to choose their own price, and they may respond to changes

in demand by expanding output. This in turn increases the demand for labor and wages, and produces a procyclical pattern in employment and real wage rates.

• You should understand the implications of the federal reserves' open market operations under "sticky wages" and "sticky price" variations in the Keynesian model.

A monetary expansion under, the condition of "sticky prices", increases the economy wide quantity of labor demanded. An increase in the demand for labor under an upward sloping labor supply curve results in an increase in the equilibrium quantity of labor input resulting in an increase in real GDP. A monetary expansion under, the condition of "sticky wages", lowers the real wage rate, raising the quantity of labor demanded and level of employment.

Key Graphs

Figure 16.1 *Effect of a Monetary Expansion in the New Keynesian Model*

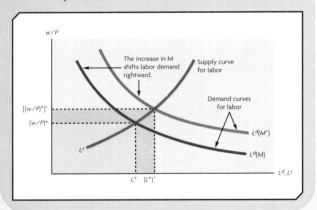

When the nominal quantity of money is *M*, the demand for labor, labeled $L^d(M)$, slopes downward versus the real wage rate, *w/P*, and is given by the blue curve. When the nominal quantity of money rises to *M'*—but the price level, *P*, is held fixed—the demand for labor, labeled $L^d(M')$ along the red curve, is larger at any given *w/P*. The supply of labor, L^s, in green, slopes upward versus *w/P*. The increase in the nominal quantity of money from *M* to *M'* raises the real wage rate from (w/P)* to [(w/P)*]' on the vertical axis and increases labor input from *L** to (L*)' on the horizontal axis.

Figure 16.3 *The Labor Market in the Keynesian Model with Sticky Nominal Wage Rates*

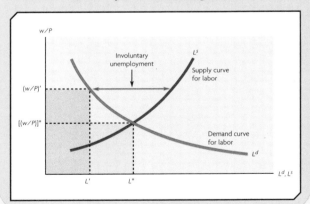

In the Keynesian model, the nominal wage rate, *w'*, is fixed above its market-clearing value, *w**. Consequently, the real wage rate, (w/P)', will be greater than the market-clearing value, (w/P)*, on the vertical axis. At (w/P)', the quantity of labor supplied, along the L^s curve, exceeds the quantity demanded, along the L^d curve. On the horizontal axis, the quantity of labor, *L**, equals the quantity demanded and is less than the market-clearing value, *L**.